CENSUS OF INDIA 1891

Census of India 1871-1951, 9 Sets In 384 Bindings (9788121258876) Rs. 700000

Census of India 1891, 28 Vols. In 49 Bindings (978-81-212-7129-5) Rs. 125000

1. General Report (9788121269834) Rs. 1450
2. General Tables For British Provinces And Feudatory States (9788121269810) Rs. 2710 (Vol. I)
3. General Tables For British Provinces And Feudatory States (9788121269797) Rs. 950 (Vol. II)
4. Assam - Report (9788121269773) Rs. 2390 (Vol. I, V.1)
5. Assam - Tables (9788121269759) Rs. 2210 (Vol. II, V.2)
6. Assam - Provincial Tables (9788121269735) Rs. 1310 (Vol. II, V.3)
7. The Lower Provinces of Bengal and their Feudatories - The Report (9788121269711) Rs. 1660 (Vol. III)
8. The Lower Provinces of Bengal and their feudatories - The Administrative Tables (9788121269698) Rs. 4200 (Vol. IV)
9. The Lower Provinces of Bengal and their feudatories - The Caste Tables (9788121269674) Rs. 2600 (Vol. V, Pt. 1)
10. Lower Provinces of Bengal - The Provincial Tables (9788121269650) Rs. 1980 (Vol. V, Pt. 2)
11. Berar or the Hyderabad Assigned Districts (9788121269636) Rs. 3360 (Vol. VI)
12. Bombay and Its Feudatories - Report (9788121269612) Rs. 4010 (Vol. VII, Pt. 1)
13. Bombay And Its Feudatories - Imperial Tables (9788121269599) Rs. 790 (Vol. VIII, Pt. 2)
14. Imperial Series - Burma Report (9788121269575) Rs. 2320 (Vol. IX-V.1)
15. Imperial Tables - Burma Report (9788121269551) Rs. 3360 (Vol. X-V.2)
16. Provincial Tables Burma Report (9788121269537) Rs. 3510 (Vol. X-V.3)
17. Provincial Tables Burma Report (9788121269513) Rs. 3630 (Vol. X-V.4)
18. The Central Provinces And Feudatories - The Report (9788121269490) Rs. 2290 (Vol. XI, Pt. 1)
19. The Central Provinces And Feudatories - Imperial tables and supplementary returns (9788121268936) Rs. 2010 (Vol. XII)
20. Madras The Report On The Census (9788121269476) Rs. 2870 (Vol. XIII)
21. Madras - Tables I to XVII-C, British Territory (9788121269452) Rs. 3490 (Vol. XIV)
22. Madras - Tables A TO E, British Territory. Tables for feudatory States and A Caste Index (9788121269438) Rs. 2820 (Vol. XV)
23. The North Western Provinces and Outh - Report and Provincial Tables (9788121268912) Rs. 3100 (Vol. XVI, Pt. 1)
24. The North - Western Provinces and Oudh- Imperial Tables (9788121269414) Rs. 2000 (Vol. XVII, Pt. 2)
25. The North - Western Provinces and Oudh- Imperial Caste Tables (9788121269391) Rs. 3020 (Vol. XVIII, Pt. 3)
26. Punjab and Its Feudatories - The Report on the Census (9788121269377) Rs. 2710 (Vol. XIX, Pt. 1)
27. Punjab and Its Feudatories - Imperial Tables and Supplementary Returns for the British Territory (9788121269353) Rs. 1370 (Vol. XX, Pt. 2)
28. Punjab and Its Feudatories - Imperial Tables and Supplementary Returns for the Native States, Together With A Caste Index (9788121269339) Rs. 4910 (Vol. XXI, Pt. 3)
29. Report on The Census of The Districts of Ajmere-Merwara (9788121269056) Rs. 720 (Vol. XXII)
30. His Highness The Nizam's Dominions - Report (9788121269315) Rs. 2240 (Vol. XXIII, Pt. 1)
31. His Highness The Nizam's Dominions - Report (9788121269292) Rs. 2410 (Vol. XXIII, Pt. 2)
32. His Highness The Nizam's Dominions - Imperial And Supplementry Tables and Caste Index (9788121269278) Rs. 3390 (Vol. XXIII, Pt. 3)
33. Baroda - Report (9788121269254) Rs. 3810 (Vol. XXIV, Pt. 1)
34. Baroda - Tables (9788121269230) Rs. 2620 (Vol. XXIV, Pt. 2)
35. Mysore - Report (9788121269216) Rs. 2590 (Vol. XXV, Pt. 1)
36. Mysore - Imperial Tables (9788121269193) Rs. 1600 (Vol. XXV, Pt. 2)
37. Mysore - Tables (9788121269179) Rs. 5320 (Vol. XXV, Pt. 3)
38. Mysore - Supplementary Tables (9788121269155) Rs. 3590 (Vol. XXV, Pt. 4)
39. Mysore- Supplement to the Mysore census report of 1891 being a list of villages in the Mysore province and : comparing the population as per Censuses of 1891, 1881 & 1871 (9788121279024) Rs. 5350 (Vol. XXV, Pt. 5)
40. Rajputana - The Report, Imperial Tables And Supplementary Returns (9788121269131) Rs. 2330 (Vol. XXVI, Pt. 1)
41. Rajputna - The Provincial Tables and Remarks (9788121269117) Rs. 550 (Vol. XXVI, Pt. 2)
42. Central India (9788121269094) Rs. 2000 (Vol. XXVII)
43. Kashmir State - The Report on the census and Imperial and supplementary Tables (9788121269070) Rs. 2290 (Vol. XXVIII)
44. The Census of Calcutta (9788121269032) Rs. 890
45. Report on the census of Cochin (9788121269018) Rs. 790 (Pt. 1)
46. Report on the census of Cochin - The Final Census Tables with Appendices (9788121268998) Rs. 910 (Pt. 2)
47. Report on the Census of Coorg (9788121268974) Rs. 730
48. Report on the census of Travancore -Report (9788121274029) Rs. 4220 (Vol. I)
49. Report on the census of Travancore -Appendix (9788121268950) Rs. 5300 (Vol. II)

Owing to the antiquity and rarity of this book, certain pages are regrettably absent, and readability is compromised due to the blurring of the original text. If you possess any insights regarding the availability of these missing sections, kindly inform us. Your assistance is crucial in ensuring the completion of this significant work for the benefit of future generations.

CENSUS OF INDIA, 1891

BOOK - 1

GENERAL REPORT

J. A. BAINES

GYAN

Published by

Gyan Publishing House
5, Ansari Road
Daryaganj, New Delhi-110002
Phone: 011-47034999, 9811692060
E-mail: books@gyanbooks.com

Distribution Network
gyanbooks.com
India, USA, Canada, UK, Australia

ISBN: 978-81-212-7129-5 (Set) 28 Vols. In 49 Bindings
978-81-212-6983-4 (PB) BOOK-1

First Published, 1893

2nd Impression 2024

Printed at: Gyan Press, Delhi.

CENSUS OF INDIA 1891

Census of India, 1891.

GENERAL REPORT,

BY

J. A. BAINES, F.S.S.
OF THE INDIAN CIVIL SERVICE.

LONDON:
PRINTED FOR THE INDIAN GOVERNMENT,
BY EYRE AND SPOTTISWOODE,
PRINTERS TO THE QUEEN'S MOST EXCELLENT MAJESTY.

1893.

PREFACE.

Some portions of the materials for this work were so late in their arrival that advantage was taken of the delay to compress as far as possible the review of the rest to within moderate dimensions. I have thus deprived myself of the opportunity, of which my predecessor, Sir William Plowden, so freely and gracefully availed himself, of showing my appreciation of the work of my colleagues, the Superintendents of the provincial census, by incorporating in my own review copious extracts from theirs. I am none the less under obligations to them for the help they have given me throughout the operations, and for which I now tender my best thanks. Rather than draw comparisons here, I prefer to leave their work to be judged by those who are in a position to view it from a standpoint less partial than that of one who has had so strong and intimate an interest in it and its authors as I have had during the last two years. I may nevertheless be allowed the personal gratification of summarising, in a few instances, what will be found expressed in a more diffuse form in the review to which these lines are a prelude.

Mr. O'Donnell's work stands by itself, as in no other case has so large a population been enumerated in such detail on the responsibility of a single and practically unaided Superintendent. That his administration was statistically and financially successful is greatly due to the unsparing personal supervision he exercised on the operations from first to last. His analysis of the movement of the population, district by district, is very valuable, and his interesting iconoclastic excursions into the domain of ethnology are by no means without justification in the information he collected. Mr. Stuart was equally successful in his handling of the Madras census, and his review of the results shows a specially keen statistical scent, if the expression be allowed, in following certain paths where one has to walk circumspectly amongst dangerously fragile premises. Messrs. Gait and Maclagan have shown throughout their work the best characteristics of that most valuable speciality of India, the district officer, namely, tact, energy and knowledge of the people. Their returns were the first to be completed, and their review, especially where they respectively tread on fresh ground. which both had good opportunities of doing, are full of remarks worth reading. Mr. Eales, too, has written a very valuable account of the census of one of the most interesting portions of the Empire, the two divisions of Burma. Mr. Drew shares with Messrs. Gait and Maclagan the honours of punctuality, and his work on Bombay was the first to reach me in its completed form. As I superintended the Bombay census of 1881, I naturally feel more than ordinary interest in this part of the operations, and must frankly acknowledge that, in my opinion, Mr. Drew managed his tabulation better than I did, though in the matter of the review, I confess a preference for my own bantling. The Central Provinces were enumerated by a Superintendent who, before he went to take up the census work, had never set foot in the Province in his life. The great reduction in the cost, and the amount of information collected in the review, speak for themselves in Mr. Robertson's favour, both as administrator and reporter. Messrs. Egerton and Hastings, too, worked well in Ajmér and Berar. Among the pleasant recollections of the census, is the cordial co-operation of the officials of some of the native States, and I must specially mention the names of Mr. V. Narsinghayangar, the Superintendent of the Mysore census, whose work was one of the first to be received by me in the Simla office, and the late Mr. Bhatwádekar, and his successor, Mr. Mulshankar, in Baroda. I have also to thank, for their interest in getting the preliminary arrangements set in proper train, Mr. Tucker, of the Central India Agency, and Mr. Erskine, in Rájputána, as well as Mr. Gunion in the former, and Colonel Abbot in the latter, for their work in connection with the operations subsequent to the enumeration.

On the other side of the account, I must express my regret at the absence of any review of the operations and results in the second province in the country in population. Whether the omission is due to Mr. Baillie or his printer I am unable to say, as I have failed in extracting any explanation of this abnormal procrastination. The reports on the census of Central India, Baroda, and Haidrabád have not been received, but the delay has in each case been explained.

I do not like to conclude this long list of those directly concerned in the operations, without mentioning the aid in connection with the arrangement and printing of forms and tables which I received from Mr. Woollam, in Simla, and Mr. Lewis in the Bengal office, at Calcutta; and also that given me personally by Mr. E. F. Augustin, whose services were lent me by the Military Department of the Government of India, and who, as head of my establishment, acquitted himself so efficiently that I felt entitled to specially refer to his services when replacing them at the disposal of the above Department.

I must acknowledge my obligations, again, to many others, not in any way connected with the operations, of whose studies and experience I have taken advantage. The census deals with so many subjects, each of which, in the present day, falls within the province of a specialist, that no single individual can safely trust to his own unaided capacity in reviewing them, but is forced, like Molière, à prendre son bien où il le trouve, and I have done my best to acknowledge such depredations at the time I have found it convenient to make them. The field covered, however, is so wide, that, in order to bring out the review before the information on which it is based is out of date, a mode of treatment in some degree superficial, cannot be avoided. On this occasion, moreover, my time has been specially absorbed by work connected with the reprint of some of the tables, and with the caste returns, which could not be completed till data had been incorporated which only reached me in the middle of May. It was only for four or five months, accordingly, that I was able to concentrate my attention on the statistics, and the amount of ground to be traversed is so vast, that I was too often reminded of the question asked of a late Laureate by his Quaker friend :—"Prythee, friend Southey, with all this writing, when do'st thou find time to think?"

For such views as I have been able to express, I am alone responsible. The work is, it is true, the review of a State operation, by a State official, but it is written at a distance from India, beyond reach of consultation with other branches of the administration. A good deal has been added, too, in explanation of the statistics, that would have been deemed unnecessary had the work been written for official readers only, but which becomes advisable as soon as a public is approached that has no experience of what is to us in India a matter of everyday observation. Whether these explanations fulfil their object, and how far we of the Census have succeeded in adequately dealing with the many important and interesting subjects thus placed within our reach, are questions that we now submit to our readers :—

Nam cœnæ fercula nostræ
Malim convivis quam placuisse coquis.

J. A. BAINES,
Census Commissioner for India.

India Office, London,
10th July, 1893.

CONTENTS.

CHAPTER I.

Introductory and Descriptive.

. . . . *Magna modis multis miranda videtur*
Gentibus humanis regio, visenda que fertur,
Rebus opima bonis, multâ munita virûm vi.—*Lucretius.*

The second general census of India was taken on the night of the 26th of February 1891, as nearly as possible 10 years after the first, which took place on the 17th of February 1881. Closer correspondence in date between the two could not be obtained, by reason of the difference in the date of the full moon, which is a factor of considerable importance in connection with an Indian census. It is essential, in the first place, that the enumerator should have moonlight to guide him round his beat, which includes, in the rural tracts, a comparatively large area; for his duties are not confined to the mere collection by day of a schedule which has been prepared for him by the householder, as in a European country. In India, the population to be enumerated contains no more than about 6 in the 100 who can read and write, so that the whole of the census record has to be prepared by special agency. As it is impossible to provide enough people of the necessary qualifications to do this in the course of a single night, the census is divided into two sections. First, the enumerator fills up the schedules of his beat with the required information for all the habitual residents therein, before the census. Then, on the appointed night, he brings this up to date by a second round, during which he strikes out all who have died or are found absent, and enters all found on the premises who were not there when the preliminary visit was paid, such as travellers, guests, and the newly born. As he is bound to visit all the outlying parts of his beat, wherever casual sojourners are likely to be found, efficient inspection is ensured and the cost of lighting saved, by the selection of a moonlight night for the operation. But, unfortunately, the night of full moon itself cannot be fixed for the census, as it is the occasion when all the principal religious gatherings of India at shrines, temples, and bathing places are held, so that a very considerable portion of the population is absent on that night from its native place. It is a matter of uncertainty how long beforehand it is the custom to start on such excursions, which constitute one of the chief pleasures, as well as the main ceremonial observance, in the life of the masses, but, as a rule, there is a tendency to return home with greater expedition than marks the journey out. It is found, accordingly, that what with the number of festivals that are purely local in their attractions, and the facilities now available for visiting the places of wider renown by rail, the third day after the auspicious occurrence will generally find the bulk of the pilgrims back in their villages, and it was on this consideration that the census night was fixed, both in 1881 and on the last occasion. A suggestion was made, again, that the census of India should be taken synchronously with that of the United Kingdom, in order to emphasize the imperial character of the operations. The conditions of India, however, rendered it impossible to fall in with this proposal. By the beginning of April, when it was understood that the census would be taken in the mother country, the hot season has set in in India, and the inspection of what has been above called the preliminary record, and also of the more general preparations for the census, could not be conducted, compatibly with other work, so efficiently as during the season when the supervising officials of the tract in question are on tour in the ordinary course of their duties, and it is to this inspection that the accuracy of the enumeration is mainly due. **Selection of date.**

The results, showing a total of about 287,000,000 persons, were compiled at various offices in the different Provinces and States with such expedition and accuracy that they were published within five weeks from the census, with a difference of only five persons in every 1,000, or ½ per cent., from the finally corrected returns. **Population enumerated.**

The figure quoted above bears a ratio to the population of the world, as at present computed, of about one-fifth, and is the largest appertaining to any single country with the exception of China. On the other hand, a map of the world on a **Diversity of circumstances in India.**

plane projection shows that of the great promontories that taper from the north down into the southern seas, India is by far the smallest. It contains, in fact, but 3 per cent. of the estimated land-surface of the globe. But in spite of its political unity and comparatively small area, India, with all the diversity of its conditions, has a good claim to be considered less as a country than as a collection of countries, or a continent. In connection with an operation like the census, this will undoubtedly be conceded. In discussing the statistics of Europe, we distinguish, as a matter of course, those of Greece from those of Holland, and Spain from Germany. Even in the case of a single empire like Russia, the circumstances of Irkutsk are not confounded with those of Kiew or Warsaw. It is equally rational, then, to discriminate between Assam and Sindh, Madras and the Panjab, to say nothing of Burma, which has so few points of contact with the rest of this great dependency. In reviewing the results of the census, therefore, it may appear that comparatively little is said of India, as a whole, for the reasons just presented, but in all cases the remarkably large numbers involved are of pre-eminent use as a centre line, from which to measure the variations of the different component parts.

Uniformity in religion and occupation.

But two of the facts that appear prominently in the returns indicate, on the surface, a significant degree of uniformity throughout the country, so it is best to bring these to notice at once. The first, then, is that nearly three-fourths of the population is returned under one religious denomination. This matter will have to be discussed in detail in its proper sequence, but, in the meanwhile, it should be understood that the apparent uniformity is little more than a concession to conventional nomenclature, and the title covers creeds as well as races as fundamentally differing from each other as any in Europe. The second point to be noticed here, is the very high proportion in all parts of the country of the population living by agriculture. Taking it as a whole, about two-thirds, and indirectly perhaps nearly three-fourths, of the community are wholly or partially dedicated to Mother Earth, and in this case the uniformity is real, not merely nominal. But it is also one which serves to throw into greater prominence the extraordinary diversity of the physical conditions under which the cultivation of the soil has to be conducted in India.

Importance and variety of physical conditions.

We have thus to look upon the great geographic and climatic features of the country in their direct and intimate connection with the predominating means of subsistence, and therefore with the distribution and circumstances of the population now existing. They have to be considered, again, historically, in their capacity of determining factors in the ethnology of that population, helping to explain the variety and fusion of the elements of which it is probably composed. Some description of the principal physical divisions of the country is accordingly necessary as a preface to the discussion of the results of their influence on its ethnology, and also on the more general subject that precedes it, namely, the ratio between population and area.

Geographical Divisions.

The Ocean, and the Himálaya.

Considering for the present India proper, excluding, that is, Burma, we find ourselves face to face with two main geographical facts, the ocean to the south, and the great mountain barrier to the north. Of the former it is enough to say that, until the arrival of the European adventurers of the 16th century, it plays little part in the history of the population, and the settlers who came by sea are scattered and insignificant. Whether it always ebbed and flowed in its present bed, or whether India is but the remnant of the submerged continent of Lemuria, it is not necessary for the present purpose to determine. The question is of great ethnological moment, especially in connection with the population of the peninsular tracts of India, but the evidence is of a sort that must be left to be sifted by specialists like Messrs. Wallace and Peschl. As regards the great mountain system of the north there is no such difficulty. As far back as there is occasion to look, they have stood between India and its neighbours, more or less of a barrier to free intercourse and colonisation. Flanked by ranges of less height, indeed, but still difficult to traverse, and backed by miles of bleak table-land and inhospitable desert, the Himálaya and its sister systems afford means of access only with great toil and hardship to comparatively small bodies of men at a time. In the extreme north-west the way is less arduous, and has been used by all the invaders of India who were able, like Alexander and his 40,000 men, to establish, as a preliminary step, their footing in the country to the west of the ranges flanking the Indus. Through these last the passes are few and narrow, so much so, that it is said that even in the present day, a body of 100,000 men moving on India from Jelálabád, through the Khaibar Pass, would find its vanguard on the Plain of Peshâwar before the rear had left the starting point. Yet it is by this route and its neighbours to the north that Irán and Turán have entered India from time immemorial, except in the few instances when the mountain range was turned altogether, and an advance in force made up or across the Indus. At the extreme east the mean elevation is less, but on passing the range, the alternative is presented of a comparatively easier progress down the valleys of the main rivers of the Burma and Siam peninsula, so that much of the immigration from the north-east has probably been deflected from India to the Golden Chersonese, by the Irrawadi and Mekong. Throughout the central Himálayan system the passes are few and of great height, and it is probable that they were not attempted until after the occupation of the Gangetic basin in force by those who had found their way thither by easier routes. So far as the census is concerned, the Himálaya and its neighbours are of little importance, since, with the exception of the Kashmér State and the southern slopes, little of the mountain tract was brought under the operations. The direct connection of the system with the present subject lies in its influence on the climatic and agricultural circumstances of the country immediately at its base, and historically, again, in its capacity of impediment to the free overflow of population from the tracts lying beyond it in the north. The former point will be noticed shortly in the course of this introduction. Regarding the latter, all that need be said is, that though the colonisation of Upper India from abroad may have been started by bodies of immigrants reaching the plains through the mountains of the Himálaya and Hindu Kush, the subsequent recruitment from that direction has been, so to speak, insignificant, and the expansion of the foreign communities thus settled in India has been due to causes arising within the country itself.

The great rivers.

The second of the main geographical divisions of India is the great river system, which covers the whole of the northern portion of the continent. The chief arteries are the Indus and the Ganges, with their tributaries, and the lower course of the stream we know as the Bráhmaputra. The last is not, however, to be compared in importance, in connection with the present subject, to the two others, firstly, because of the competition of the great rivers of the Indo-Chinese peninsula, of which mention has already been made, and, again, because the upper portion of its south Himálayan course lies in a comparatively narrow valley, cut off from the rest of the country by an intervening range of considerable elevation and width. In fact, in common parlance amongst the residents of this tract, India is held to be a foreign country. As soon as the Bráhmapútra emerges from its valley it becomes almost inextricably mixed up with the Ganges, forming one vast network of deltaic outlets. In Upper India the case is very different. Here the streams, which would naturally direct the course of the immigrants through the mountains, debouch at once into open country, affording the means of uninterrupted progress either south-east or south-west, for the watershed between the Panjab and the Gangetic system, once the Himalaya is left behind, is of insignificant height. The submontane tracts of the Panjab, with their continuation down the rich alluvial plain of the Jamna and Ganges, present the obvious outlet of a community disposed to agriculture, whilst the vast grazing grounds of the Indus valley are equally attractive to those of pastoral proclivities. Geographically, this belt of level country stretches all across India at its greatest breadth from west to east. Climatically, and from an ethnological point of view, it is by no means uniform, though for perhaps two-thirds of its extent the differences are in degree only, not in kind.

The Central ranges.

The third division is hardly as well defined as those already described. It consists of what may be called the second line of defence of peninsular India, that is, the belt of table-land and hilly country that separates the Gangetic basin from the Deccan, or great plateau of the south. Its western limits are the Aravalli hills and the rainless portion of the Indus valley. On the north it rises more or less gradually from the Ganges. It is buttressed on the south by the Vindhya and Sátpura hills, below which to the south, again, lies the tongue of flat country separating it from the Deccan. The whole of the eastern portion is a series of broken hills from the Delta and the Orissa coast line to the central plain. Strictly speaking, the western portion, or the Central India plateau, should be distinguished from the eastern, which comprises the Chútia-Nágpúr and Central Province hill tracts, at the Kaimúr range, but the line of separation is narrow and indistinct. One of the most important features of this division is its ethnological relation to the Ganges valley, on the one hand, and the plains of the south on the other, for it undoubtedly served to keep the stream of expansion of the north-western colonies within the valley, and direct it to the south-eastwards, instead of allowing its direct extension into the peninsula. So long as the fat plains along the river were available, there was no inducement to leave them in order to tempt the hardships and dangers of a trespass across the dividing ranges, so these last were left to the wild tribes, descendants of those which had been forced off the plains by the advance of the foreigner, and here they are to be found in the present day.

The central plain and Deccan table-land. From the central plain, which comprises the valleys of the Narmada and Tápti, with what is known as the Chattisgarh tract, rises the Deccan. This title is correctly restricted to the plateau rising more or less abruptly from the Tápti Valley, on the north-west; from the western coast and from the southern plains, whilst it slopes upwards much more gradually from the eastern coast. The boundaries on both east and west used to be called the Gháts, or steps, but this term is now confined by geographers to the chain on the west, because the formation to the east consists of groups of hills more or less isolated from each other, though sufficiently in line to demarcate the table-land from the plains below and along the coast: they cannot, therefore, be called a continuous range. There is thus a very gradual transition from the conditions of the latter tract to those of the uplands, a fact in strong contradistinction to the remarkable influence exercised by the western range on the climate and rain-distribution on each side of it.

The eastern peninsular coast. There remain to be described the strips of country along the coast, east and west. These vary in character very considerably. On the east, the upper portion is more or less an offshoot of the Ganges delta, but as the strip widens out from about the mouths of the Godávari, the country acquires a special character of its own, both climatic and ethnic. The name Carnatic formerly given to it, apparently by the early European settlers, is a misnomer, not recognised in philology or by the people. The derivation of the term has been often discussed, and, may, perhaps, be found in two words, received through the Telugu, meaning "black" and "country," or tract, a title very likely to be given by the denizens of the light soil of the eastern peninsula when introduced to the rich dark soil so characteristic of the western table-land. In the present day, the name is only given to a small strip along the western coast, and is scarcely recognised, even there, by the people, but owes its currency chiefly to official convention.

The western coast. The western coast-line is, as before mentioned, of a very different character from the east. For the greater portion of its length it consists of a narrow strip of level land immediately by the shore, rising by broken ranges to the foot of the Gháts. At the extreme south it may be taken to include the ranges of higher hills broken off at the Pálghát, from the main line which supports the table-land. Towards the north, the strip widens out and becomes a tract resembling in general features the central plains, gradually giving way to the conditions peculiar to the lower Indus valley. The central part of this coast-line is almost devoid of the long-shore strip, and the hills rise from the sea with but little intervening level ground, and that of comparatively low agricultural quality.

Burma. The existing administrative division of Burma into Upper and Lower serves well enough for the present introduction. If the whole of the hilly country to the north had been included in the census operations, it would have been advisable to demarcate the province more minutely, and to distinguish the circumstances of the settled portions of the country, in the plains and valleys, from the hill tracts, which differ from the rest in both climate and population.

Summary of geographical divisions. The following table summarises the distribution of area and population which has been attempted above, and as the administrative boundaries recognised in the census returns coincide fairly well with the geographical, the results are generally speaking accurate.

DIVISION.	Area in Square Miles.	Population.	Population per Square Mile.	Per-centage on total of Area.	Per-centage on total of Population.
A. Himálaya and Eastern Hills	150,570	6,542,650	43	9·68	2·28
B. Northern Plains	537,209	151,689,676	282	34·43	52·83
(a) *Gangetic System*	291,266	126,627,305	435	18·67	44·10
(b) *Indus* ,,	245,943	25,062,371	102	15·76	8·73
C. Central Hills	220,431	24,680,661	112	14·12	8·60
(a) *Eastern Group*	139,426	13,971,529	102	8·94	4·87
(b) *Western* ,,	81,005	10,709,132	132	5·19	3·73
D. Central Plain	97,390	13,738,362	141	6·22	4·77
E. Deccan Plateau	193,104	30,148,802	156	12·37	10·50
F. Southern Plain	62,494	19,862,376	318	4·00	6·92
G. N.E. Littoral	30,871	11,217,209	363	2·00	3·91
H. Western Littoral	96,581	21,648,185	224	6·22	7·54
J. Burma	171,430	7,605,560	44	10·96	2·65
(a) *Upper*	83,473	2,946,933	35	5·35	1·03
(b) *Lower*	87,957	4,658,627	53	5·61	1·62
Total, Continental India	**1,560,080**	**287,133,481**	**184**	—	—
Detached Settlements (*Aden, Quettah, Andamans, &c.*)	80	89,950	—	—	—
GRAND TOTAL	**1,560,160**	**287,223,431**	**184**	—	—

It will be seen from this table that, speaking roughly, Upper India contains 44 per cent. of the area and 55 per cent. of the population with which the census is concerned. Southern, or peninsular India, returns 24⅔ and 29, and the intervening belt, 20⅓ and 13⅓. The rest, 11 per cent. of the area and 2⅔ of the population, is found in Burma.

Before entering further into the details of the distribution thus given, some description has to be added of their climatic conditions, for without these the geographical outlines serve to denote facts mainly historical in their interest, such as the probable direction of colonising streams, and the demarcating lines of the ethnic divisions, which have to be discussed later. But on the climatic conditions, taken along with the general character of the tract, depends the ratio subsisting in the present day between the land and its population, since, as originally stated, the bulk of the latter lives by the cultivation of the former. The meteorology of India has occupied the attention of eminent specialists for a considerable number of years, and of late the area of observation has been widely extended by the establishment of new stations under efficient inspection, with an increase in the scope of record. There are six series of data available in connection with the present purpose, but most of them, for a period that is sufficient to afford trustworthy standards, are based on the observations of only a few of the principal meteorological stations. We can make use, for instance, of the record of annual rainfall, of which the data are full, whilst setting aside those of the number of rainy days, the relative humidity and aqueous vapour-tension, which are available for the principal stations only. But as regards temperature, the returns alone, without the supplement of the figures of, say, the mean Meteorological variety.

monthly range, are of little value in connection with the subject in hand. In the course of time means will be found, no doubt, to elaborate something of the nature of a "figure of merit," meteorologically speaking, for all the most typical centres of observation in India, in which attempt every one of the above data will be given its proportional weight, but in the meanwhile the annual rainfall will suffice for the general indications which are alone relevant to the question with which this chapter is concerned.

General character of the rainfall.

With respect to this rainfall, it must first be understood that though the mean for India of 42 inches, or thereabouts, is more or less what is to be expected in the tropics, the variations in its local distribution are so great that they are said by good authorities to be unparallelled in any other part of the known world,-not excepting the British Islands, which boast a high rank in this respect. There is found, for example, a fall of less than five inches in the central portion of the Indus plain, and one of over 600 on a buttress of the Khási hills, in Assam. In the peninsula, too, along the west coast, as much as 200 inches falls 40 miles from the sea, whilst at a distance of, say, 80 miles there is only a precarious sprinkling of 20. In connection with this variability there are two points that may be noted here. First, that the rainfall is subject to much variation periodically, as well as locally, and that from year to year the range of variation is in inverse ratio to the average amount, that is to say, the uncertainty, so to speak, is greater as the rainfall is less. Where an inch or two makes little or no difference to the agricultural outlook of the year, the chances of a normal fall are greatest, but in the tracts where the said amount bears a far higher proportion to the annual total, it is most likely to be in excess or defect. The second point is that, according to the observations hitherto worked up, the same feature in the rainfall does not extend over more than two-thirds of the area under record, so that, as a rule, a deficiency in one-third of India is likely to be accompanied by a fall above the average in the rest of the country. It is not to be understood that failure of the rain to the extent of causing a famine is here meant, but merely the tendency, in one or other direction, of a variation from the annual mean fall. These are both important features in regard to the numerical development of the population, a subject which occupies a later chapter.

Distribution of the rainfall, seasonal and geographic.

But for the moment, it has to be shown how far the general distribution of the rainfall corresponds to the geographical or orographic conformation of the country. This correspondence will be found to be, in the main, very close. The rainfall in India is, it need hardly be said, periodic, throughout the country, and not liable to be irregularly distributed over the year. Some tracts enjoy the advantage of two seasons of rain, but for the most part the fall for the year is concentrated into one.

Winter and spring rain.

In north-western India the season begins with the winter rains, which pass along the base of the Himálaya from west to east, getting lighter as they advance, till they cease on the confines of Bengal. Their extension southwards, too, is confined to the submontane region, and, on the whole, the advantage from them is reaped in a comparatively small tract. Megasthenes, however, judging of India from the portion of it which came most under his observation, extends the operation of this season to the whole continent as then known. It is interesting, we may remark cursorily, to find that in his time, as at present, wheat was the crop sown at this season. Before the winter rains have ceased in the north, the spring storms have gathered in the Bay of Bengal, so that the Delta of the Ganges and Bráhmapútra has the benefit of them. Their influence extends, too, though lightly, down the coast, as far as the southernmost point of India, but they do not reach the western portion of the peninsula. In their turn, they give way to the cyclonic storms so well known in the Bay of Bengal, which precede the great event of the meteorological year, the south-western rain.

Summer rain or S.W. monsoon.

This sets in about the end of May or beginning of June, in two main branches. The more important sweeps up the western coast till it fades away towards the upper portion of the north-western plain. In its course it encounters the obstacle of the Ghát line, which impedes its progress over the Deccan, whilst in the north, the hot and dry tracts of the lower Indus induce a current from the west, which is strong enough to overpower a weak one from the coast, and deflect it eastwards, thus depriving the upper Indus of its due rain. Moreover, it is almost certain that the coast current is affected unfavourably by a heavy snowfall during the winter, on the nucleus of the mountains we know as the Himálaya and Hindu Kush, so that political troubles are not the only ones in India that have their origin in the north-west. The second branch of the south-west current sets up the Bay of Bengal, and after irrigating Burma and the Gangetic Delta is deflected westward by the Himálayas. About the centre of the great valley it meets the other current from the west, so that when both are strong the fall is abundant, but if either, especially that from the west, is at all weak, it is only the south of the valley and the central belt, hills and plains, that receive their average amount of rain.

Scarcely has the south-west current ceased in the eastern portion of India, than the rain-bearing current from the north-east sets in, across the Delta and the east coast. Through this the southern plain, which receives but little rain from the south-west, and that precariously, expects its main supply for the year, but the current is by no means as strong as that from the Indian Ocean, and as the latter ceases in southern India some time before the commencement of the other rain, the earth has begun to get heated again, so the extremity of the current is weakened and the fall rendered uncertain in amount. *Autumn rain or N.E. monsoon.*

Setting aside the extreme west of India, which lies within the influence of the dry winds of the desert beyond the frontier, the minimum fall is found in the zone immediately adjacent to that region, known as the Indian Desert. But the zones of uncertainty are to be looked for round the meeting points of the main currents, at the extremities of their respective courses. The most extensive of these lies in the centre and south of the peninsula. Here the south-western current is stopped, as has been already pointed out, by the line of Gháts, so that comparatively little rain-bearing vapour escapes across the Deccan plateau. Again, though the current from the opposite quarter meets with scarcely any opposition of this sort, its direction lies more in line with the coast, so that only its skirts reach the high-lying land in the interior. Further south, again, this current has spent its force before it reaches the plain, and has but a small area of sea from which to replenish its moisture-bearing vapour. The fall is plentiful enough, when it comes, but it is wont to fail to a far greater extent than in most parts of India. The second of these unfortunate zones lies within the Gangetic valley, of which it includes the portion, roughly speaking, between the Indian Desert on the west and the Gandak on the east, situated mostly to the north of the main stream. In the tract under the influence of the same currents, but a little further south, the precipitation of rain, though not heavy, is remarkably regular. This is due, possibly, to the dampness of the land to the east, and to the shortness of the distance to the ocean on the west, at the point where the current catches the hills of the central belt. *Zones of uncertain fall.*

In connection with the relative uncertainty of the rainfall, it has been estimated from the available observations that the tracts receiving a fall averaging less than 50 inches, and with a mean deviation of about 12 per cent. above or below that average, all lie within the danger of famine. In the southern plain and the portion of the Gangetic valley that has just been described, the falls varies between 30 and 40 inches, whilst the mean range of the annual fluctuations is from 15 to 23 per cent. either above or below, or, from 30 to 46 per cent., taking both chances together. *Limit of security of season.*

Combining the two features, geographical and hydrographic, the variety of conditions under which the Indian agriculturist has to labour can be appreciated. In the first place, we find in the lower course of the Ganges and Bráhmaputra an alluvial plain, abundantly watered by the fall of two rainy seasons. Higher up the valley of the former the soil is still of the same description and the country equally open and level, but the rainfall is uncertain. Keeping on towards the north-west, we enter a submontane plain, open and fertile, with the chance of two falls of rain in the twelvemonth, one of which is fairly certain. Here we meet the Indus valley, and the circumstances are greatly changed. The country is still for the most part level, but the rainfall rapidly diminishes as the west is approached, so that the cultivation has to be to a great extent independent of it. The substitute in this case, as in that of Egypt, is the rise of a mighty river, which annually inundates the country for miles on each side. Beyond that range, again, and here the advantage is on the side of India, the five great tributaries of the Indus, supply the necessary irrigation wherever the level admits of canals. Further to the south-west, throughout the lower course of the *Summary of agricultural conditions.*

Indus, the rainfall is insignificant, but wherever water can be conducted, cultivation is possible, as the soil is naturally deep and fertile. To the south of the desert lies the tract above called the Western Litoral. The upper portion partakes of the character of the Tápti basin, in the central plain, except where it rises amongst low hills and broken ground to the central belt. But going south again, the level ground is found to be confined to the immediate coast, and inland, the country consists of series of hills trending downwards from the Ghâts. The arable land, therefore, is either on the slopes of these hills, or in the depressions between them. In the former case it is shallow in soil, in the latter, small in extent. The rainfall, however, is plentiful, though confined to a single season. In the extreme south of this strip, the arable area expands, and the rain is distributed over two seasons, so that its agricultural advantages are far greater.

In the southern plain there is abundance of arable land, and the soil is, on the whole, good, though it varies much from tract to tract. But the rainfall, as has been already observed, is very uncertain. In some measure, too, the Deccan plateau resembles its neighbour. It contains a large area of light, shallow soil in the east, where the season is proverbially fickle, since this tract lies on the border-line of the two main currents affecting the peninsula. On the other hand, the Deccan has in its west and central portions considerable tracts of the disintegrated basalt now called the "black cotton soil," of great depth and fertility, with a remarkable power of retaining moisture, said to be due to the amount of alumina amongst its component elements, without which it is probable that much of the land would not be cultivable at all. Adjacent to the Deccan on the north, lies the central plain, of great fertility, but liable in its western portion to the same uncertainty of rainfall, though in far less degree, as the north-western Deccan. The hills by which it is bounded on the other sides receive, in like manner, a plentiful rain supply from both branches of the south-west current. They contain, however, but a scanty area of level ground, so that agriculture has to be carried on in more or less of a primitive scale at present, and the collection of forest produce competes with it in favour as a means of subsistence amongst the wild tribes that form the bulk of the population of this tract. The western portion of the central hill-country forms a plateau sloping in most of its extent so gradually towards the north-east that it is almost impossible to draw the line between it and the Gangetic basin. The strip of coast land connecting the Gangetic delta with the southern plain contains a fair extent of flat country, and as it shares with its northern neighbour the benefits of both the spring and autumn rain, in fertility it is little behind that favoured tract. The greater portion of the Himálayan tracts that come within the scope of the census operations lie beyond the region of periodic rains. The southern slopes and subsidiary ranges, receive, as rule, a good fall, though in the north-western direction they are liable to the same weakness in the summer current as the region immediately below them, in the Indus valley. Further north, the Vale of Kashmér, which is the only extensive tract of arable ground in that State, has the reputation of good and certain rain, though it is not without its experience of famine within the present generation. The country surrounding it on the west and north consists of ranges of hills and mountains, where cultivation is restricted to the valleys or the portions of the lower slopes that can be terraced for irrigation. The high plateau on the east resembles its neighbour Thibet in sterility and the absence of rain. In estimating the average fall on the Himálayan tract, the whole of this portion, Kashmer, Gilgit, and Ladákh, has been omitted, as the observations have not been carried on long enough as yet to afford trustworthy returns on which to work.

Such are the circumstances of India proper, and Burma alone now remains to be described. It has been already stated that, for general purposes, the political distinction of Upper and Lower will suffice, but it may as well be mentioned here that, so far as the rainfall is concerned, there is a further and a most important distinction to be drawn between the litoral and the inland tracts of the lower division of the province. The hill-ranges along the coast exercise a remarkable influence in the distribution of the rain, and the fall, which varies from 170 to about 230 inches at the stations where the register is kept, diminishes to from 60 to 80 a few miles inland, where our record is as yet incomplete. Again, in Upper Burma, where the fall is comparatively light, there is a submontane and hilly tract to the north which attracts, undoubtedly, a far heavier fall than the open country that forms the bulk of this part of the province. Thus, whilst the whole of Lower and the north of Upper Burma fall within the region of certain seasons, there is a considerable space in the centre which must be held to be outside the limit of immunity from scarcity of rain.

Omission of certain tracts from the rainfall statement.

Owing to the curious localisation of the rainfall in the litoral tracts of Lower Burma, and to the want of accurate measurement of the areas of the subdivisions of Kashmér and Central India, these portions of India have not been included in the returns of rainfall which are discussed in connection with the distribution of the population in the next chapter.

Omissions from the census returns.

The last subject that calls for notice in this introduction is the division of the country politically and for administrative purposes, but before entering into this, it is as well to explain exactly how far the census operations extended, and what tracts that fall within the general delimitation of India have been omitted from the enumeration. In the first place, the chief Himálayan State of Nipál is excluded, and so has the corresponding State of Bhótán, further east. The small State of Sikkim, which lies between these, was only enumerated informally, though as nearly as possible synchronously with the census of the rest of the country. The population is not, however, included in the general returns, as no details beyond the actual number of each race were recorded. The same process was adopted with regard to the Cis-Sálwín Shán States, on the east of Burma, and in the rural parts of British Balochistán excluding, that is, Quettah, Lorelai and the railways. In the case of Manipúr and of a few tracts along the northern Burma frontier, the census was taken, but in subsequent disturbances the records were destroyed. In the Andamans, beyond the limits of the convict settlement of Port Blair, in the Kakhyín country, bordering on Burma and Assam, in the Trans-Sálwín Shán States, and in a wild tract in the south of Rájputána, no enumeration was attempted, though in the last case a registration by households was recorded. The marginal note shows the approximate population of these tracts. There are also to be considered the small possessions of Portugal on the west coast and the detached settlements of France, which are *enclaves* in the provinces of Bengal and Madras. By the courtesy of the French officials a census of the latter was taken simultaneously with that of British India. The population of the Portuguese territory here shown is that of the census of August 1887, which was published in October 1892. The normal population dealt with then in the succeeding review is 287,223,431, but the full detail required in the standard schedule was not prescribed for the less advanced tracts, so that from the normal figure shown above there will be found deductions made in all the more elaborate returns, and due explanation of the difference has been appended to the tables concerned.

Sikkim (*Registered*) - -	30,458
Manipur (*Estimated*) - - - -	250,000
British Balochistán (*Registered*) -	145,417
Cis-Sálwín Shán States (*Registered*)	372,969
Burma Frontier tracts - - -	116,493
Rajputána Hill tracts (*Registered*) -	204,241
Total excluded - -	1,119,578
French Settlements - - -	282,923
Portuguese Possessions - - -	561,384
Total, Foreign - -	844,307
Included in the Census - - -	287,223,431
Grand Total - -	289,187,316

Political divisions. *British* and *Feudatory*.

The results of the census are shown by political and administrative divisions, on which some explanation is necessary before discussing the statistics in detail. The first subdivision is into British and Feudatory territory. The former is the dominion of the Crown, under the sole administration of the British Government, and contains 62 per cent. of the area. and 77 per cent. of the population now dealt with in connection with the census. The remainder is under the rule of the Native Chiefs, subject to the advice and control of the British Government, in its capacity of paramount power, and includes 38 per cent. of the area and 23 of the population. The higher proportion of the area in this category is due to the inclusion in some of the States of wild tracts like the Himálayan regions of Kashmér, the desert portion of the Indus valley, and nearly all the forest-covered hills of the central belt. The first-named lies outside the turmoil of the dynastic struggles that troubled Upper India for so many years, and after its brief experience of Sikh rule, was made over by the British to the chief of a warlike clan of the outer Himálaya. The general sterility of the territory, with the exception of the Vale of Kashmér, which, as observed above, is of but restricted area, and the southern slopes of the hills that separate it from India, has been already mentioned. Rajputána, again, a country of large towns in an open plain, was obviously selected as its stronghold by a warlike race, which let the tide of invasion from the north-west roll along the frontier down the rich plains of the Ganges unheeded, so long as their desert home was unmolested. The plateau that forms the western portion of the central belt was carved out into estates by various adventurers from different parts of India, in the disturbed times preceding the establishment of the British dominion, and only the eastern and wilder portion contains dynasties of ancient lineage, strong in their mountain fastnesses. The eastern section of this tract of hills is split up into many petty chieftainships, as might be expected from the broken and difficult nature of the country. It offers no attraction to the civilised denizen of the plain, so it has been left to the scattered remains of the former occupants of the latter, driven off it to take refuge in a land that like Cameliard, before the coming of Arthur, is

> "Thick with wet woods, and many a beast therein,
> And none or few to scare or chase the beast."

On the other hand, the alluvial plains of the Ganges valley, and the equally fertile strips along the northern coast on each side of the peninsula, fall, the one entirely, the other almost so, within British territory, and contain in the aggregate more than half the population of India.

In size and population there is no more uniformity amongst the Provinces and States of India than amongst the political units of Europe. The British possessions were built up gradually, and with regard, as far as possible, to the demarcation in force under the government that preceded the acquisition. Within the last generation, at all events, the transfers of territory have been comparatively trifling in extent. Amongst the more important are those of the Delhi tract to the Panjáb from the Agra government, or what is still called by the clumsy and obsolete title of "the North-West Provinces"; and of the Surma valley from Bengal to the then newly-formed province of Assam. In the south, again, a small tract has been detached, for administrative convenience, from the Central Provinces, and added to the Presidency of Madras, whilst the still smaller Jhánsi territory was exchanged by Sindhia in 1886 for the fortress of Gwálior. The Native States exist under the guarantee of the paramount power, so their territorial limits are as they were found at the time when they entered into their agreements with the British Government. As the principle of guarantee is the same for small and great, these States vary in size from the dominion over a village or two, with a population of a few hundreds, to the lordship of more than 80,000 square miles, with nearly 12,000,000 of inhabitants. For convenience in respect to their relations with the paramount power, the smaller States are grouped into Agencies, a term applied to even those of larger size, which are either much intermingled territorially, or which are of so homogeneous a constitution that a single intermediary between them and the Supreme Government is sufficient. In both of these cases there are subdivisions of the authority of supervision, delegated to local Agencies or Residencies, but though these are recognised in the special census returns for the Agency as a whole, they do not appear in those under consideration, which deal with the aggregate as the unit. Central India, Balochistán, and Rajputána are the main instances of this. The smaller groups of States are combined in the Imperial returns according to the local government or administration with which they are politically connected. For example, those attached to Bombay appear in a single item in the general returns, and under 19 heads in the provincial volume, but individually, they number several hundreds. It is as well to note here the distinction between the position of States such as these and that of tracts in Bengal, Oudh, and parts of Madras, on the owners of which titular honours, similar to those of chiefs, may have been bestowed by the British Government. In the former case there has been the recognition of distinct political entity, whereas the second case is merely that of an estate forming part of British territory, and with nothing but a special fiscal agreement to distinguish it from the rest.

The following table shows the area and population of each of the British Provinces and States, or, as explained above, groups of States. It also includes a statement of the proportion borne by each to the total area and population respectively of India as a whole :—

Province, State, or Agency.	Area in Square Miles.	Population, 1891.	Percentage on Total.	
			Area.	Population.
Bengal	151,543	71,346,987	9·71	24·84
Madras	141,189	35,630,440	9·05	12·40
N.-W. Provinces	83,286	34,254,254	5·34	11·93
Oudh	24,217	12,650,831	1·55	4·40
Panjáb	110,667	20,866,847	7·09	7·26
Bombay	77,275	15,985,270	4·95	5·56
Sindh	47,789	2,871,774	3·06	1·00
Central Provinces	86,501	10,784,294	5·55	3·75
Upper Burma	83,473	2,946,933	5·35	1·03
Lower Burma	87,957	4,658,627	5·64	1·63
Assam	49,004	5,476,833	3·14	1·91
Berar	17,718	2,897,491	1·14	1·01
Ajmér	2,711	542,358	0·17	0·19
Coorg	1,583	173,055	0·10	0·06
Aden	80	44,079	0·01	0·02
Quettah, &c.	—	27,270	—	0·01
Andamans	—	15,609	—	—
Total British Provinces	**964,993**	**221,172,952**	**61·85**	**77·00**
Haidrabád	82,698	11,537,040	5·30	4·02
Rajputána	130,268	12,016,102	8·35	4·18
Central India	77,808	10,318,812	4·99	3·59
Mysore	27,936	4,943,604	1·79	1·72
Baroda	8,226	2,415,396	0·53	0·84
Kashmér	80,900	2,543,952	5·19	0·89
States connected with Bombay	69,045	8,059,298	4·42	2·81
,, ,, Madras	9,609	3,700,622	0·62	1·29
,, ,, Central Provinces	29,435	2,160,511	1·89	0·75
,, ,, Bengal	35,834	3,296,379	2·30	1·15
,, ,, N.-W. Provinces	5,109	792,491	0·32	0·28
,, ,, Panjáb	38,299	4,263,280	2·45	1·48
Fort Steadman, Shan Outposts	—	2,992	—	—
Total, Feudatory States	**595,167**	**66,050,479**	**38·15**	**23·00**
GRAND TOTAL, INDIA	**1,560,160**	**287,223,431**	**100·00**	**100·00**

Their distribution over the physical divisions described above is shown in the table given at the end of this chapter. The figures can also be compared with the corresponding returns for countries more widely known, so that an idea more vivid than a mere statement affords may be obtained of the relative size and population of the different parts of India. Bengal, then, to begin with the largest of the provinces, has an area equal to that of the United Kingdom, with the addition of a second Scotland, whilst the population is about that of the whole of the United States of America in 1890, together with that of Mexico. The Presidency of Madras has the area of Prussia and Saxony, and contains a population exceeding that of those two States by that of Wurtemburg, one of the smaller members of the German Empire. If the native States under this government be added, the aggregate population slightly exceeds that of the United Kingdom or of Austria-Hungary, at the last census. The North-West Provinces, with Oudh and the connected States, supports nearly the same number of people as are found in the whole German Empire, though the area is something under that of Italy. Sindh and the Panjáb are about equal in population to Austria, and with the States connected with the latter, to little below England and Wales. Similarly, Bombay and its States are comparable to Spain, Holland and Norway. The whole population of Brazil, with its 3,200,000 square miles of area, could be accommodated, with room to spare, in the Central Provinces, which extend over no more than 86,500 miles. Assam, on the other hand, shows as many people as Bavaria, but on nearly twice the area. The island of Ceylon returns about the same population as Sindh and Berar, respectively, but the former contains nearly twice the area, and the latter little more than two-thirds. The population of Lower Burma and of Ireland could exchange places, but the former would be woefully cramped in the Emerald Isle after the enjoyment of more than twice the area in its native peninsula. In the acquisition of the rest of Burma, the second bite of the cherry, which Lord Dalhousie prophesied we should have to take, there has been added to the Empire the population of Switzerland, on the combined area of Portugal, Greece, Holland, and Belgium; or nearly the area of the colony of Victoria, with more than three times the population. In the aggregate, the British territories cover an area equal to that of the whole of the Teutonic countries of Europe, with the addition of Hungary, Servia, and Bulgaria.

There is also the Feudatory territory, with more than the population of the United States, and with an area equal to that covered by the Triple Alliance, with Belgium and Servia thrown in. The two great agencies of Rájputána and Central India alone, extend over the area of the German Empire, and contain nearly the population of Austria. Haidrabád is as large as England and Scotland put together. Mysore is a little smaller but more populous than, Portugal; and, to compare mountainous countries together, Kashmer shows the population of Chilé, but on less than a third of the area.

The smaller States. *Bombay.*

Next to these large States or Agencies, come the groups connected with the various local governments, some of which deserve a few words of description before the general subject is dropped. The Bombay States form the largest group. Amongst them, the small State of Khairpur, still in possession of the late ruling family of Sindh, and the peninsula of Kachh, appertain to the Indus valley rather than to the rest of the Presidency. Then comes the peninsula of Saurásthra, now known as Káthiáwár, from one of the dominant tribes from the north that immigrated thither in years gone by. Under this general title are included many small States and four of considerable size, Junágadh, Nawanagar, Bhaunagar, and Drángadhra. On the adjacent mainland, bordering on the western hills of the central belt, are four or five smaller groups of much the same constitution. The rest of the coast strip falling within this Presidency contains a couple of small States, interesting from their connection with the former ruling races of the interior. One was the appanage of the Sidi, or Abyssinian commander of the Moghal's fleet. The other was held by a maritime chief of the Marátha race, not free from the imputation of piracy. Not to mention a few wild States imbedded in the forests at the foot of the Ghâts, where these mountains fade into the central plain, the remaining States in this part of India are mostly creations of the Peshwa's rule, with the addition of Kolhápúr, descending from Shivaji, the founder of the Marátha dynasty.

Madras States.

To the south of Bombay come the States connected with the Madras Presidency, of which there are but five. Three of them are merely small, *enclaves* in British territory. The remaining two lie along the most fertile portion of the western coast, and the larger of them, Travancore, is the more interesting, owing to the fact that from its isolated position it has been enabled to conserve features of racial and social development long since obliterated in the busier life of the tracts repeatedly overrun by foreign influences.

Central Province and *Bengal States.*

The small States connected with the Central Provinces, and also those attached to Bengal, have been guaranteed, for the most part, to the descendants of some of the chief forest tribes, displaced from the plains by various waves of more civilised immigrants. Nearly all of them are situated in the hilly country composing what has been called above the central belt, in its eastern section. In Bengal, however, there are two detached States, that of Hill Tipperah, under one of the tribes of the eastern frontier, and that now called Kôch-Behár, the appanage of a more northern tribe, which, since its settlement in the lower valley, has become incorporated in the general population of the Gangetic delta.

North-West Province States.

There is a wide expanse of British territory between the above States and the next, which are connected with the Government of the North-West Provinces. These last are only two in number, and detached from each other. The smaller but more populous Rámpúr, lies imbedded in British territory. The other, Garhwál, covers a large area, sub-Himalayan in character, between the Panjáb and the North-West Provinces.

Panjáb States.

After Bombay, the Panjáb Government has the largest and most populous collection of States connected with it. They can be divided into three sections. First, those of the plains, the largest of which, Patiála, Jínd, and Nábha, with a few others, are known as the Sikh States. Then follows the large but sparsely peopled tract under Baháwalpúr, on the Indus, between Sindh and the northern portion of Rajputána. Last come the Hill States, stretching some way into the Himálaya. These are 23 in number, but most of them are comparatively insignificant, and though, in the aggregate, of considerable area, contain but a small population. The largest, Náhan, or Sirmúr, is the best known, perhaps, from having given its name to one of the staunchest of the regiments of Hill-men that fought in the Mutiny.

In the table accompanying this chapter, which shows the distribution of the political divisions over the divisions based on geographical and climatic considerations, the territory under feudatory rule has been combined with British territory, wherever it is not recognised in the general census returns as a separate unit. Table on page 22.

The " district " in British territory.

The only topic that remains to receive notice in this introduction is the administrative subdivision of a Province. In the case of States, enough has been said to indicate the very varying character of the unit as to size and constitution, whilst the larger States are not subdivided on any uniform system. In British territory the diversity is mainly in size, as the authority and duties of the officer placed in charge are everywhere the same, in so far as responsibility is in question. From an administrative point of view the head of a State is not assumed to be beyond the influence of bad advisers, whatever be the range of his sovereignty. In Russia, again, it is said that when anything goes wrong, investigation begins at the bottom, and the tendency is to throw the responsibility upstairs, as far as audacity can carry it. But in British India, experience has dictated the judicious middle course of combining considerable power with full responsibility over an area and population within the compass of one man's efficient supervision. In detail, the size of the district differs from province to province mainly according to the system of administering the land and its revenue; but, even within the province itself there is much variety, as can be seen from the following table:—

Province.	Number of Districts.	Mean of Districts.		Extremes.			
				Area.		Population.	
		Area.	Population.	District.	Area.	District.	Population.
Madras*	24	35·4 5,882	42·4 1,465,747	Nilgiri	957	Nilgiri	99,797
				Vizagapatam Agency	12,623	Malabar	2,652,565
Bombay†	18	38·0 4,292	27·5 842,417	Broach	1,463	Panch Maháls	313,417
				Khándesh	10,907	Khándesh	1,460,851
Sindh	5	32·6 9,558	47·7 574,355	Upper Sindh Frontier.	2,549	Up. Sindh Front.	174,548
				Karáchi	14,182	Haidrabád	918,646
Bengal‡	47	43·1 3,224	38·1 1,508,520	Howrah	476	Chittagong Hills	107,286
				Lohárdaga	7,140	Maimansingh	3,472,186
N.-W. Prov. and Oudh	49	34·5 2,194	31·9 957,247	Tarai	963	Dehra Dún	168,135
				Kumáon	7,151	Gorakhpúr	2,994,057
Panjáb	31	46·3 3,570	30·1 673,124	Simla	102	Simla	44,642
				Kángra	9,574	Siálkôt	1,119,847
Central Provinces	18	38·8 4,806	42·6 599,127	Narsinghpúr	1,916	Nimád	253,486
				Raipúr	11,724	Raipúr	1,584,427
Upper Burma	17	55·3 4,910	52·5 173,349	Kyauk-sé	1,050	Ruby Mines	26,184
				Upper Khyindwin	19,000	Mandalay	374,060
Lower Burma§	18	47·0 4,885	52·4 248,795	North Arakan	1,015	North Arakan	14,628
				Amherst	15,203	Bassein	475,002
Assam	18	24·6 3,769	73·5 421,295	North Kachár	1,728	North Kachár	18,941
				Khási Hills	6,041	Sylhét	2,154,593
Berar	6	10·8 2,953	18·3 482,840	Elichpúr	2,623	Elichpúr	315,798
				Wún	3,911	Amraoti	655,645
Total, Provinces	**249‖**	**3,875**	**880,965**	Simla	102	North Arakan	14,628
				Upper Khyindwin	19,000	Maimansingh	3,472,186

* Including Madras city, and taking the three Agency tracts as distinct units.
† Excluding Bombay city and Aden.
‡ Excluding Calcutta and two suburbs.
§ Excluding Rangoon city.
‖ Including the three districts of Coorg and Ajmére-Mérwára.

The exponential figures above each item represent the percentage of the mean variation from the arithmetical mean of the province as a whole. For example, the average area of a district in Bengal is 3,224 square miles, but owing to the number of districts of considerably greater or less area, there will be found, on the whole, a difference of .43 per cent. between that figure and the area of any single district. On the other hand, in Berár, where the number of districts is small, and they are more uniform in size, the mean difference of the average is less than 11 per cent. Such additions to an average are of use in so far as they indicate whether the mean figure is typical within the province, or, on the contrary, is no more than an arithmetical expression, serving only to compare one province with another. It is clear that the figures in the margin belong to the latter class, for even in Berár we find the area of the smallest district is 2,623 square miles, and that of the largest 3,911. But the more valuable comparison is between the average of one province and that of another, and it is also interesting to set beside these averages the areas and populations of better-known tracts, such as those of an English county. For instance, the average Indian district covers an area just below that of Devon and Cornwall, or the four Home counties, whilst its population is about equal to that of the three northern counties of Northumberland, Cumberland, and Westmoreland, with that of little Huntingdonshire thrown in. Of the provincial averages, and taking into consideration both area and population, it will be seen that the heaviest charge is to be looked for in Madras, where, if the three Agency tracts are considered to be separate units, the district is about the size of Yorkshire, or of the Grand Duchy of Baden, with the population of Nottingham and Durham. If we take the Agency tracts to be part of the district to which they are subordinate, which can fairly be done, we raise the area to nearly that of Wales, minus Anglesea, with a considerably larger population than that of the "gallant little" kingdom. The provincial average that comes nearest to that of the country at large is found in Bombay, which approaches in area the three south-western counties of Somerset, Devon, and Cornwall, with a population that lies between that of Devon and Cornwall, on the one hand, and Somerset and Cornwall on the other. In some cases it appears that the discrepancy between area and population is very large. For example, in Upper Burma, the population of Tyrone is found scattered over four times the area. In the lower section of that province the area is much the same, but the population rises to more than that of Tyrone and Fermanagh together. The same disproportion is observable in Sindh, where, on the area of the four northern English counties, plus the West Riding, there is a population equal only to that of Westmoreland and Northumberland, or within a little of that of New Zealand. The contrary state of things is seen in Bengal and Oudh, where the district is small in size, but contains a very large population. The average Bengal district compares very well in both respects with Norfolk combined with Staffordshire, and one district, we may remark, in passing, contains almost as many people as the Kingdom of Saxony, within far less space. The North-West Provinces, taken with Oudh, as in the table under consideration, show an average of the area of Norfolk, and twice the population; but Oudh alone shows nearly the population of Staffordshire on the area of Northumberland. Half Wales in area, with the population of Glamorgan, about represents the Panjáb district, and that in Berár would just overlap Gloucester and Somerset, but its population is scarcely that of the latter alone. The former furnishes in population a close parallel to a Central Province district, which, however, has nearly four times the area, as is the case with Burma. With this the list closes, and enough has been said to give some notion of the dimensions of the district unit, though there is nothing in the description that serves to delineate the great importance of the position held by this division of territory in the administrative scheme of the British dominions in India. A few words, however, will not be out of place as to the part played by the district in the census operations. In the first place, it is the unit of compilation in the provincial returns, so the tables of specific population in the next chapter and of the movement of the population in that which follows it are all based on the district figure. Still more to the point is the fact that all the details of the arrangements for taking the census and for providing agency for the enumeration and also, in most provinces, for the tabulation of the results were left in the hands of the district officer, acting under the instructions of the Provincial Superintendent of the census operations, so that the accuracy of the work was mainly dependent on the efficiency of his supervision. It was directly from his hands that the preliminary totals were received in the central compilation office for India, at Simla, and as it has been already mentioned that these last were furnished in time for publication five weeks from the date of the census, it is superfluous to add comment on the admirable co-operation and energy that characterised the connection of these officers with so heavy an addition to their current duties.

GEOGRAPHICAL DISTRIBUTION OF THE POLITICAL DIVISIONS OF INDIA.*

* *See* page 17.

GEOGRAPHICAL DISTRIBUTION OF THE

(Complementary to the Table

PROVINCE AND STATE.	Total of Province and States.		A. Himálaya and Eastern Frontier Hills.		B. Northern Plains.				C. Central	
					B. (1) Gangetic System.		B. (2) Indus System.		(1) Eastern Group.	
	Area.	Population.	Area.	Population.	Area.	Population.	Area.	Population.	Area.	Population.
1.	2.	3.	4.	5.	6.	7.	8.	9.	10.	11.
Panjáb and States	148,966	25,130,127	20,615	1,645,364	21,346	5,642,878	107,005	17,841,885	—	—
Kashmér -	80,900	2,543,952	80,900	2,543,952	—	—	—	—	—	—
N.-W. Provinces, States, and Oudh.	112,612	47,697,576	18,137	1,380,376	94,475	46,317,200	—	—	—	—
Bengal and States -	187,377	74,643,366	10,669	468,042	109,448	62,919,111	—	—	59,088	7,378,819
Assam -	49,004	5,476,833	20,249	504,916	28,755	4,971,917	—	—	—	—
Central Provinces and States.	115,936	12,944,805	—	—	—	—	—	—	47,171	3,564,785
Central India	77,808	10,318,812	—	—	—	—	—	—	14,000	1,733,581
Ajmér-Merwára -	2,711	542,358	—	—	2,711	542,358	—	—	—	—
Rajputána	130,268	12,016,102	—	—	34,531	6,233,841	78,540	3,658,360	—	—
Bombay and States	133,711	23,354,216	—	—	—	—	—	—	—	—
Baroda -	8,226	2,415,396	—	—	—	—	—	—	—	—
Sindh, Khairpur and Kachh.	60,398	3,562,126	—	—		—	60,398	3,562,126	—	—
Berár - -	17,718	2,897,491	—	—	—	—	—	—	—	—
Hyderabád - -	82,698	11,537,040	—	—	—		—	—	—	—
Mysore	27,936	4,943,604	—	—	—	—	—	—		—
Coorg	1,583	173,055	—	—	—	—	—	—	—	—
Madras and States	150,798	39,331,062	—	—	—	—	—	—	19,167	1,294,244
Burma -	171,430	7,605,560	—	—	—	—	—	—	—	—
Detached Settlements	80	89,950	—	—	—	—	—	—	—	—
Total India -	**1,560,160**	**287,223,431**	**150,570**	**6,542,650**	**291,266**	**126,627,305**	**245,943**	**25,062,371**	**139,426**	**13,971,529**

POLITICAL DIVISIONS OF INDIA.

given on page 11.)

Hills.											
(2) Western Group.		D. Central Plain.		E. Deccan Plateau.		F. Southern Plain.		G. North-East Littoral.		H. West Littoral.	
Area.	Population.	Area.	Population.	Area.	Population.	Area.	Population.	Area.	Population.	Area.	Population.
12.	13.	14.	15.	16.	17.	18.	19.	20.	21.	22.	23.
—	—	—	—	—	—	—	—	—	—	—	—
—	—	—	—	—	—	—	—	—	—	—	—
—	—	—	—	—	—	—	—	—	—	—	
—	—	—	—	—	—	—	—	8,172	3,877,294	—	
—	—	—	—	—	—	—	—	—	—	—	
—	—	68,765	9,380,020	—	—	—	—	—	—	—	—
63,808	8,585,231	—	—	—	—	—	—	—	—	—	—
—	—	—	—	—	—	—	—	—	—	—	—
17,197	2,123,901	—	—	—	—	—	—	—	—	—	—
—	—	10,907	1,460,851	52,028	9,649,864	—	—	—	—	70,776	12,243,501
—	—	—	—	—	—	—	—	—	—	8,226	2,415,396
—	—	—	—	—	—	—	—	—	—	—	—
—	—	17,718	2,897,491	—	—	—	—	—	—	—	—
—	—	—	—	82,698	11,537,040	—	—	—	—	—	—
—	—	—	—	27,936	4,943,604	—	—	—	—	—	—
—	—	—	—	1,583	173,055	—	—	—	—	—	—
—	—	—	—	28,859	3,845,239	62,494	19,862,376	22,699	7,339,915	17,579	6,989,288
—	—	—	—	—	—	—	—	—	—	—	—
—	—	—	—	—	—	—	—	—	—	—	—
81,005	**10,709,132**	**97,390**	**13,738,362**	**193,104**	**30,148,802**	**62,494**	**19,862,376**	**30,871**	**11,217,209**	**96,581**	**21,648,185**

CHAPTER II.

Distribution of the Population.

. . . . . λαοὶ δ' ἔργα περιστέλλουσιν ἕκηλοι.
Οὐ γάρ τις δηΐων πολυκήτεα (Νεῖλον) ἐπεμβὰς,
Πεζὸς ἐν ἀλλοτρίαισι βοὰν ἐστάσατο κώμαις.—*Theokritus.*

The population of India, which was roughly set forth in the statements incorporated in the last chapter, has now to be considered in its relation to the land, and again, with reference to its social distribution, into rural and urban communities. As regards the former, the average number of persons to some conventional unit of area, such as the square mile, affords the best means of comparing one country or tract with another, with respect to the general distribution of its inhabitants. But we must discriminate between the density, as this ratio is called, and the pressure of the population. A low specific population may imply pressure, as much as a high one, and, conversely, great density is not incompatible with a high standard of comfort. We need not look beyond India to find two tracts with an equally small number of inhabitants per mile, in one of which the sparsity is due to some physical cause, and may thus be considered more or less permanent; whereas in the other political uncertainty alone has impeded the exploitation of what is by nature capable of supporting eight or nine times the existing population. Again, we see people crowded to a degree that in a rural community is almost incredible, but proving by their continued multiplication that the margin of subsistence has not yet been reached, whilst in other tracts, about the same specific population is only maintained by the habitual importation of food supplies from outside. These last are, however, very rare in India, where the bulk of the population is engaged in the production of food, and the preponderance of mining and manufacturing industries that is found in England, Saxony, and parts of Belgium, is unknown. The most densely peopled tracts of rural India are, as a rule, no worse off than the denizen of happy Auburn, for whom

> "Light labour spread her wholesome store;
> Just gave what life required, but gave no more."

But there is no doubt that the region of periodic rainfall is not the place for the experiment of how fine the provision of nature can be run, and apart from the tracts mentioned above, which are habitually not self-supporting, there are others in which the return from land is so near the economic limit that little more than the year's supply of food is to be expected from it. If, then, they fall within the zones of uncertain rain, described in the introductory chapter, a large number of people have to resort to the market as purchasers, and though the greatly increased facilities for transport have tended to equalise prices, there is no doubt that the normal rates have been raised throughout the country, and the agriculturist has to face the change from another point of view than that which he occupies in a good year.

But even in the parts of India thus unfavourably situated the amount of capital put by is remarkable. As in the days of Bernier, it is chiefly in the form of gold and silver ornaments; but these are now more apparent than when he wrote, irrespective of the relative amount, for it was then the object of every man to conceal the fact that he was other than a pauper, whereas now-a-days, the pendulum has swung to the other extreme, and the police courts show too frequently the temptations put before the criminal classes by the display of ornaments of value on the person of women and children when on journeys and in other comparatively unprotected situations. This form of wealth is generally kept in the family. and it takes quite exceptional circumstances to bring it into the market. A striking instance of this was afforded during the hard times of 1876–78 in southern and western India. In the early years of that decade, barring a short period in 1871, the average monthly value of the ornaments sent to the Bombay Mint was only Rs. 6,000. A rise took place at the end of 1876, and continued till it reached Rs. 1,900,000 in September 1877. With the return of good times to the south the amount decreased, but in 1878 the scarcity in some of the Native States in Gujaráth raised it again to about Rs. 700,000 till the end of the year. The rarity of these manifestations of distress indicates that the landed class generally raises crop enough to cover what may be termed normal fluctuations. There is also to be borne in mind the fact that the system of village finance adapts itself very fairly to the circumstances with which it has to deal, and often helps the raiat to tide over a crisis.

General density.

In the first statement given in the introduction there is a column showing the mean number of persons per square mile in each of the chief physical divisions. It was inserted in anticipation of the present explanations, in order to give some general notion of the different circumstances, in this respect, of the various parts of the country. For the whole of India the ratio is 184 persons. But, as has been already put forward, the mean of so many and diverse component parts is of little or no value except as a standard by which the difference of the said parts from each other can be judged. We may compare, for example, the above figure with the corresponding ratio in the case of France, which is 188; but the area of France is but about 204,000 square miles, against the 1,560,000 of India, and the population of the former is less than that of the Indian province which stands only third in this respect. To go no further than the general statement just quoted, it will be seen that this mean of 184 is exceeded in only 31 per cent. of the area, and that it is not reached, therefore, in the remaining 69. But the above 31 per cent. contains no less than 62 per cent. of the population, and when the distribution is made in smaller divisions, a rather higher proportion will be found in this category. For instance, in Statement A. below, which is compiled by districts and States, to the exclusion of the four cities coming under separate heads in the returns, the population in higher ratio of density than the average is given as nearly 67 per cent.

A.—SPECIFIC POPULATION OF INDIA.—*British and Feudatory.*

	Percentage of Variation from the mean density (184).	Area in Square Miles.	Population (1891).	Mean Density of each Group.	Percentage of each Group on total of Area.	Percentage of each Group on total of Population.
Below mean.	75 and over	329,650	8,246,950	25	21·13	2·89
	66	50,604	2,661,892	53	3·24	0·94
	50	183,277	13,644,080	74	11·75	4·79
	33	134,918	14,692,599	109	8·65	5·16
	20	248,392	33,728,984	135	15·92	11·85
	10	92,654	14,580,524	157	5·94	5·12
	1	37,934	6,532,666	172	2·43	2·29
	Total below Mean	**1,077,429**	**94,087,695**	**87**	**69·06**	**33·04**
Above mean.	1	50,406	9,631,878	191	3·23	3·38
	10	22,631	4,852,632	214	1·45	1·70
	20	57,682	13,179,523	229	3·70	4·63
	33	47,320	12,300,679	259	3·03	4·32
	50	36,956	10,737,381	290	2·37	3·77
	66	8,028	2,557,190	318	0·52	0·90
	75	23,195	8,058,854	347	1·49	2·83
	100	71,861	29,435,947	410	4·61	10·34
	150	80,022	40,714,414	509	5·13	14·30
	200 and over	84,430	59,217,349	701	5·41	20·79
	Total above Mean	**482,531**	**190,685,847**	**395**	**30·94**	**66·96**
	Grand Total	**1,559,960**	**284,773,542**	**184**	—	—

This statement is based on percentages of the mean density. The first item, therefore, represents a density per square mile less than the mean figure by 75 per cent. or more, whilst the last line but two gives the figures of area and population exceeding the mean by more than 200 per cent. The table speaks for itself, but there are a few curious coincidences in it which are worth notice. The largest item of area, for example, is equivalent, proportionally, to the largest item of population at the opposite end of the table; and, again, the proportion of population in the former group is almost exactly the same as that in the corresponding group above the mean. Then the ratios to the total of area and population respectively very nearly coincide in the groups within 20 per cent. of the mean on both sides, whilst the divergence is, of course, widest at the ends of the scale, in both directions. There is, however, a defect in this statement which must receive mention, as it affects the regularity of the distribution between the groups in the lower densities. It is due to the fact that in the case of Kashmér and Central India there are no measurements available of the subdivisions by which the returns of the census results have been compiled. Kashmér is said to contain an area of 80,900 miles in the aggregate, but it is well known that the density is much higher in the valley and the Wazirats of Jammu than it is in the highlands of Ladákh, Báltistán, or Ghilgit. By having to enter

B.—Specific Population of British India.*

	Percentage of Variation from the mean density (230).	Number of Districts.†	Area in Square Miles.	Population (1891).	Mean Density of each Group.	Percentage of each Group on total of	
						Area.	Population.
Below mean.	75 and over	28	182,740	4,378,416	24	18·45	2·00
	66	14	67,305	4,725,612	70	6·98	2·16
	50	22	105,858	10,127,884	96	10·97	4·63
	33	29	130,033	17,646,587	136	13·48	8·06
	20	15	75,657	12,586,357	166	7·84	5·75
	10 - -	10	28,834	5,649,449	196	2·99	2·58
	1 -	10	42,937	9,623,352	224	4·45	4·40
	Total below Mean -	**128**	**633,364**	**64,737,657**	**102**	**65·65**	**29·58**
Below mean.	1 - - -	7	21,096	5,190,662	236	2·28	2·37
	10 -	6	30,500	8,008,238	262	3·16	3·66
	20	8	36,020	10,454,625	290	3·73	4·77
	33 -	3	9,250	3,013,600	326	0·96	1·37
	50 -	8	24,466	9,069,745	371	2·53	4·14
	66 -	4	14,911	5,886,168	395	1·55	2·69
	75	15	32,927	14,300,585	434	3·41	6·53
	100	32	85,750	44,044,392	514	8·89	20·12
	150	17	41,333	25,507,620	617	4·28	11·65
	200 and over	18	34,302	28,730,151	838	3·56	13·12
	Total above Mean	**118**	**331,455**	**154,005,786**	**464**	**34·35**	**70·42**
	Grand Total -	**246***	**964,819**	**218,943,343**	**230**	—	—

* Excluding four seaport towns and the detached settlements, comprising 113 square miles and 2,229,509 inhabitants.
† In Madras the three Agency tracts are included in their parent district respectively, thus reducing the total number of districts to this extent.

the whole area under its general density of only 31 to the mile, the lowest group in the return is overweighted to a considerable extent. The case is the same with the group showing a density of between 20 and 33 per cent. below the mean, because in it is included the whole of the Central India Agency, in which there are several subordinate political divisions each known to present a different density, but the areas are not accurately distinguished.

British territory. Table A. can now be left, and consideration given to that on the opposite page, marked B., which relates to British territory alone. Here we are dealing with district units, so the data are on a uniform basis. In the introduction it was explained that the States included most of the more thinly populated tracts of the country, so it is not surprising that their average density in the aggregate should be no more than 111, whilst in the British provinces it is 230. In Table B., therefore, the mean taken is this last figure, but in other respects the statement is framed just in the same way as the other. As regards the distribution of the population and area, it will be seen that the proportion of the former below the mean is just below two-thirds instead of 69 per cent., whilst that of the population is also slightly less. It is worth note, too, that about 45 per cent. of the population is massed in a density of 460 and over, which is double the mean ratio of the British territory, as a whole. In Europe we find three countries with a density of 500 per mile and over; England and Wales, with 500, Belgium with 540, and Saxony with nearly 600. The aggregate population of these three is about 38½ millions. In British India there are 37½ millions of the inhabitants living in the ratio of more than one per acre, or 784, on the average, to the mile. No less than 21½ millions are packed to the extent of 877. The whole of the 37½ millions in question are to be found in the Gangetic valley and the Delta, and with the exception of 2½ millions, which may be called suburban, live, in the main, by cultivation of the soil. It will be necessary to revert to these tracts in the next chapter, when the increase or decrease of the population is in question. If we refer to the other end of the statement, we find over 182,000 square miles with an average population of 24 each. The greater part of this group falls within Upper Burma, the hill tracts of Assam, and the desert portion of Sindh. With regard to the general distribution shown in the rest of the table, it will suffice to note, first, how very small a proportion of either area or population lies within 10 per cent. of the general mean, whether we take it above or below that figure. This fact bears out in a striking manner the statement made above, that the latter cannot be used in discussing the census results as typical of the country, but only as a means of measuring divergencies in various parts of it. Again, as to the composition of the larger groups below the mean, it is worth mentioning that nearly half the Central Provinces and Berar falls within the group averaging a density of 136 per mile. To the next group, with 166, the northern districts of the Madras Presidency, and the Bengal portion of the Central Belt, separating the Ganges basin from that of the Mahánadi, are the chief contributors. The groups just noted above as lying immediately round the mean, with an average density of 224 and 236 respectively, include the remaining districts of the North Coromandel coast, and a considerable portion of Bombay. Then, crossing the line, we come to the districts of the southern plain and of parts of the Panjab. Passing over the next few groups, which are formed out of a few tracts from several provinces, we come to that of which the mean density is 434 per mile, or nearly double the general average. The bulk of this is contributed by the west-central tract of the North-Western Provinces, with the aid of a few sub-montane districts of the Panjab, and of the less thickly peopled tracts of Bengal. When we reach the higher specific rates, we find only a single district of Bombay, a couple of Madras, and five of the Panjab, standing out amidst the enormous masses of the Gangetic valley. Before entering further into the details of the provincial distribution of the population according to density, it will be interesting to deal with the subject in its more general form, in connection, that is, with the distribution of both area and population according to rainfall.

Density compared with rainfall. For this purpose, Table C. is appended. It includes the whole of India, British and Feudatory, for which rainfall returns are available to a trustworthy extent. For reasons already given in the introduction, those for Lower Burma are too partial for use, and it would be misleading to enter the whole of such widely spread tracts as Central India and Kashmér without splitting them up according to the known variety of their conditions as to humidity. The detached Settlements, again, are too small to be taken into consideration, even if full information respecting them were at hand. The omissions, being mostly those of sparsely populated country, have raised the general average of density to nearly the mean between that of India, as a whole, and that of British territory alone, as given in the two preceding tables.

C.—Mean Rainfall of India.

	Percentage of Variation from the mean Rainfall (42").	Area in Square Miles.	Population (1891).	Mean Density.	Percentage of each Group on total of Area.	Percentage of each Group on total of Population.	Mean Rainfall in inches.
Below Mean.	75 and over	123,394	6,708,577	54	9·40	2·49	7
	66	66,826	4,429,726	66	5·09	1·64	13
	50	35,708	5,658,222	158	2·72	2·10	17
	33	165,366	28,262,697	171	12·59	10·48	25
	20	184,867	36,780,747	199	14·07	13·62	30
	10	89,824	22,171,842	247	6·84	8·22	35
	1	142,898	38,102,505	267	10·88	14·12	41
	Total below the Mean	**808,883**	**142,114,316**	**176**	**61·59**	**52·67**	**26**
Above Mean.	1	85,016	25,878,282	304	6·47	9·59	46
	10	72,810	22,607,267	310	5·54	8·38	49
	20	79,970	12,832,274	160	6·08	4·76	53
	33	81,003	18,290,630	226	6·17	6·78	60
	50	44,196	12,877,074	291	2·37	4·78	68
	66	2,797	2,420,656	865	0·21	0·90	73
	75	42,125	6,590,947	156	3·21	2·44	77
	100	42,444	10,584,251	249	3·23	3·92	91
	150	39,001	10,963,712	281	2·97	4·06	115
	200 and over	15,168	4,643,949	306	1·16	1·72	140
	Total above the Mean	**504,530**	**127,689,042**	**253**	**38·41**	**47·33**	**66**
	Total	**1,313,413***	**269,803,358***	**205***	—	—	**42***

* Excluding Kashmer, Central India, Lower Burma, and the detached Settlements.

Composition of rainfall-groups. The first point to note is the large proportion of the population found in tracts with less than the mean rainfall. In connection with this there should be borne in mind what was said before, as to the relative position of some tracts with regard to the certainty of their seasons, irrespective of the amount of rain actually received. For example, in the largest group in point of population, that having an average of 41 inches of rain, we find the Hill States of Western Bengal, the submontane tracts of the North-West Provinces, parts of Oudh and Bihar, and the northern portion of the west coast, all of which enjoy comparative certainty of seasons, mixed up with others that are far less fortunate, such as parts of Haidrabad and Madras, in the Deccan, and the outskirts of the uncertain zone in the Ganges valley. On the other hand, its neighbour, just above the average, which is not nearly so populous, may be said to lie almost entirely within the lucky line of the rainfall, and contains much of the hilly tract in the Central Provinces and the eastern portions of the submontane tract of the North-West, with a good deal of the best parts of Oudh. Going back to the rainfall of about 30 inches, where the largest area in any single group is to be found, we may see that the few entries from the Panjab, Berar, and Bombay are outweighed by the number from the Deccan and the worst portions of the North-west Provinces. The most ill-situated tracts of the Deccan, however, are found in the two groups preceding this one. The groups of lowest rainfall, those with no more than 7 inches and 13 inches respectively, we find situated in a part of the country where the aid of rain is, as a rule, discounted by the extension of irrigation from rivers fed by Himalayan glaciers, or from deep wells, or, again, by watercourses led down from hill streams.

Relation between rainfall and density. A second matter to be noted in connection with this table is the sudden break in the series of increasing densities of population which occurs where the rainfall advances from 49 inches to 53. Below this, in the series, there is a continual, though irregular, rise in density from the lowest group, but the same feature does not occur again until within the three last. The explanation of the break, in the first instance, is that the group in question begins to touch the hill country of the Central Belt at its eastern extremity, where the fall of rain is comparatively heavy, but the arable area is scattered amongst forests, so that in no parts is it possible for large congregations of people to find sustenance. In the next group, the remainder of this tract has its lowering effect on the average outweighed by the inclusion of the less rainy portions of

Bengal, where the density is far greater. In the next few classes the last-mentioned province is mixed with the thinly populated Assam, and the coast tracts of Bombay, where they are least fertile, have also to be taken into account. The Malabar States and districts raise the density again in the last but one of the groups, whilst that of the highest rainfall comprises several of the Bengal submontane districts, the most populous district of Assam, and one of the corresponding class in Western Madras. Had the figures for Lower Burma been included, the group-density would have fallen to 88 per mile, instead of being 306, but the average rainfall would have risen to 170, a result which, as has been already stated, is not in accordance with the circumstances of more than the littoral portions of the tract.

The population has been considered hitherto in its distribution over the country as a whole, or at least in its two great political divisions of British and Feudatory. It has now to be treated in the greater detail of Province or State. The diversity of the distribution, even in these smaller units, has been indicated in the remarks made above in explanation of the general statements, and is illustrated in a still more striking manner in Statement D., given below, by the addition of exponential figures to the density of all provinces that contain a considerable number of districts. It has already been explained that in the case of States, or groups of States, such additions are useless.

D.—Specific Population of Provinces and States.

Province or State, &c.	Mean Density per Square Mile.	Extreme Density.			
		Highest.		Lowest.	
		Name.	Density.	Name.	Density.
Ajmér	200	Ajmér	203	Mérwára	187
Assam	$112^{68\cdot45}$	Silhét	397	Kachár Hills	11
Bengal	$471^{43\cdot99}$	Sáran	930*	Chittagong Hills	20
Berár	$163^{25\cdot80}$	Amráoti	238	Elichpúr	120
{ Bombay	$207^{35\cdot71}$	Kaira	542	Kanara	114
{ Sindh	$60^{48\cdot33}$	Haidrabád	102	Thar and Párkar	23
{ Upper Burma	$35^{117\cdot14}$	Mandalay	178	Upper Khyndwin	4
{ Lower Burma	$53^{92\cdot15}$	Thárawáddi	172	Sálwin	7
Central Provinces	$125^{29\cdot60}$	Nágpúr	197	Chánda	65
Coorg	109	——	—	——	—
Madras	$252^{49\cdot01}$	Tanjore	601	Godávari Agency	42
{ N.-W. Provinces	$411^{42\cdot09}$	Benares	914	Garhwál	72
{ Oudh	$522^{21\cdot68}$	Lucknow	800	Khéri	305
Panjáb	$188^{79\cdot78}$	Jálandhar	633	Dehra Ismail Khán	51
Total, British	**$230^{55\cdot65}$**	**Sáran**	**930***	**Upper Khyndwin**	**4**
Haidrabád	139	Bidar	216	Sirpúr Tandúr	46
Baroda	294	Baroda	438	Amréli	151
Mysore	177	Bangalore	314	Chitaldúrg	104
Kashmér	31	Ranbir Singhpúra	—	Ladákh	—
Rajputána	92	Bharatpúr	327	Jesalmér	7
Central India	133	*Baghélkhand*†	158	*Búndélkhand*	72
Bombay States	126	Kolhápúr	334	Súrgána	34
Khairpur (Sindh)	22	——	—	——	—
Madras States	385	Cochin	531	Sandúr	71
Central Province States	73	Chhuikadán	235	Bastar	24
Bengal States	92	Kôch Bihár	443	Hill Tippera	33
N.-W. Province States	155	Rámpúr	588	Tehri-Garhwál	58
Panjáb States	111	Kapúrthala	501	Bashahr	23
Total, States	**$111^{60\cdot81}$**	——	—	——	—

* Excluding the suburban district of Howrah. † The Central India return is approximate only.

In the above table, the density, taken item by item, appears to vary little more in the Feudatory than in the British territory, and in both, the extremes of crowding and sparsity of population are found very far apart. As the Provinces can be advantageously treated in greater detail, it will be convenient to deal with the States first. To begin with, the larger ones, Haidrabad, Baroda, and Mysore, are all subdivided into something corresponding to the district in British territory, so the distribution can be fairly appreciated.

Haidrabad. The first-named shows the highest density in the portion adjoining the uncertain zone of the Deccan, but as it lies more to the east, it gets the benefit of some of the autumnal rains. The lowest density is found in the north-east corner, at the edge of the southern extension of the Central Belt of hills, where it bounds the Central Provinces. In the rest of the State the density is fairly uniform.

Baroda. Baroda has the densest population of the larger States, if we except the two that round off the Malabar coast, but, as the table shows, there is considerable variety in the distribution. The greater portion of the State lies embedded in the British division of Gujaráth, the most densely peopled tract in the Bombay Presidency. In the east of the State there is a large forest area, which reduces the general average, whilst a portion of the State lies in the peninsula of Kathiawar, and is here shown as containing, relatively, the lightest population.

Mysore. In Mysore we find the heavier densities are in the south part of the State, round about the two large towns. The north-eastern tract, showing the lowest, borders on one of the least favoured districts of the Madras Presidency, Belári, and shares the physical characteristics of the latter. **Kasmér.** In dealing with Kashmér, nothing more can be said at present beyond mentioning the tracts which are reported to contain the heaviest and the lightest densities respectively. Probably the population of the portion of the valley lying immediately round the chief city, Shrinagar, is relatively as heavy as that entered in the statement, and, on the other hand, the Ghilgit region is as lightly peopled as the eastern table-lands.

Rajputána. Rajputána contains at least three well-defined regions, with very different specific populations. In the east, where the States touch the Gangetic provinces, the density is over 300 per mile in one State, and over 200 in the two adjoining it. Central Rajputána, which is combined with the eastern part in some of the returns, varies between a density of 184 in the largest State, Jaipur, and of 113 in Jhalawar, where the country trends upwards from the plains to the plateau of Central India. The southern portion is different, again, in the direction of less dense population. The only large State in this division is Mewar, or Udaipur, the premier Rajput State in India, which has a density of 145. Its neighbours are mostly small offshoots of families of chieftains who have been more fortunate in their settlements, so that the younger branches have to content themselves with the allegiance of the hill tribes of this portion of the Central Belt, who number little more than 100 per mile. Lastly, we find the sandy plains of the west. The leading State of this tract is Márwár, or Jodhpur, with its 67 inhabitants to the mile, flourishing under 13 inches of uncertain rain. Bikanér, its neighbour to the north, receives an inch less, and supports but 36 to the mile. To conclude, comes Jesalmér, with 7 inches of rain, 16,000 square miles of territory, and but seven inhabitants per mile. Yet this western region, desert, we may call it, not only breeds the finest camels in India, which might be expected of it, but sends forth to every important market in the country the keenest and the most frugal set of traders that ever drove a bargain. It is probably the large fortunes that are made by these men, and the *animus revertendi* almost invaribly maintained by them during their term of spoiling the Egyptians, that have kept up the general well-being of this tract, and the undoubted wealth of the three or four large towns that it contains.*

Central India. Passing south, to Central India, we find an increased density, on the whole, but the details of the different parts of this large agency cannot be relied on, so far as areas are concerned. The States are rarely compact, but consist of many scattered patches of territory, one within the other. But within broad lines, the two selected for the table may be considered approximately correct. The parts of Rewa that border the Ganges valley contain a population grouped in considerable density, whilst the rest of the State consists of hilly country of much the same class as that in the Búndélkhand

* There is also the tradition of safety, as these tracts have been generally avoided by Muselman, Marátha, and other marauders, owing to the absence of supplies for any considerable force, and the warlike repute of the local chieftains.

charge, where the density is probably the lowest in Central India, save, perhaps, that in a few small tracts in the extreme west, amongst the Vindhya hills.

The States in political connection with the Bombay Presidency are, for the most part, small, like those under the general title of Central India. But, unlike the latter, their territory is mostly compact and does not intermingle to any considerable extent. For the present purpose, the densities have been calculated according to the groups under distinct Agencies, as many of the States are too small to require individual recognition in the returns. The relic of the Tálpur dynasty in Sindh, found in Khairpur, has been separated from the rest, and shows a specific population even less than that of its neighbour, Baháwalpúr, across the frontier of the Panjab. Throughout the Presidency proper, the density of the Feudatory territory is greater. The lowest is in the forest States, where the Sátpuras and Ghats subside into the plain bordering on the coast. Further north, in Gujaráth, there are wide expanses of light sandy soil, as in Kachh and Pálanpur, and hilly country, such as is found in most parts of the groups along the Réwa (Narmada), and the Mahi rivers, and in the Surat Agency and its neighbours. The population thickens along the coast, falls in the Deccan, and attains its greatest density in the South Deccan, or Bombay Karnátak, of which Kolhapur is the leading State, with 324 persons to the mile. Bombay States.

The States in connection with the Madras Presidency are but five in number, and of these two are very small. They are both situated within the zone of uncertain rainfall, and have a population of but 71 and 139 per mile respectively. On the Malabar coast, the circumstances are more favourable to life, and Cochin comes high up in the scale of density. Its larger neighbour, Travancore, though returning but 380 to the mile, is really more densely populated, since behind the lowlands along the coast there is a considerable extent of hill country almost uninhabited. Madras States.

The States connected with the Central Provinces are, in most cases, little more than private estates, to which has been given the status of political units within comparatively recent times. Of those in the extreme east of the province, the leading State of years gone by is still the most populous, though the relative incidence is smaller than that found in some of the others, which have profited by the opening out of the neighbouring tracts by roads and rail. The largest State, Bastar, consists chiefly of hill and forest, with so widespread a reputation for fever and bad water that it has been left to the dark tribes, to whom alone such tracts are congenial. A few States in the centre of the province, which include within their limits a little of the plains, show a higher density, reaching in parts to 200 persons per mile and over, but for the most part, the dominion of these chiefs lies in the hill and forest, where population is necessarily sparse. Central Province States.

The circumstances of the Orissa States, of which there are 17 in political connection with the Government of Bengal, are almost the same as those of the eastern States under the Central Provinces, and show a density of 118 per mile, varying between 43 and 447, though the last figure is reached in a minute estate of little over 40 square miles in extent. The Chútia Nagpur States, which spread to the northwestwards of the last group, are still more thinly peopled, and show an average of only 55 to the mile. All of these are more or less within the domain of the dark tribes, whose mode of life, with its system of exploiting the soil, is exactly that of the "rigidi Getæ" of Horace :— Bengal States.

> "Immetata quibus jugera liberas
> Fruges et cererem ferunt ;
> Nec cultura placet longior annuâ."

A similar state of things will be found in the small State of Hill Tippera, between Bengal and Burma. If anything, it is worse here, because, owing to the universal habit of cultivating by the primitive mode of clearing a plot of forest and burning the timber and brushwood off it as manure for the one year's crop, the local resources are soon exhausted, and if virgin soil is not at hand the population has to flit a few miles to places where the forest has had 8 or 10 years rest. Thus there is little in the shape of a permanent village in the State, the only place of this character being the residence of the Chief. Lastly, we have the State of Kôch Bihár, on the Assam frontier, where the land has long been more or less brought under cultivation. Here, the density of the population has risen to 443 per mile, which is within about 20 per cent. of that of the adjacent British territory, and much above that of the eastern frontier, which divides it from its parent region, Assam.

There are only two States politically in connection with the North-West Province Government, and these two are widely separated as regards population, as can be seen N.-W. Province States.

from the table under consideration. Rámpur is embedded in Rohilkhand, and the Chief is one of the tribe or tribes from which that tract takes its name. The other State lies in the Himálaya, and is little but a succession of hills and dales, from the outer slopes to the highest peaks of the group in which the Ganges and Jamna have their sources. In the one the density is that of the surrounding portions of the rich Ganges valley, in the other no more than 58 per mile.

Panjáb States.

The States connected with the Panjáb Government may be divided into four main groups. First, those in the eastern plains, which appertain to the Gangetic system. Here the density is about 263 per mile, rising in Nábha to just over 300. This is the area formerly known in history as the Cis-Satlaj Protected Sikh States. Then come the States of the submontane tract, the most densely peopled of the whole body, though with a total population of less than one-third that of Patiala, the largest of the group just mentioned. There is one State, large in area, in the western plain, bordering on Sindh and the Rajputána Desert. Baháwalpur is a little larger than Jesalmér, one of its neighbours, but contains nearly six times the population. Even then its density is but 38. Last of all come the Hill group of States. Most of these lie amongst the lower ranges of the Himálaya, but two run up to the central mass of these mountains. In these last we find, of course, the lowest densities, as so much of their territory is little more than mere rock and snow. The population of Bashahr, for instance, is but 23 per mile; in Chamba, too, it only reaches 40, and for the whole group, the average is 77.

Comparative densities of British Provinces.

On looking at the Return B. for British provinces, to which attention is now to be directed, we find a maximum divergence of more than 700 per mile from the average, for in the Upper Khyndwin district of Burma, which, however, has not been completely surveyed, there seem to be only four inhabitants to the square mile, whilst in Sáran, a district in the Bihar division of Bengal, there are 930. It is not easy to find corresponding densities to those of many of these provinces amongst the countries of Europe, but the few that are fairly comparable are as follows. In the Panjáb the specific population is about that of France. Madras compares well with Italy, and Bombay with Austria. Hungary represents the Central Provinces. Berar comes nearest to Denmark, and Assam to Servia. The heaviest density of a province, as a whole, is found in Oudh, where it is about 20 persons per mile below that of Belgium, the second in rank in this respect of the European countries. After this we must look to fractions or multiples for our analogies. Sindh, for instance, shows double the density of Sweden, and Bengal exceeds in like proportion the density of the German Empire. In Burma, as a whole, there are about half as many people per mile as in Spain, and so on.

Use of the *weighted* mean.

But the exponential figures in the second column of the statement, taken with the extremes given in the succeeding part of that table, show how little uniformity there is in the density of the various parts, even of the same province. There is none in the list where the average divergence is less than one-fifth. Oudh comes first in this respect, then Berar, which has but six units to consider. The Central Provinces run it close, however, in spite of the great divergence of the extremes. But when we come to the Panjáb and Assam, still more to Burma, it is plain than the mean is no more than an arithmetical expression, of use only for comparison of the whole province with its neighbours. The distribution, therefore, of each province, by districts, on the same lines as have been adopted in Table B. above, is shown in Statement E. on the opposite page. In consideration, moreover, of the variety of the larger provinces in point of density and rainfall, the natural groups into which each province falls will be found specified marginally, as the province comes under review below. The reader should also note that in this review the density, and not the pressure, of the population on the land is in question.

The smaller Provinces.

It is convenient to take the less densely populated provinces first in order, especially as several of them are not subdivided. Coorg, for instance, is shown in one item in the tables, so is excluded from Statement E. The greater portion of this little tract consists of forest and hill, with clearings for cultivation interspersed. Much of the population, too, is migratory, and only inhabits Coorg during the season when the coffee and other plantations offer special attractions to field labour. Lying along the ghâts, Coorg enjoys a heavy and fairly certain rainfall, and bears with ease its light population. Ajmér, again, consists of only two divisions, Mérwára, and that which gives its name to the tract. The latter is traversed by two lines of rail, and contains two towns of considerable population, to which some of its density is due,

E.—Provincial Density Groups.

ASSAM.

	Density per Square Mile.	No. of Districts.	Area.	Population, 1891.
Below Mean.	57 and below	5	20,249	504,916
	58–75	1	3,724	254,053
	76–114	3	10,630	1,104,206
	115–152	1	2,472	367,542
	153–183	2	6,515	1,091,523
	184–206	—	—	—
	207–229	—	—	—
Above Mean.	230–253	—	—	—
	254–276	—	—	—
	277–307	—	—	—
	308–345	—	—	—
	346–384	—	—	—
	385–402	1	5,414	2,154,593
	403–460	—	—	—
	461–575	—	—	—
	576–690	—	—	—
	691 and over	—	—	—
	Total	**13**	**49,004**	**5,476,833**

PANJÁB.

	Density per Square Mile.	No. of Districts.	Area.	Population, 1891.
Below Mean.	57 and below	1	9,440	486,201
	58–75	3	14,248	1,044,047
	76–114	6	33,516	3,140,944
	115–152	2	9,158	1,385,062
	153–183	2	7,835	1,403,482
	184–206	1	4,302	886,676
	207–229	1	3,017	690,169
Above Mean.	230–253	—	—	—
	254–276	—	—	
	277–307	3	8,562	2,462,865
	308–345	2	3,781	1,259,404
	346–384	2	4,805	1,794,302
	385–402	—	—	—
	403–460	3	3,799	1,705,023
	461–575	3	5,170	2,702,458
	576–690	2	3,034	1,900,280
	691 and over	—	—	—
	Total	**31**	**110,667**	**20,860,913**
	Baloch tribes	—	—	5,934

BOMBAY.

	Density per Square Mile.	No. of Districts.	Area.	Population, 1891.
Below Mean.	57 and below	—	—	—
	58–75	—	—	—
	76–114	1	3,910	446,351
	115–152	4	29,160	3,989,527
	153–183	1	4,542	750,689
	184–206	2	6,982	1,381,217
	207–229	2	9,260	2,064,575
Above Mean.	230–253	4	14,334	3,894,059
	254–276	1	1,872	509,584
	277–307	1	3,922	1,105,926
	308–345	—	—	—
	346–384	—	—	—
	385–402	1	1,662	649,989
	403–460	—	—	—
	461–575	1	1,609	871,589
	576–690	—	—	—
	691 and over	—	—	—
	Total	**18**	**77,253**	**15,163,506**
	Bombay City	—	22	821,764

MADRAS.

	Density per Square Mile.	No. of Districts.	Area.	Population, 1891.
Below Mean.	57 and below	—	—	—
	58–75	—	—	—
	76–114	2	8,471	917,608
	115–152	3	19,972	2,880,747
	153–183	2	26,007	4,266,728
	184–206	—	—	—
	207–229	2	16,767	3,752,385
Above Mean.	230–253	—	—	—
	254–276	4	27,148	7,102,293
	277–307	2	16,424	4,788,891
	308–345	—	—	—
	346–384	2	9,018	3,288,812
	385–402	1	2,842	1,136,926
	403–460	1	5,217	2,162,851
	461–575	1	5,585	2,652,565
	576–690	1	3,709	2,228,114
	691 and over	—	—	—
	Total	**21***	**141,160**	**35,177,922**
	Madras City	—	29	452,518

* The three Agency tracts are included in their parent districts.

E.—Provincial Density Groups—*concluded.*

N.-W. Provinces and Oudh.

	Density per Square Mile.	No. of Districts.	Area.	Population, 1891.
Below Mean.	57 and below	—	—	—
	58–75	1	5,629	407,818
	76–114	1	7,151	563,181
	115–152	2	3,140	442,335
	153–183	—	—	—
	184–206	—	—	—
	207–229	3	8,475	1,885,796
Above Mean.	230–253	2	4,700	1,115,251
	254–276	1	1,480	396,361
	277–307	1	2,965	903,615
	308–345	—	—	—
	346–384	2	4,052	1,485,798
	385–402	—	—	—
	403–460	7	12,923	5,611,960
	461–575	14	29,006	14,799,734
	576–690	8	17,947	11,366,223
	691 and over	7	10,035	7,927,018
	Total	**49**	**107,503**	**46,905,085**

Bengal.

	Density per Square Mile.	No. of Districts.	Area.	Population, 1891.
Below Mean.	57 and below	1	5,419	107,286
	58–75	—	—	—
	76–114	1	1,681	170,058
	115–152	2	8,658	1,142,258
	153–183	2	14,161	2,293,206
	184–206	1	1,164	223,314
	207–229	—	—	—
Above Mean.	230–253	1	2,962	681,352
	254–276	—	—	—
	277–307	1	4,147	1,193,328
	308–345	1	5,469	1,754,196
	346–384	2	6,591	2,500,883
	385–402	1	4,993	1,944,658
	403–460	4	10,988	4,820,751
	461–575	13	44,379	23,018,046
	576–690	6	16,648	10,013,003
	691 and over	11	24,268	20,803,138
	Total	**47**	**151,523**	**70,665,427**
	Calcutta	—	20	681,560

Berár.

	Density per Square Mile.	No. of Districts.	Area.	Population, 1891.
Below Mean.	57 and below	—	—	—
	58–75	—	—	—
	76–114	—	—	—
	115–152	3	9,490	1,185,592
	153–183	1	2,809	481,021
	184–206	—	—	—
	207–229	2	5,419	1,230,427
	Total	**6**	**17,718**	**2,897,040**
	Railway Passengers	—	—	451

Central Provinces.

	Density per Square Mile.	No. of Districts.	Area.	Population, 1891.
Below Mean.	57 and below	—	—	—
	58–75	3	19,162	1,290,469
	76–114	2	8,454	730,690
	115–152	7	37,834	4,949,984
	153–183	2	7,376	1,197,267
	184–206	4	13,675	2,615,884
	207–229	—	—	—
	Total	**18**	**86,501**	**10,784,294**

Sindh.

	Density per Square Mile.	No. of Districts.	Area.	Population, 1891.
Below Mean.	57 and below	2	26,911	863,083
	58–75	1	2,549	174,548
	76–114	2	18,329	1,834,143
	115–152	—	—	—
	153–183	—	—	—
	184–206	—	—	—
	207–229	—	—	—
	Total	**5**	**47,789**	**2,871,774**

Burma.

	Density per Square Mile.	No. of Districts.	Area.	Population, 1891.
Below Mean.	57 and below	19	120,721	2,416,930
	58–75	5	21,998	1,554,677
	76–114	3	12,188	1,047,648
	115–152	5	10,149	1,303,540
	153–183	3	6,412	1,102,441
	184–206	—	—	—
	207–229	—	—	—
	Total	**35**	**171,408**	**7,425,236**
	Rangoon Town	—	22	181,324

as the surrounding tracts are not, on the whole, fertile. The smaller tract of Mérwára owes its present comparative prosperity to a single British officer, Colonel Dixon, whose personal influence during his long residence there served to reclaim the wild tribes and to establish a thriving centre of trade for the whole country round. As regards density, the table shows that in the present day, at all events, there is not much difference between the two districts. The detached Settlements of Quettah, Aden, and the Andamans require a few words here. **Aden, &c.** The area is only ascertained in the case of Aden, and for that only approximately. This Settlement consists of three small tracts. First, the peninsula, on which the main population resides. Secondly, the suburb on the adjacent mainland, including Shaikh Othman, and the Somáli quarters. Thirdly, the Island of Perim, about 90 miles up the Straits of Babelmandeb, on which there is a small detachment of military, and, of late years, a coaling depôt. **Quettah.** The census of Quettah included only the cantonment known by that name, with the adjoining town and the railway settlements, together with the outlying cantonment of Lorelai, and the camps of the political officers, who were mostly collected at the time of the census at Sibi, below the Bolán, for a horse fair. **Andamans.** Similarly, the census of the Andamans was limited to Port Blair, so we have no record of the natives, who are said to be dying out in some of the islands. **Sindh.** We then come to the five districts of Sindh, the most dense of which has only 102 persons to the mile. The lowest, Thar and Párkar, lies, as its name implies, on the outskirts of the desert, and supports its 23 to the mile chiefly on the charitable relics of the south-western rains, received up the Gulf of Cambay. This province presents no such striking differences within its limits as call for subdivision of the area, though if the tables admitted of more minute partition, no doubt it would be practicable to separate the deltaic portion, where there is a light rainfall of about 8 inches, from the upper regions, where cultivation depends upon the inundation or canal irrigation. **Berár.** *Berar*, again, is taken as homogeneous in its features, though there are small hilly tracts in both the north and south-east. The greater part lies in the Central Plain, and the density at present does not, in any tract, reach the mean of British India. The rainfall, though light, $35\frac{1}{2}$ inches, is fairly steady, and the soil famed for its growth of cotton and oil-seeds as well as of millet.

Central Provinces. Its neighbour on the east, the Central Provinces, is the first in which subdivision is necessary. The mean density of 125 per mile is composed of three main factors. First, the fertile rice-plains of the east; then the valley of the Narmada, and lastly, the belt of hills that spreads westwards from the Chutia-Nágpur plateau. North, east, and south, is found a fringe of lightly peopled forest and hilly country, where the absence of large areas of flat land prevent the formation of populous villages, in spite of the comparatively certain rainfall.

Tract.	Districts.	Area.	Density.	Rainfall.
Eastern	3	25,013	142	53"·49
Southern	4	20,988	124	54·56
Central	5	19,847	91	50·91
Narmada	6	20,653	136	46·67

Burma. Burma is the province to be reviewed next, and it is the last in which no district is found to have a population of the mean Indian density. Broadly speaking, it may be divided into no more than four tracts, two, littoral and deltaic, in Lower Burma, and two, central and submontane, in the upper portion of the province. But it has been found of practical convenience to group the districts according to the administrative divisions, as shown in the margin. Here, as has already been remarked, the mean figures help us not at all. No one of the districts comes within 30 per cent. of the general average, and the range is from 4 on the Khyindwin, to 178 in the district containing the capital of Upper Burma, and from 7, in the southern coast hills, to 172 in an older settlement of the lower portion of the province. By far the greater number of the districts lie in the two lowest groups of density, with less than 75 persons to the mile. That this light population is due to the actual want of men, not to the inability to support them, is proved by the very large proportion borne by the amount of rice exported to that grown, though it is the staple food of the whole province.

	Tract.	Districts.	Area.	Density.	Rainfall.
Upper.	Northern	5	22,580	28	47"·00
	Central	4	29,236	22	56·48
	Southern	4	18,607	42	25·13
	Eastern	4	13,050	59	40·75
Lower.	Arakan	4	14,526	46	191·11
	Pegu	5	9,299	156	65·03
	Irrawaddi	4	17,542	88	84·01
	Tenasserin	6	46,590	21	160·04

Assam.

Assam, which comes next on the list in order of sparsity of population, is really in the same category as the preceding provinces, save as regards the one district that partakes of the character of those in Bengal that adjoin it. Twelve of the 13 districts contain an average of little more density than Sindh, or about 76 per mile, whilst Silhet shows 398. We may separate, accordingly, this with its neighbour Kachár, from the rest, under the title of the Súrma valley. Assam, properly so called, consists of two divisions, the Bráhmaputra valley, and the Hill tracts, five in number. The latter fall into the lowest group as regards density, and have a specific population varying between 37 in the Gáro Hills and 1·1 in North Kachár. In the Bráhmaputra valley the extension of tea plantation, apart from the general opening up of the country, has been the means of attracting a considerable number of immigrants, chiefly from Bengal, many of whom settle on land-grants made to them after their term of service on the tea-gardens is completed. It is to be noted, too, that the eastern portion of this valley has been a frontier tract for centuries, so that till within recent times the population was kept down by war and invasion. This explains the greater density of the western districts. The river, too, has been much more used of late years than before, as the main line of communication between Assam and other parts of India besides Bengal, but the prevalence of an epidemic of fever, which has been peculiarly fatal in this valley, seems to have checked the growth of the province, as will be seen from the statistics given in the next chapter.

Tract.	Districts.	Area.	Density.	Rainfall.
Súrma Valley	2	7,886	333	146″·27
Bráhmápútra Valley	6	20,869	117	87·12
Hill Tracts	5	20,249	25	92·03

Panjáb.

Missing the main portion of the Gangetic basin for the present, we come to the Panjáb. The figures in Table D. alone show how necessary it is to subdivide a tract that exhibits so wide a divergence between the extremes of its component parts. On the other hand, Table E. shows that this province, as regards the number of its districts, lies nearly equally above and below the Indian mean, and much of it enjoys a nearly uniform rainfall. The five divisions selected, however, show where the differences are found. First, we have a submontane belt in which the density is in places nearly equal to that of the Gangetic valley, to which the eastern portion of the province may be said to belong, though the proximity of the sandy plain to the south keeps down its density. The next division is scarcely so well defined physically as racially, but is well enough described as the "Salt Range Tract," wherein the density sinks to less than half that of the submontane. The two other divisions are plainly denoted. The western plains are not in great part the desert that they seem to be from the map, or even from the small density indicated in the margin. The soil is fertile enough, but requires water to render it available for cultivation, and every decade sees irrigation canals more and more extended from the snow-fed rivers which join the Indus where it is leaving the province for Sindh. The hill tracts, which are the last to be mentioned, consist largely of the great stretches of Himálayan rock and snow, such as have been already described as characteristic of the States in these parts of the country.

Tract.	Districts.	Area.	Density.	Rainfall.
Submontane and Central.	11	26,413	381	26″·79
Eastern Plains	5	12,674	265	25·70
Salt Range Tracts	6	20,892	158	25·31
Western Plains	7	41,012	81	7·50
Hill Tracts	2	9,676	88	54·97

Bombay.

The next province that engages our attention is that of Bombay, and here, again, we find that out of the four main divisions, three are based on physical conditions, whilst in regard to the fourth, racial differences have been also taken into account. The first division is the expansion of the coast line, after the Gháts have receded into the interior. The second is the strip of coast itself. The third is, of course, the Deccan plateau, so far as it lies within the limits of the western Presidency, whilst the last is the southern part of that plateau, bordering on Mysore and north Madras. Roughly

Tract.	Districts.	Area.	Density.	Rainfall.
Gujaráth	5	10,296	301	29″·44
Konkan	4	13,639	210	104·66
Deccan	6	38,390	162	30·36
Karnátak	3	14,928	192	34·15
Bombay Island	—	22	—	74·23

speaking, the Karnátak begins south of the Bhíma river, on the east, and in the State of Kolhapur, in the west, without other marked geographical demarcation. The city of Bombay has been excluded in the tables from the Konkan, to which it belongs, so as not to disturb, with its peculiar circumstances, the general distribution of population along the coast. Considering the number of the districts and the difference of the tracts into which they are thrown in the returns, the mean figure is remarkably in accordance with the detail. Gujaráth presents the greatest density with the lightest rainfall, owing chiefly to the large area of fertile soil in the northern part of the division. The Konkan, which is the local name for that part of the coast, comes next, but here the rainfall rises, and the density recedes, by reason of the comparatively narrow area of cultivable land. In the Deccan has been classed a large portion of the central plain, included in the district of Khándesh, and the two large towns of Poona and Sholapur also tend to raise the population. The rich black soil mentioned in the first chapter as peculiar to this tract is found in the Karnátak in wider and more continuous expanse, and in the south-western portion of this last division the rainfall is heavier and more certain than to the east and north of the Deccan proper, so that the density is considerably greater.

Madras.

The Madras Presidency, with which we have now to deal, has probably the greatest number of climatic differences within its limits of any, though their range is not so wide as in the Panjáb. The districts are thus very widely distributed in Table E., but, with the exception of the Agency tracts on the north coast, which really belong to the Central belt of hills, there is little land lightly peopled. The zone of uncertain rainfall embraces the whole of what is marginally termed the Northern division, at perhaps its worst point, and owing to the protective effect of the western Gháts, the West-central division is little better off. On the other hand, along the north coast and in the South-central divisions, there are largely extended systems of irrigation from the deltas of the Kistna, the Godávari, and the Kávari, by which rice is grown enough to support a very heavy population, almost irrespective of the annual rains. The western coast districts, on the contrary, depend upon the south-western current, here at its maximum of strength and humidity, so they attain the same result by different means, and their produce, if not so near the foreign market, is probably more varied and to some extent, where spices and condiments are cultivated, more valuable.

Tract.	Districts.	Area.	Density.	Rainfall.
North Coast	5	31,464	279	48″·29
Northern	4	27,486	134	25·47
East Central	3*	10,487	359	39·51
West Central	3	16,346	249	30·45
South Central	3	12,557	458	44·48
Southern	2	14,195	319	32·46
West Coast	2	9,487	391	117·17

* Including Madras City.

Last of all, the task remains of reviewing the manifold conditions of the Gangetic valley, as comprised within the two great provinces of the north-west, with Oudh and Bengal. What has been said already of these tracts in connection with different subjects, has indicated the remarkable density of the valley as a whole. Even taking into consideration, as is done in the table under review, the outlying territory included in each of the two provinces, the specific population of Bengal rises considerably above, and that of the other province comes not far below, double the mean of British territory, as a whole. In the former, 76, and in the latter 72 per cent. of the population exceeds that average.

N.-W. Provinces and Oudh.

Taking the two political divisions of the Upper provinces separately, it will be found that in the North-western division the density is only 411 per mile. In Oudh, however, it rises to 522, a ratio unparalleled over so large an area in any Indian province except Bengal. The density of the combined Provinces is 436. The latter has been divided into seven physically different tracts. One of these, situated amongst or just below the Himálaya, is thinly populated by reason of the scarcity of arable land. There are parts, indeed, of this tract that are deep in snow most of the year, so that the population descends for the winter into the grazing country at

Tract.	Districts.	Area.	Density.	Rainfall.
Himálayan	3	13,973	81	62″·13
Submontane	7	18,202	486	46·43
Upper Doáb	5	10,133	509	31·25
Central Doáb	6	10,139	470	28·38
North Central	7	14,116	499	38·29
South Central	15	25,300	652	38·42
Southern	6	15,639	221	37·51

the foot of the hills and returns only for the four or five months when cultivation is practicable. This migratory population, therefore, was added at the time of the census to that of the submontane tract, but the total number of persons thus displaced was comparatively insignificant. At the opposite side of the province, to the south, lies another tract that shows a density which, though it is not far below that of British India, as a whole, must be classified as sparse when considered in relation to the rest of the province. It consist largely of broken ground, forming the outworks of the Central belt of hills. Between these extremes, the valley rarely supports a population of less than 460 per mile. The exceptions are found in tracts along the base of the Himálaya, where, for some reason or other, there has been a good deal of malarious disease of late years, and in the central portion of the Doáb, or tract between the Jamna and the Ganges, which is said to have got water-logged of late.* Even here the density is comparatively high, and we find about 375 persons to the mile in the former tract, and between 400 and 450 in the latter. The more thickly peopled part of the province lies first, along the line of rail, in the upper Doáb, and still more remarkably in the South central group of districts, which includes all of Oudh lying to the west of the Ghágra river. In Table D., the two districts mentioned as containing the most dense population are Benares, in the North-West Provinces, and Lucknow, in Oudh. Both these, however, are peculiar in being more or less appanages of great cities, and include, accordingly, a comparatively high proportion of urban and suburban inhabitants. We may take, therefore, as illustrations, more rural tracts, and in Balia, Ázamgarh, and Jaunpur, we find three, in none of which is the density less than 800 per square mile.

Bengal.

Crossing into Bengal, we find the same high ratio. In dealing with this immense population, the historical divisions of Bengal, Bihár, and Orissa, are found unwieldy, save in the last instance. Bihar has accordingly been split into two, and Bengal sub-divided into three parts. But for old association's sake, it is worth while to give the population of so well-known tracts. In Bengal, then, the population is returned as 40,398,265. Bihar returns 21,265,150, and Orissa 4,047,352. To these must be added the later acquisition of Chútia Nágpúr, the Feudatory States in which have been described above. The population of the British portion of this tract is given in the marginal table, since it is sufficiently well marked off from the rest of the inhabitants of the province to warrant the distinction. In the first place, of the seven districts containing a population less dense than the general mean, four are in this division. It is fortunate, again, in lying almost entirely within the zone of light but certain rainfall. Lastly, as has been said in the Introduction, the hilly tract of which it is chiefly composed is the last refuge of the dark races that were expelled from the plains by the foreigner, or absorbed into his ranks, if they elected to stay there. Two of the three remaining districts of light population are of a similar description. One is in Orissa, and is the inheritance of the Khond tribe, of whom much has been written since the British occupation of that tract and the adjacent Madras districts. The other lies in the wild country separating Bengal from Burma, and consists of a series of forest-clad hills and deep valleys, of which the latter only are under cultivation. The remaining district in this category is Darjiling, originally part of the Sikkim domain, now a flourishing tea-planting centre, with a favourite sanitarium, and a considerable trade with the tribes of the surrounding Himálaya to the north. But the arable area, except in the submontane tracts, is scanty, and the population sparse, as it is in the district touching Darjiling, in the plains. But the rest of the division specified in the marginal table as Northern Bengal, lies in a partially alluvial tract, with a density of more than 500 per mile. Here, however, begins the influence of the great rivers, which by the gradual shifting of their course, have wrought most serious damage to the country, both in respect to its fertility and to the health of its population, through the obstruction of the natural drainage. The next division, Eastern Bengal, is still more subject to the river influences, and

Tract.	Districts.	Area.	Density.	Rainfall.
Northern	8	19,253	459	85"·73
Western	11	26,491	562	58·11
Eastern	10	32,165	531	82·59
North Bihár	5	17,515	667	51·82
South "	5	19,300	520	45·14
Chútia Nágpúr	5	26,966	134	46·84
Orissa	4	9,853	411	58·86

* The remarks on these two tracts must be taken as subject to correction, since they are based on the provisional report of the Census Superintendent, whose final work has not yet been submitted.

throughout the littoral tracts, communication is chiefly by boat, all the year round. This continuous supply of fresh deposit, with the abundance of wholesome water, make the tract one of health and plenty. It not only feeds its own population of over 500 to the mile, and annually augments it, but it exports also large quantities of rice both to the less fortunate parts of Bengal, and to Madras and elsewhere in India and abroad. It has been epigrammatically stated that in Bengal the population is in exact proportion to the productive power of the soil, measured in rice, and there seems good ground for the saying. As regards the density of this tract, however, we must make allowances for the inclusion of the hill tract of Chittagong above mentioned. The deltaic waste-lands of the Sundarbans, which fall within it are apparently excluded. Its limits, too, are being gradually restricted by the encroachment of the estuaries of the Ganges and Bráhmaputra to the eastwards. In Western Bengal the metropolitan area has been included, with its population of nearly a million. There is not here and in Madras, as in the case of Bombay, that great distinction between the two classes of population which would affect the ratios of the whole surrounding tract. In the latter, the mainland is comparatively sterile and thinly peopled. It is not so in the other two instances. The great distinction found in this division, and it is one that justifies still further partition, ethnologically, is that between the country on the east and that on the west of the estuary we know as the Hughli. Even in connection with the present subject, there is a noteworthy rise in density as we pass over to the eastern bank, and the western portion tends towards the characteristics of the Central Hills, both physically and in point of racial admixture. Orissa, apart from the hill tracts, consists of two belts; one salt and less fertile, the other, one of superb rice-growing soil. The density varies, accordingly, a good deal in small patches throughout the plains, but in the main supports the same specific population as the North-West Provinces, without Oudh. Bihár has here been divided into the two main sections of north and south, but there appears to be fair ground for further sub-division, as each of the above contains a zone of extremely dense population, lying along the Ganges, with a fringe of comparatively lightly-peopled country, situated under the Himálaya on the north side of the river, and along the foot of the Chútia Nágpúr plateau and in the Rájmahál hills with their surroundings, on the south. North Bihár contains the highest densities in the whole province, and in some places these have crept up almost to the sub-Himálayan forest. In the southern division, except for the influence of the great towns, there is a lower specific population, and the belt of almost thinly-peopled country is far wider, and is continuous throughout the tract. It is here that the population has to some degree outgrown its means of livelihood, and the seasonal migration to Calcutta, with the importation of large supplies of rice from Eastern Bengal, shows this. On the other hand, north of the river, in all places where there are no special disturbing causes, such as river changes or malarious outbreaks, the greater density seems to be supported without difficulty, and, as will be shown in the next chapter, it has not reached its limit. It is as well to mention this fact here, as otherwise the density might seem incompatible with the prosperity, or even the maintenance, of the population at its present level.

Pressure of population.

The whole country has now been reviewed with reference to the density of its population, that is, merely the number of people to the square mile. Behind this, however, lies the more important question of the pressure of this population on the land. In order to appreciate this it will be necessary to travel considerably beyond the mere census record, so that the subject can only be treated here in the barest outline. There are instances in which the temporary migration of a portion of the inhabitants, together with the continuous inward course of the traffic in food supplies, are facts which need no corroboration. But in most of the cases which call for examination, the existence or the absence of congestion of the population depends upon many less patent factors. For example, there is the ratio of the inhabitants to the arable area, which in its turn is qualified by the relative facilities of communication with local markets for agricultural produce, the capabilities of the soil, the character of the cultivating classes, and the relative variety of the field of employment. As to the first and main point, even in British India, to which the following remarks are confined, the record of arable land, especially if that in occupation be distinguished from the remainder still available for fresh tillage, is by no means complete, owing to differences in the tenures prevalent in the various provinces, and in the system on which the unoccupied arable area is administered by the State. The figures of population can thus only be applied to the statistics of agricultural areas by experts in matters of land-revenue, and on this consideration the census authorities deprecated the inclusion in their returns of any statements in which the two were combined. The omission has been supplied, as was suggested, by special investigations through experienced local officers, from the results of which much more useful information has been obtained than can be incorporated in the present work. The general statement made at the beginning of this chapter, regarding the divergence of pressure from density, is borne out in several remarkable instances. The most striking, no doubt, is that of Bengal, where we find a very dense population supported in the eastern division with ease, for the soil is alluvial, continually renewed, well watered with a rainfall distributed over nearly three-fourths of the year. Passing over the tracts accidentally afflicted of late years by epidemic, we reach, in Bihár, one tract with a density of 930, of almost proverbial prosperity, due not only to its natural fertility but also to the admirable system of roads by which it is traversed, to the capabilities of the tract for specially remunerative crops, such as indigo and the poppy, and last, but most of all, to the very high class of its agriculture. Adjacent to it are two districts with densities of 902 and 840 respectively, in which there is, no doubt, congestion, due to the subdivision of the arable area beyond the capacity of the cultivator to get a living out of it. It is said, however, that the competition for field labour is keen, so that one of this class, whether he is landless or not, is better off than a man who confines his attention to a patch of loss than four acres for the support of five or even six persons. There is one district here, however, Champáran, which is reported to be still under-peopled, though it returns 526 persons per mile. To the south of the Ganges we come to another congested tract, distributed, however, over parts of three districts, where many of the holdings are of two-and-a-half acres only. Here migration for a part of the year is habitual to a considerable part of the population, who find a living in the Calcutta mills and the rice fields of the east, and even return with savings from their annual trip.

Bengal.

N.-W. Provinces and Oudh.

In the North-West Provinces and Oudh it seems difficult to point to any special local congestion; but if there be any, it is most probably amongst the higher social grades of small cultivators in the central parts of Oudh. The case of the less fertile districts in the central Doáb is hardly one of congestion so much as of bad luck, susceptible of remedy. But the main point in connection with these provinces is the possibility of general congestion, since the area available is comparatively small, the population is large and very evenly distributed in the plains, so that it is necessary for the total annual surplus of food stock to rise proportionally with the increase of the people, as importation of food to an agricultural community of this size is almost out of the question. The contingency, however, has not yet arisen.

Panjáb.

In the Panjáb there seems to be no congestion, except in a few parts of the submontane tract. Four districts show a remarkable density of population on the arable area, Hoshiárpur, Jálandhar, Sialkot, and Amritsar; but all are within reach of the new field for cultivation thrown open by fresh irrigation projects. In two other districts the ratio to the arable area is very high, but it appears that these tracts, Hazára and Kángra, are largely pastoral, for which pursuit the vast expanse of hill-slope affords ample room.

Sindh and Bombay.

Sindh, with its system of cultivation by irrigation, is not likely to feel pressure of population so long as the Indus continues to run from lake and glacier to the sea. In the Bombay Presidency there are two tracts that may be said to feel the pressure of their population, and neither is densely peopled. In the Ratnagiri district, below the Ghâts, there is congestion of the sort mentioned in connection with some tracts of South Bihár. The area suited for cultivation is small and nearly all taken up; millets are imported from the adjacent Deccan tracts along the top of the Ghâts, and a considerable number of the lower agriculturalists annually migrate to and from Bombay, where there is always work for them in the cotton mills and docks. The density, however, is but 282 per mile. In the case of the Deccan, the primary cause of the pressure is the uncertainty of the rainfall. There is also the fact that the richer classes of soil are comparatively small in area, and are occupied, for the most part, by the better class of cultivators. There is thus a goodly proportion of the population that lives off the lighter class of land, and is accordingly very sensitive to the variations of the season. The condition of the people of the northern part of the Deccan was made the subject of a special inquiry last year (1892), and confirms the above view regarding the influence of the season on the finances of the cultivator. The density of the tract in question lies between 245 per mile in the most westerly district, and 140 in the north and east. In Gujaráth, the more densely populated division of this Presidency, the pressure is said to be scarcely felt.

Madras, too, has its most unfortunate tracts on the Deccan plateau, and the remarks about the Bombay portion of this tract apply to Karnul, Anantapúr, Belári, and Kadapa, where, in Karnul, the density of 109 is too great, as 134 is in Anantapúr. On the other hand, Tanjore, with 600, does not yet show signs of pressure, owing to the extensive and fertile rice tracts under the Kávari irrigation system, and the facility of making short and lucrative trips to Ceylon for labour during the season when the fields do not require the raiats' áttention at home. Madras.

The Central Provinces have generally been regarded as a field for immigration from the more densely peopled tracts of Bengal and the North-West Provinces. But if we deduct from the area surveyed the 20,000 square miles that are included in State forests, the density rises to very nearly that of Bombay. Taking, as has been done in the recent inquiry into the condition of the people, only the area which is under cultivation, it will be found that in the so-called "black-soil" tracts, where, as a rule, only winter cropping is practicable, there is but little room for expansion, and this tract extends over much of the north and west of the province. In the rice districts, as in Bengal, the densities are far higher and the pressure less. Central Provinces.

The general statistics of Berar seem to speak for themselves. There is comparatively little arable land outside forests that is not taken into occupation, but less than 40 per cent. of the area under crops is devoted to the growth of the staple food of the province. The out-turn, even in a year of short rainfall, is enough to supply the whole population, and in an ordinary year over 40 per cent. of the crop is available for export, in addition to the produce specially grown for the foreign market, such as cotton, wheat, and oil-seeds. Berár.

The two small provinces of Ajmér and Coorg need few remarks. In the former the railway has largely increased the town population and the means of feeding it. In the rural tracts the precarious rainfall and the small area of arable land not taken up seem to indicate a certain amount of pressure, but on the other hand the reports on the appearance and the fécundity of the cultivating classes prove that the limit has not nearly been attained. In Coorg, too, in spite of the area under non-food crops, the native population is easily supported on the plots of hill land that alone are available in much of the province, but during a good part of the year the immigrants from Mysore and the coast are numerous, and the local supplies turn out insufficient. Pressure, however, cannot be said to exist at present. Ajmér and Coorg.

In Assam proper there is rather a want than an excess of population on the land, and even in Sylhet, with its 398 persons to the mile, there is no pressure, and food leaves the district every year. In Burma, as in Assam, there are thousands of acres of rich soil awaiting cultivation. The annual exports from Lower Burma include as much rice as is used by the whole population, including the supply occasionally required for the central districts of the Upper Division, when the rainfall is short there, which is a not uncommon occurrence. There is not, however, any sign that the agricultural population is pressing at all on the arable area. Assam and Burma.

From the above sketch it may be gathered that the agricultural class, that is, the bulk of the population of British India, is not pressing too closely on its means of subsistence, except in a few special localities. In a part of Bihár, and in a small tract on the Bombay coast, the local produce is insufficient for the inhabitants every year, and migration is adopted as a mode of relief. In parts of the Deccan the uncertainty of the season makes a pressure felt in circumstances where otherwise the land could bear the burden with ease. In the centre of the Gangetic valley there is a zone in which the margin of subsistence has been nearly reached, owing to not simply the weight of numbers thrown on to the land, but in part also to the liability of the tract to failure of rain. With these exceptions, the local resources suffice, and in several parts of India are year by year in excess of local needs, so that a large stock is always available for transport to places where it is wanted. Such is the problem in the present day, so far as the great mass of the people is concerned, and its further development will be discussed, so far as the census returns afford grounds for conjecture, in the next chapter. General conclusions.

It may be noted that in the foregoing review the pressure of population has been regarded from the standpoint of the agriculturist, and looking at the heavy preponderance of this class with that immediately allied to it, the village menials, the attitude is justifiable. The two together comprise little less than three-fourths of the whole community. But setting aside the trading class, which rises and falls in great measure with the condition of the masses, it is necessary to add a few words as to Pressure in the non-agricultural occupations.

those of the professional classes and such artisans as are not semi-agriculturists under the village organisation so common throughout India. There is no doubt that the general rise in prices of food, which is to the gain of the cultivator, has hit these two classes rather hard, and what with the supply of the former being in excess of the present demand for professional services, and the concentration of much of the textile and metal industry into the large factories in the towns, there is the possibility and likelihood of both professional and artisan falling back on the land for support, not so much as agriculturists as exploiters of such estates as they may be able to obtain. In connection with what has been said above on the pressure on the land in some parts of the country, this prospect is not to be regarded as of no significance, though it may happily still be very remote.

Town and Country.

Definition of urban population. The stage of social aggregation at which a community ceases to be rural, and passes into the category of urban, can nowhere be sharply defined. In no two countries is the line drawn on the same principle, so that comparison of the respective classes has to be confined to the places the population of which is assumed to be universally a guarantee of their urban character, and the respective proportions of urban and rural, as a whole, have been voted to be beyond the scope of international statistics. As regards the smaller aggregates, the population standard is liable to be as delusive as the constitutional test, for their size depends very much on the density of the country and the physical resources which determine the bent of the occupation of its inhabitants. The title of town, again, is conventional in most countries, and applied in consideration of varying constitutional distinctions, such as those of city and borough, in England. In India the difficulty of classifying these small places is peculiarly felt in the present day, when the rapid extension of railways and other means of communication brings with it a very considerable amount of shifting of the trading and mechanical communities from place to place. It becomes necessary, therefore, to adopt three general tests with reference to the smaller units of population. First, that of constitution, that is, has the place been established as a municipality, or brought under some similar regulation for police and sanitary purposes? Secondly, if neither of these methods of local government has been applied, is the proportion of the trading and industrial population to the total equal to, or greater than, that of the agricultural? In the latter case the general numerical standard of 5,000 inhabitants was prescribed, as experience shows that taking the whole country together, this represents about the limit of urban preponderance. If the numerical standard alone had been adopted, many of the smaller municipalities and other towns in Northern India and Mysore would have been dropped out of the category of urban, and, on the other hand, a considerable number of the large aggregates of homesteads on the Malabar coast, which are merely revenue units of a purely agrestic nature, would have come on the list. The system of classification of these comparatively small places obviously leaves the door open to a good deal of variety of interpretation of the term "urban" as applicable to the population thereof, but, on the whole, the results show that local experience, at all events, in British territory, was usually right as to the preponderance of non-agricultural occupations in the places determined to be towns, and the return shows that no less than 505, or nearly 25 per cent., of the total number of towns fall below the prescribed standard in point of population. The adscription of so large a proportion of the people of India to the soil, a point that has already been brought prominently forward in the foregoing part of this chapter, is in itself a sufficient explanation of the remarkable sparsity of the urban population. The village system of organisation will be treated of below, and where the rustic finds a scheme of existence so thoroughly adapted to his wants and aspirations, where rank is hereditary, and custom provides a regulation for every contingency, the city offers no attractions, save to the Adullamite and Nonconformist, and the average villager sticks to his surroundings,

Forumque vitat, et superba civium
Potentiorum limina.

Distribution of urban population. We find, then, out of the 717,549 places returned at the census, only 2,035 classed as towns, and the rest under the head of villages. The urban population is in the proportion of 9·48 per cent. to 90·52 of rural. In British territory, the proportion falls to 9·22, and in Feudatory States it rises to 10·38 per cent. The probable explanation of the difference will be found in the following statement, F, where a summary is given of the main features of the urban population in the different parts of India :—

F.—Distribution of the Urban Population.

Province or State.	Urban Population. Total.	Urban Population. Percentage on Total Population.	Percentage of Urban Population in Towns of 50,000 and over.	20,000.	10,000.	5,000.	Under 5,000.	Mean Proximity in Miles of Towns of 20,000 and over.*
Madras	3,406,105	9·56	29	24	22	23	2	68
Bombay	3,116,304	19·49	43	13	22	17	5	75
Sindh	342,295	11·92						125
Bengal	3,443,876	4·82	44	24	22	9	1	78
N.-W. Provinces	4,352,573	12·70	38	11	17	21	13	56
Oudh	961,755	7·60	36	7	22	25	10	75
Panjáb	2,413,704	11·56	41	15	15	22	7	81
Central Provinces	739,952	6·85	27	20	23	30	—	149
Upper Burma	371,404	12·60	51	—	17	27	5	168
Lower Burma	575,245	12·35	41	21	20	13	5	
Assam	102,074	1·86	—	—	24	43	33	—
Berar	360,711	12·45	—	25	28	47	—	83
Ajmér	118,631	21·87	58	36	—	6	—	32
Coorg	15,511	8·96	—	—	—	45	55	—
Haidrabad	1,090,129	9·45	38	10	17	35	—	138
Baroda	483,515	20·02	24	11	30	31	4	56
Mysore	626,558	12·67	41	—	9	18	32	127
Kashmer	197,743	7·77	60	18	5	17	—	216
Rájputána	1,530,087	12·73	26	14	25	35	—	117
Central India	964,538	9·34	28	25	17	30	—	87
Bombay States	1,177,422	14·61	5	29	26	31	9	—*
Madras States	175,125	4·73	—	29	42	29	—	—*
Central Province States	38,656	1·79	—	—	—	100	—	—*
Bengal States	16,542	0·50	—	—	69	31	—	—*
N.-W. Province States	103,188	13·02	74	—	—	16	10	—*
Panjáb States	456,544	10·71	12	9	24	39	16	—*
Detached Settlements	71,349	—	—	—	—	—	—	—
Total India	**27,251,176**	**9·48**	**35**	**16**	**20**	**23**	**6**	**90**
Number of Towns	2,035	—	78	149	407	896	505	30

* The smaller groups of States are in this column included in the Government with which they are connected.

Proximity of towns.

One striking comparison suggests itself which is not brought out in these figures. It is that whereas in England 53 per cent. of the whole population is found in the 182 towns of 20,000 and upwards, in India, though there are 227 such towns, only 4·84 per cent. of the population reside in them. The limit of 20,000 has been selected as being about the smallest that may be presumed to have any considerable influence on the rural tract of which it is the centre. The last column of the statement, accordingly, shows the average distance between one of these towns and the next, on the assumption, of course, of equal distribution, as is the rule in such computations. It thus appears that, taking India as a whole, we shall find a town of not less than 20,000 inhabitants every 90 miles. If we exclude the larger States, the distance is somewhat less, owing to the removal from the calculation of the large areas of Mysore and Kashmér, which boast only two towns each of this size. Burma and the Central Provinces then show the worst provision in this respect, but it must be remembered that in the latter the outlying States have been taken into consideration, since most of them use the towns in British territory. In the case of Bombay, the difference caused by the addition of the States is hardly felt, as the latter contain a fair number of towns of the requisite population, whereas there are none in the small States of the Central Provinces. Baroda and the North-West Provinces are the best off for large towns, since Ajmér may be left out of the account, as its circumstances are peculiar. Madras, too, comes high up in the scale. Bombay, Oudh, and Bengal, are all much on an equality.

Proportion of urban population.

The next point is the proportion of urban population to the total. Again omitting Ájmér with its three railway markets, the highest percentage is that of Baroda, which, in addition to the capital of the State, has a fair number of small towns. Bombay is the next in order, and, with its States, is considerably above the rest. Sindh, which has been taken with it in the table, shows only 12 per cent., in spite of its four large towns. The proportion in the Panjáb, too, is much the same. In Bengal the urban population, which is of itself considerable, is utterly swamped when taken alongside of the enormous mass of rustics in this province. The proportion in Upper Burma seems high, but half of the number returned is found in Mandalay, and there is a long drop from the capital to the next town. It would be much the same in Lower Burma, but for the influence of Maulmain, the younger sister of Rangoon. Kashmér, too, shows in the return the predominating position of Shrinagar in its urban element. On the other hand, Madras, without any specially large town besides the capital, has a wide distribution of middle-sized places, including several flourishing seaports. The North-West Provinces do not appear to due advantage in the return, since the proportion of their numerous large towns is outweighed by that of the still more numerous small ones, which have been of late years brought under the local regulations regarding police and sanitary provisions without being constituted municipalities. In Mysore, too, it seems that something of this sort has been done. In several of the States we find one large town with a few much smaller ones. This is especially the case in Rámpur, of the North-west group, in a few of the Panjáb States and in most of those in Rájputána, and finally in Haidrabád. The urban element, in conclusion, is at its lowest ebb in Assam and the small Hill States of the central belt.

Large towns.

Another feature in the return is the comparative paucity of towns of large size. Out of the total tale of 2,035, there are 1,401 which do not contain as many as 10,000 inhabitants. Between this and 20,000 there are 407, whilst above this limit there are, as we have seen, 227. The towns of 100,000 and over number only 28, or 30, including two of the suburbs of Calcutta to make the total completely in accord with the general tables. The following statement shows these places, in order of magnitude :—

Town	Population	Town	Population
1. Bombay	821,764	15. Pátna	165,192
2. Calcutta, &c.	741,144	16. Poona	161,390
3. Madras	452,518	17. Jaipúr	158,905
4. Haidrabád	415,039	18. Ahmedabád	148,412
5. Lucknow	273,028	19. Amritsar	136,766
6. Benáres	219,467	20. Baréli	121,039
7. Delhi	192,579	21. Meerut	119,390
8. Mandalay	188,815	22. Shrinagar	118,960
9. Cawnpore	188,712	23. Nágpúr	117,014
10. Bangalore	180,366	24. Howrah	116,606
11. Rangoon	180,324	25. Baroda	116,420
12. Lahore	176,854	26. Súrat	109,229
13. Allahabád	175,246	27. Karáchi	105,199
14. Ágra	168,662	28. Gwálior	104,083

The great gap between the three Presidency towns and the rest is filled, it appears, only by Haidrabád, in which is included the large suburban cantonment of Sikandrabád. As regards the claim to be the first city in India in population, it must be considered that Bombay is under one municipal body, and contained within well-defined boundaries, and has no suburbs on the island itself, which means none within about 12 or 14 miles. On the other hand, the extension of Calcutta is like that of London, laterally ; so that whilst the nucleus of the metropolis is much as it was 10 years ago, the outskirts are growing into suburbs in all directions. There is, again, the large town of Howrah, across the Hughli, which, though in another district and under separate municipal government, is as much a part of the city as Southwark is of London. Taking all these straggling units together, the metropolitan population rises to 961,670, under no less than six municipal bodies, with three different

Presidents. Irrespective, therefore, of the outskirts, Calcutta must be content with the second place, both in population and in homogeneity of administration. Madras covers a large area, and comprises within its limits several collections of houses that are almost separate units; but the whole is under one municipality, and there is no question of suburban aspirations. The floating population, too, is small compared to that of the other two cities, since there is little of the manufacturing industry on a large scale that attracts so many of the labouring class to Bombay or the banks of the Hughli. The shipping trade, too, in Madras is by no means large. Haidrabád includes, besides Sikandrabád, a considerable suburban population, but it is in itself a very large city of quite the native Indian type. Lucknow, like the rest of these large towns, includes a considerable cantonment population, and in several other respects resembles Haidrabád, in spite of a generation of British occupation. The population of Benares, its neighbour, fluctuates considerably from month to month, as a large proportion of it consists of pilgrims. It is not necessary to go through the rest of the roll in detail. Bangalore, Agra, Poona, Baréli, and Meerut, are largely maintained directly or indirectly, through their position as great military depôts, or as the head-quarters of civil administration of a considerable tract. In some degree this may be said of Lahore and Allahabád. Mandalay, Jaipur, Gwalior, Shrinagar, and Baroda, owe their position to the fact of their having been for so long the capitals of wealthy States. Nagpur is fortunate in having no rival near it, and in being surrounded by a fertile country, the produce of which finds its chief outlet through this town. Karáchi and Rangoon are practically the creations of British trade. Cawnpore and Ahmedabád may be bracketted together as combining to a great extent commerce, of the more extended kind, with manufacture on the modern system. Delhi is the admitted metropolis of the north-western and larger portion of the Gangetic basin, as Lucknow is of the north-eastern. The former has, moreover, entered into the movement of modern industry, and is not entirely given over to the system on which it grew up under former dynasties. We have, finally, Patna and Súrat, both formerly provincial capitals of note, but failing to keep up the population of 10 years ago.

Townward tendencies.

Their condition will fitly serve as an introduction for a few words on the difference between the nature of the tendency to town-formation that we find in operation at the present day, and that in pursuance of which most of the older cities of India were developed. The extent of the tendencies and the degree in which they are now in action are matters which appertain to the dynamics of society, which will be treated of, so far as they fall within the scope of the census, in the next chapter. But as offering explanations of the existing condition of things they are relevant to our present subject. In the minds of the great majority of the masses, city life and its attractions are no more than a "nebulous hypothesis," and the town might just as well not be in existence. To the upper classes it is distasteful, saving to a native Chief in his own capital, of which more anon. The local magnate in his own domain is a Triton amongst minnows, by hereditary right, but in the city the equality of all before the law, a feature in British administration which he despises, is at its full height, and liberty lords it over birthright. Thus the field is left open to the trader, the professional, and "business man" generally, and under the influence of railways and foreign commerce his horn has been greatly exalted, to the prejudice of the others into whose presence, a few generations back, he could not have hoped to be admitted. There is also to be considered the stimulating presence of the foreign element found in the centres of trade, which is thrown into the scale in favour of the middle classes. On the whole, then, the main factors in the development of the cities of the present day, such as the seaports, Presidency towns, and the few trading and manufacturing centres in the interior, have been foreign capital administered by foreigners, and the scope given to the talents of the native trading classes. To a minor degree, too, the artisan and professional has contributed to the growth of such towns.

Court stimulus.

Let us now turn to the conditions of town life in India before British influence began to make itself felt, or to where, in later days, it is confined to merely the protective functions of a paramount power. In former times, whatever the theory, in practice the State existed for the maintenance of the Chief, and his duties began at the outer edge of the frontier. The public revenue was sucked into the treasury, and the expenditure was limited to the army and the personal tastes of the chief, or the embellishment of his palace and capital. It has been said by Jacquemont, that in India the authority of the Chief "décroît au moins comme le cube de la distance du lieu où il se trouve," so that what with the quasi-feudal relations of the clansmen amongst the Hindus, and the system of payment by "jágir," or the assignment of tracts to skin, by the Moghals, there was little temptation to amass wealth that could not be protected, except under the immediate wing of the chief's courtiers. This state of affairs was fatal, of course, to any growth of the smaller towns,* but excessively stimulating to the congregation in the capital of such professions and industries as ministered to the requirements of the court and army. The sole chance for an aspiring author or artisan was to attract the attention of the Chief or Emperor, as the case might be, or of the reigning favourite. To do this, he was obliged to go to the court, and, if lucky, to remain there till he had buried an ample fortune in some wall or garden. In fact, as Bernier says, "From the nature of the government of this "country, a capital city, such as Delhi or Agra, derives its chief support from the "presence of the army, and the population is reduced to the necessity of following "the Moghal whenever he undertakes a journey of long continuance. Those cities "resemble anything rather than Paris; they might more fitly be compared to a camp. "The king's pay is the only means of sustenance." We thus see how the dialect of Hindi spoken round the head-quarters of the Moghal came to get the name of Urdu, the *camp* language. It is not probable that in the older States, especially under the Rájpút clans, the concentration of trade was as great as is pictured by the genial physician, as the petty sub-chiefs each made a point of establishing a little court in imitation of their superior, but outside these cities of refuge, the trader had no protection and but little business. Then, again, looking at the nature of the demand in these towns, it appears that the greater and more lucrative traffic was in arms, ornaments, fine fabrics, cloth of gold, illuminated manuscripts, and other objects of what economists call unproductive expenditure. So factitious a stimulus could not long survive the régime under which it flourished, nor was it likely to be continued under the plain utilitarianism of the British system of government. Nowadays, whatever may be said by the denizens of the Presidency towns regarding the annual "exodus" of the Government to hill stations, the support, such as it is, to commerce, which is thus withdrawn, is insignificant in the mass of new openings that have sprung up independent of it.

In proof of this the general condition of the chief towns may be brought forward. The seaports and the manufacturing centres, and the great produce-markets in touch with the coast, all of recent birth or regeneration, are flourishing. Of the former capitals, apart from the presence of military forces, inferior in number and luxury, perhaps, to those of yore, but better paymasters, Delhi, which, as above mentioned, has entered into the race on the new conditions, is almost the only one that holds its head up. Vijianagar lies in a boulder-strewn waste. Bijapur, that once sucked in the wealth of the Deccan for miles round, is now but a skeleton into whose dry bones life is just returning under the magic touch of the iron horse. Agra and Dacca just hold their own, and that is all. Patna fails to do this, and Murshidabád is little more than a large village, overshadowed by the palace of those who were once graciously pleased to allow Calcutta to exist, but forbade it to grow. Lastly, look at Surat, the port of the Empire, the Gate of Mecca, which, with its foreign relations, was the only place that showed signs of taking rank with modern emporia. Its river has played it false, and it is now hopelessly stranded in the backwater of commerce. Of the latter-day towns that are still in motion, more will be said in the next chapter.

The village system.

A wider, and a more important subject is opened out in the consideration of the distribution of the rural population. There are few topics connected with India that more repay investigation than the different systems on which this population has formed itself into the microcosm which we know by the generic title of village, but it will be out of place here to enter into more than the outlines of it. In the first place, it should be explained that for the purposes of the census, the term village is used in most parts of India to denote the unit of administration of the land revenue, and this implies, as a rule, the existence of a congregation of the inhabitants on a fixed site, with occasionally some outlying hamlets. It is not so, however, in parts of Lower Bengal and of Assam, where the land settlement, not being subject to periodical revision, does not require the maintenance of minute administrative records, and the population scatters itself as it pleases within the limits of the village. It is not so, again, in most of the hill tracts, where the boundaries of the village, as a unit, may be surveyed or not, but the inhabitants thereof are not to be bound down to a fixed site, the spirits attached to which may at any time turn out suddenly malignant, leading to unexplained death or sickness in the resident families, or, still worse, to the loss of some of their fowls or cattle. In such localities, therefore, the tie to the site

* As this was passing through the press, Hofrath G. Bühler, C.I.E., to whom I referred this point, communicated a few instances, such as Páli, Nágara, and Siddhapur, in Western India, where a town flourished otherwise than under a local chief. There are doubtless others, but they seem to make the general rule stand out all the more clearly.—J. A. B.

is a very lax one, and it takes little to break it. Then, again, on the Malabar coast, the village, such as it is on the plateau above the Ghats, is almost unknown, so the unit taken is the collection of separate homesteads, known as the *Desham*, which corresponds to the *Deh* in the desert tracts of Sindh. When, too, we come to the constitution of the village, we find as much difference as there is in appearance between the walled and castellated mass of buildings that repels outsiders in the Panjáb and Deccan, and the unprotected bamboo-covered group of cottages that rises out of the rice swamp of Lower Bengal. The title of village community, which may be used of all, must not be held to imply that all possess the special feature so thoroughly described by Sir H. Maine in connection with the corresponding communities in the west, namely, the joint property of the whole body in the lands of the unit. This exists, though often in some modified form, in the north of India, and is the predominant form of village organisation in most parts of the Panjáb. Here the question of race comes in, as the communities from the north-west who have from time to time made their way into India across the mountains, have generally colonised the frontier Province in force, but have not strayed, save in small bodies, further into the plains. The great exception is that of the race known as the Aryas, who avoided the Panjáb and fixed their abode lower down the Ganges valley. Lastly, there is to be considered the race, or races, of darker colour and lower civilisation who were displaced by the immigrants, whether Arya or other. Inquiry stops here. Amongst these, who are generally called the Dravidian race, a term which may be used here for want of a better, it appears that the joint proprietary village was scarcely, if at all, recognised, though there were leaders of the community who held a predominant position in the village without interfering with individual property in the lands thereof, but who regulated the dealings of the community with the waste land and uncleared forest. It is possible that in most instances to this class was originally given a colonising or clearing lease of the village by the superior agent of the tribal Chief, who had the grant of a larger tract, which was subdivided as above. This is very different from the position of the joint owner of the northern frontier. Here, he is in most cases the sharer of all the land of the village, waste and occupied. In others, though the greater part of the land may have been partitioned off into individual holdings, it is subject, it is said, to occasional re-division, so as to give each cultivator of the village-family the chance of a share of the choicest soils, or, as is more probably the origin of the custom, to prevent any single set of occupants from gaining a permanent superiority over the rest of the sharing clan. It appears, however, that in this part of India, either the Dravidian element was not in existence, or that the repeated waves of immigrants of various races obliterated it in pre-historic times.

In the tract occupied by the Arya, on the other hand, which lay to the east of the Five rivers, there are, no doubt, traces of the imposition of hereditary proprietary right above the right of individual occupants; but in the present day, partly owing to more modern influences, the joint or landlord system of village property is universal throughout the North-West Provinces and Oudh, excepting, perhaps, in some of the hill tracts. Still further to the east, again, there is in Bengal, though not in Bihár, a village system created within the past century by the early British administrators, which, in the sense in which the term is used in connection with our present subject, is no system at all. The archaic form of holding these estates was stamped out wherever the Moghal got a fair grip on the country, as was the case with the half of Bengal that was populated at the time it passed into the hands of the British. In this province, accordingly, we do not find the more or less complete village organisation that distinguishes this community in the rest of India, whether joint or individual. In the Central Provinces, too, the system of village tenure is in great measure the creation of British administration, but differing from that in Bengal in the very important provisions made at the later settlement for the maintenance of the rights of the individual occupants against the encroachment of the newly-made proprietary title. Further south, the iron heel of the Marátha was exercised, like that of the Moghal in the north, in equalising subordinate rights, but the destruction of the former system was by no means so complete as under the more scientific procedure of the foreign absorbent of the revenue. Isolated instances of joint property are found in the west of India, one of which, in the north of Gujaráth, resembles in almost every particular the joint system of North-west India, whilst another is singular in the fact that the sharers are not necessarily connected by caste or blood. In a third we find the revenue system of the Maráthas perpetuated by the creation of what has now been confirmed as a proprietary title, that is, of a kind of farm of a village, or collection of villages, with the preservation, as in the Central Provinces, of tenant rights to occupancy at settled rates, instead of at will. One of the last distinctions between the joint and the individual system of village tenure which it is necessary to mention here, is the existence in the latter of the headman, as the leader of the community, and not, as in the former, as merely a State official for the collection of revenue and the minor duties of administration. Under the joint system such an exaltation of the *status* of any one member of the proprietary body, would be inconsistent with the oligarchical rule implied by the tenure. In the southern system, on the other hand, the post belongs, if not hereditarily, at least by convention, to certain families, on the condition that the occupant of the post is in possession of a landed estate in the village.

The village community. Such is the constitution of the village community, and the next point is its internal organisation. The Government is practically oligarchical, whatever it may be in name. If there be a headman, he acts as one of a body of "leading families." Where there is a coparcenary body, the village affairs are managed by a jury of the heads of the sharers. Megasthenes, on his travels, says that he found the institutions of the Panjáb democratic, and perhaps they were in those days, so far as the outside world is concerned. But the ambassador had been bred under democracy, and was predisposed by his training to find traces of it everywhere. We only see what we have been taught to look for, and the first judges of the Calcutta Supreme Court found in the absence of clothes on the part of the boatmen who carried them on shore, a proof of the poverty of the country, which poverty it was their duty to eliminate, whilst the British soldier is apt to attribute the want of muscle amongst the Indian peasantry to the unsatisfactory distribution of butchers' meat. But in fact, to the average villager, the notion of equality is scarcely "thinkable," and to those of higher rank it is abhorrent. If there chance to be a storm in the even tenor of country life, directed against the ruling body of the community, it will generally be found that the motive was, as Sully put it, not *l'envie d'attaquer*, but *l'impatience de souffrir*—some violation of the immemorial custom of the village.

In its economic aspect, the village aims at being self-sufficing, as may be assumed from its history. For not so very long ago, relatively to the life of a people, every village had to be in a state of continual preparation for defence against its neighbours. Community of interests was confined to the walls of the village, at least in the plains, and the ruling sentiment was towards peace internally, with distrust, if not actual hostility, in respect to all outside. No doubt, at a comparatively early stage in the development of the village in India, the local market was established for barter of surplus produce against articles of domestic use or convenience not to be made in the village itself, and these markets were regarded, according to Sir H. Maine, as the neutral ground of the inhabitants of the whole tract round. By-and-by, as matters settled down, room was made for the vendors of such articles within the village as residents, but not as members of the inner circle of the community, though they took rank above the groups of helots, who represent the displaced tribes found on the soil by the immigrant foreigners, and who were compelled to live in hamlets immediately outside the village site. Taking the "village community" of Sir H. Maine to refer to only the joint or northern Indian type of village, his work is still the standard authority on the subject, but, as shown by Mr. Baden-Powell, it should not be taken as of universal application to the whole country.

We find, then, that the community in question, in its normal stage, included only the differentiation of function necessary to supply the wants of an agricultural community, and, in the climatic conditions of India, these wants are few and simple. The spread of railways and other means of communication, and the general development of the trade of the country, have largely helped to add to the variety of the village population, but, as was remarked above, the new comers, in spite of their often greater wealth, occupy a social position considerably below that of the older members of the community. They make, accordingly, for the market town, so that out of the nine-tenths of the people of India, who, as shown above, dwell in villages, four-fifths at least belong to the classes that composed the original village community.* This is a matter that will have to be noticed in connection with the distribution of the population by occupation, but it is so far relevant to the present subject that it shows how, with the growth of the village in wealth and population, there is but little tendency towards extension laterally, as it were; in the direction, that is, of needs of a sort unknown to their forefathers.

* Where the tradition of hereditary title to the village lands is in its vigour, the rank of a well-to-do cultivator hailing from another village is far below that of the poorest of the "Old Standard." In the Deccan, for instance, there is a proverb that "the Pálki (marriage procession) goes to the door of the moneyless Mirásdár (hereditary landholder), past that of the Upri (new-comer) who has his five fingers in ghi (is rolling in wealth).—J. A. B.

The Statement G. on the next page, includes both towns and villages, but the marginal note gives the latter separately, but without territorial sub-division. It will be seen, however, that there are hardly any places of 10,000 inhabitants and over which are not classed as urban in character. The few in the highest group are almost entirely confined to the coast States of Madras, where the unit has been taken to be, not the Desham but the collection of Desham, known as the Provarti, a system of grouping which renders the return valueless for comparison. It must also be noted that the villages of the small State of Hill Tipperah, under Bengal, are omitted, for the reason already given. As regards the factors that determine the size of a village unit, a very few words will suffice. In former days the insecurity of a great part of the country no doubt led to the formation of comparatively large aggregates. In the north-west Panjáb, again, the tribal character of the occupation of the soil tended in some places to large, in others to small, villages. Thirdly, the fertility of the tract and the facilities for getting water where the rainfall is scanty, result in the establishment of small villages in favourable circumstances, and of large elsewhere. In the hill tracts, such as those of Assam, the Central Provinces, Bengal, and north Madras the want of arable land limits the village population to a very low figure. In some tracts, again, the custom of splitting up the original community into detached hamlets is increasing, now that life and property are secure, especially where the soil is so light that large holdings have to be taken up in order to provide for the family wants, and the cultivator would have to go long distances daily if he adhered to his ancestral homestead.

Varying size of the village.

Group.	Population.	No. of Villages.
20,000 and over	314,481	17
10,000–	1,455,214	109
5,000– -	3,883,938	606
3,000– -	12,854,322	3,469
1,000–	70,025,695	45,830
500–	67,475,109	97,846
200– -	71,180,018	222,996
Under 200	32,625,858	343,052
Unclassed -	20,478	—
Total -	259,834,813	713,925

Such offshoots are not, as a rule, counted as distinct villages, except in Bengal, east of Bihár, where the circumstances, as explained above, have been adverse to the formation of large communities. Then, again, in the Himalayan tracts of the Panjáb, the village, in its ordinary sense, is not to be found, the hamlet taking its place. Thus the return shows that whereas in the British portion of this tract, the revenue unit has been used, in the Hill States the return recognises only the *tika* or hamlet. On the whole, the latter seems to be the preferable course to be taken in future, as the members of the *tika* are usually connected by some bond or other, but the village, consisting of a number of hamlets founded by entirely independent sets of cultivators, is a mere unit of record, the collective name of which is not always even known to many of the inhabitants, and certainly is not in colloquial use. At the other extreme of India, in Assam, there is the revenue unit in the Bráhmapútra valley and in the upper portion of the Súrma; but elsewhere the people have squatted according to the convenience of their field work, and the village, as a community, is unknown. In the hills, too, there is only one large tribe that dwells in fortified units of population, and the rest move about in the forest, as need or inclination dictates. In Kashmér, we find much the same tendency as in the adjacent Panjáb hills to fix the abode close to the field, and as in such a hilly tract the area of land fit for cultivation is scanty and scattered, there is nothing in the shape of a large village except in the valley. In parts of Sindh, again, where the distances to be traversed are very great, the village unit occasionally includes from 10 to 20 hamlets, distributed over many square miles of almost desert country. With the above explanations Statement G. can now be examined.

Mean population of the village.

The general mean population per village in India, as a whole, is 363. In British Provinces it rises to 374, and falls in the States to 330. But the exponential figures added to the mean of the chief Provinces prove that except in Oudh, the Central Provinces, and Berar, that mean is the result of very considerable district variation. In the case of the States, where such aid is wanting, one or two leading points of difference have been already explained. For instance, the high average of 2,727, in Madras, as compared with that of 567 for the British portion of the Presidency, is due to classification only. The same may be said of that in the Panjáb States, which is 190, as compared with 532, for the divergence is greater in the Hill tracts than elsewhere, the reason being the different treatment of the *tika* or hamlet.

TABLE G.—Showing the GENERAL DISTRIBUTION of TOWNS and VILLAGES.

Province or State.	Average			Per-centage of Population contained in Places of							Per-centage of Places containing a Population of					
	Population per Unit.	Rural Population per Village.	Proximity of Villages in Miles.	Under 200.	200.	500.	1,000.	5,000.	10,000.	20,000 and over.	Under 200.	200.	500.	1,000.	5,000.	10,000 and over.
Madras	624	567 [56·26]	1·69	5·3	12·9	20·9	47·7	5·8	2·3	5·1	40·2	24·3	18·3	16·4	0·6	0·2
Bombay	845	605 [30·57]	2·05	3·8	15·9	22·0	37·8	5·4	4·7	10·4	24·6	35·4	23·3	15·7	0·6	0·4
Sindh	766	644 [31·83]	3·75	3·0	14·1	25·3	38·4	8·5	2·1	8·6	22·1	31·2	27·5	18·0	0·9	0·3
Bengal	314	299 [41·13]	0·88	16·7	30·4	24·0	23·4	1·1	1·1	3·3	53·6	30·8	10·9	4·6	0·1	—
N.-W. Provinces	418	367 [29·97]	1·09	10·0	25·1	25·3	28·2	3·1	2·1	6·2	44·6	32·4	15·6	7·1	0·2	0·1
Oudh	519	481 [10·39]	0·34	6·1	24·1	31·3	31·5	2·1	1·6	3·3	28·5	37·6	23·3	10·3	0·2	0·1
Panjáb	599	532 [32·33]	1·92	5·5	19·1	23·9	38·5	4·4	2·2	6·4	31·3	34·5	20·5	13·1	0·4	0·2
Central Provinces	314	298 [15·35]	1·71	16·1	35·2	25·4	16·1	2·4	1·6	3·2	50·0	34·8	11·9	3·2	0·1	—
Upper Burma	268	235 [29·36]	2·96	22·3	36·3	19·0	10·5	3·4	2·1	6·4	58·8	31·4	7·8	1·9	0·1	—
Lower Burma	262	230 [27·82]	2·39	22·9	39·9	17·7	7·9	1·5	2·5	7·6	57·4	33·9	7·2	1·3	0·1	0·1
Assam	319	313 [60·70]	1·82	12·9	45·1	23·0	17·6	0·9	0·5	—	40·2	45·2	10·9	3·7	—	—
Berar	496	439 [13·21]	1·87	7·6	23·0	25·8	31·1	5·8	3·5	3·2	37·4	34·7	18·4	8·9	0·4	0·2
Ajmér	728	572	2·05	4·9	13·8	18·6	35·1	7·0	—	20·6	33·3	32·2	19·5	13·8	0·8	0·4
Coorg	348	320	1·92	11·2	32·9	33·7	18·1	4·1	—	—	45·5	32·6	17·5	4·2	0·2	—
Total, Provinces	**411**	**374**	**1·44**	**11·0**	**24·8**	**23·8**	**30·3**	**3·2**	**1·9**	**5·0**	**46·2**	**32·0**	**14·2**	**7·3**	**0·2**	**0·1**
Haidrabád	573	522	2·18	5·3	20·8	29·1	35·4	3·3	1·6	4·5	27·8	35·5	23·9	12·4	0·3	0·1
Baroda	793	643	1·78	3·6	12·5	21·9	41·9	7·1	5·9	7·1	26·3	29·6	24·5	18·4	0·8	0·4
Mysore	293	257	1·37	19·3	34·3	21·0	17·6	2·5	1·2	5·1	55·6	32·1	9·3	2·9	0·1	—
Kashmér	306	282	3·36	17·3	31·5	23·5	19·8	1·9	—	6·0	54·8	30·7	10·5	3·9	0·1	—
Rajputána	395	346	2·24	11·8	24·4	22·6	28·6	4·4	3·2	5·0	50·0	30·2	13·0	6·4	0·3	0·1
Central India	317	289	1·68	16·6	31·2	21·5	22·5	2·7	1·6	4·9	54·0	31·6	10·1	4·1	0·1	0·1
Bombay States	522	449	2·29	7·5	20·2	25·2	33·0	4·9	4·1	5·1	38·5	32·1	18·9	9·9	0·4	0·2
Madras States	2,831	2,727	—	0·4	2·5	5·8	22·0	25·1	34·9	9·3	8·8	20·6	22·7	30·0	9·4	8·5
Central Province States	207	204	1·80	27·6	41·0	20·2	9·4	1·8	—	—	65·4	27·0	6·3	1·2	0·1	—
Bengal States	175	174	1·49	32·0	35·6	18·7	12·2	1·1	0·4	—	71·6	21·6	5·3	1·5	—	—
N.-W. Province States	442	298	1·60	12·0	45·1	19·2	11·9	2·1	—	9·7	38·2	49·1	9·8	2·8	0·1	—
Panjáb States	212	190	1·48	18·9	20·7	21·2	30·0	4·3	2·6	2·3	76·0	13·6	6·4	3·8	0·1	0·1
Total, States	**367**	**330**	**1·83**	**12·7**	**25·7**	**22·4**	**26·6**	**4·7**	**4·1**	**4·8**	**53·1**	**28·7**	**12·1**	**5·8**	**0·2**	**0·1**
INDIA	**400**	**363**	**1·59**	**11·4**	**24·8**	**23·5**	**29·4**	**3·5**	**2·4**	**5·0**	**47·9**	**31·1**	**13·7**	**7·0**	**0·2**	**0·1**
Villages only	—	363	1·59	12·6	27·4	26·0	31·8	1·5	0·6	0·1	48·1	31·2	13·7	6·9	0·1	—

Panjáb.	British.	States.
Hill Tracts	828	60
Submontane Tracts	516	474
Salt Range Tracts	547	—
Western Plains	440	616
Eastern Plains	666	419

Panjáb. But in other parts of the Panjáb, also, there is little agreement between the two, except in the submontaue tract, in which the village is less populous than where the arable area is less productive.

Baroda. Baroda, again, shows the high average of 643, the same as that of Sindh, but the cause is less artificial, as the size of the village seems determined chiefly by the circumstances of the northern division of the State, the soil of which is light, and the area under each unit relatively large. In the most fertile division, omitting the capital city, the mean is a little below that of the adjoining British districts, where the forest belt along the eastern edge, is narrower, and has less lowering effect on the average.

Baroda.	State.
Southern	535
Northern	853
Western	485

N.-W. Provinces and Oudh. In the case of the two States under the North-West Provinces, we find a curious coincidence of the averages, in spite of the very different density of the two. As, however, the British hill tract shows only 106 per village, and the Hill State gives over 300, it is clear that the method of classification differs, as in the corresponding tract in the Panjáb, only here, the *tika* is apparently recognised in British territory, and the village in the State. In the rest of the province the mean of different tracts is less uniform than usual. It is low in the southern hills, rises a little in the densely peopled south-central division, and very considerably in the Upper Doáb, where the population, though still thickly spread, has to undertake the cultivation of a wider area.

North-West Provinces and Oudh.	British.	States.
Hill Tracts	106	301
Submontane Tracts	375	—
Upper Doáb	565	—
Central Doáb	501	—
North Central	416	297
South Central	425	—
Southern	363	—

Bengal. The Bengal States are chiefly in the hill tracts above mentioned, where land is scarce, and the population is obliged to move about more frequently than in the plains, in search of fresh fields. On the eastern frontier, too, shifting cultivation is the rule, and when a forest tract has been wastefully burnt down for ash manure, by which the harvest of a single year is raised, the whole settlement migrates elsewhere for perhaps 10 or 12 years, by which time the low scrub has probably grown up again sufficiently for a second course of destruction. In the British portion of the hills and on the plateau of Chútia Nágpúr, the average size of the village is a trifle less than in the States. The highest average of the Province is found in North Bihár, where the village organisation is on the same footing as that of its neighbours in Oudh and the North-West Provinces. The high average of Eastern Bengal is in part attributable, probably, to the paucity of elevated building sites available for that amphibious population. In the only State found in the plains, Koch Bihár, the average is higher than even in Bihár itself, a result due, perhaps, to classification of hamlets in the sub-Himalayan portion of the State, but no explanation is given in the returns.

Bengal.	British.	States.
Northern	268	492
Western	240	—
Eastern	388	86
North Bihár	489	—
South Bihár	329	—
Orissa	216	149
Chútia Nágpúr	170	189

Assam. The case of Assam requires little comment. The two valleys, in spite of their different densities, show nearly the same average population per village, but in neither is the village a compact unit, as in the rest of India. In the hill tracts, the size of the village is determined, as in the hills of Bengal, by the necessities of agriculture, and is very nearly equal to that for Chútia Nágpúr, as given above.

Assam.	British.
Súrma Valley	348
Bráhmapútra Valley	353
Hill Tracts	155

Bombay and Sindh.

The four tracts included in the Bombay Presidency, excluding, of course, Sindh, show very different figures. The averages of Gujaráth and the South Deccan, or Karnátak, are both high, but in the former the aggregate is that of a generally homogeneous community, on a single site, in the midst of a comparatively small area of irrigable land. In the latter, on the other hand, hamlets are common, since the black soil, though fertile, is not irrigable to any great extent, and thus necessitates the occupancy of larger areas for dry-crop cultivation. The States falling within these two divisions show a different distribution. In Gujaráth, the average is below that of British territory, by reason of the wide belt of forest-clad hills that is included in the Eastern States. In the South Deccan the villages are a little larger than in the surrounding British districts. In the northern portion of this division, which includes Khándesh, and the forests at the foot of the Ghâts, the States, which lie for the most part in the latter, show, as a rule, smaller villages. Along the coast, on the other hand, owing possibly to a different treatment of hamlets, the reverse is the case.

Bombay.	British.	States.
Gujaráth	748	403
Konkan	483	541
North Deccan	588	345
South Deccan (Karnátak)	715	752
Sindh	644	849

Madras.

The Madras average, on account of the very different tracts into which the Presidency is divided, is by no means a useful one. Allowing for the special constitution of the unit on the western coast, we find the largest villages on the Deccan plateau, where, as in the case of the Bombay portion of that tract, the congregation is due to the large holdings necessitated by the lightness of the soil, with the consequent growth of hamlets, subordinate to the main village. A third very distinct class of village is found in the Agency tracts of the east coast, which form a continuation of the hill-belt of Orissa and the Central Provinces. Omitting this, the provincial average rises to 692, the highest in India. This is probably the true light in which the distribution should be regarded; for throughout the rest of the province the average is remarkably above the general mean. The Malabar States have been already discussed in connection with the present subject, and the rest are so small that they need no special comment here.

Madras.	British.	States.
North Coast Tracts	674	—
Agency Tracts	106	—
Northern Tracts	891	545
East Central	476	—
West Central	708	—
South Central	653	1,164
Southern	707	—
West Coast	982	3,469

Burma.

Burma comes last of the British provinces. It has not much of the village organisation of the rest of India, in which caste, from which this province is free, plays a considerable part in holding together the community. A trace of the village system is to be found, though slightly developed, in Upper Burma. The distribution in the different divisions calls for no remark, save that it does not seem to follow at all the density of the population in general.

Burma.		British.
Upper.	Northern	203
	Southern	286
	Central	237
	Eastern	194
Lower.	Arakan	172
	Pegu	247
	Irawádi	254
	Tenasserim	228

Haidrabád.

There remain the larger States and agencies about which a few words are required. Haidrabád is returned in three linguistic divisions, the Maráthi, the Kanarese, and the Telugu-speaking tracts. There does not seem to be much difference between them so far as the village average is concerned, and the two first agree in this respect pretty closely. In the north-east corner of the last there is some hilly country that contains a number of small villages, but the average is raised by the size of those in the plains.

Haidrabád.	State.
Maráthwáda	523
Karnátak	423
Telingána	537

Mysore.	State.
Eastern	265
Western	241

Kashmér.	State.
Kashmér	221
Jammú	320
Hill Tracts	354

Mysore presents no special features, except a generally small village. In Kashmér, the unit apparently varies in definition, so comparison is out of the question. Mysore and Kashmér.

In Rájputána, the three divisions are very different from each other. In the desert the villages are large, as they are in Sindh and the lower Panjáb, and for the same reason. In the south the Hill tracts are still in the occupation of wild forest tribes, who are averse from populous settlements, and so disperse by clans all over their territory. The Eastern States form the mean. They include more than half the population, and the extreme divergence between the other two gives them the preponderating influence in the general average. Rajputána.

Rajputána.	State.
Western	468
Southern	243
Eastern	351

The Central India Agency is such a mixture of race, jurisdiction, and geographical subdivisions, that the differences in the size of the village in the three great sections into which it is alone practicable to divide it may be purely arbitrary. The tract bordering on the Gangetic basin contains the largest villages, and Rewah, where the population lies thickest, comes second in order. The extreme west, like the south of Rájputána, is the refuge of the wilder tribes driven out of their former haunts in the valleys of the Tápti and Narmada, and their villages are little more than small collections of huts scattered over clearings in the forest. Central India.

Central India.	State.
Western	256
Northern	385
Eastern	287

In a former part of this chapter the mean proximity of towns to each other was shown, and in the statement now under review, the corresponding figure will be found for the villages. It may be worth while, perhaps, to explain that the proximity is a function of the square root of what Dr. Farr calls the areality of the unit selected. For example, in Sindh, where cultivation is sparse, each village, assuming equal distribution, is the centre of 12·17 square miles of country, and the average distance between it and any one of its neighbours is found to be about 3¾ miles. On the other hand, in Oudh, the villages are but 2⅔ furlongs apart, and in the North-West Provinces, just over, and in Bengal just under, a mile. The three tracts last mentioned contain over 46 per cent. of the total number of villages, which are there so closely packed that they determine in great measure the general mean, which is a little under 1½ miles. Table G. shows that in all other provinces this mean is exceeded. In the States, the average distance is greater, and falls just short of two miles, but Haidrabád, Rajputána, Kashmér, and the Bombay States, all show a higher mean. Mean proximity of villages.

The remainder of this table is given up to the proportional distribution of the places, whether town or village, according to population groups, and also of the population under the same groups. Nearly one half the total number of places contain less than 200 inhabitants. In British territory the proportion is a little lower, but in the States it rises above that figure. If we raise the limit to 1,000 inhabitants, it will be found that 93 per cent. of the places, with 66 per cent. of the population, falls within it, and the admission of the smaller towns makes but an insignificant difference. The table shows how this ratio varies in the different Provinces and States. Omitting the exceptional cases of Ajmér and the Malabar States, nowhere does the proportion of population in villages of less than 1,000 inhabitants fall below 38 per cent., whilst in some, as in Assam, Burma and the small States of Bengal and the Central Provinces, it rises above 80, and even to 89, facts which speak for themselves when the rural element of the population is in question.

House-room.

In discussing the density of the population it is usual to treat, also, of the question of house-room, in connection with either the inhabitants or the area. In the one case, the mean number of persons per house is generally taken as the subject for comment. In the other, either the mean number of houses per square mile, or the mean area of which, on the assumption of equal distribution, each house is the centre. The proximity, too, which has been shown above to be a function of the areality, to use the nomenclature of Dr. Farr, is also in some cases a matter worth consideration. But it is with reference to urban tracts, principally, that these statistics are of importance, and to render the data complete, information is necessary regarding both the inhabited and the empty houses. In India, as we have seen, the conditions of town life affect but a small fraction of the people, and looking at the heterogeneous items of which a town in that country is often composed, and the large area of open land generally included within the municipal limits, it was held to be superfluous labour to do more than register the unoccupied buildings at the enumeration, without compiling the results. For the same reason, the areality of occupied houses is not a point, at present, of moment, except, perhaps, in two or three of the largest cities. On the other hand, it must be pointed out that where it is the custom to build the village in a compact mass, often surrounded by a high wall of masonry or hard mud, the sanitary conditions are deteriorated to the level of those in a large town, and if the commingling indoors, on intimate terms, of human beings and cattle, be an evil, the village is even at a disadvantage; for the measures of purification introduced into the former on the initiative of British administrators, is highly honoured in the breach in rural India. But the compact, or castellated, type of village is confined to the dryer tracts of India, and throughout Bengal, east of Bihár; in Assam, Burma, the hill tracts, and along the coasts, the structure of the houses, as well as their arrangement on the village site, is quite different. The material is lighter, and the distance between the buildings is usually considerable, so that air circulates more freely than where the street, or continuous block of buildings, is the rule; but the habits of the people are the same, and the drainage, especially in the comparatively level tracts, is very obviously deficient. The heavy rainfall seems to counteract a good deal of the effect of this negligence, but when an epidemic has once got a lodging in one of these places, it is, no doubt, harder to dislodge than in the dry dirt of the north and centre of the country.

Definition of house."

After it was decided to restrict the census inquiry to a return of the inhabited houses only, the usual difficulty arose as to the definition of a house. In England, after the matter had been discussed at an International Congress of Statists, the house was held to comprise by definition "all the space within the external and party walls of the building." The committee of the aforesaid Congress that reported on the question, was unanimously adverse to the substitution of a proposed restriction of the term to what may be generally called a "tenement." In Scotland, and now in England, the latter term has been recognised, but subordinate to the general definition of the house. In India, the variety of structure with which the census has to deal is so great that it has been found impossible to frame a definition that would meet all the cases that would occur in the process of registration. In the Hill tracts one meets with collections of leaf huts that are here to-day and gone to-morrow, because, perhaps, the *genus loci* has brought about the untimely death of some of the family poultry, or a forest-guard has threatened a visit of inspection to the adjacent reserve. In Haidrabád, on the other hand, there are the residences of the high officials, or connections of the Chief, covering several acres of ground, with numerous courtyards and detached buildings, into some of which none but a member of the household is permitted to go, and the whole is surrounded by what would be the "external wall" of the English definition. Between these, come numerous varieties of house or hut. First, the portable arrangement of matting and bamboo that is slung on a donkey by the vagrant classes, though sometimes stationary on the outskirts of a village for months together, according to the patience of the permanent inhabitants. Then, the more stable erection for the cultivator whilst engaged in watching his crops; and so on, to the really permanent abode of the lower grades of village menials, with wattle and daub walls, which last for years, and a roofing of thatch or palmyra leaves, renewed as necessary, before each rainy season. The house, properly so called, is equally varied. In some parts of India it is the practice to wall in, with a thick hedge of thorn or rattan, a considerable space, over which the family expands in separate buildings as the sons marry; but all is considered to be a single "house." In the north of India, where family exclusiveness is carried to the highest pitch, all well-to-do people adopt the walled enclosure, with a courtyard or yards, and a small room or verandah along the outer wall in which to receive visitors and strangers. In Peshávar, for instance, which is a city pre-eminent in this respect, and, in a lesser degree in Lahore, there is street after street with hardly a single window in it. In the centre and south of India publicity is less disliked, and the house, both town and country, presents a less forbidding aspect. The material, too, is less solid, and, as a rule, the buildings seldom run to more than one story in the village, or two in the town. Pitched roofs, tiled or thatched, are usual in the moister tracts; flat-topped mud or brick buildings are almost universal in the dry plains of the Deccan and Upper India.

Extremes of climate.

One great cause of this diversity, and probably the most important, is the variety of climate that is experienced. The range of rainfall has received due attention in the introductory chapter, but in connection with the housing of the people, the average range of temperature has also its value. From the following table it will be seen that in the drier parts of the country the range of temperature is considerably over 20 degrees, whereas the mean temperature is not excessive, as compared with that of the moister tracts.

TABLE H.—Showing the Temperature and its Monthly Range.

Range of 20° F. and over.

	Station.	Average Monthly Range of Temperature.	Mean Monthly Temperature.
Panjáb	Dera Ismail Khán	28·3	74·3
	Multán	26·7	76·3
	Ráwal Pindi	27·2	69·2
	Peshâwar	26·9	70·6
	Lahore	26·7	73·3
Ganges Valley	Meerut	24·3	75·0
	Agra -	23·4	77·8
	Lucknow - -	24·5	77·7
	Allahabád - -	23·3	77·8
	Benares	23·0	77·8
Deccan	Poona -	23·5	75·8
	Sholápur -	25·0	79·0
	Belláry	22·7	80·6
	Karnúl -	22·6	81·8
Central Plains	Khandwa -	25·0	78·0
	Jabalpúr - -	23·8	75·5
	Nágpur - -	23·3	79·5
	Amraoti -	23·6	78·2
Indus Valley, &c.	Haidrabád - -	24·7	79·3
	Jacobabád	30·3	78·7
	Bhúj -	22·3	78·3
	Deesa - -	26·3	79·7

Range of less than 20° F.

	Station.	Average Monthly Range of Temperature.	Mean Monthly Temperature.
West Coast	Cochin	12·5	80·3
	Mangalore	12·6	78·6
	Kárwár	13·5	78·6
	Ratnagiri	14·5	79·2
	Bombay	10·8	79·5
	Karáchi -	17·2	77·2
East Coast	Negapatam	13·7	81·5
	Madras	15·9	81·8
	Masulipatam	16·1	81·2
Bengal and Assam	Calcutta	15·8	77·8
	Dacca	16·1	77·8
	Chittagong	14·8	76·3
	Dhúbri	14·8	74·2
	Sibságar	16·3	72·3
Bihár	Darbhanga	17·0	76·7
	Patna	19·7	77·3
Lower Burma	Akyáb	14·0	78·5
	Rangoon	16·4	78·8
	Maulmein	16·0	78·5
	Mergui	15·6	78·5
	Toungú	19·8	78·1

In these last the range is very slight, especially along the sea coast. The result is that in the region of great extremes, in the north of India, the houses have to be built to keep out the burning heat of the summer and also the biting frost of the winter. In the Deccan, though the heat is great, the winter is mild, whilst the Central Plains furnish a very fair example of the medium between the two. Now, along the coasts and in the Delta, even up to the Assam valley, the people enjoy a hot but equable climate, and have thus only the rain to guard against. But as soon as we get into Bihár, the extremes recede from each other, and a more substantial class of residence becomes desirable.

The above is the principal physical cause for the diversity of building in India, and another is the material that happens to be most convenient. But, what with the climate that allows the people to spend most of their time out in the open air, and their main occupation, which compels them to so spend it, the house comes to be but a relatively insignificant item in the domestic comfort of the masses. In the dry season, as soon as it begins to get hot, shelter at night is considered in many parts of the country a troublesome and ridiculous excess, and the open spaces outside the houses are covered with cots or mattresses. In crowded streets, even, the footways are blocked by rows on rows of long white bundles, giving it the appearance in the moonlight of an exaggerated edition of the slab at the Morgue. But with the upper classes throughout the country, and with the middle also in the north, custom prohibits to the women any participation in this freedom, so the roof of the house has to be specially protected for their use, and in a large establishment, sometimes a small courtyard affords the means of taking the air, with such exercise as is held to be necessary for the fair sex.

Social custom. Social custom, too, has a good deal to do with the construction and arrangement of the dwellings of the people in more ways than the above. The relative prevalence, for instance, of what is known as "joint" or "divided" family life amongst the Brahmanic classes, that is, the bulk of the population of India proper, determines the partition of the house inside, or even the number of doors. Then again, there are numerous degrees of detachment. If the link is only severed so far as property is concerned, the family often continues to eat together, and to cook at the same fireplace. But it may be deemed necessary to reverse the operation, and then the property remains in its integrity, but the family adds to its fireplaces, and eats in separate messes. The due arrangement of these fireplaces, too, has to be considered, as there is risk of offence to the supernatural if the mouth does not open towards a certain point of the compass. In many parts of the country, in the present day, it is said to be the custom for the younger branches to build themselves entirely separate houses, and to leave the paternal nest altogether, on which matter the provincial census Superintendents have in some instances found evidence in the returns. Amongst certain classes, again, chiefly in the Central Belt of hills, there is a general refectory or meeting-room for the whole unmarried population, and the spinsters are sent off after the evening meal to a dormitory at one end of the village, and the bachelors to one at the other, the houses of the Benedicts of the community intervening. The results of this arrangement are not said to be different from those of any other.

Varying definition. Upon considering all this variety, and the difficulties in getting a uniform interpretation of a general definition that arose in 1881, it was decided to prescribe a standard on which the provincial census Superintendents were to engraft special additions to suit the circumstances of the different parts of their charge. It was the object to thus obtain a return that would be uniform for the province or State, though it might be inconsistent with that of other parts of India. Clearly, therefore, the subject had to fall out of the ranks of the Imperial series. So far as the latter is concerned, the chief aim was administrative; namely, to show the enumerator what buildings he had to visit. It has, however, been treated provincially in all the reports, so that a certain amount of useful information has been recorded on it. It is not proposed to review the return generally, though this work would be incomplete without the quotation of the figures for the different provinces and States that have compiled them. For the sake of comparison, the corresponding return of 1881 has been added. The reduction of the average number of persons per house from 5·8 to 5·4 is due to the changes in Bengal and the North-West Provinces, and these, in turn, are clearly attributable in great part to a change in definition. In the last-named province there are numerous cases in which a courtyard surrounded by many separate tenements opening on to it is entered by a single gateway. These were formerly treated as one building, but on this occasion they were enumerated by tenements. In Bengal, again, the test on this occasion was the custom as regards eating together, or what the Provincial Superintendent calls by the convenient name of the commensal test. Each separate cooking place was counted as a house wherever the building was obviously outside the standard definition. In the city of Bombay, too, it is plain that the enumeration must have been by tenements on this occasion, probably counting as such those which had an independent entrance from some space either public or common to all the residents of the building in question. For further details the reader is referred to the provincial reports on the census.

TABLE J.—Showing the Average Number of Persons per House.

Province, &c.	1891.	1881.	State, &c.	1891.	1881.
Ajmér	5·2	5·3	Haidrabád	5·1	5·3
Assam	4·8	5·4	Baroda	4·5	4·6
Bengal	5·4	6·3	Mysore	5·5	5·7
Berar	4·9	5·7	Kashmér	5·7	—
{ Bombay	5·6	5·6	Rajputána	5·5	4·9
{ *Sindh*	5·6	5·5	Central India	5·3	5·6
{ Upper Burma	5·3	—	Bombay States	5·0	5·1
{ Lower Burma	5·4	5·5	Madras States	5·1	4·9
Central Provinces	5·0	4·2	Central Province States	5·3	4·6
Coorg	7·0	7·9	Bengal Province States	5·3	5·6
Madras	5·3	5·5	North-West Provinces States	6·0	5·8
North-West Provinces	5·8	6·8	Panjáb States	5·8	5·9
Oudh	5·5	5·5			
Panjáb	6·9	6·7	Madras City	7·5	8·4
			Rangoon Town	6·4	6·5
Calcutta	9·6	11·6			
Bombay City	14·4	26·3	**India**	**5·4**	**5·8**

CHAPTER III.

The Movement of the Population.

The true greatness of a State consisteth essentially in population and breed of men.—*Bacon.*

In the foregoing part of this work the population has been regarded as stationary, that is, as it existed at the time of the census was taken. It has now to be considered as in motion, in its relation, that is, to what it was 10 years ago, on the one hand, and, on the other, to the general change that, judging from recorded experience, is likely to have taken place in it by the time the next statement of account is obtained, at the beginning of the 20th century.

General conditions.

In this, its dynamical aspect, a population is the resultant of certain opposing forces, whose combined action tends ultimately to equilibrium. In the present stage, however, of the world's development, there is an almost rhythmic variation in the intensity of each, effecting continuous change, the bias of which is just now in favour of the positive, as distinquished from the preventive, elements. There are various ways of grouping these elements, and, on broad lines, we may adopt the two classes of the physical, or domestic, and the political, or foreign. Under the former head come the natural forces of birth and death ; in the latter we place war and migration. Underneath these general combinations, again, may be distinguished influences that are practically constant from those which are accidental or temporary. The reproductive instinct, for example, is constant, but its results are stimulated or repressed by artificial considerations, such as, amongst others, the prevailing views on marriage or inheritance. It may even be qualified, some hold, by a modification of type in a community which has reached a certain stage of development, in which case the restriction borders on the permanent. Death, again, is a debt due by all, though most of us are like Falstaff, loth to pay it before its time; but is liable to receive the fortuitous assistance of war, pestilence and famine. The change, too, resulting from migration may be accidental, or else part of the ordinary process of internal expansion.

The conclusions arrived at by Malthus on this important subject have been severely criticised, and often misquoted or misapprehended, but, in the main, they have not been disproved. In certain particulars, no doubt, his deductions were too sweeping, and in others, modern science, in the progress of physiological investigation and in the experience drawn from a wider field of observation, has had to introduce qualifications derived from sources of which Malthus was ignorant. For instance, in estimating the means of subsistence, he seems to have depreciated the results of an increased and improved application of human industry to the production of food from natural sources, and to have laid too little stress on the power of dispersion in sustaining any particular population. His view, too, that the power of multiplication was only restrained by what he termed the preventive checks, appears to be controverted by what we know has happened since he wrote. For, allowing that the proportion of married women of the reproductive age is the main factor in the natural increase of the population, we find that instead of the maximum number of children that could be produced during the 20 years included, as a rule, in this period, the average, even under highly favourable conditions, physical and moral, is about four per marriage, and only six at the maximum. We see, also, that in countries where every circumstance is in favour of multiplication, unrestricted by either postponement of marriage or abstinence from it, by war, starvation or disease, and stimulated, perhaps, by the immigration of adults of both sexes, the rate of increase is considerably below that which might, *ex hypothesi*, be possible. There is every reason to suppose, accordingly, that Malthus' view ignores some important physiological sequence that has not even yet been ascertained. We have, however, the suggestion, to call it by the least assumptive title, of Mr. Herbert Spencer, that pressure of population consequent on excessive fecundity, tends to provide, in some degree, its own corrective. For this pressure implies an increased demand upon the intellectual and nervous qualities of life to meet it, and the stock of nutriment being the same, these latter can only be satisfied at the expense of the reproductive faculties. The more the former are brought into play, the less there is left for the sustenance of the others. Life may be, and probably is, lengthened, but the community is neither so numerous or so physically well equipped as the well fed savage. If this doctrine be correct, and it has much to recommend it, one of its consequences may fitly be mentioned here. It is, that according to the theory, every community has to pass through a stage of what we may call probation. Between races and even the larger political entities, such as nations, a higher type of civilisation in the one and of character in the other, is pretty sure to prevail, and this is apparently what Bacon implied in the latter portion of the phrase quoted at the head of this chapter, and what one of our greatest modern statists, Dr. Farr, meant when he said that the "character of every race of men, "allowing for accidents of position and time, is the real limit to its numbers in the "world." But in the case of smaller aggregates than the above, where, that is, competition lies within narrowed limits and is actuated by more individualised impulse, intelligence and what are called the social virtues, must be, for a time, and a considerable one, at a discount. For, by the hypothesis, they result in diminished fecundity, so that, until they have permeated widely through the community, the class which exercises them must inevitably fade into numerical insignificance relatively to the reckless prolificity of those who have nothing to lose by the indulgence of their strongest instinct. This is an aspect of the population question which it has luckily not been necessary to take into consideration hitherto in connection with India, but the peculiar social organisation of the great mass of the people of that country renders it impossible for enlightenment to progress at anything like the rate of its numerical growth. The period of probation, therefore, during which these multitudes will have to be passing through the discipline of hardship before they are mentally adapted to their new circumstances, must be a peculiarly long and trying one. Luckily it seems to be still far off, and the approach to it is by steps almost imperceptible. For before pressure of the character above described can be felt by a community it is necessary that dispersion should have reached its limit. By dispersion is not here meant solely the migrations of a single community, but the corresponding movements of all communities to tracts which allow of their providing food to supply the wants of others, over and above the stock raised for their own maintenance. It is the facility of this transfer of the results of labour together with the greater industry and intelligence brought to bear on the soil where the arable area is fully occupied, that makes it possible to say that in the present day the food supply has increased not only in line with, but even in advance of, the growth of the population, and, other things being equal, this will continue to be the case, so long as there is land to be found on the globe fit for remunerative tillage.

Conditions in India.

We can now consider the part respectively played in the movement of the population of India by the birth-rate, by famine, by epidemic disease and other causes of death, and by migration. War has happily been, for this generation, a factor in abeyance. Of the rest, the natural causes of change, that is, the birth and the normal death rates, are necessarily entitled to the first place in the list, and in connection with them, the special causes of mortality, by epidemic and famine, will have to be discussed. Migration will then be treated separately.

Marriage customs.

Now, the number of births depends, as was remarked above, very much on the proportion of married women of the reproductive age, so we are here brought face to face with the marriage customs of the people and the tendency towards matrimony prevailing in India. In anticipation of a more detailed examination of this wide subject, which will be specially handled in a later chapter, a few general observations must suffice to explain its connection with our present topic. We should omit Burma, for the present, from the question, since the social system of that province is entirely different from that of the rest of the country. In India, as thus restricted, marriage is regulated by a few leading principles which nominally prevail amongst at least three-fourths of the population. Strict conformity with all is probably confined to a not very large minority, but such is the pervading influence of the system indigenous to the country, that a good many of its special tenets have been adopted by most of those communities that are brought into close contact with it, even though the orthodox prescriptions of their own system may be opposed to them. One of the most prominent universal duties imposed by this heterogenous public opinion is that of marriage. In the case of the Brahmanic community this is intelligible, as their current system dooms a man to a particular region of pandemonium unless he leave a son to perform the proper obsequies for his release. The duty is also connected with the law of inheritance which is, to some extent, binding on the masses. The forest tribes conform as they become civilised and are incorporated with the rest. The Musalmáns, who are, for the most part, converts from the ranks of Brahmanism, have not abandoned it, and the rest of the denominations of Indian growth equally observe the obligation. Then, again, amongst the higher and middle classes of all denominations there is the general feeling that the paternal hearth is disgraced by the presence of a girl who has arrived at womanhood unmarried. Polygyny, too, though undoubtedly rare, is allowed to all, whilst polyandry is confined to two or three comparatively small communities. It is scarcely necessary to dwell on the main fact indicated by these tendencies, that is, the enormous number of births that is likely to result from them. At the same time, it must be pointed out that it is the universality of marriage, not the early age at which it is contracted, that is here in question. The latter has sometimes been erroneously put forward as one of the causes of an increase in the child population, whereas its chief and direct effect in India seems to be only to shorten the mean lifetime of a generation, and not to increase the number of births per marriage, possibly owing to the physiological cause mentioned above, the nature of which has not yet been ascertained. Furthermore, the relative age at marriage is largely a matter of local custom, as well as of social position, and in certain tracts the upper classes marry, as a rule, at a higher age than the lowest in others. It should also be borne in mind in regard to this part of the subject, that the term marriage includes both the formal betrothal, which is the principal ceremony, and the subsequent handing over the bride *in manum viri*, the interval between the two being, as above mentioned, dependent on the local custom or the rank of the contracting parties, as the case may be. Amongst the Hill tribes and many of the labouring classes, the ceremonies are not distinguished, as girls are not married in either sense till they are grown up. In its ceremonial aspect, the betrothal is the binding and more important part of marriage, but from our present standpoint it is superfluous to pay attention to more than the later stage of this social arrangement. Thus we find that 94 per cent. of the unmarried females are below 15 years of age, and that though the proportion of women between 15 and 40 years of age is but a trifle in excess of the corresponding ratio in European countries, in India, no less than 84 per cent. of them are married, whereas in Europe, if we omit Hungary, where the ratio rises to more than 63, the average is not above 40.* The period in question, too, contains in India about 70 per cent. of the total married female population, but in Europe, excluding Hungary, as before, the average is only just above one half. This fact takes us a step further in the analysis of the return, for if we sub-divide the period into two, it seems that of women in India between 15 and 25 years old 87 per cent. are married; but in Europe the highest proportion, to the west of the Leith, is in France, where it is only 22. In the remaining period, from 25 to 40, the ratio of wives in India falls to 81 per cent., whereas in the West, it advances to about 70. The divergence is here due to the Indian custom as to widow-marriage. The orthodox Brahmanic view, whether it be well founded or not we need not inquire, absolutely prohibits the marriage of females whose husbands are dead, so that a girl betrothed in infancy, whose affianced happens to die before the latter part of the ceremony has taken place, is as much a widow as she who enters that condition at the decline of life. This rule is only strictly observed amongst the comparatively small communities of the upper classes, and throughout the masses there is great variety of practice. The lower and lower middle classes are, on the whole, influenced chiefly by local opinion on the matter, and where adult marriage is the rule, there is generally found no objection to the "maimed rites" and less expensive procedure involved in bringing home a housewife at second-hand. On the other hand, the general tendency of social aspirants to adopt the customs of those immediately above them, is extended to the case of the widow of course, and when a man of this class has, as the French say, "arrived," he makes the fact apparent by secluding his womenkind and abjuring widow-marriage. The above remarks apply to the Brahmanic community only, or, at most, to the fringe of Hill tribes that border on the plains. The Musalmáns have no prejudice in the matter, *teste* the first matrimonial venture of the Prophet himself, but even amongst them the pervading atmosphere of Brahmanism has had a certain effect. On the whole, the proportion of women who are returned as widows is 17·6 per cent. of the total of the sex, or about 3·5 to every widower. In Europe, the average ratio is about one half the above, and there are only about 106 widows to 100 men in the same condition. To some extent, therefore, we may take into consideration this rejection of second marriages amongst females as a check on the number of children that might be brought into the world under the operation of the great stimulus given by the religious sense of the majority to the indulgence of the strongest animal instinct of humanity. But, looking at the prevalence of marriage, it is clear that more than the existence of a few millions of widows, more

* The more correct period for Indian women would be from 13 to 35 years of age, but for the sake of comparison the higher limitation has been adopted.

or less, is required to account for the comparatively slow growth of the population under the impetus of so enormous a number of births. The clue is to be found in the accompanying high mortality. The birth-rate is indeed very far above that of any European country, if we except Russia, and reaches nearly 48 per mille on the whole country. But the death rate is equally abnormal, even if we omit the more frequent occurrence of famine and epidemic disease in India, and may be taken to reach, on an average, 41 per mille. This matter will be discussed in its due sequence, but, speaking generally, it can be attributed to an excessive mortality amongst infants of both sexes, a large mortality amongst young mothers in childbirth, and a general want of "staying power" after about 50 years of age. Of these factors, the first is the most prominent, as about 26 per cent of the children born do not live to the end of the first year of their life. In England the rate is not higher than 15·6. The operation of the second cause is more difficult to determine, as the return is complicated by the admitted repugnance in some parts of the country and amongst certain classes to communicating any information about the married or nubile women of their household. As to the last, the returns as they stand uncorrected indicate more than five per cent. deficiency of persons of 40 years old and upwards, as compared with the age-tables of Europe. The general divergence of the constitution and age distribution of the two communities can be appreciated to some extent from the average duration of life, which is little more than 24 years in India, against nearly 44 in England. These figures are given merely for the purpose of comparison. They do not show the actual mean age of the population, as it stood at the census, but the higher estimate obtained by considering the community as stationary. The former averages would, necessarily, in the case of increasing populations be some years lower. Still, the fact is made prominent by them that in India the generations must succeed each other with much greater rapidity than they do in the West.

Approximate birth-rate.

In estimating the growth of the population of India by what we have termed the natural increase, that is, by the excess of births over deaths, we are without the aid of complete registers of these occurrences. Registration has been in force for a considerable time, and a good deal of attention has been paid to it, but the circumstances of the country are against it. In municipalities, especially where town-duties are levied on imports, the deaths are registered with approximate accuracy, as the corpse has to be carried out to the cemetery or burning-place past one of the toll-bars. Births, however, even here escape registration to a very considerable extent. In the rural tracts, where the country is open, the villages close together, and their staff of officials fairly complete, the results are, on the whole, very good; the births, indeed, are probably as correctly entered as in the towns. But in the hill tracts, where locomotion is difficult and the villages far apart, even if stationary, and the people not only illiterate, but suspicious of everyone who is not equally so, the returns are too often altogether neglected, or kept by the headman by means of knots in a piece of string hung up to a beam in his roof till the next visit of the accountant or other officer, who writes up the register from dictation. In many parts of Bengal, too, the absence of a village staff placed registration for a long time in the hands of the lower grades of the rural police, so that the return was trustworthy in towns only. Then again, there are tracts where registration is not even attempted, owing partly to the density of the forest and the sparsity of the inhabitants, or again, to the nature of the tenure, which varies greatly in its degree of independence of State control. The large area under the feudatory Chiefs is excluded from the returns. In a few cases, such as Mysore and Baroda, there is a system of registration, but in most of the larger States information of this sort is not available. Finally, we come to the personal grounds of objection to the system. The householder of rank dislikes inquiries of any sort as to his family affairs. The rest do not fall in with the official idea of its utility, even if they understand the question. The death of an adult male member of a family is an event known to the whole village, and is registered accordingly, so is the birth or the death of a son. But mothers, wives, and daughters pass away without leaving a ripple on the surface of village life, and it is with respect to them that registration is most deficient. It is plain, however, from the returns, that greater accuracy is annually being obtained, and in one or two provinces, as was remarked above, the results for the 10 years that elapsed between the two enumerations so nearly coincided with those of the census that both operations may be congratulated on their successful issue. Elsewhere, the latter is the only means of, as it were, taking stock of the population. Even in England, where registration of domestic occurrences has reached so high a degree of accuracy, the last census showed that the results, apart from migration, were not quite what were expected. There is

Birth and death registration.

another point in connection with these returns for India that requires notice. The increasing accuracy of the registration, especially where the latter has been hitherto backward, is likely, if not duly discounted in the returns, to lead to the assumption that changes are taking place in the birth and death rates which, in fact, are not taking place. This is the more noticeable when the population on which the rates are calculated is maintained, as it often is, at the figure of the last census throughout the decade, so that even though the registration may have been uniform in its degree of accuracy during the whole interval, there is a sudden descent in the rates when the increase of perhaps 10 or more per cent. in the population, shown by the census, is brought into the returns. With all their deficiencies in respect to the absolute figures, these returns afford most useful data in comparing one year with another; for the error to be found in them is in all probability constant and uniform throughout the whole series. It is in this capacity that they have been used in preparing the corrections to be applied to the age-returns, which, as will be shown in a later chapter, enable us to dispense, to some extent, with the actual numbers.

Epidemic disease.

Having thus disposed of the main normal factors in the natural increase of the population, it is necessary to refer to those which we may call incidental, the first of which is the check on the increase produced by the prevalence, in annually varying proportionate strength, of certain epidemic diseases. It is not easy to treat this subject otherwise than very generally, for the diagnosis of the village accountant or the local constable is very liable to error, and except in the hospitals and dispensaries, the classification of the causes of death leaves much to be desired. Small-pox and cholera, however, if, indeed we may call them epidemics in India where they are always present, are probably more correctly registered than most other fatal maladies. The symptoms are too well known, and the disease, too, in both cases, is under the special control of a certain female divinity, who is to be propitiated only through the mediation of the classes descended from the pre-Aryan population. The rest of the ills to which Indian flesh is heir to, excepting accidents and snake-bite, mostly come on to the returns under the generic title of fever. Taking the return for what it is worth, we have had, during the past 10 years, a population under observation averaging about 197¼ millions, with a mean annual number of deaths amounting to 5,140,000, which seems to indicate an omission of at least one in three. Of those registered, the 10 years' average includes about 309,000 deaths from cholera, yearly, with the maximum of 475,600; 126,750, from small-pox, the highest number being 333,380, and 3,397,300 from fever, with the corresponding limit of 4,110,000. Of the remainder, a number just short of a thousand is unclassed; and accidents and what are grouped under the head of bowel complaints, account for the rest. Thus, to fever are attributed 66 per cent. of the deaths, to cholera, 6; to small-pox, 2; to bowel complaints, 5; and 21 to injuries and unclassified causes. The latter include, roughly speaking, 60,000 accidents, of which a considerable proportion are due to drowning, and 20,000 deaths from snake-bite.

Cholera and small-pox.

Cholera and small-pox are the two main causes of abnormal mortality in India, apart from famine and certain special outbreaks of fever, which will be noticed below. Not a year passes without cholera in some part or another of the country, and there seems to be no sign of its becoming rarer or less fatal. Whatever may be its origin, its dissemination is no doubt largely due to the immense congregations of pilgrims at certain seasons of the year, especially about the hottest time, to bathe and drink at one of the many sacred rivers or pools of the country, just about the month when the water is at its lowest. In spite of all the sanitary precautions adopted, the outbreak is still a matter of chance, and once it happens there is no limit to its local extension. As to small-pox, though it cannot be said to have been stopped by the greater prevalence of vaccination nowadays, it is said to be of a milder type in some parts of the country where it was formerly frequent and severe. The returns of blindness seem to indicate this to a slight extent.

Fevers.

Fever, as has just been remarked, includes a variety of diseases, amongst others, influenza, in the form in which it was prevalent during the past three years. There are, however, certain classes of fever that seem confined to special localities, which they ravage for a few years, and often disappear as unexpectedly as they broke out. For instance, in the Bráhmaputra valley of Assam, the "black sickness" (kála azár), that broke out some years since, has been peculiarly destructive to life along the southern bank, and has also crept across to a few tracts on the northern. For some time it baffled medical research, but its nature was thoroughly investigated in 1890 by a competent expert, who found the disease to be largely due to the insanitary habits of the villagers. The name he proposed for it was parasitic anæmia, or anchylostomiasis. Whatever it may be, its results are painfully apparent in the two districts where it has been rife for the longest period, and the Provincial Superintendent of the Census attributes to it a loss of over 100,000 people during the decade. Another instance of epidemic fever is that popularly known as the Bardwán outbreak, from the name of the district where it was specially prevalent some years ago. The tract, however, has obtained this bad eminence unjustly, for it seems that the disease originated further in the delta, about Midnápur, where it is attributed to the water-logging consequent on the choking of the natural drainage channels of this part of Bengal, by reason of the gradual changes in the course of the main estuaries. This process has been in operation, too, high up the delta, even to the border of the submontane tract, and affects the returns of four large districts. It is not only in the lower part of the Gangetic basin that water-logging has occurred. In the south-east of the Panjáb the natural drainage has been obstructed to some extent, and portions of the Karnál and Dehli district have passed out of popular favour, apparently for good sanitary reasons. Remedies have been tried, and others are about to be applied to the condition of the tract by Government. The case of the southern portion of the Ganges Doáb was mentioned in the last chapter. Here, however, there does not seem to have been so much an increase of mortality as the abandonment of the soil because it deteriorated for agricultural purposes. Along the borders of the Tarai, or sub-Himalayan forest and grazing tract in Rohilkhand on the other hand, fever has increased in prevalence during the last decade or so, though it is not said to be of so special a type as that of Bardwán or Assam. On this point the report of the Provincial Census Superintendent, which has not yet been submitted, will no doubt contain full comment. In other parts of the country there have been outbreaks of fever due to some local cause, such as that in Amritsar in the Panjáb, where the city population fell off by 11 per cent., whilst the rural tracts surrounding it continued to increase. In other cities, too, the malady we now call influenza grew to the intensity of an epidemic, and carried off numbers of the inhabitants in a few weeks. These examples, though not covering the whole field, suffice to show that in India the abnormal influences affecting the death rate are by no means as rare as the equable climate and the healthy outdoor life of the population at large would lead one to suppose they would be.

The next of the influences that we have to consider is that of famine, with which we have in India always to reckon. Most fortunately, the 10 years under review have been almost free from this calamity, and the one or two cases of serious failure of crops that did occur were purely local and restricted to very narrow limits, both territorially and with respect to the population affected. In fact, the only occurrence of this description worth mentioning is the scarcity that prevailed in the northern portion of the east coast of Madras, in 1889, and even here the direct effects were comparatively small. The season following the census, however, was unluckily marked by distress in the south-east Deccan, as well as in Rajputána, and by scarcity of a milder type in Bihár, but this is a period falling beyond the limits of the present subject. It is otherwise with the great famine of 1876–78 in the Deccan and South India, which has impressed itself rudely on the census returns. Here, as in the case of Orissa, in 1886, and Rajputána, two years later, and again, of the North-West Provinces, in 1861, the effects will be marked out in the age-tables until the generation that suffered them has passed out of life. But for the present, we have only to consider famine as one of the checks on the growth of the population, not in its detailed action on the latter. That check is exercised in a twofold manner, directly and indirectly. It not only increases the number of deaths, but it tends to diminish that of births otherwise than by merely destroying possible parents, as was the case in Thebes of old, Famine.

. . . . οὔτε γὰϱ ἔκγονα
Κλυτάς χθονὸς αὔξεται οὔτε τόκοισιν
Ἰηίων καμάτων ἀνέχουσι γυναῖκες.

As regards the first, the number of people who die from actual want of food is probably small compared to the deaths which result from the greater hold which disease gets on those who are enfeebled by diminution of their usual supply of nutriment. Thus, in times of scarcity, the mortality from ordinary causes, such as bowel complaints and intermittent fever, rises considerably above the normal rate, since many succumb who would in ordinary times offer a successful resistance. The second of the results just mentioned was very prominent in the age returns at the census of 1881 for the Deccan and Southern India, and reappears at the age of 10 to 14 in those of 1891. From these data it is clear that famine is most felt in the first four or five years of life. It then seems to pass lightly over the adults, and to fix on the aged, but only where the distress is acute, for the evidence on this point is not conclusive, as it is on the other. Now, as the reproductive ages are the least affected, one would expect to find the process of replenishing the gaps in the depleted population in full operation within a year of the return of normal prosperity. But even where the famine was followed by a bumper harvest this did not happen, and the cause of the check in reproduction was undoubtedly physical weakness, resulting from the long spell of insufficient nourishment endured by the masses. It took from three to four years, according to the returns, to restore the vitality of the worst tracts, but the marginal table shows that since then a considerable amount of lee-way has been made up. In regard to this table, it should be borne in mind that the famine was far more severe and of longer duration in Madras than in Bombay. There is also an indication that the resistance offered to distress is greater on the part of females than of males. On the whole, we have only to read of the terrible mortality that accompanied the historic famines of 100 or 150 years ago to appreciate the advance that has been made within the present generation in administrative experience of how to deal with these calamities, so that their effects may be mitigated, though to prevent them is impracticable. By the aid of lines of railway and telegraph, the tract threatened with scarcity is brought into speedy communication with those in which the harvest has been abundant, so that from the latter food pours in as long as the prices at the markets of the former keep the transport remunerative. The case of the classes thrown out of work by a failure of the crops, who have neither grain of their own nor cash in hand to buy what is physically within their reach, has been duly considered, and so far as a crisis of this sort is concerned, the problem of State aid for the unemployed has been solved. An estimate based on local inquiry, collated with the census returns of caste and occupation is prescribed for each district, showing the approximate numbers of the community that are most prone to suffer, classified according to the order in which they are respectively likely to be thrown upon State support. Estimates and plans of undertakings of public utility involving the employment of the requisite amount of unskilled labour are kept in readiness by the Public Works Branch of the Local Government, and by each of the latter a code of rules regarding famine administration has been framed, which includes minutiæ of sanitary arrangements, daily tasks, the laying out of camps of work and refuge, with other measures of relief that the experience of the last 30 years has proved to be the most efficient in the circumstances of the tract and population to which they are to be made applicable. The loss of life which is inevitable in time of famine is thus likely to be reduced to a minimum.

TABLE A.

—		Males.		Females.	
		Famine.	Normal.	Famine.	Normal.
MADRAS	Total increase	20·56	11·20	19·58	12·10
	Increase of children under 5.	72·83	19·69	71·82	19·14
BOMBAY	Total increase	20·03	10·05	19·11	10·63
	Increase of children under 5.	66·34	15·87	66·60	16·97

Probable diminution of normal mortality.

The present system of administration is conducive also to the preservation of life in less abnormal circumstances. The spread of vaccination, though uneven, is doing much to mitigate the ravages of small-pox. Cholera, which it seems impossible to prevent altogether, is localised by segregation, or by the strong measure of prohibiting religious gatherings, whenever they are likely to lead to an outbreak of this scourge, and in all such cases the sanitary arrangements of the locality are placed under the control of special Superintendents. As for normal disease, every year sees an increase in the number of dispensaries, which are, in fact, small hospitals under trained men, scattered about the rural tracts, whilst in larger towns the lower grade of medical practitioner, turned out by the Universities, is growing in popular favour against the rivalry of the herbalist and exorciser. There seems, again, no immediate prospect of any general amelioration of the views of the populace respecting marriage, which will continue, therefore, to be one of the chief duties of man, whilst the extension of trained obstetric aid of late years will in time probably do something to counteract the results on immature mothers and their progeny of the ruthless empiricism of the barber's wife, who at present is the chief officiator in this capacity. But can there be any doubt as to the result towards which all these provisions tend?

In countries where there are no large tracts of unoccupied arable land, the rate of increase of the population is, other things being equal, inversely as its numerical growth. Every census shows that in compliance with the tendency noted in an earlier portion of this chapter, as a country fills up, the annual rate of increase diminishes.

The conditions on which that rate can be maintained at a uniform level are either the increase of return from the cultivated land, to which the limit is soon reached, or dispersion of one of the two kinds already specified. The community must betake itself to occupations other than food-producing, and indent for their nutriment on other parts of the world, where the products of their industry are in higher demand than food; or the dispersion must be over fresh land in their own country. Whilst and where this last is to be got, pressure of population amounts to no more than local congestion, for so long as there is room, actually or potentially productive, relief is only a matter of time, more or less according to the character of the people concerned, their adaptability to change, and the nature of the tract within their reach.

Quality of agriculture.

Now, in India, there are several tracts where the agricultural skill and experience of the people have been said by experts to get the maximum yield out of the soil. In others, the harvest does not respond so thoroughly to the care bestowed on it owing to the scanty or uncertain rainfall, but the aid of irrigation can be called in to preserve the crops. In most parts of the country there is a great waste of the material available for fertilisation. Cattle are very numerous, but they are turned out to stray over waste land, or where they can pick up a little grazing more or less scanty, so that their droppings are either wasted or collected only for fuel, and their bones are being exported for use in Europe in increasing quantities. In some parts of the country sheep and goats are systematically hired out to be penned at night on the field, but this practice can affect but an insignificant portion of the dry-cropped area. As to rotation, experts have a good deal to say against the somewhat primitive cycle received by the Indian husbandman from his forefathers, and it may, perhaps, be possible to increase or sustain the productiveness of the soil by a change in system, but this, like so many other suggestions in the same direction, is at present a matter of conjecture. The variety of character amongst the cultivating classes, too, is a factor in the situation, as well as that of the soil. The chance, under the present conditions, of many more tracts in India rivalling the fertility of Oudh and the great deltas is about equal to that of the scratcher of the hillside in the forests, or the many-acred driver of the Maratha plough, settling down into a market gardener. So far as lies within our present purview, neither one nor the other is probable or impossible.

Prospects of dispersion.

It appears from what has been sketched above, that throughout the greater portion of India the occupied land has, probably, not yet reached the limit of its productiveness, and in the preceding chapter it was shown that congestion of the population was at present found to comparatively a small extent. We have to consider now the question of dispersion, whether vertically, by change of occupation or produce, or laterally, by change of locality. As to the former, circumstances seem to point to a long continuance of the present position of India as a self-sustaining country. With its existing population it manages to set aside very considerable areas for the production of raw material other than food, and throughout the decade under review, the outturn of this class of produce seems to have increased rather than to have been restricted by the growth of the population. From one quarter, cotton and wheat, from another, indigo, jute and tea; rice from a third, and oilseeds and opium impartially, pour into the seaports, in close response, apparently, to the opportunities offered in foreign markets. The easier task for the cultivator would doubtless be to confine his efforts to the growth of food-grain or pulse, so his free adoption of the alternative proves that he appreciates its superior advantages. As for manufacturing industry, its progress, though rapid of late, has not been diverse enough, either in kind or locality, to make much impression on the country at large. It has certainly hitherto won only a comparatively small portion of the community away from the agriculture to which the letter is traditionally devoted. For one thing, India is at present at a disadvantage in comparison with many of its compeers as regards a sufficient native supply of good coal and iron. Its labour is plentiful enough; whether it is cheap or not depends on its quality relatively to that of the more highly paid wage-receiving class elsewhere. Some branches of industry, it is true, have taken root to an extent that seems to open out the way for the transfer of capital to India from countries where, for various reasons not yet prevalent in the East, profits are, to put it mildly, uncertain. Amongst these are, of course, cotton and jute works, to which may now be added paper-making and articles of leather. The wider extension of any of these operates towards the dispersion of the population from the land, and so far tends to lighten the burden as it becomes heavier in the course of years.

Finally, there is the question of lateral extension. To measure the possibilities in this direction it is necessary to ascertain the area of arable land still available for cultivation, and this, as was shown in a previous chapter, we are unable to do, with even approximate accuracy, for the country at large. It will be more convenient, therefore, to touch briefly upon the point in connection with the provinces for which the best information is available. For our present purpose, the returns of birthplace, which form part of the general series, will enable us to appreciate to some extent the tendency towards migration within India. This tendency, it is clear from the tables, is at present remarkably weak; and that this should be the case is no more than is to be expected from a community so devotedly agricultural, a class invariably opposed—

Migrare vetusto
De nemore, et proavis habitatas linquere silvas.

Migration. In India, too, there is the additional attractive power of the village organisation and the prevalent connubial system. With regard to expansion within the limits of the land appertaining to the village itself there is no difficulty, but cultivators from outside are, as a rule, only admitted with considerable reluctance, and in many parts of India would not obtain land at all. Then, too, where the available waste land lies in a compact tract within an easy distance of the ancestral village, the population is able to advance on it, as it were in line, and is thus in a position to form fresh communities on exactly the old model, and to keep in touch also with the home and tradition of their forefathers. The objection to agricultural migration begins where the tract to be occupied is separated from the native land of the emigrants by a population differing from the latter in race or language, and except in a few special cases, attempts at migration of this sort, to any great extent, have not yet been successful. In Assam, a good many of the immigrant labourers on tea plantations have settled down on plots of land near the scene of their work, made over to them for home cultivation. In the west of the province, too, there is a flourishing colony of the same class, under missionary supervision. An attempt to relieve parts of Bihár by means of State grants of land in Burma has been made within the last few years, and though it is too soon as yet to judge of the results, the progress made on a small scale seems encouraging. The difference in race and language, however, will probably be found an obstacle to any great extension of the movement. Temporary displacement of the population, however, both agricultural and other, is by no means rare, and is increasing in both number and variety. The movement is not yet extending to any significant degree to foreign countries. For instance, during the last 10 years, the number of emigrants registered was only 130,483, the greater portion of whom were bound for the West Indies and Guiana. But to Burma and Ceylon from Madras, and from Bengal to the tea gardens of Assam, the annual movement is considerable. The docks and mills of Bombay and Calcutta, too, and the wheat harvests of various parts of northern and central India, and the plantations of Coorg, attract a considerable number of extra hands, the proceeds of the labour serving to sustain the whole family during the period when the cultivation of their plot of land at home does not entail their presence.

Immigration. There is then to be considered the accretion to the population due to immigration from beyond India. This movement is mostly confined to the tracts immediately bordering on Nipál and the north-west frontier, and most of the immigrants come from the first-named State and from Balochistán, Afghanistán, and the strip between the last and the Panjáb, called Yághestán, or the independent territory. We have no corresponding returns from these countries to show how far the inward movement is balanced by one in the opposite direction from India, but where the boundary is merely political, and denotes no distinction of race or customs, the larger proportion of the movement is probably restricted to villages immediately contiguous to the frontier line on both sides.

The marginal statement shows how small a part immigration plays in the constitution of the population of India. Taking 10,000 of the people at random, only 23 will be found to have come from across the frontier. Of these last, the nine from Nipál are chiefly along the frontier of Bengal and the north-west, and the rest in the Native Army. Balochistán supplies only Sindh, except for a few Mekránis and others entertained as guards in native States. The natives of Afghanistán and its neighbour are mostly on the Panjáb frontier, or scattered in small bodies of pedlars all over

Birthplace.	Number.
British Provinces	7,708
Feudatory States	2,269
Total within India	**9,977**
Balochistán	2
Afghanistán	3
Yághistán	3
Nipál	9
Asiatic Countries remote from India	2
Elsewhere	4

northern and central India. Of the other Asiatics, one will probably be a Chinese, and the other an Arab; the former in Burma, the latter in Aden. There are, of course, numbers of other birthplaces returned, but under none but the United Kingdom do the figures approach the proportional limit above given, of one person in 10,000. The statement B, below, shows the main facts ascertained with regard to the birthplace of the foreign population.

The full return at the present census will be found in Table XI. (A. and C.) of the general series. It should be remembered that in this statement we are dealing simply with birthplace, not with nationality. Though the relative numbers involved are insignificant, it is worth while to compare them with those of the census of 10 years back, so the returns for Kashmér and Upper Burma are not included in the marginal table. On the last occasion, Yághistán was not distinguished from its neighbour, and there were, no doubt, good reasons at that time for the population to refrain from entry into India. The increase of people from Nipál is mostly due to immigration into Dárjiling and the adjacent territory, for work on tea gardens. There are settlements, too, of this race in the North-West Province Tarai, as well as in Benares, the object of the aspirations of all devout Gúrkhas. Passing over differences which are probably due to classification, we come to China, which has furnished a comparatively large contingent to Rangoon since last census. The addition to those from Arabia is due, chiefly, to the development of Aden, which accounts, too, for the great number of those born in East Africa. The bulk of the persons returning birthplaces in Europe beyond the United Kingdom, is to be found in the centres of commerce and missions. The Scandinavians, especially, affect the seaports. Of the rest, the Germans and French are the only nations strongly represented, though most of them show a slight increase since 1881. The return for America is obscured by the confusion between the States and Canada, more especially in the army and railway schedules. Australia contributes a good many more

TABLE B.

Birthplace.	Number returned.	
	1881.	1891.
ASIA.		
Afghanistán and Yághistán	125,141	158,655
Belóchistán	60,318	61,433
Túrkestán	429	977
Thibet	2,756	1,641
Bhotán	4,964	4,353
Nipál	135,166	233,553
Ceylon	2,774	5,574
Further India, &c.	4,662	8,259
Arabia, &c.	23,430	28,065
Persia, &c.	3,501	4,386
China and Japan	12,783	19,704
EUROPE.		
United Kingdom	89,015	97,921
Gibraltar, &c.	171	302
Germany	1,208	1,439
France	1,131	1,230
Italy	812	878
Austria	350	414
Sweden, Norway, and Denmark	586	540
Holland and Belgium	261	335
Spain and Portugal	240	376
Greece	212	236
Russia	205	262
Turkey, &c.	379	295
Europe unspecified, &c.	869	851
America and Canada	1,504	2,325
East Coast of Africa and Mauritius	3,537	9,568
Other places in Africa	1,194	1,997
Australia	378	503

than it did 10 years ago; probably the horse trade has something to do with this, but there seems also a tendency to settle in the south on the part of people who have long worked in India. The rest of the table needs no special comment.

We can now deal with the return as a whole, and to facilitate reference a proportional summary is given below :—

TABLE C.

Province or State, &c.	Born in India.			Born in Asia beyond India.		In other Continents.	Mean Number of Females per 1·000 Males.	
	In District or State where enumerated.	In contiguous Districts or States.	In non-contiguous Territory.	Contiguous Countries.	Remote Countries.		Born in District, &c.	Born in contiguous District, &c.
Madras and States	9,601	313	83	1	—	2	1·011	1·221
Bombay and States	8,808	683	496	2	3	8	·946	1·452
Sindh and Khairpur	8,824	809	325	25	5	12	·854	·727
Bengal and States	9,142	391	442	23	—	2	1·025	1·044
N.-W. Provinces and States	8,910	885	200	1	—	4	·860	1·926
Oudh	8,911	933	152	1	—	3	·902	1·565
Panjáb and States	8,692	922	320	56	—	10	·899	1·218
Upper Burma	9,289	365	307	9	20	9	1·136	·860
Lower Burma	8,141	499	1,293	17	38	12	1·002	·664
Central Provinces and States	8,664	1,079	254	1	—	2	·996	1·108
Assam	8,868	262	845	23	—	2	·980	·665
Berár	7,678	1,814	505	3	—	—	·925	1·159
Ajmér	7,996	1,382	612	2	—	8	·832	1·425
Coorg	6,942	2,768	280	2	1	7	·950	·552
Haidrabád	9,054	575	362	2	4	3	·952	1·211
Baroda	8,629	1,026	343	1	—	1	·868	1·720
Mysore	9,219	533	241	—	—	7	·994	1·062
Kashmér	9,726	262	4	8	—	—	·877	1·089
Rajputána	9,120	724	155	1	—	—	·840	1·902
Central India	9,271	609	116	1	—	3	·899	1·218
Total India	**9,038**	**623**	**316**	**17**	**2**	**4**	**·947**	**1·370**

Interchange of wives between contiguous villages.

Now, the important feature in the above is the fact that no less than 9,661 persons out of every 10,000 were born in or touching the district or State where they were enumerated, and that by far the larger proportion of these were natives of the place in which the census found them. Then, again, the movement from the contiguous territory is not migration, in the ordinary sense. Instead of being the transfer of families, it is mainly the interchange of children in marriage, a practice which obtains to a greater or less extent according to the predominance of the influence of Brahmanic prescription, with its strict observance of endogamy, as it is usually termed, within the caste or tribe and the accompanying prohibition of marriage within certain degrees of relationship, of which some are, according to western motions, rather remote. In order to make this clear, two columns have been added to the statement, giving the ratio of females to males, first, amongst the district-born, and, again, in the case of those who come from other parts of the country, but touching the unit of tabulation. There are, of course, other factors that enter into the proportion, such as the complexity of territory with other districts or States, which is the case in Bombay and Baroda. But, on the whole, the marriage system is at the bottom of the divergence. Thus, in Bengal, where it will be noticed that the difference in this respect between the two groups is small, it appears from the more detailed tables of the Province that the ratio is but 687 females to 1,000 males in the eastern division, though there, too, the females are on the whole, in excess. But here the bulk of the people are Músalmán, on whom the strict marriage law of the Brahman is not binding, and we find in all the rest of the province a proportion varying from 812, in the north, where women are altogether in defect as compared with men, to 1,934 in Orissa, the population of which is wholly Brahmanic in belief. It is the same, though to a smaller degree, in Bihár, where society and the village are organised very much as in the neighbouring territory to the west. In this last, the proportion of females from across the district border is remarkably high, and for this the small size of the unit may be to some extent accountable. Not to dwell too long on this point, it will be seen that in Burma, where the Buddhist form of faith is predominant, the ratio is low, and the same feature results in Assam and Coorg from the prevalence of male immigration to the plantations.

Migration from a distance.

Outside the above two categories, there remains but 3⅛ per cent. of the population, and of this, again, 3·16 per cent. comes from tracts within India which do not actually touch the district of enumeration. There must be, accordingly, a good deal of accident connected with entry in this group. For instance, most of the immigrants into Berár that do not come from territory immediately adjacent, are probably from parts of the Deccan not far off, as the population there is very homogeneous in structure. So, too, with Baroda and Haidrabád. In Bengal and Bombay, the internal migration of the temporary character that has been described above raises the average proportion that is there found in this group, for in the former province the migrants place central Bengal between their home in Bihár and the scene of their labours, and in Bombay, too, the recruits are mostly from a distance, whether in the capital or in the wheat fields of the North Deccan.

Variation in migration.

On the whole, then, permanent migration outside the district and State unit is very rare, and the only question regarding it that need be here discussed is its relative prevalence now and 10 years ago. This point is dealt with in the marginal table, so far as British provinces are concerned. Any slight difference that may be found between the figures given in the last column and those in the more general tables quoted hereafter is due to the exclusion in the former of the number of persons who did not return their place of birth. In the case, too, of Madras and Bombay, it has been thought advisable to separate the famine area of 1876–78 from those in which the circumstances of the last 15 or 20 years have been normal, in order to show, to some extent, how much of the replenishment that has been going on of late is due to births within the district, and how much to immigration. The data are not, however, sufficient to distinguish, in the case of the latter, between those who have come in as new men from outside and those who left the district during the time of distress, but who have returned since the last census. There can be little doubt, however, that the primary factor is the first, as is indicated in the age-returns for the two enumerations. The return of the temporary migrants is a feature in the increase in some of the Bombay districts, but is not mentioned in the report on the corresponding tract in Madras, where it was no doubt less marked, though not entirely absent. In the former, the hill-lands of the west and north were comparatively near the affected tract, and as fodder for the cattle was to be got there, many of the inhabitants accompanied their flocks and herds to these favoured parts of the country, and there was also a slight movement in the direction of the central plains of Berár and Khándésh, on the part of agriculturists in search of fresh land under better auspices. In Madras, the area affected was larger, and the lands of promise further off. On the other hand, there seems to have been a considerable increase in the latter Presidency of migration to Burma and to Mysore. The former

TABLE D.

Province.	Per-centage of the District-born.		Per-centage of Increase amongst the	
	1881.	1891.	District-born.	Total Population.
Madras — Normal	95·16	95·76	12·27	12·21
Madras — *Famine*	*96·22*	*96·01*	*19·84*	*20·11*
Bombay — Normal	84·81	84·21	9·35	10·13
Bombay — *Famine*	*90·63*	*90·60*	*19·50*	*19·54*
Sindh	87·10	87·89	20·05	18·97
Bengal	92·54	91·75	5·98	6·88
North-West Provinces	88·23	89·04	5·51	4·56
Oudh	88·05	89·11	12·42	11·08
Panjáb	87·56	87·49	10·66	10·74
Lower Burma	78·93	81·22	28·19	24·59
Central Provinces	88·17	90·12	12·03	9·61
Assam	92·48	89·39	7·58	11·30
Berár	76·59	76·77	8·66	8·40
Ajmér	74·59	79·96	26·21	17·72
Coorg	58·01	69·42	16·11	— 2·94

is but the continuation of a tendency of some standing, but the latter is a new departure. It is attributable, it is suggested, in some degree, to the opening offered by mining enterprise in this State, and this is most likely true, since the chief mining district runs far into British territory on three of its side, so that change of domicile to one of the labouring class, is a matter of little difficulty. Of the increased number of natives of Madras found on this occasion in Haidrabád, the Provincial Superintendent finds no explanation. It seems, however, that the increase is but small, and deducting the probable figures due to frontier marriage transactions, the rest may be easily absorbed by the large cantonment of Secandrabad, which returns a large Madras-born population, or by the attractions offered to the enterprising labourer of the south by the mining works in hand in the north of the State. Until we have the detailed account of the Haidrabád Superintendent, however, which is not yet published, conjecture is at a discount.

Some of the other provincial figures present no complications. In Sindh we find the growth to be nearly entirely that of the home born, and by this term we mean no more than those born in the district where they were enumerated at the census. In Lower Burmah the same feature is very apparent, in spite of the great absolute growth of the immigrant labouring population. The case is the same with Berár, Oudh, the North-West and Central Provinces to a less extent, and with Ajmér to a greater. On the other hand, Assam, it will be seen, depends very largely on immigration for the increase it shows as a whole, a fact which is partly connected, of course, with the bad health of some of the districts during the decade, as has been mentioned above. Coorg presents the unusual feature of a large increase of its native population with a falling off in the total, the result being partly due to the early season on the plantations in 1891, and partly, perhaps, to a decline in the labour market. The Panjáb shows very small divergence from the figures of 1881 in regard to the ratio of its home-born population. There is a good deal of difference, however, between the east of the province and the west in the character of what movement there is. In the former, the reciprocal marriage system is in vogue, so that the figures tend to approach those of the North-West Provinces. But in the west, the ethnological differences are more striking, and the tribal system of connubium does not entail so constant a search for a wife at a distance. The settlements, too, are further apart, owing to the nature of the tract, and, altogether, the migration that is apparent here seems due mainly to special causes, such as the opening of new irrigation works, of a new railway, and so on. It is remarkable to find that in the congested districts of the submontane tract, emigration has advanced by only 17 per cent. in the 10 years, whilst immigration shows an increase of 23 per cent. It is true that much of this movement is merely that of brides from neighbouring villages, but the fact remains that the proportion of females to males entering the tract is on the increase, whilst in the other direction the reverse is the case. The continual demand for females in this tract gives rise to suspicions of infanticide, as the Provincial Superintendent has hinted in dealing with the population in connection with the subjects of age and sex distribution. In both Bengal and Bombay the tendency to migrate seems a little more pronounced than it was 10 years ago, but in the latter province the real movement is confined to a few districts, notoriously those of the Deccan and the coast, where life is hardest to the lower class of the agricultural population, whether small landholders or merely field labourers. The way the districts in this province are mixed up with small States, especially in the north and south, reduces the proportion of the district-born, owing to the custom of reciprocity in disposing of marriageable children. The return shows some noteworthy differences in the case of the migrants to and from parts of India outside the Presidency, as compared with the corresponding figures for 1881. The most instructive, perhaps, are those for Berar. After the famine of 1876–77, the movement from the Deccan to the plain was largely composed of males, but in the interval, though the males still preponderate, it is in a much smaller proportion, whilst the return from Berar is almost doubled in number, and the sex-proportion shows that it is chiefly based on marriage considerations. Something hitherto unexplained seems to have happened in regard to the connubiality of the Haidrabád frontier, for whilst the Bombay receipts have risen, the gifts of the province to the State have declined by more than 40 per cent. Baroda, on the other hand, keeps up its reputation, apparently, for both wives and husbands. The returns for Bengal have been minutely analysed by the Provincial Superintendent of the census, owing to the great importance in so dense a population of a knowledge of local movements. It seems, to speak generally, that the course of migration is almost entirely from west to east, but the sex-proportions indicate that the transfer of the family, or permanent migration, is confined to very small limits. It is curious to see that the Bihár labourer is very averse from venturing further south than the Ganges into the Delta, whilst all round Calcutta and in the inland districts of Eastern Bengal both he and his neighbour from across the Ghágra are comparatively numerous.

Migration to Feudatory States.

In concluding this portion of the subject, a few words may be said about a matter that has sometimes been brought forward in connection with internal migration in India. This is an alleged tendency, due either to the greater arable area available or to political motives, according to the predilection of the writer, for agriculturists to leave British territory and to settle in the Native States. It is difficult to deal with this point so far as the smaller States and groups of States are concerned, for in many cases birth within them is returned under some general term, or by the name of the adjacent and probably better known British district. But the following table gives the more important data regarding the principal States :—

TABLE E.

State.	Gives to British Territory.		Receives from British Territory.	
	Males.	Females.	Males.	Females.
Haidrabád—Total	**167,557**	**201,314**	**152,583**	**166,955**
Bombay	74,406	100,968	69,250	90,478
Berar	53,264	57,641	19,650	24,194
Madras	27,023	30,437	46,642	44,458
Baroda—Total	**64,774**	**101,596**	**75,555**	**106,209**
Bombay	64,384	101,414	67,143	103,740
Mysore—Total	**69,280**	**68,833**	**103,848**	**83,213**
Madras	45,458	48,350	89,487	71,268
Bombay	8,591	9,156	11,652	9,474
Coorg	14,413	10,726	775	996
Kashmér—Total	**38,857**	**46,875**	**32,173**	**34,465**
Panjáb	36,415	46,158	31,375	34,237
Rajputána—Total	**270,644**	**259,245**	**106,012**	**153,301**
Ajmér	34,707	46,800	18,261	31,702
North-West Provinces	54,178	71,880	40,820	58,577
Panjáb	69,685	87,413	35,159	52,537
Bombay	38,379	13,147	7,491	6,767
Central India—Total	**197,948**	**258,212**	**231,676**	**265,962**
North-West Provinces	79,529	145,865	109,576	156,702
Central Provinces	95,402	95,428	52,884	64,983
Bombay States	220,973	254,224	232,682	320,336
Madras States	13,387	18,908	45,702	54,391
Central Province States	11,446	13,837	287,733	287,634
Bengal States	40,106	46,383	269,099	257,447
North-West Province States	25,544	36,786	28,350	39,388
Panjáb States	149,986	283,569	175,671	266,395

Haidrabád, it appears, gives Bombay and Berar more than it takes, and in both cases the female element predominates. As to its dealings with Madras, the gifts seem to be those of intermarriage, but the movement from the Presidency in question includes a superfluity of males, attributable, as has been already suggested, to the attractions of a large cantonment to a class very numerous in Madras, that of domestic servants and town labourers. Baroda is so mixed up, territorially, with British districts, that the interchange across the ever recurring frontier, is prevalent throughout the State. Here, as in similar tracts elsewhere, the larger choice is on the side of the British, so fewer are taken from the State than are given to it. The case of Mysore is, so far as Madras is concerned, like that of Haidrabád, and the State receives from Bombay, too, rather more than it returns. The latter fact is partly due, possibly, to a real immigration of cultivators of the predominant caste in the South Deccan State, who took advantage of the gap left by the famine of 1876–77. The Kashmér movement is affected in part by the famine of 1878, previous to which emigration from the State was forbidden. On the removal of the embargo, numbers rushed into the Panjáb, many of whom have now returned, though the balance is still against the State. In Rajputána we have an instance of a heavy exportation of the inhabitants, whilst the opposite movement is almost entirely that of intermarriage, regarding which the rules are closely observed by the orthodox of these States. Apart from the military classes who are in service away from their native place, Rajputána furnishes India with a large proportion of its traders, as was mentioned in the first chapter of this work. Central India apparently loses population to the Central Provinces, and gains it from the North-West. As neither the first nor the last have submitted reports on the results of the census, explanation is not available. As to the Central Provinces, the inroad seems to have followed the scarcity of 1877–78. All the rest of the groups, except the Pánjab, seem to be affected by the return of the birth-place under the title of the Province, instead of the State. This is very marked in the Central Province group and that under Bengal. In the Panjáb, the Superintendent points out that the immigration from the States to British territory exceeds that in the reverse direction, and the balance is due to the omission in the North-West Province return, to distinguish between the States of the Panjáb and British territory. In any case, the females outnumber the males, so the movement, as a whole, is insignificant. Taking the feudatory territory all round, it is clear, according to the above statement, that there is no general tendency to migrate from British dominion, and in some cases, it is a pity that it is so. In Mysore there are special attractions, and, to a less extent, in Haidrabád, but they are not agricultural, so they can do little to relieve the soil of the relatively more burdened tracts. Taking the return of birthplace, as a whole, it will be seen from the marginal statement that British territory gives to the feudatories about 916,000 above the number received from the latter; and that the excess contains about 24,000 more males than females; but looking at the large omissions in the returns of the immigrants from the smaller groups of States, such as those under Bengal, Madras, and the Central Provinces, it is clear that the difference is but nominal. It is to be expected that between now and the next census there will be a larger transfer of population from one political section of the country to the other, for there is no doubt that unoccupied land of good quality exists in the States in far greater quantity than is left in the provinces. The actual assessment in the former is said to be higher, but the system of realisation is less efficient and more elastic, a difference which has its recommendation in the eyes of the peasant. The administration in some of the larger States no doubt leaves much to be desired, especially in the rural tracts at a distance from the chief town, but in all will be found the greatest boon yet conferred by the strong hand of British rule—Peace.

TABLE F.

——	Total.	Males.	Females.	Females to 1,000 Males.
Migration from Provinces to States.	3,776,780	1,741,084	2,035,696	1,169
Migration from States to Provinces.	2,860,784	1,271,002	1,589,782	1,250
Difference	915,996	470,082	445,914	948

Pace Ceres laeta est; et vos optate, Coloni,
Perpetuam pacem.

Summary of conditions.

Summing up what has been said above as to the conditions that affect the growth of the population of India, it seems first that the number of children annually born into the country is a very high one, and that there is no prospect of its speedy or extensive decrease. Then, again, that the tendency of British administration is to prolong the normal life, and to protect it, as far as possible against the abnormal attacks to which it is there liable. As regards provision against the contigencies to which the above conditions give rise, there is, first, the prospect, of, for a time, at least, increasing the yield of food supply from the soil. Secondly, the resources for the purchase of food may be increased by the production of material in demand abroad, or in home manufacture. Thirdly, the growth of the non-agricultural industries, and, fourthly, the increase of the area of land under tillage, due to either the extension of irrigation or, still more, to the slow migration of the surrounding population, as pressure increases, to land as yet untouched by the plough. Thus, in brief, may be stated the population question, as it exists at present in India, and after the statistics bearing on the movement that has taken place within the last 10 years have been discussed, there may be room for a few words on the question of how far, up to the present date, has the growth of the resources of the country been commensurate with that of the people.

General variation in population.

The second table in the general series gives the figures showing the variation in population that has taken place since 1881. It is divided into two sections; first, the tracts for which returns at both the enumerations are available, and, again, the total accretion to the population in the decade, both by growth and addition. In the last category will be found Kashmér, which was not enumerated in 1881, and the Quettah settlements, as well as Upper Burma, Fort Steadman, and North Lushai land, which are new acquisitions. Internal modifications, such as transfers or exchanges, will be found noted on the fly-leaf of the table. The remarks that follow refer, of course, only to the nett variations, and exclude the increase that may be called accidental. The territory that was enumerated in 1881 returns an increase during the decade of 27,821,420, a number exceeding the whole population of England, and nearly equal to that of the kingdom of Italy. The British Provinces account for 19,294,509, nearly the population of Spain and Norway together, and the Feudatory States for 8,526,911, a little short of that of Scotland and Ireland. But, large as this growth seems in absolute numbers, if we take it with reference to the population to which it has been superadded, it shrinks into very moderate proportions. In British provinces it amounts to 9·70 per cent., and in the States to 15·52 or to 10·96 for the whole country. It is composed of an increase of 11·52 per cent. over 94·56 per cent. of the population of 1881, accompanied by a decrease amounting to 2·40 per cent. over 5·44.

The annual rate of increase is thus 9·3 per mille. That this is but average is shown by the marginal table, in which, out of 28 countries, India comes 20th. It is indeed an open question whether the actual rate is not a little below this. The details of age and sex indicate a certain growth of confidence, as well as of population, so that there are persons, especially amongst the forest tribes, who now appear for the first time in the return, though, no doubt, they should have been in that of 10 years back also. Then, too, the return of girls between the ages of 10 and 15, or even 20, is considerably better than it was in 1881, but it still affords evidence that reticence about this portion of the household is by no means uncommon, more particularly in the north of India. There the example of the Musalmán conquerors, and the traditions of the military tribes of the Arya and some of the other settlers, are all in favour of the strict seclusion of women of the upper classes, and the middle, as is its wont, follows suit. In other parts of the country the practice is common, but as an imitation, not an indigenous growth, so that there, it seems, the objection to the census inquiry regarding the females of the family stops at a demand for inspection. This demand was specially prohibited in the rules, and the head of the family manifests, as a rule, no unwillingness to dictate to the enumerator all particulars about the secluded class, barring their names, though, of course, all information thus obtained has to be taken on trust. In the north, where the custom is of immemorial standing, or is a point of racial distinction, it is too probable that

TABLE G.

Country.	Annual increase per cent.*
1. New South Wales	5·10
2. Queensland	4·39
3. Victoria	3·22
4. United States	2·48
5. Saxony	2·00
6. New Zealand	1·70
7. Algeria	1·56
8. South Australia	1·40
9. England and Wales	1·28
10. Egypt	1·25
11. Holland	1·18
12. Prussia	1·15
13. Portugal	1·14
14. Hungary	1·08
15. Germany	1·07
16. Canada	1·07
17. Greece	1·05
18. Belgium	0·99
19. Denmark	0·99
20. *India*	*0·93*
21. Austria	0·76
22. Switzerland	0·64
23. Bavaria	0·64
24. Italy	0·62
25. Norway	0·60
26. Spain	0·55
27. Sweden	0·50
28. France	0·06

* Between the last Census and that which preceded it.

an inquiry. even as to the bare numbers, would meet either with no response, or a denial of the existence of such persons. On these considerations, the omissions at the census of 1891 may be to some extent set off against those of 1881 which were repaired on this last occasion. But the general ratio of females to males at the two enumerations, in the absence of special cause for disproportion, such as may be found, for example, in famine tracts, is a measure of some value of the confidence of the people in the intention of the State in making the inquiry. Judged by this test, the census under review brought on to the register a greater number of those left out in 1881 than it omitted of those concealed till they creep out 10 years hence. Instances of this will be seen in the returns for Rájputána, Central India, and some of the smaller groups of States, of which mention will be made below.

Variation by density-groups.

Before entering, however, into the discussion of the figures piecemeal, it will be as well to show how the variation is distributed over the whole country with reference to the specific population. For this purpose, portions of tables embodied in the preceding chapter are reproduced below for convenience of reference.

TABLE H.—SHOWING the INCREASE of the POPULATION according to DENSITY-GROUPS.*

Per-centage of Variation from Mean Density.	1. Provinces and States.			2. Provinces only.		
	Population (1891).	Group-density.	Per-centage of Increase of Population.	Population (1891).	Group-density.	Per-centage of Increase of Population.
75 and under	5,075,771	25	25·06	3,151,519	24	17·75
66–74	2,062,222	53	20·57	4,062,242	70	14·66
50–65	13,469,447	74	21·29	9,776,473	96	14·17
33–49	13,725,889	109	13·65	17,271,758	136	14·40
20–32	32,521,492	135	14·68	12,212,297	166	13·00
10–19	15,539,809	157	16·40	5,649,449	196	14·02
0–9	6,158,606	172	12·12	9,623,352	224	10·69
Total below mean	88,553,236	87	16·28	61,747,090	102	13·64
1–9	10,426,794	191	11·99	5,190,662	236	10·24
10–19	4,057,716	214	11·61	8,008,238	262	15·95
20–32	13,179,523	229	12·18	10,454,625	290	15·64
33–49	12,300,679	259	14·10	3,013,600	326	9·05
50–65	10,737,381	290	15·42	9,069,745	371	8·37
66–74	2,557,190	318	14·30	5,886,168	395	8·73
75–99	6,686,137	347	10·00	14,800,585	434	4·99
100–149	30,808,664	410	6·17	44,044,392	514	6·68
150–199	40,714,414	509	7·00	25,507,620	617	7·00
200 and over	59,157,765	701	7·48	28,670,567	838	8·06
Total above mean	190,626,263	395	8·78	154,146,202	464	8·19
Total	**279,179,499**	**184**	**10·96**	**215,893,292**	**230**	**9·69**

* This statement does not include Upper Burma, North Lushai-land, Kashmér, and the detached Settlements, or the four towns of Calcutta, Bombay, Rangoon, and Madras.

In both sections of the statement the most distinctive feature is the way the rate of growth decreases as the density rises. But in the first portion of the table, that dealing with both Provinces and States, the irregularity of the unit of compilation in the case of the latter somewhat obscures the fact. In the remarks that follow, therefore, only the British section will be discussed. Here, with a few exceptions, such as the groups with a density of from 10 to 33 per cent. above the general mean, which contain several of the famine districts of Madras, where the increase has been abnormal, the rate of increase varies with remarkable regularity inversely as the specific population. The most thinly-peopled tracts, such as those of Sindh, Lower Burma and the Assam Hills, show a rate nearly double the mean. This diminishes to about one and a half times that rate as the North-West and Central Province hills, the western plains of the Panjáb, and the southern portion of the Bráhmapútra valley in Assam, come on to the list; and here it remains, until the mean density is nearly reached. Just above that point, there is a drop, caused by the preponderance of the Berar districts with a few of those in the south of the North-West Provinces. The fall continues through the next group, where the non-famine districts of Bombay are strongly represented. Then follows the rise consequent on the rebound from scarcity in Madras. The decline then continues, and takes a sudden drop again where the average density is 434, that of the water-logged tract of the North-West Provinces, where there has been a slight recession of the population. In the groups where the density is more than double that of the average there is a curious rise, though not quite as high as that in a few groups above on the list. It is worth noting that the rate of the last group but one is determined by districts of the Upper Ganges valley, with three out of the four in Bengal that have lost ground since 1881, whereas the last group includes the pick of Oudh, Bihár, and the Delta. Calcutta and its detached suburbs are excluded, so it is a remarkable testimony to the fertility of these tracts that, starting with 767 people to the square mile, they have managed in the decade to pile on about 70 more. In Eastern Bengal the fishing industry is perhaps sufficiently prevalent to add materially to the food resources of the people, and a portion of the burden on the land, too, may be only temporary, and removed after the cultivating season is over. But in North Bihár and the Ghógra tracts immigration is insignificant, and agriculture engrosses nearly the whole of the labour supply. Fortunately, in some of these districts, special products, such as indigo and opium, are largely grown. These are highly remunerative to the cultivator, and the advances made on account of them come in just at the right time to help him to tide over the interval between one harvest and the next. This resource is not within the reach of the peasant of the decreasing tracts in Bengal, where there is only jute to fall back upon. Here, a tract of 14,252 square miles, with a population in 1881 of about 592 to each, has been reduced by 1·40 per cent., owing, as previously mentioned, to the deterioration of the drainage. Nor are the waterlogged tracts of the North-West Provinces more fortunate. Over an area of 5,162 square miles, with a specific population of 477 per mile ten years ago, the decade has resulted in a decrease of 5¾ per cent. But these instances are exceptional, and the detailed return from which the statement under review was compiled, shows that in the case of the higher densities there are comparatively few districts that have approached near to the stationary stage, though the present rate of increase will probably not be maintained through the next decade. The variations in the various Provinces and States, and their main physical divisions, are shown in the Statement J. on the next page, about which a few words of comment are necessary.

In the North-West Provinces the highest rates are in the Himálaya tract, where the census on this occasion was probably more correct than before, and in the submontane districts, where there is more waste land available. Then comes the south-central division, throughout which there is an average density of more than one person per acre. In Eastern Bengal, which supports 531 per square mile, the rate of increase is higher than in any other part of this large and varied province. It is of no consequence, in connection with this question, that the presence of a considerable temporary labouring population is indicated by the returns, since these are regular annual visitors, and are supported out of the produce they are called in to garner just as much as the residents, and most of them come from tracts in the same province where the mean density is 667 per mile. Take Tanjore, again, in the Kávari delta, where the increase has been only 4·56 per cent. in the decade, according to the returns as they stand. But, looking at the migration figures, it will be seen that a nett population of nearly 100,000 has to be accounted for, and will be found in Ceylon or Burma. Thus, the real rate of increase is set down at 9·12 per cent. If we go northwards, again, we find that in the Panjáb submontane tract, where the density is 381 per mile, the rate of increase is 11¼ per cent., which, though not quite equal to that in the west of the province, is above the rate in the Himálaya tract and the eastern plains. In the latter there is even a decrease in one district, attributed to the attraction of the town of Dehli, and the unhealthiness of the surrounding country. In Assam, again, and in the Central Provinces, the rate of growth is highest in the most densely peopled divisions. In the former this is perhaps accidental, as, had it not been for the effects of the epidemic with the

Table J.—Showing the Variation in Population since 1881 in Provinces and States, according to their Main Physical Divisions.

Province.	Mean Density.	Variation per Cent.		
		Total.	Males.	Females.
Madras	**252**	**15·58**	**15·48**	**15·68**
North Coast	279	13·55	12·73	14·38
„ Agency	68	24·17	23·04	25·38
Northern	134	18·32	18·53	18·14
East Central	359	17·43	18·11	16·76
West Central	249	21·07	22·44	21·40
South Central	458	11·66	11·08	11·83
Southern	319	16·98	17·51	16·40
West Coast	391	11·55	10·85	12·23
Bombay	**207**	**13·71**	**13·97**	**13·44**
Gujaráth	301	8·41	8·22	8·61
Konkan	210	9·50	8·73	10·28
Bombay Island	—	6·28	11·47	*−1·54*
Deccan	162	17·01	17·33	16·67
Karnátak	192	19·88	20·37	19·38
Sindh	**60**	**18·97**	**19·12**	**18·79**
Bengal	**471**	**6·89**	**7·10**	**6·67**
Bengal { Northern	459	4·69	5·66	3·66
Bengal { Western	562	5·34	6·56	4·14
Bengal { Eastern	531	11·81	12·69	10·92
Bihár { Northern	667	6·35	5·13	7·53
Bihár { Southern	520	2·79	2·08	3·47
Orissa	411	6·79	6·14	7·42
Chutia Nágpúr	134	9·53	8·79	10·25
N.-W. Prov. & Oudh	**436**	**6·23**	**5·96**	**6·52**
Himálayan	81	15·58	15·47	15·84
Sub-Montane	486	12·06	12·18	11·94
Upper Doáb	509	3·32	2·88	3·59
Central Doáb	470	*−1·40*	*−1·72*	*−0·97*
North Central	499	6·50	6·45	6·54
South Central	652	6·77	6·46	7·08
Southern	221	3·22	3·15	3·90

Province.	Mean Density.	Variation per Cent.		
		Total.	Males.	Females.
Panjáb	**188**	**10·74**	**10·32**	**11·23**
Himálayan	83	4·25	3·95	4·56
Submontane and Central.	381	11·29	11·23	11·36
Salt Range	158	12·58	11·19	14·24
Western Plains	81	13·40	12·57	14·37
Eastern Plains	265	6·36	6·06	6·72
Central Provinces	**125**	**9·61**	**8·83**	**10·40**
Eastern	142	13·76	12·85	14·66
Southern	124	7·51	7·42	7·60
Central	91	10·23	9·70	10·76
Narmada	136	6·24	4·98	7·58
Lower Burma	**53**	**24·67**	**23·67**	**25·81**
Arakan	46	14·36	12·33	16·75
Pegu	156	24·59	22·92	26·68
Irawádi	88	33·68	33·46	33·91
Tenasserim	21	19·41	19·52	19·28
Assam	**112**	**11·30**	**11·71**	**10·88**
Surma Valley	333	11·46	11·99	10·90
Bráhmapútra	117	10·8	10·54	9·59
Hill Tracts	25	11·32	11·27	11·36
Berár	**163**	**8·41**	**8·06**	**8·78**
Ajmér	**200**	**17·72**	**15·86**	**19·89**
Ajmér	204	17·55	16·02	13·32
Mérwára	187	18·30	15·31	30·67
Coorg	**109**	*−2·94*	*−4·51*	*−0·92*
Aden	—	**26·44**	**35·97**	**8·57**
Port Blair (Andamans).	—	6·70	5·80	12·37
Total, British Provinces.	**230**	**9·70**	**9·63**	**9·80**

TABLE J.—SHOWING the VARIATION in POPULATION, &c.—*continued.*

State, &c.	Mean Density.	Variation per Cent.		
		Total.	Males.	Females.
Haidrabád - -	**139**	**17·18**	**17·41**	**16·94**
Telingána -	111	21·11	21·93	20·27
Maráthwáda -	145	13·26	13·13	13·40
Karnátak - -	141	26·96	27·17	26·75
Haidrabád City, &c.	—	12·96	15·14	10·68
Baroda	**294**	**10·54**	**9·96**	**11·18**
Southern	263	8·22	7·49	9·03
Northern -	349	11·15	10·47	11·87
Western -	152	22·18	21·79	22·61
Baroda City -	—	9·30	10·78	7·61
Mysore -	**177**	**18·09**	**19·06**	**17·13**
Eastern - -	191	20·7	21·8	19·6
Western -	149	11·7	12·5	10·8
Rajputána	**92**	**20·22**	**17·56**	**23·34**
Western -	45	46·53	38·05	57·12
Southern -	131	33·84	19·12	24·36
Eastern	181	9·15	8·43	9·99
Central India -	**133**	**9·92**	**9·00**	**10·95**
Bombay States -	**116**	**16·35**	**15·59**	**17·16**
Gujaráth - -	110	17·00	15·89	18·18
Konkan - -	184	9·42	8·02	10·81
North Deccan -	106	11·33	11·14	11·53
South Deccan -	243	18·28	18·56	17·99
Sindh (Khairpur) -	22	2·15	2·80	1·36

State, &c.	Mean Density.	Variation per Cent.		
		Total.	Males.	Females.
Madras States -	**385**	**10·63**	**11·51**	**9·77**
Northern -	110	13·55	14·26	12·84
South Central -	339	23·48	24·57	22·51
West Coast	405	9·30	10·23	8·37
Central Province States.	**73**	**26·36**	**25·51**	**27·25**
Eastern	118	22·02	21·23	22·82
Southern	27	51·33	49·40	53·43
Narmada -	120	10·64	9·59	11·73
Bengal States	**92**	**18·30**	**17·75**	**18·87**
Koch Bihár -	443	*−3·9*	*−2·9*	*−4·9*
Tipperah	34	43·71	39·13	49·04
Orissa Group	118	20·31	19·21	21·44
Chutia Nágpur Group.	55	30·28	30·25	30·32
North-West Province States.	**155**	**6·84**	**6·44**	**7·27**
Rámpúr -	583	1·72	3·09	0·23
Garhwál - -	57	20·71	15·67	26·01
Panjáb States	**111**	**10·42**	**10·05**	**10·87**
Hill Group -	77	9·54	8·39	10·87
Submontane -	349	16·58	16·01	17·28
Eastern Plains -	263	8·71	8·66	8·78
Western „ (Baháwalpúr).	38	13·34	12·96	13·81
Total, States -	**111**	**15·52**	**14·81**	**16·29**
Total, India -	**184**	**10·96**	**10·77**	**11·16**

fromidable Greek name, the upper valley, where there is so much waste land available would no doubt have outgrown in this respect its elder sister. The eastern division of the Central Provinces has been connected during the decade with the outside world by a through line of railway, so that its surplus produce, much of which used, it is stated, to rot on the ground for want of carriage, is now sold by the cultivators to foreign dealers. The whole division, too, is the most fertile in the province. At the same time, the sex proportions indicate that some of the increase must be attributed to better enumeration, especially in the extreme east. The same remark applies to the hill country in the centre of the province. Bombay, on the other hand, shows the lowest rate in the most densely populated division, that is, in Gujaráth, and not along the coast strip, where, as before stated, the population approaches nearest to the sustaining power of the land. On comparing the details of the last two enumerations, it seems that the rate in the latter division is in part nominal, for, owing to local causes, the women who used to accompany their male relations to Bombay for the working season, now stay at home in the Konkan. The Deccan and Karnátak rates represent, it is needless to point out, the rebound after famine, and in both cases the males have outgrown, relatively speaking, the other sex. We are justified in attributing this fact to the greater vitality of the latter in time of distress, and partly also to the return of some of the adult males that left their home for the hills in 1876–77. The corresponding tracts in the Madras Presidency indicate the same influences, though none of them returns the astonishing rate of increase, or rather replenishment, of one or two of the Bombay Deccan districts. Moreover, except in the west central tract, the divergence between the rates for the two sexes is not so marked, a fact which appears to show that in the northern tracts of the Deccan, immigration, or the return of the native, was a more prominent feature than it was further south. In the Agency tracts, or the south-eastern slope of the Central Hills, the increased proportion of females is entirely due, no doubt, to more accurate enumeration. The Berár return shows simply a slow rate of increase, with one instance of recession. A part of this is attributed to the return of immigrants from Bombay and Haidrabád to their native districts after the famine. But the local authorities seem to think, too, that all the best portions of the arable area have now been taken into occupation. Such immigration as there is, therefore, will be confined to the labouring classes, and not be more than seasonal. Coorg has been already dealt with, and Ajmér owes its increase mainly to railway extension, and in part to the better enumeration of Mérwara. The rural part of the little province is probably nearly filled up. We then reach Lower Burma, which returns the highest rate of increase of all the provinces. The average annual addition to the cultivated area during the 10 years has been 159,000 acres, or $4\frac{1}{2}$ per cent. on that cultivated in the first year of that period. The estimated yield of husked rice per annum is about 1,940,000 tons, and the quantity required for the support of the population is said to be 1,050,000 tons. The average exports for the 10 years have been 1,003,000 tons, so that obviously a short crop only reduces the latter, and there is no question of want of sustenance for the home population, or even for that of Upper Burma, where failure of this harvest has sometimes occurred. The average provincial rate of growth is found in the delta, but the highest is to the north-west, where, in Thongwâ, many acres of rice land have been reclaimed of late from the sea by dykes to keep out the high tides. The littoral districts of Arakan and Tenasserim show the lowest rate of expansion, but even here the growth has exceeded that of most of the Indian provinces.

Variation in Feudatory States.

As regards the progress of the States, in five, no doubt, the census was as well taken on both the last occasions as in British territory, whilst in the other six a good deal of the increase returned in 1891 is attributable to greater accuracy rather than to actual growth. A glance at the figures for Rajputána, for instance, will show this. The males have increased by $17\frac{1}{2}$ per cent., whilst the females are more numerous by over 23. In the desert tracts the increase amounts to 38 per cent. of males, and 57 for the fair sex. The hill tracts of the south, too, exhibit similar vagaries, though to a less degree. The rate in the case of the eastern division is about normal, but here, too, the female rate is in excess of that of the males to an unusual extent. One State only, Bharatpúr out of the whole group shows a decrease, and of this exception no explanation is recorded. For Central India details are not available. The tract was enumerated by States, but tabulated by Agencies, and as the larger States are scattered over several Agencies, comparison is not at present practicable. The report, which is not yet to hand, will probably supply the defect as far as possible. The tract, as a whole, shows a normal rate of increase, though with a leaning towards excess in that of the females, which, as in other instances cited, is apparent only.

It is the same with the Central Province group, but to an exaggerated degree, and in a lesser one with the States under Bengal. Here, however, we have one, Kóch, Bihár, which has receded to the extent of 3·9 per cent. This is probably due to the same causes that have affected the neighbouring British districts, as mentioned above. In the North-West Provinces, the Himálayan State of Garhwál shows the usual feature of a better census, namely, the high rate of increase unequally shared between the two sexes. The small State of Rámpur is practically stationary. As regards the Panjáb group, the most interesting fact is that whereas migration is flowing out of the States into British districts in the eastern and Himálayan portions of the province, in Baháwalpur, on the western plains, the reverse is the case, and from both the southern Panjáb and from Sindh there is a tendency to settle in that State. The general result of the movement is to keep the rate of increase very much at the level of that in the British districts. There are signs of the effects of the famine in the small States in the north of the Deccan portion of Madras, but on the west coast only Cochin shows an expansion similar to that of the neighbouring British district, and the Provincial Census Superintendent gives reasons for doubting the accuracy of the enumeration in Travancore, where the female increase is in a lower ratio than that of males, without the influence of famine to account for the discrepancy. In Baroda and Mysore, on the contrary, the results are thoroughly trustworthy. In the former the growth during the decade was normal, and the relatively greater increase of the females is much the same as is found in the surrounding tracts of British Gujaráth, where there has been a movement of males to Bombay. Mysore was severely dealt with by the famine of 1876–77, and the changes in the 10 years have most of the characteristics noted in the case of the similarly afflicted tracts in Madras and Bombay. Last comes Haidrabad with a very high rate of increase, attributable partly to the recovery from the famine of 1876–77, and partly, as indicated by the sex-proportions, to immigration. We have already seen that this is the case as far as the movement to and from the Mádras Presidency is concerned, and the fact receives confirmation from the great disproportion between the rates of increase in the two sexes in the chief town and its suburbs, which are places of great resort for the servant class from the south. In the Telugu-speaking division, too, immigration has been probably instigated by railway and mining enterprise, but for the full explanation we must await the report of the local Census Superintendent.

Urban increase.

Such has been the growth of the population of the country, as a whole, and the last question that needs comment here is the attraction of the town relatively to what it was 10 years ago. The marginal statement, in which are summarised the figures found in full in Table IV., Parts 1 and 2 of the general series, shows the progress of the urban population, classified according to the size of town. The relative number of females to males is added, as the change therein is a matter of considerable importance in connection with the migration in question. In comparing the figures with those of the general population, it must be borne in mind that in the latter the mean rate of increase is 10·77 per cent. for males, and 11·16 for females, or 10·96 for the whole. Again, the proportion of females to the other sex throughout India was 954 in 1881 and 957 at the last census. In the urban, as previously in the general, comparison, all areas not included in the census of 1881 as well as in that under review, have been omitted from consideration, so that the town limits are identical in both years. In special cases, where the distinction between certain transferred areas was not preserved for the purpose in hand, the town has been left out of the comparison, as will be seen from the full Table IV. above mentioned.

TABLE K.

Group of Towns.	Increase since 1881.			Females to 1,000 Males.	
	Total.	Males.	Females.	1881.	1891.
I. 100,000 and over.	10·58	12·89	7·68	798	707
II. 75,000 -	6·54	8·41	4·46	931	868
III. 50,000 -	13·60	15·00	12·05	898	875
IV. 35,000 -	9·48	11·12	7·74	943	914
V. 20,000 -	11·58	12·98	10·07	926	902
VI. 10,000 -	10·66	11·21	10·08	953	944
VII. 5,000 -	7·54	7·31	7·78	953	957
VIII. 3,000 -	1·54	1·47	1·62	929	31
IX. Under 3,000 -	0·86	0·28	1·53	862	873
Total	9·40	10·44	8·24	903	886

The statement, taken with the above qualifications and explanation, shows that the urban population has increased, on the whole, at a rate less by 1½ per cent. than that of the population at large, whilst that of females, instead of being the higher, is lower than that of males to a considerable extent. The growth of the larger towns, of those of middle size, and of the larger market towns, seems to have been the greatest. The rate declines suddenly in the case of those below 10,000, and the smaller groups are practically stationary. The last group comprises all the small places that have gained the title of town from some special cause, so their case is altogether exceptional. On the whole, the sex proportions are considerably below the normal in respect to the number of females, showing a good deal of immigration. But where the town contains less than 10,000 inhabitants, it will be seen that the proportion of females has risen since 1881, instead of falling, as it has done in the larger town groups. The relative increase of the male element in the population is highest in the two first groups, and in the fourth, where the supply of labour is required to be on a high scale. The causes of this have been generally described already. In the case of the first three classes, it is due to commerce and manufacture, with the trade that is accessory to the establishment of large military garrisons. The next two classes are largely the creation of new lines of railway. Before entering upon the statistics of individual towns, selected as examples of the general tendencies towards aggregation, it is convenient to give, as in the following statement, the figures of the urban growth in the different Provinces and States, as compared with that of the whole population thereof :—

TABLE L.

Province.	Increase per Cent. of Population.		State, &c.	Increase per Cent. of Population.	
	Urban.	Total.		Urban.	Total.
Madras	10·75	15·58	Haidrabád	11·09	17·18
Bombay and Sindh	10·29	14·51	Baroda	7·02	10·54
Bengal	7·37	6·89	Mysore	13·55	18·09
North-West Provinces	2·32	4·55	Rajputána	12·22	20·22
Oudh	6·18	11·09	Central India	7·27	9·92
Panjáb	7·93	10·74	Bombay States	12·67	16·85
Lower Burma	17·86	24·67	Madras States	0·85	0·63
Central Provinces	7·11	9·61	Central Province States	12·09	26·36
Assam	10·37	11·30	Bengal States	8·85	18·30
Berar	8·49	8·41	North-West Provinces States	2·01	6·84
Ajmér	22·44	17·72	Panjáb States	6·77	10·42
Coorg	*−7·36*	*−2·94*			

As regards the generally low rate of increase in the towns, as compared with that prevailing in the Province or State as a whole, it may be observed that in the former the nominal increase due to greater accuracy at the later census is reduced to a minimum, as in towns the enumeration blocks are smaller and more compact and the supervision more close, owing to the better supply of trained and competent men that is available. But this is not enough to account for the whole of the difference between the rural and the urban rates of increase, for the statement shows that in all, except Berar, where the difference in favour of the towns is trifling, and in Bengal, where the scale is probably turned by three or four of the larger items, the towns are considerably below the general population in their rate of expansion. The case of Ajmér is peculiar, and due to the dominating position of the chief town in the centre of Rajputána, as well as to the increase of traffic that has been drawn to both Ajmér and Beáwar by the through line of rail that had not been yet developed at the time of the last census. In the case of the Madras States, the return is available for only two or three of the towns, because the population of certain areas which were included in 1881, but have been since excluded from town limits, is reported to be not now ascertainable. In other respects the return offers no features requiring special notice here.

We can pass on accordingly to the consideration of the change in the population of some of the more representative of the larger towns. These are mentioned in the following table:—

TABLE M.

A. Commercial or Manufacturing Towns.		B. Military Stations or Provincial Capitals.		C. Capitals of States, past or present.		D. Religious Centres.	
Name.	Percentage of Variation.	Name.	Percentage of Variation.	Name.	Percentage of Variation.	Name.	Percentage of Variation.
1. Bombay	+ 6·28	1. Lahore	+12·44	1. Haidrabád	+16·92	1. Benares	+ 2·19
2. Calcutta	+ 8·25	2. Allahabad	+ 9·45	2. Lucknow	+ 4·49	2. Gáya	+ 5·19
3. Madras	+11·50	3. Bangalore	+15·72	3. Patna	− 3·20	3. Amritsar	− 9·96
4. Rangoon	+34·89	4. Poona	+24·38	4. Agra	+ 5·28	4. Mathura	+ 6·00
5. Karáchi	+43·01	5. Meerut	+19·91	5. Súrat	− 0·56	5. Násik	+ 2·79
6. Cawnpore	+24·61	6. Baréli	+ 6·72	6. Jaipúr	+11·45	6. Mádura	+13·78
7. Dehli	+11·06	7. Nágpúr	+19·04	7. Baroda	+ 9·30		
8. Ahmedabád	+16·29	8. Jabalpúr	+11·59	8. Gwalior	+18·19		
9. Howrah	+10·83	9. Peshâwar	+ 5·26	9. Dacca	+ 4·10		
10. Trichinopoly	+13·71	10. Ambála	+17·53	10. Mirzápúr	− 1·44		
11. Sholápur	+ 3·38	11. Bellary	+11·24	11. Rámpúr	+ 3·34		
12. Calicut	+15·75	12. Ráwal Pindi	+39·30	12. Jodhpúr	+ 8·10		
13. Cocanáda	+33·22			13. Tanjore	− 0·65		
14. Maulmain	+ 5·04						
15. Negapatam	+10·13						
16. Mangalore	+27·49						
17. Ajmér	+41·26						
18. Hubli	+43·40						
19. Bhaunagar	+20·68						

Modern or commercial centres.

Taking first the modern or commercial towns, there is a point that must strike one as remarkable at the very outset. This is the small increase in the two leading cities of India. Whilst seaports like Karáchi and Rangoon, which are centres of distribution and nothing more, have increased by 43 and 34 per cent. respectively, Calcutta and Bombay, which are not only great centres of trade, but also manufacturing towns of notable prosperity, have only an increase to show of 8¼ and 6¼ per cent. The explanation is the same as could be given for London, so far as Calcutta is concerned; namely, that the tendency is now to live in the suburbs, where rent and food are cheaper, taxes less burdensome, and with the extension of railways, access to the city within the reach of all. Bombay is not so fortunate in its surroundings as Calcutta, but the middle classes engaged in that city have betaken themselves to residences some distance out of the town in far greater numbers than were shown at the census of 1881. But the main cause of decrease, or rather of the reduction in the rate of increase, is the withdrawal of women from Bombay in the decade. Whether there is less demand for their labour in the cotton and other mills, or whether the greater facilities of intercourse with the coast have induced men to keep their wives at home during the open season, and to indulge in an occasional run to visit them, instead of bringing them up with their children to the more expensive life in the city, is not stated in the reports hitherto received. But, at any rate, the fact remains that a considerable number of the women who were to be found in the city in 1881 were located in the Ratnagiri district at the time the last census was taken.

The marginal statement will serve to show clearly the difference between the four chief cities in respect to their relative attractiveness to outsiders. Madras, for instance, in spite of its large increase, is chiefly maintained by local prolificity, whilst Bombay breeds only a quarter of its population, and neither of the others more than a third. But it is only in Bombay that the home-born show a decrease. In Madras there is a tendency towards immigration, but the natural increase has nearly kept up with the total growth. In Rangoon, on the other hand, the former is remarkably high in rate, but the immigration from outside the province quite outtops it. The figures for Calcutta are open to doubt, as the areas have been much changed since 1881, and the last column clearly refers to the old city alone, irrespective of the suburban portion that has since been included. But the increase of the relative strength of the city-born is not affected by this change, and it is here that this town differs from the rest. The other towns in this class may be dealt with more generally. Cawnpore is the rising commercial centre of the fertile tracts under the government of the North-West Provinces. It is increasing, too, in manufacturing importance. Amongst other innovations it has taken the lead in the leather trade of India, and with such success that much of the work that used to be done for the army and police in England has been assigned to the manufactories here. Dehli, too, is not left stranded by the stream of modern commerce. Like Cawnpore, it is the great wheat market of the surrounding tract, and manufacturing industry also is alive there. It has, moreover, the prestige of former metropolitanism, and is well known to many of the country folk all over north and central India, to whom Calcutta and Bombay are names of no significance. Calicut, Cocanada, Mangalore, and Negapatam are all seaports of rising trade. Maulmain has been outshone by its younger sister Rangoon. Bhaunagar is not only the chief port of the peninsula of Káthiawár but the seat of a wealthy feudatory Thákur, or Chief. It has thus the advantage of both commerce and patronage. Húbli and Trichinopoli resemble Ajmér in owing much of their prosperity to the extension of railways. Howrah is part of Calcutta, and Sholápur, which began well as a cotton centre, seems not to have recovered from the results of the famine, which pressed very severely on the weaving classes of the Deccan.

TABLE N.

City.	Per-centage of City-born.		Per-centage of Variation.	
	1881.	1891.	City-born.	Total Population.
Bombay	28·41	25·10	− 4·17	+ 6·28
Calcutta	27·42	30·49	+15·67	+ 4·10
Madras	72·68	71·97	+10·40	+11·50
Rangoon	36·41	33·68	+24·29	+34·39

Provincial and military centres.

About the second group of towns there is little to be said. Poona has the advantage of being both a political and a military centre, and has a good deal of the prestige of former times, like Dehli. Ráwal-Pindi, which shows so large an increase, is purely a military station, and probably some of its rise accounts for the comparatively small increase of Peshâwar, which has a good deal more trade but less garrison, now that Pindi has been found more advantageous from a military standpoint.

State-centres.

The third class of towns can be taken with the remarks made in the last chapter as to the position of the capital of a Native State. Patna, Súrat, Mirzápur, and Tanjore, which have descended from that eminence, are all on the wane. Lucknow, Agra, and Dacca show less than half the general rate of increase. There are, no doubt, special reasons to account for the slow progress of Rámpur and Jódhpur, since the latter at all events might have been expected with the increase to have been more in sympathy with the surrounding State. Finally, the centres of religious pilgrimage claim a little comment. Of the six given in the table, Madura, perhaps, should hardly be taken in the same line as the rest, since it has its reputation as a place of trade as well as its sacred associations to support it. If we exclude it, the general rate of growth of the class is very slow. In the case of Amritsar, there is, as has been already mentioned, a special cause for the falling off in population, and it is possible that in addition to the epidemic of fever nine years or so ago, there may have been a loss by the return to Kashmér of some of the artizans who fled that State in the famine of 1878. On the other hand, as regards all towns of this sort, it may be said that no rapid increase is to be expected, since there is a temporary influx of purchasing power at periodic intervals, perfectly well known beforehand, so that the vendors of

Religious-centres.

all goods that can be easily transported merely join the throng of visitors at the times in question, and do not waste their time in residing permanently in a place where trade is so spasmodic.

Parallel movement of population and material prosperity.

The increase of the population has hitherto been discussed merely in its relation to the number of people who were enumerated 10 years ago, and this is, of course, the only aspect with which the census has to deal. But there is another of equal importance, but which, as the facts concerning it do not arise out of the operations under review, can be only treated here in the barest outline. Still, it will not be altogether out of place, as it bears on the question of the probability of the continuance during the current decade of the rate of growth that has prevailed in that which has just passed. The point is, whether, judged by the facts by which the progress of a country from a material standpoint is usually tested, it can be fairly assumed that in India the increase of the population has been accompanied by a parallel development of its resources. The simplest way of treating so complex a mass of statistics is to make use of a base-line or index-year. It may be admitted at the outset that for anything like a detailed examination of the conditions such a method is faulty, but our present object is to give a sketch only. The table given on the next page, then, shows the figures for each year of the decade in their relation to those of the year which immediately preceded that period. For instance, taking the first column, the land revenue of 1880–81 being 100·00, that for 1881–82 is represented by 103·96, and the average for the decade by 107·94. On the other hand, the imports of kerosine oil were only 90·96 in the first year of the decade, but rose to 542·30 in the last. To save space, however, the 100·00 has been omitted in favour of the appropriate sign. Now, the increase of the population in British provinces is 9·70 per cent., and what with recoveries from famine and the greater accuracy of the returns, it may be safely assumed that this rate is above the normal, and the latter can be set down at about 8·50 for this territory as a whole. This, then, is the ratio with which the figures should be compared in the several columns relating to revenue, post, and currency. In the case of the States the rate is no doubt higher, and may approach 10·00; and with the latter we may take the figures regarding railways and trade generally, since the whole country contributes to their support. In the former case, that of the Provinces, it appears that the increase, except in the assessment on the land which, for reasons that are too lengthy to be stated here, moves slowly, is generally above that of the population. Salt, for instance, the only tax paid by the lower classes, shows a remarkable increase in the amount consumed as compared with the revenue from it, taking the whole of the 10 years together, though the two last years of the period indicate a less satisfactory divergence, which proved, however, only temporary. The postal system shows a marvellous development, especially in the matter of cards; and telegrams, too, are now sent to an extent unheard of even 10 years ago. In connection with the railway passengers, it must be noted that in India the traffic by the upper classes is comparatively insignificant, so that the bulk of the growth is to be set down to the third. It is also noticeable that the rate of increase in both passenger and goods traffic is considerably above that in the open mileage, and the same remark applies, though less forcibly, to the net earning of the lines.

With reference to the trade returns, it is perhaps advisable to present the actual as well as the proportional figures, so as to indicate the general distribution of the whole amount entering and leaving the country. This is done in the marginal table, which represents the average values for the 10 years in question. Speaking generally, the import branch is so much more varied than the other, that the articles mentioned, though the most important, form but two-thirds of the whole value. On the other hand, the chief articles of export leave a comparatively little remainder. In the proportional tables quantities, it should be mentioned, are taken instead of values, owing to the complications introduced into the latter by the vagaries of exchange of late years. On the whole, it will be noticed that as to merchandise the increase in

TABLE O (1 = 1000).

Imports.		Exports of Indian Products.	
Total.	Rx. 57,787.	Total.	Rx. 86,491.
Cotton Goods	23,732	Raw Cotton	14,762
Cotton Twist	3,650	Cotton Goods	2,437
Hardware	921	Cotton Twist	3,601
Iron	2,110	Hides	4,731
Copper	1,837	Wool	1,302
Oil	1,470	Opium	10,786
Silk Goods	1,393	Tea	4,668
Sugar	1,866	Oil Seeds	9,225
Woollen Goods	1,403	Raw Jute	5,958
Others	19,405	Jute Goods	1,734
		Wheat	7,172
		Rice	9,162
		Others	11,058

Table P.

Variation per Cent. from the Returns for 1880–81 of Main Items of Revenue, Commerce, &c.

Year.	State Revenue from: Land.	State Revenue from: Stamps.	State Revenue from: Salt.	Consumption of Salt.	Post and Telegraph Transactions (Non-Official Correspondence only): Letters.	Post Cards.	Private and Inland Telegrams.	Value of Currency Notes Issued.	Railways: Miles Worked.	Passengers.	Goods.	Net Earnings.	Private Trade (Value): Merchandise: Imports.	Merchandise: Exports (of Indian Produce and Manufactures).	Treasure: Imports.	Treasure: Exports.	Ratio of Net Excess in value of Exports over Imports including Treasure.
1881–82	+ 3·96	+ 4·02	+ 3·52	+ 3·46	+ 7·97	+ 47·68	− 0·86	− 1·16	+ 4·16	+ 12·61	+12·28	+ 9·80	− 6·59	+10·12	+ 25·97	−23·65	+66·26
1882–83	+ 3·61	+ 3·97	−13·18	+ 8·52	+ 17·62	+100·77	+ 13·92	+11·11	+ 7·80	+ 24·51	+29·36	+21·21	− 0·61	+11·98	+ 49·68	−27·66	+28·25
1883–84	+ 5·92	+ 8·08	−13·63	+10·32	+ 28·16	+169·82	+ 18·39	− 2·02	+12·54	+ 41·18	+26·13	+13·77	+ 4·76	+18·22	+ 43·28	−29·86	+36·53
1884–85	+ 3·41	+10·95	− 8·56	+13·66	+ 38·87	+227·60	+ 30·72	+ 6·42	+17·00	+ 54·67	+43·25	+31·26	+ 5·65	+11·59	+ 54·52	+36·81	+ 0·78
1885–86	+ 7·01	+12·69	−10·83	+12·03	+ 53·20	+295·92	+ 46·34	+ 7·67	+28·07	+ 69·15	+48·18	+40·57	+ 2·99	+12·17	+ 72·20	−23·06	−13·78
1886–87	+ 9·20	+15·40	− 6·44	+16·05	+ 63·60	+355·81	+ 61·26	+ 3·94	+42·72	+ 82·49	+52·87	+34·69	+16·60	+17·97	+ 22·98	+19·44	+ 6·40
1887–88	+ 9·83	+19·25	− 6·26	+16·06	+ 72·94	+410·29	+ 78·18	+18·29	+46·11	+ 97·30	+69·50	+42·25	+24·00	+20·00	+ 53·82	+11·40	−24·85
1888–89	+ 9·02	+20·81	+ 7·86	+17·66	+ 84·80	+477·96	+102·65	+20·26	+46·76	+111·64	+68·41	+45·50	+32·32	+28·72	+ 54·03	+23·88	−16·83
1889–90	+13·59	+25·76	+15·06	+16·88	+ 96·63	+535·30	+109·90	+18·21	+70·64	+118·26	+71·16	+49·02	+32·30	+37·69	+ 94·25	+32·44	− 3·79
1890–91	+13·89	+25·18	+19·78	+18·29	+105·01	+579·80	+126·51	+67·53	+79·16	+133·22	+96·77	+82·50	+37·22	+33·25	+144·04	+47·40	−64·25
Mean of Ten Years	+ 7·94	+14·61	− 2·23	+13·54	+ 56·31	+319·11	+ 58·70	+15·02	+34·86	+ 74·50	+51·79	+37·06	+14·86	+20·17	+ 61·47	+ 6·70	− 1·83

Year.	Imports (Quantities): Iron.	Hard-ware.	Copper.	Kerosine Oil.	Sugars.	Cotton Piece Goods.	Cotton Twist and Yarn.	Exports (Quantities), Indian Produce or Manufacture: Raw Cotton.	Rice.	Wheat.	Oil Seed.	Raw Jute.	Raw Wool.	Cotton Twist and Yarn.	Cotton Piece Goods.	Jute Manufactures.
1881–82	− 7·99	+ 13·40	−11·42	− 9·64	− 21·33	− 8·56	−11·15	+23·96	+ 5·95	+167·33	+ 1·73	+ 29·27	+ 3·92	+ 14·44	− 1·63	−19·69
1882–83	+18·25	+ 43·36	+17·92	+105·36	− 31·80	− 7·58	− 2·22	+35·86	+14·64	+ 90·66	+27·60	+ 78·13	+ 2·46	+ 68·68	+ 36·69	+27·40
1883–84	+32·94	+ 47·29	+38·92	+ 35·28	− 25·29	− 2·95	− 1·09	+31·83	− 0·83	+182·11	+68·46	+ 20·80	− 1·99	+ 85·41	+ 82·87	+21·49
1884–85	+35·14	+ 52·84	+44·73	+171·34	+ 63·93	− 2·39	− 2·35	+11·63	−19·12	+112·92	+77·22	+ 44·04	− 0·85	+144·96	+ 57·67	+58·02
1885–86	+31·05	+ 40·54	+71·08	+ 81·54	+ 18·74	− 1·86	+ 0·08	− 7·71	+ 3·51	+183·02	+68·09	+ 33·95	+21·67	+190·85	+ 69·58	+21·71
1886–87	+23·06	+ 56·62	+61·14	+219·47	+ 77·38	+21·35	+ 6·83	+19·69	− 1·42	+199·07	+54·38	+ 42·98	+31·07	+241·26	+ 75·62	+23·26
1887–88	+62·12	+ 97·98	+39·55	+211·59	+ 83·36	+ 3·52	+12·35	+18·35	+ 4·65	+ 81·86	+56·08	+ 65·99	+36·26	+321·73	+128·52	+41·96
1888–89	+50·17	+ 99·47	−74·20	+295·01	+ 64·01	+19·70	+14·63	+17·40	−15·12	+136·57	+51·18	+ 81·64	+36·39	+379·18	+131·18	+90·49
1889–90	+35·37	+ 88·39	+49·05	+434·85	+ 74·70	+12·42	+ 1·10	+39·23	− 0·61	+ 85·40	+53·32	+ 76·53	+48·64	+427·67	+ 95·70	+85·90
1890–91	+45·43	+116·74	+16·97	+442·30	+197·26	+13·39	+11·10	+30·46	+28·23	+ 92·37	+43·65	+106·30	+32·57	+529·24	+122·61	+88·50
Mean of Ten Years	+32·56	+ 66·66	+26·68	+198·77	+ 50·10	+ 4·71	+ 2·93	+22·07	+ 1·99	+133·13	+50·16	+ 57·96	+21·01	+240·34	+ 79·88	+43·91

the exports has been continuous, and in rate above that of the imports, whilst, including treasure transaction, the balance is inclining a little in favour of closer correspondence. But here, as in the case of the post, telegraph, and railway, one of the main points worthy of note is the increase in the apparent reserve available for spending on what are to the masses of India, objects of luxury. Then again there is to be noted the growth of the export trade in raw produce, though it is here as everywhere else, subject to annual variations of a somewhat irregular character. Lastly, the competition between imported piece-goods and yarn and that made in India. As to the first, the marginal table O shows that the absolute quantities manufactured abroad and sent to India are very largely in excess of the others, but the proportional statement indicates the relatively far higher increase that has taken place in the exports of this sort of goods from India in the 10 years under review. The yarn from abroad, again, is being beaten in the race, just now, by that made in the country, but there is probably a check to be expected in this rapid increase of foreign demand, as there has been to a slight extent in the jute trade of late. Finally, a few words must be said about the absorptive power of India for the precious metals, which, in discussing the circumstances of the country, is a point too often overlooked. In the last 10 years India took in an amount of gold which is valued in what is known as Rx, or "tens of rupees," at no less than 44,051,255, whilst it disgorged in the same time only 3,144,069. Simultaneously, the corresponding amount of silver introduced into the country was 101,086,766, of which only 12,225,899 has left it. Thus there remains in round numbers, the equivalent of Rx. 41,000,000 in gold and 89,000,000 in silver, which has been added to the hoards already in the possession of the people previous to the period under review. We have every reason accordingly to assume that the present rate of increase amongst the people of India is well within their means of subsistence. If maintained, which of course it will not be, it would be 75 years before the population doubled itself, and the problem of their support would then, no doubt, be a hard one for our successors.

CHAPTER IV.

The Occupation of the Population.

> "By ceaseless action all that is subsists.
> Constant rotation of the unwearied wheel
> That nature rides upon, maintains her health,
> Her beauty, her fertility. She dreads
> An instant's pause, and lives but while she moves."—*Cowper*.

The statistics that have been dealt with in the foregoing chapters of this review are of a comparatively simple character. In some particulars inaccuracy is admittedly present in the returns, but it is not difficult to trace, and it can be localised within certain fairly well defined limits, so that its effects can be adequately discounted in discussing the points in question. Uncertainty, therefore, as to the true meaning of the statistics prevails to but an insignificant extent. For example, the deliberate omission of adult females is attributable to a single cause operative amongst certain classes or within certain tracts. The return of birth-place, again, is well known to be often characterised by excess of minuteness on the part of the native of India who happens to be sojourning at a distance from his home, and by equal want of definition on that of the foreigner. The one insists on entering his native village, without adding the name of the State or district in which it is situated, whilst the other too often considers that the name of a continent is sufficient to satisfy reasonable curiosity on this matter. A still more striking case is that of the age-table, with which we have yet to deal. Here, the prevailing ignorance is so uniform and so widely spread, that the error tends to group itself into certain easily recognisable forms throughout the whole country, so that in accordance with the general tendency of such large aggregates, the very irregularity of the figures becomes, to a considerable extent, the test of their accuracy.

Special difficulties met with in enumerating occupation.

But with regard to occupation, the conditions are more complicated and the opportunities of going wrong proportionately increased. To begin with, the difficulty in formulating the question is considerable, for the circumstances are so various that it is hopeless to attempt to frame instructions or illustrations comprehensive enough to cover the whole subject. Then, too, there seems to be in all countries alike a tendency towards certain classes of error, generally in the direction of the use of terms too indefinite to indicate sufficiently the precise nature of the occupation, or which bear a special local signification alien to the usual meaning. Lastly, owing partly to the difficulty of the subject itself, partly to the defects above mentioned in the original record, a return of occupation may be, and too often is, grievously handicapped by the system adopted for the grouping and classification of the enormous amount of detail that has to be thus worked into shape.

Scope of the inquiry.

As regards the first difficulty, the main point is to settle exactly what is to be the scope and extent of the inquiry and this necessarily differs in every country, according to the stage of its development. In all cases it is held necessary to ascertain the numerical proportion of the main classes of occupation, such as agriculture, manufacture, mining, commerce, or the liberal professions, not to mention the less definite category of the unskilled, which has sprung into such prominence in some countries within the last few generations. In most instances, too, it is advisable to estimate the relative strength, in the majority of the above classes, of possession and proletarianism, the wage-paying and the wage-receiving population. But the question then arises whether the return is to be that of the working members of the community only, or that of the supporting power of each means of subsistence at the time of the census. In the first case, it would include only those who actually work, or who are in the immediate receipt of the means of livelihood which render them independent of work. In the other, the scope is widened so as to comprise not only the working members of the household, but all who immediately depend upon them for their support. Similarly, in the case of those who have the means of living without the need of working for them, the return would include, in addition to the person actually in possession of the income, those supported out of it by him, otherwise, of course, than by way of charity or wage for special service rendered, since the last named are not indissolubly connected with the income in question, but constitute independent means of livelihood. The relative advantages of these two rest mainly on local considerations. The reason for selecting the latter, or wider, system for India will be found later on in this chapter. Another question under this head is the amount of detail in returning the occupation that should be asked for. Whether, that is, a general title or class is considered enough, or whether greater accuracy should be demanded. The answer to this depends, obviously, on whether the object is to get a complete industrial survey, or merely a general view of the distribution of occupation on broad lines. Connected with this point, too, as we are on the topic of difficulties, is the much vexed question of how to deal at the census with the numerous instances in which a single individual or family, as the case may be, has more than one means of livelihood, or where, as frequently happens, and not in India alone, the return is that of a title that may include all or any of several occupations.

Inaccuracy in the entry of occupation.

The second of the above mentioned obstacles to a complete return will be found well illustrated in the course of examining the details of the figures for India, though, as was hinted before, the inaccuracy in question is by no means confined to that country. A few entries of this sort, however, may be here quoted in explanation of the difficulty. We have thus a lot of people returned as "shopkeeper," without any guide as to the goods sold. "Labour," again, leaving it uncertain whether it is agricultural that is meant, or the general unskilled labour that chiefly haunts towns and extensive public works. "Service," is another term that is used without qualification, more often, probably, in India than elsewhere. It may there be that of the State, or of the household, or of the shop, or in a merchant's establishment. The profession of a "writer," is as common in India and as various in its application as that of "mechanic" in England. It has no connection, however, with authorship. Numbers of others of the same description suggest themselves, but it is superfluous to quote them.

Objects of classification.

The general question of the classification of occupation is a highly complicated one, so it is not proposed to enter into it minutely in the present work. The distribution of industry varies from country to country so much that comparison is both valuable and interesting, but the field of inquiry is so extensive and full of detail, that however desirable it may be to make such a comparison, for which, of course, a general scheme of classification is essential, it has been found impracticable hitherto to carry it out in a trustworthy manner on the basis of a census return alone. The subject, therefore, has not been recognised as one falling into the category of international statistics, and there seems abundant reason for not placing India side by side with western countries in such a return. If once we abandon the idea of international comparison, the object of classification is confined to the exhibition of the leading characteristics of the local population with reference to their occupation, irrespective of the sociological considerations of a general nature to which weight has to be attached when the field of comparison is enlarged. How many of these have been dropped out of sight in dealing with the returns for India on this occasion will be seen from the comments made below on the system of arrangement herein adopted, but, so far as the main purpose, that of indicating the general features of the social organisation of the country, will admit, the obvious advantages of theoretical consistency have been retained.

General value of the returns.

It may be gathered from these remarks that a high value is not attached to the results of the census of occupation. This is true, and the opinion is not confined to those who have had the administration of the operation in India alone. In some of the countries of Europe the subject is excluded altogether from the enumeration, and in one, at least, which need not be named, much forethought and many elaborate instructions were rewarded by results which the census authorities thought it advisable not to mislead the public by including with the rest. In Germany as well as in the United States, it has been decided that a comprehensive industrial survey, obtained by dint of detailed inquiry spread over a considerable time, is preferable to the rough and ready return which is all that it falls within the capacity of a synchronous census to furnish. The elaborate and in many respects admirable tables that contain the results of the occupation return at the last census of England and Wales have been shown by experts in industrial economics to be incomplete in several important particulars. Italy, on the other hand, is a staunch supporter of the census of occupation, and the opinion of a statist of the eminence of Commendatore Bodio, who has brought his country's statistics to such a pitch of efficiency, carries great weight. Still, he would be, no doubt, the first to admit that the section in question of his Confronti Internazionali can only be digested with a copious sprinkling of explanatory salt. This usually takes the shape of the enumeration of the various ways of going wrong, as above, which has the further advantage that many minds of a complacent order take the admission of statistical error as incense offered in some way or other to what they speak of as common sense. India, it is true, is, in its present stage, at an advantage in respect to the enumeration of occupation, as compared with countries which are more adapted by situation or natural products to commercial or manufacturing development, since, in the former, the specialisation of functions is, relatively speaking, in its infancy; the organisation of labour is of the simplest, and the multiplication of the various means of subsistence proceeds at a rate barely perceptible, except at considerable intervals of time. But, from a census point of view, the very simplicity of this almost exclusively agrestic community has its drawbacks, and the complication that arises is largely due, not to the manifold differentiation of occupations, as it might be in England, but to their combination; as, for instance, when one individual lives by the exercise of several which are otherwise totally unconnected with each other, and he is probably unable to specify which of them may be by preference termed his chief means of support. In fact, in the most favourable circumstances, the completeness and accuracy of the enumeration is a matter of very considerable uncertainty, and to those who have acquired knowledge of the subject by experience, it is scarcely possible to conceive a state of society at all above that of primitive savagery in which it would be otherwise.

System of enumeration. Before discussing the results of the enumeration of India by occupation, as qualified by the above general admissions of imperfection, some explanation is necessary of the scope of the returns and of the system on which they were prepared, because important innovations have been introduced into both since the preceding census. It has been stated above that the object of the present census was to obtain a view of the supporting power, at the time of the census, of each means of livelihood, whereas in 1881 the return was that of workers only, and persons of, so to speak, independent means. Thus no less than 53 per cent. of the population, or, as the return was by sexes, 37½ per cent. of the males, and 69½ of the females, was excluded. If, therefore, the total strength of any particular group was in question, such as, for instance, the agricultural or the artisan class, recourse to approximation was necessary, and this had to be based on estimates of the probable number of heads of families, and of the numerical strength of their respective households. As there was no general tabulation of occupation by age, except in a few of the larger towns, the above computations had to be purely conjectural, and the postulates and methods of calculation differed in each province. But even as a record of the working population only, the results, in the opinion of the Superintendents of the census operations, in their respective provinces, were very defective, and so far as the return of working females is concerned, the figures were found by Sir W. Chichele Plowden, the then Census Commissioner for India, to be unworthy of examination. A few facts in confirmation of this view may as well be cited, which will show that the abandonment of the former system was neither premature nor based on inadequate grounds. First of all, of course, stands the inconsistency of practice in regard to the entry of the occupation of women, which is based to a great extent on social considerations. Where there is a strong and well defined line drawn between the upper and the lower grades of society, owing to distinctions of caste or race, the women who actually do work are generally returned as workers in the lower section only, although they may be similarly engaged in various occupations in many of the higher classes. On the other hand, there is noted a general tendency to return the women of the middle classes, all over India, as following the occupation of the head of their household, whether they actually do so or not. This last fact was one of the inducements to adopt the scheme of return indicated by this inclination. Then, again, the distinction between the principal and his dependents or sharers is much valued in certain occupations, so the chief worker, especially the artisan, is disposed to ignore, in making the return, the aid rendered by the others with whom he may be connected. There is a similar inconsistency with regard to occupations dependent on the land. In some cases, the nominal occupant will alone be recognised, and the rest of the family returned as labourers, whereas in others, where the participation of the soil is based on different principles, the number of occupants or sharers will include all who have any interest therein, irrespective of the position of the patriarch. The young children of agriculturists, too, are as often as not entered as graziers, though their attention is gratuitously devoted to the family live-stock only. Elsewhere, they will be found to have been omitted from the workers altogether, or returned, in some instances, as farm servants. Other cases of a similar tendency can be adduced, but, on the whole, they reduce themselves to the above categories of inconsistency of treatment of subordinate or subsidiary interest in the family means of livelihood.

Now, under the present scheme of enumeration, though the number of workers is ignored, the whole population is accounted for under some head or other, with the exception of about $1\frac{1}{2}$ millions, who either did not fill up the column at all or returned some term which was unintelligible, or, as is more frequent in India than in the West, frankly disreputable. The object of the return renders the distinction of sex immaterial, since man, woman, and child are alike supported by the occupation in question. From the provincial returns, however, it is possible to get the number of adult males under each head, since in these the detail of both age and sex has been retained. In the Imperial series of tables it has been omitted, first, because for a considerable portion of the population in the Feudatory States and for some in Southern India the age was not tabulated for occupations; secondly, because, as will appear in a later chapter of this review, the ages, in the crude state in which they are extracted from the schedules, are by no means correct in two, at least, of the periods selected for the occupation table; thirdly, because the detail of age and sex, added to that of rural and urban population for British and Feudatory territory, would swell the return to the dimension of a considerable volume with incommensurate advantages; Lastly, because, as shown above, these details are irrelevant to the general purport of the statistics in question. But although the distinction between worker and dependent is obliterated in the final results of the census, it was retained, as will be seen from the instructions quoted below, throughout the enumeration. This, however, was done merely as a measure of administrative convenience, not with the view of tabulation. There are numerous prejudices on such matters amongst the people in India which deserve consideration, and by prescribing the addition in this column of the schedule of the word "dependent" to the entry of occupation made against such as do no work, the awkardness was avoided of appearing to attribute to these persons the exercise of various functions which are impossible or prohibited to those of their age or sex. Had the distinction been carried into the tables, it is very plain that the defect that vitiated to such an extent the results in 1881 would have been perpetuated, and casual readers would have been liable to be misled by assuming the number of the active members of the population to be that set forth as such.

Instructions to enumerators.

The instructions for filling up the occupation column were the fullest and most elaborate in the code, for it was decided that as this was the most difficult portion of the task imposed on the enumerating agency, it was only fair to carry the explanations of what was wanted as far as the time available for their instruction and the limits of their intelligence would allow. It was also held desirable to obtain in the first stage of the operations as much detail as possible, so that any reduction that might seem advisable could be postponed till the whole field of the subject came under the eye of the Provincial Census Superintendent during compilation. If general terms, or classes of occupations, had been considered sufficient, the instructions could easily have been curtailed into a few lines. In order to show precisely the nature and scope of the inquiry under this head, and the difference between it and the corresponding procedure at the census of 1881, the heading of the column in the schedule and the rules for filling in the entries to be made on the two occasions are here reproduced:—

1891.	1881.
Occupation or Means of Subsistence.	Occupation of Men, also of Boys and Females who may do work. N.B.—Boys at School, Girls, Small Children and Women who perform no regular Work, should not be shown at all in this Column.
Instructions:—Enter here the exact occupation or means of livelihood of all males and females who do work or live on private property such as *house rent*, *pension*, &c. In the case of children and women who do no work, enter the occupation of the head of their family, or of the person who supports them, adding the word "dependent," but do not leave this column unfilled for any one, even an infant. If a person have two or more occupations, enter only the chief one, except when a person owns or cultivates land in addition to another occupation, when both should be entered.	*Instructions*:—Only such persons are to be shown in this column as actually do work contributing to the family income. Mere employment in such domestic occupations as spinning will not entitle women to be shown in this column, unless the produce of their labour is regularly brought to market. When a person has two or more occupations, he should be entered as following the occupation whence his income is chiefly derived, but if he combines agriculture with any other profession or trade, such as that of vakil or money-lender, carpenter, or smith, both occupations should be shown.

1891. (*continued.*)	1881. (*continued.*)
No vague terms should be used, such as ***service, Government service, shopkeeping, writing*** and ***labour***, &c., but the *exact* ***service***, the ***goods sold***, the ***class*** of ***writing*** or of ***labour*** must be stated. When a person's occupation is connected with agriculture it should be stated whether the land is cultivated in person or let to tenants; if he be an agricultural labourer, it should be stated whether he be engaged by the month or year, or is a daily field labourer. Women who earn money by occupations independent of their husbands, such as ***spinning, selling firewood, cow-dung cakes, grass***, or by ***rice-pounding, weaving***, or doing house-work for wages should be shown under those occupations. If a person makes the articles he sells he should be entered as "maker and seller" of them. If a person lives on alms, it should be stated whether he is a religious mendicant or an ordinary beggar. When a person is in Government, railway, or municipal service, the special service should be entered first, and the word Government, railway, or municipal, &c., after it as:—clerk, ***Government;*** sweeper, ***municipal;*** labourer, ***railway***. If a person be temporarily out of employ, enter the last or ordinary occupation.	General terms, such as servant, workman, dealer, must not be employed. In each case the specific service or trade in which the person is engaged must be named, *e.g.*, watchman, office-messenger, digger, ploughman, cloth-seller. General expressions [such as ***pesha-i-khúd***] must not be employed. In every case the occupation must be indicated by the common vernacular term by which it is known [and not by the Persian name; thus ***Kumhár*** for potter, not ***Kasgar***].

The changes made in 1891 are chiefly in detail, always excepting that shown in the beginning of the rules. One or two points were treated at greater length, where it had been found that the first code led to misunderstanding. For instance, the phrase "regularly brought to market" is said to have excluded a good number of the class to whom it was intended to apply. Again, in some few but important cases, the name of the caste is a better indication than that of the principal occupation, so the penultimate provision of the older code was omitted. The greater detail as to the connexion with the land was intended to serve as a guide to the relative strength of the cultivating class and the non-agricultural proprietor or occupant, and a special provision was held necessary in order to prevent the entry of "household work" against those who were not getting their living by it as an independent source of livelihood. The bulk of the rest of the modifications simply met cases of doubt that had arisen in the course of the operations of 1881. It should be mentioned, by the way, that the new rules were framed for the sanction of the Government of India by a Committee of the census Superintendents of 1881, appointed for the purpose on the suggestion of Sir W. Chichele Plowden, the Census Commissioner on that occasion, as affording the best means of making use of the experience then gained. There are two points, besides that of the obliteration of the distinction of the dependent classes, which are of sufficient importance to justify a few explanatory words in this place, as they appertain to matters of somewhat wider interest than those above-mentioned. The first is the application of the final sentence of the 1891 rules to the inmates of prisons or asylums. The general instructions, as they stand, seem to imply that at all events temporary prisoners and inmates of asylums should be returned according to the means whereby they lived before their withdrawal from public life. On the other hand, the special rule issued to those in charge of the census of the above institutions prescribed that the inmates should be returned as such, irrespective of their former or ordinary employment. The discrepancy is based on two arguments. First, that the results of the census represent, so to speak, the people photographed at a given time without reference to that which preceded or was to follow it. Clearly, therefore, the persons in question were not at that time exercising any occupation by which they lived, but were, for the moment, withdrawn from the active section of the population. Then, again, we should look at the source of their means of support, which is the taxation of the public, or private charity, as the case may be, but not the result of their own labour. They are thus in an entirely different position to that of the free agent temporarily out of employ, who is presumably living on the proceeds of previous work of the sort he intends to resume. A somewhat kindred point which has occasionally arisen is that of the entry of the original occupation by those who have ceased to exercise it. Here, too, there is a withdrawal from work, and the means of subsistence are either investments or, at best, capital derived through a past occupation, just as, with reference to the present question, the officer of the State is in a different position when he is in receipt of salary from that he occupies when on pension, quite apart from the celebrated definition of the latter in Dr. Johnson's Dictionary.* The second matter which seems to be open to comment is the way of dealing with the people who have more occupations than one. It will be seen from the rules that only one class of such cases has been recognised, namely, where the second means of livelihood is connected with the land. This is in India by far the most prevalent form of such pluralism; the next to it is, perhaps, money-lending, which is practised to a greater or less extent, by most men of substance, except Musalmán, and then comes a miscellaneous group of occupations which are associated under the name of the caste which exercises them. Both these last have been lost to us in the census return, owing to the selection of the main employment only, and as regards the first of the two, it is very doubtful whether the return would have been anything like complete had it been prescribed, because the inquisitiveness about subsidiary sources of income would possibly have raised suspicions connected with taxation, from which, as it was, the proceedings were fortunately free. The omission of the second is undoubtedly to be deplored. As to the general question, it must be admitted that the rule followed in England, of entering all the occupations in their order of importance to the total income of the family or householder, is the best, though for the reason above given, it may seem inadvisable to apply it at present to India.

Abstraction of the results.

Such was, in brief, the scope of the information it was sought to obtain. After the census, the abstraction from the schedules was effected for the rural and urban tracts respectively by sexes, showing for each the distribution of every occupation by three age periods; first, those under five, which would include all who are too young to work; secondly, between five and fifteen, an interval which covers the school-going age of those of the upper classes, and that of casual help in the home occupation on the part of the youth of the lower and middle. The third, which includes all over fifteen, though it contains probably a good many of both sexes who are either still at school or who are not engaged in regular work, represents, as fairly as can be expected, the working age of the masses. A subsidiary object in selecting these periods should not be forgotten, and this was the check afforded by this independent tabulation on the age tables. It has been stated above that in the Imperial tables no use has been made of the details of sex and age, but in most of the Provincial reports comments have been made on them by the census Superintendents. It requires note, too, in connection with the present topic, that under the general instructions for abstraction, the whole of the detail found in the schedule was recorded, so that all grouping could be handled by more experienced agency at a later stage in the operations. Lists of all doubtful cases were sent for decision to the Census Commissioner, and in several Provinces the complete index was so treated.

Classification.

The object of the above provision was obviously to ensure as much uniformity in the final return as the nature of the information allowed. To further this end, the scheme of classification, which is explained below, was accompanied by a lengthy list, showing under their correct classification all the occupations and means of livelihood that were either returned at the census of 1881 or had been noted down in the course of tours of inspection from the schedules of that under review. They were also indexed alphabetically, in pursuance of the system adopted in such cases in the English census. The grouping and distribution by class are inevitably elaborate, but it is satisfactory to find that the scheme was found workable and convenient by those who had the duty of applying it to their results. It is undoubtedly nearer to what was wanted for India than the scheme on which the returns of the preceding census was based, but it is admittedly far from being completely adapted to its object, and the experience gathered from its use shows plainly that so far as the return of caste for occupation is concerned, and this is one of the main difficulties to be met, the practice in one part of India is so different from that in another, that it is out of the question to deal with the matter under a single set of rules. In the Panjáb, for example, the Superintendent found from the returns that the number of caste entries in the occupation column were so few compared to that which returned one or other of the actual means of subsistence, that no difficulty was experienced in classifying them. On

* "An allowance made to anyone without an equivalent. In England it is generally understood to mean pay given to a State hireling for treason to his country."

the other hand, the Bengal Superintendent writes of Orissa that about 20 per cent. of the population seem to have returned their caste instead of some form of agriculture, by which they really live. Thus, instead of the almost purely agricultural character of the people of this division of his charge being shown in the returns, Orissa is the only part of the province in which more than half the population are entered as non-agricultural. He points his comments by comparing the general results in this respect of the occupation census amongst a Musalmán population, where caste is not functional to any preponderating extent, with those of a purely Brahmanic population, such as is found in Orissa.

The best and shortest way of explaining the system of classification seems to be to reproduce *in extenso* the instructions regarding it. These, then, ran as follows:—

"The object in view is to group the entries in the census schedules as far as possible in accordance with the distribution of occupations in India in general, and at the same time to allow room for the designation of special features found only in certain provinces. It is superfluous, therefore, to discuss the classification in use at the census of communities further advanced in economic differentiation, or one based simply on the abstract laws of sociological science. The classification now published is not altogether scientifically correct, but it will serve its purpose if it collects under one head occupations known to be akin to each other, and keeps apart others which are but nominally related.

"2. There are certain classes of occupations in India which require a few general remarks before the details of the scheme are reviewed. In the first place, Government service is so comprehensive a term in this country, that for the purposes of classification it is necessary to restrict its application to the functions which cannot be dissociated from the main end of administration—protection and defence. Thus, special functions undertaken by the State in India beyond the primary duties above quoted are to be classed, not under the head of Government service, but under their special designation. Public instruction will come under education, and engineering, meteorology, agricultural training, medical practice, and administration under these heads respectively. It will be almost impracticable to affect a complete separation from the general title to which objection is raised above, as the combination of these special functions with that of the military or civil service of the Crown has been retained too closely in the schedules to admit of discrimination; but, as far as possible, the principle above ennunciated should be rigorously applied. It is the same with the service of local and municipal bodies, where only persons actually engaged in administration should be entered under those titles. Engineers and road overseers or supervisors, sanitary inspectors or surveyors, schoolmasters and vaccinators, all have their special groups, irrespective of the source from which their salary is drawn. If the extent to which in India the functions of the State are exercised beyond the limits of protection be in question, the better source of information will be the periodical lists published by Government of its employés, rather than a census return.

"3. A second class of occupations needing special treatment is the very large one of what have been called "Village Industries," one great characteristic of which is that the same person both makes and sells. Amongst the most important of these come the brass-smith, blacksmith, cotton weaver, potter, tanner, carpenter, and the like, representing, with their fellows, the bulk of the artisan class throughout the country. Owing to the extension of towns, it is misleading to group such occupations under what would be otherwise an obviously suitable title, and some artisans indeed may have totally changed the character of the occupation on emigrating from the simple community to which they originally ministered. It has, therefore, been thought advisable to make no difference in the classification between those who make and those who sell special goods, though in the sub-divisional groups there is room for the general dealer, the commercial agent, and other middlemen, and also for that class of dealers known by a special name in each province, which supplies certain articles which are almost invariably associated together throughout the country.

Classes.

"4. After the above general remarks, the scheme may be taken up in detail. In the first place, the aggregate of the various means of livelihood are divided into the following main classes:—

"A.—Government.
"B.—Pasture and agriculture.
"C.—Personal services.
"D.—The preparation and supply of material substances.
"E.—Commerce and the transport of persons, goods, and messages, and the storage of goods.
"F.—Professions, learned, artistic, and minor.
"G.—Indefinite occupations, and means of subsistence independent of occupation.

"Of these, the first and fourth are the most complicated, though, making allowances for the defective return in certain cases, the former should be nearly freed from all but those who can rightly be classed in it. The fourth has had to be minutely sub-divided lest confusion should arise.

"5. Subordinate to the seven classes come 24 Orders, as shown marginally, bracketted according to their respective main heads. The first few explain themselves. As regards the seventh, eighth, ninth, tenth, and eleventh, the object the article or service is intended for is placed more prominently than the material dealt with. On the other hand, from the twelfth to the seventeenth, the latter is regarded as more characteristic of the occupation than the object for which the prepared article is intended. The distinction is, of course, conventional only and not economic, as in both Orders the makers and the sellers of an article are combined, and it is only in the eighteenth that special mention is made of those who return themselves as exclusively engaged in distribution.

ORDERS.

Class	Order		Class	Order	
A.	I.	Administration.	D.	XV.	Wood, cane, and leaves.
	II.	Defence.		XVI.	Drugs, gums, &c.
	III.	Foreign and feudatory State service.		XVII.	Leather.
B.	IV.	Cattle-breeding, &c.	E.	XVIII.	Commerce.
	V.	Agriculture.		XIX.	Transport and storage.
C.	VI.	Personal services.	F.	XX.	Learned and artistic professions.
D.	VII.	Food and drink.		XXI.	Sports and amusements.
	VIII.	Light, firing, and forage.	G.	XXII.	Complex occupations.*
	IX.	Buildings.		XXIII.	Indefinite occupations.
	X.	Vehicles and vessels.		XXIV.	Independent of work.
	XI.	Supplementary requirements.			
	XII.	Textile fabrics and dress.			
	XIII.	Metals and precious stones.			
	XIV.	Glass, pottery and stone ware.			

* In the Imperial Returns this has been omitted, and Order XXIII. divided into XXII. General labour, and XXIII. Indefinite or disreputable.

"6. The classification next passes into sub-orders, and where still further definition is thought necessary, into groups below the sub-orders. Of the latter there are 77, which are shown, with their groups, in Appendix A. In some respects they are the most important items of the scheme, and it is possible that with careful classification, the Imperial tables may be based on them, leaving detail below groups for supplementary or Provincial returns. At all events, beyond a few generally prevalent occupations, it is probable that each Province will be best served by being given discretion to select under each group the items it considers most typical or otherwise important in the constitution of its population. Before this is done, however, every occupation and means of livelihood returned will have to be catalogued for classification, so that uniformity up to the point mentioned above may be ensured. Sub-orders and groups.

"7. In Appendix B. is given a sample of the application of the scheme to a collection of items found in two or three of the Census Reports of 1881. It is not to be confounded with a complete index, such as was attempted on the last occasion, but will nevertheless serve as a general guide in preparing the detailed catalogues prescribed for the present census in Appendix B., page 12 of Circular M. Occupations.

"8. A very important point to be dealt with in connection with the tabulation of occupations in India is how to deal with an occupation shown conjointly with some description of agriculture or with the possession of land, or, again, which is locally known to be always combined with another non-agricultural occupation, of apparently quite a distinct character. It seems advisable to show all of the former class in the main return under their respective special headings, and in a supplementary return to show them with the agricultural connection as the main head, and the special occupation subordinate to each several sub-division of the former. For example:—We may have a pleader who is a non-cultivating landowner, a money-lender who is also a non-cultivating landowner, a carpenter who is a cultivating tenant, and so on. In the general return these will appear under the items of pleader, money-lender, and carpenter respectively. In the supplementary return, after the total number of non-cultivating landowners who have no other occupation returned against them, will come the pleader, and after him the money-lender, whilst the carpenter will occupy a corresponding position under the head of cultivating tenant. In this way the total number of landowners and tenants and their families, so far as the census return is correct, will be obtained without detracting from the roll of the occupations which probably take up an equal or greater portion of the time of the person returning both. As regards the second-class, no general heads can be prescribed, as the combinations may differ in every province. Notorious instances are those of the tanner and shoemaker, shepherd and blanket-weaver, and, as shown by Mr. Ibbetson for the Panjáb, the fisherman, water carrier, and public cook. Where the caste is used to denote the occupation, there need be no difficulty in providing a special heading for the complex functions in question. In other cases, local knowledge should be called in to point out which are the occupations almost always combined together, and these can be demarcated by a special note to the return. The instruction, however, that only the main occupation should be entered in the schedule, is against the chance of obtaining a complete return of non-agricultural combinations. All the same, provincial Superintendents should suggest as soon as possible the heads of this class which they find can be distinguished in their respective Provinces." Combined occupations.

It will now be well to indicate in what particulars the above prescriptions failed in their object. This can be done in very general terms. In the first place, the vague title of "service" was not entirely driven out of the field, in spite of all the precautions taken against it, so that the groups of State employ and domestic work must be somewhat intermingled, to the detriment, possibly, of the commercial groups. Then, again, the provision of food is understated, since many of those purveying grain and pulse are to be found amongst the shopkeepers, in the trading class, because their entry was of a general nature, wanting the specification of the article in which they dealt. Fishermen, too, cannot be always distinguished from boatmen and sea-faring workers, whilst there is even more confusion between the sellers of milk, who are often residents of the town, and the rural dealers in cattle. Often where the head of the family is a man, the entry is of the latter, but if he be away, his wife will return herself as a milk seller, and so on. Scavenging, which figured in the returns of 1881 to a great extent under the honorific title of "municipal service" seems to have been more correctly allocated in the present tables. But agricultural labour has suffered grievously from its dangerous proximity to the class of the "general unskilled." On the whole, the artisan and professional classes appear to have been the most correctly returned, or the easiest to classify, though in the case of the former, the details indicate in several places the want of uniformity of return; but their grouping is not deficient in general accuracy. Defects in enumeration.

The scheme of classification can be seen in operation, first, on the broader lines of the functional Orders, in Summary Table XIII., on page xii. of the first volume of the Imperial Returns, and again in detail, in Table XVI., on page 455, &c. of the same volume. In the Provincial volumes, the serial number of the latter return is XVII., but for the Imperial series, the delay in furnishing the returns of caste, &c. rendered it advisable to transpose the two, and to complete the first volume with the material in hand, rather than delay its publication. In commenting on this return, it is convenient to reproduce the figures only in their relation to the general total, and to refer the reader to the original for the absolute numbers. The latter, however, will be quoted when any special group is under discussion. In Table B, at page 99, the percentage of each Order and sub-Order of occupation on the total population is shown, and to avoid the repetition of so long a statement, later on, the respective prevalence of the occupation General results of the Census of occupation, &c.

in urban and rural tracts is added, in the same proportional form. There is one feature in this last series to which attention may as well be called at once. This is, that though the general ratio of the urban population to the whole is about $9\frac{1}{2}$ per cent., in the case of occupations, this proportion is exceeded in every one of the Orders and sub-Orders, except those relating to agriculture, pasture and village service. It nearly recedes to it in the case of general unskilled labour, which has been mentioned as probably recruited very considerably from the ranks of field and farm hands, and again amongst the potters, cane-workers, and the purveyors of minor forest produce, such as leaves, honey, rubber, lac, and so on. This fact shows the remarkable simplicity of the industrial structure of the community in India. A little has been said on this point already, but before entering into the examination of the general return, it is worth while to dwell upon it in a little more detail.

Village industries.

In respect to the relation of the village community to the land there is a different system to be found in nearly every Province and large State, and in detail, too, the respective social grades are diversely arranged. But on the whole, the component parts of the society considered as an economic unit, are wonderfully uniform throughout India. This, however, cannot be held to include Burma or several of the hill tracts, since in the latter the community is hardly a settled one, and in the other, the caste system, as has been mentioned in a former chapter, does not prevail, so the facilities for separation are greater. The marginal table shows the relative strength of these component parts. Speaking generally, the village community consists, firstly, of the cultivating class, and, secondly, of those who minister to their most pressing wants. A cross division exists, on one side of which stand those belonging to the inner circle of the society, that is, the occupants of the land and the artisans or menials to whom tradition assigns a cognate racial origin; and on the other, the lower village menials, the agrestic serfs, and others whose occupation, in the present day, as in the time of the Chinese pilgrims, relegates them to an inferior position, and who are, no doubt, also separated by their direct relationship to the races displaced from the ownership of the land by successive waves of aggressive immigration from the north. The former are admitted as residents within the village site, but the latter must dwell without those limits, or on a special site of their own. In the process of evolution there have been successive passages upwards from the one to the other, but the transformation is a matter of many generations; this is a question that will have to be treated in connection with the ethnology of the people, in a later chapter of this work. We have it then, that the backbone of the village is the agriculturist, or he who holds the village lands. The labourer is found generally in the ranks of the helots above mentioned, or of others a little higher in the social scale. The pastoral class is to be distinguished first as the nomad, with which we are not at present concerned, but which occupies itself chiefly with sheep and goats

TABLE A.—Showing the main occupations returned.

Occupation.	Per-centage of each Occupation on	
	Total Population.	Rural Population.
1. Landholders and tenants	52·98	57·06
2. Agricultural labourers	6·50	6·92
3. General labourers	8·87	8·77
4. Graziers, shepherds and wool-workers.	1·45	1·49
5. Cotton workers	3·07	2·75
6. Goldsmiths	0·62	0·50
7. Blacksmiths	0·55	0·52
8. Brass and coppersmiths	0·14	0·10
9. Carpenters	1·06	0·96
10. Masons	0·36	0·24
11. Barbers	0·90	0·89
12. Washermen	0·72	0·71
13. Fishermen	0·95	0·94
14. Oil pressers	0·69	0·69
15. Potters	0·82	0·81
16. Village servants	1·07	1·13
17. Leather workers	1·14	1·09
18. Scavengers	0·40	0·35
19. Priests	0·60	0·56
20. Mendicants	1·95	1·78
Total, Primitive	**84·84**	**88·26**
21. Milk sellers	0·35	—
22. Grain and pulse dealers	1·10	—
23. Shop keepers	0·88	—
24. Money-lenders	0·34	—
25. Grocers	0·74	—
26. Tailors	0·42	—
27. Piece-goods dealers	0·32	—
28. Toddy drawers	0·35	—
29. Cane workers	0·50	—
30. Grass and firewood sellers	0·47	—
Total, Supplementary	**5·47**	—
Others	*9·69*	11·74
Grand Total	**100·00**	**100·00**

throughout the greater part of India, and with camels in the west and north-west only. Secondly, there is the settled section, busied mainly with milch and plough cattle. This attaches itself, as a rule, to the outskirts of the towns and larger villages. In the ordinary village, the milk of the family is supplied by the livestock of the household, as the practice of keeping a cow or two is very widely spread. We may even quote on this point the title of daughter in support of it, for though, as Dr. Max. Müller allows, the derivation from "duh" may seem too pastoral or idyllic, it may be said, as Dr. Boteler said of the strawberry, that no better has been found. On the other hand, in the Dravidian country, where the practice is the same, it is not recorded that any connection has yet been traced by philologists between "milk" and "múlgi" or "makkalu." The great majority of the population is mainly granivorous, so that it grows its own supplies of food. Fuel is only required for cooking, save in the extreme north for a few months, and if not to be got from a neighbouring forest, or on the household estate, it is provided by the cattle, which are generally stabled in the back yard, or on the ground floor of the family abode. Thus, too often, especially in the open champaign of the Deccan and the plateau of Central India, household requirements entrench seriously upon what ought by rights to be returned to the soil. The regular purveyors of these cowdung cakes and firewood are to be found chiefly near towns, and are a section of the ordinary labouring population of those tracts. There come next the personal servants of the community. Of these the most important is the barber, who exercises various functions in the village besides that of shaving. His wife, too, plays a leading rôle in certain not unfrequent domestic incidents, a fact which was mentioned in the last chapter. The washerman is also to be found in most villages of any considerable size, though he is hardly a member of the original community, but has grown on to it from lower rank, in the progress of civilisation. We then reach the artisans. The first of these, the goldsmith, cannot be considered to belong to the original community, any more than the washerman, though he probably joined it earlier. The habit of not only investing cash in ornaments, but still more, of constantly having the family ornaments re-fashioned, is of great antiquity, and though in a Deccan proverb the goldsmith is grouped with the accountant and the tailor as one of the people to be avoided by the agriculturist, there is no doubt that the first named enjoys a settled and not dishonourable place in the village organism. As regards his colleagues there is no question. The carpenter, who is also joiner and plough maker, and the blacksmith and the mason, who are on much the same level, are found amongst the recognised members of the community in question nearly everywhere. The brass and coppersmith is of more recent affiliation, and is comparatively rare in places of a purely rural character. But he deserves mention here, because throughout the south of India the trade is combined in common parlance with the four others, and the whole group is known as the "pánch-kalsi," or the five arts, so that they are exercised indiscriminately by the same caste. The remarkable extension of the brass and copper trade that has taken place within the last 20 years or so, is a sure indication of the prosperity of the masses; for, as soon as a family can afford it, the earthen vessels in household use are replaced by those of a more durable material. Ceremonial purity has been found to be not incompatible with the great saving effected by the adoption of the foreign article. The Potter, however, flourishes, as he has done since the dawn of Indian history, and has added brickmaking to his original trade. In certain offices and in certain parts of the country his wares are still absolutely necessary for household use. But he is an exile from the aristocratic portion of the village site, not only by reason of his trade, but because of his association with that unjustly aspersed quadruped, the ass. He and the washerman are the only people in India, except, perhaps, a few of the lower vagrant tribes, who drive donkeys. The Oil-presser comes considerably above the potter, and is also one of the regular village staff. His products are in demand for social ceremonial, as well as for cooking and lighting. In the latter respect, however, he has been hard pressed of late by the importation of cheap mineral oil from America and the Caspian, an innovation by no means to be welcomed in a dry atmosphere, where the ordinary building materials are of a highly inflammable nature. The Fishermen belong to the village community in a certain sense, though they usually form into bodies by themselves, independent for the most part, except in Eastern Bengal, of cultivation. But in many parts of the country they combine several non-piscatorial functions, such as that of carrying palanquins, of bringing water from the village well, and even of keeping cookshops and parching grain. In one division of the west coast, where tiled roofs are in fashion, the fishermen have the monopoly of the duty of annually turning the tiles as a substitute for their ordinary employment which ceases just at the time when the approaching rainy season involves their engagement in the other capacity. The next group to be specially mentioned in connection with the present subject is that of the village menials. Now, in a certain sense, all the community, except the agriculturists—or rather the landowners—are the menials of the latter. This is especially the case where the original settlement of the village was on a tribal or family basis, not immediately under the Crown. In such cases, no doubt, the original settlers selected their site, partitioned their land, established their staff of serfs, where they had any to bring with them, built the village temple and dug the well or tank, and then invited artisans from other parts of the country to come, on the offer of a house and probably an allotment of village land. But the case was different with the class ascribed to the soil or devoted to the functions rejected by the rest of the community. These hewers of wood could not, under the Brahmanic system, be drawers of water also. They have the disposal of cattle that have died, and the privilege of removing the hides and horns. They are, accordingly, the leather workers of the village, and make all the shoes, and also the water-bags used in well-irrigation wherever the Persian wheel, which requires the aid of the potter, is not preferred. It is said that they are too apt, in some cases, to take care that the material of their trade does not run short, especially when there is a feud between them and the cattle-owning classes. This group supplies the Village Watchmen, who are by no means all of the leather-working castes. It is also the acknowledged authority on the details of the boundaries of fields and of the village as a whole. Then, again, the ministers at the shrine of the malignant goddesses of disease and the like are taken from the same class, a fact which supports the view that they are of an older stratum of settlement than the rest and so more conversant with the ways of propitiating the local divinities. The Scavengers, as a rule, are a lower section of the same class, but are found chiefly in the larger villages and in the towns. Amongst the village servants, however, as returned at the census, are two classes far above the menials in standing. The Accountant is, comparatively speaking, a modern innovation, and can hardly be said to belong to the village community. He is a State functionary who looks after the revenue due to the public treasury, and collects also all the statistics required for general use in connection with crops, births and deaths, &c., in fact he does all that entails a knowledge of reading and writing, and this by itself is enough to differentiate him from the bulk of his neighbours. The Headman, on the other hand, though probably in many cases not an original institution, is one of the landholders. His position in the north of India differs from that in the south and west. In the former he is a mere Government official, like the accountant. But in the latter he is what his name implies, the leader of the community. In much of this tract the office is hereditary, and the families entitled to furnish the officiator constitute the governing body in the village in all social and ceremonial affairs.

Modern additions to village occupations.

There remain a few cases which are more or less offshoots of the original village constitution, but which are, in the present day, practically incorporated in it. In the first place, the Weavers, especially those of cotton, have, as it were, risen from the ranks, and, though their status varies with the kind of article they turn out, turbans, for instance, ranking before waistcloths, and coloured goods before plain white, they are all in the village, but on sufferance. Silk is worked in towns alone. Hemp and flax are relegated to the lower grade of village menial; in the west of India, the latter supplies the only caste which will officiate as hangman. Spinning cotton yarn as a domestic industry may be added to the class of respectable ways of living, and this swells to a considerable extent the sum of the workers in this material. Last in the roll of what may be termed primitive occupations, or those of the village proper, is that of the Priest, or religious adviser and performer of rites and ceremonies on domestic occasions. Under this general title come a very large number of functions, which need no special mention here, as they can be easily conceived. Hanging on to the skirts of faith is a body, which in India is particularly numerous, of Ascetics, Devotees, or religious mendicants. Some of these are nomad by prescript of their order. Others settle themselves in shrines, and many more form part of the general community, but subsist on the charity of their neighbours. The distinction between the class that base their demand for support on religious considerations, and those who claim the substantial pity of others on account of infirmity, or simple poverty, is not accurately maintained in the census returns, in spite of all the instructions that were issued on the point. The confusion of the two is of less consequence in India than in the West, since in relation to the motive, the merit of the act of giving is the same in both cases to a great extent, and the number of the former can be approximately estimated from the return of castes.

Before considering the rest of the occupations, that conclude the table, there is one point in connection with the group already discussed that needs some comment, and this is the absence of competition that prevails in all the non-agricultural services rendered to the village community. In the great majority of instances, and the remark applies, it is believed, to the whole of India, wherever the village system is in force, such services are repaid either by the grant of a certain portion of the village lands, when each of the allotments is called by the title of the service rendered, or by a certain quantity of grain and so on from each harvest, to be provided by every landholder. In cases where cash passes the price is regulated by custom, which is of course, slow to change, rather than by any considerations of the value in open market. There is no inducement held out to new men to come forward and undersell the old. It may be that with the improvement of communications and the general safety of the road in the present time, what is known in the well worn phraseology of political economy as the "higgling of the market" has found its way into the Indian village, but, as a rule, what is made in the village itself and not imported or taken to the inter-communal market for sale, is disposed of on a non-competition basis, in accordance with the understanding in force at the original colonisation. Custom, as in the day of Pindar, is lord of all where, as in rural India— Absence of competition in village industries.

"Das ganz
Gemeine ist's, das ewig gestrige,
Was immer war und immer wiederkehrt,
Und morgen gilt weils heute hat gegölten.
Denn aus gemeinem ist der Mensch gemacht,
Und die Gewohnheit nennt er seine Amme.
* * * * * * * *
Das Jahr übt eine heiligende Kraft;
Was grau für Alter ist, das ist ihm göttlich."

But when we come to the dealer in imported commodities and to others not included in the original organism, who reached village life after that institution had closed its gate, to use the phrase of Sir H. Maine, to outsiders, the conditions are different. They are, in fact, those of the market, which was, to quote the same author, the neutral ground assigned for the meeting of the surrounding mutually exclusive communities. In the present day these occupations are found in every village, and to the superficial observer are established on the same basis as the rest of the inhabitants. But they form no part of the community proper, and on the occasions of village ceremonies, wherever, that is, the system is strictly maintained, they find themselves without any assigned place. These remarks apply to the general shop-keeper, the grocer, the grain dealer, the money-lender, who may be any one of the above, and the tailor, whose work is not required by most of the inhabitants, save in the north, where the waistcloth and sári give place largely to trousers in both sexes. All these are in the village, but not of it. There are a few other cases which are mentioned in the table under discussion for special reasons. In the first place, they are some of the most numerously represented. The toddy drawers, again, constitute a large portion of the village population in Southern India, where they are also cultivators, whilst the grass and firewood sellers, as has been said above, form part of the regular labouring community found attached to nearly every village. The cane workers owe their recognition to their numbers. They are mostly nomads, but are often settled within reach of large towns, where their custom is likely to be brisk. The milk sellers, too, congregate near the town and mainly for the same reason. They have not, therefore, been included amongst the original village population, though from their caste-names and the nature of their employment, they must always have been an important item in the community at large. Megasthenes clubs them with other nomad tribes, such as hunters and fowlers; with these they would hardly like to be classed nowadays, though a certain portion of them are still constantly on the road with their stock. Semi-urban and competitive occupations.

The table we have been discussing, then, shows that the 20 village occupations in the first section, that of the more primitive modes of life, comprise no less than 88 per cent. of the rural population, and nearly 85 per cent. of the whole of the inhabitants of India. Furthermore, if we add to the category 10 more occupations, which are mostly of a semi-rural character, we account for over 90 per cent. of the whole. We have thus no more left than about the population of England, distributed amongst all the rest of the 500 heads found in the general tables. There are comparatively few large aggregates to be seen in this miscellaneous balance. Domestic service, which, as The small proportion of the remaining occupations.

already explained, includes a good deal of the unspecified class of salaried employment, shows about 5,300,000. The service of the State and of local authorities contains some 2,420,000, and the army and navy, with the service of foreign States, about 1,650,000. Transport, in which group the largest item is that of cart drivers, who are semi-agriculturists, accounts for nearly 4,000,000. Professions, with the deduction of Religion, the largest, has left about 2,500,000. We have then to seek below the million, with the exception of the combined trade in tobacco with betel-leaves and the areka nut, which just passes that figure. The sale of vegetables is said to support about 700,000; that of sweetmeats, 580,000. The preparation of garlands, necklaces, armlets, &c. gives employment and food to 586,000. Brokerage and so on is returned at 463,000, and the only large item left is that of the miscellaneous and disreputable, which numbers 658,000. Most of these, it must be explained, belong to the former category. The employments that are usually held to be disreputable in India are generally found disguised under "non-committal" titles. At the same time, it may be admitted that there is a good deal more candour in this respect in the East than in the West, and allowing, in some cases, for private malice on the part of the enumerator, and the strange sound in others of the terms in their English dress, such entries as the following are probably rare in other countries. "Idler," "hanger-on," and "living happily," are probably meant to convey simply independence of work. "Living on loans" and "debtor" are open to suspicion. "Thief," "gambler" and "Dacoit," are probably from the jails, but "village" thief savours of malice. "Giving daughters in marriage" is intelligible enough in the eastern part of India, but "earnings of daughters" are a doubtful source of income, like "making presents," and "well wisher of the public." The "marrier of female servants" is peculiar to the Surma valley, where it apparently denotes a domestic function of the sort that Gringoire at first thought he was destined to perform for the pious king Louis XI. A "free girl" is one who is exempted from school fees. Nor does the term "Trash-seller" imply disparagement of the wares in question, but merely means a miscellaneous stall by the roadside. As means of livelihood, however, we must allow that "guardian of minor," "honorary magistrate" and "witness in court for wages," are such as might have been discreetly veiled in the schedule, in spite of the statutory privilege given to entries made at the census.

We may now pass on to the general Table B, on the opposite page, which can conveniently be taken in the serial order of its sub-divisions.

ORDER I.—*Administration.*—This comprises occupations connected with the administration of the State, of local bodies, and of the village. Most of what has to be said about the last will be found above, but it has still to be pointed out that it includes a number of Headmen and their families, who are probably cultivators, but have selected the more dignifying appellation. The Accountants and those they support are a little more numerous than the above. In all three sub-orders the menials form by far the bulk of the return, and in the service of the State are nearly three times the number of the clerkly contingent. The defects in detail in connection with this Order have been noted already.

1. State service - -	2,395,162
2. Service of local bodies -	118,135
3. Village service - -	3,086,856
Order I. - -	5,600,153

ORDER II.—*Defence.*—People supported by occupations connected with the Army form the bulk of this group, and the only noticeable point about it is that the Feudatory States contribute nearly as much as British territory, and if the military group in the next order be included, their aggregate is in excess of that of the larger political section of India. Of course a considerable number even of the adult males in this category cannot be held to be troops, in the ordinary sense of the term, but a sort of irregular escort to the Chief and his principal relatives or officials, such as Dryden considered a part of the English so-called force to be in his time—

4. The Army - - - -	663,271
5. The Navy, &c. - -	1,151
Total, Defence -	664,422

Mouths without hands, maintained at vast expense.
In peace a charge, in war a weak defence.

The Navy and Indian Marine are represented but sparsely. Of the Feudatory entries under this head, 200 are from the inland State of Haidrabad, about which explanation will no doubt be forthcoming in the report on that census.

TABLE B.—SHOWING the GENERAL DISTRIBUTION of the POPULATION by OCCUPATION, &c.

Order and Sub-Order.	A. Per-centage on Total Population.	B. Per-centage in each Order of	
		Urban.	Rural.
I. ADMINISTRATION	**1·95**	**25·61**	**74·39**
1. Civil Service of the State	0·83	49·51	50·49
2. Service of Local Bodies	0·04	79·15	20·85
3. Village Service	1·08	5·03	94·97
II. DEFENCE	**0·23**	**70·88**	**29·12**
4. Army	0·23	70·92	29·08
5. Navy and Marine	—	48·56	51·44
III. SERVICE OF OTHER STATES	**0·18**	**45·28**	**54·72**
6. Civil and Unspecified	0·13	40·78	59·22
7. Military	0·5	56·67	43·33
Total, Class A. Government	**2·36**	**31·51**	**68·49**
IV. PROVISION, &c. OF CATTLE	**1·27**	**6·13**	**93·87**
8. Cattle-breeding, &c.	1·25	5·44	94·56
9. Training and Care of Cattle, &c.	0·02	46·86	53·14
V. AGRICULTURE	**59·79**	**2·72**	**97·28**
10. Landholders and Tenants	52·20	2·42	97·58
11. Agricultural Labour	6·50	3·74	96·26
12. Growth of Special Products	0·79	8·56	91·44
13. Agricultural Supervision, &c.	0·30	15·81	84·19
Total, Class B. Pasture and Agriculture	**61·06**	**2·79**	**97·21**
VI. PERSONAL, HOUSEHOLD, AND SANITARY SERVICE	**3·91**	**22·78**	**77·22**
14. Personal and Domestic	3·48	22·65	77·35
15. Non-domestic Entertainment	0·02	52·86	47·14
16. Sanitation	0·41	22·71	77·29
Total, Class C. Personal Services	**3·91**	**22·78**	**77·22**
VII. PROVISION OF FOOD, DRINK, &c.	**5·07**	**19·94**	**80·06**
17. Animal Food	1·41	16·17	83·83
18. Vegetable Food	1·88	24·73	75·27
19. Drink, Condiments, &c.	1·78	17·88	82·12
VIII. LIGHT, FIRING, AND FORAGE	**1·23**	**16·26**	**83·74**
20. Light, &c.	0·76	12·90	87·10
21. Fuel and Forage	0·47	21·62	78·38
IX. BUILDINGS	**0·50**	**35·47**	**64·53**
22. Building Materials	0·14	24·74	75·26
23. Artificers in Building	0·36	39·77	60·23
X. VEHICLES AND VESSELS	**0·05**	**37·72**	**62·28**
24. Railway Plant	0·01	72·90	27·10
25. Carts, &c.	0·02	39·57	60·43
26. Ships and Boats	0·02	9·56	90·44
XI. ARTICLES OF SUPPLEMENTARY REQUIREMENT	**0·40**	**36·12**	**63·88**
27. Paper	0·03	40·66	59·34
28. Books and Prints	0·03	87·75	12·25
29. Watches, &c.	—	85·29	14·71
30. Carving and Engraving	0·02	55·80	44·20
31. Toys and Curiosities	0·02	36·46	63·54
32. Music and Musical Instruments	0·01	19·78	80·22
33. Necklaces, Armlets, &c.	0·20	25·80	74·20
34. Furniture	0·01	60·90	39·10
35. Harness	0·01	61·56	38·44
36. Tools and Machinery	0·06	25·72	74·28
37. Arms and Ammunition	0·01	52·44	47·56
XII. TEXTILE FABRICS AND DRESS	**4·39**	**22·66**	**77·34**
38. Wool and Fur	0·21	15·81	84·19
39. Silk	0·11	46·46	53·54
40. Cotton	3·07	18·92	81·08
41. Hemp, Jute, and Coir	0·16	16·66	83·34
42. Dress	0·84	35·92	64·08

Order and Sub-Order.	A. Per-centage on Total Population.	B. Per-centage in each Order of	
		Urban.	Rural.
XIII. METALS AND PRECIOUS STONES	**1·33**	**23·46**	**76·54**
43. Precious Metals and Stones	0·62	26·96	73·04
44. Brass and Copper, &c.	0·14	35·41	64·59
45. Tin, Zinc, and Lead	0·02	66·12	83·88
46. Iron and Steel	0·55	14·80	85·20
XIV. GLASS AND EARTHENWARE	**0·82**	**10·60**	**89·40**
47. Glass and Chinaware	—	70·72	29·28
48. Earthen and Stoneware	0·82	10·23	89·77
XV. WOOD, CANE, AND MATTING	**1·50**	**15·18**	**84·82**
49. Wood	1·00	17·21	82·79
50. Cane, Matting, and Leaves	0·50	11·08	88·92
XVI. DRUGS, GUMS, &c.	**0·14**	**24·91**	**75·09**
51. Gums, Resins, &c.	0·03	9·89	90·11
52. Drugs, Dyes, &c.	0·11	28·53	71·47
XVII. 53. LEATHER, HIDES, &c.	**1·14**	**13·97**	**86·03**
Total, Class D. Preparation and Supply of Material Substances	**15·43**	**20·32**	**79·68**
XVIII. COMMERCE	**1·63**	**30·42**	**69·58**
54. Money and Securities	0·39	27·91	72·09
55. General Merchandise	0·41	27·56	72·44
56. Dealing—unspecified	0·67	28·36	71·64
57. Brokerage and Agency	0·06	52·39	47·61
XIX. TRANSPORT AND STORAGE	**1·38**	**30·16**	**69·84**
58. Railway	0·10	55·93	44·07
59. Road	0·63	25·03	74·97
60. Water	0·28	28·28	71·72
61. Messages	0·11	38·19	61·81
62. Storage and Weighing	0·26	31·21	68·79
Total, Class E. Commerce and Transport, &c.	**2·91**	**30·30**	**69·70**
XX. LEARNED AND ARTISTIC PROFESSIONS	**1·97**	**26·56**	**73·44**
63. Religion	1·11	20·05	79·95
64. Education	0·17	33·11	66·89
65. Literature	0·10	53·98	46·02
66. Law	0·08	62·56	37·44
67. Medicine	0·18	29·69	70·31
68. Engineering and Survey	0·03	50·55	49·45
69. Other Sciences	0·07	20·76	79·24
70. Pictorial Art and Sculpture	0·01	52·31	47·69
71. Music, Acting, and Dancing	0·22	23·57	76·43
XXI. SPORT AND GAMES, &c.	**0·05**	**18·19**	**81·81**
72. Sport	0·02	19·79	80·21
73. Games and Exhibitions	0·03	17·48	82·52
Total, Class F. Professional	**2·02**	**26·35**	**73·65**
XXII. 74. EARTHWORK AND GENERAL LABOUR	**8·87**	**10·46**	**89·54**
XXIII. 75. INDEFINITE AND DISREPUTABLE MEANS OF SUBSISTENCE	**0·54**	**15·48**	**84·52**
XXIV. INDEPENDENT OF LABOUR	**1·66**	**19·69**	**80·31**
76. Property or Alms	1·50	15·90	84·10
77. Supported by the State	0·16	54·72	45·28
Total, Class G. Indefinite and Independent	**1·66**	**12·10**	**87·90**

ORDER III.—*Service of other States.*—This head was intended for the persons employed in one State but who happened to be in another at the census. It has been construed however, in some cases, as including those of the State furnishing the return.

6. Civil officers - - - - - -	358,079
7. Military, &c. - - - - - -	141,951
Total, Foreign States - -	500,030

ORDER IV.—*Pastoral Occupations, &c.*—It was found advisable to considerably subdivide this order. First, the number of those concerned with horses and horned cattle had to be distinguished from those who dealt with smaller cattle, who form a totally different class of the community. Then an intermediate group was suggested for the breeders and catchers of other draught animals, the use of which is practically confined to certain parts of the country. Camels, for instance, are principally to be found in the dry plains of the west. Elephants on the other hand, haunt the moist jungle of Assam, Mysore and Burma. Asses, as has been already mentioned, are the adjunct of the humble potter and washerman, and mules appertain chiefly to the military establishments of artillery and commissariat. To the number of those occupied in the breeding of small cattle are to be added most of the blanket weavers, now under the head of textiles, as the occupations are exercised by the same class. Lastly, there are the farriers, veterinary surgeons, and so on, with a small contingent, under a separate head, of those who live by catching monkeys, crocodiles, and other noxious animals.

8. (*a*) Horses and horned cattle	2,950,649
8. (*b*) Other draught animals	33,067
8. (*c*) Sheep, goats, pigs, &c. -	971,682
Total, 8 -	3,585,398
9. (*a*) Training and care of cattle - - -	54,467
9. (*b*) Vermin catchers, &c. -	5,984
Total, 9 -	60,451
Total, Pastoral	3,645,849

ORDER V.—*Agriculture.*—Of this great class the subdivision is all that needs comment here. The return includes, under the first head, 97,674,965 tenants holding under an intermediary, and 51,592,844 occupants holding under the State, but there is some reason to suppose that in Feudatory territory these terms are not uniformly applied. Under the second head we find 4,699,897 supported by farm labour, that is, by field work of a more or less permanent character, as by the year or for life. There are, moreover, 13,973,309 given as ordinary field labourers, a number which, as before mentioned, has to be supplemented by perhaps as many as 18,000,000 more, out of the class entitled general unskilled labour, that comes towards the end of the return. The third subdivision comprises a considerable number of persons who ought to appear under the first, such as market-gardeners and those who live by growing spices, betel, areka, and so on. The 560,000 planters, too, of tea, coffee, and indigo, with their staff and labourers are here included. As to the care of trees, which forms a part of this section, the main items are the employés of the Forest Department of the State. The last subdivision consists chiefly of the agents and managers of estates, who are most numerous in Bengal and Madras, where the permanent settlement of a great part of the province has stimulated the growth of absentee landlords.

10. Landholders and tenants	149,931,159
11. Agricultural labour -	18,673,206
12. Growth of special products and of trees -	2,261,481
13. Agricultural supervision, &c. - -	869,544
Total, Agriculture	171,735,390

ORDER VI.—*Personal, Household, and Sanitary Services.*—The main items of this group have been already mentioned in various parts of the introductory remarks to this chapter. We have, in addition to the Barber and Washerman, 2,492,544 indoor servants, and 1,241,521 persons living by service, but of what description is not specified. Water-carriers support some 900,000 persons, and cooks a little over a quarter of a million. Some of the latter are no doubt keepers of cookshops in the larger towns, especially in

14. Personal and domestic services - -	10,008,387
15. Non-domestic entertainment - -	47,803
16. Sanitation - -	1,163,882
Total, Personal, &c., Services -	11,220,072

the north-west of India, where there is a large population not so addicted to officinal purity that they cannot take advantage of such services. The second group under this order, too, is a very restricted one, and is largely recruited from the north. The mass of the people require no inn or refreshment-room when they go on a journey. They bathe in the nearest pond or river, and sleep on a chance verandah, or in the village or town meeting-shed. In the north of the country, where life and property is supposed to be in greater danger of attack, and distances are longer, the rest-house or Saraí is a recognised institution, and the bath-house introduced by the Musalmán is found in every large town, though not perhaps in the perfection of luxury described by Lady Mary Wortley Montague. Sanitation, finally, is an item divided between the scavengers, who are, as above stated, a village institution, and those who supervise their labours in the towns.

ORDER VII.—*Food, Drink, and Condiments, Stimulants, &c.*—This order is a large one, and if we allow for the number of fishers and milk-sellers who are probably to be found under other headings, the three divisions are fairly equal. In the first, the butchers are remarkably few, only 274,282 being returned as supported by this trade, which is widely spread over the north of India. The supply of vegetable food is, as is to be expected, the largest of the three. The chief items have been discussed already. Next to the grain and pulse dealers come the grain parchers, an important section of the community in towns, who return 795,177 persons. Sweetmeat selling is an allied occupation, and comes after the former in numerical strength. The sellers of fruit and vegetables, who are mixed up between this class and that of agriculture, are the only others that need be mentioned. In the matter of drinks and condiments we have a very varied selection. The grocer holds the first place with over two millions depending on his business. The consumption of betel leaf, areka nut, and tobacco is almost universal, but the persons who subsist by the exclusive sale of these products number only just over the million. Many of the first named, however, are growers as well as sellers, and are therefore to be found amongst the landholders. Throughout the coast districts, and in many inland tracts, the juice of one or other of the palm tribe of trees is habitually drunk by all the middle and lower classes, and the class known by the general term of Toddy-drawers is returned at nearly a million. The distiller and vendor of country-made spirits, who comes from the same section of the community, where he is not a Parsi, is returned at only a third of the above number. The number of those depending on the sale of opium for their living is remarkably few, considering the wide distribution of the classes that use the drug. It may be borne in mind, however, that in British territory the sale of opium is restricted to shops licensed in the larger towns, whilst in Rajputána, where every house of good social position amongst the dominant tribes begins the day with an aubaine of Kúsumba, the decoction is prepared like any other portion of the family food, so that no special occupation is attached to its manufacture or sale. The small return of the purveyors of preparations of hemp and their dependents, amounting to 17,881 only, cannot be so explained, but no doubt a good many are to be found in the category of Farmers, in Order XVIII. In fact, the whole of this group suffers from the confusion between the dealing in a special product and dealing in general.

17. Animal food -	4,045,165
18. Vegetable food	5,397,113
19. Drinks, condiments, &c.	5,133,315
Total -	14,575,593

ORDER VIII.—*Light, Fuel and Forage.*—The first of the two subdivisions is mainly occupied by the oil presser and his companions, under various titles. Gas and candles only provide for some 1,233 of the lieges, but there is an abundance, *valdé deflenda*, of the dealers in the mineral oil that is expelling the native product from the market. We have, however, a trace of primitive custom in the 4,060 people who trust for their bread to the manufacture of torches, useful though malodorous, on a dark journey. In the other section of this Order, forage and fuel are combined in the item which furnishes the bulk of the persons concerned, because the class that brings in grass for sale is equally disposed, according to the season, to provide firewood, the main object being to get a head-load to the market. The prevalence of the use of cowdung fuel has been mentioned above. As this is a pure

20. Light - -	2,163,593
21. Fuel and forage - -	1,358,664
Total - -	3,522 257

product, ceremonially speaking, most families prepare their own cakes for burning or selling, so the occupation is not specialised. But near a town the cowkeepers seem to have a monopoly, or nearly so, and the south walls of the houses in their Ward are often decorated all over with rows of these solid brown wafers, smacked on to dry. On the approach to the Táj at Ágra, there is usually a peculiarly extensive display of this sort.

ORDER IX.—*Buildings.*—The first section under this head is a very small one, since most of the brick burners are returned as potters, from their main business, and also from the habit of returning the caste for the occupation. The lime burners, too, do not confine their labours to this commodity, but combine it with saltpetre digging and other cognate trades. In the second section the masons, mud-wall makers, and stone cutters fill nearly the whole tale. The number of builders is understated at 17,678, as the majority are, in the the villages, merely carpenters.

22. Building materials	410,142
23. Artificers in building	1,027,597
Total, Building	1,437,739

ORDER X.—*Vehicles and Vessels.*—We have here a still smaller class to deal with, as the railway establishments are confined to a few large towns, and some of the original work is brought out from Europe, and a good deal of the rest is done by people who return their general occupation as blacksmith or carpenter, not the special branch of it. The cart-makers are merely a branch of the carpenters, and are not specially devoted to the manufacture of articles for which the demand in their own village is small, though, in the aggregate, considerable. Much the same may be said of the boat-builders, but the canoe-diggers, where those vessels are in fashion, are duly returned as such.

24. Railway plant	42,529
25. Carts, &c.	47,728
26. Boats and ships	56,251
Total, Vehicles, &c.	146,508

ORDER XI.—*Articles of supplementary requirement.*—This rather clumsy title includes what is, for the most part, in demand after the first wants of social man have been satisfied. Paper, to take the first item, is made to a considerable extent in India, on two systems. In a small way, the native hand-worker holds his own, but his occupation is restricted to comparatively few places and families. The larger operator uses machinery, and his employés are probably returned under the head of labourers, to some extent. The largest works are near Calcutta, and from them, it may be remarked, *en passant*, most of the paper, amounting to about 290 tons, more or less, was obtained for the census schedules. In Gwalior, too, where there is abundance of the special quality of grass required for tough paper, mills have been erected. There are others in Poona and Lucknow. To pass on to books, we may note that with a population of whom only six in a hundred can read and write, authorship is not likely to be widely adopted as a means of livelihood; so the amount of work thrown on the press is executed by about 12,000 people. Watchmaking, again, is not yet an acclimatised industry, as the mass of the population require no more accurate timepiece than the sun, with whose movements they are remarkably familiar. In the carving and engraving line it seems that there are a good many carpenters and turners who have preferred the general title. In the next section, the toy makers, especially those who deal in kites and clay dolls, or images of the more popular deities, are found in towns generally, but in the country, only in certain parts of India. Possibly kites are often home-made, otherwise it is not easy to account for the numerical deficiency of those who further so very popular a recreation, and one, too, that has certainly in some tracts, if not universally, a religious sanction. Next to the kite-maker, the maker of pipe-stems is most numerous. This, too, is somewhat of a local industry, as the north patronises it in preference to the shorter smoke of the centre and south. The bowl, it must be remembered, is not made by the same person. In regard to music, it is

27. Paper	78,153
28. Books, &c.	94,277
29. Watches, &c.	11,638
30. Carving and engraving	44,336
31. Toys, &c.	69,747
32. Music and musical instruments	21,397
33. Armlets, necklaces, &c.	586,739
34. Furniture	15,616
35. Harness	17,406
36. Tools and machinery	173,593
37. Arms and ammunition	42,365
Total, Supplementary	1,155,267

as well to point out that, though in the upper classes a stringed form of instrument may be the favourite, the national instrument of India is the drum, and its usual accompaniment is a long brass horn. As a rule, the performers make their own drums, and will appear, therefore, either in Sub-order 71, or, as they belong generally to the village menial class, some of them are sheltered under that title. The next group is the largest in the Order. The makers of armlets are not accurately distinguished according to the material of which their wares are composed, as was intended, but they form in the aggregate the main portion of this section. Beadmakers are closely allied in caste to the workers in glass bangles. Rosaries, or to speak more correctly, chaplets, and flower garlands, are the articles next in favour under this head, and there are 8,007 people returned as dependent on the fitting on of armlets, a process of some nicety. Furniture is not a section calling for remark. The chief item in the house of the masses is the bedstead, which does not appear in this group, as its legs are turned by a carpenter, and it is strung by another artificer. Outside offices, tables are required only by the literate minority, and chairs, though more common, perhaps, are not a regular article of use in any household native to the country. The report as to the use of these articles by the inhabitants of Káfiristán requires confirmation. Harness making is probably carried on to a considerable extent by the leather workers, and only the embroidery of the saddle-cloth and the adornment of the cotton or woollen reins fall into this section. The next section, referring to tools and machinery, is shared with the carpenters, who make the ploughs and also part of the looms, and these are the main items here. The knife grinder is an itinerant, as in England, and when he settles, he adopts a fresh trade, such as that of blacksmith, or, in a small way, cutler. The makers of sugar presses, too, come into this group. The carpenter makes these also, so it is probable that the 1,149 under this head are concerned in the production of the iron press, which has come into fashion during the last 10 or 12 years. It has been said that in some parts of India the adoption of this form of press, which gets more but impurer juice out of the cane, is the prelude to the use of mineral oil in the house. The first step on the path of innovation leads to others. The last subdivision of the Order is that of the provision of arms and ammunition. There are only two items under this head that require mention. First, the manufacture of powder for blasting purposes, which is carried on very sparsely, and, next, the preparation of fireworks, which, as conducted in India, is a higher branch of the same trade. Fireworks are an accompaniment of most festivals, domestic or public, but the articles are usually of a simple character, though there are masters of the craft in some of the capitals of native States who enjoy a great and deserved reputation for their skill. The swordmaker and those who provide the forest tribes and the watchmen with bows and arrows are in a majority in the native States, or possibly the latter trade is better regarded there than under British rule.

ORDER XII.—*Textile Fabrics and Dress.*—This large group is subdivided according to the material used. The woollen workers consist mainly of the blanket weavers and wool spinners, who number 411,269, and belong to the pastoral class. There is a largish item, too, of cloth sellers, which means, in all probability, sellers of cotton piece goods, as the vernacular term may apply to both. Shawl weavers come next, with a dependent population of 41,831. Of these 30,000 are in Kashmér and over 9,000 in the Panjáb, where Amritsar has secured a regular colony of both shawl and carpet makers. The section dealing with the silk workers contains two very diverse elements. First, there are some 87,400 silkworm rearers and cocoon collectors. The latter are members of the forest tribes who make it their business to look for the Tassar moth and bring in the cocoons to the dealers in the plains. Most of the former are in Bengal and the rest in Burma, Mysore, and Assam. In the first named they are located chiefly in the Múrshidabád, Rájsháhi, and Máldah districts. In the other provinces they are probably collectors. Then come the workers in silk. These constitute an honourable offshoot of the great weaver class. The differentiation must have taken place many generations back, as they are mentioned with commendation for their piety towards the sun and the general respectability of their behaviour, in an ancient inscription of the time of Kumára Gúpta in Mandesúr, a town of Central India. In the extreme south-east of the Madras Presidency they form an independent community, who have within the last

38. Wool and fur	587,701
39. Silk	319,397
40. Cotton	8,820,466
41. Jute, hemp, &c.	461,193
42. Dress, &c.	2,422,510
Total, Textiles, &c.	12,611,267

few generations established a priesthood of their own, in defiance of the Bráhman of the neighbourhood. The census return shows only 204,000 of them, however, and it may be that some have been returned as embroiderers. Apart from articles made entirely of silk, they are much engaged in working at the edging of cotton garments of the better sort and in braid. The cotton industry has been already characterised as a village occupation, but there are 1,668,895 persons in towns who return it. The main body are found under the head of spinners or weavers, the distinction not being well drawn. These, with the factory hands, reach a total of 7,380,278. There are also the calenderers, printers, and dyers, numbering nearly half a million. One of the questions of the day is whether importation and the establishment of machine-driven cotton-works in the larger towns, especially in Bombay, has not tended to drive the industry out of the hands of the home-worker into those of the general labourer, who soon picks up one of the special branches of mill-work, on the one side, and into those of the foreign operative on the other. It is impossible for the census to adequately deal with this. As to the first point, however, it seems both from the census and the trade returns that not more than 120,000 hands, maintaining, say, 600,000 persons altogether, were employed in the factories in 1891. The competition of the European operative is, of course, more serious than that of an infant enterprise. Twist, as we have seen, is more than holding its own, but this does not affect the village weaver. The question is, what room for his wares is left by the Rx. 23,750,000 worth of piece goods annually imported, on the average, during the last decade? The only provincial Report on the census in which this question is dealt with is that of Mr. Stuart, for Madras. He shows that the occupation has slightly increased in the last 10 years, and by comparison with the caste-return, he finds reason to believe that it is recruited to some extent from those beyond the pale of the castes with whom the function is traditional. He assumes, accordingly, that there is something to be gained by engaging in this pursuit, though the improvement is but slight. On the other hand, if we recognise the chances of the entry of some weavers under a more general title, as is not uncommon with Musalmáns in the north, and the difficulty experienced by an artisan, especially one of so technical a class as the weaver and a member of a community, to boot, with whom occupation is generally hereditary, in changing his trade, it is difficult to accept the numerical test as entirely disposing of the question. There is this to be said, that the competition between him and the foreigner is less than the above figures might seem to denote. For the home product, strong and coarse, but genuine and durable, still holds the agricultural market amongst the lower classes, and, indeed, amongst the raiats generally, a fact that is obvious to any one who goes about amongst the country people. In the towns, the competition is beyond a doubt severe, for the finer fabrics of the home-loom must be more expensive than the machine-made product of Europe, now that processes are so much improved and freights so low, and it is the townsman that takes first to a novelty. On the whole, therefore, looking to the very small proportion of the urban population, and of the wearers of fine raiment amongst the rustics, it does not appear that the field of the ordinary weaver is yet usurped by any competitor. The manufacturer of muslin and "woven-air" and so on, is the one to suffer. The next sub-order is a composite one. The persons depending on jute production and working are mostly to be found in Bengal, where the industry supports, or helps to support, a good many more than the 120,000 or so who have returned it as their special industry. It has been said in the last chapter that on the whole this occupation is a very thriving one, though perhaps in the present season it may have been temporarily depressed. Along the west coast as far north as Bombay, the preparation and manufacture of coir, or the fibre of the husk of the cocoa-nut is a recognised industry amongst the fishing and other classes of similar position, but it is returned as the sole or principal means of livelihood by only 108,169 persons. The ropemakers and workers in hemp and flax are nowhere devoted solely to this occupation, but undertake it as an adjunct to village service or some other means of subsistence. This accounts for the fact of the return being limited to 192,000 people. Finally we have the tailors and their comrades to consider. The former seem to have originated from the calenderer or weaver class. Many are mere dealers in cotton piece-goods rather than actually makers of clothes. Thus there are but 1,209,343 dependents on tailoring, and 915,796 vendors of piece-goods in the return. But to the former there may be added some 160,000 who return special branches of the trade, such as cap, bodice, or sári-making. Turban-binders again are an offshoot from the sartorial mystery. Embroiderers, on the other hand, form a distinct class allied to the finer weaving industries. There are returned of them only 44,548, so elsewhere but in the great towns of the north, they have evidently given some other title. Lastly, we may throw in a word for the makers of umbrellas, since they, like the weavers, have probably suffered from foreign competition. The indigenous article of waxed calico is being displaced by the more durable gingham of Europe, and it is only along the coasts and where there is the heaviest rainfall that the clumsy but efficient arrangement of leaves on bamboo framework holds its own. Like brass or copper pots the imported umbrella is usually taken to be a symptom of improved circumstances.

ORDER XIII.—*Metals and Precious Stones.*—Nearly the whole of the first subdivision is absorbed by those who live by working on personal ornaments, for the number assigned to assayers should, no doubt, come under the general heading of Goldsmith. Of the rest we need only draw attention to the manufacture of gold wire, lace, and braid, numbering 47,000, and the 23,676 persons living by washing out the refuse of the goldsmith's shop, and recovering from it the minute particles of the precious metal that have been clipped or filed off in the course of the day's work. Of the precious stone dealers, only those in pearls and rubies, in both of whom divers and miners are probably included, show any significant figure in the return. Coral dealers, like those in pearls, are most numerous in the Madras Presidency, where the fisheries are situated. Those persons who come under this head on the west coast are probably connected with the Bahrein fisheries in the Persian Gulf, residing in the Indus delta, at Tatta or Karáchi. The brass and copper workers must be taken in the lump, as the detailed heads are probably not mutually exclusive, and a large proportion of the entries do not specify any particular branch of these industries. Tin-working is an important town industry, though but sparsely represented here. Some of the workers in this metal are to be traced into the heading of Lampmakers, for, since the introduction of mineral oil, the tall and graceful brass lamp has given place to the cheap tin product of the local bazar. The cans, too, in which this oil is brought into India are much appreciated by the people, owing to the varied uses to which they can be put after a little manipulation by the tinman. For instance, probably half the watering-pots in the country consist of one of these cans, stiffened with a rough wooden bar or two, and adorned with a rope or wire handle. The supplies of vegetable oil and even of clarified butter, or ghi, that have to be sent from the market town to the city, are put into the dead shells of their rival. In architecture, too, the can has introduced a new feature, surpassing even the corrugated iron plate in unsightliness, for it is flattened out for roofing, made into spouts, or arranged along the pediment. As regards iron-workers, enough has been said in connection with the village organisation. With the exception of the smelters, who form a small section of the hill population in the Panjáb and other parts of India, the same person combines all dealings with this metal, so the sub-divisions shown in the return are but partially representative.

43. Gold, silver, and stones	1,783,874
44. Brass and copper	405,600
45. Tin, &c.	59,048
46. Iron and steel	1,572,911
Total, Metals, &c.	**3821,433**

ORDER XIV.—*Glass, Earthenware, &c.*—The workers in glass are prone to return themselves under the title of bead or armlet makers, so very few come under the heading appropriated to the material in which they work. The second sub-division of this order is composed of two main pursuits; first, the potter, who has been described above, and then the makers and rougheners of the hand-mills used in every household in the preparation of meal, and of the flat stones for the mixing of the condiments that go to flavour it.

47. Glass and china	14,419
48. Earthen and stoneware	2,346,204
Total Glass, &c.	**2,360,623**

ORDER XV.—*Wood, Cane, and Matting.*—In the first section here there are three main occupations. First, the carpenter, then the sawyer, his inferior, and lastly, the man who deals in timber and bamboos. As to the last item, it must be understood that he is altogether different from the worker in cane, who comes in the second section. In towns, the occupation of providing wood and the bamboos that are so much used as lathes for roofing is quite a special one, and it was

49. Wood	2,868,433
50. Cane, &c.	1,424,579
Total	**4,293,012**

desirable, therefore, to try and distinguish it. The cane-worker, under a variety of titles, is generally, as he is, or was, in England, a vagrant of shady repute. Some inquirers have sought to identify him with the gipsy of Europe, and quote Changár, the Panjáb variety, as the origin of Zingári, Tsingáne, and so on, as well as Dóm, who performs similar functions further to the east, and is, they say, the Rôm of Borrow, Leland, and other gipsyologists. This, however, is a matter to be considered later. In this group there is one occupation which we must dissociate from its companions. This is the manufacture of leaf-plates, which is the function of a special class in Bengal and Bombay. The purveyors of these articles, which are in much request at caste-feasts and the like ceremonies, are not nomads, and in the west of India they combine with the above occupation that of temple-ministrants.

Order XVI.—*Drugs, Gums, Dyes, &c.*—The first section is confined to the collectors or preparers of minor forest produce, of which the chief representatives are lac and catechu, or cutch, as it is called in Burma, where, and in Bengal, the industry seems most to flourish. In Burma, however, it is combined with wood-cutting, so the number is thereby reduced in the return. The central hills of Bengal and the North-West and Central Provinces yield most of the lac-workers. There are also returned 26,144 collectors of honey and similar wild produce. In the category of drug and dye sellers, the perfumer comes next to the saltpetre digger and the chemist, or rather, the person who deals in the ordinary village medicines. This last represents about 14,000 families, which seem hardly sufficient to supply the whole demand for opium throughout the country, as has been suggested, even if we grant that any of them, except the few in the largest towns, know anything of pharmacy in the English sense of the term. Some of the dealers in dyes ought clearly to have been classed in Order XII., as they probably use the dye, and do not merely prepare or sell it. Amongst the minor items in this class it is not altogether satisfactory to find about 300 dealers in aniline dyes returning themselves as such, without shame or fear. In Persia, it is said, the trade amounts to felony.

51. Gums, &c.	76,186
52. Drugs, dyes, &c.	315,389
Total	391,575

Order XVII.—*Leather, &c.*—The first four items in this group, which amount to 3,131,156 persons, represent the members of the village staff, as already described, who have extended their original functions so as to include more than the mere tanning of the hides of the dead cattle of the neighbourhood. The enlistment of a good body of this class into the factories established in Cawnpore on the European system has been already mentioned. The demand for hides, horns, and other *exuviæ* of the sacred animal has increased considerably of late. In 1881–82 the number of hides and skins exported was 24,802,043, and in 1890–91 it was 32,742,431. The value of the horns for the two years was respectively Rs. 1,329,150 and Rs. 2,077,190. Bones, again, were exported to the value of Rs. 1,327,500 in 1887–88, and of Rs. 2,309,570 last year. All this is favourable to the exchequer of the village tanner, but as to the last, the benefit to the country at large is less than doubtful, since the soil of India thereby loses nearly 44,000 tons of fertilising material which it cannot spare.

53. Leather, &c.	3,285,307

Order XVIII.—*Commerce.*—Dealings in money are naturally the subject with which this order opens. Taking the bankers and money-lenders together, the persons supported by them is very nearly a million. It should be understood that in the term money-lender, we include that of pawnbroker, for the business done in the village is largely in advances on ornaments pledged. The only other considerable item in this section is that of money-changer and tester, with 93,233 against it. The function is often mixed up with lending, so the above figure is probably below the reality. General merchandise, as we have seen, includes many of the village shops which deal in a variety of articles in general demand. There are 1,494,165 persons set forth against the term, unqualified by further description, and 1,028,980 come under the head of general merchants. Hawkers and pedlars are understated at 145,000, as many purvey food: others are merely the

54. Money, &c.	1,128,283
55. General merchandise	1,186,892
56. Dealing, unspecified	1,907,555
57 (*a.*) Brokers and agents	259,726
57 (*b.*) Contractors and farmers	203,123
Total, Middlemen, &c.	462,849
Total, Commerce	4,685,579

travelling members of a shop in the market town, and return themselves there. The sub-order relating to middlemen, such as brokers and the like, has been split up into two. The first, which includes mere general intermediaries, shows 240,592 brokers and agents, and 19,000 auctioneers, &c. The second group relates, or was intended to relate, to those who take a share in the business and live on profits, not merely on commission. The numbers in it are not accurately distributed between the items, and there are too few farmers with an excess of contractors not otherwise specified.

ORDER XIX.—*Transport and Storage.*—Here it appears that the railway, in its capacity of carrier, and irrespective of mechanics, feeds some 285,000 people, mostly, of course, in the lower ranks of employ, such as porters, pointsmen, signallers, clerks, and so on. The next section is a large one. The persons connected with carts are almost entirely of the agricultural class, whilst the bearers of palki, or palanquins, a mode of conveyance rapidly falling into disuse, hail from amongst the fishers. It is a common practice for both to engage in their ordinary occupation for most of the year, and take their cart and bullocks, or their thews and sinews, as the case may be, to some large town during the agricultural recess. The pack-animal drivers are very widely distributed, but, as a rule, the bullock traffic that used to be so celebrated is now confined very much to Rajputána and Central India. The camel driver, who is also the breeder of the animal, flourishes all over the west of India, north of the Gujaráth division of Bombay, and the elephant is mostly found in this capacity in Assam and Burma. The third section, which contains those who go down to the sea in ships, is shared by the return of fishers, as above stated. In other respects no comment seems necessary. It is much the same with the sub-order relating to the conveyance of messages, which is sub-divided into telegraphy, &c., and postal and others. The unclassified is here, again, the largest item. In the last section of the order, we have the class of worker attached mainly to grain and other produce warehouses, and thus differing to some extent from the ordinary unskilled labourer. The weighmen, also, are in the same position, and these two cover nearly the whole field of the sub-order.

58 (*a.*) Railway administration	29,169
58 (*b.*) „ working staff	231,040
Total, Railway	285,187
59 (*a.*) Carts, &c.	1,126,847
59 (*b.*) Pack animals	676,339
Total, Road	1,803,186
60 (*a.*) Ship and boat owners	92,701
60 (*b.*) Tailors, &c.	697,051
Total, Water	789,752
61 (*a.*) Post, &c.	307,903
61 (*b.*) Telegraph, &c.	19,171
Total, Messengers, &c.	327,074
62. Storage, &c.	747,794
Total, Order	**3,952,993**

ORDER XX.—*Professions.*—We have now reached an order where the range of interpretation is at its maximum, and every single sub-division seems to require a good deal of explanation. The term Profession is held to include both the liberal and the artistic branches, and each of them, in India at least, contains a very heterogeneous collection of professors. Then, too, it must be borne in mind that most professions are of comparatively recent development in India, always excepting that of religion. Education was confined, till the advent of British rule, to a small class of Bráhmans, and during the Musalmán period, to a still smaller group of hereditary clerks. Literature, therefore, was equally circumscribed, and restricted chiefly to theology, mythology, astrology, and the chronicle of the deeds of chiefs and their ancestors, which went by the name of history. Law, as a profession, was practically unknown, though there

63 (*a.*) Priests, &c.	1,721,487
63 (*b.*) Subsidiary religious services	1,463,273
Total, Religion	3,184,760
64. Education	486,497
65. Literature	280,705
66. Law	226,163
67 (*a.*) Medical practice, &c.	469,895
67 (*b.*) Subsidiary medical services	44,179
Total, Medicine	514,074
68 (*a.*) Engineers, &c.	22,217
68 (*b.*) Draughtsmen, surveyors, &c.	72,053
Total, Engineering, &c.	94,270
69 (*a.*) Astronomers, botanists, &c.	1,354
69 (*b.*) Astrologers, &c.	198,656
Total, Other Sciences	200,010
70. Painters, &c.	35,788
71. Music and dancing, &c.	649,926
Total, Professional, &c.	**5,672,191**

were learned expounders of the hieratic systems of Brahmanic origin and of the Kurán and its commentators, as we find is the case in the Rajputána of the present day. Medicine was in the hands of the barber-surgeon and his wife, with a sprinkling of herbalists and a larger throng of the possessors of charms, spells, and amulets. In the towns could be found, no doubt, some of those who found their system on the Vedas, or, rather, the later Brahmanic literature of the orthodox period, and others owning to the name of Ionian (Yunáni) physicians, to whom some of the present-day *laudatores temporis acti* ascribe a wonderful and elaborate scientific body of doctrine, apparently not far below that of which we read in certain plays of Molière. Architects and engineers of indigenous birth and training were probably as few as they would be now, were it not for the institutions established by the British Government for their education. Of pictorial art there is little to be said, and of music and the drama the less said, perhaps, the better.

Religion

We may begin the comments on this class with the occupations connected with religion, which, as shown in the marginal table, comprises considerably more than half the professional class. The two main items, priests and religious mendicants, are hardly to be distinguished, except in the case of foreigners and Buddhists. In the Brahmanic system, the person actually officiating in a temple is a group comparatively sparse, and lower in rank than the spiritual adviser and reciter of texts, whilst charity to a Bráhman is a duty imposed on all alike. Amongst the Musalmáns, too, the extension of religious asceticism is one of the peculiarities of the faith that has sprung up in India. In Burma the distinction was drawn between Phongi, persons actually received into a religious order, and Upázin, or novices, with a further division of the unaffiliated mendicants, who are only bound by vows of poverty. There is a considerable number shown under the subsidiary services of religion, as is to be expected from the addiction of the masses to pilgrimage and the adoration of relics or the images at particular shrines. Of these functionaries there are several different grades, as there are of the reciters of the semi-theological poems, but it will be out of place to enter into detail here, where only the general class of occupation is in question.

Education

The section connected with education comes next in serial order, though owing to the prevalence of the herbalist, it is numerically inferior to the sub-order of medicine, and the drummer and dancer exalt over it the category of music, &c. It contains but one large item, that of teachers and their families, amounting to 476,216 persons. This includes, of course, the village school as well as the college, since any distinction between the two can be better obtained from the special returns of public instruction than from a census schedule.

Literature.

Literature is not a large class, and even as it is, the number is swelled unduly by the addition of all who returned their occupation under the general term of writing, by which they mean the traditional pursuit of their caste in some cases, and some post of a clerical nature in the rest. With so restricted a public as is before them in India, the chance of making a living by literature occurs but to few.

Law.

The law, too, though largely recruited from the colleges in the present generation is not as well represented as we should expect from the continual complaint of increasing litigation and of the British exaltation of the toga over arms, through which—

> "Encounters at the bar,
> Are braver now than those in war."

There are nearly as many unaccredited practitioners as there are of the orthodox. The petition writer, for instance, on whose labour 29,348 depend, is often the standing counsel of the poorer litigant for the whole street. The Kázi, who is here entered to the number of 13,389, is in reality far more numerous, but as his functions are scarcely separated from those of religion in the law he professes, part of the class is probably to be looked for in Sub-Order 63 (*a*).

Medicine.

Of medicine and its votaries we have already spoken. The bulk of the section is comprised under the head of Practitioners without diploma, a conveniently comprehensive title, represented by no less than 353,295 persons. The midwives and their families come next with 82,589. The superior class of practitioner supports only 16,494, but, no doubt, looking to the tone of recent representations on the subject, there must be several families of this sort which are returned under the title of military officers. The last section of this sub-Order includes the comparatively numerous and worthy class of hospital assistants and other attendants at the dispensaries and other institutions of the class which have sprung into existence with British rule, in both Crown and Feudatory territory.

Engineering, architecture, and surveying.

Engineering and Survey are titles that explain themselves. The section comprises mainly, no doubt, the persons in the employ of the State or Local bodies in this capacity, with their establishments. For instance, the world-famed Trigonometrical Survey has under it a considerable number of employés who are far above the rank of mere labourers, though coming below that of surveyors. There are, again, the Revenue Survey of each of the larger provinces, the Archæological Department, and several others.

Other sciences.

The last section of the learned professional class is that of the branches which are represented very sparsely in India, save in one direction. The astronomer, indeed, is to be counted by units, but of the domestic diviner there are 198,656. But a good portion of the latter is no doubt attributable, not to prophecy, but to the pedigree-keeper, a man of considerable merit and dignity, especially in Native States of the west of India, where family is all important.

Painters, &c

The 30,056 painters returned in the next section are far from being of Academy* rank, and many are probably artists in house-walls rather than in more moveable material. The photographer, as is only to be expected, has invaded India with some profit, and his art supports nearly 3,000 persons.

Music and the drama.

We have, finally, the large body of musicians and dancers. Of the former there are returned 372,561, and of these most are, no doubt, village performers on the drum and certain wind instruments. The dramatic arts are mixed up with other professions, and a good many of those who exercise them are entered under some euphemistic title of the less reputable branch of their functions. It is impossible to separate the two in the returns, any more than is done in the course of the education of the class in question. The Chinese pilgrims noticed the combination, and in their day, the singer and courtezan were compelled to reside outside the village walls, along with the fisherman and scavenger. History seems to indicate that she was not kept out long, at least when the village grew into a town. As far as the dramatic part of the occupation goes, however, there are numerous degrees of proficiency distinguished in practice, though not in the returns, in which last the general notion of the employment is that expressed in one of the schedules from a town in the north, as "singing and enjoying sensual pleasures!"

ORDER XXI.—*Sport.*—This is a very brief record, in spite of its comparatively minute sub-division. The people who make it their business to search for game, large and small, constitute the chief item in the first section. Then come the minor performers, such as puppet-showers and buffoons, not to mention the largest class of all, the conjurors. Exhibitors of trained animals, and the so-called snake-charmers, return some 10,500. Acrobats and tumblers are from the various gipsy bands, and are found all over the country in small parties, each professing kinship of some sort or other with the rest. There are the professional wrestlers, too, many of whom are permanently on the establishment of the State, as in Baroda and Mysore. Others, as in the Panjáb and the South Deccán, keep schools for the training of champions, and much is the ingenuity exercised to keep and to discover the secret of some special wile invented by one of these trainers for the discomfiture of the pupils of his rival at the next village festival of the neighbourhood. Lastly, there are the people entertained in the institutions for the exercise of Occidental athletic or outdoor games, of which cricket, at all events, has been successfully acclimatised in one section of the community. Billiards, too, is not without its votaries, who seem to have taken to it to some purposes, as while this is being written, the current journals contain a notice that "in consequence of Mr. * * * (a Músalmán) having won the All-England Amateur Spot-barred Championship, telegrams of congratulations are pouring into London from all parts of India."

72. Sport, &c. - - -	43,919
73 (*a.*) Trained animals - -	12,448
73 (*b.*) Conjurors, buffoons, &c.	36,453
73 (*c.*) Acrobats, tumblers, &c.	42,184
73 (*d.*) Athletic sports, games, &c.	6,176
Total, Games, &c.	97,261
Total, Sport - -	**141,180**

* If recent criticism is to be trusted, we ought to interpolate here the word "even."—J. A. B.

ORDER XXII.—*Earthwork and General Labour.*—In the provincial series of returns this figures as Order XXIII.; but it was found that the Order assigned for the caste or complex occupations, which it was expected to find in the schedules, was not required, so the series in the Imperial return was increased by the sub-division of the former Order XXIII. into two, that under consideration and that of the indefinite occupations. In the former we have one or two very distinctive occupations, but the bulk is included under the general title of unskilled labour, of which, as before observed, much is simply agricultural. Amongst the special branches of earthwork we may mention the well-sinkers, a peculiar class, originating, it is said, in the eastern part of the Deccan, but found all over central and north-western India. The process by which they live does not involve the selection of the site for their operations, as this has to be done under the sanction of spells or divination by more learned people. But once the spot pointed out, this class not only excavate and pass out the earth quicker than others, but they are experts, too, at setting the rings of pottery or other material, by which the soft earth is kept from falling in. The tank diggers and probably most of the railway labourers returned are of this class, as it is said that there is the same difference between their power of work and that of the ordinary day labourer as there is between the efficiency of the latter class in England and that of the trained "navvy." The rice-pounder is here entered wherever it is a special occupation, as in Bombay, Bengal, and Madras. In Burma, where it provides for numbers of temporary immigrants from the last-named Presidency, it is returned under the general head.

74 (*a.*) Earthwork, &c. -	1,647,740
74 (*b.*) General labour -	23,820,277
Total	25,468,017

ORDER XXIII.—*Indefinite and Disreputable Occupations.*—Of these the former, as returned, is by far the more numerous, as it includes those who returned themselves simply as "dependent," without specifying the occupation concerned, and also those who did not return occupation at all, as amongst some of the wild tribes of Rajputána, Assam, and the Bombay States.

75 (*a.*) Indefinite - -	1,395,348
75 (*b.*) Disreputable, &c. -	167,633
Total, Indefinite, &c.	1,562,981

ORDER XXIV.—*Independent of Occupation.*—Of these we have four sections. First, those who have property which makes it unnecessary for them to work at any occupation for their bread, of whom only 193,291 are returned. Secondly, those subsisting on alms, of whom, first come the people enjoying scholarships and so on, and, secondly, the army of mendicants, which, as before remarked, must be taken with the class demanding alms as a religious obligation on the part of the giver, based on the sectarian or ascetic character of the applicant. Taken in this way, the mendicant band amounts to about five and a quarter millions of persons.

76 (*a.*) Property -	193,291
76 (*b.*) Alms - -	4,115,243
Total, 76 - -	4,308,534
77 (*a.*) Pension -	360,293
77 (*b.*) Prisoners, &c. -	105,166
Total, 77 -	465,459
Total, Independent of Work	4,773,993

In another sub-division we find those supported by the State, of whom we have already spoken. First, the pensioners, numbering with their dependents 360,293; then the prisoners and inmates of asylums. Of the latter there are very few, 4,783 in all. The number of prisoners is admittedly incomplete at 80,500, and many mus have been assigned to the occupation habitual to them when not incarcerated.

The next subject for consideration should rightly be the extent to which the above sub-divisions of non-agricultural occupation are respectively combined with some form of agriculture, but as the return bearing on this point does not include the whole of India, it will be better to take up first the wider subject of the distribution of function between

TOWN AND COUNTRY.

It has been already pointed out that, according to the last column of the general proportional table we are now considering, the only Orders of occupation in which the share of the urban population is not greater than that of the rural, relatively to their respective masses, are pasture, agriculture, and the sub-division connected with village service. Next to these comes the category of Labour, which is semi-agricultural. The Potter is but slightly ahead, and then approach the other main village occupations of the Tanner, the Carpenter, and the Oilman. The small group of the exhibitors of animals, &c. is the only one of the Orders which does not show an urban proportion of more than double that of the general ratio of urban population as a whole. If we go into a little more detail and consider the sub-Orders, it will be seen that the growers of special products bear a slightly higher proportion than the other agriculturists, indicating the admixture of sellers of such wares, and also, probably, the growth of the latter on plots of land within municipal limits. In the next order, the supply of places of entertainment is very much more urban than the distribution of the personal services. The reason has been already given. Fuel, again, provides subsistence for relatively more in the town than lighting. Of vehicles and boats, only the last are built in nearly even proportions in town and country. Supplementary requirements are naturally more frequent in the former, where tastes are wider, and only the drum-maker, the tool-maker, and the purveyor of armlets and flower garlands and the like, reduce the general group-average. The Order of textiles varies much in detail, and silk and dress are apparently the items most favoured by an urban community. Cotton, jute, and wool are, from the character of their operatives, more prevalent than the above in villages, though the proportion is still much in favour of the town. Iron we may class in the same category in this respect as pottery and wood-working, and it comes fairly between the two. The collection of forest produce is, of course, a rural industry, and cane-work is but a little less so. The commercial element, owing to the misnaming specified in an earlier part of this chapter, is relatively less of an urban pursuit than might have been expected, but the middleman rises in the scale considerably above the rest of the group. In the matter of transport, though even cartage is attracted to the town to an extent a good deal above the normal proportion, there is evidence in the return to show that both this and transport by boat are largely recruited from the village and fishing classes respectively. Amongst the professions, the priest and mendicant, the astrologer, the hail-averter, and our constantly recurring friend the drummer, are the only instances in which the urban proportion is not three times that of its total strength. This, of course, is only to be expected. In the village, where all is ordered by custom, and position is hereditary, there is no room for what Plato calls Timarchy, or the uprising of the ambitious. But in the town, the professional has now full scope for the exercise of his faculties,—

> Notæque per oppida buccæ
> Munera nunc edunt, et verso pollice vulgo
> Quemlibet occidunt populariter.

He who formerly had to blow the trumpet for others can now blow his own. He heads deputations and gets put on the committee of agricultural exhibitions, and is even eligible for the jury which may perhaps convict his higher caste neighbour. The last sub-order but one, were it concerned with property alone, would, no doubt, show a high superiority on the part of the town, but the preponderance of mendicants in the rural tracts drags the ratio down to a comparatively moderate figure.

City distribution of occupation.

In supplement of the above general comment, it will be interesting, perhaps, to compare with the distribution of occupations of the province as a whole, that of the capital town, in the case of four or five of the chief urban centres of India. This is done in the following statement:—

TABLE C.—SHOWING the DISTINCTIVE FEATURES in the DISTRIBUTION of OCCUPATION in FIVE LARGE TOWNS.

Order.	INDIA.		BOMBAY AND SINDH.		BENGAL.		MADRAS.		BURMA.		HAIDRABAD.	
	Rural.	Urban.	Total.	Bombay.	Total.	Calcutta.	Total.	Madras.	Total.	Rangoon.	Total.	Haidrabád.
I. Administration	1·60	*5·26*	3·25	*3·20*	0·98	*3·87*	2·45	*4·98*	1·36	*4·34*	4·69	*14·13*
II. Defence	0·07	*1·73*	0·23	*0·76*	0·02	*0·47*	0·09	*1·46*	0·41	*1·63*	0·55	*9·75*
III. Other States' Service	0·11	*0·88*	0·04	*0·03*	—	—	—	*0·01*	—	*0·06*	0·04	*0·86*
IV. Pasture, &c.	1·32	*0·82*	1·37	*0·21*	0·64	*0·17*	2·01	*0·32*	0·09	*0·50*	2·46	*0·25*
V. Agriculture	64·26	*17·13*	58·24	*6·94*	63·19	*2·79*	58·81	*3·62*	03·44	*2·24*	44·88	*2·53*
VI. Personal and Domestic Service.	3·83	*9·38*	2·55	*8·95*	3·51	*15·08*	2·96	*9·66*	0·78	*8·71*	5·65	*24·87*
VII. Food, &c.	4·49	*10·67*	7·56	*6·02*	4·96	*7·51*	5·90	*10·13*	9·93	*13·24*	5·70	*7·27*

TABLE C.—*concluded.*

Order.	INDIA.		BOMBAY AND SINDH.		BENGAL.		MADRAS.		BURMA.		HAIDRABÁD.	
	Rural.	Urban.	Total.	Bombay.	Total.	Calcutta.	Total.	Madras.	Total.	Rangoon.	Total.	Haidra-bád.
VIII. Light and Fuel, &c.	1·13	*2·10*	1·52	*0·59*	1·06	*1·04*	1·26	*1·07*	0·91	*1·43*	0·80	*1·08*
IX. Building	0·36	*1·87*	0·80	*1·51*	0·28	*2·12*	1·00	*2·37*	0·64	*0·93*	0·53	*1·13*
X. Vehicles and Vessels	0·04	*0·20*	0·08	*0·36*	0·06	*0·17*	0·05	*0·32*	0·19	*0·36*	0·03	*0·12*
XI. Supplementary	0·28	*1·53*	9·65	*2·76*	0·43	*3·48*	0·28	*3·66*	0·43	*1·35*	0·28	*1·05*
XII. Textiles and Dress	3·75	*10·49*	5·42	*15·82*	2·60	*4·47*	4·71	*6·71*	4·93	*5·67*	6·28	*3·41*
XIII. Metals, &c.	1·13	*3·29*	1·51	*2·62*	1·13	*3·09*	1·38	*4·07*	0·91	*3·12*	1·49	*2·16*
XIV. Earthenware and Glass	0·81	*0·98*	0·62	*0·24*	0·67	*0·43*	0·61	*0·30*	0·50	*0·29*	0·81	*0·37*
XV. Wood and Cane	1·40	*2·39*	1·74	*3·20*	1·17	*2·12*	1·73	*2·74*	2·36	*6·40*	1·42	*1·13*
XVI. Drugs, Dyes, &c.	0·11	*0·36*	0·12	*0·15*	0·17	*0·30*	0·12	*0·40*	0·15	*0·27*	0·17	*0·14*
XVII. Leather	1·09	*1·68*	1·28	*1·15*	0·48	*2·32*	1·38	*0·66*	0·26	*0·77*	1·37	*0·92*
XVIII. Commerce	1·25	*5·23*	2·12	*11·28*	1·58	*8·63*	0·97	*5·59*	1·73	*7·94*	1·53	*4·78*
XIX. Transport, &c.	1·06	*4·38*	2·02	*8·66*	1·27	*10·08*	1·49	*7·15*	2·54	*13·59*	0·72	*2·54*
XX. Professions	1·60	*5·53*	2·13	*5·16*	1·92	*7·01*	1·95	*10·08*	2·74	*4·61*	1·19	*3·93*
XXI. Sport, &c.	0·05	*0·09*	0·08	*0·06*	0·03	*0·05*	0·06	*0·08*	0·07	*0·18*	0·10	*0·14*
XXII. General Labour	8·77	*9·78*	4·54	*15·45*	12·51	*7·50*	8·41	*17·59*	3·99	*18·50*	12·09	*8·73*
XXIII. Indefinite, &c.	0·51	*0·89*	0·17	*1·40*	0·21	*13·63*	1·16	*1·38*	0·04	*0·82*	3·82	*1·25*
XXIV. Independent, &c.	1·48	*3·45*	1·96	*3·85*	1·13	*3·68*	1·17	*5·45*	0·49	*2·62*	2·80	*7·48*

It is worth while, also, to note the two first columns, relating to the rural and urban distribution of the whole country, both as a standard by which to measure the special instances in the later portion of the table and in connection with the remarks made on the general subject above. It can thus be seen at a glance that, speaking generally, the town differs from the country in its higher proportion of servants, food-suppliers, textile-operatives, traders, professionals, and the class that is independent of work, not to mention those engaged in administration and defence. It is also important to note how the introduction of the small town raises the proportion of agriculturists, for amongst the urban population, as a whole, the cultivator is still the best represented of any individual class.

Passing on to the more special portion of the table, we may just touch upon the main points of difference between the five cities selected as most in contrast with the rural part of the Indian community. First, as to the agricultural element. Herein Bombay stands out high above the rest, since the municipal limits, being coterminous with those of the island, include a considerable area of "batty" or rice land. Similarly, this isolation from the neighbouring mainland and the general character of the cultivation on the latter, which is confined to one or two products, and no large surplus of those, seem to be the causes of the comparative paucity of the oil-pressing class and of those who bring in fuel and forage by headloads. The high ratio of the suppliers of food in Rangoon, and perhaps in Madras also, is apparently due to the number of the fishermen. The extension of textile industry in Bombay is well shown in the table under review, where the proportion stands at 15·82 per cent., as compared with 6·71 in Madras, which comes next to it. The latter, however, has a slight pre-eminence in metal-working. Rangoon, with its large teak yards, stands first as regards dealings with wood and timber, and it is in the same position in respect to transport, since its shipping connection has of late years tended to outgrow the development of the permanent or shore population. In the matter of commerce, or to put it more correctly, with respect to the proportionate number of persons supported by that class of occupation, Bombay exceeds the rest considerably, with 11·28 per cent. against the 8·63 in Calcutta, but in transport the latter outshines it. Madras stands first in its predominance of the professional class, with 10·08, against 7·01 in the City of Palaces, and only 5·16 in its western sister. The great influx of labour from Madras gives Rangoon the lead in this respect, but Madras itself is not far behind, so it is fair to presume that some of the contingent in the latter case are really debitable to some more special head. There is a considerable number coming under this class in Bombay, where the dock-works absorb, no doubt, all that the cotton mills can spare, but the relative paucity of the general labourer in Calcutta, together with the remarkable proportion of the entries grouped as indefinite, which is 13·63 per cent. against 1·38 in the next highest case, leaves room for the supposition that the tabulation, not the class itself, is deficient. This assumption receives some confirmation from the equally remarkable proportion of the order relating to domestic service and so on, in which the head "Indoor Service" includes more than double the number found under it in the far more populous city of Bombay, so that it is probable that a good deal of clerical or general service has been thus disposed of.

The great difference in some respects between the four cities of British India and Haidrabád, the capital of the dominions of His Highness the Nizam, will not have escaped attention. In the first place, there is the very large excess in the proportion of the administrative element, which is 14·12 per cent. on the total population, as compared with 4·98 in Madras, the highest rate in the selected cities, and 5·26 for the whole urban population of India. Defence, again, is 9·75 as against 1·75. Private service is 24·87 per cent., and in the other cities, as we have seen, the highest ratio is that in Calcutta, where it stands at 15·08. Lastly, the independent classes in Haidrabád bear the proportion of 7·48 against 5·45 in Madras, and a general ratio of 3·45. Looking into details, it appears that pensions and mendicancy are responsible for the greater portion of the Haidrabád figure. On the other hand, the trading, professional, labouring, and some of the commoner artisan classes are curiously deficient in Haidrabád. The weavers and carpenters, for instance, are in proportion fewer than in the surrounding rural tracts, instead of being in excess, as they are in the other cities. These divergencies are in accordance with what was said in a former chapter regarding the predominance of the official element in the constitution of the capital of a native chief. The main classes to be considered are his immediate *entourage*, his troops, and the couriers, with all their servants and dependents. Even in certain branches of luxuries, recent events have shown that in these days of rapid communication encouragement is not always given to local talent, as it was of yore.

The alternate columns of the table under review afford the means of estimating the difference between the distribution of occupations in the town in question and the total of the territory of which it is the capital. It is not worth while to comment on this in detail, as the figures mostly either explain themselves or can be explained from what has been said already.

Occupations combined with Agriculture.

Information on this point has been collected, as observed in an early part of this chapter, for most of the larger provinces, though in many cases the results are evidently incomplete. This is not altogether due to defect in the original record, but partly, also, to negligence in tabulation. It is clear that in every rural enumerator's block there are likely to be duplicate entries of all the main occupations; namely, that of the occupation itself, and that of the same in combination with some form of cultivation or tenure of land. To save trouble in abstraction and subsequent addition, the latter was ignored by a lazy operator in the census centre, and amongst some 15,000 of such employés the proportion of the unjust is naturally high. This accounts, it appears, for the difference, in Table D opposite, in the proportion of the semi-agriculturist in Berár, where the staff was chiefly of temporary hands, and Bombay, where the work was done by the more experienced agency of village accountants. In the case of Assam and the North-West Provinces the results show that trouble was in no ways spared to get out the full tale of this class of occupations, and here, too, the supervision seems to have been efficient, and the proportions are the highest in India. Comparison was made above, however, with Bombay, because the village system in Berár is practically identical with that of the western Presidency, and differs from that of the north and east. There are other instances in which the results are deficient, not because there is less addiction to these quasi-agricultural pursuits in the Provinces or States in question, but from defective tabulation. On the whole, we may accept the returns of Assam and the North-West as very nearly representing the actual facts, and Bombay as approaching accuracy in a less degree, whilst the rest are decidedly below the mark. The omission of Bengal, the largest Province, should be explained. The Census Superintendent of that heavy charge states that owing to one reason or another this return was so incorrect for a considerable portion of the Province that he thought it waste of space to include it in his series of tables.* He comments, however, in his Report on the details of about half the population, for which he considers the return is satisfactory, and, as the proportions he quotes are in general accordance with those for most of the rest of India, his assumption is

* He seems, however, to have printed a return of some sort, but it has not yet reached the Imperial Office.

TABLE D, showing the Per-centage on each Order of the Persons returned as also partly Agricultural.

Order.	BRITISH PROVINCES.								FEUDATORY STATES.					
	Madras.	Bombay and Sindh.	N.-W. Provinces and Oudh.	Panjáb.	Central Provinces.	Berár.	Assam.	Ajmér.	Haidrabád.	Baroda.	Bombay States.	Panjáb States.	Central Province States.	N.W. Province States.
1.	2.	3.	4.	5.	6.	7.	8.	9.	10.	11.	12.	13.	14.	15.
I. Administration	18·01	33·44	19·90	17·40	12·60	2·90	44·08	5·62	28·56	18·79	14·24	4·75	37·67	3·49
II. Defence	1·07	1·19	7·02	7·55	4·52	0·05	3·03	3·57	0·01	0·50	1·73	0·75	10·25	—
III. Other States' Service.	26·85	6·33	5·44	4·96	0·19	—	9·00	1·39	0·50	—	5·50	21·17	—	—
IV. Pasture	6·89	5·64	14·27	7·04	3·24	0·94	16·60	3·07	0·58	3·90	2·98	0·28	4·03	2·28
V. Agriculture*	—	—	—	—	—	—	—	—	—	—	—	—	—	—
VI. Personal and other Service.	11·20	10·14	20·39	4·71	8·70	2·65	32·49	4·66	4·24	7·58	6·47	2·50	13·35	5·18
VII. Food, &c.	7·08	4·55	8·40	6·32	6·02	1·07	50·21	2·13	1·89	2·23	3·11	0·83	12·11	7·05
VIII. Light and Fuel, &c.	5·15	11·56	28·99	8·06	9·17	3·97	43·54	21·69	2·58	2·80	4·92	1·88	27·03	10·48
IX. Buildings	5·66	5·21	9·70	4·24	1·57	1·10	34·19	1·97	0·41	3·25	2·42	0·22	2·88	2·52
X. Vehicles and Vessels.	8·42	3·26	9·28	1·75	0·94	0·34	75·50	—	—	7·37	3·58	0·25	—	—
XI. Supplementary	5·67	5·80	18·59	2·00	3·66	1·21	26·01	1·35	0·26	0·65	3·74	0·95	2·06	3·28
XII. Textiles and Dress	4·73	4·08	13·04	5·65	3·77	2·16	42·90	4·39	0·35	2·11	2·09	1·06	11·03	4·80
XIII. Metals, &c.	8·95	12·07	23·78	9·31	10·28	2·76	40·45	5·87	10·46	10·40	4·60	2·16	9·12	8·87
XIV. Earthenware and Glass.	14·42	15·36	33·67	6·56	7·03	1·64	47·09	20·41	18·47	10·47	5·80	1·67	31·66	36·73
XV. Wood and Cane	3·43	13·94	27·33	20·20	5·80	2·72	63·70	21·62	20·85	10·41	9·46	4·27	3·71	8·74
XVI. Dyes, Gums, and Drugs, &c.	5·15	4·44	12·24	8·69	4·55	0·42	51·70	—	0·09	—	1·86	0·26	6·02	2·90
XVII. Leather, &c.	9·05	15·34	21·86	7·75	7·04	1·31	14·66	21·12	20·46	10·24	4·59	2·21	13·06	25·13
XVIII. Commerce	8·96	11·56	31·79	12·08	17·99	10·28	39·92	9·40	9·01	2·60	2·14	1·16	13·48	8·91
XIX. Transport, &c.	4·79	7·93	28·45	6·40	4·54	1·32	28·96	2·10	2·06	2·53	2·99	1·75	5·78	2·52
XX. Professions	12·25	11·07	19·35	14·42	7·74	3·78	40·98	7·40	3·03	6·64	5·48	3·77	14·35	13·24
XXI. Sport and Games	2·77	5·97	10·68	6·18	3·66	0·37	29·53	—	—	1·80	2·10	—	1·11	4·08
XXII. General Labour	0·34	2·05	14·97	2·42	0·52	1·01	16·90	1·88	0·19	0·71	6·93	0·40	1·28	3·40
XXIII. Indefinite, &c.	0·46	2·96	18·65	1·03	1·48	1·37	0·22	—	0·72	—	0·47	—	0·84	—
XXIV. Independent	3·33	7·03	10·06	7·69	2·71	2·82	7·22	7·08	0·13	2·57	1·47	1·07	2·47	1·60
Total	**6·54**	**9·24**	**18·28**	**7·96**	**5·56**	**2·54**	**38·02**	**6·38**	**5·21**	**5·68**	**4·29**	**1·96**	**10·82**	**6·65**

* Order V. and the occupations combined with it are excluded.

probably correct. Having regard to the varying degrees of accuracy admittedly to be found in the statistics on this matter, it is useless to review the return in detail. But there are a few interesting points that are brought out in the figures as they stand.

The classes that most largely combine some form of agriculture with their special occupation are, first, the village menials, such as watchmen, then the artizans we have grouped under the head of the normal village community; the carpenter, for example, and blacksmith; still more the potter and the oil-presser. The barber, too, is not an unfrequent landholder in some parts of India, and the tanner, the cart owner, and even the general labourer, eke out their income in this way. The weaver, another of the large rural industries, seems to be somewhat averse from this pluralism, and his own occupation, indeed, is hardly one that would fit him for strenuous outdoor work, so that unless he can get hold of a plot of land and let it out to others, it is difficult to see how he could make anything out of his possession. In fact, the proportion of weavers, as it is, must be largely recruited from the class who work, not in the more respectable fabrics of cotton and silk, but in the humble hemp or flax, which is, as we have seen, the monopoly generally of the watchmen class, who are all semi-agricultural by tradition and predilection. Next we find a few professionals in the field, for instance, the proportion of the priestly class is high in the following cases:—Bombay, 17·26 per cent.; Madras, 18·84. Central Provinces, 22·33; North-West Provinces, 32·21; Panjáb, 23·51, and Assam, 45·66. Even in Berar, it is considerably above the general proportion of the non-agricultural community. The religious orders, it is to be understood, are prohibited but to a small extent from worldly pursuits, and to a still smaller from the acquisition of property, in India. In Burma it is different, and the Buddhistic system is more severe in its restrictions. The Brahman, however, may do practically anything but hold the plough, and the very wealthiest are not debarred from receiving the alms to offer which is an act of religious merit. At places of pilgrimage, where the right to receive the offerings of the faithful is distributed according to hereditary position, a Brahman rolling in wealth will pursue, even to the High Court or Privy Council, a claim to the coppers of the potter or oilman—*non olet*. The lawyer, again, has his eye on land in the present day, and the fact that so shrewd a class should think it worth while to invest in this form of property is a testimony in favour of the current system of assessment and administration. In the following Provinces, various kinds of limbs of the law are returned as interested in the land:—Assam, where, however, they are comparatively scarce, 41·75; North-West Provinces, 15·16: Bombay, 13·51, and Madras, 18·98. Lastly, we come to a question of considerable inportance, on which the evidence of the census as it stands is not at all re-assuring. This is the extent to which the land is passing into the hand of the money-lender. It must be understood that the subject is a widely spread one, on which but superficial evidence can be obtained from the data before us, but in nearly every province that has sent up fairly trustworthy returns, the proportion of quasi-agriculturists is higher amongst the money-lenders than any other class, save, perhaps, village menials. It may be that some of the persons included are really of the land-holding class, for, as has been already remarked, it is a very ordinary custom for a man, not of Islám, who has surplus cash in hand, to lend it on such security as he may think proper, whatever his special occupation; and as such transactions would have been set forth in his income-tax return, it is probable that he thought it consistent to enter the same at the census. On the other hand, the wide extent of the high proportion, and the remarkable difference between it in British Provinces and in the two large Feudatory States, where, for the most part, the transfer of land to a creditor is unusual, if not unlawful, seem to indicate a real advance of the commercial class engaged in this particular branch of transactions on the land, as occupants, *de jure* or *facto*. The following are the instances in point:—

Province.	Per-centage of Landholders, &c., amongst		State.	Per-centage of Landholders, &c., amongst	
	Total Non-Agricultural Population.	Money-Lenders.		Total Non-Agricultural Population.	Money-Lenders.
Bombay -	9·24	31·22	Haidrabád -	5·21	15·31
Madras -	6·54	17·77	Baroda - -	5·68	2·60
Central Provinces	5·56	36·74	Bombay States -	4·29	5·51
Berar	2·54	23·21	Central Province States.	10·82	13·48
Assam	38·02	67·65			
N.-W. Provinces	18·28	46·57			
Panjáb	7·96	18·37			

The excess in this special instance over the general proportion of semi-agriculturists in the provinces is a very noteworthy feature in the return.

Provincial Returns.

To conclude this chapter, a table is given on page 119 in which the relative strength of the 24 orders in the different Provinces and States is shown. The most convenient way to treat these details in the cursory examination which alone is necessary in this work will be to deal with each in its serial order, instead of taking the Province or State as the unit of comparison.

The first Order will be seen to be high in British territory, according to the relatively complete equipment of the village staff. In Bombay, Berar, and Madras, the proportion is high, but in Assam, Bengal, and Burma it falls. In Feudatory States, on the other hand, the proportions are usually high. In the case of Central India and the Madras group, Order III., should be added to this head, as it clearly belongs to it, but has been misplaced by a misinterpretation of the meaning of the headings. In the same way, Order II., Defence, has got mixed with the first in some of the States, owing to the adoption of the title of Service, unspecified. In British territory, this Order is mostly insignificant, save in Ajmér, where there is a large cantonment in a small province; in the Panjáb and in Burma, where the number of troops is always considerable. In the North-West Provinces the case is the reverse of that of Ajmér, and the very considerable garrison is swamped by the enormous rural population.

Pasture calls for few remarks. It is apparently most frequently returned in the Central Provinces and Madras of the Provinces, and Baroda, Haidrabád, and the Bombay States, of the rest of the country. Rajputána, too, shows a good proportion, whilst it is singularly weakly represented in the damper climes of the west coast, Assam, Bengal, and Burma.

Agriculture has been sufficiently dealt with above, but attention should be again called to the fact that in the Madras States, Haidrabád, Ajmér, and Central India, the field-labourer has been very largely relegated to the category of general labour, a fact sufficiently obvious from the return now under review. The very high proportion of agriculture in Assam, Coorg, and the small States under Bengal and the Central Provinces may be noted.

Order VI., dealing with service of various sorts, has been described already as unduly comprehensive. The proportion is high in the Panjáb and in northern India generally, and is at its minimum in Burma. It is above the average, too, in some of the larger States, so presumably the proportion is dependent upon general service, as well as upon the special attentions of the village class of functionaries. As regards the supply of food and drinks, &c., we may note the high rank of Burma, where the fisher holds his own well, and in the Madras States, where he is likewise a great feature in the community, with the supplement, in this group, of the toddy-drawer. The proportion in Assam and Bombay is affected in the same way, the former by the fisher and the second by both.

The provision of Light and Fuel, &c. is remarkably evenly represented throughout the larger items, but the proportion falls in Coorg, Burma, and some of the smaller groups of States.

Building seems to be chiefly returned as a separate occupation in Madras, Bombay, the Panjáb States, and Ajmér. The next Order, too, is too small to need much comment. In Assam and Burma the canoe digger and boatbuilder, respectively, are the main items, and Ajmér apparently owes its predominance to a colony of people on the railway. Supplementary occupations are too varied and too small to require notice here. Textile industries are proportionately high in the Panjáb, the Central Provinces, and Haidrabád, and low in the more primitive communities of Assam, the smaller States of the Central belt of hills, and in Coorg. Nor do they flourish to any considerable extent in Bengal.

Metals occupy a singularly even proportion throughout, except in Assam and Burma. It may be remembered that this group includes two or three of the main village industries, which accounts to some extent for the uniform distribution.

The potter, too, is fairly distributed between a maximum of 1·83 per cent. in Rajputána and 0·26 in the North-West Province States. He is at a discount, too, in Coorg and Burma.

The order connected with working in Wood and Cane is a very varied one as to distribution, in spite of its prevalence as a village industry. This is due to the inclusion of timber-dealing and work in cane and leaves. The former predominates in Burma, the latter in the coast States of Madras, and here the general ratio is highest. In Mysore there is a singular deficiency of carpenters. In the Central Province States, where huts are the usual form of dwelling, the absence of this artisan is intelligible.

The small group of those working in connection with minor Forest produce and Dyes, &c. can be passed by. Then come the leather-workers, who seem to be in force more in the north of India than in the Deccan and south or east. In Assam and the small Central Hill States, indeed, the tanner and shoemaker is but a minute element in the community, and in Burma and Coorg he stands relatively little higher.

Commerce, a mixed group, as has already been stated, is at its maximum in Ajmér and the Madras States. The former is essentially favourable to trade, from its position, and its proximity to the refuge of the most enterprising class of traders in India. But the secluded coast States of Madras seem hardly to compete in this respect, and the high proportion there is possibly due to some error in classification, as in the case of the agriculturists. The census administration of the largest State in the group, Travancore, showed signs of originality in several respects, of which is this probably one.

Under the head of Transport we have to consider that by water and that by road or rail. Bombay and Burma come first with respect to the former, and Rajputána, where the railway is of comparatively recent introduction, shows a high proportion of road-carriers, and also, as we have said above, of porters and warehousemen. Professions, which to a large extent means priests and so on, are pre-eminent in Baroda, the Panjáb, Burma, and Rajputána. Then comes Bombay, British and Feudatory. Except in the small States under the Central Provinces, they do not fall below one per cent., and on an average, they reach nearly double that proportion.

Passing on to General Labour, we may note that this item is almost absent in Assam and the Panjáb, and exaggerated, as we have described, in several of the States, if not in Bengal also, at the expense of the agriculturist. The indefinite group is recruited largely from Rajputána, where a good many entries were omitted, and from Madras, where there was a superfluity of entries of "dependent," without further qualification. In Haiderabád, too, this class is strongly represented, but in the absence of the local Report, explanation is not possible. Those who are supported by other than their own work vary greatly in distribution. On the whole, they are in greater force in the States than in the Provinces. Rajputána takes the lead, followed by Haiderabád and the Panjáb. Ajmér, Central India, and Kashmér all show a high proportion. In most cases the ratio no doubt depends on the number of those supported by charity. In and near Ajmér, for instance, there are several places of pilgrimage, which form an outlet for almsgiving. In Rajputána the community is highly orthodox, and the numerous Chiefs' courts are therefore much affected by the medicant orders, whether devotees or others. The Panjáb has to support two religions, each with its separate train of claimants for the charity of the faithful. Presumably, the corresponding class in the Madras States has been endowed with land or some other means of livelihood, as the proportion shown is remarkably low, considering the number reported to be dependent on the royal bounty in the "Land of Charity" along the Malabar coast.

With this comparatively brief summary of the diverse conditions of occupation in India, in its various sub-divisions, this review must conclude. The reports of the Provincial and State Superintendents of the Census contain much detail that will repay perusal, but which it is impracticable to incorporate in a general work such as the present.

TABLE E.—Showing the Per-centage of the several Orders in each Province, &c.

PROVINCE OR STATE, &c.	Administration. I.	Defence. II.	Other States' Service. III.	Pasture, &c. IV.	Agricultural. V.	Domestic and Other Service. VI.	Food, Drink, &c. VII.	Light and Fuel, &c. VIII.	Building. IX.	Vehicles and Vessels. X.	Supplementary Services. XI.	Textile Fabrics and Dress. XII.
1. Ajmér	1·28	1·06	0·41	1·21	48·40	6·37	2·36	1·07	0·77	1·16	0·56	5·66
2. Assam	0·67	0·17	0·01	0·28	76·91	1·62	6·87	1·24	0·27	0·20	0·21	1·37
3. Bengal	0·98	0·02	—	0·64	63·19	3·51	4·96	1·06	0·28	0·06	0·43	2·60
4. Bombay and Sindh	3·25	0·23	0·04	1·37	58·24	2·55	7·56	1·52	0·80	0·08	0·65	5·42
5. Berár	2·98	0·07	—	1·21	68·55	2·50	2·90	1·54	0·62	0·01	0·35	3·87
6. Burma	1·36	0·41	—	0·69	63·44	0·78	9·93	0·91	0·64	0·19	0·43	4·93
7. Central Provinces	1·82	0·11	—	2·47	64·04	2·44	4·10	2·00	0·40	0·05	0·47	6·74
8. Coorg	2·20	0·01	—	0·72	72·00	2·39	5·62	0·30	0·38	0·02	0·19	1·15
9. N.-W. Provinces and Oudh	1·80	0·15	0·02	0·83	60·81	5·41	4·90	1·64	0·32	0·03	0·66	4·67
10. Panjáb	1·79	0·52	0·08	1·29	55·65	6·73	5·16	1·04	0·59	0·04	0·24	7·56
11. Madras	2·45	0·09	—	2·01	58·81	2·96	5·90	1·26	1·00	0·05	0·28	4·71
12. Haiderabad	4·69	0·55	0·04	2·46	44·88	5·65	5·70	0·80	0·53	0·03	0·28	6·28
13. Baroda	3·56	0·82	0·03	2·27	57·76	2·98	4·12	1·45	0·58	0·02	0·28	5·14
14. Mysore	4·32	0·45	—	0·47	66·61	2·21	1·27	0·47	0·62	0·02	0·20	2·94
15. Kashmér	2·25	0·42	0·03	1·18	68·12	3·33	2·38	0·59	0·12	—	0·16	5·73
16. Rajputána	2·67	1·23	0·21	2·34	52·69	5·26	2·66	0·93	0·49	—	0·24	3·03
17. Central India	0·74	0·17	3·38	0·94	48·12	5·10	2·31	1·05	0·32	—	0·34	3·21
18. Bombay States	3·55	0·25	0·11	2·63	57·33	2·35	4·02	1·53	0·68	0·02	0·27	5·72
19. Madras States	0·01	0·04	1·90	0·30	43·27	2·99	8·54	1·26	0·64	0·03	0·11	3·45
20. Central Province States	1·85	—	—	2·72	70·62	1·47	3·50	0·81	0·07	0·01	0·37	7·68
21. Bengal States	1·18	0·01	—	1·87	69·19	2·20	2·59	0·55	0·11	0·02	0·13	2·97
22. N.-W. Province States	1·94	0·76	0·02	0·41	69·94	4·91	4·26	1·09	0·30	—	0·29	4·51
23. Panjáb States	1·97	0·46	0·05	1·30	64·55	4·56	4·25	0·83	0·87	0·04	0·15	5·48
INDIA	**1·95**	**0·23**	**0·18**	**1·27**	**59·79**	**3·91**	**5·07**	**1·23**	**0·50**	**0·05**	**0·40**	**4·39**

Table E.—*concluded.*

Province or State, &c.	Metals, &c. XIII.	Earthenware and Glass, &c. XIV.	Wood and Cane. XV.	Gums, Drugs, and Dyes. XVI.	Leather. XVII.	Commerce. XVIII.	Transport, &c. XIX.	Professions. XX.	Sport. XXI.	General Labour. XXII.	Indefinite, &c. XXIII.	Independent of Work. XXIV.
1. Ajmér	1·47	1·20	1·18	0·06	2·45	5·63	1·75	3·64	0·08	9·87	0·08	2·38
2. Assam	0·75	0·55	1·04	0·04	0·11	0·82	0·80	1·87	0·02	1·94	0·82	1·42
3. Bengal	1·13	0·67	1·17	0·17	0·48	1·58	1·27	1·92	0·08	12·51	0·21	1·13
4. Bombay and Sindh	1·51	0·62	1·74	0·12	1·28	2·12	2·02	2·13	0·08	4·54	0·17	1·96
5. Berár	1·32	0·65	1·66	0·13	0·82	1·82	1·02	1·26	0·12	4·58	0·22	1·80
6. Burma	0·91	0·50	2·86	0·15	0·26	1·73	2·54	2·74	0·07	3·99	0·05	0·49
7. Central Provinces	1·57	0·56	1·35	0·11	1·37	1·04	0·79	1·18	0·05	5·96	0·14	1·24
8. Coorg	1·59	0·49	1·72	0·01	0·22	0·37	1·32	1·73	0·09	6·76	0·16	0·56
9. N.-W. Provinces and Oudh	1·37	1·01	1·35	0·13	0·77	1·03	1·47	1·64	0·04	8·44	0·04	1·47
10. Panjáb	1·64	1·10	1·96	0·21	2·74	1·76	1·78	3·12	0·05	2·02	0·98	2·82
11. Madras	1·38	0·61	1·78	0·12	1·38	0·97	1·49	1·95	0·06	8·41	1·16	1·17
12. Hyderabad	1·49	0·81	1·42	0·17	1·37	1·53	0·72	1·19	0·10	12·69	3·82	2·80
13. Baroda	1·51	1·46	1·69	0·05	1·54	1·82	0·55	3·92	0·04	6·62	0·06	1·73
14. Mysore	1·49	0·55	0·67	0·06	0·49	3·26	0·33	1·56	0·06	9·99	0·06	1·90
15. Kashmér	1·00	0·52	1·02	0·04	1·27	2·42	0·88	1·79	0·08	2·94	1·07	2·66
16. Rajputána	1·22	1·83	1·62	0·03	2·50	3·26	2·92	2·67	0·06	5·88	2·71	3·55
17. Central India	1·27	1·04	1·50	0·15	2·21	2·65	0·34	1·11	0·07	21·26	0·04	2·68
18. Bombay States	1·57	1·18	1·85	0·13	1·72	2·74	1·13	2·77	0·06	5·79	0·37	2·23
19. Madras States	1·71	0·32	2·40	0·08	0·13	4·76	0·71	1·98	0·04	24·39	0·51	0·43
20. Central Province States	1·25	0·71	0·58	0·12	0·32	0·52	0·58	0·52	0·05	5·42	0·14	0·69
21. Bengal States	1·41	0·69	1·19	0·10	0·14	0·74	0·39	1·17	0·02	12·16	0·10	1·07
22. N.-W. Province States	1·40	0·26	0·89	0·04	0·60	0·84	0·65	1·54	0·02	4·25	—	1·08
23. Panjáb States	1·51	1·12	1·51	0·19	2·84	1·08	0·98	3·21	0·07	0·92	0·04	2·02
INDIA	**1·33**	**0·82**	**1·50**	**0·14**	**1·14**	**1·63**	**1·38**	**1·97**	**0·05**	**8·87**	**0·54**	**1·66**

CHAPTER V.

Ethnographic Distribution of the Population.

Language, Religion, Race, and Caste.

Δεῖ δ' εὐγνωμόνως ἀκούειν περὶ τῆς 'Ινδικῆς· καὶ γὰρ ἀπωτάτω ἐστί . . . οἱ δὲ καὶ ἰδόντες μέρη τινὰ εἶδον, τὰ δὲ πλείω λέγουσιν ἐξ ἀκοῆς . . . διόπερ οὐδὲ τὰ αὐτὰ περὶ τῶν αὐτῶν ἐξαγγέλλουσι . . ἀλλ' ἕκαστος ἑκάστῳ τ' αναντια λέγει πολλάκις· Ὅπου δὲ περὶ τῶν ὁραθέντων οὕτω διαφέρονται, τί δεῖ νομίζειν περὶ τῶν ἐξ ἀκοῆς ;—Strabo.

In preceding chapters it has been sufficient to treat of the population as ethnically uniform. In most of the statistics that follow, however, discrimination becomes necessary between the various component parts that go to form that vast mass. It is well to begin by clearing out of the way the notion that in the Indian population there is any of the cohesive element that is implied in the term nationality. There is, indeed, an influence peculiar to the country, but it is adverse to nationality, and tends rather towards detachment without independence. It is as difficult to define as that by which the land of the Lotus was protected,

Breathing like one that hath a weary dream ;

but like that, too, it is subtle and all-pervading, and no social institution brought within its range seems able to completely withstand it. In treating of the religious and social divisions of the people this influence will be found traceable throughout the whole course of their development. To put it generally, it is that of an excessive devotion to heredity and custom, manifested in the inclination to exalt the small over the great, and to exaggerate the importance of minor considerations, and thus obscure that of the more vital. For example, in religion, abstract or elemental conceptions, as shadowed forth in the earlier Vedic compositions, rapidly give place to the tutelary deity of the village or the forest tribes, elevated to a seat in the Puránic Pantheon. The strict monotheism of Islám is dissolved into the adoration of the personality of the Prophet, or that of the miraculous powers of locally-canonised ascetics. In some instances Christianity has been similarly interpreted. In all, liturgy and ceremonial observances usurp the place of moral and spiritual ideas, with the inevitable result that the sanction of religion is applied to all the regulations of social intercourse. Rank and occupation are thus crystallised into hereditary attributes, a process which ends in the formation of a practically unlimited number of self-centred and mutually repellent groups, cramping to the sympathies and to the capacity for thought and action. Within these groups, it is hardly possible to speak too highly of the charity and devotion of the members of the community to each other; but beyond them, the barriers on all sides preclude co-operation and real compassion, and stifle originality and invention. It is inadvisable to further anticipate a subject that must be dealt with in detail later on, and enough has been said about it to indicate the incompatibility of a social system of this sort with the homogeneity of structure involved in the conception of a nation. To some extent, too, an explanation has been thus obtained of the combination under one head of matters apparently so distinct as religion and the social divisions known as race, tribe, or caste. In dealing with each in its present condition, that is, with the actual statistics collected at the census, the two are kept apart, but in the historical summary, which is essential to a complete view of the subject, however general it may be, the connection of the supernatural with every-day life, in the case of the majority of the classes that come under review, is too close to admit of separation. The caste-spirit.

A few words of explanation, too, seem necessary in connection with the inclusion of the return of languages in the present section of this work. In the first place, though there may be no intention of overrating the value of the information afforded by differences of language with regard to the sub-division of a population, it seems injudicious to eliminate it altogether. Again, without condoning what Dr. M. Müller calls the "unholy alliance" between Comparative Philology and Ethnology, it is permissible, under due safeguard against misconception, to make use in the one of certain highly convenient terms invented or usually applied in connection with the other. In other respects, the return of language serves merely philological purposes, and represents only tho distribution of mother-tongue in India, according to the views of the people on the subject at the time of the census.

Ethnic isolation of India.

In treating of the ethnological history of the population it is as well to distinguish Burma from India proper, and to deal with the former separately. As regards the latter, what was said in the introductory chapter about the physical divisions of the country should be borne in mind. The Himálaya and Hindu-Kush, though a barrier to any extensive colonisation, have been passed on several occasions by comparatively small bodies of immigrants or invaders, in pursuance of what seems to be the general and irresistible tendency of northern races to seek the southern extremities of the old world. The fertile plains that awaited the new-comers on their passage of the mountains, were bounded on the extreme west by desert, and probably by swamps also; on the east by a delta that was, till within a period which counts but as short in the history of a country, a marshy waste. To the south a barrier of hills closed the way of free intercourse with the plains and coasts beyond.

Absence of historical information.

The materials for the history of early days in India are singularly defective. In the case of one, and that the most important community, we have, indeed, a certain body of literature and tradition, but dating from a period long after that to which it purports to relate, and compiled at various times, but always later than the establishment of a hieratic influence in the community. The curtain of myth, to use Grote's metaphor, is thus far less instructive than that drawn before the early annals of Greece, and the historical period begins at least 450 years later than in that country, with much occasional dropping of the curtain after it first rose. Chinese and Greek travellers managed, it is true, to get in by a stage-door, but only in time, as a rule, for an interlude, or afterpiece. Attempts to reconstruct the ancient history of India from the literature that has come down to us, judging from the want of harmony amongst the experts who have made them, are remarkable only for their brilliant failure. From out of the mass of hieratic myth and the latter-day glorification of the eponymous heroes of the different clans of the immigrants of the class in question, we may select a few indications that are probably less untrustworthy than the rest.

The Árya occupation.

To begin with, it seems clear that the first historical movement into India was that of a race from beyond the Himálaya, hailing from the temperate zone, where they had differences, of which more must be said hereafter, with another section of the same race. The name they give themselves is that of Árya, but it is shared by their rivals, from whom they split off to tempt the snowy passes of the mountain barrier. As the others did not come into contact with India till many centuries later, by which time they had acquired for themselves a new appellation, it will be convenient to restrict the term Arya to the community that found its way to India. Some objection has been raised to the use of the term at all for other than a class of language, but the question arises what is the alternative? Linguistically, no doubt, Greek, Briton, German, Swede and Russian are all Aryan, but in the community that we are now discussing, the term is used as a distinctive title, and their legends all point to their foreign origin, whereas the Greeks, for example, never fail to hold themselves autochthonous. By Árya, then, we mean, in this work, the people who entered India from the north-west, leaving a larger community of the same race who seem to have kept a south-westerly course along the opposite side of the mountains. It is open to question whether the Arya entered the country by the Hindu-Kúsh, down the Kábul River, or by the Upper Indus. Probabilities seem slightly in favour of the latter, though the migrants must have had time to spread about considerably during their sojourn in the hill country. But they debouched upon the plains of India, apparently, to the east of the Panjáb, so that it is not improbable that their course was from what is now Ghilgit and Chitrál, to the valley of Kashmér, where a colony was formed. There is no doubt that they avoided the western portion of the Panjáb, and the most likely reason is that they found it already in the possession of an earlier wave of immigrants from the north, who were too much on a par with the Arya themselves in point of strength and civilisation to render conflict advisable. It is in this region probably that they found the first enemy of foreign race to themselves, for they mention hostile serpent worshippers of a yellow complexion, and from other sources we learn that very early in history there had been movements amongst the light tinted race of West-Central Asia, that went by the generic title of Skythian, and that these were being gradually extruded from the east towards the south-west by the encroaching hordes of Mongol or kindred origin. In later days, too, we hear of serpent worship in Kashmér, even to the present time, and the Indian legends contain numerous references to serpent races, and to the death of Arya kings from the bites of these reptiles, and, on the other hand, even to intermarriage with them. We may take it as probable, then, that the Arya avoided the Five Rivers, and made for the Jamna, or, rather, the tract of land lying west of the upper course of that river, after it has left the mountains. This seems to have been their first settlement, and here they remained for a long time. But here, too, they meet with the second of the foreign races against which they had to make head. This was a race black in skin, low in stature, and with matted locks; in war treacherous and cunning; in choice of food, disgusting, and in ceremonial, absolutely deficient. The superior civilisation of the foreigner soon asserted itself, and the lower race had to give way. The first object seems to have been to get possession of the land; the next, after securing their cattle and families against those whom they had ousted, to establish the members of the lower race on it as helots or agrestic serfs. This process went on at least as far as the confines of Bengal, where the Central Belt of hills, on the one side, and the swamps of the Delta on the other, stopped the eastward movement for some generations. As to the tribes met with in the Tarai, and the lower belts of hills parallel to the Himálaya up to the confines of the present frontier of the Panjáb, it is apparently doubtful whether at the time of the advance of the Arya they were not branches of the serpent-worshipping races from the north-east of the Himálaya, who are still represented in these tracts.

The Pre-Árya race or races.

But the most interesting and important questions with regard to the foe of darker skin, are, in the first place, whether it was autochthonous, or, like the Áryas themselves, immigrant; in the second place, whether it consisted of a single race or of several. On the first point, we have, first, the theory that the race in question is the remnant of the inhabitants of a continent now submerged, connecting India with Africa or Madagascar on the one side, and with Melanesia on the other. This view is based partly on physiological grounds and partly, in a less degree, on philological. Next, we find supporters of the hypothesis that, like the Árya, the darker race came into India from the north-west. This rests chiefly on philological grounds, as no physiological investigation has apparently thrown light on the causes for so complete a change of type in all its details. On the second point in dispute there is now but little evidence. The old traditions make no distinction between the dark races, if, indeed, there were any, but rest their classification entirely on the colour of the skin. Philology indicates a fairly well marked distinction between the languages of the tribes of the Central Belt, and groups one section, mainly those to the southward, under the head of Dravidian, and the other under a title which has remained, for want of a better, in its primitive and not very correct form of Kolarian. Physiology, however, has been busy amongst these tribes, and discovers no trace of distinction between the two groups. The view, therefore, that one stream entered India from the north-west, as already stated, whilst another came round by the Bráhmapútra valley, may be considered in abeyance. There is a third group, probably of later growth, to the extreme east of the Gangetic valley, where the Árya did not penetrate till many centuries after the original tradition had been lost. This group is apparently an offshoot of the great wave of Mongoloid immigration southward, part of which found its way into the upper portion of the Bráhmapútra valley, but more sought the sea in the Burmese peninsula, or were content with the table-lands of Thibet and the higher cultivable vales of the Himalaya. Their contact with the Árya and the other occupants of the plains of India was accordingly less close than that of the race or races we have mentioned above, and as it took place at a later date, when the colonisation of the open country had been completed, so far as social organisation is in question, the results of the connection were very different from those which followed the intercourse of the Árya with the tribes they dispossessed.

The Árya movement one of occupation not conquest.

In regard to the latter, one of the facts most important from an ethnological standpoint, is that the foreign movement was that of occupation, or colonisation, not of invasion and conquest. The newcomers had to deal with opponents far inferior to themselves in civilisation, and with only a very rudimentary political organisation, so that the opposition to be overcome before the Árya could take possession of the soil was of the feeblest. The advance down the valley of the Jamna and Ganges or across the plains of what is now Rájputána was no more than the growth of pastoral and agricultural settlements, expanding as they waxed and multiplied beyond the means of support of the tracts that first fell into their hands. Anything more different from the process of invasion and conquest that characterised most of the later inroads from the north-west it is hard to conceive. On the one side we have the constant burden of such portion of the Vedic Hymnal as may be attributed to the earlier period of the Indian enterprise, which consists in the strenuous demands for an increase of the material wealth of a peaceful community :—

Da fortunare Penates !
Da pecus et gregibus foetum !

The military element is in the background, or prominent only as the means of defending their precious cattle. On the other side we have, for example, the ruthless slaughter and rapine of the Makedonian expedition under the great Alexander, to whom friend and foe seemed to stand on the same footing when his own interests were concerned, and whose operations may be summed up in the pithy phrase so often recurring in Thukydides as characteristic of the Greek mode of procedure, "the men "were put to the sword, and the women and children sold into slavery." All the "fine hysterics" of the epics of India and the later hymns regarding the pitched battles and deeds of heroism of the Árya against the swarthy foe, appear to be the inventions of a far more settled age, when it had become the duty of the court singer to glorify his patron in the person of those of old time, to whom the former had been duly affiliated. It does not seem to be too wide a hypothesis to presume that the early Árya were of a temperament, for that age, peaceful, and their military prowess was not stimulated until they had enough political units of their own race in the land to induce them to engage in internecine strife. The bearing of this characteristic on the development of the community is easy to conceive. The opposing races were not exterminated, and, in fact, it appears that they were not in all cases even driven away, but became the adscripti glebæ of the stronger race. In accordance with the usual tendency of human nature in such circumstances, interbreeding was only a matter of time, and as a penal rule presupposes a corresponding offence, the fulminations of the hierarchy a few centuries later against this practice, and the barbarous penalties attached to it in the academic productions that embodied the priestly notion of what ought to be the law, show that the Árya had virtually abandoned the notion of maintaining the purity of his foreign blood. The social system of the majority, even to the present day, owes much of its adaptability and fissiparous tendency to this fact. In connection with it, too, may be borne in mind the comparative isolation of the Arya from their native country and traditions after they had once crossed the mountains. The difficulty of the routes allowed of no free recruitment of the population from the north, and, moreover, the only other branch of the Árya family of which there is any mention in the Vedic lore, is that with which those who came to India had apparently had a bitter feud. It has been stated that the mention in the Hymnal of the former of the Seven Rivers is a proof that the two branches "lived side by side" for some time after the separation, but it seems far more probable, from the context, that the passage in question * referred to the days of the first Darius, who added the Panjáb to the Persian Empire. By that time the tradition of common ancestry had apparently been lost, or at least, was devoid of vitality.

Skythian immigration.

But there were other races from the north that had found their way to Upper India, as has been mentioned, before the Árya, and these were succeeded by more from the same stock. In the course of time some of them occupied the whole of the north-western Panjáb and spread down the Indus to the sea. Others obtained possession of what is now Kábul. There is evidence, too, that the Árya, many generations after their first settlement on the plain of Dehli and Karnál, broke back to the Five Rivers, and ousted the tribes we may agree to call Skythian, and spread also through Rajputána to the western coast. A race either identical with, or very closely allied to them, occupied parts of what is now Afghanistán, whilst another section, that may have strayed from the larger settlements in Kashmer or Swat ensconced itself in the valleys, difficult of access, at the southern foot of the Hindu-Kúsh. Changes in religion, changes in dynasty, and the frequent passage of invading armies have confounded tradition in these tracts, and obliterated ethnological traces. In the term Pathán, for instance, the Pakhtuwán, or speaker of Pashtu, are now included not only the ancient, and probably Indo-Arya, race mentioned in the books of the Bráhmans and the Greeks, but the Syro-Arabic Áfghán and the Central Asiatic Ghilzai. The small tract known as Kafiristán is still a *terra incognita*, and contains,

* The first Fargard of the Vendidád, where the term is used, enumerates, apparently, only the 16 lands subject to the Persian King, with the exception of the mythical Aireyanam Vaejo.—J.A.B.

according to one conjecture, the last relics of the pre-Indic Árya, and, according to another, the offspring of the Makedonian garrison left by Alexander the Great. But this much may be safely asserted, that, west of the Jamna, the blood, however it may be composed, is of a far purer northern strain than to the eastwards of that river, so that, whether by reason of constant petty incursions from across the snows, or because the dark races of the rest of India did not tempt the desert, the mixture of breed in Rajputána and the Panjáb, and perhaps in Sindh also, is totally different from that prevalent between the Doab and the Hughli. Here we again find a river as an ethnologic frontier, and it may be said, in general terms, that the further we get from the possibility of northern influence, the higher the proportion of lower blood, but that the mixture changes its character in the extreme east to semi-Mongoloid, instead of the semi-Dravidian, or Negrito, of the rest of the Ganges valley.

Before concluding this sketch of the chief ethnological features of Upper India, some comment is necessary on a few other foreign influences which have in time succumbed to that of the majority, and been absorbed in the masses without more than a faint historical trace being now discernible. Of the Skythians enough has been said already, particularly as it is uncertain, save from verbal coincidences, what are the communities in which their blood can be found. There is no doubt that their main strongholds were in the Panjáb alone, and that the bodies that moved southwards were soon melted up in the fusion of races under Brahmanic influence, though traces in the local nomenclature are still to be found. General Cunningham is the chief authority on the Skythic element in the Panjáb and its western neighbourhood, but except in tribal names, such as that of the Takka, Ghakkar, Gujar, Megh, and, above all, Jat, racial distinctions seem to have vanished.

Greek influence in India.

A good deal has been said of late about the Greek influence on India, so this sketch would be incomplete without some mention of the subject. The leading factor in the connexion between the two races was, necessarily, the expedition of the Makedonians under Alexander. This was a purely military enterprise, undertaken in pursuance partly of the conqueror's dream of universal empire, partly, too, because India, or rather the north-western portion of it, formed a part, and that the richest, of the dominion of the late Darius. The system followed by the king was to establish a small body of his own nation in every one of the large cities or important posts he passed. The native chiefs who submitted were rewarded by the gift of some of the territory wrested from those who were less prudent. He also established independent outposts, garrisoned by his own troops, to guard his new acquisitions, but, considering the number of his trustworthy adherents, such detachments must have been very small. It is this practice that is dignified in the oration of Plutarch* by the name of the "foundation of cities." In reality, they scarcely survived the departure of the king from the shores of India. We hear of the revolt of the Panjáb chiefs whilst Alexander was still in Sindh, and little trace was left of his foundations by the time the ambassador of his successor visited India five-and-twenty years later. Even the sites of the most celebrated are matters of dispute, and no tradition of his two years' stay in the country is on record. It is the same with the cities, so called, that he founded in Kábúl and Bálkh, Alexandria of the Paropamisus, and that called the "Uttermost." The character of his expeditions left no room for the introduction of the arts of peace, and if any Greek influence entered India at all, it was owing to the efforts of him to whom fell the eastern portion of the house of cards left by Alexander. The permanent record of the connection of the latter with India consists of the discovery of the first chronological fact in the history of that country, the date of Chandragupta. The weakness of Seleukus and the strength of this native potentate seem to have been the means of bringing the two into peaceful relations with each other, and the Greek withdrew altogether from his Indian pretensions. But, on the rise of architecture amongst the Buddhist monarchs of the Maurya dynasty, Greek influence undoubtedly made itself felt, though only to a small extent, and over a very restricted area, practically the north-west of the Panjáb. It has been questioned, indeed, whether even these traces are not due to a much later period than that of the rule of the Diadokhi. Ethnologically, there was no regular Greek connection. Alexander married, it is true, a wife from Badakshán or the neighbourhood, as he did a Persian afterwards, but his proclivities were altogether towards the intermarriage of his officers with the latter, as the stronger, race. Seleukus, too, seems to have given his daughter to Chandragupta as

* This lucubration has been treated by some authors as of historical value, but when compared with the accounts of other writers, it is clear that Grote is justified in regarding it as no more than a rhetorical essay.—J.A.B.

an act of policy, but the Greeks left behind in India are not heard of amongst the tribes of the Panjáb, and the term Yavana, as afterwards used, seems to indicate any Western Asiatic. Kafiristán, as has been remarked, still keeps its secret. Finally, the short reign of Menander seems to have been destitute of permanent results, though he got farther into India than any other sovereign of his race before he succumbed to the usual Skythian attack from the north. In the Christian era, the connection between India and the west was insignificant till the arrival of the Musalmán zealots and the historic inroads of the Mughals. We here enter a fresh phase of Indian ethnology, but one confined to the north-west, like so many more of the movements that have been mentioned. The number of families of the foreign races in question that actually settled in India is nowhere great except in the Panjáb and its neighbourhood. We find, indeed, a vast collection of people in the census tables, 34⅓, in fact, out of the 57 millions of Musulmáns, returned under the appellations of distinctly foreign races, such as Shaikh, Mughal, Patháns, and so on, but the greater portion of them are local converts to Islám, who have taken the title of the person of highest rank amongst those by whom they were converted, or who have affiliated themselves to these races on grounds even less relevant.

Race in the Peninsula.

Comment has hitherto been confined to the upper, or continental, portion of India, so it is now time to treat briefly of the ethnic features of the peninsula. Here we have a few small communities of foreign origin, who have settled in India within historical times, but the mass of the people is without even a tradition of migration from any other country. Physiology and philology both agree in the indications they afford of the identity of the race with that of the dark population driven off the land of Upper India by the Árya migration, but developed under far more favourable conditions. This is due, perhaps, to the strength of the position they occupied behind the Central Hills, which constitute, as it were, a second line of defence against inroads from the north. The base of the hills, too, was flanked on both sides by dense forest, and, inexperienced as the Árya were in navigation, the greater part of the coast was inaccessible to them in any force. Thus the people to the south of the Central Hills were left undisturbed for many generations after their kin that lay in the track of the foreign occupation had succumbed, and they had time, therefore, to organise themselves into communities of considerable political strength. It is clear that no hostile demonstration was made against them from the Ganges basin so long as the Árya were engaged in the colonisation of that more desirable locality, and it seems probable that the only connection between the two races was through stray visits paid by ascetics or other men of peace to the regions on the other side of the Vindhia Hills. The intercourse was thus solely religious, and continued to be so, as we hear of the Bráhman as an honoured guest at the courts of the southern Chiefs. The result was finally the reception by the latter of the hieratic system of the Brahmanic tribes, and the inclusion of the local religion in the pale of orthodoxy. It is a question whether the gradual process of absorption took place before or after the suppression of the Buddhistic reformation, but probabilities are in favour of the later date.* At all events, it may be taken for granted that the tales of the foundation of dynasties in the south by offshoots of the more renowned Árya lines of the north are fictions attributable to the inventive power of some latter-day laureate of an indigenous court. The Aryá-bred influence in certain directions is incontestably predominant in the south, but the Arya blood is conspicuous by its sparsity.

Áryan and other colonies on the west coast.

Along the west coast, however, traces of it are to be found, but mainly in the priestly class, so that the exception is probably due to the selection of the Konkan as a place of refuge after the early inroads of Musalmán iconoclasm. Earlier colonies of northern race, too, are traceable further south. The same reason accounts, in all probability, for the appearance there of small branches of the Jewish community, at Cochín and in the neighbourhood of Bombay, and it certainly explains the settlement of the remnants of the Zoroastrians, driven out of their native country to seek shelter amongst the earliest schismatics of their race. Western Asia is there represented also by an undoubted infusion of Arab blood amongst certain classes of the Malabar coast; but the greater part of this element that appears in the returns of the census is to be found in the detached Settlements of Aden and Perim, where alone, too, the African contingent is in any strength.

---

* According to the code of Manu, Áryas, who go to live in Dravida, the Tamil country, are *ipso facto* cut off from their brethren.—J.A.B.

Another question arises in connection with the composition of the southern Indian community, that is, the identity in race between the mass of the population and the lower grades, known by the names of Paraiya, Pálla, Mála, Púlaya, and so on. As in the north of India, these classes are relegated to hamlets of their own, outside the village site occupied by the rest. In the same way, too, they are the professional drummers of the community, and take special parts in certain religious ceremonies which are invalid if performed by anyone else. By analogy, therefore, it is fair to assume that they are the relics of a race still lower than that which now possesses the soil, but on this point physiology has by no means said its last word. The religious system introduced from Upper India did not reach the south until it had been highly developed along the Ganges, so that in the former country a much greater value was set by its missionaries on ritual, ceremonial, and caste, with all the other elaborate devices of its hierarchic paternity, than was possible amongst those who had assisted at its development. For this reason, the position of the lower castes was much more minutely defined than in the north, and this may, perhaps, account for their long period of debasement and their segregation from other than menial occupations, which distinguishes them from the corresponding class in Upper India. The whole question is intimately connected with that of the origin of the general mass of the people of the peninsula. If they can ever be traced from the north of the Himálaya, which is very doubtful, there is no difficulty in accounting for the existence of a servile class, and it only throws the investigation a stage further back, to the origin of the classes thus enslaved. Philology finds no difference between the speech of the masters and that of the servants beyond what can be accounted for by the ordinary processes of vulgarisation. But the assignation to the lower of special and very important ceremonial duties seems to afford strong proof of the recognition of their position as more influential in the eyes of the local divinities. In the same way the proudest chief in Rájputána to this day does not consider his coronation complete until the caste-mark on his forehead has been applied by the head-man of one of the Hill tribes, whose touch on any other occasion would be utter pollution. Obviously, the assumption is, that the older the race in occupation of the locality, the better its acquaintance or credit with the spirits who watch over it, whether for good or evil. *Agrestic serfage in South India.*

Between the differentiation of the two classes in southern India and that in the north there is one very remarkable distinction. In the latter, the question of colour was never out of mind. The gods were adjured to protect the Árya colour, and the epithet most often applied to the opposing race is that of dark-complexioned. Thus, the old name for race, or, as subsequently interpreted, caste or order, connoted, at the time it originated, that is, at the first contact of the Árya with a lower race, a real ethnic difference, as Mr. Risley has pointed out. But in the case of the southerner, we find no distinction, either in fact or fiction. The colour and general type of feature, where there is no suspicion of northern blood, are just the same in high and low, nor is there any indication in ancient literature that it was ever otherwise. It is here that further investigation is necessary, especially in the direction of scientific physiological measurements. Till these have been made, and the results collated with those on the same lines in other parts of the country, the question of the unity of the Tamil, or Dravidian, race can prudently be left open. The argument from colour alone, though a remarkably strong one, is not perhaps decisive in the present day, when no theory to account for its distribution or variation is safe against attack. *Caste and colour.*

We may sum up the ethnological position in India somewhat as follows:—In the extreme north-west the predominating element in the population is a strain from West Central Asia, but received at different times, and probably from different sources. Adjoining it, along and across the frontier, comes a community of still more western origin, but much mingled with the former. The Himálayan tracts bordering on the plains of the Panjáb and North-West Provinces also preserve a considerable element of northern origin, but in the same tracts further to the north and east, the population owes its ancestry to the eastern side of Central Asia, which seems to have peopled the whole range along the British frontier, and, in the eastern section of Upper India, the greater part of the valley also. Across the Ganges basin, the predominant element is that of a lower race of darker complexion and different physiognomy, which stretches, with few interruptions, to the point of the peninsula, and over the north of Ceylon. The strain from West Central Asia first mentioned is found in more or less purity in the Panjáb. It rapidly deteriorates from admixture with dark blood the further it gets eastward of its first settlement on the plains, *Summary.*

until it meets the north-eastern strain in the Delta. Admixture with the yellow races seems confined to a few submontane tracts along the central Himálaya, where special influences have been at work, and to the eastern portion of the Delta. The strain of northern blood south of the Central Belt of hills is of the thinnest, and hardly extends into the plains at all. On the west coast, however, specimens may be found in which it is probably pure, and the general average of the dark type throughout the peninsula has apparently been raised by prosperity and long-settled quiet considerably above the level in which we find it amongst the tribes that have been content to remain in the hills and forest.

Burma. The ethnology of Burma has this feature in common with that of peninsular India, that in both all native tradition has been equally tainted by the attribution, under hieratic influence, of descent from the ruling races of Aryan India. On the Bengal side of the northern frontier, the settlers from Arrakan are known as Maghs, said to be derived from Mágadha, the middle kingdom of Árya supremacy, but the title is not recognised in Arrakan itself. The Burmese call the Môn race Talaing, from a certain colonisation from across the Bay of Bengal under a Telanga leader, but the Môn themselves repudiate the term. Finally, we have the Burmese themselves, whose name is derived by some from Brahma, but is far more likely to be no more than a corruption of Myánma, the Man, a title we find arrogated to itself by tribes all over the world, especially when the distinction it denotes has been intensified by contact with an inferior race. **Early inhabitants.** There is, again, the same uncertainty as in India with regard to the earliest races inhabiting the peninsula. Physiology most distinctly points to the common origin of most of the races now in Burma and of the Himalayan tribes which have been called, by a conventional use of the term, "Mongoloid." Philology, in spite of the adoption of a modification of the Aryo-Indian character in the prevailing tongues, and of the introduction of much of the vocabulary required in connection with religious doctrine and ceremonial from the same source, confirms these conclusions. But though these races were, at the beginning of the historical period, in a very backward stage of civilisation, there is no evidence of their being, or claiming to be, autochthonous. The most important, indeed, as has been stated above, puts forward quite contrary pretensions. It is thus fair to assume that the general process of occupation of the peninsula has been on the same lines as that in other parts of the world, and that the direction of the movement has been invariably from the continent to the coast. The Malay element, which is now confined to the extreme south of Burma, is not without its traits of resemblance in language and physiognomy to that found in the lower grades of the Dravidian or south Indian population, and it may have spread once considerably more inland than its present sphere. Above the Malay **The Môn.** comes the Môn, which clearly once occupied the whole of the deltaic portion of the Golden Chersonese with its four rivers. They have now been split into two by a stream of immigration which undoubtedly came from the north. This consists of the southern branch of the Shán race, known amongst themselves as the Htai, or freemen. The Môns in Burma hold a portion of the Irawádi delta, and though the census under review indicates a certain revival of race-sentiment, there is reason to think that as a distinct community the Môn will soon cease to exist.* The only other remnant of the race within British territory is the small tribe of the Palaung in Upper Burma. The **The Karén.** question of the priority of occupation between the Môn and the Karén, which is probably the only rival barring the Malay, seems to be decided by tradition in favour of the Môn, for whilst these have no reminiscence of ever having been elsewhere than where they are at the present time, the Karéns trace back their origin to beyond a "river of sand" in the north, which seems to indicate a home in the eastern part of Central Asia, on the border of the great desert. The Karéns, too, do not appear to have advanced far below the hill country which they still hold, and into which they were penned by the tide of Burmese that rolled across the peninsula in later days. Their language, moreover, is peculiar in its more complete preservation of the tonic system characteristic of the Chinese dialects which probably originate from about the **The Burmese.** same region. The Burmese have similarly the tradition of a northern origin, though the latter may not have been so far to the west as Oudh. But leaving this part of their story out of the question, their movements after they entered Burma seem to point

---

* There are curious coincidences between the vocabulary of the Môn and that of the Múnda, a forest tribe of the Central Belt, but not enough to form the grounds for concluding that the race is an Indian offshoot. The Môn tradition only extends to the immigration and reception amongst them of a chief from across the water, and does not ascribe to him the paternity of the race.—J.A.B.

to their entry down the Khyíndwín River, and subsequent migration into the Irawádi valley. Here they established themselves for some generations and spread downwards till they met with the Mōn in the delta, or Pegu, who resisted their advance more or less successfully for a considerable period. Before the Burmese had established their power in more than a few isolated principalities, they were subjected to attacks from a kindred race hailing from the same direction as that by which they themselves had come. The Shâns, however, arrived in the peninsula by a route different from that followed by the Burmese, and established themselves to the east and north of the territory occupied by the latter. In several of their attacks they were more or less successful, and even obtained possession for a time of the Burmese capitals of Ava and Sagaing. But the main stream southwards was diverted from Burma by the course of the Mekong, which they followed to the sea, and thus, separated into two communities, the intercourse between which grew less and less. Later on, a branch of the greater Shâns, the Htai-Long, made its way into Assam, and colonised the upper portion of the Bráhmapútra valley, which they wrested from the local tribe of the Chutia. This detachment, again, led to stoppage of intercourse. The captured community, in the course of years, converted its conquerors to its language and religion, so that the connection of the Ahóm with the Shán race is now but historical. The main strength of the race is located in the hilly country to the north and east of Burma, in two political divisions, known as the Chinese and the Burmese States, and between the latter and the residents of the valley of the Irawádi there seems to be a fairly close intimacy. The comparatively numerous hill tribes of Burma differ from the corresponding class in India by being, in all probability, offshoots of the same race as the denizens of the plains below. They thus resemble rather the small remnants of the class to be found in the extreme south of the Indian peninsula. It is difficult in the present stage of our information regarding them to discriminate accurately between the various tribes in respect to race and origin; but, to speak generally, there seems to be a line drawn between those of the western hills and those of the northern. The former are called by the Burmese by the comprehensive name of Khyín, or wild man, just as in parts of the plains of India the forest tribes are known as Pahári, Mallé, and so on, meaning a hill man, or Wanwási, the forest people, irrespective of tribal distinctions. From Arrakan to Manipur, the whole tract is in the possession of various denominations of Khyíns and their neighbours to the north, the Taungthá or Kúki, all of whom seem to be no more than a link in the chain that once bound the Burmese to their kin in the Central Asian plateau. The second division of this class of people inhabit the hills all across the north of Burma, stretching a good way into Assam. The collective name for them is Kakhyin, within the Burmese limits, and Ching-pau, corrupted into Sing-phó, in Assam. But the latter title, meaning, as usual, the "men," is that which alone they recognise amongst themselves. It is not yet settled whether the Nága, and, perhaps also, the Míkir tribes, each occupying separate ranges of hills in Assam, should not be affiliated to the Kakhyín stock. Linguistically, the tribe about Bhamó, on the Upper Irawádi, seemed to be connected with the Karén rather than with the Burmese, so that possibly the race is an isolated portion of the body that swept down from the desert towards the south, which has been cut off from its fellows by the occupation of the intervening valleys. On the other hand, the Nága have a tradition of migration from the Manipur tract, which would connect them with the Khyín and Taungthá of the more southern ranges. It is as yet too early to consider any of these questions otherwise than as still open. Our occupation of the tracts held by the tribes is comparatively recent, and only a few of them have as yet been opened up by communications with the plains on either side. Much has been done by the military and civil officers employed there to collect information, and what has been published by them gives promise of valuable results, both from a philological and ethnological standpoint. For example, the Notes on the Nagas, by Mr. Davies, and that on the Kakhyins, by Mr. George, appended to the Assam and Burma Census Reports respectively, bring to light much that is entirely new regarding the dialects and the customs of these tribes, so that by the time the next census is taken what is now mere conjecture will have been proved or disproved, as the case may be, and the question of race will thus be settled.

The Shâns.

Hill tribes of Burma.

Khyín.

Kakhyín or Ching-pau.

Nága and Míkir.

The sketch that has been now given of the main ethnologic features of the population with which the census has had to deal will suffice as a general introduction to the separate branches of the subject. Where a mere outline covers so much ground, it can easily be conceived what an enormous field is open in India for the expert in such matters. This review has to be limited to the statistical side of the questions involved, that is, the relative strength and the local distribution of the numerous component elements of this heterogeneous community. There remain untouched the more interesting topics of customs and folk-lore, information on which forms the most valuable contribution that India can make to the study of ethnology in the present day. For, as has been pointed out of late more than once, speculations on these subjects have been too often based on the comparatively unverified accounts of customs observed amongst the lowest type of savage, whilst in India there lie ready to hand abundant instances of all sorts of custom, barbarous and otherwise, in every stage of transition or development. During the last 20 years some advantage has been taken of these stores, as can be judged from the works of Mr. Campbell in Bombay, Mr. Risley in Bengal, Messrs. Crooke and Kitts in the North-West Provinces, and the ethnological chapters, still unrivalled, in Mr. Ibbetson's work on the Panjáb.

In the light that it has been possible to throw on the general ethnographic position in India by the foregoing remarks, there can now be considered the distribution of the population according to, first, language; secondly, religion; and lastly, race, caste, or other social subdivision.

A.—The Distribution of the Population according to Mother Tongue.

Ἐστι δὲ πολλὰ ἔθνεα Ἰνδῶν, καὶ οὐκ ὁμοφωνά σφισι.—Herodotus.

Scope of the inquiry.

The committee which drew up the scheme of statistics for the Census of 1881 recommended that a return of mother tongue should be obtained, which might serve, in combination with another of birthplace, as an indication of race, in cases of foreigners and those of mixed blood. The results are to be found in the report on that census. For 1891, an expansion of the schedule was proposed, to allow for the separate entry of race in the cases in question, but it was thought advisable to retain the column for parent tongue, not so much for comparison with that of the preceding census as to serve as an aid to future philological inquiry. The off-hand inquisition, which alone is practicable at a census, is, admittedly, not much of a step in this direction, still, a step it is, and the object in view was to get, as in the case of occupation, a photograph, as it were, of the existing distribution of language in India, from the popular standpoint, which might, to some extent, guide the more leisurely and comprehensive researches of competent specialists. In accordance with this view, the instructions issued regarding language ran as follows :—

Enter here the language ordinarily spoken in the household of the parents, whether it be that of the place of enumeration or not.

General results.

The question put to those enumerated was, no doubt, simple enough, but even to the most optimistic Superintendent of census, this is no reason for expecting a straight answer. In accordance with the general tendency noted in the introductory portion of this chapter, the first impulse, in many cases, is to return the name of the caste as that of the language. For example, the potter gives "potterish," the tanner "tannerish," or the weaver "weaverish" as his mother tongue, especially if he be either a member of a large caste or a stranger to the locality where he is being enumerated. In other instances, the name of the District or State will be returned. The defect is no doubt on the right side, though the superfluous detail tends to complicate the process of compilation, and there are cases, too, where the tribal designation indicates a real distinction. But a further difficulty arises when the name mentioned happens to be not in accordance with the enumerator's notion of what is fit, or where official views on matters philologic may have filtered down to him. In that way a good deal of valuable information may have been lost in the course of the census; as where, for instance, a general term, such as Hindi, was substituted for some name locally recognised. But, on the whole, a very fair delimitation has been obtained of the various language fields of the country, and it can be seen how far the accepted scientific nomenclature is in accordance with the usage of the masses. So far, the attempt has been successful, if only as an aid towards getting a complete and scientifically conducted survey of the whole field of investigation. An operation of that description can only be conducted by a skilled philologist, who knows exactly the lines on which information should be collected, so that the results may be susceptible of comparison over the whole of India. It is hardly necessary to add that he must have a practical knowledge, too, of the country and its inhabitants, and should not work from books alone. Then, again, an inquiry of this sort should be commenced, if taken in hand at all, without further delay. In the plains, old linguistic landmarks are being rapidly obliterated by the advancing tide of popular instruction. The Hill tribes of the central belt are being brought more or more under the influence of a vernacular too far from their own in construction and dialectic variety to amalgamate with it, so, ultimately, the weaker must give way, and the tongue of the Korwa, like that of the Cornishman, will become a tradition in the mouth of a single tough old woman, and a debased vernacular from the plains will reign in its stead. Many a dialect, which may be, as Sainte Beuve puts it, "une ancienne qui a eu des malheurs, "ou bien une nouvelle qui n'a pas fait fortune," will ere long be beyond the reach of investigation, in the process of opening out the Hill tracts. It is not the intrinsic merits of these rude forms of speech that makes one regret their decay, but the links they afford between the tongues of localities far apart from each other. The languages of the eastern frontier are only now being brought under observation by the industry and experience of officers working independently. By the time the results of their labours have been collated, not only with each other, but with the corresponding out-turn of those working on the same lines in distant fields, who can tell how much that is of value in the dialects may not have fallen into disuse? For this task a single inquirer, and he a specialist, seems necessary, for the path of the philologist in India is so full of the pitfalls of incomplete data, false analogy, question-begging titles, and imposing speculation, that only a highly competent scholar can expect to thread his way by it successfully.

Tracts not enumerated by mother tongue.

As regards the geographical scope of the inquiry, it was thought that as in some of the less advanced Feudatory States the agency available for enumeration would be inferior in experience and supervising power to that of British Provinces, it was inadvisable to throw upon it the burden of collecting detail which would probably turn out untrustworthy. The schedule for use in such tracts was therefore limited to the more general points on which statistics were wanted for the Imperial returns, and along with the columns that were thus thrown overboard, went that relating to language. So far as this part of the inquiry is concerned, the loss is not great in Rajputána, where the dialect is fairly uniform. In Central India, however, there are wild tracts in which the Hill tribes use forms of speech that are said to be dying out, so it is a pity that the opportunity was lost of getting a record of them whilst they were still current. The omission of Kashmér is far more to be regretted, as there is much room for information about the dialects prevalent amongst the tribes inhabiting the outskirts of the State and its encircling mountains. Philology requires something wider regarding the archaic tongues of the recesses of the Hindu-Kúsh and the Thibet frontier than the indications, often meagre and inconsistent, of chance travellers. Then, again, we have to do without statistical information about the linguistic distribution of the population of the interesting State of Nipál. This is the more to be deplored as it is probable that there has been considerable change in the relative prevalence of the numerous dialects since Mr. Hodgson published his valuable studies on them many years ago. Finally, Manipur, where the census was duly taken, cannot be brought on to the returns, because, as stated in the introductory chapter, the records were destroyed in the deplorable outbreak of March 1891. A similar misfortune happened to those of the census of some of the small States on the frontier of Burma. This is a pity, as what was said in the preceding section of this chapter on the variety of tribe and race to be found in that part of the country, and our general ignorance of it at present, shows what a field lies open there to the philological investigator.

Margin notes: Rajputána and Central India. — Kashmér. — Nipál. — Manipur, &c.

Variety in the results.

The omissions above mentioned include a population of over 26 millions, but we still have left the return for 262 millions, or about 90 per cent. of the population dealt with at the census. The titles of the languages returned, as culled direct from the schedules, numbered many hundreds. Even after sifting out synonymous entries, and grouping under main heads dialectic variations which it was not thought worth while to distinguish in the general return, it has not been found practicable to reduce the latter to less than about 150 items, though some 50 may have been relegated to the provincial portion of the table. In the majority of the reports by the superintendents, the details are fully shown, and the final selection is embodied in Table X. of the Imperial series. But the main value of this information, as in the case of so much of the material collected at the census, lies in the variety of its component parts, not in their numerical bulk. India is, indeed, the happy hunting ground of the philologist, as it ought to become that of the ethnologist, for here we find language in every stage of its development; or, to put it otherwise, forms of speech are here current which appertain to nearly every one of the main classes recognised in philology. Its geographical isolation, almost as much as its political history, have contributed to this, as can be judged from the general sketch of the ethnography of the country above given. Especially in the case of language have the influences to which it has been subjected been peculiarly local and restrictive. A mountain range, a belt of dense, dank forest, the deep gorges of the Himálaya, so completely separate the respective inhabitants of their flanks that communities which have split off from the same tribe but three or four generations ago are often unable to understand each other's tongue. Politically, again, the spread of the more civilised along the plains and great river basins has driven a considerable portion of the older population to the shelter of the hills, which thus stand out like patches of cover in the midst of cultivation, affording a place of refuge to all the wild animals that have been expelled from the rest of the country. Nor was the immigration itself more favourable to the maintenance of the integrity of the languages thus introduced into the country. Setting on one side the Skythians, of whose tongue practically no trace remains, the only movement of importance, from our present standpoint, is that of the Arya. Now the progress of this community was not that of a united race or nation, but of various collections of clans which were disintegrated with great rapidity into small independent bodies. The growth of the community, therefore, numerically, seems to have been in advance of that of their civilisation, and by the latter alone can a language be spread uniformly through the mass of the population. Then, again, the intercourse with the darker race must have had its effect on the tongue of the immigrant, and its influence is likely to have been far greater than that which is usually assigned to it. But the establishment of a number of separate States and free admixture with the daughters of the land were not the only influences that helped to break up the unity of the language brought with them by the Arya. The firm establishment of that race in the plains was followed by a highly peculiar ecclesiastical development, which will be noticed in its place in the next section of this work. But as it had a direct influence on the linguistic tendencies of the community, its general features must be briefly described here, in anticipation of a more complete account. It began, then, with the elevation of the family priest into the member of a hierarchy, so that, from being the agent of the tribal or family patriarch, in the ceremonial of sacrifice, he became the controller of all social as well as religious ritual. The sacred formulæ became his monopoly instead of the special appanage of the chief, and it is not difficult to conceive how this change weakened the hold of the original language amongst the other classes. For the farther the latter spread over the country from the primary settlements, the more exaggerated was the value the priest was able to place on the exact knowledge of the sacred words, and the closer was the restriction of that knowledge to within the hieratic class that he was able to impose. There was accordingly no linguistic standard available to the masses, and, in the end, it was made penal for any but the upper classes to even listen to the recitation of the texts. A survival of this triumph is found in the present day, when in some parts of India it is the practice of the impure castes of the Bráhmanic system, who are the direct descendants of the helots mentioned above, to get an ecclesiastical sanction for their unions by performing their wedding within sight of, though at a distance from, the corresponding ceremony amongst the orthodox, who are being tied together with full rites. Until comparatively modern times, the prohibition in question amounted practically to the denial of instruction of any sort to the masses, since the greater part of the learning here, as in so many other countries in the corresponding stage of their development, consisted solely of expansions of various forms and uses of the ritualistic texts, known only to the ecclesiastical body.

Disintegrating influences on language in India.

Influence of an exclusive literary class.

Results of Buddhism on language distribution.

A temporary break in the continuity of this system was caused by the rise of Buddhism, a sect which repudiated the monopoly of the key of salvation by the priestly class, and was the means of diffusing a certain amount of instruction amongst the middle classes also. There were, about the time of this reformation, two main offshoots of the original tongue of the Arya current in India, the Mágadhi and the Sauráséni. It is an open question, perhaps, whether these divisions represented real distinctions in the vernacular, or were only the creations of the grammarians of a later period. At all events, the new faith was preached in the Mágadhi dialect of what is known as Prakrit, which was prevalent, it is said, in the east and north of the rallying point of Brahmanic civilisation, that is, the middle tracts of the Ganges and Jamna

Doáb. This dialect was thus carried by Buddhistic missionaries far into the Himálaya and Hindu-Kúsh, and it is possible that it may have been the foundation of those now current in the outlying portions of Kashmér and in Afghánistán. In the latter, however, the original tongue of the Paktæi of the Greek writers, the modern Pakhtwán, of Pathán, as they are termed in India, has been overlaid to a great extent by a veneer of Persian received from the west, so that its construction alone remains to indicate its Arya origin. In another direction, it penetrated into what is now Nipál, where the religion it served took so strong a hold of the higher valleys that in later years, when the Bráhmans, driven out of the plains by the Musalmán invasions, fled into this part of the country, they were able to make an impression only on the lower valley. Here, however, they found consolation of a worldly character, and started a colony of mixed blood, which became a power in the land, and in the whirligig of time managed to incorporate the ruling race into the orthodox pale, as being of the warrior caste of that system. The language introduced by them, with the invariable local modifications by the masses, became in time the court dialect, and obtained possession of the whole of the lower portion of the State.

Influence on southern Indian language.

It has already been stated that a somewhat similar process of incorporation was adopted in the southern part of India, though here, as there does not seem to have been any mixture of blood, at least at the time in question, the local dialect assimilated only the vocabulary required in ritual and in social ceremonies. It is not improbable that the intercourse with the south did not grow really close until the wave of Buddhistic monasticism spread over the peninsula, and crossed the straits into Ceylon. If this were the case, it would account for the peaceful nature of the conversion of the Tamil races, for the expulsion of Buddhism from India seems to have been a merely sectarian measure, and owed its completeness to the superior social attractions held out to the masses by the general lowering of the Brahmanical tenets to nearer the pre-Aryan level. The structure of the language remained unchanged, and the vocabulary received useful additions, as was the case in Burma, to which country the Buddhist missionaries proceeded after their success in Ceylon. The Hill tribes of the south followed the same course as their compatriots of the Central Belt, with whom they are physiologically and otherwise inextricably mixed.

Later foreign influences.

The subsequent political changes that have occurred in India consist of either the short and sharp impact of alien races from the more temperate regions of Asia, or movements of sections of the people of the country itself, neither leaving any marked imprint on the language of the community as a whole. We have, again, the occupation of the country by foreigners from a distance, who, whether they share the honour of philological Aryanism or not, are still farther from the parent stock than even the denizens of India at the present day, and come in such small numbers that even if they had the intention of permanent colonisation of India, instead of the reverse, they could only have an insignificant effect on the language of the places they thus favoured.

Musalmán influence.

On the invasions by land a short comment is all that is required in this section. The Musalmán dynasties imported with them a foreign element that settled in the country and administered its resources. They thus set their mark on the vocabulary, but left the rest of the language untouched. The dialect known as Úrdú, from the Túrki name for the citadel, or chief's camp, consists of the vernacular of the tract round the seat of government, interlarded with large numbers of Persian words, or of Arabic words received through the Persian.* There has been no introduction of the Persian construction, nor are the Arabic terms inflected according to their own rules, but they have to conform to the grammatic system of their host. Of Túrki there is but a very slight trace in the vocabulary and none elsewhere in the language. But some of the conquerors sought to propagate their creed amongst the people under their rule, and the results on the language of the latter is curiously varied. In the north, where the conversion has been on a large scale, the vernacular has suffered no change. For instance, in Báltistán or Little Thibet, where the population is Musalmán almost to a man, the language is the same as that of their Buddhistic neighbours in

* The account given by Bernier, of Dehli and Agra, which cities he describes as moving almost *en masse* when the Emperor shifted his quarters for the summer, has been quoted on page 46.

Ladákh, and only the special terms required by the new faith are introduced, and these are modified to suit the local pronunciation. In Kashmér, where again the masses are Musalmán, it is the same with the Áryan vernacular. No change, too, is noticed to follow conversion in the Panjáb. In its neighbour, Sindh, and in the Laccadiv Islands and with the Máppila of Malabár, it is the same, though for correspondence the Arabic character has been adopted with a few modifications. There are, similarly, certain well-known mercantile bodies in the west of India who are all Musalmán, but though they study Arabic for religious purposes, they have remained staunch to their native Gujaráthi or Kachhi in all besides. So, too, the converted cultivators of Gujaráth are undistinguishable in speech from their Hindu neighbours, and the colonies of probably Arab blood that have settled there, have adopted the same vernacular. On the other hand, there is all over India a numerous class of Musalmán converts, especially in the towns, comprising artisans, domestic servants, and those who largely swell the bodies of the police and the native army, who have not only abandoned their original caste titles, and, as already stated, have affiliated themselves to foreign tribes, but regard the dialect of Hindi known as Úrdú as the peculiar appanage of their faith, and adopt it, accordingly, with a strange and varied garnish of the local vernacular.

Sikh and Marátha influences.

As to the movements amongst the inhabitants of India itself, those of the Sikhs and the Maráthas may be briefly noticed. One of the results of the success of the Sikhs in emancipating themselves from Brahmanic orthodoxy was the erection of Panjábi to the position of a separate language. This was an accident, like the establishment of Vraj or the Dehli Hindí as the court language of the Moghals, with this difference, that the latter had already an established position, whilst the former cannot be even now said to have any recognised standard. Then, again, as the Panjáb tongue was so nearly related to its eastern rival, there was no occasion for an aggressive propaganda on the part of the new State across the Jamna, and the Lower Indus valley did not tempt occupation. In the case of the Maráthas, too, no attempt was necessary to extend their language. The object of their expeditions was mainly gain, where it was not to obtain possession of territory already inhabited by their own race under foreign domination. The invader took what was to hand, and left a sufficient establishment of his own adherents to ensure the due realisation of future benefits, when the time came. In the meantime he was called to distant duties, and when ousted in his turn from his new nest, naturally nothing would be found of a permanent character in his arrangements, still less in the effect of his occupation on the language of the conquered tract. For instance, in Orissa there is no trace of Maráthi in the language, though the Marátha domination lasted over 50 years. In Tanjore, the Deccani is a myth save in the precincts of the late court.

Influence of caste on the Indian languages.

This summary of what may be called the dynamics of Indian philology, can be fitly brought to a close with a few remarks on the results of the influences above described in the present day. The particularism that has been noted as the leading tendency pervading the atmosphere of the country, has prevented the evolution of anything in the nature of a *lingua-franca*, current throughout the continent. What is termed Hindustáni is generally the addition of a few conventional terminations to the local vocabulary, with the introduction of some Persian words. The language of the ruling race is known as a working means of communication to a few residents of the larger towns, and these belong to a very restricted class. The vernacular is apt to change, not only territorially, as it does from county to county in England, but by classes also. Then, again, the gap between the literate and the rest is so great that it can hardly be appreciated from the mere repetition of the fact that only six per cent. of the population is not wholly illiterate. It will be seen in a later chapter of this work that a very high proportion of this small number is found in three or four groups numerically insignificant, compared to the predominating interests of the country. Thus, it is not only the want of a standard in language that is felt, but the absence of root or depth. The expanding needs of the tongues in modern times are supplied not from the living language, but by reference to a classic, whose scope was for ages narrowed down to a few academic uses by a class desirous above all things to prevent its vulgarisation in the mouths of laymen. The diction of the literate bifurcates, accordingly, on all important points from that of the masses, on which it lies like an artificial stratum, stifling the natural capacities of the "voice of the people."

"Et sua mortifera est facundia."

On this point the words of the late Mr. Lowell are well worthy of consideration :—

"It is only from its roots in the living generation of men that a language can be reinforced with fresh vigour for its seed. What may be called a literate dialect grows ever more and more pedantic and foreign till it becomes at last as unfitting a vehicle for living thought as monkish Latin. That we should all be made to talk like books is the danger with which we are threatened by the universal schoolmaster, who does his best to enslave the minds and memories of his victims to what he esteems the best models of composition; that is to say, to the writers whose style is faultily correct and has no blood-warmth in it. No language that has faded into diction, none that cannot suck up the feeding juices secreted for it in the rich mother earth of common folk, can bring forth a sound and lusty book. . . . There is death in the dictionary, and where language is too strictly limited by convention, the ground for expression to grow in is limited also, and we get a "potted" literature, Chinese dwarfs instead of healthy trees. . . . The schoolmaster has been busy starching our language and smoothing it flat with the mangle of supposed authority."

Mongoloid influences.

So far as to the languages of India proper. The description of the remaining linguistic divisions will occupy but a short space. In the Himálaya and the high lands that they support to the north, the Buddhistic propaganda secured a certain stability of language, by the medium of monastic institutions, but the basis of the tongues were unaltered. So, too, in Burma, where the same system, through its teaching agency, has given a power to the language of the majority that seems to enable it to absorb gradually most of the local distinctions of dialect prevalent amongst the minor tribes. The gap between the Burmese races and those of the central Himálaya is difficult to fill from the material to be found in the Delta, but some connection no doubt there was in times long past. The general course of the population of Assam has been already sufficiently described, and the tribal languages thus introduced seem to have remained undisturbed in the hills first occupied. On the descent of a community to the valley, however, freedom of communication seems to have been fatal. The Kóchh, for instance, has given place to Bengáli; the Ahóm substituted for their own language that of their conquest, the Chutia, and now the few relics of the former language can hardly be deciphered, even by the tribal priests, and are used only on great occasions, such as for rain in time of drought. The Chutia, in turn, have fallen before the Assamese of the valley, and in their case, too, the original tongue is known only to a few priests and exorcists. But in the Hill tracts agglutination is left to work out its own reformation.

Linguistic classification.

Reviewing the whole position from a philological standpoint, it will be seen that India is hemmed in on the north and east by forms of speech of what is known as the Tonic class; in some parts, too, in the agglutinative stage. The central belt of hills has been left to forest tribes using an atonic form, rudely agglutinative; and the south of the peninsula is almost entirely Dravidian in language, that is, the agglutination has reached a stage in which it is scarcely distinguishable from the Inflectional or Synthetic class. This last forms the basis of the language of the whole of the northern plains and the base of the Himalaya, with the Gangetic delta, the whole course of the Indus and the upper coasts of the peninsula, both east and west. It stretches, too, beyond the British frontier towards the west. The influence of the displaced Dravidian, however, is traceable throughout in the degradation of both construction and vocabulary from the Arya original, but in the highest stage of the latter, that is, in the region round its traditional centre, it is the least inflectional, or the most analytic, of all this class, approaching the western languages of Europe in its tendency in this direction. It meets in this stage the lagging Hill dialects above-mentioned; and what with the opening out of the country by roads and railways, the administration of the forests on the modern economic system, and the reluctant advance of the village schoolmaster, even the wildest of those tribes are being brought within touch of the outside world. Means of livelihood are being disclosed to them of which a few years ago they never dreamed, and each step forward is accompanied by the acquisition of something fresh in the way of vocabulary, even if the adventurer does not pick up an entirely new dialect, with which the philologist of the future will have to wrestle, even as his predecessors strove with the mongrels of their day.

The general classification of the language return is as shown in the following table:—

TABLE A.—Showing the GENERAL LINGUISTIC DISTRIBUTION of 10,000 of the POPULATION.

Language and Class.	Number per 10,000.
A. Indic-Aryan	**7,460**
Hindi	3,269
Bengáli	1,578
Maráthi	721
Panjábi	676
Gujaráthi	405
Úriya	344
Úrdú	140
Sindhí	99
Western Pahári	58
Assamese	55
Central Pahári	44
Márwádi	44
Kachhi	17
Halabi	6
Kashméri	1
Goanese, &c.	1
Eastern Pahári	1
Minor Languages	1
B. Dravidian	**2,021**
Telugu	759
Tamil	581
Kanarese	371
Malayálam	207
Gónd	53
Túlú	19
Oráon	14
Kandh	12
Kodagu	2
Mal-Pahádia	1
Bráhui	1
Minor Languages	1
C. Kolárian	**113**
Santhál	65
Múndá and Kól	25
Kórwá and Kúr	7
Bhíl	6
Sáwara	4
Kharria	3
Baiga, Bhinja, &c.	2
Gadaba	1
D. Gipsy Dialects	**15**
E. Khási Dialects	**7**
F. Thibeto-Burman	**278**
Burmese	212
Arakanese	14
Kachári	8
Nipáli dialects	7
Gáro	6
Tippera	5
Khyín	5
Nága dialects	4
Míkir	4
Méch	4
F. Thibeto-Burman—*cont.*	
Kathé (*Manipuri*)	3
Miri-Abor	1
Kúki	1
Lálúng	1
Lúshai	1
Thibetan	1
Minor Languages	1
G. Môn-Annam	**9**
Môn (*Talaing*)	9
H. Shán (Tái)	**7**
Shán (*unspecified*)	7
J. Malayan	—
K. Sinitic	**27**
Karén	26
Chinese	1
L. Japanese	—
M. Eránic-Aryan	**51**
Pakhtú	41
Balóch	9
Persian	1
N. Semitic	**2**
Arabic	2
O. Turánic (*Úgrian*)	—
P. European-Aryan	**9**
English	9
Q. Basque }	
Hamitic }	1
Not distinguishable or not returned }	

First of all come the tongues which are traceable to an origin amongst the immigrants that have been termed the Árya, which are returned by about three-fourths of the population. Secondly, in numerical sequence, though *longo intervallo*, comes the Southern or Dravidian group, in which are included the languages of the Hill tribes of the central ranges which form the northern frontier of the Deccan on the eastern side. They are almost isolated geographically from their comrades, and much intermixed with the next class. The northern but entirely separate language, Bráhui, since it has been admitted to be morphologically of the south, has also been included, though with considerable diffidence. Sinhalese, too, and its offshoot Máhl, or the tongue returned by the inhabitants of the lonely little island of Minikoi, midway between the Laccadiv and the Máldiv groups, have been similarly treated, swelling the total to about one-fifth of the population. The small remains of an older type of language, restricted to the tribes of the hill tracts of Western Bengal and Central India, with a branch or two running west and south has been denominated Kolarian, though there are no doubt good objections to that name. It has been adopted, however, by so many distinguished writers on Indian philology and ethnology that though it may be wrong it is quite intelligible. The whole group bears a proportion of but a trifle over 1 per cent. of the total, and contains only two items of any considerable prevalence. Aryan and Dravidian groups. Kolarian group.

There are two groups statistically insignificant, but having special interest of their own in other ways. The first is the tongue of the inhabitants of the Khásia and Jaintia Hills, between the two main valleys of Assam. It has not been affiliated to any of the surrounding languages, whether of the Áryan or the Tonic families. Till recently it was unwritten, but now, owing to the study and enterprise of the Welsh missionaries, the Roman character has been generally adopted. The whole community, however, with its three dialects, only numbers about 178,000 souls. The second of these groups is that of the many tongues spoken by the wandering or Gipsy* tribes of the plains of India, and numbers just over 400,000. It is out of the question to distribute these languages amongst those having fixed dialects, as their character changes with the locality most favoured by the tribe using them, and, whilst retaining a backbone peculiar to itself, freely assimilates the local vocabulary and pronunciation. The most prevalent of these dialects is that of the Brinjáras or Lambáni, the carriers of Upper and Central India, which is based on a sub-Himalayan Hindi vernacular. The tribe, however, is found as far south as the Madras table-land, and it is not improbable that the Lambáni of the Deccan could hardly make himself understood by the corresponding caste farther north. Again, the earth-workers called Od or Waddar, carry a language of their own from Pesháwar to the sea, using a vocabulary less and less Dravidian as the tribe frequents tracts farther away from the East Deccan, from whence it probably originated. More difficult still, as regards classification, are the dialects used by the less reputable tribes of wanderers such as the nominal Hindi of the thieving and mat-weaving castes of Hindustán, and the Telugu and Maráthi of the acrobats and pickpockets of the Deccan. All these can doubtless be generally divided into degraded forms of either Hindi or Telugu; but in doing so we have to disregard the local characteristics just mentioned, so they have all been taken under a heading of their own, namely, Gipsy dialects. Khási, and the gipsy dialects.

We pass now into the Tonic zone of language, which comprises in all its branches just over 3 per cent. of the population. As in the case of the regions of India linguistically Áryan, this proportion would be higher if the whole of the races using language of this formation had been brought under enumeration. But a large tract on the borders of Burma and Assam had to be omitted from the census, owing partly to the unsettled state of the tribes just included within our territory, and partly to the difficulty of getting competent enumerators for a population not only entirely illiterate, but using a language in most parts which has never been reduced to writing. In tabulating the information obtained, it has been found convenient to group this otherwise unwieldly class by geographical position, beginning with Thibet, and working eastwards through Assam down into Burma, where the largest of the component units are found. Here the main group, called in the return the Thibeto-Burman, is touched by three smaller groups of a kindred class, though differing Thibeto-Burman groups.

* The term Gipsy is here used conventionally, as the equivalent of vagrant. The only class to which it now applies in its European signification is that mentioned at the end of this paragraph, the subdivisions of which are very numerous.

enough to be separately shown. These have been already mentioned as the Tai or Shán, the Môn, and the Karén. The two first appear in the tables to a very small extent compared to the total number of the races by whom they are spoken. The Tai group, for instance, includes a small colony or two in East Assam, and a few more representatives in Burma, but the bulk of the Shána are found either in the border States, where language was not returned, or in the neighbouring kingdom of Siam. The Môn language, too, is returned only in Lower Burma, and in an isolated tract occupied by the Palaung on the frontier of Upper Burma; but the greater portion of the Môn race lies in Anam and Cambodia, or Khmér. The Karéns are chiefly confined to Lower Burma, and their language has been classed with the Chinese, to which, according to the best authorities that have been consulted, it can be most safely affiliated. The Japanese language is hardly represented. The Malay class is chiefly interesting, from an Indian point of view, on account of the curious group of sea-gipsies called Salôn, inhabiting the Mergui Archipelago in the south of Tenasserim. The Nikobári was returned by one individual only and as its correct allocation has been yet satisfactorily settled, its single representative has been allowed to bring up the rear of the Burman group, though possibly he would be more congenially mated with the Malays.

Minor Tonic groups.

Other groups of language.

On the same grounds as those on which Chinese has been grouped with Karén, though the bulk of those who use it are foreign to India, this survey may include the Eránic section of the Arya language, which is represented by a considerable number of border tribes on the north-west; and the Semitic, because Aden shows the majority of its small population to be speakers of Arabic. The Skythic or Turanic group is a very small one in the return, and the Hamitic, like Arabic, is almost confined to Aden, where the settlers or sojourners from the opposite coast are relatively numerous. As for the European element, all that need be said is that the whole tale is about 246,000 persons, of whom 238,000 return English. To conclude the list, one person returned Basque as his parent tongue.

The statistics of language.

The languages have now to be reviewed in detail. It is as well to begin within the largest group, which is also the most advanced, namely, the Indic-Aryan, or the Inflectional or Synthetic class. This has been subdivided into three geographical sections, the northern, the western, and the eastern. The first is by far the largest, as it includes Hindí, which predominates throughout Hindustán and Bihár, two of the most thickly peopled tracts in India. This title is admittedly a comprehensive one, and includes all the varieties of Aryan speech between the Jamna and Rajmahál. It has thus absorbed such distinctions as *Vraj*, *Baiswári*, and *Bhojpúri*, as well as *Maithili* and other Bihár varieties of

Language.	Population returning it.
Hindi	85,675,373
Western Pahári	1,523,249
Central*	1,153,233
Eastern	24,262
Panjábi	17,724,610
Kashméri	29,276
Hindu-Kúsh dialects	17
Total, Northern Group	**106,130,020**

* Garhwáli, 647,739; Kumaoni, 505,494.

Hindi.

Hindi. The same is the case in the south and west of Hindustán, where *Búndéli*, *Bághéli*, *Rángadi*, and *Nimádi* were returned by but a small fraction of the persons known to use a local variety of the standard language. On the other hand, *Lária*, the last form of Hindi found in the south-east, was returned pretty completely. A want of detail of this sort is often attributable to the absence of literature in those tongues, a fact which led to the enumerator's hesitation to give them official recognition in a formal document, such as he considered the schedule to be. It is noticeable, too, that most of the returns of dialect were made by persons not belonging to the place where they were enumerated, so the census agents, having foreigners to deal with, thought it most prudent to accept the term dictated to them rather than betray their ignorance by contraverting its use. Then, again, as far as Hindustán proper is concerned, that is, the present North-West Provinces and Oudh, the language of the plains is officially "Hindustáni," so it is not likely that any attempt would be made through the medium of the census to contravene this authoritative decision.* On all these considerations, therefore, all such sporadic entries have been absorbed into the general title, lest the separate recognition of such small and scattered numbers should give a misleading notion of the actual prevalence

* It is a question, too, whether the distinctions are recognised at all, otherwise than by grammarians.

of the dialects in question. It should be pointed out, too, that west of the Jamna, the boundary between Hindi, Panjábi, and Marwádi is scarcely distinguishable; and similarly, on the east, the tongue of North Bihár becomes gradually more and more Bengali in construction as well as vocabulary and pronunciation. In South-West Bengal, too, Hindi is returned by many of the Hill tribes, who have abandoned their own tongue in favour of a very vulgarised form of the language of the plains. The variety of dialect prevailing in the submontane tract and lower valleys of the Himálayas west of Nipál requires a few words of explanation. The term "Pahári," or Hill tongue, has been taken as distinctive of the whole body; but as the dialects are by no means uniform in detail, the tables show them in three sections, the Western or Panjáb, the Central, including Garhwáli and Kumaoni, and the Eastern, which is practically equivalent to the Nipáli dialect of the south-western portion of that State. The title of Nipáli is not available for this last, as it has been appropriated by the regiments of Nipál soldiers collectively known as Gúrkhas, whose language is very largely of the Thibetan type. At the same time it is said that owing to the adoption by the ruling families of the Khas or Parbatia dialect, which, as has been already stated, is based on Hindí, there is a tendency on the part of the tribes of the higher valleys to abandon their own tongue as they enter more intimately into the military system of the State. But until Nipál is brought under the census operations we are without clear information on this point. As regards the territorial distribution of Hindí, it may be observed from the table on page 364 of Vol. I. of the Returns that though this language was returned in every one of the main divisions of India, out of the 85½ millions of *soi disant* Hindi-speakers, 77 millions were enumerated in Hindustán, Bihár, and the Panjáb, and seven millions more in the Central Provinces. **Pahári.**

In connection with the statistics of Hindi, a few remarks are needed about the Urdú form of that language. As to Upper India, it may be broadly stated that no line can be drawn between the vernacular and the Persianised speech of the larger towns, where, as before observed, the foreign element has been assimilated to the local construction. South of the Vindhya range, in places where the Musalman element is in a considerable minority, and has been recruited in such a way that the converted communities do not retain their original *status*, there is in use a distinctive dialect, based on the Dehli dialect, largely tempered with vernacular words. This was returned as Musalmáni or Deccani, and it has been taken to be the equivalent in the south of the Urdú, or *lingua franca* of the foreign settlers in the north. It must be distinctly understood, therefore, that the 3¼ millions entered under this designation by no means represent the relative prevalence of the diction of the Bágh-o-bahár and the Prém Ságar. **Urdú.**

Next in order of the Northern group comes Panjábi, which differs from Hindi rather in vocabulary and pronunciation than in any other particular. It owes its position as an independent language more to political causes than anything else, and throughout the tract of its adoption shows variety every few miles. The three main branches are the south-western, called Jatki or Multáni, the Dógri and the Pahári. The first is returned by 1¾ million persons, all from the plains of the Indus and the borders of Sindh.* The second is the lower hill dialect of Jammu westward, so it is represented more in the Kashmér State than in our returns, and is, moreover, lapsing into Panjábi, where it meets the tongue of the plains. The third, which has been noticed above, shows over 1½ millions of representatives. In the south of the province the language is mixed with Bágri, here classed with Marwádi though in the eastern districts the latter element is very weak. Curiously enough in the west there is no trace of Sindhi. Owing mainly to the number of recruits furnished to the native army by this province, Panjábi is found represented widely over India and Burma, but as a vernacular it is confined to the land of the Five Rivers. **Panjábi.**

Of the other languages in this group there is little to say. Kashméri, the most interesting and inportant, has strayed but a short way out of its native valley, and is spoken chiefly by the colonies of weavers and carpenters in the Panjáb, and by wandering shawl-merchants elsewhere. The falling off since the last census is probably due to the temporary immigration in 1879 of people then allowed for the first time to **Kashméri and the Hindu-Kús dialects.**

---

* The tongue of the Jats, *Getæ* (*Xanthii*), through whom we derive probably our words Egyptian, Gipsy, Gitano, as it was a colony of this tribe which was first transported from Western India to Persia and Asia Minor, and spread thence into the Lower Empire and through Rúmelia up the Danube.

leave their country under the pressure of famine, and who have now returned. The small settlement of Kashméri in the North-West Provinces is a permanent one, consisting apparently of the Hindu or literate class, not of Musalman artisans. There are but few instances in the census record of the languages of the Hindu-Kúsh. In the Panjáb a few families of Ghilghit, Chitrál, and even of Káfiristán and Húnza, or Borishka, origin were found, but the bulk of the population of those tracts was altogether outside the census. There is no need, therefore, to enter into the discussion of the correct nomenclature or classification of this group of little known but philologically interesting languages.

The Western group includes nearly $33\frac{3}{4}$ millions. Taking the languages in their geographical order, Sindhi comes first. Philologically, it is a more backward language than Hindi, having retained far more of the inflections it derives from its Sanskrit parentage. On the other hand, owing to its frontier position, it has borrowed freely from the languages of the Persian Gulf. Indeed, since the country has passed under British rule, a modification of the Arabic character has been adopted in place of the local combinations of debased Devanágari letters. These last, both here and in parts of the Panjáb, only serve to record personal memoranda or accounts, and can hardly be called a means of correspondence, since one of the main objects of the scribe is to keep his production legible by no one but himself.

Language.	Population returning it.
Sindhi	2,592,341
Kachi	439,697
Márwádi	1,147,480
Gujaráthi*	10,619,789
Marátbi†	18,892,875
Goanese, &c.	37,738
Total, Western Group	**32,729,920**

*Patnuli, 77,534. †Konkani, 314,435.

Sindhí. Sindhi is not at all a widely spread language, and most of those speaking it beyond the province are to be found in the two States of Kachh and Baháwalpur, contiguous to Sindh, where the proportion of the sexes amongst those returning it shows that the migration is only the ordinary interchange of children in marriage between adjacent villages. Like the Kashmér trader, however, the merchant of Sindh is met with in most of the large towns of India, and, if a census were taken of Russia, he would be found in the far-off markets of Bokhára and Samarkand, and even in Nizhni-Novgorod, or, rather, he would have been so found at the time of the Indian census, for there is a report that this race has since received notice to quit the territory of the white Tsar.

Kachhi. The connection between Kachhi and Sindhi is very close, and were it not that the parent State of the former is politically and geographically more in touch with Gujaráth than with Sindh, it would be hard to say that Kachhi was not still a dialect of the latter. In the present day, however, the vernacular is receiving a strong tinge from its southern neighbour. As Kachhi is the home of a large body of the most enterprising merchants of Western India, it is not surprising to find their language returned from nearly all parts of the country.

Márwádi. The case of Márwádi, again, is one in which it is hard to say whether a distinction should be drawn, as with Panjábi, or whether the language thus returned should not be absorbed, like Búndéli, Maithili, and so on, into the general term Hindí. We have not, however, the advantage of seeing from the census of Márwár what is the opinion of the people of that State and Bikanér, or rather, that of their enumerators, on this question. At any rate, Márwádi approaches very near Gujaráthi as the latter is spoken on the south border of Rájputána; so it is taken as forming a link between Gujaráthi and Hindí. Like Sindhi and Panjábi, when written by Hindus, Márwádi has no graphic merits, and several good old tales are current as to the consequences of extending its use to correspondence, a purpose for which it was never intended. As regards its local prevalence, it is superfluous to state here that Márwádi is a widely spread tongue. As we have seen in the second chapter of this work, the thrifty denizen of the sands of Western and Northern Rájputána has found his way to fortune all over India, from the petty grocer's shop in a Deccan village to the most extensive banking and broking connection in the commercial capitals of both East and West India. The census returns show us Márwádi as a vernacular only in the tracts immediately adjacent to Rájputána, but it appears largely in Berar, where the race has established itself in the villages and in connection with the cotton trade, and also in Bombay and the Central Provinces, for much the same reason, with additional attraction in the case of the former, of the grand field of speculation in rain, grain and silver afforded by the circumstances of the chief town. Relatively to the population, and the distance of the region from their native land, the Márwádi is strong in Assam, but Burma is a country which he has not yet begun to tap. To a peaceful man, whose inclination is to start life in a village remote from competitors, commercial existence in rural Burma is too full of the unexpected to be palatable.

Gujaráthi, in like manner, has become the commercial language of Western India. But as it is also the vernacular of a considerable area of British territory as well as of Baroda and many of the States connected with the Bombay Presidency, it appears in the returns to be nearly ten times as prevalent as Márwádi. In reality, it may be about thrice as numerously represented, if the whole country be taken into account. Gujaráthi is one of the main offshoots of the Prakrit of Northern India, and differs little, save in detail and its more complex inflection, from vernacular Hindi. It is almost free from dialect, but as it is the language of commerce, it acquires modifications according to the class using it. For example, the Musalmán trader combines it with Kachi, and the Parsis, who have abandoned their original tongue in favour of it, have engrafted certain peculiarities of their own. One very remarkable offshoot of Gujaráthi is found in the Patnúli or Sauráshtri dialect of the silk weavers of the Deccan and Madras. The migrations of this class have not been clearly traced, but probably it was first brought above the Gháts through one of the many local courts of old time in the Deccan.* The descendants of the original silk weavers are now found exercising the same trade in Mysore, the Deccan, and in quite the south of the peninsula. The dialect they use is peculiar to themselves, and is not current amongst them when dealing with other communities, though it has taken the colour of the countries through which the caste has passed, and is at present mainly Telugu, whereby it has lost its northern twang. The reason for this segregation may be found, perhaps, in the fact that a class of this sort, especially when engaged in a lucrative industry, raises its demands for social recognition as it recedes farther from its place of origin. We thus find the Sauráshtri weaver of the south employing priests of his own caste, who claim Brahmanical honours and ignore connection with a region where silk-weavers are not in such a high position. This leads them to neglect or depreciate their former tongue. There are, nevertheless, over 77,000 Patnúli in the Madras province who still return their language as of yore. In addition to the extension given to the Gujaráthi language by traders and artisans, there has been a considerable movement up the Tápti valley, in the shape of agricultural colonists, from the plains below, and Sindh, too, has received its share from across the lower desert. Then, too, there is the well-known class of domestic servants, called Sùratis, who were returned in most provinces in India. Gujaráthi.

Maráthi is the chief language in the Western group. In structure and vocabulary it is remarkable for its adherence to the later Sanskrit dialects of North India, and may be called particularly Brahmanic in all its elements. It has suffered less change than the rest of its companions, and retains much of the complexity of grammatical form that has been sloughed off by Hindi and Gujaráthi. The Bráhmans of Western India have for generations borne a high reputation for scholarship, and as the region under their influence was late in receiving the shock of Musalmán invasion, and more or less successful in repelling it, the Hindu character of the language has been well maintained, whilst its fertility has enabled it to develop without the expedient of continually taking to itself fresh grafts from the Sanskrit. It is what some writers have called a "playful" tongue, abounding in jingles and alliterations, such as "ándhala-pángala," a blind and lame man; "dagad-gigad," a stone; "lagbag," close by, and "jat-pat," quickly. Foreign words, too, are not respected, for we find "bandhuk-enduk," a gun; "pádri-widri," a missionary; "ardóshi-pardóshi," the neighbours, and so on. The Maráthas have named their hill-forts and any villages that have anything striking about their position on the same principle, and their tongue has struck out, it is said, more diminutives and secondary words than any other of the Prakritic derivatives. Setting aside the variety of pronunciation, Maráthi is singularly uniform throughout the Deccan. There are, it is true, certain entries Maráthi.

* Hofrath Dr. Bühler has directed my attention, since this was first written, to the Gupta Inscription, translated at page 79, vol. iii., of the *Corpus Inscriptionum*. In this, the colony of silk weavers which immigrated to Dasápur (Mandesúr) from Central and Southern Gujaráth, are praised for their industry and piety; the latter being shown by the erection of a temple to the Sun in the time of Kumára Gúpta.—J.A.B.

from the north of that tract giving Ahiráni as a distinct language, but this is the result of caste, not linguistic, difference. It may be recollected that the later Prakrit grammarians applied the ancient name Apabhransha specially to the language of the Ábhira or Ahír, the cattle-grazing communities of the north-western plains, and there has always been some jealousy between the agricultural classes and those of nomad stock who settle down amongst them at a later period. A real distinction is drawn, however, on the other hand, between the Maráthi of the table-land and that of the Konkan, or the strip of country between the coast and the foot of the Ghâts. As far south of Goa this distinction is not recognised, except amongst a small community of native Christians, who entered that fold under the auspices of Portuguese missionaries, and have adopted the language of their instructors from Goa; for in the latter territory there is a decidedly Portuguese element in the vernacular, due probably to the discouragement of native studies and to the destruction of the records in the vernacular when the western Christians first occupied the coast and took in hand the propagation of their religion. The basis of the language, however, is distinctly Maráthi. Farther south, the foreign element changes to Kanarese, which is more perceptible as we approach Mangalore, where Konkani gives way to pure Kanarese and to Túlú. But wherever Konkani is the vernacular it may be held to be a variety of Maráthi. The language spoken by the Christian natives of Goa, who are found nearly all over British India, is usually given as Goanese, but so many have returned it as Portuguese that to avoid misconception the two have been combined, and are placed after Maráthi in the Indic, not the European, section of the tables. The return of birthplace shows that only 168 persons were born in Portugal, and whatever may be the language used by the class in question in their correspondence, the proportion of Portuguese in the spoken dialect is insignificant. The geographical distribution of Maráthi remains to be noticed. Its covers a wide area, including, as it does, the whole of the North Deccan plateau, the Konkan coast, Berár, the western portion of the Central Provinces, and the greater part of the western districts of the Nizam's dominions. It is met above the Ghâts by Kanarese in the south and Telugu in the south-east. On the coast, as just stated, it merges through Konkani into Kanarese or Túlú. In the north, it meets Hindí and Gujaráthi, without mixing with either. Settlements of Maráthas are to be found in Mysore, and there is the small Tanjore colony in the south of Madras; but, as a rule, the language is not found much in tracts where it is not the vernacular. In Baroda, for instance, which is a Marátha State, there are only about 52,000 Maráthi-speakers, mostly confined to the south division of the State, where there is a forest tract in which it is the vernacular, and to the troops and retinues of the Gaikwár and his officials. In other parts of the west and centre of India, those who return this language are chiefly in the native regiments, or engaged on railways or as clerks, and in the north as priests.

Halabi. Crossing India from the Deccan, only one Aryan language is met before we enter the Eastern group of that family. This is the Halabi, which is prevalent only in the south-eastern portions of the Central Provinces and the tracts adjacent thereto. It has been grouped with the eastern Aryan tongues from its position, although in structure and vocabulary it is more akin to Hindi. In fact, it seems doubtful if it is not mainly a dialect of the latter adopted by the Hill men on coming into contact with others from the plains, like the cases mentioned above in connection with the Gangetic valley. On the other hand, it is surrounded by Dravidian Hill languages, and the people by whom it is spoken are not reputed to have made such an advance in civilisation as would lead to the improvement of their former language. Their whole strength is only 143,000 souls.

Language.	Population returning it.
Halabi	143,720
Uriya	9,010,957
Bengáli	41,343,672
Assamese	1,435,820
Total, Eastern Group	51,934,169

Uriya. The Eastern group proper begins with Úriya or Útkali, the least advanced of the Prakritic tongues. The country of its adoption is difficult of access, and the hilly tracts that protect it on the west bear an evil name for air and water, the two elements of comfort in a residence that a native of India first values. They have been left, accordingly, in the possession of a collection of tribes of the race either Dravidian or Kolarian. The language of the Hindu population of Orissa, therefore, has retained a good deal of its archaic form and vocabulary. It is also peculiarly free from dialectic variation. In addition to geographical isolation, Úriya has the drawback of a remarkably complicated and awkward character, attributed by several good authorities to the use of strips of the leaf of the Palmyra (*borassus flabelliformis*) as writing material, on which the local scribe performs with a sharp steel stylus, in place of the reed pen common to most of Áryan India. Thus the horizontal line which keeps together the Devanágari characters and their immediate descendants is here out of the question, as it would split the leaf along its fibre, so the top stroke is omitted. Again, it appears that in writing, the style is worked on the left thumb as a fulcrum, a process which imparts a circular form to the results. Mr. Beames, from whose work the above explanation has been taken, adds, "Perhaps the above account may not "seem very convincing to European readers, but no one who has ever seen an Úriya "working away with both hands at his style and strip will question the accuracy of "the assertion, and though the fact may not be of much value, I may add that the "native explanation of the origin of their alphabet agrees with this." It should be mentioned in confirmation of the above that the same explanation has been adopted by Dr. Caldwell, the chief authority on Dravidian language, the southern forms of which are always written on the same material as Uriya. Mr. Beames states also that when he wrote in 1871, the extension of the use of paper was leading to the abandonment of the round top to the Uriya letters; but judging from the census returns, the fashion is certainly dying hard. The literature of Orissa is neither extensive nor valuable, except as showing the little change the language has undergone in the last few centuries. As to the geographical prevalence of Úriya, it appears that this tongue is practically confined to the tract from which it takes its name and the bordering districts and States of Madras and the Central Provinces. Its representatives found at the time of the census elsewhere in India belonged probably to the class of palki-bearers and domestic servants, for which Orissa and the north-east coast generally are famous.

Bengáli. Bengáli is the largest in point of numbers in this group, and is surpassed in this respect by Hindí alone. Though it has no distinct dialects, it resembles Panjábi in having no standard, so that it varies from place to place more probably than any other of the Aryan tongues. It is true that some years ago an attempt was made to degrade Úriya into a dialect of Bengáli, so as to exclude it from schools and public offices; but fortunately history and philology prevailed over political ambition, and the elder language has held its own against its hybrid sister. For Bengáli has no doubt been unfortunate in the circumstances that have attended its development. The latest of all the Prakrit offshoots to be recognised as a language at all, it dates in that capacity only from the decay of the Dehli empire. Bengal, too, is the province of all others in which there is the widest gap between the small literary castes and the masses of the people. One of the results is that the vernacular has been split into two sections; first, the tongue of the people at large, which, as remarked above, changes every few miles; secondly, the literary dialect, known only through the press, and not intelligible to those who do not also know Sanskrit. The latter form is the product of what may be called the revival of learning in Eastern India, consequent upon the settlement of the British on the Hughli. The vernacular was then found rude and meagre, owing to the absence of scholarship and the general neglect of the country during the Moghal rule. Instead of strengthening the existing web from the same material, every effort was made in Calcutta, then the only seat of instruction, to embroider upon the feeble old frame a grotesque and elaborate pattern in Sanskrit, and to pilfer from that tongue whatever in the way of vocabulary and construction the learned considered necessary to satisfy the increasing demands of modern intercourse. He who trusts to the charity of others, says Swift, will always be poor; so Bengáli, as a vernacular, has been stunted in its growth by this process of cramming with a class of food it is unable to assimilate. The simile used by Mr. Beames is a good one. He likens Bengáli to an overgrown child tied to its mother's apron-string, and always looking to her for help, when it ought to be supporting itself. For instance, when the instructions for filling up the census schedule had to be translated into the vernacular for use in this province, the local Superintendent of the operations, a civil servant of much experience of men and cities, obtained versions, not from the men of light and leading in the capital, but from officers administering districts, who knew what the lieges can and will understand. A good working translation was thus obtained, which, when read over to a Calcutta scholar, no doubt made him stare and gasp, and mourn over the opportunity thus lost of giving the widest possible dissemination of culture in style. It is to be feared that not Bengáli alone is passing into the hands of official scholarship, though this language is probably the least unwilling captive. Bengáli, in whatever form it may be, is spread all over the southern valley of Assam, which was till 20 years ago a part of the province of Bengal. In Arrakan, too, this language has made some way, but elsewhere it is confined to a few colonies, at religious centres, and to persons employed in offices of Government or the railway companies, both of which look largely to Bengal for their supply of clerical labour.

Assamese. Assamese, which concludes the list of Áryan vernaculars, has had, like Úriya, the experience of resisting the attempt of the ambitious Bengáli to reduce it to a patois, and thus open a wider field of employment to the studious youth of the Lower Provinces; and, like Úriya, too, Assamese has been hitherto successful.* Possibly the political separation of the province from Bengal may have helped on the declaration of independence, for the tongue of the eastern and northern districts of Bengal bears scarcely greater resemblance than Assamese to the euphuistic speech of Calcutta and Nadiya. Assamese is hardly found out of its native valley and the immediate neighbourhood.

Sanskrit. In bringing to a close this review of the Aryan tongues of India, the fact should be mentioned that 308 persons returned the language habitually spoken in their parents' household as Sanskrit. This survival of 25 centuries is a thousand less than the corresponding tale in the last census returns; still it is hardly expected that the ladies, at all events, of the households in question spoke in a classical language. The truth seems to be that in the south of India the term *Nágaram* is used by the priestly families of the Gujaráthi silk weavers to denote their divergence from the ordinary language of their caste, whilst in the rest of the country, the entries may be set down to schoolboys or undergraduates studying the rudiments of the ancient tongue of their faith.

In dealing with the Dravidian section of the subject, two groups have been formed. The first or southern covers nearly the whole field occupied by this class of languages, but the balance, which is here called the northern, comprises tribal forms of speech differing from the rest, except in general structure; so it has been thought best to keep them apart.

Tamil. The first language to be mentioned is the Tamil, not because it is numerically or geographically the most important, but by reason of its being the most cultivated and the best known of the Dravidian group. It has, indeed, given to the latter its original name.† Two dialects are by some attributed to Tamil, but these seem rather caste varieties than those of special tracts; so both *Irulár* and *Kúrúmbar* have been included under the general head, whilst *Yérukala*, which has been in some cases separately tabulated, has been added to the Gipsy dialects, of which mention has been made above. Tamil, then, may be taken to be a homogeneous language, covering the whole of Southern India up to Mysore and the Ghâts on the west, and the Ceded Districts, as they are called, on the north. It is disseminated, however, as widely as any tongue in India by special classes, such as labourers, who flock chiefly to Ceylon and Burma, and domestic servants, who are found hailing from the Tamil country in every large town and cantonment in India. The Madras servant is usually without religious prejudices or scruples as to food, head-gear, or ceremonial, so he can

Language.	Population returning it.
Tamil*	15,229,759
Telugu	19,885,137
Kanarese†	9,751,885
Kodagu	37,218
Malayálam	5,428,250
Túlú‡	491,728
Tôda	736
Kôta	1,201
Sinhalese	187
Máhl	3,167
Total, Southern Dravidian Group	**50,829,268**
Gônd	1,379,580
Kandh (Khond)	320,071
Oraon	368,222
Mal-Pahádia	30,838
Kharwár	7,651
Brahui	28,990
Total, Northern Group	**2,135,352**
Total, Dravidian	**52,964,620**

* Kúrumba, 5,288. † Badaga, 30,656. ‡ Koragu, 1,868.

* There is a tendency, however, towards assimilation, I understand, in the present day.—J.A.B.
† Dravid is said by Dr. Caldwell to be a corruption of Tamir.—J.A.B.

accommodate himself to all circumstances, in which respect he is unlike the northern Indian domestic.

Next to Tamil comes Malayálam, or the language of the Malabár coast. This is an offshoot of Tamil, and has maintained a close relationship with its parent. Its name is derived from "mala," the local term for a hill, and an abstract noun signifying possession, like the Persian *dár,* so that it means the "mountain tract." The term Malabár is comparatively modern, as the last syllable is probably the Arabic for a coast or roadstead. Malayálam has been closely hemmed in by its neighbours, and, indeed, the whole tract in which it is spoken has been peculiarly secluded from the foreign influences which have swept over the table-land overhanging it. Those returning this language in Coorg and Mysore are probably settlers just within the frontier, or temporary sojourners who have gone above the Ghâts for the coffee season. In other parts of India there is reason to suspect that, except at the seaports, the entry really means Malabári, a vulgar name for Tamil, originating with the early Portuguese travellers. Malayálam.

I come now to Kanarese, the north-western representative of the Dravidian group. As stated in the introductory chapter, its name seems derived from the Telugu words for *black* and *country,* a title that the denizens of the light soils of the eastern table-land would not improbably apply to the rich western tracts of what is now known as "cotton soil," but other derivations have been suggested. The language itself, however, has a far greater affinity with Tamil than with its neighbour on the east. The only form of speech that can be called a dialect of Kanarese is that of the *Badaga* tribe on the Nilgiris, called by our early historians the *Burghers.* If this be admitted, it seems not unreasonable to attribute to *Kodagu,* the dialect of Coorg, a like relationship. Both communities have been shut off by their hills and climate from Brahmanising influence, and seem to have preserved in their speech the older forms of Kanarese, which have been rubbed off that language in the busier life of the plains. The tract held by Kanarese is very compact. It includes Mysore, most of Coorg, and a strip of the coast between the Túlu and the Maráthi. Above the Ghâts, it stretches eastwards well into the Nizam's territory, and northwards to the Kistna river. Kanarese.

Its neighbour, Túlu, is confined to a small area in or near the district of South Kanara in Madras, and it is doubtful if it ever prevailed far beyond its present limits. It has the curious feature of linguistic independence without a character or literature of its own. Dr. Caldwell regards it as a very interesting and highly developed tongue, bearing but a distant relationship to Kanarese and Kodagu, still more distant to Maláyalam, which presses on it from the south, and most distant of all to Tamil. The Kanarese character has lately been adopted in printing modern Tulu works, and it is likely that Tulu will ultimately give way to that language. But as it is, it shows an increase of 10¼ per cent. over the return of 1881. Túlú.

The last of the chief Dravidian languages is Telugu, which is also the most numerously represented at the census. It is said to be the most euphonious, and, next to Tamil, the most ancient and advanced of the whole class. There are no dialects returned under it, for the languages returned as *Yánádi* and *Chentsu* in 1881 are said to be merely tribal corruptions of the standard language, and in no way distinct. On the other hand, the language of certain wandering tribes, such as the *Waddar* and *Kaikádi,* though no doubt of Telinga origin, suffers such change in the course of the peregrinations of these earth-workers and mat-weavers, that in provinces beyond Madras it has been grouped with the Gipsy tongues instead of with Telugu, wherever it has been returned under a tribal designation. The Telugu character has been adopted for Kanarese, as the latter has carried it on to Túlu. Like the Tamil, Malayálam, and probably the ancient form of Kanarese, it has been modified from the Devanágari of the Southern Asoka inscriptions, curved at top to suit the palm-leaf book which is current here as in Orissa. A very ancient form is still occasionally used in Malabar for formal documents, but, for the most part, the resemblance to the original is scarcely traceable. A counter theory has been adopted by some writers, namely, that the Asoka character is based on Dravidian forms; but though the question cannot be considered yet closed, the balance of evidence and probability seems rather on the side of an Aryan ancestry. Telugu.

As a vernacular, Telugu is more widely spread than Tamil. We find it not only all over the eastern coast of Madras, but throughout the Ceded Districts above the Ghâts and in one half of the Nizam's territory. It has also gained a considerable footing in Mysore and in a corner of the Bombay Karnátak, with branches in Berár, the Central Provinces, and Orissa. Although only the inhabitants of the North Coromandel coast have any right to the name of Kling, that title is applied on the other side of the Bay of Bengal to labourers from both Kalingapatam and Negapatam. During the rice-shipping season, and now, in fact, throughout the year, Burma is thronged with labourers from this part of the peninsula, who have almost monopolized the hard work so distasteful to the Burmese. It was noticed that in some of the schedules filled up by or for this class, the antiquated term of Gentoo was used to denote caste or race. This word was introduced by the Portuguese, to whom all Hindus were Gentiles, even as to the British soldier all natives of India, whether Musalmán or not, were collectively Moors. In the present day Gentoo means a Telingáná man.

Tóda and Kóta. There are a few of the minor Dravidian languages belonging to the Southern group which require a word or so of comment. First, the Tóda of the Nilgiris. The tribe has received a great deal of attention, ethnological, phrenological, social, and linguistic, mainly because it resides within an easy walk of a favourite hill resort. One member of the tribe has even been distinguished by temporary incorporation into the establishment of the greatest showman of the world, the late Mr. P. T. Barnum, of New York. Tôda is returned by 736 persons, instead of 673 as in 1881, and the members of the tribe are only more numerous by three than those who return the tribal tongue. This last is of similar origin to the Tamil and Kanarese, and was kept from advance by the secluded life of the tribe in the hills. The Kôta is another of the Nílgiri tribes, lower in position and occupation than the Tôdas, and speaking a dialect of archaic Kanarese, like that of the Badagas or Northerners mentioned above. Neither of these languages extends beyond the limits of the eponymic community.

Sinhalese and Mahl. A few entries of insular languages of this class may as well be noticed here. The Sinhalese is included amongst the Dravidian, since it shows morphological peculiarities which distinguish it from the Aryan class in which, owing perhaps to the cultivation of Páli by the literate classes of the island, it used to be placed. Then, again, the Máhl is returned only by the inhabitants of the little island of Minikoi, situated almost midway between the Máldiv and the Laccadiv archipelago, and belonging politically, though not linguistically, to the latter. The language in question is allied to the Sinhalese, it is said, though the Arabic character has been introduced, as in the Laccadiv, to suit the Musalmán proclivities of the people.

Gónd. The Northern group of Dravidian languages comprises one large item, which includes the various dialects spoken by the numerous Gónd tribes of Central India. These dialects, which are all unwritten, differ considerably in detail from each other, but are all Dravidian in their main characteristics. The Gónd tract, entered in the old maps as "Góndwána—Unexplored," radiates from the Central Provinces into Bengal, Berár, Madras, and the Nizam's dominions, and the tribes therein are suffering much change, in the course of which their tribal dialects will infallibly assimilate a great deal of the vernacular of the encircling plains.

Kandh. The Kandh or Khond of the hills of Orissa and the neighbourhood has, like the Tôda, attracted more attention than was perhaps his due, owing to his persistent attempts to keep up the habit of human sacrifice as a means of securing a good harvest. The language is localised to his native hills, and the only wanderers found on the census roll are in Assam, where, if the return be not due to clerical error, the Kandh speakers must be immigrant labourers who have joined a gang of adventurers from Orissa. It is the same with a few of the Kolarian tribes, which have been found even in Burma, though not retaining their tribal language there.

Oráon and Kharwár. Farther north, we enter the region of the Kolarian languages, and the distinction between them and the Dravidian becomes much weakened. The Oráon, however, and the Kharwár may be said to present decidedly Dravidian features. As to the language of the inhabitants of the hills of Rájmahál, who hold that tract against the Santháls, there seems to be less information available. Following such authority as seemed trustworthy, a Dravidian ancestry is attributed to the language of this curiously isolated community. If this be correct, the survival of this relic so far from its fellows seems to indicate the former existence of a considerable Dravidian colony between the Kolárian and the mixed races of Eastern Bengal, though the two former may have been identical in blood.

Last of the Dravidians has been placed the Bráhui, though the link attaching it to the rest is of the thinnest. There are, however, curious features in common which can hardly be ignored. Ethnically, there seems to be absolutely no resemblance between the tawny cattle-graziers of the Khelát desert and the squat dark cultivators of the peninsula or the mountain tribes of Central India, any more than can be found between the former and the Mongoloid settlers of the north-east, to whom Signor Finzi would, on linguistic grounds, attach them. The bulk of Brahui speakers dwell in Balóchistán, a tract which was not enumerated at the census, and the traditions of the race as to their migrations have yet to be satisfactorily investigated. The language of a good number of the Brahui tribes would no doubt be returned as Balóch, to which their own tongue is rapidly approaching in the frontier districts, so here again we have an instance of the obliteration of valuable philological evidence. Bráhui.

The Kolarian class, to which our attention is now directed, is small, but considerably subdivided amongst tribal dialects. The chief is the Santhál, which includes nearly three-fourths of the whole. This language, like so many others, owes its reduction to grammar and writing, to the labours of missionaries, chiefly Danes and Germans, who have devoted their lives to the study of this race. It is widely disseminated over Bengal, as the Santháls are first-rate labourers, and show no reluctance to leave their native country for work at a distance. They are found even in Assam, both as settlers and as temporary hands on tea estates. Kolarian Class.

Language.	Population returning it.
Santhál*	1,709,680
Múndá or Kôl	654,507
Kharria	67,772
Baiga and Bhúnjia	48,883
Korwá or Kúr	185,775
Bhíl	148,596
Sáwara	102,039
Gadaba	29,789
Juáng and Malér	11,965
Total, Kolarian	2,959,006

* This figure for Santhál has been since reduced, on final revision of the Bengal return, to 1,642,154, the balance being distributed apparently between Bengáli and Hindí.

The Mundá, in which returns of Kôl and Hô have been included, has apparently a somewhat wider range, but this is probably due to the partition of their tract amongst three provinces. Like the Santhál, the Mundá has taken kindly to foreign labour. The language seems to resemble Santhál in its main features, but its local varieties are frequent, and each main clan returns a separate designation to both itself and its language, and also, by the way, to its religion. The Kharria is on the same pattern. The Baiga, Bhinjwa, or Bhúnjia is probably a tribe of earlier date in the country than the Mundá or the Dravidians of these hills, judging from the fact that amongst the other tribes the name is used for a priest or exorcist, even if the functionary is not of the Baiga tribe. In the Central Provinces, the Baigas are said to speak Hindi to a large extent, but whether their women do or not is a more important point, on which information has not been furnished. The Kúr, Kórwa, or Kurku reaches across the hills to the west of the Kolarian tract, and joins the Bhíl, which carries the class on nearly to the sea. The former varies in detail throughout its length, and is different in Berár, for instance, from what it will be found to be in the Chútia Nágpúr division of Bengal. As to the Bhíl tongue, it has been adulterated to such an extent that it retains little but corrupt Hindi, Maráthi, or Gujaráthi, according to locality, in its vocabulary, though its construction, at all events in the eastern portions of the tract it occupies, is still agglutinative. Múndá and allied tribal dialects. Kúr and Bhíl.

The most southerly forms of Kolarian speech are the Sáwara and Gadaba, both of which are almost confined to the hills bordering on Orissa, in the Madras Presidency. The former may have extended nearly to the sea in earlier days, as it is said that the *Suaroi* of Greek geographers are the ancestors of the present Sáwara. The last of this class of languages which has to be noticed is the Juáng or Patua, spoken by a tribe which Colonel Dalton, in his work on Bengal Ethnology, considers the lowest of all found within the tract he describes. It is but within the last few years that either sex wore clothes at all. The women were till then content with bunches of leaves tied round the waist in front and behind, and renewed, as required, when the fair wearer went to fetch in the cattle from the wood which provided her millinery.* With the Juáng is grouped the Malér, which is not returned by more than a few hundred persons. Sáwaru, &c.

* An attempt was made some years back to introduce waistcloths, which were distributed gratuitously, but it is reported, I believe, that, as a rule, the innovation did not outlast the material.—J.A.B.

Gipsy dialects.

The group entitled Gipsy dialects contains many items which are in use only amongst a single caste or tribe. The chief of these, the respectable body of carriers and cattle-breeders, called Brinjáras, is a community which is spread all over Northern India as far as the Deccan, where many have permanently settled as landholders, speaking Maráthi only. In the south of the latter tract it gives place to a similar tribe, known as the Lambáni, which is the term used, too, in the Panjáb. In both provinces the tribe has an evil repute. There are also the numerous tribes of wandering artisans, such as knife-grinders, grindstone-makers, and matting-plaiters; the last of whom alone is held popularly to be of bad character, wherever in India it is found. Perhaps, as formerly with the broom-making trade in England, the facility of the occupation makes people regard it as only a cover for nefarious but more lucrative means of livelihood. Then come the tumblers, rope-dancers, and acrobats, with the castes which unabashedly maintain the name of cut-purse (*Ganti-chor*), all notorious evil livers, each with its special form of thieves' Latin unintelligible to respectable people. Jugglers and snake-charmers, who are equally nomad in habit, are not invariably regarded malevolently, though open to suspicion. These tribes collectively represent the class from which originate the Róm or Gipsy of Europe and Asia Minor and the Lúri of Persia. Their name of Gipsy is probably a corruption of Zotti, or Jat, as already mentioned, which became "Egyptian," either by misnomer, or because, as some say, Nikomedia, through which they reached Europe, was sometimes called "Little Egypt." The other term for them, Zigane, is probably due to their capacity for music, *Chang* being a stringed instrument in Persia, and *Tchingián* or Tsigán, the musician, in Western Turkey.

Khási.

There remains the small group of Khási dialects (178,637) between the above and the enormous field of the Thibeto-Burman tongues. It has been stated already that this group cannot be affiliated to any of its neighbours, and it is confined to the range of hills that separates the two valleys of Assam. There are three tribal dialects the Lyngám, Dýko, and Sýnteng. Through the efforts of the Welsh missionaries in this tract, the Roman character is now used in all three, and the census was taken in it. It seems thoroughly established, and as the surrounding languages are different in structure, Khási will probably withstand their influence.

Thibeto-Burman languages.

The Thibeto-Burman group, which is the first and largest of the Tonic class with which the census has to deal, has been subdivided, chiefly for convenience in treatment, into geographical sections, in the same way as the Aryan. The first of these comprises not only the Thibetan of the region immediately to the north of the Himálaya, but the language of the Mongoloid tribes of the higher valleys on this side of the range, and those of Sikkim and Bhotán, none of which regions were included in the census. We are thus dealing with immigrants, except in the comparatively insignificant case of Kanáwari, or the language of the higher valley of the Satlaj, where it passes through the State of Bashahr, between Thibet and the Panjáb. The Thibetan was found chiefly in the valleys of the Panjáb Himálaya, in the neighbourhood of Sikkim and the Bengal Himálaya, and in the Tarai of the north-west, which is the winter resort of the inhabitants of the upper valleys of Kumaon and Garhwál. The Rong or Lepcha is nearly allied to the Thibetan, like the Bhotáni, or the tongue of that portion of the Himálayas known in India as Bhótant, or the end of Bhót, Thibet. The former language is found only at Darjiling, and the latter either there or amongst the winter traders in North Assam. Most of the languages of Nipál of

Thibetan dialects.

Language.	Population returning it.
Thibetan	20,544
Kanáwari	9,265
Nipáli, unspecified	141,273
„ Múrmi	20,597
„ Mangar	11,281
„ Limbu	12,605
„ Newári	5,217
„ Sunuwár	4,236
Other Nipáli dialects	657
Lepcha	10,125
Bhotáni	9,470
Total, Himalayan Group	**245,270**
Bôdo (Kachári)	198,705
Gáro	145,425
Lálúng	40,204
Kôch	8,107
Mêch	90,796
Tipperah	121,864
Other Bôdo dialects	4,314
Total, Bôdo Group	**609,415**
Miri-Ábor	35,703
Other Frontier dialects	1,282
Total, N.E. Frontier Group	**36,985**

Language.	Population returning it.
Nága dialects* - - - -	102,908
Míkir - - - - -	90,236
Kákhyín and Lisháu - - - -	5,669
Total, Nága-Kákhyin Group	198,813
Manipuri (*Kathé*) - - - -	88,911
Kuki - - -	18,828
Zhô (*Lúshai*) - - - -	41,926
Khyín - - - - -	126,915
Total, Khyín-Lúshai Group -	276,580
Arrakanese (Magh) - - -	366,403
Burmese - -	5,560,461
Total, Burmese Group	5,926,864
Nikobári - -	1
Total, Thibeto-Burman Group -	7,293,928

* Seven, but not completely distinguished in the returns.

the Tonic class are the mother tongues of people living beyond the British frontier, and many of those mentioned by Mr. Brian Hodgson, the chief authority on the subject, were not represented at the census at all, either because the tribes had not penetrated down to India, or, having got there, were confounded by a Hindu enumerator in the general term Nipáli. In addition to the recruits in our infantry regiments, Nipál furnishes a fair number of immigrants of Himalayan race to the adjoining hill country in Bengal and the west of Assam. The Gúrúng and Mangar are the main languages returned by the former class, and Múrmi, Limbu, and Newári, by the latter. It is remarkable that we find hardly any trace of the great Nipáli family of Kiránti languages in the schedules, and none of those of what Mr. Hodgson calls the "Broken tribes" of the lower portion of the State. The Nipáli soldiery as often as not had their language set down as Gurkháli, a title to which probably very few of them would have advanced a claim in their own country. Nipál dialects.

Keeping still to the east, we enter the thorny path of Assam Hill philology, which requires as cautious treading as those of the country itself, where stockades, pitfalls, and bamboo caltrops beset the unwary at every turn. The languages of the western and southern tracts are comparatively easy to classify, as they have been studied for some years. Following the practice of local experts, they have been formed into a separate group, called, from the leading dialect, the *Bódo* or *Kachári*. This last has been fully examined in the works of Messrs. Hodgson and Endle. It is spread widely over the tract in question, and holds nearly the whole of the north-west of Assam. There is no literature or means of keeping up a standard of Bódo, and variations are therefore frequent. It is curious that no trace of the allied language, Dhimál, mentioned by Hodgson, should appear in the Assam return, nor in Bengal are there more than a couple of individuals returning it. It is probably confined to the Eastern Tarai, within Nipál territory. So the two persons just mentioned have been included under the Nipál troup. The Gáro language is current in the Western Assam Hills, and is said to be closely allied to the Bódo. The Méch, Rábha, Hajong, and Hojai, with the Lálúng, are all more or less local forms of the same family, and prevail respectively in small tracts along the Bengal and Assam border-land and the north bank of the Bráhmapútra. There are two other languages of this group worth note. The Kóchh, which includes the so-called Páni-Kóchh, belongs to an early tribe of settlers along the great river, which has been almost entirely converted to Bráhmanism. They number no less than 2,364,000, but the vernacular has been abandoned for Bengali towards the west, and the small State which represents the former Kóchh domination found no more than a dozen in it to return the ancestral tongue. The Tipperah language is found almost contiguous to the south-eastern branch of the Bódo, with which it is closely connected. It is returned chiefly from the State bearing this name on the Bengal frontier. The repelling force of the Hill tribes of a more northern descent has proved sufficient here, as farther south, to keep the dialects of the plains strictly within their political limits. Bódo dialects.

Of the curious group of Tonic languages spoken amongst the wild tribes of our north-eastern frontier, we have but little on the census record. The Aka, Daphla Abor, Miri, and Mishmi inhabit the lower valleys of the Himálaya and send but few offshoots into what is known there as the "inner belt" of our influence. There is a settled colony of the Mishmi, however, in British territory, and some progress has been made with the investigation of the languages of this and the neighbouring tribes by frontier officers, to whom we have to look at present for our knowledge of the subject. Probably better acquaintance will lead to the discovery of more links between Miri-Abor group.

the various forms of speech amongst them; for in this corner of the empire tribal hostility is the leading feature of intercourse, and the mere fact of separation is reason enough for considering a neighbour a natural enemy, and in disclaiming, of course, any former connection with him.

Nága-Kákhyîn group.

Between the above group and the next in order lies a small wedge of the Tai or Shán family, which will be dealt with in connection with the languages of Burma later on. The Nága group is not confined to the tribes which bear that name, but, as stated in the introductory section of this chapter, includes the inhabitants of the Mikir hills to the north-west, and the tract stretching east, probably along the whole of the northern frontier of Upper Burma, which is in the hands of the people collectively known as Kákhyîn. There are seven tribal languages of the Nágas returned at the census, but unfortunately there is also a large body of people who are shown as speaking Nága only, without the distinction that could easily have been obtained had the enumerators been warned to look out for it. We have, for instance, a fair approximation to the number of the Angámi and Á-o Nagas, but the Kácha or Empe-o, the Kezháma, the Lho-tá, the Séma, and the Rengámá are but poorly represented. The language of the main Nága tribes on the western slope of the Indo-Burman watershed has been reduced to more or less grammatical form by Mr. Davies, the officer in charge of the Hill tracts, who is at present the best authority on the subject; and when similar work has been accomplished for the language of the Burmese tribes of the same race, the two results will be a very valuable contribution to philology. The curious off-shoot of the Kákhyîn race in the north-east corner of Assam has been already mentioned under the name of Sing-phô, or, more correctly, Ching-pau. It had its centre at Mogaung on a tributary of the Irawadi, near which the fighting took place last year, and established itself in Assam near the end of the last century, and made slaves of a good many of the Assamese of the neighbouring tribes. A mixed race, the offspring of this connection, is in existence, but returns the language of the country, not of the foreigner. The whole community is very small, just over 2,000 in all, of whom two-thirds are Sing-phō, and the rest, Duánia, of half-breeds.

Kúki-Lúshai group.

The next group of languages on which comment is required comprises the languages of the tribes of the range of hills separating India from Burma. In their northern extension these tribes are collectively known as Kúki. The term Lúshai, which is applied farther south, is not recognised by the people themselves, who use the name Zhô. Shendú is also a synonymous title for the Lúshai tribes. The tribes of the country between Bengal and Burma are known collectively as Khyîn in the east, and by a variety of local names in Bengal. The whole lot was left very much to itself in former years, as the inhabitants of the plains hold such races in considerable respect, and, trading on this feeling, the mountaineers have manifested their superiority over the peaceful communities they overhang in ways that the British had to stop with some vigour. It is hardly necessary to point out that with so many tribes close together, each under hereditary obligations to lay by a store of the skulls of its neighbour, the diversity of language is as great as in the tract across the Bráhmapútra. Information on these dialects has not yet been obtained, as the hills have but recently been permanently occupied. The only civilised community is that of the valley of Manipur, which acquired so painful a notoriety from the disturbances of March 1891. The language of this tract is called Manipuri in Bengal and Assam, and Kathé or Ponnú in Burma. The returns available relate only to the colonists or visitors in the adjacent portions of Assam, and the *entourage* of the late chief in Bengal and Mathura. In Mandalay there is still a considerable colony, descended from prisoners or slaves brought over during the wars of the late dynasty. In Lower Burma the number is decreasing, owing either to cessation of immigration or to the adoption of the Burmese language by the settlers, since there is no single colony in that part of the province like that in Mandalay, where the similarity of fortune and intimacy of intercourse has helped to keep up the original language. The cultivated dialect of Manipur has been studied and described by Colonel Lewin and Mr. Brojonáth Sháha, according to whom it shows a great advance on the rest of the tribal dialects. It is said to have had a special character of its own, which, like that of Malayálam, is now only used occasionally in formal deeds. For ordinary purposes it has been superseded by Bengali, introduced by the officials and settlers from that province. Manipur, like Nipál, has had its Bráhman invasion, with its concomitant traditions of the orthodox descent of the ruling family from the demigods of Bindraban on the Jamna, and there is a good deal of mixed blood in the central valley, which accounts for the relatively high culture of that tract. The hills are still held by Kúki and other tribes of the same stock, and it is doubtful, therefore, if the language of Imphál is current far beyond the immediate influence of the court and its Hindu officers.

Khyin dialects. Between the Zhô country and Arrakan the tribal languages are badly mixed at the census. We have, however, grammars and vocabularies of the dialects current on the Burma side of the Yóma hills, amongst the Southern Khyíns, but the literary Burman, in his contempt for the men of the mountain, avoids discrimination of the rest of these tribes, and to him all Khyíns are one, or nearly so. We find, however, a few tribal languages set down, such as Mrô (15,891), Khwé-mi (14,126), and Daignét (856), from Northern Arrakan, but some of the races returning these are doubtless more numerons than the above figures would imply. Possibly, therefore, as the tribes expand beyond the shelter of the hills, they are absorbed linguistically into the gulf of Burmese.

Arrakanese. We then come to Burma itself, and here it has been found advisable to show the main language under the two heads of Burmese and Arrakanese. Historically and philologically they are the same, but geographically it is possible to distinguish them. Arrakanese is the older form of the language, and has preserved features, especially of pronunciation, which the soft and indolent inhabitant of the rest of Burma has been willing to let drop. But there are still dialects outside Arrakan which belong to it rather than to the inland tracts. *Tavoyer*, for example, the special dialect of Tenasserim, and *Chaungthâ*, a vanishing relic, may be cited in proof of this. On the Bengal side of the bay, north and east of Chittagong, the language is returned as *Magh*, a name unknown to Arrakan, and, like the Goanese of the western coast, calling to mind the modern kitchen rather than the ancient kingdom from which it is derived, for the Magh and the Goanese furnish European India with the best of its *chefs*.

Burmese, &c. In Burmese we have the language most numerously represented at the census of all the Tonic class. We have had occasion to mention already the tradition that this tongue came from the west, but, in fact, the only impression received from India viâ Ceylon is the alphabet in a very modified form, and a comparatively small vocabulary relating to the Magadhi-born religion. On the other hand, the appearance of the people betokens a far more northern origin. Within historic times Burmese has proved itself a great absorbent of local dialects, either owing to political influences from Pegu and Mandalay or to the prevailing ecclesiastical system, which includes monastic training and education. *Yebein*, a tongue held to be distinct from the Burmese, and which was represented by 436 persons in 1881, has vanished from the returns, though there are nearly 2,300 of the tribe left. *Kádu*, *Dánu*, and *Yau*, too, are well on the way to the same fate, and show signs of decrepitude in the last 10 years, though the tribes are flourishing. But however strong the Burmese may be in its own country, it spreads but little into India. With the exception of the Maghs of Chittagong, most of the Burmese speakers who are to be found across the sea have strayed thither against their will, and include the late King and his establishment, and the "true patriots" scattered amongst the Indian jails—

> "For be it understood,
> They left their country for their country's good."

Môn group. The Môn or Talaing languages may be mentioned here, though little more need be said about them than is to be found above in connection with the general subject of classification. The language is found in Anam and Cambodia, though in the latter case the influence of Chinese is very marked. It is worth noting, too, that the same tradition as to the advent of a prince from across the Bay of Bengal is current in all three communities. The only link between Pegu and the Môn colonies of the far east is found in Palaung, a language spoken by a small and isolated tribe in the north-east of Upper Burma. In the time of the late dynasty the Môn language was almost obliterated in Lower Burma, owing to the discouragement of it by the Burmese rulers and their officials, and it was expected to become extinct in a generation or so. Now, however, the census returns seem to

Language.	Population returning it.
Môn - - - -	226,495
Palaúng - - - - -	2,847
Total, Môn Class - -	229,342

indicate that this language is either reviving, or that persons who were reluctant to return it on former occasions have taken heart, for there were only 154,553 returning it in 1881: but it is imprudent to prophecy that it will ever resume its position as one of the leading vernaculars in Amherst and Pegu. As yet, it is returned by little over one-half of the Môn-Talaing community in Lower Burma.

Shán or Tai group.

Between the two branches of the Môn there has been thrust a long belt of the Shán language, called in the centre and south Láo, or, by Europeans, Siamese. It has already been pointed out that the Ahôm or Shán settlers of Upper Assam failed to preserve their language in their new circumstances, so we find no entries of that tongue amongst them; and the Aitôns, a more modern tribe, are returned as mostly speaking Shán only, which is very likely due to mistake on the part of Hindu enumerators. The two other Shán colonies in Assam return a few entries of Khámti and Phakiál respectively, but the tongue does not extend beyond the limits occupied by those tribes. Khámti has been investigated by a frontier officer, and a grammar written of it; but there is a gap between this tract and the Láo or Htái of the Siamese kingdom, in which the intervening linguistic changes have still to be investigated. This cannot be done until the cis-Sálwîn Shán States have been brought into closer touch with the new administration of Upper Burma. By next census, therefore, more information will have been obtained, even if the States be not completely enumerated.

Language.	Population returning it.
Shán	174,871
Láo (*Htai*)	4
Aitôn	2
Khámti	2,945
Phakiál	625
Total, Taic Class	**178,447**

Malay group.

The Malayan class of languages is represented chiefly in the south of Burma, where there are a few settlers from the peninsula. The Sea-Gipsies or Salôn of the Mergui Archipelago, too, speak a tongue of this class, and owing to more careful enumeration, show nearly double the number that appear in the returns of 10 years back. The rest of the Malays are seafaring people, enumerated at the ports of India. As this class of languages does not really prevail within the sphere of the census operations, no more need be said about it.

Language.	Population returning it.
Malay	2,437
Salôn	1,628
Javanese	19
Total, Malay Class	**4,084**

Japanese.

Japanese can be disposed of in the same way. A few residents of the chief towns are all that return this language, and as the women returning it are more numerous than the men, its introduction is probably due to the fame of the Musmé of the baths and tea-houses of the Far East, which has been productive of emulation.

Chinese.

The Sinitic class is represented by two languages, Chinese and Kárén. The former is scattered nearly all over India, since merchants, carpenters, and cane-workers of this race are to be found in most large towns and cantonments. In Rangoon and Upper Burma there are regular communities from the Flowery Land, though in the latter the number of immigrants seems to have decreased since the country became British. In nearly every district, however, there are a few Chinese. They belong mainly to two classes. First, the merchant who hails from Canton or the east, and who comes round by sea; secondly, the people from Yún-nán, who come across by land to trade in petty wares and forest produce, and whose language is different from that of the former.

Language.	Population returning it.
Chinese	38,504
Kárên	674,846
Total, Sinitic Class	**713,350**

Kárén.

Kárén has been classed with Chinese on the authority of Dr. Cushing and other missionary scholars. The Kárén tract has been for some years the main field of missionary labour in Burma, and the results are to be found in most districts of the lower division of that province. The three chief dialects of this language differ considerably from each other, owing probably to much the same reason as is found operative in the case of the Lushai group, namely, the dispersion of the tribe over wide tracts of difficult country, after the first arrival from the north. The Pwô dialect was returned by 449,450 persons, though only about 27,000 are given as of that tribe. The Sgáu shows 225,193. The Bghái or Kárén-ní was returned under these titles by no more than 16, so is evidently included in the first-named dialect. Taungthû, Mópghâ, and so on, are said to be only local names for one or other of the above three dialects. The Kárên does not extend much beyond the tract occupied by the tribes themselves, and some of the outskirts are said to be getting rapidly Burmanised in speech.

Eránic-Aryan languages.

We can here take leave of the languages of India, and discuss the return of other Asiatic tongues. First comes the sister branch of the Aryan class, which may be called the Eránic, because, whatever its origin, the few representatives we have to deal with are well under the influence of Persian.

Language.	Population returning it.
Persian	28,189
Armenian	833
Pakhtú (Pashtú)	1,080,931
Balôch	219,475
Total, Eranic-Aryan Class	**1,329,428**

Persian

As regards this last, in spite of the connection of India with Iran, and the settlement of natives of the latter in the north and west of the country, the language has obtained, as a parent tongue, little footing within the empire. It is still the language of polite society and of *belles lettres* amongst the educated classes of Musalmáns, but those to whom it is the only or the most familiar language are but few. In Bengal and Rangoon there are remnants of the old ruling families of Dehli and Lucknow; in the Panjáb, traders and immigrants are found, and the refugees from Afghánistán; and in Bombay, horse-dealers and emigrants from Persia, who have settled down in the chief towns. Beyond these centres there is hardly any real Persian spoken, and a good deal of what is returned as such is but the better sort of Urdu.

Armenian.

Armenian is the parent tongue of a small colony of that race in Bengal, Lower Burma, and a few other parts of India. The persons returning it are permanently domiciled in India, and probably use English more and more each generation.

Pakhtú.

Pakhtú or Pashtu, the language of the Pathán (Pakhtwán), belongs, as has been said, to the Indic-Aryan class in its structure, but to the Eránic in much of its vocabulary. It has been grouped under the latter, as it is geographically beyond India, and Persian of a sort is undoubtedly the vernacular of the north and west of Afghánistán. Most of the Pashtu-speakers are located in the Panjáb, either as settlers or amongst the retainers of the refugees. There is another class which travels over nearly all India peddling rugs and fruit, and sometimes selling horses brought down from their native land. They leave the latter in the autumn, perambulate the genial plains of India during the winter, and return to Ghazni, or wherever it may be, in the late spring, in time to resume their home occupation of agriculture and fruit-growing. Year after year they do this, and many tribes of the Sulaimán and Kharoti map out India into regular divisions, one of which is assigned to be exploited by each company. There are a few who do not return at all, but remain all the year round in India, varying the monotony of commerce, according to the police, with exploits less legitimate.

Balôch.

Balôch, again, is a language of Persian affinity, used as a vernacular only in the frontier districts of the lower Panjáb and in Sindh. The prevalence of this tongue, according to the returns, in some of the native States, is due to the number of mercenaries of Balôch race entertained by the chiefs as personal retainers and treasury guards. They are usually Makránis, speaking that dialect of Balôch. They have a strong strain of African blood, and are not of the pure type of the north.

Turánic languages.

Next to Erán, we naturally come to its enemy, linguistically known as Turán, but the latter is very poorly represented in India linguistically. The majority of Túrki speakers come from Turkestán, and there are a few Osmánli settled in Bombay and Haiderabád. It is not worth while for so small a number to distinguish the various entries of Uzbegi, Yárkandi, Chagatai, &c., from the cultivated dialect of Stamboul. The Finn entries are from the vessels in port on

Language.	Population returning it.
Túrki	607
Finn	10
Magyár	42
Total, Turánic	659

the census night at Calcutta and Rangoon. Magyár is returned by a few merchants and travellers, and by artisans on the railways, where nearly all the tongues of Europe are to be found. The term Turánic has been reserved for this class of languages, instead of being extended, as is sometimes done, to the whole of the Tonic and Agglutinative languages of Burma and the Himálaya, for which the title selected above raises, it is to be hoped, fewer questions.

Semitic languages. Arabic.

The Semitic is the last of the Asiatic classes with which the census is concerned. It is made up mainly of Arabic, the vernacular of Aden, which Settlement furnishes nearly half the return. Most of the rest of the entries are returned from Haidrabád, where a portion of the Nizám's force and the body-guards of his chief nobles are recruited from Arabic-speaking tribes of Africa and the coast of the Persian Gulf.

Language.	Population returning it.
Arabic	53,351
Hebrew	2,171
Syriac	12
Total, Semitic	55,534

Hebrew.

Hebrew was returned by a number of Jews, much on the same principle that Sanskrit was put down by Bráhmans and Arabic by Musalmán teachers of the Kurán. It is the distinctive language of their faith, though it can hardly be called a mother tongue, so it is considered dignifying, if the head of the house is at all conversant with it, to have the fact recorded. The entries were chiefly from Jewish colonies where Arabic, Maráthi, or Malayálam would be the correct return. Turkish Arabia supplies a good number of Israelitish settlers. In Cochín there are two permanent colonies, one of which is certainly of foreign origin, whilst in the coast district round Bombay the class of rural Jews habitually use Maráthi in their households. In Aden, too, the colony is permanently settled, and speaks a dialect of Arabic. No definite information has been recorded about the few entries of Syriac which are found here and there. Possibly they are traceable to Nestorian priests, of whom there may be some in Cochín and other parts of the country.

Negro dialects.

From Africa we get a number of dialects, found mostly in Aden, where there is a constant stream of migration to and from the opposite coast. The Somáli and Swahíli tribes furnish most of the entries. The negroes who are employed on board the steamers trading with India are often called Sidi or Habshi, which, strictly speaking, is Abyssinian. They are from farther south, however, and usually take ship at Zanzibár, or come from the Persian Gulf ports, such as Mascat. It would be incorrect, therefore, to class their languages as Abyssinian, which would bring them into the Semitic class. It may be remembered that in the early days of operations against the slave trade on the east coast of Africa, vessels full of boys and girls were captured, and the children made over to certain missionary orphanages and other institutions in Bombay. They were trained to a mechanical trade or to domestic service, and thus remained in the country of their adoption. Another class found in the households of chiefs and rich nobles is still recruited in less reputable ways, mainly on account of the high character for fidelity to their employer borne by men of this race.

European languages.

We have now to consider the return of the languages of Europe and the west. Of these there is a great variety, though none but English is strongly represented. This last, which, for census purposes, is held to include *Scotch*, though not Gaelic, is returned by 100,000 or so born in the United Kingdom, by scattered denizens of Australia, the United States, and Canada, &c., as well as by the increasing class of Europeans of British descent born and domiciled in India, and the Eurasians. Of the other languages returned, German, French, Italian, and Greek may be taken as those of commercial sojourners, and Welsh, Gaelic, and Irish are recruited from the regiments that happen to be on service in India. In the same way, the Scandinavian languages depend on the number of vessels in port on the census night for their representatives.

Language.		Population returning it.
Teutonic	English	238,499
	German	2,215
	Dutch	119
	Flemish	22
Scandinavian	Danish	94
	Swedish	187
	Norwegian	152
Keltic	Welsh	245
	Gaelic	264
	Irish	299
	Keltic (*unspecified*)	2
Mediterranean	Greek	380
	Latin	1
	Italian	690
	Maltese	32
	Roumanian	22
	Spanish	159
	French	2,171
Slavonic	Russian	95
	Polish	46
	Czech	1
	Bulgarian	49
	Slavonic (*unspecified*)	1
	Basque	1
Total, European		245,746

Comparing the return of these languages with that of the preceding census, it will be seen that the Europeans have increased by some 37,000, out of which number more than 35,000 are amongst the English speakers. Changes in the garrison, as well as the natural increase amongst the domiciled population and Eurasians, sufficiently account for the latter. Of the foreigners, the three commercial classes, German, French, and Greek, have all largely increased, but the Italian-speaking population has fallen off, owing partly to the disappearance of a colony of that nationality from Rangoon, where it was established during the existence of the kingdom of Upper Burma. The Scandinavians were much fewer, and the Celts many more, than in 1881, owing to the temporary causes just mentioned. Looking up some of the details, it appears that the priest who returns Latin as being the tongue of his mother, the Church, has safely weathered the intercensal decade; so, too, have the two Kelts and and the single Slavonian, who still refrain from further particularising their mother tongue; but the Lapp has given place to a Basque, and representatives of Bohemia and Iceland have appeared, besides various Bulgarians.

Comparison of Tribal languages with Tribal population.

No general comparison between the returns for the two enumerations has been attempted, since, partly owing to the wider scope of the present operations, partly perhaps, to the better understanding of the rules by the enumerators, it is only in the purely localised or tribal dialects that such comparison could be practicable. But there is a certain interest, connected with what has been said regarding the prevalence of tribal dialects, in comparing the return of languages in this table with that of the tribe in Table XVII. The following statement, accordingly, gives specimens of the results of this comparison, the population where language was not returned being deducted in all cases:—

	Tribe, &c.	Numerical Strength.		Difference of B. from A.
		A.—By Tribe.	B.—By Tribal Language.	
N. Central Belt.	Santhál	1,494,045	1,642,154	+ 148,109
	Bhíl	933,512	148,596	− 784,916
	Baiga, Bhinjwa, &c.	1,030,332	48,883	− 981,449
	Múndá, Hó, Kól, Kur, and Korwa	1,109,157	840,282	− 268,875
	Kharria	68,425	67,772	− 653
	Kharwár	112,298	7,651	− 104,647
Central Belt.	Oraon	523,258	368,222	− 155,036
	Gond	2,897,591	1,379,580	− 1,518,011
	Sáwara	438,317	102,039	− 336,278
	Gadaba	34,127	29,789	− 4,338
	Kandh	627,388	320,071	− 307,317
	Mal-Paháḍia	18,506	30,838	+ 12,332
	Juang	9,179	11,171	+ 1,192
Nilgiri.	Irula	58,503	1,614	− 56,889
	Tóda	739	736	− 3
	Kóta	1,201	1,201	—

	Tribe, &c.	Numerical Strength.		Difference of B. from A
		A.—By Tribe.	B.—By Tribal Language.	
Assam.	Miri-Abor	36,738	35,703	− 1,035
	Khási	172,150	178,637	+ 6,487
	Kachári	243,378	198,705	− 44,673
	Kóchh	2,364,365	8,107	−2,356,258
	Gáro	150,227	145,525	− 4,702
	Méch	96,873	90,796	− 6,077
	Nága	101,568	102,908	+ 1,340
	Manipuri	84,540	88,911	+ 4,371
	Kúki	25,940	18,828	− 7,112
	Lúshai	43,840	41,926	− 1,914
Nipal.	Murmi	21,889	20,597	− 1,292
	Mangar	19,383	11,281	− 8,102
	Limbu	15,079	12,605	− 2,474
	Sunúwár	5,210	4,236	− 974
	Newár	4,979	5,217	+ 238
Burma.	Burmese	5,408,984	5,560,461	+ 151,477
	Arrakanese	452,164	366,403	− 85,761
	Karén	540,876	674,846	+ 133,970
	Món	467,885	226,495	− 241,390
	Chinese	41,832	38,504	− 3,328

The general drift of the statement is to show how the tribal tongues are falling before the general dialects of the plains. This is marked out very plainly in the figures for Bhíl, Gónd, Baiga, with its companions, and Kharwár, in the case of Hindi, and equally well in that of Uriya, amongst the speakers of Kandh and Sáwara. A

TABLE showing, proportionally, the LANGUAGES prevalent in each PROVINCE, &c.

Province and Language.	Per-centage on Total.
1. **Ajmér**:—	
1. Hindi	56·58
2. Marwádi	42·20
Others	1·22
2. **Assam**:—	
1. Bengáli	50·06
2. Assamese	25·82
3. Hindi	4·20
4. Kachári	3·59
5. Khási	3·25
6. Gáro	2·19
Others	10·89
3. **Bengal**:—	
1. Bengáli	52·89
2. Hindi	36·65
3. Uriya	6·46
4. Santhál	1·99
Others	2·01
4. **Bengal States**:—	
1. Uriya	45·21
2. Bengáli	19·72
3. Hindi	15·29
4. Santhál	8·25
5. Tippera	3·34
6. Mûndá, &c.	3·19
Others	5·00
5. **Berár**:—	
1. Maráthi	79·46
2. Hindi	9·67
3. Gónd	3·24
Others	7·63
6. **Bombay**:—	
1. Maráthi	53·82
2. Gujaráthi	20·78
3. Kanarese	15·59
4. Urdú	5·62
Others	4·19
7. **Bombay States**:—	
1. Gujaráthi	60·68
2. Maráthi	22·19
3. Kanarese	7·25
4. Kachhi	4·73
5. Urdú	3·20
Others	1·95
8. **Sindh**:—	
1. Sindhi	83·00
2. Balóch	6·20
3. Márwádi	4·74
Others	6·06
9. **Baroda**:—	
1. Gujaráthi	93·00
2. Urdú	3·39
3. Maráthi	2·11
Others	1·50
10. **Central Provinces**:—	
1. Hindi	60·26
2. Maráthi	19·61
3. Gónd	9·32
4. Uriya	6·35
5. Urdú	1·48
Others	3·04
11. **Central Province States**:—	
1. Uriya	42·41
2. Hindi	36·06
3. Gónd	8·47
4. Halabi	6·48
5. Kandh	3·06
Others	3·52
12. **Upper Burma**:—	
1. Burmese	92·91
2. Shán	2·68
Others	4·41
13. **Lower Burma**:—	
1. Burmese	60·49
2. Karén	14·28
3. Arakanese	7·41
4. Món	4·85
5. Bengali	3·50
6. Khyín	2·15
7. Shán	2·02
Others	5·30
14. **Coorg**:—	
1. Kanarese	43·99
2. Kodagu	20·40
3. Tamil	9·36
4. Malayálam	6·47
5. Túlú	6·94
6. Urdú	3·99
7. Telugu	2·14
Others	6·71
15. **Mysore**:—	
1. Kanarese	73·94
2. Telugu	15·19
3. Urdu	4·73
4. Tamil	3·22
Others	2·92
16. **Madras**:—	
1. Tamil	39·51
2. Telugu	38·32
3. Malayálam	7·54
4. Kanarese	4·06
5. Uriya	3·63
6. Urdú	2·29
7. Tulu	1·34
Others	3·31
17. **Madras States**:—	
1. Malayálam	73·54
2. Tamil	22·86
3. Telugu	1·54
Others	2·06
18. **Haidrabád**:—	
1. Telugu	43·61
2. Maráthi	30·28
3. Kanarese	12·58
4. Urdú	10·38
Others	3·15
19. **North-West Provinces**:—	
1. Hindi	97·06
2. Kumáoni	1·46
3. Garhwáli	1·19
Others	0·29
20. **N.W. Province States**:—	
1. Hindi	69·58
2. Garhwáli	30·32
Others	0·10
21. **Panjáb**:—	
1. Panjábi	63·13
2. Hindi	17·63
3. Jatki	8·43
4. Pakhtú	5·06
5. Western Pahári	3·54
6. Bágri (*Márwádi*)	1·50
Others	0·71
22. **Panjáb States**:—	
1. Panjábi	60·40
2. Western Pahári	18·39
3. Hindi	11·21
4. Jatki	3·27
5. Marwádi (*Bágri*)	5·61
Others	1·12

few items seem to be capable of special explanations. For instance, the Khási speakers include those returned as Christians, not under the tribal name. The Manipuris, too, use the title of Kshatria, or the warrior caste of Brahmanic society, to some extent. Assamese, moreover, seems gaining ground amongst the Kachari tribes and their fellows, as Burmese is further south. The discrepancy between the two returns of Karéns is not explicable on the surface, as the Christians who have returned that as their race are included for the purposes of this table under the tribal head. The Chinese have the peculiar custom of attributing their own nationality to the male children of mixed parentage, but of returning the females as Burmese, a fact which seems to account for the difference noticeable in the table. The Irula tongue is no more than a rude dialect of Tamil, so there is no reason to expect its return under a distinct head. In the case of the Nipál tribes the mother-tongue was mostly entered simply as Nipáli or Pahári. The figures for Mal-Pahádi are clearly confused with those of other tribes. There is no more detailed explanation available as to the rest of the discrepancies in the statement.

The third part of Table X. in the Imperial series shows the linguistic distribution of the population of each province and State. A proportional summary of it is shown opposite. It seems to require no special comment.

B.—The Distribution of the Population by Religion.

"One religion after another may fade away, but the religious sense which created them all can never become dead to humanity."—*Richter*.

The various forms of religious profession current in India bear, as a rule, very distant relationship to the ethnic distribution of the population, as each includes recruits from nearly every section of the community. But all bear traces of the general influence mentioned in the opening section of this chapter. That influence, indeed, finds perhaps its strongest manifestation in the hold still universally retained over the beliefs of the masses by concrete notions regarding the relationship between man and the supernatural, such as are associated with the very earliest stages of organised Animism. The subject is, from its very character, too wide to be discussed here, but it is impossible to deal adequately with the statistics given in Table VI. of the Imperial series without considerable explanation of the scope of the nomenclature adopted, and this entails something in the way of a disquisition on the development of the various component elements of the general titles which have been thus brought into the service of the census.

To begin with a term just used above, it is necessary to show what is here meant by Animism. As the word is extensively used by Dr. Tiele in a sense somewhat wider than that which other writers on the subject have given to it, his own interpretation, which is that adopted for the purposes of the present work, may as well be quoted:— **Animistic religion.**

"Animism is the belief in the existence of souls or spirits, of which only the powerful—those on which man feels himself dependent, and before which he stands in awe—acquire the rank of divine beings, and become objects of worship. These spirits are conceived as moving freely through earth and air, and, either of their own accord, or because conjured by some spell, and thus under compulsion, appearing to men (*Spiritism*). But they may also take up their abode, either permanently or temporarily, in some object, whether lifeless or living it matters not: and this object, as endowed with higher power, is then worshipped or employed to protect individuals or communities (*Fetishism*). Spiritism, essentially the same as what is now called Spiritualism, must be carefully distinguished from Fetishism, but can only rarely be separated from it."

Such is the general conception of Animism, but, as we have no occasion to treat of it in its more primitive form, it has been used above with the addition of the word organised. By this is meant that in the stage of development in which we find it in India, it has passed from its archaic and indeterminate shape into a collection of polydaimonistic tribal religions, in which spells, magic, and exorcism are all prominent. It is relevant to what has to be said a little later, to point out that in this stage the malevolent spirits are considered the more important, and little notice is taken of the good. The main object, in the first place, is to get power over the spirits by magic. and, in a higher stage of belief, to propitiate them by gifts or homage. These notions are to be found in every stage of evolution in different parts of India, but the term Animistic has been restricted, in the census tables, to a certain class of the community. As in the case of several other forms of creed in that country, it is necessary to define the scope of the title negatively, or by explaining what is not included under it, rather than what is. In anticipation, therefore, of an explanation of the term Hindu, it may be stated that it was the intention of the framers of the rules for enumeration that under the head of Animistic should come all members of the forest tribes who were not locally acknowledged to be Hindu, Musalmán, Christian, or Buddhist, by religion. No general title for the religion of such communities was prescribed, but the enumerator was instructed to enter in the column reserved for this information the the name of the tribe, and the compilation under the above-mentioned head was made at the Central office of the Provincial census. The distinction between the tribal form of faith and that of the lower grades of the Bráhmanic community is very elastic, as will be shown below, so that the application of the rule on the borders of the hill tracts was no doubt arbitrary. It is well known, too, that the process of Brahmanising has been long and continuously in progress amongst these tribes, where, indeed, the latter religion is said to find the only fields left for its propaganda, so that very probably the more advanced branches of one of these tribes, who presumably dwell in closer proximity to the plains, are in fact affiliated to the Brahmanic faith, which makes but small demands upon their capacity for change, whilst their fellows in the remote valleys and forests continue in their former unregenerate condition. In this way we can account for the fact that out of 15,922,000 members of the forest tribes, only 9,280,000 are returned under their tribal form of religion. But the distinction is really of little moment, because, as was mentioned in the beginning of this section, every stratum of Indian society is more or less saturated with Animistic conceptions but little raised above those which predominate in the early stages of religious development.

Hinduism. We can pass on, therefore, to the next form of creed, which, under the title of Hinduism, is returned by more than 72 per cent. of the population of India. The clumsy name is only justifiable by convention, and only definable by the same process of successive exclusion as was used above with reference to the application of the term Animism. Primarily and historically, it is the antithesis of Islám, and thus includes all Indian forms of faith in which the uncompromising Unitarianism of the adherents of the Prophet detected signs of the worship of idols. But for the present purpose greater discrimination is necessary, and internal dissent is entitled to recognition. For example, there are two purely Indian offshoots from the parent stock, the systems adopted by the *Sikhs* and *Jains* respectively, that have been, on the whole, sufficiently differentiated to form distinct professions, although, in the present day, the dividing lines are anything but clearly denoted, owing to the confusion between social identity and doctrinal diversity. *Buddhism*, again, originally a manifestation of nonconformity arising almost in the centre of the orthodoxy of the day, received a new set of characteristics when allowed to develop *in partibus infidelium;* and even in the few tracts within the borders of its native land where it still prevails, little affinity is traceable between it and the religion in the bosom of which it was nurtured. There are two modern schools of doctrine to each of which the name of a separate religion is sometimes given, Brahmoism and Aryanism, but neither is current beyond a section of the community numerically insignificant, or differs sufficiently from the vital tenets of orthodoxy to be entitled to such a distinction. In the return under review, accordingly, they are shown subordinately to the general title, and in the other returns in which religion is specially recognised, they are included in the latter. The confusion between Hinduism and the lower or tribal forms of religion has been sufficiently mentioned in the foregoing paragraph. And in some parts of the country, as, for instance, the Panjáb and Central India, there is a marked disinclination to apply the term Hindu to members of the lower and impure castes, such as sweepers and village menials. In the Panjáb, however, such returns have been added to the Hindu, but in Central India many have been classed as Animistic which are shown elsewhere as within the pale of orthodoxy. Thus, by the process of exclusion, we reach the conclusion that Hinduism is the large residuum that is not Sikh, or Jain, or Buddhist, or professedly Animistic, or included in one of the foreign religions, such as Islám, Mazdaism, Christianity, or Hebraism. Thus limited, a more applicable title for it would be Brahmanism, which connotes its two chief characteristics in the present day, the recognition of inherited social status and the authority of a hereditary sacerdotalism. It must be understood, however, that this use of the term does not imply that absolute supremacy of the priestly class which induced M. Barth, a leading authority on the subject, to restrict the term to the earlier stage of the faith, before the Buddhistic schism, nor does it imply that the sacerdotalism in question is invariably that of this class, for we have instances where the office is undertaken by those of other sections of the community, such as the Jangam, amongst the Lingaiat heretics, and the Gosains of the quasi-orthodox converts of the Assam valley. The expansion of the creed consequent on the recrudescence of Brahmanic influence that succeeded the decay of Buddhism in India has induced the authority just cited to employ the term Hinduism for the present system, but as the latter is the work of the Bráhman, and the entire tendency, whether of orthodoxy or dissent, is in the same direction as during the earlier development, it seems inadvisable to ignore in the nomenclature the main factor in the actual conditions.

In few, if any, other parts of the world can be found so apt an illustration of what Gibbon puts as an *obiter dictum* into the mouth of the Roman magistrate, that in every country the form of superstition which has received the sanction of time and experience is the best adapted to the climate and its inhabitants. Religion, in the etymological sense of the word, it is not, and never was. The binding element is only educed by active opposition on the part of some other form of faith, such as Islám, and is generally confined to that part of the country where the two communities are separated by race as well as doctrine. Elsewhere, if there be any general feeling at all, it is limited to sectarian disputes, subordinate to social considerations. Its extraordinary vitality is due, obviously, to its power of adapting itself to many new circumstances, to the elasticity that accompanies the absence of dogma in the faith taught to the masses, and to the relegation of ceremonial and liturgy to social observances, and equally concrete worship. To quote Gibbon, again,—

> "The superstition of the people was not embittered by any mixture of theological rancour, nor was it confined by the chain of any speculative system. . . . The deities of a thousand groves and a thousand streams possessed in peace their local and respective influences. . . . Such was the mild spirit of antiquity that the nations were less attentive to the differences than to the resemblances of their religious worship."

This applies very fairly to the state of feeling in India in the present day. The faith of the masses is purely local, and Brahmanism, as a whole, is absolutely restricted to the Indian continent, from the Himálaya to Rámnád, and from the Indus to the borders of Arrakan. Here it lies, as has been said, like a lake, in gentle motion within its banks, from local ferment below, or as its surface catches some stray gust of fresh ideas. Every now and then an island of Animism is sapped and crumbles into the depths till no trace of it remains, but beyond this there is no accretion affecting the dead level of the contents.

The process by which the community has reached this stage of, so to speak, marking time in its religious development, is highly instructive, for, as its recent historian, M. Barth, writes :—

> "Nowhere else do we meet with circumstances, on the whole, so favourable for the study of the successive transformations and destiny, so to speak, of a polytheistic idea of the universe. Among all the kindred conceptions that we meet with, there is not another which has shown itself so vigorous, so flexible, so apt as this to assume the most diverse forms, and so dextrous in reconciling all extremes, from the most refined idealism to the grossest idolatry ; none has suceeded so well in repairing its losses ; no one has possessed in such a high degree the power of producing and reproducing new sects, even great religions, and of resisting, by perpetual re-genesis in this way from itself, all the causes that might destroy it, at once those due to internal waste and those due to external opposition."

Of the religion brought by the early Arya into the plains of India, little, if any trace is left. By comparison of the more archaic conceptions of the Mazdaistic creed with those of the same class in the Vedic, it seems that the worship of the elements was one of the chief features in both. But the earliest utterances on the subject in the collections that have come down to us are clearly stamped with the mark of their sacerdotal origin, and can only be accepted as the productions of an age far more advanced in religious conception than that in which the Arya crossed the mountains, leaving their nearest kin in possession of the field in Central Asia. In the Vedic literature there are invocations, no doubt, parts of which are far older than the rest, which were pieced together after the sacrifice with which they were connected had grown into the appanage of a hieratic body, and from these some notion of the Vedic theology may be obtained ; but this is very different from what must have preceded it, and between the two is drawn a curtain which bears no sign or representation of what it conceals. Modern investigators, however, are satisfied that alongside of the higher Animistic ideas that are shadowed forth in the Vedic, or sacrificial literature, there must have been an exoteric, and lower, stratum of beliefs, of much the same sort as are found amongst undeveloped communities in other parts of the world. As the immigrants advanced eastward, this lower influence asserted itself, and the superstition of the dark races came into contact with that of the foreigner. The sacrifice, as a means of securing the material favours of the gods, had by this time become the main feature in the religion of the Arya, and it is curious to note that even in this early period the religious element was egregiously restricted, for the altar of each clan or family had, by special prescription, to be erected as far as possible from that of any other member of the community. This is, perhaps, only what is to be expected from the very practical bargain which the sacrifice was the method of concluding with the supernatural powers, the benefits of which could not possibly be shared by any besides the provider of the oblation. From the time when the sacrifice passed from being an office undertaken by several of the leading classes of the community into a mystery in the hands of a special body, the liturgy naturally closed upon what it had already acquired, and the production of fresh invocations ceased, lest the monopoly of the sacrificing priest should be endangered. Thus a close body of literature was created, and the text grew in importance over the spirit, as the conceptions of the community were popularised away from their original tradition, and all participation in communion with the supernatural was withdrawn from the bulk of the population. The effects on the language of the Arya has been already mentioned. On the hieratic body the results were more direct. The whole duty of the Bráhman was held to lie in the preservation of the verbal accuracy of the ancient invocations, and in the interpretation thereof as the original tongue fell more and more into disuse. With the exception of the metempirical speculations that began to be rife soon after the class had outgrown the duties imposed on them in connection with ministration, the whole course of study was directed to the ritual, in which their male progeny were trained by long and arduous instruction. Women and the lower orders were excluded from this course, and, in fact, no class but that of the priests was admitted to what was at the time the only learning. Ere long, too, the Bráhman abandoned the practice of the sacrifice in favour of study and devotion, with a view to his own personal salvation. The hereditary sub-division of society was also developed so as to ensure the permanent debasement of the masses of the people, as seems to have been the intention of the later authorities amongst the Jews, in the Levitical stage of their history. But the impassable gulf between the hierarchy and the rest, the restriction to the former of all knowledge, study and ritual, still more, the selfishness of their system, under which all effort was centred in the thaumaturgical storage of merit for personal use only, to the exclusion of others—all these are traits that inevitably lead to a reaction.

Buddhism.

This came in the shape of Buddhism. Regarding the question whether such a person as Sákya Muni ever existed, there is this to be said, that there certainly was a personal head to the movement, and that to this fact is due a great deal, in fact, most, of the success that attended the propagation of the new creed in later years. On the other hand, there is no doubt that, as pointed out by M. Senart, most of the legend that attached itself to this personality in the hands of the proselytes who were not with the Founder from the beginning, is little more than can be attributed to the ordinary glamour of a solar myth. But the main point to be noted in reference to our present subject is that the reaction grew out of the system itself, leaving much of the latter unaffected. The great change lay in the substitution of the merit of the good life for that of cult, theological lore, or asceticism. There was no overt opposition offered to the current creed, but the flank of the priestly class was completely turned by the new doctrine. The monopoly of the knowledge of the sacred works of Vedic literature by the Bráhman was not impugned, but Buddhism explained that such knowledge was not essential to emancipation. The practice of asceticism was not deprecated, provided that it was accompanied by active benevolence to others. Worst of all, as a good life is within the capacity of all, the merit thereof could be reaped by anyone, irrespective of social position, so that salvation was placed within the reach of the lowest caste as much as within that of the Bráhman or warrior. In the monastic discipline, which was described as the first step towards that object, caste distinctions, and afterwards those of sex, were obliterated. Human nature, however, was probably not so very different then from what it is now, so there is no reason to conclude that this equality was at once carried to its extreme, save in theory; and as many Brahmans are reported to have joined the monasteries, it is more than probable that the impure castes, from long habit, held aloof till the new religion had made considerable way. Just so, in the present day, we find that in spite of the theoretical equality of all castes before the governing power, it has been found impossible to mix together the middle classes and the helots in the same school. The latter are either not admitted into the same building at all, or, where they are provided with a separate quarter, the teacher is said to provide himself with a supply of clay pellets as instruments of chastisement, to avoid the pollution of the orthodox rattan by contact with their bodies. But in this monastic discipline lay, in the first instance, the strength of the whole Buddhistic system, and its weakness in the end. The object was to train people to disseminate the principles of the faith by exhortation in the tongue of the masses. All was on a popular basis, and in the teaching there was nothing esoteric, but much morality and little or no spiritism. Buddhism made way slowly but steadily at first, without fanaticism or aggressiveness towards the Brahmanic tenets and practice. But, in accordance with the tendency, we have already had more than once to notice, the founder received the honour of apotheosis at the hands of his disciples; miracles were attributed to him, and on the recognition of his system as the State church of the only consolidated monarchy in India at the time, the new faith enjoyed for rather over a century unprecedented opportunities of expansion. There was evidently opposition of some sort from without, and schismatics and Laodiceans crept into the fold, but all this, so long as the path lay upward. only served to strengthen the faithful, and dissent was subdued by a General Council held under royal auspices. Selected missionaries were sent abroad with instructions from the king himself to see that the doctrine was made available to one and all in their respective vernacular languages. This last provision, however, was apparently disregarded in later years. But at all events Buddhism was conveyed across the Vindhya through the Deccan and the south to Ceylon. The mission to that island had the honour of being conducted by the son of the king in person, and from thence it spread later on to Burma, Java, and the surrounding country. The advent to power in the north of monarchs of considerable strength, both Skythian and Greek, gave an opportunity of diffusing the creed over the trans-Himalayan tracts bordering on India, and from thence into the north-east. Menander himself is claimed by the Buddhists as a convert, and there is no doubt that the human element in the creed carried it where the narrow doctrine of Brahmanism would receive no hearing.

We have now to look briefly at the causes which led to the decline of Buddhism. We have seen that in the first instance it was the founder's intention to run parallel with the orthodox faith, and even to retain caste, where conduct was in conformity with Buddhistic prescription. But there was the obvious denial of the right of the Brahman, as such, to assume superiority over the rest, and this was the thorn that rankled. Harmony was outwardly maintained, however, until the favour of the monarch began to divert the stream of charity, which, under the old system, to be meritorious had to flow into the coffers of the Brahmans, to whom a gift was personal, into the laps of the monks, who by their vows endowed their monastery with all the largess they might receive. The results, apart from the effect on the Brahmanical mind, were twofold. In the first place, the monastic orders rapidly increased and throve, so as to be able to provide the army of trained missionaries of whom we spoke above, and again, the establishment of these large bodies of more or less educated men in fixed situations, gave rise to architectural art in India, to the enrichment of the simple ritual of the founder, and, finally, to the erection of gorgeous temples and shrines over his relics. For, following on his canonisation came, of course, the desire to perpetuate his miraculous powers by the distribution of portions of his clothing, his begging bowl, and even his hair, teeth, and other terminals. But the tide of Buddhism as professed in India did not remain long at the full. We have no trustworthy or complete account of the causes that led to its decadence. It is plain, however, that soon after its accession to power as a State church it began to temper propaganda with persecution. One of the passages in the inscriptions of King Asoka puts this point with Thukydidean terseness:—

> "In less than two years the gods that were worshipped as true in Jámbudvípa have been rendered false, the result, not of my glory, but of my zeal."

Then, too, in the monastic system it was forging the means of its own extinction. The number of monks increased till they formed a society of their own, apart from worldly interests and from the lower sympathies of the community. When the zeal of conversion and exhortation had spent itself, the monks had nothing left to do but what is their fate in all countries where they exist, to withdraw from active life, and pass their time in discipline, introspection, and what Bacon calls vermiculate discussion. Thus their hold over the people and over their creed as a working religion, weakened. The Brahmans, during their period of depression, had laid to heart the methods of their adversaries. Theological teachers arose who enrolled bodies of disciples, in rivalry of the monasteries of Buddhism. Their tenets were popularised, their ritual enriched and modified, temples were built with public and gorgeous ceremonial, and, more important than all this, the Brahmanic pantheon was avowedly opened to the most widely popular of the local deities, male and female. Thus the regenerated and transformed Brahmanism was very soon in a position to gain an easy victory over their enervated rivals. The rapidity and completeness of the decay of the faith of Buddha, in spite of the short and partial revival under Shiláditya, is one of the most remarkable features in the history of Indian religion. Not that it has not left a praiseworthy mark on the latter-day Brahmanism that succeeded it, for no doubt the charity and tenderheartedness with the disregard of sacrifice that characterise the latter, are indirectly due to the lessons learnt by the masses whilst under Buddhistic influences, as they are alien to both the older Brahmanism and the Animism with which it is mingled. But as a religion, it has completely disappeared from the continent. We find the north-eastern portion of Kashmér and of the Panjáb, the Lepcha and Bhótia of the eastern Himálaya, and a few tribes in eastern Assam still acknowledging the creed of Buddha in its northern development. In Nipál, too, it holds the higher valleys, though the lower have succumbed to the social attractiveness of Brahmanism. Omitting this last-named tract, the Buddhists of India number but 243,000, of whom, again, one-half are found in the border land of Burma and Arrakan. When we take into consideration, moreover, the number of Chinese traders and of Burmese convicts in Indian prisons, the actual Buddhist population becomes very small indeed, and of the Aryan community professing this faith not a single representative remains. All that are not Burmese are of Thibetan extraction.

Jainism.

A second offshoot from the earlier Brahmanism is found in the Jain, a form of belief that still subsists and flourishes in India to this day. Its origin is veiled from us, but it bears a strong family likeness to the earlier form of Buddhism, and it is a question amongst scholars whether it rose about the same time or a little earlier. At all events it seems to have been unpopular with the Buddhists, and to have diverged less from Brahmanic orthodoxy. The monastic system was not countenanced, but ritual was simplified and women were allowed to share in it. As in Buddhism, however, the larger section of the Jains decline to allow that women can attain Nirvána. The latter, however, is with them perpetual bliss, instead of complete annihilation. Caste, amongst the Jains, is maintained, and though they have no special reservation of the priesthood to a class, there is a general tendency in that direction, and in some cases Bráhmans even are employed. In later years the Jains seem to have competed with the Bráhmans in literature and science, so that they fell into disfavour, and would very probably have succumbed, but for the advent of the Musalmán power. In the north and west of India they are still a cultivated class, mostly engaged in commerce, whilst in the south, where they share with the Buddhists, who preceded them, the credit of forming the Kanarese and Tamil literature, they are as a rule, agriculturists. Except in a few of the larger cities of the north there seems to be little sectarian hostility between them and the orthodox; and in the west, where they are still closer in customs and observances, the line of division is scarcely traceable. In parts of both tracts there is, in the present day, a tendency for Jainism to regard itself as a sect of Brahmanism, in spite of the non-recognition of the divine authority of the Veda. It is probable that in compliance with this tendency many have returned their religion as Hindu of the Jain sect, so that where sect is not separately compiled, as in the Imperial series of returns, the total of the Jain religion is reduced by that number. As it is, the number of Jains is given as about 1,417,000.

The Neo-Brahmanism.

To describe in other than very general terms the religion that superseded the Buddhism of about the first century before and after the Christian era is a task that would require a volume to itself of very considerable size. It will be sufficient to give a mere sketch of its more prominent characteristics. In the first place, the Bráhmans, in whose hands the whole of the reconstruction rested, had to reconcile the popular element implanted by Buddha's teaching with their own supremacy. The first method adopted was the incorporation into their system of the local gods and goddesses, which seem never to have been ignored by the masses, whatever may have been the views taken of their power by the educated portion of the population. These divinities were accordingly proved to belong to the Vedic pantheon. The Veda was held up as the key of all knowledge, and the knowledge of its prescriptions alone gave man the power of controlling the supernatural. These notions were adapted to the popular understanding by means of the later Brahmanic literature, epic and Puránic. By the term used here it is not, of course, meant that the authors were all of the Bráhmanic caste, for it is well known that the most celebrated works of this class are attributed to others, but it is essential that all should bear testimony to the authority of the Veda.

Now the knowledge and interpretation of the latter was the monopoly of the Bráhman caste, and we have seen that this fact was not disputed by even the most strenuous opponents of the orthodox system as a whole. It is immaterial, accordingly, to what number of deities the pantheon is opened, so long as they derive their recognition from, and are alone approachable through, the Veda. In the actual ceremonial of worship the Bráhman takes no part, according to strict interpretation of the later Vedic prescription, and those that are occupied about a temple, either as ministrants, or as guides to pilgrims, administrators of bathing-places, or other offices of a like character, are regarded as of a very inferior type of Bráhman, and scarcely recognised as of the caste at all by the higher grades of the hierarchy. In fact, there are many functions which in the eyes of public opinion are not acceptable to the divinity, if undertaken by a Brahman, another testimony to the non-Aryan origin of the present theology. But the authority of the Veda is found in all social ceremonies or those unconnected with worship. Here, the sacred text is all important, and only a Bráhman is competent to enunciate it. That is, it has become the spell by which the local deities are influenced, and public opinion, which is that of the caste, demands that the precautionary measure implied by its use shall not be disregarded. It has fallen a victim, in fact, to the particularism of which religion in India furnishes so many examples. Caste has been called the stronghold of the Brahmanic religion, in spite of its apparently purely social attributes, and it is to caste uses that the Veda has been inextricably bound. Sect, again, of which there is so much heard in the accounts of the Neo-Brahmanic system, begins, where it constitutes a radical reformation, in declaring itself open to all castes. Very shortly afterwards, it finds it has to except the leather-worker and the watchman, and, if it does not become a shadowy figment of doctrinal hair-splitting, turns into a caste, with all its exclusiveness, and its tendency to sub-division, as its number waxes. Next to caste in their hold on the minds of the masses, and it is of them alone, not the educated few, that we speak, come pilgrimage and the deification of the teacher, or spiritual guide, both of which owe their origin, in all probability, to the doctrine of faith current in this later form of religion. Into this it is out of place to enter, save to point out that it is itself a derivative, apparently, of the direction of worship to a special protective divinity. From the general conception, it was very soon detached in favour of the concrete figure of an incarnation, and from the adoration of the latter at the most efficient shrines, it is a short step to that of the mortal to whom is due all the knowledge one possesses of that worship, more especially as the age of miracles is by no means past and the canonised teacher is as competent to perform them as any god in the pantheon. As an act of faith is in itself an absolution, pilgrimages are the substitutes for most other religious observances, always excepting those connected with the propitiation of local spirits, whether family or attached to the house or village. It may be worth remarking, too, that in south India, where some local form of belief must have attained considerable development before the Árya influence on it began to be felt, and perhaps in Lower Bengal, also, for the same reason, the number of local deities, especially those requiring to be attended by people of the helot class, is much larger than in Upper India, and the propitiation of the malevolent spirits holds a far more important place in the popular ceremonial. The Brahmanical faith, too, was more developed when it reached the south, and as its greatest influence was probably exercised after it had begun its reconstruction on the new plan, the Dravidian element that it had to assimilate was proportionately high. The decline of a polytheistic religion, too, it has been said, is traceable in the exaltation of female deities, as well as in the multiplication of those of the other sex, and in both Madras and Bengal we find this feature very prominent. It almost seems, moreover, that in India, at all events, the weaker the race, the more numerous and more bloodthirsty are its gods, and the greater the influence of the sacerdotal system of caste. In connection with the present development of Brahmanism there is no need to speak of the contact with it of foreign religions, since whatever its effect on them may have been, they have made no impression on it, though the progress of conversion in one or two cases has been considerable.

Neo-Buddhism.

As regards Buddhism, the greatest, if not the earliest, of the offshoots from Bráhmanism, there is but little to add to the historical summary above given, except in relation to local developments. In the Himálayan form of this creed, which received its shape from the daimonolatry of the Skythian races which it replaced, the original tenets have been quite overlaid by the incorporation of former Animism. The Lama has become a priest and exorcist, instead of being a monk and preacher, and where the Indian frontier is approached the caste system of modern Brahmanism has attacked the tribal communities of the Buddhists. In one valley, for instance, the census shows that the inhabitants are in doubt as to what their religion may be, for in 1881 they were all set down as Hindus, and on this occasion they appear as Buddhists. In the eastern Himálaya the Lamaism is more restrictive, and of Nipál there is no occasion to speak. In Assam there has always been a suspicion of serpent worship and other forms of Animism, and the Buddhism of the days of the Chinese pilgrim bore but a poor character, as the inhabitants were, he says, addicted to the worship of Deva, or local gods, and to sacrifices. In the present day the Buddhism is confined to those who have apparently brought it with them from the north-east, so that it was altogether obliterated for some centuries, even if it ever had a firm hold of the wild tribes of the valley. The only country, therefore, of those with which the census has to deal, in which Buddhism still flourishes, is Burma, where it is the religion of about 90 per cent. of the population. But even here, as Mr. Eales points out in his report on the census, the popular belief is little but Animism, and the attachment to the higher creed is largely due to the educational influence of the religious orders, because every boy has to be sent, if only for a short period, to one of the monasteries as a novice or lay brother. Like the Neo-Brahmanism, too, it is gradually absorbing within its sphere the forest tribes who are professedly Animistic in their belief, and, like its former rival, it places no embargo on their tutelary gods, whilst as above stated, through the monastic system, it tends to raise them in the social scale. Considerably more than half the males in Burma can read and write, a feature in which the difference between the two systems is very clearly denoted.

Sikhism.

Of Jainism as a present-day religion we have said enough above. Sikhism was not specially mentioned in the general sketch of the Brahmanism from which it is derived, as it is a comparatively modern movement, and one that is not connected with the general history of the later development of its parent, since it has been confined to a single province and almost to a single community. It originated towards the end of the 15th century, and seems to have been due to the teaching of one of the most influential of the sectarian leaders of a quasi-Unitarian revival amongst the lower classes of Brahmanism. Kabir, the leader in question, was very appreciative of the tenets of Islám, on which ground he was alleged to belong to that faith, but in all other respects his doctrine and practice was that of Brahmanism, and there is no doubt that though he wished to combine part of Islám with the teaching he founded on the Veda, his views of the Kurán were anything but orthodox. The founder of the Sikhs, or disciples, Nának by name, seems to have rejected both Kurán and Veda, but maintains Brahmanic practice in social matters, and still employs that caste in ceremonial. The influence of Islám, however, as was natural to one of the frontier province, is traceable not only in his doctrine, but in the conception of the virtue of aggressive hostility towards dissentients, which was not brought to its full significance until the fifth Gúru from the founder espoused the side of the emperor's son in one of the numerous family disputes amongst the Moghals. He was promptly thrown into prison and died there. From that date the Sikhs became a political force, and have never since relaxed their hostility towards the Musalmán. The conversion was completed by the 10th Guru, Govind Singh, who died early in the 18th century, and under his guidance the separation of the disciples from the Brahmanic community was effected. But the new departure seems to have been largely nominal only, and a good deal of orthodox practice remained intact. The political objects of the Sikh leaders obscured the doctrinal, and culminated in the establishment of the kingdom of Ranjit Singh. In the present day, peace has relaxed the bonds of discipline, and the distinction between Sikhs and the rest of the Brahmanic community is mainly ritualistic. For example, it was found by experience that at the census, the only trustworthy method of distinguishing this creed was to ask if the person in question repudiated the services of the barber and the tobacconist, for the precepts most strictly enforced nowadays are that the hair of the head and face must never be cut, and that smoking is a habit to be absolutely avoided. The observance of these two injunctions, writes Mr. Maclagan, the Census Superintendent for the Panjab, is the best practical test of true Sikhism, "without any further rigmarole about sects"; for not only is a true Sikh generally called a Hindu in common parlance, but many of those who are spoken of as Sikhs are not true Sikhs, but Hindus. It is this confusion between the sectarian and the ceremonial elements that makes the return of Sikhs liable to correction, and instead of the number shown in Table VI. of the Imperial series, which is 1,907,833, the Panjáb Superintendent estimates that, so far as his Province is concerned, which is the only one in which this religion prevails to any significant degree, about 85,000 should be added from the Brahmanic total, and that 488,000 should be deducted from the Sikhs and added to the latter. The first item, he adds, is fairly accurate, but of the so-called Nánakpanthi, or sectarian Sikhs, it is possible that some may be true Sikhs as well.

Modern reforms. It is as well to complete this review of the Brahmanic and quasi-Brahmanic religions by adding a few lines on the two modern developments of Bráhmoism and Aryanism. The former is more or less known in Europe from its adoption by the scholar Rám Mohan Rai, who came to England, and died there in 1833. It originated in Bengal, and whatever stimulus it has since received has been due to teachers belonging to that Province. Some 30 years after its foundation the usual detachment took place of a party that desired greater communion with the orthodox Brahmanism from which they started, and the younger spirits that proposed independence, based on the eclectic assimilation of what they thought applicable from other religions. The leader of the innovators lost his influence, in great measure, by his approval of the marriage of his infant daughter with Brahmanic rites to a young *parti* of considerable mundane attractions, and on his death shortly afterwards, another split took place, in consequence of the disputed succession to the post of leader. The movement is purely local, and confined to the literate classes of Bengal Hindus, with a few converts, it is said, from Islám. The total number of those who returned this form of faith, either as their religion or as a sect of Brahmanism, is 3,051, out of whom 2,596 are in Bengal, 239 in Assam, and 128 Bengalis serving in Government or railway employ in the Panjáb. The sporadic entries under this head in other parts of India are generally debitable to the somewhat similar sect of the Aryas, which is noticed below. As regards the number of the Brahmoists, it is highly probable that there are many more sympathisers with the doctrine than are shown in the census return, but, owing to the natural dislike to break from their social moorings in the haven of orthodoxy, a result which might follow on open sympathy, they adhere to the original term, and hold their creed to consist of a sectarian distinction, which commits them to nothing when marriage or caste ceremonies are in question.

The Áryan schism is based on much the same lines as the Bráhmo as regards its relation to Brahmanic orthodoxy. Doctrinally, it seems to be something in the nature of the "Veda up to date," and finds that these sacred works contain all the discoveries of modern sciences, including electricity and natural selection. In theory, the study of the Veda is opened by them to all, but in practice, caste is maintained in all its strictness, and, as most of the adherents of the Neo-Arya faith are of the Writing or Trading class, a line is drawn below these, but none between them and the Bráhman. The census return shows the number of this sect to be just under 40,000. It was founded about 1877, in Lahore, by a Bráhman from western India, who retired to Ajmér, where he died in 1883, some say by poison. Most of its adherents are found in the Panjab, North-West Provinces, and the surrounding tracts in which the clerical agency required in State or railway offices is recruited from those provinces. It is interesting, as a study of the results of western instruction on a hereditary literary body in social subordination to an equally inaccessible hierarchy. It makes no appeal to the masses, and as the female element in the return is mostly illiterate, and the founder has not yet been canonised, it does not seem likely to supersede orthodoxy at the family hearth, and will probably manifest no more vitality or influence than any other of the almost innumerable sects of the Neo-Brahmanism. It has achieved the first step towards success in the possession of an adversary, a "religion" started by a personal enemy of its founder. The new faith was proclaimed on the occasion of the Jubilee of Her Majesty, at Lahore, and is now estimated to have 190 followers. It publishes three periodicals and a shower of tracts, mostly directed against its rival. The latter is not slow to retort, and as both parties are recruited chiefly from the officio-cleric community, to whom composition is a recreation, the amount of literature produced, in proportion to the number of the faithful, is enormous.

Mazdaism (*Pársi*). We have now to consider the religions foreign to India. First of these may be placed that of the Pársis, entitled Mazdaism, from the name of its supreme deity, or Zoroastrianism, from the Greek rendering of Zarathústra, the reputed founder of the creed. Its claim to be treated of next after the religions that have taken their rise in India rests upon the common origin of Mazdaism and Brahmanism. In both cases we find the same gods named, but as the community split into two branches before the religion had been at all organised, it is impossible to trace more than a vague outline. As is usual in such cases of early dissent, the gods of the one branch became the devils of the other, but whether, as some think, the Indian branch went south and kept on attacking the Eránic branch from their standpoint on the upper Indus, or whether the two quarrelled on the north side of the mountains, and separated in consequence, seems an open question, and likely to remain so. In the reign of the Persian monarch, Darius the First, the two resumed contact, as the former obtained possession of the north-west corner of India. But his hold was slight, and the intercourse, even if not barred by the intervention of more than one chief of Skythian race, was barren of results. By this time, moreover, the religion of the Eránic branch had been moulded in quite a different form from that taken by the early Arya of India. It is another open question whether the founder of the former, Zarathústra, had any more real existence than Buddha, but it is certain that in the time of Darius, the religion attributed to his agency was established as that of the State, throughout Persia. The invocationary literature, as with that in the Veda, consists clearly of compositions of very different age. Most of it bears the trace of the influence of the forms of belief that prevailed at the time in Mesopotamia, that great birthplace of creeds, under which influence it diverged completely from the luxuriant growth taken by the Aryan mind in the more genial conditions of the south. The Greek invasion drove the Mazdian religion into temporary obscurity, but during the rule of the dynasty of Sásán it achieved a temporary revival, and to this period is due the greater part of the Mazdaistic liturgy, which is in the Pahlavi language, in contradistinction to that of the Avasta, or original scripture. Then came the flood of Islám, which directed all its force to the extirpation of what it denominated fire-worship, with such efficiency that only in the north-west corner of what is now Erán was any remnant left of the Eránic faith.* This brings the history of that faith down to the point with which we are chiefly concerned. A portion of those who preferred exile to either the abandonment of their creed or massacre, left their native country by the Persian Gulf for Ormuz, where they resided for some years. In the year 717 they reached India, debarking at Sanján, a small place some 60 miles north of Bombay. Here they settled, and four years later built their first place of worship in the land of their adoption. It would be pleasant to be able to attach thorough credence to the legend that with them they brought the sacred fire from their home in Erán, as Æneas conveyed his household gods from the flames of Troy to their new home in Latium. For several centuries the Parsis, as we may call them in their new domicile, peacefully waxed and multiplied. On several occasions they rendered important services to the local chief, who requited them with grants of land for settlements. Some of their number even visited the court of the Moghal Emperor, Akbar, who favoured Mazdaism with the affectation of temporary adhesion. Up to the middle or end of the 18th century, Súrat and Nausári were their headquarters, with colonies all over Gujaráth and even in more distant parts of India. They have ever since that time been gradually transferring themselves and their interests to the city of Bombay and its suburbs, on account of the opening they found there under British auspices for their great enterprise and commercial talents. Their religion during the early years of their residence in India suffered from the influence which must be exercised over a small and foreign body, numerically weak, by a strong Animistic atmosphere, combined with that absorptive power which is, as we have seen, one of the most prominent characteristics of the Brahmanism of the day; and from the accounts of contemporary travellers it appears that at one time it was barely distinguishable from the surrounding form of worship. But reinforcements arrived from Erán, and race-feeling has since served to keep it unmodified in all main doctrine, so that the lower influence is now confined to social and semi-religious ceremonial. On the other hand, the long period of political extinction in such a small community, jealous amongst foreigners of the tenets of the faith they had taken such pains to preserve, checked the development of their creed beyond the limits of the scripture and ordinances of rite and ceremony to which they attached so patriotic a value. In the present day the Parsi is a completely Indian community. The language they brought with them from Erán has been relegated to their liturgy, where it is studied like a classic by the scholars of their race. The mass of the Parsis in speaking and writing use Gujaráthi, the vernacular tongue of the tract where they first landed, and which is said to have been imposed on them as a condition of residence. In certain circles, especially in Bombay, the census shows a considerable tendency to return English as their mother tongue, a statement which

* Some writers have said that the Eránic religion was destroyed by the Túrk invaders, and that those under Abu-Bakar alllowed its exercise in peace, but there must have been strong grounds for the voluntary exile of so small a band, and the cessation of communication on their part with their native country.

will be by no means improbable in a few years, when the girls of the present generation arrive at the dignity of maternity, for this race has shown a remarkable aptitude for assimilating the lighter tints of western life, so that it will be interesting to those of a few generations hence to see in what way this occidentalisation has affected the religious development of the community. Taking the whole of India together, the Parsis number just under 90,000, but on looking into some of the details, it seems likely that a few Persians may have been here included, owing to the similarity of the names in some of the vernacular characters. The grounds for this supposition is that there are a few Parsi entries under the Musalmán religion, and if there are any two creeds in India the votaries of which are absolutely antagonistic to each other, they are Islám and that which it did its best to destroy. On the borders of the Caspian and a little to the south, in Yezd, there are still some of the ancient fire temples, with a congregation estimated at from 6,000 to 10,000 souls, with whom, during the last 20 years or so, the Parsis of Bombay have re-opened communications, so that when a famine took place in 1871, or thereabouts, a considerable number were brought down from Yezd to Bombay, where they were maintained by their more fortunate co-religionists.

Judaism. Of the Jews and their religion little need be said here. Apart from the modern immigration to the chief commercial cities, such as Bombay and Calcutta, there are two colonies of this race, both on the west coast. It seems probable that both arrived by sea, and though the date of their anabasis is not known, there is no doubt that they are of very considerable antiquity. In both cases are there two sections in the community; one, called the white, the other that of the black. The former justify their title by the tradition that they have kept aloof from intermarriage with the daughters of the land, whilst the others, like the Árya, have fallen victims to native alliances. In addition to these, though not strictly speaking within India, we find a colony of traders of this race in the settlement of Aden. These, being nearer to their native country, are of purer race and less tainted with local custom in their religion. They speak, too, a northern dialect of Arabic. The whole number, including these last, is only about 17,200, and of these 10,500 are found in Bombay, 2,800 in Aden, 1,300 in Cochin, and 1,450 in Calcutta. The rest are scattered over India, both in trading centres, and, in the case of the Bombay coast colonists, in the ranks of the native army. These last, whilst maintaining the main principles of their faith intact, have adopted the language and much of the social custom of the Marátha population by whom they are surrounded. It is much the same with the Israelites of Cochin.

Islám. One fifth of the population of India is returned as of the faith of Islám, but these 57 millions, like the 208 millions of Brahmanism, though to a less degree, contain an extraordinary collection of heterogeneous elements. In the first place we must divide the community into those of foreign race, who brought their faith into the country along with them, and those who were converted from one of the previous creeds of the country itself under various inducements and at many different periods of history. Not counting the teachers of Islám, who are scattered pretty numerously over India, the foreign colony, speaking generally, consists of three main bodies; first, and numerically the most important, are the immigrants from just across the north-west frontier, who are found chiefly in Sindh and the Panjáb. Next come the descendants of the court and armies of the Musalmán dynasties, who are also centred in upper India, with considerable offshoots in the large feudatory States of the Deccan; lastly, we have all along the west coast, settlements probably of Arab descent, who arrived by sea. Some of these, especially those who took to agriculture, appear to have mixed with the natives of India, and to have adopted a good deal of the social system of the latter, whilst others, including the trading classes, who could keep touch more easily with their country of origin, are decidedly of purer descent, and have preserved, moreover, their faith in much more of its primitive form. As regards the converts, no such subdivision is practicable. It is true that the process of conversion in India was of two very different characters, only one of which is still extant; but at the present time we cannot distinguish, at least in the parts of the country where both have prevailed on different occasions, the results of the one from those of the other. It seems probable that the first in the field was the method of peace introduced by those from over sea. Omitting considerations of doctrine, the new faith held out inducements of great worldly attractiveness, especially to those whom the Brahmanic régime had chained to a position of perpetual subordination. We find this along the west coast, and it is in full operation in the eastern division of Bengal at this moment. The official propagation of Islám does not seem to have been undertaken for several reigns after the establishment of the Musalmán power in northern India. The early monarchs, though no doubt they took no steps to quench the iconoclastic ardour of their followers, had their attention fully occupied by the novelty of their administrative task; and it is also fairly plain that Bábàr and his family were not troubled with much anxiety for the salvation of their infidel subjects, since they were by no means convinced of the exclusive merit of the substitute they had to offer. It was not until the tolerance of Akbar and the indifference of his two immediate successors had given place to the zeal of Aurangzib that the diffusion of the faith of the Prophet was taken in hand with real fervour.

From this time downwards we hear of wholesale conversions, some to avoid the alternative of death or confiscation of property, others to gain the favour of the great. The same system was pursued later on in the Deccan, when the Sultán of Mysore was seized by the desire to add to the number of the faithful. It does not appear that more than the public profession of belief was required, with the requisite punctuality of attendance at the Friday service and the observance of the prescribed fasts, so that all that is of the more vital importance to the masses in India—especially to the women—was left as before. The simplicity of the Kurán made but a feeble appeal to the mind of those accustomed to the sensuous rites of the new Brahmanism and the neighbourly proximity of the supernatural in the Animism that governed the life of the people at large. Hence arose the remarkable differences that demarcate the Islám of India from that of the population amongst whom the religion originated. In the former the "mild spirit of antiquity," as we have seen above, mitigated the asperity of sectarian hostility, so that Shíah and Súnni joined issue in doctrinal discussion without recourse to arms. The good men amongst the teachers received divine honours as if they had never left the Brahmanic fold, and in default of the pilgrimage to Mecca, which was beyond the reach of the majority, resort was had to the tombs of the canonised, where fruit and flowers are offered, as to one of the orthodox pantheon and often by Hindu and Musalmán alike. Saints are the special feature of the Indian development of Islám, and the worship of relics follows. In some places there is a hair or two, in others a slipper, elsewhere a footprint, of the Prophet, to which the devout pay homage and are rewarded by miracles. Even where the two religions do not participate in the same festival, the more simple has borrowed for Indian use some of the attributes of the more elaborate, as in the case of the procession of the tombs at the Muharram, and the subsequent dipping of the imitation fabrics in water, as in the Dúrga Púja of Bengal. In many instances, where the two forms of faith exist more or less in numerical equality side by side, the Brahman officiates at all family ceremonial, and, as it has been put by a local writer, the convert to Islám observes the feasts of both religions and the fasts of neither. This state of thought is very much like that described by Lady M. Wortley Montague as existing amongst the Makedonian Arnauts of her time, who, living between Christians and Mahomedans, and—

> "Not being skilled in controversy, declare that they are utterly unable to judge which religion is the best, but to be certain of not rejecting the truth, they very prudently follow both. They go to the mosque on Friday and to the church on Sunday, saying for their excuse that at the day of judgment, they are sure of protection from the true Prophet, but which that is, they are not able to determine in this world."

Compare with this the following experience in the present generation as having occurred in the eastern plains of the Panjáb:—

> "A traveller entering a rest-house in a Musalmán village found the headman refreshing the idol with a new coat of oil whilst a Bráhman read holy texts alongside. The pair seemed rather ashamed at being caught in the act; but, on being pressed, explained that their Mulla (priest) had lately visited them, and being extremely angry on seeing the idol, had made them bury it in the sand. But now the Mulla had gone, they were afraid of the possible consequences, and were endeavouring to console the god for his rough treatment."

On the frontier of this province, where the bulk of the population is Musalmán, and fanatically devoted to that faith, the Animism takes a different shape, and the Mùlla is simply a magician. In the southern tract the spiritual guide is valued, it is said, by his supposed ability to procure the object of the vows of his disciples. In the north, the description given by Sir Herbert Edwardes is so graphic that its reproduction will be excused:—

> "For the Bannuchi peasant the whistle of the far thrown bullet, or the nearer sheen of his enemy's sword, had no terrors; blood was simply a red fluid; and to remove a neighbour's head at the shoulder as easy as cutting cucumbers. But to be cursed in Arabic, or in anything that sounded like it, to be

told that the blessed Prophet had put a black mark against his soul for not giving his best field to one of the Prophet's own posterity; to have the saliva of a disappointed saint left in anger on his door-post, or behold a Háji who had gone three times to Mecca, deliberately sit down and enchant his camels with the itch, and his sheep with the rot; these were things that made the dagger drop out of the hand of the awe-stricken savage, his knees to knock together, his liver turn to water, and his parched tongue to be scarcely able to articulate a full and complete concession of the blasphemous demand."

To find a parallel to this feeling, one has almost to go west of Bantry Bay. But the above remarks refer mainly to the rural population, and in the towns, where the masses of the Musalmán community are equally converts from Bráhmanism, the standard of doctrine and practice is better maintained. In the tracts, too, where conversion is still going on, and the bulk of the surrounding population is Brahmanic of the lower polydaimonic type, as in Bengal and the Malabar coast, the antagonism is sufficient to keep Islám alive. In the Panjáb, on the other hand, the caste is weak, tribe and race are strong, the power of the Bráhman is in abeyance, and religion is altogether on a popular basis, where supernaturalism is strictly localised, so as to be under the control of special persons or agencies. Conversion and reversion, therefore, amongst the lower classes are here common. Where the caste system is very strict, on the other hand, the lower orders, instead of retaining their social titles on conversion, affiliate themselves to one of the foreign tribes, Shaikh, by preference, as has been mentioned in the introduction to this chapter, so that they obliterate the traces of their origin, and, if lucky in their worldly affairs, become the social equals of the best. One point regarding Islám in India may as well be noted here, as it is of considerable interest in connection with the general results of conversion; it is that the prejudice against postponing marriage till the girl is grown up is very much weakened, even if not altogether obliterated, and this, as well as the absence of prohibition against widow-marriage, seems to account, according to the views of Mr. O'Donnell, the Census Superintendent for Bengal, for the better lives of the Musalmán population, and the consequent greater rapidity of its growth in that province. Something, too, may be due to the diet of the Musalmáns, which in Bengal is more varied and nutritious than that of the Brahmanic castes, whilst in the Panjáb, on the contrary, the restrictions on the Musalmán are greater than those on his rivals, so that a year of high prices or scarcity is said to drive many of the lower class of the former into the ranks of Brahmanism, for the time being, to revert to the more liberal creed when its rules as to diet press less harshly on their resources.

It is thus plain that in India the religion of the Prophet is in practice by no means the uncompromising Puritanism it is found to be in, say, Arabia, whatever may be the theoretical identity of the two forms. In the towns, indeed, antagonism between it and the local religions is always smouldering, and if the strong hand were to be lifted for a moment, there would be no loss of time in finding an excuse for collision. To the Musalmán, Hindu, Sikh, and Parsi are alike obnoxious, as he to them, and against another religion, Sunni and Shiah fight shoulder to shoulder, leaving their own sectarian differences to be settled after the disposal of the common enemy.

Christianity.

Christianity was probably the latest of the great religions to be disseminated in India. It is true that a small settlement of early Christians was established on the west coast within the first two centuries of that era,* but the real spread of the creed dates from the 16th century, when the Portuguese navigator, Cabral, was instructed by royal commission to conquer territory and to promote Christianity, beginning the latter task "with preaching, and proceeding, if that failed, to the sharp determination of the sword." The methods adopted were, in fact, political, and the support of the Portuguese power was the reward of profession of Christianity by any of the petty chiefs of the tracts surrounding the European settlements on the western coast. A generation later, with the arrival of St. Francis Xavier, missionary enterprise was not only extended, but took a milder shape, detached from the polemic zeal of the first Portuguese Crusaders. The missionaries assumed the habits, dress, and often the titles of Brahmanic ascetics. It being their avowed object to build on an indigenous foundation, in order that the priesthood might be recruited from amongst the people themselves, they recognised much of the local Brahmanic customs, such as that of

* The arrival and death of St. Thomas on the east coast of Madras is probably apocryphal, as it seems that his labours terminated in the Skythian or Indo-Baktrian territories of Gondofares, apparently in lower Sindh. But there were Christians whose conversion was attributed to his influence settled on the Malabar coast at the end of the second century, who were visited by a Roman navigator about the year 190.

caste. The upper orders were separated in church from the lower, and intermarriage between castes was not sanctioned. Then, again, the creed had its miracles and martyrs to hold up to their congregation, its relics and acts of faith. Pilgrimages are still made to the tomb of St. Francis Xavier in Goa, on which occasions devout aspirations are fulfilled and fleshly ills are cured. These manifestations are probably now confined to the faithful, but in old days, Hindu and Musalmán joined at the tomb of Albuquerque in imprecations against his successors. In Upper India, the mission of the Jesuits and others, though less fruitful in numerical results, were apparently subjected to less opposition from the local rulers, as was to be expected from the policy of Akbar and his son towards the creed of any denomination. In the present day, the missions of the Roman Church are widely spread over India, but their chief strongholds in British territory are found in the extreme south and on the west coast of the peninsula. Recently, too, their propagandist zeal seems to have been remarkably successful amongst the dark tribes of the hills of western Bengal. Missionary enterprise on the part of the reformed churches of Christianity was two centuries later in its inception. Its pioneers were Danish Lutherans, who began work in the tracts surrounding Tranquebar on the south east coast, just above the Roman field of labour on that side of India. At the end of the century, too, the English mission to Bengal established itself under Danish protection, on the Húghli, and there carried out the literary work which has made the name of Serámpur so famous. In 1813 the Established Church of England entered the field. A bishopric of Calcutta was established, with archdeaconries for the two other Presidencies. In the next year, missionaries were sent out, followed, 12 years later, by another society. Since then bishops and societies have greatly multiplied. Some of the latter spread themselves all over the country, others settle down in selected localities, and confine their labours to it. We find amongst the nationalities represented, not only the principal ones recognised at the Sacred College, by whom the various ecclesiastical divisions of the Roman Church in India are respectively manned, but the Reformed Church comprises English, Welsh, Scotch, Irish, American, Swiss, German, Danish, Moravian, and Swedish. The various denominations represented are given in Supplementary Table A., at page 495 of the first volume of returns, for in the case of this religion, the tabulation of sects was prescribed as part of the Imperial scheme, instead of being left, as in that of the other religions, optional with the provincial authorities. Unfortunately, for spite of special instructions to secure accurate nomenclature, the results show that for a considerable proportion of the Christian population, the denomination was not returned at all, or else entered under the general title of Protestant. Thanks, however, to the courtesy of the Secretary of the Church Missionary Society, reference has been made practicable to a volume of Statistical Tables of Protestant Missions for 1890, through the aid of which the mission to which the above indefinite entries should, from their locality, be probably assigned, has been ascertained. Taking into consideration this adjustment, the return shows that out of a total of 2,284,380 Christians, 57½ per cent. belong to the Roman Church, 8¾ to the Jacobite or Syrian Church, 33 per cent. to the various denominations of the Reformed Church. The rest comprises the unspecified, and a few members of the Greek and Armenian forms of creed. The details will be considered below, where the statistics of each religion are dealt with in more detail.

Minor forms of religion.

In every enumeration of forms of faith room has to be found for a residuum of special classes of belief which cannot be fitted into any of the corners of those more generally prevalent. In India this residuum is small but varied. It is not, however, complete, for we find samples of Unitarians, Theists, and Agnostics included with Christians, probably because the enumerator found them mostly in the schedules of Europeans. Similarly, there were a few instances, altered on scrutiny, of Buddhists amongst European and Eurasian Christians. Some of these related probably to the professors of the new Theosophy; others may be set down, perhaps, to the example of a high official, who pronounced for Buddhism, on the ground that there was less to be said against it, he thought, than against any other form of religion. The number of persons from whom the return of religion was not required, or who did not fill in the column reserved for it, was remarkably small, so that no more than 42,578 people are excluded from the table. These are not to be confounded with those who positively assert that they have no religion, of whom there appear to be 18, including one whose attitude was further emphasised by the entry of "indifferent."

We have now to deal with the returns which are to be found in Table VI. on page 87 of the first volume of the Imperial series, and in a summarised form on page vi. of the same volume. The three aspects in which they are to be regarded are their respective and local prevalence, and their variation, wherever it is possible to ascertain it, from the corresponding return in 1881. The marginal table summarises the first and last, and in the table on the next page will be seen the proportion borne by each to the total population of the Province or State. Wherever there are special features to be noted with regard to the territorial distribution, mention of them will be found in the text. Comparison between the two years is in some cases little better than approximately correct, as has been admitted in the heading of the marginal table, since to uncertainty as to the exact limits of the tracts not enumerated by religion in 1881, there is added that regarding the identity of the definition and application of the nomenclature on the two occasions. On looking over the provincial details for the purpose of compiling this statement, the latter defect was found very prominent in the case of Sikhs, especially in Sindh, and of Jains, in most of those parts of the country where they are only found as exotics. The territories not brought under the census of 1881 have been, of course, excluded in making the comparison, but, in the case of Brahmanism, there may possibly be a little excess in the 1891 return, as compared with the one preceding it, owing to the inclusion of some parts of the wild tracts of Rájpútána, Madras Agency, and Eastern Bengal, but looking at the numbers dealt with, the difference in the proportional figures will be insignificant.

Statistics.

Religion.	Population (1891).	Per-centage on Total Population.	Approximate Per-centage of Variation since 1881.
Brahmanic	207,731,727	72·33	+ 10·82
Animistic	9,280,467	3·23	
Sikh	1,907,833	0·66	+ 2·12
Jain	1,416,638	0·49	+ 14·86
Zoroastrian	89,904	0·03	+ 4·91
Buddhist	7,131,361	2·48	+ 24·46
Jew	17,194	0·006	+ 20·93
Christian	2,284,380	0·80	+ 21·85
Musalman	57,321,164	19·96	+ 10·61
Minor forms	185	—	—
Unreturned	42,578	0·014	—
Total	**287,223,431**	**100·00**	**+ 10·98**

Territorial distribution of religions: Brahmanists, or Hindus.

The mean proportion of the Brahmanic to the total population is $72\frac{1}{3}$ per cent., and the table under review shows that this ratio is exceeded in all parts of India, except Burma, the Panjáb, Kashmér, Assam, Bengal, and Sindh. The detached Settlements also show greater variety of creed, as is to be expected, and the small State of Rámpúr, under the North-West Province Government, reduces the proportion in that group, owing to the preponderance of the followers of the faith of the ruling family. In the case of Kashmér, Sindh, and Bengal, too, the main competitor in popular favour is Islám, but in the Panjáb and its States, the Sikh faith, and in Assam, tribal Animism, are considerable factors in the distribution. Burma is almost exclusively Buddhist, but it is interesting to note the difference between the prevalence of that creed where it has been for generations the State religion, as in the Upper division ($96\frac{1}{2}$ per cent.), and where non-sectarian administration prevails, as in the lower, and it has had to compete with the local Animism on the one side and Christian missionary enterprise on the other, not to mention a considerable admixture of Brahmanism casually introduced by the labouring population from Madras and Bengal, all of which reduce its proportion to 86·8 per cent. It may be remarked, in passing, that in Kashmér a purely Brahmanic administration is placed over a population of which but 27 per cent. profess that creed, whilst, on the other hand, in Haidrabád, a strictly Músalmán régime presides over the destinies of a community of which 90 per cent. are, in its eyes, doomed to perdition. Taking Brahmanism as returned in the tables, its greatest relative prevalence is found in the south of India, Mysore, Coorg, Madras and Haidrabád; Bombay, Berár, and Baroda follow close behind, and eight other Provinces or States, including Rajpútána and the populous tracts of Oudh and the North-West, shows this creed in a proportion of over 80 per cent. of the total population. It has been sufficiently shown in the foregoing portion of this section that the identity of the title does not imply anything like identity of doctrine or practice, except in regard to caste and pilgrimage, and the variety is on the whole local rather than dogmatic. Certain sects attain popular acceptance throughout a certain class of the community, not always in the tract in which they originate, and are there localised.

TABLE showing Territorial Distribution of Population by Religion.

Province or State, &c.	Brahmanic.	Animistic.	Músalmán.	Sikh.	Jain.	Buddhist.	Zoroastrian.	Christian.	Jew.	Minor.	Unreturned.
	Proportion of each Religion to 10,000 of the Population of the Province or State.										
Ajmér	8,075	—	1,369	4	497	—	4	50	1	—	—
Assam	5,472	1,771	2,710	—	2	14	—	31	—	—	—
Bengal	6,338	322	3,285	—	1	26	—	27	—	—	1
„ *States*	7,899	1,391	670	—	1	17	—	5	—	—	17
Berár	8,738	473	717	1	65	—	1	5	—	—	—
Bombay	8,814	85	805	—	150	—	45	95		—	—
„ *States*	8,414	121	1,060	—	391	—	3	10	1	—	—
Sindh	1,976	271	7,714	3	3	—	5	27	1	—	—
Aden	616	—	7,984	—	—	—	72	682	641	—	—
Burma, Upper	98	66	144	9	—	9,653	—	30	—	—	—
„ Lower	306	320	452	1	—	8,680	—	240	1	—	—
Central Provinces	8,189	1,476	276	—	45	—	1	12	1	—	—
„ „ *States*	7,675	2,266	55	—	3	—	—	1	—	—	—
Coorg	9,063	—	732	—	7	—	2	196	—	—	—
Madras	8,981	133	631	—	8	—	—	243	—	—	4
„ *States*	7,456	—	609	—	—	—	—	1,931	4	—	—
N.-W. Provinces	8,579	—	1,380	3	24	—	—	14	—	—	—
„ „ *States*	6,935	—	3,060	—	3	1	—	1	—	—	—
Oudh	8,708	—	1,281	1	2	—	—	8	—	—	—
Panjáb	3,711	—	5,575	666	19	3	—	26	—	—	—
„ *States*	5,850	—	3,006	1,127	15	1	—	1	—	—	—
Quettah	4,291	—	4,170	414	—	—	14	1,103	—	8	—
Andamans	6,044	15	2,551	253	2	826	—	309	—	—	—
Haidrabád	8,941	25	987	4	24	—	1	18	—	—	—
Baroda	8,850	124	781	—	208	—	34	3	—	—	—
Mysore	9,384	—	512	—	27	—	—	77	—	—	—
Kashmér	2,720	—	7,051	45	2	116	—	1	—	—	65
Rajputána	8,483	342	825	1	348	—	—	1	—	—	—
Central India	7,496	1,857	551	2	87	—	1	6	—	—	—
Provinces	**7,016**	**264**	**2,240**	**64**	**22**	**321**	**4**	**67**	**1**	—	**1**
States	**7,958**	**520**	**1,176**	**76**	**140**	**5**	**2**	**120**	—	—	
INDIA	**7,233**	**323**	**1,996**	**66**	**49**	**248**	**3**	**80**	**·6**	—	**1·4**

We find, for instance, the greatest tendency to sectarian fissiparity amongst the imbellic Dravidians of the south, and the maximum of eclecticism or indifference, whichever it should be the more correctly termed, amongst the hardy and oft-invaded tribes of the Panjáb. In the former, a doctrinal schism, such as the Lingaiat, for example, led to a completely separated section in every caste that joined in the movement. In the Panjáb, the sects, though equally numerous, bear no relation to the life of the community, and the Brahmanic and Musalmán sections, whether of the same tribe or district, pay their respects to the same shrine. In the eastern portion of the Central Provinces, again, the lower classes, such as weavers and tanners, have joined in large numbers the Kabirpanth and the Satnámi, a couple of sects of the sort described earlier in this chapter, which begin with universal brotherhood and end in becoming a somewhat enlarged caste. The former of the two, though not indigenous to this part of the country, is found but sparsely represented elsewhere, and the latter also is almost entirely local in its development. In 1881 they were shown in the returns as separate religions, like Sikhism and Jainism, but on this occasion they have not been so distinguished, as it appeared that beyond their acceptance mainly by low castes, they had no better title to such treatment than many other well-known modern sects, such as the Wallabhachárya, Mádhwa, Swámi-Náráyan, Sákta, and so on. In the provincial volume, however, the numbers of their followers are given, from which we can presume that they are not at all falling off, though the increase may not be so large as that represented by the figures for the adherents of the doctrines of Kabír. As regards sect in the Panjáb, where the subject was dealt with at a census for the first time, the remarks of the Superintendent are well worth perusal, and show clearly the Animistic origin of the most popular beliefs, as distinguished from those inculcated by sacerdotalism. In the adjoining province, too, of the North-West and Oudh, the subject has been taken up, but no report on it is at present available. The development of Bráhmanism in Assam is well described by Mr. Gait in his Provincial Report, and seems in the Bráhmaputra valley to present the peculiarity of dispensing largely with the Bráhman and substituting the efficacy of the influence of the Gúru, or teacher. The progress and distribution of the small sects of Bráhmo and Arya need no more comment than has already been given to them, but before quitting the subject of the Brahmanic religion a few words are necessary regarding the confusion between its statistics and those of Animistic religions. It has been before remarked that the application of the two terms in tracts where the hill population is closely connected with that of the plain was very arbitrary. For instance, in one district, the whole of certain tribes which were shown as Animistic in 1881, appeared as Brahmanic in 1891, though in the next district the same communities were returned under their former appellation, and in neither had any material change been effected in their creed during the decade. Conversely, the opportunity offered by an alternative title was eagerly seized by the enumerators in Central India as a means of stigmatising as outside the Brahmanic communion, if that term be admissible, all the class of village menials, whose touch is doubtless polluting to the higher castes, but whose religion is but a trifle lower in Animism than that of the society they serve. Thus, in estimating the prevalence of Animism in this part of the country, a deduction of probably nearly one-half should be made, referring to the class of people whose beliefs are elsewhere included under the title of Brahmanism. This reduces Central India from its place as second in the order of prevalence of tribal religions, to fifth, or thereabouts, below the Central Provinces and their States, Assam, and the Bengal States, in all of which the definition has been probably applied as accurately as the state of religious practice will at present allow. In the extreme east and west, that is, in Burma, and in Bombay, Sindh, Baroda, and probably Rajputána, the line between the two is very ill-defined, and the distinction, consequently, of little value. In Ajmér and the North-West Provinces the tribes shown as of an Animistic form of religion in the neighbouring territory are returned as Brahmanic. In the Panjáb, where there is but one tribe thus diversely treated, it is almost certain that the form of religion has really changed in proportion to the distance between the northern settlements of the tribe in question and the hill tract from which it originally came, and where its fellows still reside. The distinction, therefore, is actually in existence, and is not the arbitrary creation of a Brahmanic enumerator. It is not proposed to enter into any discrimination between the different forms assumed by what is here classed under the general head of Animism. There are certain layers of belief throughout the community which are all susceptible of classification into groups now recognised in ethnology, some of the items being tribal, others local, in their prevalence. The task of examination and description has been

Animism.

undertaken by various investigators at different times, and Bengal, the Central Provinces, Berar, Bombay, and a portion of Assam have been fortunate in the results, but no general collection of the results has yet been attempted, nor can it be successful until the inquiry has extended over the whole field open to such a survey. Steps in this direction are now being taken by Messrs. Gait and Crooke, in Assam and the North-West Provinces respectively; and in the Panjáb, where Animism in its tribal form has been beaten out through the whole community, so that it can no longer appear under that title, the subject has been well worked by Mr. Ibbetson and others.

Músalmáns. The next religion to come under review is that of Islám, which is taken here on account of its numerical importance. The Músalmán population of the world has been roughly estimated at various amounts from 70 to 90 millions, so that whatever the real figure may be between those limits, the Indian Empire contains a large majority of the followers of the Prophet. No Province or large State, and probably few districts or other subdivisions in the plain country west of Burma, is without a certain number of Musalmán inhabitants. We find them relatively most numerous, of course, in the north-west, where Sindh and Kashmér head the list, with 77 and 70 per cent. respectively. In the former there is a considerable foreign element, consisting of Balóch and Bráhui from across the frontier, but the bulk of the population has been converted from a lax form of Brahmanism. For a short period in its history the province was under a Bráhman régime, centred about Haidrabád, where it was disturbed and afterwards confirmed by Alexander the Great, but was overthrown not long afterwards by one of the numerous waves of Skythian origin that broke upon the west and north-west frontier of India before and shortly after the beginning of the Christian Era. According to the Chinese pilgrim Hiuen Tsang, Sindh was in the seventh century both barbarous and superstitious, and orthodoxy of any sort sat lightly upon its unscrupulous population*, as it is said to do even now. In Kashmér, the present population, whether Skythic or Árya, has been addicted within historic times to serpent worship, Buddhism and Brahmanism, by turns, before its conversion to Islám was undertaken by the Moghals during their summer visits to the valley. The Sikh rule succeeded, but left both Músalmán peasant and Bráhman professional alike untouched, except that the privileges of the latter were confirmed. In the north-west the tribes were probably converted from the side of Afghanistán, not from India, and their example was followed by the Mongoloid Thibetan races to the north along part of the upper Indus. On the east, however, in Ladákh, the sparse population is still Buddhist, and along the south range intervening between the valley and the Panjáb, there is a considerable Bráhmanic element of comparatively pure Árya descent, but, on the whole, 70½ per cent. of the population of the State is Musalmán. In the Panjáb we have samples on the largest scale of both foreign immigration and local conversion. In the British portion of the province, 55¾ of the population professes Islám, the proportion rapidly rising towards the west and gradually falling as the Jamna is approached. On the States, the largest of which, with one exception, are under Sikh rule, Islám has made, of course, less impression, and it is returned by only 30 per cent. As has been said above, the outward observances of the faith are more or less strictly regarded where the religion is that of a large majority of the people, but left in abeyance where the conversion was effected by force or worldly pressure and without the example of foreign zealots to sustain devotion. The more martial races are converted to the extent of at least one half, and the lowest class of the Brahmanic community favours alternatively Islám and Sikhism. Passing eastwards, we find the proportion of Musalmáns high in the submontane tracts of the North-West Provinces, but below the average in the province as a whole. In Bengal, as we had occasion to note in connection with the density and migration of the population, there is a strong Musalmán element, exceeding one half the population, nearly all over the whole of the eastern division, and the same remark applies to the Súrma Valley, now included in the Assam Province. It is in this part of the country that the results of conversion are more marked in the circumstances of the population than anywhere else in India. We have seen that the growth of the population here has been more rapid than in any other division of the province, and the Provincial Census Superintendent attributes this in a great degree partly to conversion and partly to other ecclesiastical factors as they are understood in India. In the first place there is the rise in *status*, then the range of diet is

* "The cattle-breeders are of an unfeeling and hasty temper, given only to bloodshed. They have no masters, but shave their heads and adopt the mendicants' robe."

greater than amongst the Brahmanic classes. Thirdly, not only is marriage deferred till the bride is grown up, but there is no prohibition of widow-marriage, both of which are facts tending towards a longer life on the part of the women and a healthier offspring. In connection with this part of the country, we may mention the Musalmán population of Lower Burma, which is largely indebted to Chittagong and its neighbourhood for its recruits, chiefly sea-faring people, supplemented by a certain influx of the trading Musalmáns of Bombay and Madras, and the followers of the last Dehli princes, who were assigned a residence at Rangoon. The high proportion of Musalmáns in the Bombay States and in Baroda is, in its turn, partly due to the number of traders in Kachh and other Gujaráth States, partly to that of the cultivators mentioned already—both foreign converts—who abound in that division of the Presidency. It must be remembered, too, that Gujaráth was the seat of a considerable Musalmán power in the days of Moghal rule in Upper India, and Cambay, Júnágadh, Pálarpur, Rádhanpúr, and Balásinur, testify to the extent and durability of its authority, as Sachín and Janjíra do to the influence of the same religion amongst the foreign employés of the Marátha chiefs. We can now turn to the parts of India where the proportion is the lowest. The Nadir of Islám, numerically speaking, is found in the Hill States under the Central Provinces, and, with the exception of Upper Burma, where there are now fewer immigrants of the Pánthé class, in those provinces themselves. Next to these comes Mysore, in spite of its former period of Musalmán rule. In fact, it nowhere appears that rulers of that faith, when detached from its centre in Upper India, surrounded themselves with large numbers of their co-religionists. Witness the case of Haidrabád, where, though the whole administration is in the hands of Musalmáns, less than 10 per cent. of the population is of that faith, or only 2 per cent. more than in the neighbouring province of Bombay. The proportion in Madras would be very low, as it is in other parts of Southern India, were it not for the trading community of the Labbé on the east coast, and the semi-trading semi-agricultural Mappila of Malabar and its two adjacent States; for the local convert, in spite of the zeal of Tippoo, is not a considerable feature in the general population, though he is in sufficient force in the larger towns, as shown some years back at Salem, to present a strong front to infringement on what he considers his privileges by Brahmanical neighbours. The Músalmán element in Central India is singularly low, seeing that it was the refuge for many years of wandering bands of marauders of considerable strength. But the strong hand of the two great Marátha powers and the exclusiveness of the Brahmanic chiefs of comparatively pure race in the south-east of the Agency, tend to confine the foreign religion to the Musalmán States, of which only one, Bhopál, is of considerable size. As regards the progress of the faith of Islám, little need be added to what has been already written above. It has been undoubtedly rapid in Eastern Bengal, and has been perceptible, though on somewhat an uncertain basis, in the Panjáb. Elsewhere, the increase seems to be mostly that due to normal growth. But so far as regards the large and heterogeneous class of urban Músalmáns found all over the country, it is possible that that growth may have been actually impeded by the difficulty found in getting a living under the new conditions of British rule. For the minimum of literary instruction required now as a passport to even the lower grades of middle-class public employ is decidedly higher than it used to be, whilst the progress of learning amongst this class of Musalmans has not proportionately advanced, and with the comparatively small number of recruits for the army, police, and menial offices that is now found sufficient, few outlets remain available. It is possible that some such reason as this accounts for the fact that the general rate of increase outside the tracts above mentioned is a little below that found to prevail amongst the population as a whole.

Buddhists.

In the course of the general sketch of the history of Buddhism, it was mentioned that outside Burma and the Himálayan valleys and table-lands this religion was no longer prevalent in India. The few specimens we find of it in the returns for Madras, the Central Provinces, the Andamans, the North-West Provinces and so on, are chiefly from the jails, where Burmese convicts were drifted temporarily to relieve the local prisons during the days of dacoity. There are also Chinese shoemakers and carpenters, found at Calcutta and other large sea-port towns. Finally, we have from one district in Bombay a relic of the time when in statistical returns Jains and Buddhists were combined, for a small colony of the former were set forth as the latter by some enumerator whose memory was apparently more accurate than his eyesight, or his perusal of his instructions. The increase of the religion, as a whole, is determined, of course, by the actual growth of the population of Lower Burma, which is, as we have seen, the most rapid in rate of any part of the country. In the Himalayan tracts, too, a little more accuracy in regard to Thibetans has been observed, but still, it is said, a good many of the Bhótia, or Thibetans of the northern uplands of Kumaon and Garhwál, return their religion as Brahmanic, when they are in the submontane grazing grounds for the winter.

Jains.

The Jains are widespread over India, though they form an appreciable numerical element in the population only in Rájputána, Ajmér, and Western India, and nowhere reach 5 per cent. of the total. It is worth notice that they seem to flourish most where they have devoted themselves to trade and commerce, and are weak in number where they have become agriculturists. In the latter capacity they are found in Madras, but only to the number of 27,400, in Mysore, where there are 13,300, whilst the Bombay Karnáták returns about 46,000, the bulk of whom are evidently cultivators. This is a very different state of things from that of the early centuries of the Christian Era, when the ancestors of these communities were leaders of literature and art in the south. Of the trading communities a good deal has been said already in different parts of this work. There are large colonies along the Jamna and in parts of Central India, but except in Dehli, they do not much effect the Panjáb. In the Gujaráth division of Bombay they flourish exceedingly, with headquarters in Ahmedabád and settlements at their mountains of pilgrimage in the Káthiawár peninsula, Palithána and Girnár. Between them and their co-religionists in Upper India come the best known, perhaps, of the whole body, called by the generic name of Márwádi. In Assam and Upper India they are stigmatised as Káya, a term of uncertain etymology, but vulgarly attributed to their inquisitiveness, as it has an interrogative sound about it. Perchance it will occur to philologists at some future period to connect it with the nick-name Kaitoukeitos, given to one of the Deipnosophists of Athenæus, in consequence of his aggressive thirst for information. The Jains of the Central Belt and the north Deccan are of this race as well as of Gujaráthi origin. It is remarkable that in the country of its birth, Párasnáth in South Bihár, there should be no more than 1,487 of this religion returned at the census. From evidence indirectly afforded by applications made from the neighbouring tract just before the census, it seems highly probable that in this part of the country, instead of desiring to emphasise the distinction of their religion from Brahmanism, as was the case at Dehli, &c., the Jains are anxious to efface it, as their social position is evidently based on caste orthodoxy within the Bráhmanic fold. If this tendency be true, it will account for the disappearance of the Jains into the general sea of Hinduism.

Sikhs.

The Sikh religion may be considered as localised in the Panjáb, for though there are members of this faith in most provinces, 98 per cent. of them are returned from its birthplace. The bulk of those in the North-West Provinces are colonists or soldiers, and in the rest of India and Burma, the latter only. In Kashmér, of course, there are some belonging to the Panjáb, who have been permanently settled in Jammu or the valley ever since the time of Goláb Singh, or of the Sikh domination that preceded the assignment of the State to him. The Superintendent of the Panjáb census shows in his report that in British territory the Sikhs have increased by 24 per cent., whereas in the States under that Government, their numbers have declined to the extent of 19 per cent. He attributes the latter fact to greater accuracy of definition only, and it is probably due in great measure to the exclusion of the Brahmanic classes returning the Nánakpanth, &c. as their sects. Undoubtedly this is the cause of the notable decrease in the number of Sikhs returned from Sindh, where there are few, if any, of the true, or Govindi, Sikhs, outside native regiments. Mr. Maclagan summarises the effect of the change of definition as tending to increase the Sikhs on the return where they are few and to diminish them where they bear a high proportion in the population.

Zoroastrians or Pársis.

As the Sikhs appertain specially to the Panjáb, so the Zoroastrian religion is almost confined to the Western Presidency and States surrounding it. The early settlements of the Pársis at Nausári, in the Baroda State, and in Súrat and Broach, still contain about 30·4 per cent. of the entire community, and their original fire temple at Udwáda on the Súrat coast has maintained its supreme repute. But the head quarters of the race have been gradually shifted to Bombay, where there are now 52·8 per cent. returned. Colonies of some strength are also to be found in Karáchi, Aden, the Haidrabad State, and in Poona. Elsewhere, small detachments, sometimes consisting of one or two families only, are settled in military stations, or along the lines of rail. In Upper Burma, the flag was soon followed by the Pársi, and the enterprising Zoroastrian settled himself down in Mandalay on its occupation with the same promptitude and confidence in British protection as his forerunners showed in Aden and Quettah. The only province into which he has not yet penetrated seems to be Assam. Here, apparently, trade is not yet sufficiently extended to invite competition, and perhaps, too, the small and isolated European community, for whom the Parsi is always glad to cater, has placed co-operative institutions already in the field. The numerical progress of the Pársi community is a matter of some uncertainty, owing to the migratory habits of the race. Unhampered by caste rule as to food or clothing, the Parsi is free to seek employment all over the world, and many leave Bombay for years together, to work in China, England, or even more distant countries. The census Superintendent for Bombay finds in the age tables reason to think that in 1881 the young children were over counted, so that the increase is really greater than that shown in the tables. On the other hand, temporary causes are manifested in a small community with unwonted prominence, and the conditions of the case, apart from emigration for a certain time from the native country, seem to point to the probability of a slow growth. The community is a small one, and in spite of its general prosperity and the probable infusion of fresh blood from time to time from various local sources, the marriage field is a restricted one, and domestic ceremonial which is very strictly observed, weighs with undue severity on the weaker sex. Hence, especially amongst the wealthier families, who all belong to the professional and higher commercial classes, there seems to be a tendency towards deterioration in both prolificity and physique, which is not counteracted, as in the case of the middle and the rural classes, by outdoor life and the relaxation of caste rule amongst the latter, or by the energy and success with which the former have of late betaken themselves to athletic sports and exercises.

Jews.

Of the Jewish community, as in the case of the Jains and Sikhs, there is little more to be added to what has been said above. The returns do not discriminate between the various classes of the race, so we are not in a position to exactly demarcate the foreign element from the local. The chief seaport towns, such as Bombay and Calcutta, contain a small and wealthy community which came thither from Baghdad or other places in Turkish Arabia, but which is now domiciled in India. The Aden colony, too, is domiciled there, and seems to flourish and multiply greatly under local auspices, as in 1881 there were but 2,121, and 10 years later the number had risen to 2,826, an increase of 33 per cent. Lastly, there are the two purely Indian communities of the Beni-Israel, on the Bombay coast, and the Cochin Jews, further south. The former, in which the local element predominates, shows a tendency to migrate, but does not increase very rapidly. In Malabar, the white Jew, with his small endogamous circle, is apparently stationary, or even on the wane; nor does he travel far from the places where he first settled, whereas the Beni-Israel is more enterprising, and forms a small, but intelligent and valuable, fraction of the native army in the Western Presidency.

Christians.

In the returns of the Christian population, the distribution by race is given, in addition to that by territory and denomination, and it will serve as a sort of introduction to the rest. From Supplementary Table A, at page 496 of the first volume of the returns, the community will be seen to be composed of 89·1 per cent. of natives of India, including a few negroes; 7·4 per cent. of Europeans, including Americans and those from Australasia, and 3·5 per cent. of a mixture of these two, known by the general title of Eurasian.

Europeans.

The foreign element is composed of, first, the military, next the civil employés of the State, thirdly, those engaged on railways or mines, and then the professional and commercial classes chiefly congregated at the seaports and provincial capitals. There was also, at the time of the census, a considerable contingent of seafaring people on board vessels in harbour. It is not practicable to separate these groups in the general return. Speaking roughly, the military section amounts to a little over one-half. At the time of the census the strength of the European troops was about 67,800, with 2,550 officers, 3,120 women, 5,900 children, and approximately, 800 people engaged on the staff and in various military avocations in India. To these can be added about 1,200 wives and children of officers and those on the staff, &c., with 2,530 European officers attached to the native army, and about 1,100 persons representing their families, making in all about 85,000 souls. As to the other classes, we have still less of a foundation to build on. A recent estimate gives the civil employés and their families 10,500, and the railway servants 6,100, leaving about 66,400 to be distributed over the other groups, but this is admittedly no more than an approximation. Then, again, the distinctions between the three races is very shadowy, and there is a tendency for Eurasians to enter the European group, and for native Christians to be returned as Eurasians. As the return stands, however, the influence of the army is visible in the number of Europeans found in the Panjáb, which heads the list. On the other hand, Bombay, which follows very closely, there being a difference of less than 200 people, is recruited chiefly from the non-official civil element, including seafarers. The North-West Provinces and Oudh come third, owing, again, to large garrisons, such as those at Meerut, Lucknow, Bareli, &c. Bengal follows with a fall of nearly 4,700. In the case of this Presidency the civil element is relatively considerably higher than in Bombay, as there are no large garrisons, and, in addition to the mercantile and professional population, and the large port of Calcutta, there is the planting colony in Bihár, East Bengal, and the sub-montane tracts, to be included. Madras and Burma come next, though at the very wide interval of 9,800 in the first case, and of 10,900 in the second. In Burma both trading and military population prevail. In Madras the latter is less prominent, perhaps, and the resident European more so. The number of Europeans in places like Quettah, Haidrabad, Mysore, and Central India depends obviously on the strength of the garrison in Belóchistán, Sekandrabád, Bangalore, and Mhow respectively. The marginal table gives the European population of a few of the chief towns, exclusive of the stations purely military.

Town.	European Population.
Bombay -	11,458
Calcutta - -	11,914
Madras -	4,200
Rangoon - -	4,120
Karáchi - -	3,182
Total -	34,874

Eurasians.

Assuming the Eurasian return to be correct, Madras heads the list with 26,600 out of the total of 79,790. Bengal, which comes next, returns only 15,000. Bombay shows 8,500, amongst whom there are no doubt a good many Goanese or others with Portuguese patronymics. The North-West Provinces have always been remarkable for the number of their Eurasians, and Burma, which, in spite of its small population has nearly the same number, owes its pre-eminence to its peculiar domestic institutions which foster the supply of children of mixed race. Haidrabad and Bangalore follow Madras in the frequency of the entries of this class. It would be interesting to compare the returns of the two last enumerations, so as to see if this community is numerically on the rise or not, but owing partly to defects in the schedules filled up, partly to the number in 1881 not filled up at all as regards race, the census operations give little help in this direction, and the matter can only be satisfactorily dealt with through special investigation. Since the community is mostly congregated in the chief towns such an inquiry is not difficult, and can be made to include within its scope valuable details, such as the number of children per family, the age of parents at the time of marriage, and so on, which are impossible at a census.

Indian converts.

The bulk of the Christian community is, as we have seen above, of native Indian origin, and out of the 2,036,600 souls of which it consists, no less than 1,538,800 are found in Madras and the Malabar States. It includes, also, 152,500 in Bengal, 122,600 in Bombay and Sindh, and 101,300 in Burma. The rest are scattered about in comparatively small societies, such as 23,400 in the North-West Provinces, 19,600 in the Panjáb and about 43,400 in Haidrabád, Mysore, and Coorg, where the Madras influence makes itself felt. Its greatest development is thus found where the Brahmanic caste system is in force in its fullest vigour, in the south and west of the peninsula, and amongst the Hill tribes of Bengal. In such localities it is naturally attractive to a class of the population whose position is hereditarily and permanently degraded by their own religion, as Islám has proved in Eastern Bengal and amongst the lowest class of the inhabitants of the Panjáb. We have seen that in the early days of Portuguese missionary enterprise, it was found necessary to continue the breach that Brahmanic custom had placed between certain grades of society and those above them, but in later times, and in foreign missions of the Reformed Church, the tendency has been to absorb all caste distinctions into the general communion of the Christianity of that form. The new faith has thus affected the lower classes more directly than the upper, who have more to lose socially, and less to gain, and a good deal of its early spread in the Malabar States seems to have been due to the success achieved by the missionaries in their efforts to mitigate the rigour of the local rules and customs towards those classes.* In Burma, again, the chief success has been amongst the Karén races, who are dwellers in the hills and forests, of Animistic proclivities, who, before the arrival of the British in this province had been grievously oppressed by the Burmese. The instruction placed within their reach by the missionaries enables them to take their place in society on a level with their former tyrants, who refused them that means of rising; but though Christianity has, doubtless, got a footing amongst these tribes, the present conditions in Burma seem favourable to the extension amongst the Karéns of the local Buddhism rather than of a more advanced form of belief. It is a question whether amongst the converts in the south-east of the Indian peninsula caste has not still a considerable attraction, for we find that when one of the lower caste converts has prospered in his worldly affairs, he manifests a tendency to dub himself one of the warrior-caste of the Brahmanic system, and to appear in the census returns as a Christian Kshatría; and in another part of the country the same class, on conversion, considers himself justified in attempting to avail himself of wells, the use of which had been prohibited to him by public opinion whilst he was in his unregenerate stage, thereby causing a village commotion. For the same reason as affects the return of Eurasians, namely, the number of Christians not returned by race in 1881, there can be no estimate formed from the census figures of the general increase in the ranks of native Christians on the last 10 years. Taking special localities, such as the south-east of Madras, the district of Lohárdaga in Bengal, and of Siálkot in the Panjáb, the variation is very large, and due probably exclusively to the growth of the active community. But even with these remarkable cases of increase the Christian native is but in the ratio of seven in a thousand of the whole population, and of these about five would belong to the older churches and the balance to the reformed. The remark, accordingly, made by the Roman Bishop of Ágra to Jacquemont, is as applicable now as it was in 1828: "La caldaja è molto grande, ma la carne è molto poca."

Christian denominations.

The return of Christian sects is not altogether complete, for we find in the original tables no less than 60,350 persons who omitted to fill in this column of the schedule, and 60,700 more who returned their sect simply as Protestant. With the help of the volume of Missionary Statistics before mentioned, these figures were finally reduced to 9,350 and 14,200 respectively, as shown in the following statement:—†

Denomination.	Total Number.	Distribution by Race.		
		European.	Eurasian.	Indian.
A.—Church of England, with Churches of India, Ireland, America, Anglican, and Episcopalian churches.	340,613	103,145	29,922	207,546
B.—Church of Scotland, Presbyterian, United Presbyterian, Reformed Presbyterian, American or Irish Presbyterians, Irish Presbyterian Mission.	46,351	10,581	2,440	33,329
C.—Baptist	202,746	2,907	2,352	197,487
D.—Wesleyan, Wesleyan Methodist, Methodist, Primitive Methodist, Episcopalian Methodist, Bible Christian.	32,123	5,362	2,349	24,412
E.—Congregationalist, London Mission, Independent, Calvinist, Welsh Calvinist.	48,036	1,285	742	46,009
F.—Nonconformist, Dissenter, Puritan	557	230	180	147
G.—Plymouth Brethren, Open Brethren, Swedenborgian, New Jerusalem, Catholic Apostolic, Quaker, Friend, Salvationist, Anabaptist.	1,445	178	38	1,229
H.—Lutheran, German Mission, Swedish Church, Reformed Dutch, Zwinglian, Moravian, German Church, Evangelical, Evangelist Church, Evangelical Union, Reformed Church.	69,405	1,285	195	67,925
J.—Protestant	14,213	3,938	4,052	6,223
Total, Reformed Church	755,489	128,912	42,270	584,307
K.—Church of Rome	1,315,263	35,645	36,089	1,243,529
L.—Syrian Church (*Jacobite Section*)	200,467	15	3	200,449
M.—Greek, Abyssinian, and Armenian	1,258	726	275	257
Total, Older Churches	1,516,988	36,386	36,367	1,444,235
Unsectarian and Unreturned	11,903	2,702	1,153	8,048
Grand Total	**2,284,380**	**168,000**	**79,790**	**2,036,590**

* Linschoten, for instance, writes "As these Nayros (*Nairs*) go in the street they use to cry 'Po, Po,' "which is to say 'Take heed, look to yourselves,' or 'I come, stand out of the way,' for that the other sort "of people, called Polyas, that are no Nayros, may not once touch or trouble one of them . . . . . . for, if "any of the Polyas should chance to touch their bodies, he may freely thrust him through, and no man ask "him why he did it." There are also strict sumptuary laws regarding the dress and habitation of this class, which are only now in abeyance during the rule of the British, and would be reimposed, with the acquiescence of those subjected to them, within a week from the removal of the foreign hand. *See* Mr. Mateer's Account of Travancore.—J.A.B.

† The grouping was suggested by Sir T. C. Hope, K.C.S.I., whose help in this portion of the work I have the pleasure of gratefully acknowledging.

The most striking feature of the return is that 76½ per cent. of the Europeans return some denomination of the Reformed Church, whilst 71 per cent. of the Indian converts appertain to the Roman and Syrian denominations of Christianity. It may also be noticed that the last term includes a considerably smaller number than in 1881, the reason being that in the latter year the section of the Eastern Church that had been combined with the Roman on the arrival of the Portuguese was shown under the same head as the Jacobite section, which has remained independent. The marginal table gives the above statement in a proportional form, so as to show the per-centage of each race returning each denomination. The Eurasians are fairly equally divided between the two sections of the Church, but the proportion of the unspecified, such as Protestants, is relatively higher than in the case of the two other races. The ratio of the Roman to the total, in the case of the Europeans, depends first upon the strength of Irish in the regiments serving in India, and next upon the number of Goanese, &c. who have been returned as Portuguese. Next to the Church of England, the native Christian shows a partiality for the Baptist denomination of the Reformed Church, which seems to have achieved its numerically greatest results in the northern districts of Madras and amongst the Karéns in Lower Burma. The latter field has been in the hands of this denomination for many years, but the latter received its great impetus during the famine of 1876–78, where it afforded a refuge for orphans and other destitute persons. The Church of England societies are found in most parts of India, but by far its largest congregations are in the southern districts and the Malabar States of the Madras Presidency. There is also a nucleus of this denomination in the hill tracts of Western Bengal, and in the Karén tracts of Burma. The Congregationalists, too, are mostly found in the Malabar States and in North Madras, whilst the Methodists chiefly haunt the North-West Provinces. The Lutherans, who, as seen above, were the first of the Reformed Churches to systematically take up the evangelisation of the natives, have nearly 68,000 converts, chiefly in Madras, where they began, and amongst the hill tribes of Bengal. A branch is settled also on the western coast to the north of the Malabar missions. In fact, as a rule, the different bodies of this section of Christianity seem to map out the field pretty definitely to meet each other's convenience, though there are, no doubt, instances of aggression. We find, for instance, that the newly arrived "Salvation Army," wherever it is in force, is in or near the nests of an older denomination, whose "fort" has been duly stormed like Jericho of old, by the aid of the instrument which, as we have seen, is the most popular one in India, and whose efficacy in the service of sectarianism is attested by no less an authority than Hudibras.* The Roman Church, though the great bulk of its native adherents are found in Madras and in the neighbourhood of that Presidency, has a strong foothold in Burma, but its greatest success during the last decade has been in the Lohárdága district of Bengal, where the wild tribes came over in numbers during an agrarian crisis a few years ago. In other parts of Bengal, too, as well as here, the census Superintendent points out that there have been reprisals from the Baptist and Lutheran denominations to a considerable extent. The Goanese element, together with the curiously isolated community of native Christians on the island of Salsette, near Bombay, is the main factor in the Roman Church of the Western Presidency.

Denomination.	Total Christians.	By Races.		
		European.	Eurasian.	Indian.
Church of England	14·9	61·4	37·5	10·2
Presbyterian	2·0	6·3	3·1	1·6
British Nonconformists	12·4	5·8	7·0	13·2
Lutheran	3·0	0·8	0·2	3·3
Protestant, unspecified	0·6	2·3	5·1	0·3
Total, Reformed	32·9	76·6	52·9	28·6
Roman	57·6	21·2	45·2	61·0
Syrian, &c.	8·7	0·4	0·3	9·8
Total, Old Church	66·3	21·6	45·5	70·8
Others and unspecified	0·8	1·8	1·6	0·6

It is worth while to compare the returns furnished to the census enumerator with those in the missionary publication already more than once quoted, though this can only be done in a very general way. The figures for the Roman Church agree very

* "We'll beat a drum, and they'll all follow.
A drum, quoth Phœbus, 'troth that's true,
A pretty invention, quaint and new!"

fairly with those given in the year book called "Missiones Catholicæ," the difference being a trifle in excess on the side of the census. In the case of the Reformed Church, too, the total results are biassed in the same direction, but in some of the details there appears a great difference. In the course of the preparatory operations before the enumeration, a circular was issued by the Superintendents to all missionary agents suggesting that the Societies concerned should issue cards to all native householders of their denomination, with the name of the latter legibly entered thereon in the vernacular character of the district, so that it might be copied into the schedule with as little danger of error as possible. This course was evidently not universally followed, and in default of such a guide both enumerator and enumerated were at a loss to get at the correct entry. The neglect of such a precaution seems to indicate a dislike on the part of the leaders of the congregation, similar to that which prevails in Great Britain, to the return of denomination. On the other side of the question it may be pointed out that a good deal of the missionary statistics is admittedly approximate only, and in some cases is based on the simple rule of multiplying the number of communicants by 2½ to get that of the whole denominational community. Taking Indian converts only, we find the main differences between the two returns to be as shown in the marginal table; some of the discrepancy is attributable, no doubt, to defective nomenclature. For instance, the group marked F. should be distributed, apparently, in the case of the mission return, between Lutheran and Baptist, and the census return under group C. includes, probably, some Congregationalists. The Salvation Army, again, claims considerably more than are assigned to it in the census schedules, and may possibly be confused with the Presbyterians, alongside of or amongst whom it works in some parts of the Bombay Presidency. As regards the variation from the 1881 return, the scrutiny of denomination shows that the only figures coming under identical heads are those for the older churches, which, too, omitting the small number of the Greek and Armenian sections, must be taken *en masse*, on account of the confusion between the Roman and the Jacobite sections of the Syrian Church, which occurred in 1881. Thus taken, the increase is about 19·2 per cent. If the above items be deducted from the grand total, the increase of the remaining denominations, representing the Reformed Churches, amounts to 28·6 per cent. The "Protestant" and other unspecified entries numbered 189,692 persons in 1881, and 142,925 in 1891, a difference which affects a considerable proportion of the detailed entries of denomination. It should also be mentioned that there is a discrepancy between the number of Christians by race, as shown here and as shown in Table XVII. In the case of Europeans, the difference amounts to 1,572 in favour of the return under review, whilst the Eurasians are here shown as fewer by 1,954. The discrepancy is chiefly in Madras and Rangoon, and is apparently attributable to the revision of the tables after the Imperial series had been completed. The entry of Goanese as Portuguese, and the return by Eurasians of non-Christian religions accounts for part of the confusion. As to the Indian converts, who are here returned in excess of the other table by no less than 200,742, the explanation obviously is that in the latter there is no distinction by religion shown, so that much of the Christian community has been compiled under the caste or tribal name which they returned in the portion of the schedule assigned for that detail. We have mentioned above the case of the toddy-drawers of the south of Madras, who return themselves as Christians of the warrior caste of Brahmanic orthodoxy, and many other Christians will be found under the lower castes. These are mentioned in the provincial reports, but in accordance with the general scheme of the Imperial return, the distinction is ignored in the latter. Moreover, as there was no requisition on

Denomination.	A.—Census.	B.—Mission.	C.—B. compared with A.
A.—Church of England	207,546	194,482	—13,064
B.—Presbyterian	33,329	34,979	+ 1,650
C.—Baptist	197,487	133,762	—63,725
D.—Wesleyan, &c.	24,412	33,058	+ 8,646
E.—Congregationalist	46,009	78,132	+32,123
F.—Indefinite Nonconformist	147	23,794	+23,647
G.—Miscellaneous (*chiefly Salvation Army*).	1,229	2,491	+ 1,262
H.—Lutheran	67,925	63,251	— 4,674
J.—Protestant	6,223	—	— 6,223
Total	584,307	563,949	—20,358

Christian converts to return the caste to which they belonged before their conversion, and the general feeling is adverse to the recognition of that caste, except in special instances, chiefly found on the Malabar coast and near Bombay, the return is necessarily only partial, and most of the community appear under the collective title of Christian.

C.—The Distribution of the Population by Race, Tribe, or Caste.

Πατρίους παριδοχὰς ἅς θ' ὁμήλικας χρόνῳ
Κεκτημέθ' οὐδεὶς ἀντι καταβαλεῖ λόγος,
'Ουδ' εἰ δι' ἄκρον τὸ σοφὸν ἥυρηται φρενῶν—*Euripides.*

Nature and origin of caste.

In this section we have to deal with the last and the most important of the ethnographic elements included in the census scheme; and, it is also, unfortunately, that of all others which it is most difficult to treat adequately within the limits of the present review. Philology, as we have seen above, is of little help in the demarcation of the ethnic distinctions amongst the people of India. As to religion, again, what has been said already is enough to show its imperfection as a guide, and of all the erroneous methods of discriminating between the divisions of the community, that which assigns any ethnic value to the terms Hindu and Musalmán is the most misleading. It is true that very high authorities have described caste as the "express badge of Hinduism," and M. Barth, whose testimony has been already cited more than once in the course of this chapter, considers that this institution is not merely the symbol of Hinduism, but its stronghold, and a religious factor of the very highest order. To a very great extent, so it undoubtedly is, but what has been said in the foregoing pages justifies, perhaps, a wider view of caste, by which term, it is as well to explain, is here meant the perpetuation of *status* or function, by inheritance and endogamy. For caste is a development of the special tendency to which the social atmosphere of India is abnormally favourable, and is not, therefore, the peculiar attribute of the Brahmanic form of religion, whatever it may be, so much as of the circumstances of which the Bráhman had the opportunity of moulding in days long gone by. For example, we find that where tribal pride is strong, and the social position good, the change of faith involves no alteration in either nomenclature or social custom. Where, on the other hand, the community in question is in a depressed condition in the Brahmanic system, conversion to another faith is used as an opportunity to slip out of the hereditary yoke. Thus we find the various tribes of Jat and Rájpút, in the north of India, contain nearly an equal number of Bráhmanic and Musalmán members, not to mention the Sikhs that prevail in certain localities. Amongst the Jains, again, of Western India intermarriage is not uncommon between the Brahmanic and Shráwak sections of the same community. In another direction, fiction assigns to the leaders of a forest tribe the position and honours of the warrior caste when they enter the fold of orthodox Brahmanism, whilst the rest of the tribe retains its original designation, and sometimes, as we have seen in the preceding section, remains even professedly Animistic, or, as in Assam takes a special title conventionally allowed to those who join the Brahmanic community. The case of the eastern Bengal Musalmáns has already, too, been quoted as an example of social rise on conversion, since they all assume the honorific designation of Shaikh, implying admission into the Arab fraternity. The Christian converts of Southern India may be cited since a further instance of this tendency. The Shánan, or toddy-drawers, with the corresponding class on the western coast, hold but a very low position in the Brahmanic system, as it is in force in Dravidian lands. When, therefore, they become Christians, most of them abandon their caste name, but as they rise in worldly circumstances, the tendency comes out, as has been mentioned at the end of the last section, to arrogate to themselves the title of the warrior caste, like the wild tribes of the Central Belt. But under the early Portuguese missionaries, higher up on the Malabar coast, the distinctions of Brahmanic caste were always recognised on conversion, as the object was to provide the church with a class of convert who was fit by position, rank, and education, to take up an influential position in the priesthood.* Numbers of similar instances can be cited of the independence of the obligations of caste from the elastic bondage of what, with the masses in India, passes for religion, *a non religando.*

---

* As this is going through the press, I see that this point has been noticed in a leading Indian journal in the following fitting phrase:—"The multiplicity of Hindu castes is such that some have even assimilated the terminology of the Christian faith."—J.A.B.

But granting that there is something inherent, as it were, in the conditions of life in India that fosters the sentiment of which the caste system is the expression, and granting again that the form, or collection of forms, that this expression has taken is the outgrowth of the Brahmanic creed, it seems within the bounds of reasonable hypothesis to attribute to its present development an origin distinctly racial. We have seen the origin of that creed in the necessity of keeping the gods on the side of the Árya, in the struggle of the latter with the dark races they found in possession of the tracts they coveted. We find the germs of the caste system in the subsequent contact of the foreign race with their late opponents, when actual hostilities had closed. The Bráhman had already developed into a hierarchy, and by their influence over the supernatural, could easily prevail on the Arya laity to exclude the subject races from participation in what seemed to be the peculiar privilege of the superior. There is thus an ethnologic justification for the use of the Vedic term "colour," in the sense in which caste or race is now used, as has been pointed out by modern writers. But here the racial element seems to cease for the moment, for inside the community of the Arya themselves, assuming that the fulminations of the Brahman had any effect, the development of function must have proceeded on caste lines. That is, the right to sacrifice, and to perform the other offices of the priesthood having been established on a hereditary basis, the natural tendency would be to extend the principle to those who supported the priesthood, namely the warrior chiefs. So, too, within the circle of the Vaishya, or colonists of Árya descent, function became hereditary, through trade guilds, in imitation of the higher classes, and with the growth of the settlements of the race, the hierarchy separated from the commonalty, so that practice was less supervised, and the non-Arya undoubtedly entered by the lower gate, even though interbreeding was not prevalent till a later age, which is a doubtful assumption. The literature of the Brahmanical revival, after the downfall of Buddhism, is practically devoted to caste, that is, to the support of the Brahmanic pretensions, and on this is based the system that prevails in the present day. The process of absorption of the Hill tribes, mentioned in the preceding section, necessarily tended to obliterate the line of demarcation between the Árya Kshatria and the black chieftains now admitted to the title. Indeed, according to the orthodox doctrine, the whole of the Kshatria caste, which apparently was found inconvenient in the new order of things, was destroyed to a man, by the Brahmanical creation named Parasu-Ráma, but this is a difficulty that no hierarchy would fail to solve.* Then with regard to the Bráhmans themselves, who may be assumed to have done what they could to defend the sacerdotal body from recruitment from outside, we read of instance upon instance of the creation of the class by royal edict, and of others where the Bráhman, having descended to temple ministration, is degraded from the hierarchy. In one province alone there are over 150 divisions of Bráhmans, none of whom will intermarry with each other or sit down together at a ceremonial banquet. If this be the course of events at the root of the tree, it is hardly necessary to descant upon the chances of genealogical purity amongst the branches. The Arya entered India, no doubt, white in colour, and more hardy and advanced in the arts of war and husbandry than his antagonists, but not so far removed in race as to prevent successful interbreeding. Then, too, being an Asiatic, albeit of the temperate zone, he was able to settle in Upper India, beyond the tropic, with as little inconvenience as regards climate as the Burman in the neighbouring peninsula. There was no question of physical deterioration, as in the case of the European and those crossed with him in India and corresponding climates. As the settlers receded further from the north-west of the country, their touch of the fathers of their race, and the chances of recruitment from across the mountains, grew less, until there is no basis for even a reasonable pretence of Árya blood. The case is often cited of the importation of a few families of Bráhmans into Bengal from the centre of Brahmanic orthodoxy, to restore the decaying practice of the faithful in the Deltaic marshes, and the consequent repeopling of that tract, even unto the present day, with the pure blood of Kanaujia. But from the original tradition, it appears that only the first wives of these prolific teachers were of the Bráhman caste, and that the rest were daughters of Heth. It is the same in Nipál, the most orthodox tract in India, and the only one wherein the Musalmán has never set his conquering foot. The ruling family was found by the refugee Brahmans to be

---

* The new race of chiefs, according to the Puránic and Epic literature, resembles the Levitic conception, given in the Chronicles, of the Kings of Israel, who war for, and at the command of, the priesthood, with minds filled, says Renan, with nothing but priests, Levites, and poets.—J.A.B.

of Rájput blood, and the Bráhmans themselves laid the foundation of the well-known Khas tribe, of mixed blood, who now constitute the predominant community in the whole of the lower valleys. In this tract, by the way, it is said that there is the only opportunity to be found in the present day of judging of Brahmanism where its development has been absolutely unchecked; and something very like the code of Manu is in force in its unmitigated bigotry. It is only within comparatively recent times that the racial distribution of the population has been investigated on the line of modern science. Previous to that time philology had held the field unchecked by observations from other standpoints. A beginning has been made in Bengal by Mr. Risley, who has published anthropometrical data from about 6,000 persons. Most of them are from Bengal, but some were made in the North-West Provinces and the Panjab. Such an extensive field of survey, comprising over 146 millions of inhabitants, cannot, of course, be appreciated from the results of measuring one person in 24,000, but the results show the value of the method, and it is to be hoped that more material of the same sort may be made available. It is imprudent to base any general conclusions on this small foundation, but so far as the local circumstances of Bengal are concerned, it may be inferred that the population consists of a mixture of two breeds, first, the western, in which the Arya is an element, especially in Bihár, but mixed with the dark races of the Hill tracts. Secondly, the eastern, where the predominant factor is the Mongoloid of the north-east, mixed with the dark races of the plains and marshes, and with a slight tincture of Aryan blood in a portion of the upper class. One valuable feature in the measurements is the apparent identity they establish between the two families of the dark inhabitants of the Central Belt of hills. The distinction, as a purely linguistic one, is still untouched, but physiology has pronounced against any difference between the Kól and the Oráon or Gónd. Taking the measurements of the Panjáb for what they are worth, it appears that the lower castes in that province possess a higher type of feature than the higher castes of the Lower Ganges valley. This conclusion jumps with what is known of the history of the population of the north-west corner of India, where not only has recruitment from the hardy races of Central Asia been going on within a far later period than any that can be assigned to an Árya movement from the same direction, but, moreover, the dark or Dravidian race does not seem to have ever been prominent in the land of the Five Rivers, so that the development of caste in the latter region, wherever it obtains, must have been mainly tribal or functional. The alternative hypothesis, to which the existence of the village helot in the centre and east of the Province gives colour, is that the race that preceded the Skythic tribes who were found in possession by the Arya were of a northern stock; or, again, that the race had been long enough in India to change the type in the different physical conditions of the peninsula. But it seems very doubtful whether such migration would affect more than the skull-shape, and would not leave unaltered the other facial measurements and the colour. All that can be said safely is that whatever the mixture, the race type of the north and west of India differs from that in the south and east, and that of the Arya type, whatever remains, must be sought in the Ganges Doáb. On the west coast there are a few curious distinctions that indicate, apparently, difference in racial origin. The first of these instances is that of the Nair, the military caste of Malabar. Their traditions point to the north as their native land; they are light in colour, in very great contrast to the rest of the castes of the tract, have retained the custom of polyandry, with a good deal of serpent worship. It appears that they advanced upon their present tract by way of the coast higher up, but how they got there does not appear. As with the Árya, they found a dark race in possession and enslaved them on their estates, where they labour to the present day. In the same tract, too, there is a class of Bráhmans, the Nambudiri, of remarkable fairness of complexion, and noted for their rigid ceremonial puritanism. Then, again, in the track of the Nair's alleged progress, we find a peculiar caste of Bráhmans, partly occupied in the cultivation of spices and betel nut, but settled mostly above the Ghâts, and not therefore so well sheltered from foreign influences as the Nair, who sought the coast. These Havig or Haiga Bráhmans show their connection with the Túlu country in their speech, and, like the Nairs, attribute to their caste a serpent origin in Rohilkhand, a statement borne out by their title. Between these we have a class of female temple servants of an equally light complexion amidst a universally dark population. Further north come the well known Konkanasth Bráhman, sometimes called Chitpáwan, who gave to the Maráthas their line of Peshwás. Their traditions point to an origin beyond the sea, and they have certainly preserved a complexion and features in marked contrast to those of their neighbours. It is not proved, however, that the sea they crossed was wider than that between Sindh or Káthiawár and their present settlements in Ratnagiri, so that they may well be the remnants of one of the really Árya clans of Northern India; either that harried by Alexander on his voyage down the Indus, or that which was the appanage of the Rájpút courts of Saurâshtra or south-western Rájputána. At all events, these curious instances of an evidently northern community embedded in a purely Dravidian entourage show that a good many links in the ethnological history of the country are wanting.

So far as race is concerned, then, India has a north-western or Skythic element in the Panjab, fringed by the semi-Arab blood of the Afghán and Balóch along the west. It is impossible to say where the former influence ends towards the south and east, but it probably reached as far as the peninsula of Káthiawár, in one direction, and nearly to the Jamna in another, but all along the border line the demarcation has long been obliterated. There is then the Mongoloidic element in the Himálaya and the eastern valleys, stretching down to the sea at the extreme east, and much mixed up with the population of other races throughout the trans-Gangetic tracts of the Delta. Burma may be said to be entirely Mongoloidic. Along the west coast there are traces here and there of Skythic blood, and even of that of races still further removed from India, who have settled there, however, within historic times. In Kashmér, the lower valleys of the Panjáb and Garhwál Himalaya, the central portion of the Upper Ganges basin, and, probably, the eastern part of Rajputana, the prevailing racial element is as nearly Arya as in any part of India, the tinge getting darker as the hill country is approached. In the latter we have the Dravidian, or whatever the appropriate title may be, and with the exception of the few communities along the west coast already mentioned, this race predominates throughout the peninsula, the hills everywhere standing out with special purity of blackness. It is not possible to give accurate statistics regarding the relative prevalence of these races, owing to the assumption of membership of well-known social orders to which the newly-enrolled have no racial title, nor can any approximation be made that is not likely to turn out fallacious, owing to the great confusion of blood in every part of the country, except Burma and the Hill tracts.

Development of caste.

The evolution of caste from the comparatively simple basis of race and function into its present complicated shape is a subject of which it is impossible to give here more than a bare sketch. The supersession of racial by tribal feeling is not an unusual feature in any country where the two are found, and in India, no doubt, it has been helped by change of religion in the more frequent cases of widespread conversion. Of castes of political origin instances have been already given, and more can be obtained on reference to any of the census reports of the last two enumerations. The most striking example, however, seems to be that of the Hill tracts of the Panjáb, where the Rája is the fountain of honour to an extent unprecedented, probably, in other parts of India, for by his word he creates, enlarges, and restricts the castes of the population of his realm. Elsewhere, the process of creation is, as a rule, confined to the two upper classes, Bráhman and Rájput. We have, then, the incorporation, by fiction, as it has been called, of members of the forest tribes, of which enough has been said above. The gradual acquisition of a higher caste by the lower seems not confined to any particular locality or system, for in Assam Mr. Gait has well described it as becoming almost a rule amongst certain classes. In the Deccan, again, the acquisition of wealth by a landholder often carries with it a rise in caste, of which the first manifestations are the seclusion of the female members of his family and the abjuration of widow marriage. In the next generation the family becomes Marátha, and then proceeds to Rájpút. The Christian aspirations after the latter title have been mentioned already, and in one instance a Madras apothecary of this faith applied for a wall round the yard of the dispensary of which he was in official charge, in order that the women of his family might take exercise in the seclusion due to their caste. But the great majority of the new formations on social considerations seem to be in the direction of degration rather than of usurpation. Some violation of caste ceremonial or etiquette is met with excommunication by those who have not yet tripped, and the peccant community at once forms a subdivision of the old, intermarrying only within itself. In this way, the semi-agricultural grower of fruit, generally a suburban resident, has declined communion with his fellow who devotes himself to the provision of vegetables. The carpenter, again, will have no companionship with him who repairs the carts used in municipal conservancy. Other instances are found scattered throughout the caste history of every province. We then come to territorial divisions, which are often based on difference of language. The functional castes, of course, furnish the bulk of these, and it is rare that there is *connubium* or *confarreatio* between the two sections. Sectarian differences, too, are fruitful sources of new caste growths. Some instances have been given in the section of this chapter which treats of the development of religion, and the process is pretty generally on the same lines in all. There is a sort of revolt against the Brahmanic authority, which attracts people of different castes. If it involves nothing but dogma or academic principles, caste is not affected. If, however, social orthodoxy is impugned, the adherents have to retire from the fold and form a new community. Thus, the Lingaiat sect of the South Deccan includes a number of different castes, all receiving separate recognition within the sect, and all prohibited from intercourse by marriage at all events, with the castes from which they have respectively seceded. In a number of cases, too, the name of the sect was returned as a caste without further discrimination, and, as in other instances, such as those of the goldsmiths and silk-weavers, the spiritual guides of the community have laid claim to the title of Bráhman. The communities in question are all in good circumstances, and it is noticeable that whereas all the great Nonconformist movements of India, involving, that is, large numbers, have been in a direction extra Brahmanic, and patronised by the lowest sections of the population, the numerically smaller have been taken up by the well-to-do and directed, ultimately, to the advance of the community within the system to which they originally belong. For, to quote Butler again,

> "Gain has wonderful effects,
> To improve the factory of sects."

Thus, in spite of the theoretically immutable barriers of caste, it is plain that the community which acknowledges them is constantly leaping over or creeping under them, or adding to their number, but in all this change steadily adhering to the main and vital principles of the institution. It is of the highest interest to trace the various influences that seem to pervade the caste system of the different parts of the country, but space does not allow of it,* and in addition to the chapters on the subject in the provincial and State reports on the census, both on the present occasion and in 1881, works are available for reference, such as Lyall's "Asiatic Studies," Risley's work on Bengal castes, Crook's and Nesfield's on those of the North-West Provinces, and the "Bombay Gazetteer," with many others, from which the chief features can be learned, with much valuable folk-lore into the bargain.

We have now to consider the results of the enumeration of caste, and it is necessary, accordingly, to show, as in the case of occupation, what was the scope of the inquiry. The following statement, therefore, gives the heading of the schedule and the standard instructions :—

1881.	1891.
Column Headings { Religion { 6. Religion. 7. Caste, if Hindu; Sect, if of other Religion.*	*Column Headings.* { Religion { 2. Main Religion. 3. Sect of Religion. Caste or Race. { 4. Main Caste, Tribe, &c. 5. Sub-division of Caste, Tribe, &c.
Instructions.—Col. 6. Here enter the main religious denomination to which each person belongs, as [Hindu, Muhammedan, Christian, Sikh, Jain, Brahmos, or other religious division of Hindus not mentioned above, Buddhist, Jew, Pársi]. If a person belongs to some aboriginal or non-Hindu tribe, enter the name of his tribe, as Gáro, Khásia, &c. Col. 7. In the case of Hindus, here enter the caste, as Brahman, Rajput, &c. If the name of the sub-division of the caste be entered, you must also enter the general name of the caste, as a whole. In the * In this column such details of tribes, clans, and sects, as the Local Government may direct, should be introduced.	*Instructions.*—Col. 2. Here enter the main religion which each person returns :— As *Hindu, Musalmán, Jain, Pársi, Christian.* Forest tribes who are not Hindu, Musalmán, &c., should have the name of their tribe entered in this column, as *Bhil, Gond, Gáro,* &c.; low castes, such as *Chamár, Dóm, Pária, Mahár,* &c., should be entered by the religion which they themselves return, and no dispute about it is to be raised. Col. 3. Enter the sect of religion followed by each person as they return it :— As *Smárth, Vaishnav, Walabhachárya, Lingaiat,* &c., for Hindus; *Sunni, Shiah,* &c., for Musalmán; and for Christian enter whether *Church of England, Roman Catholic, Presbyterian, Baptist, Lutheran, Methodist, Episcopalian,* &c. If the sect cannot be stated, enter "Not returned" in this column, but do not leave it blank.

* For example, the curious division in the Tamil country of the castes, other than Bráhmans and Kshatria, into those of the right hand and those of the left, unknown in any other part of India; and the still more curious custom of the males of the leather workers and females of the Polya (menials) being on the left, whilst the other sex of those castes is dignified by a place on the right. During factional warfare conjugal rights are suspended, and resumed when peace again reigns.—J. A. B.

1881. (*Continued.*)	1891. (*Continued.*)
case of Musalmans, state whether they are Shiahs, Sunnis, Farazis, or Wahábis. Christians should be shown as members of the Church of England, Roman Catholics, Presbyterians, Baptists, Wesleyans, Armenians, or as belonging to the Greek or Syrian rite, or, if not belonging to any of these denominations, under the general head of "others."	Col. 4.* Enter the caste if Hindus or Jains, and the tribes of those who have not castes, and the races of Christians, Buddhists, &c. :— As *Brahmán, Rájput, Bania, Kúnbi,* for Hindus; *Pathán, Moghal,* &c., for Musalmán; Eurasian or Native Christian for Christians; do not enter vague terms, such as *Hindustáni, Márwádi, Panjábi,* &c. Col. 5.* If the caste has been entered in col. 4, enter here the sub-division, as *Kanaujiá, Nágar,* &c., for *Bráhmans, Osvál* for *Banias,* &c. If *tribe,* enter the *clan,* if race, enter the tribe or nationality. Some races or castes may not return sub-divisions, and in their case the entry in col. 4 should be repeated, but this column must not be left blank. *Native Christians,* for instance, may be returned as *Portuguese, East Indians, Madrási,* or by their caste, if recognised. *Karéns,* as *Sgau,* &c.; *Bhils* as *Tadwi, Páwada,* &c.; *Gónds* as *Ráj,* &c. * The drafting of illustrations in the instructions for cols. 4 and 5 was left to the local census Superintendent.

As to the main points of difference between the two sets of rules, it will be seen that in the later code the caste was separated entirely from the religion, and the sect, accordingly, kept equally distinct. In other respects, the difference is merely in the greater detail of the illustrations, a matter that was left largely to the discretion of the local census Superintendent. The first mentioned change was made in order to get rid of the notion that the caste, or social distinction, was not required for Musalmáns, Sikhs, Jains, and so on, or was held to be subordinate in any way to sect of religion. With respect to the greater detail, it was thought that with plenty of discretion allowed to those who knew the special ways in which the enumerators were most likely to err, delegation was, on the whole, better than reservation, as in some cases on the last occasion prohibition of certain entries had been found to be taken as prescription. On the whole, too, the separation of the four items of religion, sect, caste, and sub-caste, &c., was found to make the notion of what was required more easily intelligible to the enumerator. Mistakes in abundance there were, of course, and the chronicle of these can be read in the provincial reports, where they are duly noted; but, speaking generally, the detail was more correct than on the former occasion, and justified the greater elaboration of the instructions.

Then came the process of abstraction, in which the main chance of error arose from the misreading of badly-written titles, more especially in the case of names of cases foreign to the district, of which alone the clerk had experience. When the heavy task of checking and tabulating the district totals was completed, there remained that of classification. It will be as well to explain this process by reproducing the Census Commissioner's Circular Order on the subject, as was done with reference to the corresponding process in the case of occupation.

On the Abstraction and Tabulation of Castes, Tribes, &c.

The Abstraction should include every caste, &c., and every subdivision, found in the schedule. From the Abstraction sheets an Index is to be prepared in which each caste, &c., with its subdivisions, should appear in alphabetical order. In a province such as the Panjáb, where the question of caste distribution was fully dealt with in connection with the last census, it has been found unnecessary to tabulate more than certain locally important subdivisions, after abstracting and indexing the whole. Elsewhere, it will be advisable for a complete table, showing the strength of each item, to be recorded for further inquiry.

2. The form of the Index has been already given in Appendix B. of Circular M., and the present Note supplements the above instructions with the scheme of classification therein mentioned. Generally speaking, the method of grouping is a rather more comprehensive form of that adopted by Mr. Kitts in his Compendium of Castes, but, instead of following closely the order and detail of the Occupation table, an attempt has been made to arrange the groups more or less in accordance with the position generally assigned to each in the social scale, as suggested by Mr. Ibbetson in his Panjáb work. A class has been added, too, for those who do not belong to the Hindu, Jain, or Musalmán communities or to Forest tribes, which addition will include, also, converts to Christianity who do not retain their original caste or tribe. No sample list has been prepared, as there is danger of confusion between the nomenclature of different provinces; but Mr. Kitts' list affords a general indication of the application of the scheme, though, no doubt, the detailed knowledge of provincial Superintendents will enable them to make corrections in certain points of detail. The main object is to ensure uniformity of classification, so that the circumstances of the provinces in respect to sex-distri-

bution, education, and marriage customs, where abstracted, and the prevalence of the selected infirmities, &c., may be accurately compared, in spite of the local name borne by the same caste in different parts of the continent.

3. For Imperial purposes, therefore, the numerical table required should include every distinct caste or tribe under its appropriate class and group. In several provinces the main castes are divided by religion, so that the latter fact should be recognised, as well as the social distinction.* Rájpúts and Jats, for instance, in the north, are found to be Hindus, Musalmáns, and Sikhs. Baniyas are both Hindu and Jain. Forest tribes return themselves as Hindus, and of the tribal religion, and in several important cases as Musalmán and Christian also. The provincial form of this table should, moreover, mention such sub-castes, &c., as may be recorded in tabulation; and on the subject of arranging and defining these subdivisions useful hints will be found in a paper by Mr. H. H. Risley, printed at pages 343–352 of Volume I., No. 6, of the Journal of the Anthropological Society of Bombay. In the Imperial Return for India the number alone of such subdivisions is sufficient, and a further selection will be made in the Central Office of the castes in each class or group which will have to be separately named.

* This refers to the provincial series of tables, as it may be worth while in special cases to see if conversion works any change as regards education or marriage.—J. A. B.

The scheme of classification mentioned in the above circular is as follows; the serial numbering, however, is that finally adopted for the Imperial Return for India, which differs a little from that originally prescribed, and which will be found in use in the provincial volumes:—

A. Agricultural and Pastoral.
- I. Military and Dominant.
- II. Other Agriculturists.
- III. Cattle Graziers.
- IV. Field Labourers.
- V. Forest Tribes.

B. Professional.
- VI. Priests, &c.
- VII. Devotees and Ascetics.
- VIII. Temple Servants.
- IX. Genealogists.
- X. Writers.
- XI. Astrologers and Herbalists.
- XII. Musicians and Ballad Reciters.
- XIII. Singers and Dancers.
- XIV. Actors and Mimes.

C. Commercial.
- XV. Traders.
- XVI. Pedlars.
- XVII. Carriers by Pack Animals.

D. Artisans and Village Menials.
- XVIII. Goldsmiths.
- XIX. Barbers.
- XX. Blacksmiths.
- XXI. Carpenters, Masons, &c.
- XXII. Brass and Copper Smiths.
- XXIII. Tailors.
- XXIV. Grain parchers and Confectioners.
- XXV. Perfumers, Betel-leaf, &c. Sellers.
- XXVI. Weavers and Dyers.
- XXVII. Washermen.
- XXVIII. Cotton Cleaners.
- XXIX. Shepherds and Wool Weavers.
- XXX. Oil Pressers.

D. Artisans and Village Menials—*cont.*
- XXXI. Potters.
- XXXII. Glass and Lac Workers.
- XXXIII. Salt and Lime Workers.
- XXXIV. Goldsmiths' Refuse Cleaners.
- XXXV. Gold Washers and Iron Smelters.
- XXXVI. Fishermen, &c.
- XXXVII. Domestic Service, &c.
- XXXVIII. Distillers and Toddy Drawers.
- XXXIX. Butchers.
- XL. Leather Workers.
- XLI. Village Watchmen, &c.
- XLII. Scavengers.

E. Vagrants.
- XLIII. Grindstone Makers.
- XLIV. Earth Workers, Stone Quarriers.
- XLV. Knife Grinders.
- XLVI. Mat and Cane Workers.
- XLVII. Hunters and Fowlers.
- XLVIII. Miscellaneous Vagrants.
- XLIX. Jugglers, Acrobats, &c.

F. Races and Indefinite Titles.
- L. Musalmán Foreign Races.
- LI. Himalayan Mongoloids.
- LII. Burmese and Chinese Mongoloids.
- LIII. Western Asiatics.
- LIV. Burmese, &c. Mixed Races.
- LV. Indefinite Indian Castes.
- LVI. Europeans, &c.
- LVII. Eurasians.
- LVIII. Native Christians.
- LIX. Goanese and Portuguese.
- LX. Africans.

This grouping, it will be seen, is based mainly upon function, but it was further explained to the classifying officers that the occupation to which the caste in question was to be credited was not necessarily that actually exercised by the caste in the present day but that which was assigned to it by tradition, and generally implied in its current appellation. There is thus no connection between this return and that of occupation. Again, towards the end of the classification, a set of groups will be found in which race is the predominant feature. It has been explained above that the Músalmán titles that appear in Group L. do not, except in the Panjáb, necessarily imply foreign origin. In Group LVIII., too, the term Native Christian only covers those of this community who returned themselves under no other title. As pointed out in the circular, what was aimed at in prescribing the classification, was as much uniformity as the nature of the statistics will allow, so that the returns of each province might be dealt with on the same basis. This was especially necessitated by the tabulation of caste or race, as the case may be, in combination with such details as literacy, infirmities, and, where undertaken by the local authorities, with marriage and widowhood also. The index sent up from most of the provincial census offices enabled this object to be fairly fulfilled, but owing to the absence of such a guide in the case of the two largest provinces, comprising more than half the population of British territory, the returns for which did not reach the Imperial office until six months after all the rest had been compiled and worked up, inconsistency could not everywhere be avoided. In the summary statement, called Table XVII.—A., with which Volume II. begins, the more important adjustments that seemed advisable have been made, at the cost of discrepancy with the succeeding tables. The general scheme of arrangement is admittedly devoid of pretension to ethnological order, since in the chaotic condition of the population at the present time an attempt to achieve such would inevitably be a failure. On the other hand, an arrangement purely according to the position occupied by the caste in social estimation would only be possible for each Province or State taken separately, as there is but little uniformity in this respect if we regard the circumstances of the country as a whole. The general rule, therefore, has been to place the caste concerned in the group to which it is assigned in the part of the country in which it most prevails, so as to get at least approximate accuracy. There are, however, obvious flaws in the grouping itself, due in great measure to the adoption of functional classification to an excessive extent. For instance, amongst professions we have the arts of singing, dancing, and acting, which in India are anything but reputable in public estimation. Again, in the large class of agriculturists are included the field labourers, who are, in many places but little more than agrestic serfs, and the forest tribes, who, though chiefly agricultural, no doubt, are lower in the scale than the village artisan. Thus, every one of the chief Classes must be taken by itself, and the relative positions of the groups in it considered as subject to this limitation. But for the purposes of the present review, a little more detail seems advisable in the combinations, and as the recognition of function in connection with caste has been already carried so far, there is no sufficient reason for seceding from it, on Luther's principle of *pecca fortiter*, if the principle be a wrong one. In the table on the next page, accordingly, the 60 groups of the original distribution have been collected into 21 classes, and against each is shown the ratio borne by it to the total population dealt with in the return, which amounts to 286,900,000. Taking the return as a whole, the two points that are most prominent are, first, the indication given by the small proportion of the purely agricultural castes of the extent to which other classes join in cultivation, and then, the fact that nearly 16½ per cent. of the population is returned on other than functional considerations, thus showing the inutility of comparing this return with that of occupation. In fact, in all cases above those of the lowest, the members of the caste have diverged widely from the means of subsistence from which they respectively take their name, and the divergence is very often indicated by the establishment of a fresh subdivision, higher or lower, according to the occupation in question. In some of the provincial returns the several subdivisions have been compiled into an index, and in others the more important have been shown in the return subordinate to the main caste. This detail, however, was beyond the scheme adopted for the Imperial tables, which deal accordingly with the latter only.

It is now proposed to consider Table XVII.—A., re-grouped as described above.

Agricultural groups.

The agricultural class then contains nearly 30 per cent. of the population under three groups. The first, that of the military section, includes those castes and tribes which have risen to power at different stages in the history of their province. Amongst them the largest, that of the *Rájpút*, is spread all over India, but to a far less extent to the south than in the continental portion. The title is an extremely comprehensive one, as must have been seen from what has been said regarding the

TABLE

Class and Group.	Proportion to 10,000 of Population.
I.—Agricultural	**2,988**
1. Military and Dominant	1,025
2. Other Cultivators	1,670
4. Field Labourers	293
II.—Pastoral	**583**
3. Cattle Graziers'	403
29. Shepherds and Wool Weavers	180
III.—5. Forest Tribes	**551**
IV.—36. Fishers, &c.	**288**
V.—Artisans	**1,007**
18. Goldsmiths	58
20. Blacksmiths	91
21. Carpenters and Masons	120
22. Brass and Copper Smiths	11
23. Tailors	26
26. Weavers and Dyers	327
28. Cotton Cleaners	30
30. Oil Pressers	163
31. Potters	122
32. Glass and Lac Workers	5
33. Salt and Lime Workers	53
34. Goldsmiths' Refuse Cleaners	—
35. Gold Washers and Iron Smelters	1
VI.—Personal Services and Food, &c.	**488**
19. Barbers	130
24. Grain Parchers, &c.	49
25. Betel-leaf, &c. Sellers	8
27. Washermen	98
37. Domestic Service, &c.	15
38. Distillers and Toddy Drawers	167
39. Butchers	21
VII.—Leather Workers and Lower Village Menials.	**1,073**
40. Leather Workers	488
41. Watchmen and Village Menials	446
42. Scavengers	139

Class and Group.	Proportion to 10,000 of Population.
VIII.—Traders	**428**
15. Traders and Shopkeepers	424
16. Pedlars	4
IX.—Professionals	**755**
6. Priests	539
7. Devotees, &c.	95
8. Temple Servants	11
9. Genealogists	21
10. Writers	89
X.—Arts, &c.	**40**
11. Astrologers and Herbalists	11
12. Musicians and Ballad Reciters	22
13. Singers and Dancers, &c.	5
14. Actors and Mimes	2
XI.—Carriers and Pack Animals	**34**
XII.—Vagrants	**121**
43. Grindstone Makers	1
44. Earth Workers, &c.	39
45. Knife Grinders	1
46. Mat and Cane Workers	22
47. Hunters and Fowlers	33
48. Miscellaneous Vagrants	14
49. Jugglers and Acrobats	11
XIII.—Indefinite Indian Castes	**107**
XIV.—Indian Christians	**64**
58. Native	63
59. Goanese, &c.	1
XV.—Musalmáns bearing Foreign Titles.	**1,197**
XVI.—Himálayan Mongoloid	**8**
XVII.—Burmese and Chinese Mongoloids	**254**
52. Burmese, &c.	253
53. Mixed Races	1
XVIII.—Western Asiatics	**4**
XIX.—Eurasians	**3**
XX.—Europeans	**6**
XXI.—Africans	**1**
Total	**10,000**

extension of Brahmanism by fiction of common origin, in which the warrior caste plays a leading part. Practically it is not the caste, but the tribe of Rájpút that is regarded in the present day, so the general term has fallen into the hands, more or less, of the lower grades of social aspirants, whose acquaintance with the intricacies of Kshatria genealogy is of the slightest. In the *Jat*, again, we find a caste which is so divided internally that the tribe has taken its place in social estimation. It is still more of a northern denizen than its predecessor, and is mainly found in the Panjab and the adjacent tracts of Rajputana and the upper Jamna. In fact, it has strayed but little from the tract it occupied on its entrance into India from the north. The ethnology of the tribes that compose it is most interesting, as they contain better trace of their origin in the Caucasian region of

Class I.	**85,729,227**
Military	29,393,870
1. Rájput	10,424,346
2. Jat	6,688,733
3. Gújar	2,171,627
4. Maráthа	3,324,095
5. Bábhan	1,222,674
6. Nair	980,860
7. Kalla	410,983
8. Marawa	313,881
9. Velláma	479,783
10. Khandait	671,272
11. Awán	616,328
12. Káthi	41,996
13. Méo	365,726
14. Kodagu	32,641

ancient history than any other, but this is not the place to enter upon the subject. The *Gújar* is another northern tribe, but more like the Rájpút than the Jat; it is composed of varied elements. In the Panjáb it is mainly agricultural, though it tends towards cattle grazing in the southern plains. Elsewhere in India the title generally implies the latter occupation. Going further south, we meet the division of the Bombay Presidency to which it gives its name, and from this point southwards the latter almost invariably implies a trader from Gujaráth, without any reference to the northern origin of the caste. It is undoubtedly the relic of one of the later Skythian waves that flooded upper and western India, and many of the old forts and caves of the Sátpura and north Deccan are attributed to rulers of this race. We then pass to the *Marátha*, the ruling caste in the Deccan proper, who exceed the Gújar in numbers, but not in expansion. The number is swelled, no doubt, by the use of the term in contradistinction to a linguistic or sectarian community with which the Maratha speaker is brought into contract. Thus, wherever there are many Lingaiats, the north Deccani will call himself a Marátha, though amongst his own people he would be a Téli, Kúnbi, or some inferior caste. The *Bábban* is a caste confined, according to the returns, to Bihár, but the *Bhuinhár* of the adjacent territory of the North-West Provinces should, no doubt, be added. It is an offshoot of a community of fairly pure Arya blood, descended from some of the earlier settlers of Hindustan. The *Áwán* is a Panjáb caste, said to be one of the branches of the earliest Arya dispossessors of the Skythic races, and, like the rest of its compeers in that corner of India, its tribes are more cohesive than the caste as a whole. The *Káthi* seems to be descended from the Kathaei who defended their country against Alexander, and who afterwards migrated, whether voluntarily or not is uncertain, to the south-west, where they give their name to the province of Sauráshtra. The *Méo* is an interesting caste of the northern tracts of Rájputána and the south of the Panjáb. It is mostly converted to Islám, but seems to have been originally a wild tribe of the Central Plateau. The *Khandáit* is the military caste of Orissa, and is said to be of the same stock as the Bhuiya, a Hill tribe of the central belt. From constant employment in military service, and intercourse with the warrior caste from Hindustán, who conquered this tract, they have made a decided advance in appearance and general civilisation since they took service with the foreigner in a strange land. We have now left the military classes of the Dravidian country, of which the *Nair*, who has been mentioned in a preceding part of this section, is the most numerous. The *Kalla*, or thieves, are, with the *Marava*, the ruling class of the extreme south-east. The former are the Colleries so often mentioned by Orme in his account of the British operations in these parts. The *Vellama*, or Yellama, for the initial is interchangeable all over the Deccan, consider themselves, from their title, autochthonous in Telingána and the Kanarese Deccan. It is a question, and an interesting one, whether these frequent instances in India of caste names meaning "those of the soil" signify title to the possession of the land or those bound down to it. Examples of both usages can be found. Presumption seems rather in favour of the interpretation that these classes represent the pre-Aryan inhabitants who were not driven off the land in the Gangetic basin and western India, but were ascribed to it as serfs in the plains, and left as occupants in tracts which did not tempt the foreigner. In the case of the Yellama, probably they were fixed in possession long before the stray Bráhman began to thread his way through the Kaimúr or Vindhia. The last name that requires comment is that of the inhabitants of Coorg, the *Kodagu*, a peculiar and warlike race, secluded from much of the influences that have caused the general fissiparity of the Dravidian population of the plains.

2. Cultivators	**47,927,361**
1. Kunbi, &c.	10,531,300
2. Máli	1,876,211
3. Lódhá	1,674,098
4. Káchhia	1,384,222
5. Koeri	1,735,431
6. Vellála	2,254,073
7. Vakkiliga	1,360,558
8. Lingaiat	655,491
9. Panchamsáli	482,763
10. Kaibartta	2,298,824
11. Náma Shadra	1,948,658
12. Kóchh	2,364,365
13. Kóli	3,058,166
14. Reddi	2,665,399

Group 2 of this class is, necessarily, the largest and perhaps the most miscellaneous of all, though in the latter respect the group of Musalman who own to foreign titles approaches it. First of the castes that are here included comes that of the *Kúnbi* or *Kúrmi*. The former designation is that of the Deccan and west of India; the latter is used in the Gangetic valley. Both mean no more than tiller of the soil, and are therefore minutely subdivided. The Kurmi is returned from the North-West Provinces and Bihár chiefly, but he is found, too, in the north of the Central Provinces. Closely allied to this caste, in fact, in some parts of the country, almost subdivisions of it, are the *Káchhia*, and *Kúnjra*, market gardeners, and the *Kóeri*, the *Lódha*, and the *Máli*, cultivators. All but the Máli are chiefly found in Hindustán and its neighbourhood. The Máli is so bound up with the Kúnbi in the Deccan that the ordinary term for an agriculturist is the combination of the two, Kúnbimáli. We find names of the same comprehensive character amongst the cultivators of the south, as, for instance, *Vellála*, the Tamil equivalent for the Kunbi class, and the *Wakkaliga*, which corresponds to it in Mysore. The *Lingaiat*, too, of which something was said above in connection with sect, is shown without distinction, and the *Panchamsáli*, which is one of the terms included in the former, appears independently to nearly the same extent as the parent. Here we begin to find discrepancy of function, for the Panchamsáli must, from his name, have once been a weaver, or sprung from the village menial class, whereas he appears here as a cultivator and generally is one. Again, to cross India, the *Kaibartta*, the great agricultural caste of Bengal is, or was, entirely devoted to fishing, and it is even stated that his name is derived from his acquatic tendencies, but he is now rooted to dry land for his main livelihood, whilst the Bihár caste, that is said to have once been a branch of the Kaibartta, has changed its name to Kéwat, and will be found amongst the fishers. Take the *Námashúdra*, again, the lowest caste, or very nearly so, in eastern Bengal. Here they are cultivators, probably because there has been no ruling class from the west to oust them from the soil, and the proprietary right belongs in great measure to non-agriculturists, who require their property to be worked by other classes. But in Assam they are fishers. Amongst the more interesting castes in this group are the *Kóchh*, originally a Mongoloid tribe that came down the Bráhmapútra valley. They are now completely Brahmanised in title and certain portions of their domestic ceremonial, and have abandoned Assam for the submontane tracts of Bengal. The *Kóli*, who is returned in the largest numbers from the Western Presidency and the States of Haidrabád and Central India is not a homogeneous caste by any means. The philological connection between this appellation and that of Kól, and similar terms in more eastern parts of the continent, has not been established, but there is evidence, nevertheless, of the pre-Aryan existence of a race corresponding to it. In Gujaráth, where it forms the bulk of the lower cultivating community, it is called "the local," though there are several endogamous subdivisions, chiefly territorial. Along the Gháts there are other Kóli of an entirely different community in the present day but of the same stock. On the coast, again, the Kóli represents the early fishing interest, like the Kaibartta on the other side of India. Everywhere he is dark, and of the same physique as the Hill tribes of the Central Belt, except on the plains of Gujaráth, where the mixture with the higher races from the north seem to have improved his appearance as well as his intelligence. It is a question how far the Kóri, or low class weaver of the north, is allied to the Kóli of Central and Western India. Etymologically the titles are the same, but socially the former is an offshoot of the village menial of impure habits in connection with leather, whereas the Koli does not by his touch pollute the twice-born. But so far as the census is in question, the Kóri is classed with the weavers, whilst all the others appear under the present head. The only other large caste that is not purely provincial in its dispersion is the *Reddi*, or Kápu, the great cultivating caste of Telingána.

3. Field Labourers	8,407,996
Músáhar	622,034
Bágdi	804,960
Báwari	612,430
Dúbla	172,052
Pálé	2,242,499
Palla	814,989
Mála	1,365,520
Chéruma	523,744

The third group of agriculturists is anything but well-defined, as the boundaries between it and the lower grades of landholders and Hill tribes on the one side, and of village menials on the other, depend simply on local conditions. In the open country the position seems to be, generally speaking, the lower, and rises as the tract falls in futility or ease of access. The bulk of the group is found in the Madras Presidency, where the agrestic serf is an actual though unrecognised institution along the Malabar coast.* It is probable that the tradition of the Nairs is fairly trustworthy, and that they displaced and enslaved the

* Camoens mentions the distinction—

"A nobre
Naires chamados são; e a menos dina
Poleás tem por nome; a quem obriga
A lei não misturar a casta antiqua."

Chéruma and others, such as the Pulya, who are of an inferior race, and still practically bound to the estates on which they labour. In other parts of Southern India it is doubtful whether the corresponding castes do not belong to the group of village menials, in which they have been included in the neighbouring provinces and States. At all events the difference between the *Pálé*, the *Mála* and the Paraiyan, which may be linguistic only, does not seem to quite justify the separation of the two in classification, as was done on the above analogy, in default of local knowledge.* In the west of the Bombay Presidency there are two distinctly agrestic classes of labourers confined to one or two districts. These are the *Dúbla* and the *Dhódia*, who were ascribed to the soil by a class of agricultural Bráhmans who colonised the southern portion of Gujaráth. It is curious, by the way, to note that where Bráhmans take to colonisation there are always predial serfs attached to the estates, as in the tract now in question, on the Malabar coast and in Kanara and in Orissa. In the North-West Provinces and Bihár we find the agricultural labourer but little reclaimed from the tribes of the lower hills of the central belt. The *Bágdi* and *Báwari* and *Músáhar* are all instances of this, and with the Rajwár, a smaller caste of the same sort, are all related to the Bhuiya, Saharia, Chéro, and Khéro of Class III. below. The village watchman, such as Dhákar in the west and Dhánuk in the centre of Hindostán, is confounded partly with these functionaries, as he is in Madras.

The next class in the list is that of the castes accredited to pastoral occupations, of which the group engaged with horned cattle is the most numerously represented. The Ahír, under this title, is chiefly found in North-Western India, where he has, in his time, given more than one dynasty to local thrones. To him is attributed a Skythian origin, and there is no doubt that the Ahír once prevailed a little way south of the Vindhia range, and was in the Indus Valley at a very early period in the history of India. The largest subdivision of the caste, known as the Goálwansh, extends from Oudh far into Bihár. The next caste mentioned in the margin is probably only functionally connected with it, though the etymology of the title is the same. The *Goála*, *Gauli*, or *Gôlla*, is the Ahír of the south and east, and spreads all over Bengal and the peninsula.

Class II.—Pastoral	16,721,494
Group 1. *Cattle graziers, &c.*	11,569,319
1. Ahir	8,155,219
2. Gauli, Goála, &c.	2,237,323

The second group in this class comprises those castes who specially attend to sheep and goats, and who also are engaged in the preparation of wool and the coarse blankets universally worn in wet or cold weather. In the north of India the *Gadaria* represent this class and the *Dhangar* of the Deccan is nearly akin to them. The Hatgar is a subdivision of the Dhangar, but more specially devoted to weaving and the spinning of black yarn from the fleeces of their charge. The *Kurubar* are the shepherds of the South Deccan and Telingána generally, whilst the *Idaiya* and Kurúmba are the Tamil, or South Dravidian, representatives of the group. Of the larger provinces, Bengal and Burma have the smallest proportion of this class, owing to the comparative scarcity of grazing land in the former and the damp in both. The latter reason, with the great amount of forest, probably accounts for the absence of the shepherd from Assam. In Western India, Rajputána and Gujaráth, the Rabári and Bharwád are the chief shepherd classes. Nearly all are, from the nature of their calling, nomad for most of the year, though some of the larger clans keep up connection with some headquarter village or district.

Group 2. Shepherds, &c.	5,152,175
1. Gadaria	1,294,830
2. Dhangar	1,305,583
3. Kúrnbar	1,059,185
4. Idaiga	665,232
5. Rabári	434,788
6. Bharwad	128,271

It is impossible to enter into the detail of the heterogeneous class of Forest Tribes; so, for convenience of review, the chief items have been collected into territorial groups, several of which denote, also, racial distinctions. The marginal table over page shows the main results of this arrangement. The largest group is that of the tribes of the north-eastern hills of the Central Belt, amongst whom, however, we must include the detached

* The caste chapters of the Superintendent's Report have not yet been received.—J. A. B.

colony of the Santháls, further north.

Class III. Forest Tribes	15,806,914
1. Santhál	1,494,045
2. Kól	474,969
3. Korwá	158,700
4. Hó	150,262
5. Munda	410,624
6. Bhuiya, &c.	909,822
7. Pán	341,740
8. *Kharwár*	112,298
9. *Oraon*	523,258
10. Baiga	136,478
11. Kúr	155,831
12. *Gónd*	3,061,680
13. Bhil	1,665,474
14. Bhilála	175,329
15. *Kirar*	175,508
16. *Ména*	669,785
17. *Káthodi*	77,705
18. *Wárli*	168,631
19. *Ghát-Thákúr*	130,481
20. *Naikada*	74,479
21. *Dhánka*	67,451
22. Kandh (Khónd)	627,388
23. Sáwara	438,317
24. Halaba	102,643
25. Gadaba	34,127
26. Yanádi	84,988
27. Játápu	81,152
28. Tóda	739
29. Kóta	1,201
30. Irula	58,503
31. Khási	172,150
32. Kachári	243,378
33. Gáro	150,227
34. Méch	96,873
35. Tippera	99,395
36. Mikir	94,829
37. Nága	101,568
38. Ching-pau, &c.	3,483
39. Kúki	25,940
40. Lúshai	43,840
41. Kathé (*Manipúri*)	84,540
42. Khyín (*Unspecified*)	82,710
43. Khyín Khwé-mí	14,200
44. Khyín Mró	15,666

The whole group may be conventionally termed Kolarian, as the language of all but the two last belongs to that family. But they are, nevertheless, of the same ethnic stock as the bulk of the next three groups. They furnish the bulk of the labourers who migrate into Assam for a term of service on the tea estates, &c., and in Eastern and Central Bengal, too, are found in considerable numbers as general labourers, wherever strength and endurance are required. The discrimination noted in the margin between the *Hó*, *Múnda*, *Kól*, and *Korwá*, is by no means accurate. The term Kól, for example, seems to have been applied to certain tribes by outsiders, as the people concerned recognise no name but that of Hó, or Múndá. The *Bhuiya*, again, is not a homogeneous body, but includes Bhúmij, Bhinjwa, Bhúnjia, &c., and the term Baiga, which is that of a tribe in the Central Provinces, is applied by some people in Chutia Nágpur simply to the magician of the community, possibly because he belonged to a tribe preceding, in occupation of the place, that which now employs him in the above capacity. The second group appertains more especially to the central ranges of the Hill Belt, the *Bhil*, *Bhiláta*, and *Kúrku* being found to the westwards, and the *Baiga* in the middle. The *Gónd*, who, as shown in the language section of this chapter, gave their name to the whole tract, are still spread all over it, north and south. They do not come much within the Chútia Nágpúr districts, Berár, Haidrabad, or North Madras, though all these tracts contain certain of their tribes, but are chiefly found in the Central Provinces and the Orissa hills. The subdivisions are very numerous, and in some cases amount to a completely separated community. The *Kúr* spread from Chutia Nágpúr, across the south of Central India into the hills which bound Berár on the north. The *Bhils* there meet them, and carry the race on to the western extremity of the Sátpura and Vindhia. Here they seem to have founded the now separate tribes of Bhilála, Páwada, Dhánka, Naikada, and Tadwi, of whom the third and fourth are the Gujaráth representatives of the great tribe, and the last has become Musalmán. The *Kirár* is almost confined to the hills where the Central Provinces, Central India, and the North-West Provinces meet. It is doubtful whether it is an independent tribe or an offshoot from one of the larger ones. The *Mena*, or Mina, are the originals of the Méo, who have moved into the northern plains adjoining the Jamna and have embraced Islám. From their title it might be thought that, like the Kaibartta, they were connected with fishing, either by profession or by tribal symbol, but their gods are those of the landholding classes, and there is no tradition of other occupation than those of cultivation and robbery, for they formerly kept the whole country round their settlements in terror of marauding expeditions. It is doubtful whether they are properly classed as forest tribes, and whether they should not rather be placed amongst the Skythian wanderers, like the Ahír or Káthi. In the next group, Nos. 17 to 21, the two last have been mentioned above as offshoots of the Bhil and the three others are confined to the country immediately above and below the Ghát range. The *Káthodi*, or Kátkari, get their name from the occupation of preparing catechu from the tree, to which they were originally addicted. The *Wárli* are hill cultivators of a low type, and the *Thakúrs*, a branch of the same race, specially distinguished by this honorific designation, and in position and habits somewhat above the others. We then cross to the Orissa hills and their western extension. Here we have the *Kandh*, or Khónd, of whom much has been written, and the *Sáwara*, mentioned, it is said, by the Greek geographers, both being confined to the eastern ranges. The *Halaba*, probably allied to the Gónds, succeed them towards the west, and the *Gadaba* are also adjacent to the south-west. The *Yanádi* are the tribes of almost detached masses of hills in Telingána, like the still smaller tribe of the Chentsú. The Nilgiri group of hills is represented by the *Tóda* and *Kóta*, who have been already mentioned as small or local tribes, curiously isolated from the rest of the Dravidians, and by the *Irulas*, who spread down the slopes on the Mysore side. There are other tribes of much the same class occupying the Ghát forests, Malabar, and the Annamallai and other groups of hills in the extreme south, but they are of small numerical extent, and have not had the advantages in the way of advertisement enjoyed by the Tóda. The three remaining groups are Mongoloid in race, and chiefly Assamese in habitation. The *Khási*, though linguistically distinct, are racially allied, in all probability, to their neighbours in the hills east and west of them. The rest belong to the great Bódo group of the Assam valley and the hills to the south thereof. The *Tippera*, it is true, is now separated from the parent stock by sundry tribes of *Zhó* and *Kúki*, but its language shows that the separation is of comparatively recent date. The small tribes of the Abor and Mishmi have not been specially mentioned, because, like their western neighbours, the Akka and Dafla, the majority of the community dwells outside the British frontier, and the population found within the red line consisted partly of offshoots settled there within the few last generations, or casual families or gangs come down to market. The Nága, Mikir, and Singphó, or Kakhyìn, have been mentioned in connection with their respective languages. The first is the subject of an interesting memorandum by Mr. Davies, appended to the Assam Census Report. The Burmese tribes belonging to the last-named family have likewise yielded a corresponding contribution to the Report on the Census of Burma. As regards the last group, very little, as has been stated above, is at present known. The Manipuri, however, has his tradition of ancestry from the demi-god Arjún, and Bindraban, the scene of the youthful frolics of Krishna, is the goal of his aspirations, as Benares is to the devout Khas and Gúrkha of Nipál, who are more Kshatria than the Kshatrias of the plains. But the mass of the population of Manipur is Mongoloid, even in title, and Brahmanic proclivities are confined to the court and its *entourage*. The forest tribes of Burma, when not returned as Khyìn or Kakhyìn, have been absorbed into the general titles of Burmese or Karén.

Class IV. Fishers	8,261,878
1. Kahár	1,943,155
2. Mállah	1,147,544
3. Kéwat	989,352
4. Bhoi	606,190
5. Jhinwar	489,819
6. Dhimár	287,436
7. Gaurhi	317,111
8. Máchhi	260,496

The class of fishers is broken up into a large number of small castes. Those given in the margin are the best representatives, either of the group as a whole or of a special province, but they are probably mixed up together in the returns. For instance, the Dhimar and Jhinwar are probably the Panjáb and Central Indian equivalents of the Kahár, from whose ranks they sprang. Looking at the peculiar position occupied everywhere by the class of fishers, especially those who are very largely engaged in non-piscatorial work, it is clear that there is some racial basis for the anomalous rules and privileges attached to this caste. The fisher will carry any burden that is supported on a pole across his shoulder, but may refuse a head load or knapsack. He can give water to men of far higher caste, and become a servant in the recesses of their establishment; he can even knead dough, &c. for their bread, but must not lay a finger on it once it has been put into an oven or on the baking-plate. Yet he is allowed to indulge in ardent spirits and to eat strange food on which the orthodox may not even look, and is admitted to functions from which far more wealthy and reputable castes are rigorously excluded. As regards the nomenclature of the castes selected for mention, the *Kahár* is the form adopted throughout the North-West Provinces and Bihár; the *Jhinwar* is the Panjáb equivalent, and the *Dhimar* that adopted in the Central Provinces and its neighbourhood. In Assam we have seen that the two castes, which are classed in Bengal as agricultural, constitute, with the Kéwat, the bulk of the fishing class, whilst the *Kéwat* of Hindustán is probably the Kaibartta of the Lower Ganges. The *Mallah* is prevalent in both these provinces. In the table, some of this caste are attributed to Haidrabád, but it seems very likely that they belong to the agricultural labourers, called Mála in the Madras Presidency. Amongst other widespread castes of this group comes the Bhói, which is apparently the Telingána version of Kahár, and is spread also over the Western Presidency and Rajputana, and the Béstá, which prevails still further south. The rest are almost entirely local. Muháno is the Sindh fisher caste, Máchhi is only found on the Indus and in Gujaráth, and Sembadáwan, Mogér, Pallé, &c. appertain to the south of the peninsula, east and west respectively.

The functional classes contain little but linguistic or territorial groups, which only need comment in special cases, or where there may have been confusion in nomenclature or tabulation. The first four groups are taken together, because, in popular estimation, they are the special care of Viswakarma, the Hephæstus of the later Vedic theogony, and in the south of India are almost invariably taken as constituting a single caste, though with five non-endogamous subdivisions. Elsewhere, however, the latter only are recognised, and the five vary respectively in rank according to locality. The function of the gold and silversmith has been described in an earlier chapter. His aid in making and remaking ornaments is constantly in request where capital invariably takes this form of investment. Owing to the majority of the members of all five groups being returned in Madras under the general title of "the five arts," the number there has been distributed according to that of the portion of each class which was separately returned, so that the division is partly arbitrary. The three castes shown in the first group are simply the general title, with its Kanarese and Tamil equivalents, and a good deal of the second has doubtless passed into the first. The second group, again, consists of two linguistic groups. The first, Luhár, is a general term, though, as explained above, the Luhár of the Panjáb will decline *connubium* with him of the Deccan, as will the Kammar of Madras with his namesake of Bengal. The carpenters, again, comprise six groups, none of which, save for differences in language and locality, are mutually exclusive. The original carpenter caste was the Sutár, or Sutradhár, but the Barhai, from *vardh*, to cut, is equally Sanskritic, as is Káthi, Kháti, from either *Káth*, timber, or *Kháti*, a wooden bedstead, &c. Badagi and Asári are the Dravidian versions. The mason is poorly represented. In the Deccan he forms a separate caste, but the Ráj of Upper India is probably more comprehensive, and includes all who work at masonry. In some provinces or tracts, of course, his services are scarcely required by the great bulk of the population, and in all, the carpenter undertakes most of the building, aided by unskilled labour. The brass-smith is growing annually in wealth and importance, but his functions are not yet so specialised as those of the carpenter or blacksmith. Of the two main castes mentioned, the first carries on the whole business in most parts of the peninsula, and sells what he makes. In the Panjáb, however, the Thathéra sells and the Kaséra makes, and in the North-West Provinces the latter moulds and the former polishes the vessels and platters, &c. There is a curious affinity between brass-ware and Brahmanism. The great centres of brasswork in India are also the Brahmanic centres of pilgrimage, such as Benares, Násik, and Madúra, or political centres where Brahmanic influence is supreme, as Poona and Tanjore. Then, again, in all the temporary bazárs that are set up during the time of pilgrimage at shrines and bathing-places, the booths of the seller of brass vessels, images, lamps, and so on, are perhaps the most conspicuous of all in number and variety, for the commercial element is as prominent at these gatherings as the sacerdotal. It is, therefore, plain that the production of these wares must be carried on by a great many more than the relatively insignificant number set forth in the return.

Class V. Artisans	28,882,551
Group 1. *Goldsmiths, &c.*	1,661,088
1. Sonár	1,178,795
2. Aksále	307,670
3. Tattan	56,044
Group 2. *Blacksmiths*	2,625,103
1. Luhár	1,869,273
2. Kammar	666,887
Group 3. *Carpenters and Masons*	3,442,201
1. Sutár	681,790
2. Barhai	932,718
3. Tarkhán	696,781
4. Badagi	452,339
5. Asári	100,409
6. Kháti	301,476
7. Gaundia, &c.	76,995
8. Raj, &c.	19,770
Group 4. *Brass and Coppersmiths*	301,519
1. Kaséra, &c.	161,596
2. Tathéra	60,837
3. Bogár	37,002

The next section of the class under review is that of the workers in textile fabrics. This, as has been said in a former chapter, is an occupation evolved out of the dregs of the village population into comparative respectability, and in the case of certain articles, such as silk, gold braid, and coloured goods, into a decidedly good position. But the mass of the castes are still not far above the village menial. The Kori, for example, is often returned as a Chamár or leather worker, to which tribe he once belonged. The workers in hemp and in coarse, undyed cotton cloth are elsewhere set far below the ordinary toiler at the loom. The latter is said to be occasionally ambitious of rising in the social scale, but circumstances are against all but perhaps the silk-weavers, whose wares are less affected by foreign competition. The castes mentioned in the margin are mostly provincial and linguistic, except the three last, of which the first represents the high-class weaver of silk, &c., the second the Gujaráthi weaver of the finer class of wearing apparel, from which the former sprang, and the last is the dyer, who, like the Joláha, is both Brahmanic and Musalmán, sometimes even according to the material he works in. The *Darzi*, according to his modern and Persianised appellation, or the Shimpi, in the older version, is somewhat of the rank of the middle-class weaver, and is developed from the calenderer, Chhipgár or Bhausár caste, which, again, is allied to the weaver. It is more or less of an urban growth, however, and is not much found in villages. The cotton-cleaner is usually a Musalmán, and is found all over the country, wherever cotton is grown and weavers work in it. The general name for the caste is *Pinjári*, or Penjá, but the Musalmán improves it into the Persian title Nadáf, or Dhúnia, and the Brahmanic cleaner in Hindustán and the Central Provinces calls himself *Kadhéra*. In Bengal there are several local titles in both religions.

GROUP 5. *Tailors*	735,548
1. Darzi and Shimpi	710,092
GROUP 6. *Weavers and Dyers*	9,369,902
1. Juláha	2,660,159
2. Kóri	1,187,613
3. Tanta	483,942
4. Júgi	424,219
5. Balai	305,635
6. Sáli	394,064
7. Kaikola	316,620
8. Tatwa	328,778
9. Koshti	225,019
10. Gánda	291,768
11. Patnúli	96,443
12. Khatri	116,880
13. Rangréz	187,698
GROUP 7. *Cotton Cleaners*	859,288
1. Pinjári	753,675
2. Kadhera, &c.	105,613

The two next groups, those of the oil pressers and the potters, are very simple, the different items representing simply linguistic variations of the same functional group. The Téli is the general title. Ghánchi corresponds to it in Gujaráth, and Ghániga in the South Deccan. Vaniya is the Tamil equivalent, and Kalu is a Bengal subdivision, based on some inferiority of process in extracting the oil. As to the potters, the only variation from the general caste is in the shape of a few who have returned their function as brick-making, which in some parts of the country has been differentiated from the rest. The second item is merely the southern title of the potter.

GROUP 8. *Oil pressers*	4,672,907
1. Téli and Ghánchi	4,147,803
2. Ghániga	142,374
3. Vaniya	186,297
4. Kalu	191,395
GROUP 9. *Potters*	3,497,306
1. Kumbhár	3,346,488
2. Kúsuvan	138,097

The glass workers are mainly makers of beads and bangles. The class that work in lac is very closely allied to them in rank, but are not so largely recruited from Islám. There are numbers of small castes returned under special or local titles which come under the general head of Káchári. Those mentioned in the margin are chiefly in Bengal and Hindustán. The salt and lime workers belong to castes nearly allied to each other. The *Lúnia* are the prevailing caste of this group in Northern India. The *Ágri* are found along the west coast.

GROUP 10. *Glass and Lac Workers.*	155,003
1. Chúrihár	55,618
2. Lahéra	32,139
GROUP 11. *Salt and Lime Workers.*	1,531,130
1. Lúnia	796,080
2. Uppár	267,715
3. Ágri	241,336
4. Rehgár	77,856

Group 12. *Goldsmiths' Refuse Cleaners.*	6,363
1. Niária	5,808
2. Jhálgár	555
Group 13. *Iron Smelters and Gold Washers.*	24,893
1. Jhora	7,337
2. Dhangari	3,672
3. Asuri	3,552
4. Deoli	2,289

The *Uppár* are the Dravidian equivalent to the Lúnia. The *Rehgár* are confined to Rajputána, where the Sámbhar Lake gives employment to a considerable number of this class. The next group, that represented by the Niária and Jhálgár, two names for the same small community, busies itself with recovering the chips and filings of precious metal from the refuse of goldsmiths' workshops. The iron smelters are found in some of the Hill tracts of the Panjáb, the Central Belt, and the Gháts of Bombay. They are a small and scattered community. The gold washers, too, are very low in both numbers and rank. Most provinces have a stream or two, in the bed of which minute portions of gold are found mingled with the sand, and by careful panning the outturn is just enough to support the family of the operator. The heavy mining work in Mysore is largely in the hands of European labourers.

The position of the two first groups of the class of personal servants have been described in a previous chapter. The Nái, Nápit, Nhávi, &c., besides shaving, which is a ceremonial of considerable importance, acts as formal messenger and go-between in cases of betrothals, &c., and is also a leech of empirical skill. The *Hajám* is the same caste under its Musalmán title. *Ambattan* and *Mangala* are found in the south and south-east of the peninsula, and Bhandári in the Central Provinces. The *Dhobi* shares the low rank of the potter, partly owing to his use of the donkey in his profession. The second name in the group is that used in the Kanarese and Telugu country. The two next appertain to further south, and the last is purely Marátha. The group of other servants is a miscellaneous one, many of the items in which are scarcely entitled to the name of caste, as they are not all endogamous or otherwise distinct from each other socially. The first on the list, *Gólá*, is the rice pounder of Western India. The second, the water bearer, is returned as a separate caste chiefly in Hindustán, and enjoys the name of "Paradisaic" from the boon he carries. The other two are simply hereditary domestic servants of the courts of the chieftains of Rajputána and Central India, some of them, no doubt, blood relations of their master.

Class VI. Personal and Domestic Service, preparation of Food, &c.	**14,019,626**
Group 1. *Barbers*	3,729,934
1. Nái, &c.	2,532,067
2. Hajám	605,721
3. Ambattan	186,187
4. Mangala	154,438
5. Bhandári	103,026
Group 2. *Washermen*	2,824,451
1. Dhobi	2,039,743
2. Agasé	126,710
3. Vannan	258,508
4. Sákala	327,720
5. Parit	60,129
Group 3. *Service, &c.*	430,065
1. Golá	33,804
2. Bihisti, &c.	98,824
3. Khás	215,200
4. Chákar	25,706

Most of the fourth group are connected with the great fisher caste of the Kahár, or some corresponding division. They are most strongly represented under the titles selected in Hindustán and Bengal. The first-named, Bhadbhúnja, is found, also, far to the south and west of those provinces, but usually asserts an origin in the north or along the great rivers. The next group is very undermanned, considering the extensive and, in fact, universal consumption of the articles in which they deal. But in many parts of the country the sellers are also growers of the leaf, and thus appear under the head of agriculturists. The *Támbóli* is a distinct caste in Central India and the North Deccan, but in Hindustán and Bihár it is probably a sub-caste of the Barai, a large cultivating class, affiliated in some parts of the country to the Káchhia, and thus finally thrown back on the great Kúrmi stock.

Group 4. *Grain Parchers and Confectioners.*	1,407,169
1. Bhadbhúnja	343,308
2. Kándoi	524,155
3. Halvai	260,801
4. Gúria, &c.	141,628
Group 5. *Betel Leaf Sellers and Perfumers.*	236,507
1. Tambóli	222,048

The class that traditionally lives by toddy drawing and cultivating the palm tree is a very large and varied one. The items selected, too, are somewhat peculiar in not being, in most cases, linguistic variations of the same caste. By far the largest number of the communities belong to the coasts of Madras. The *Bhandári* prevails on the Bombay coast, and the *Sháha*, or Sunri, in Assam and Orissa, whilst the *Gaundla* is returned only from Haidrabád. The *Kalál*, or *Kalwár*, is the general distiller of spirits, as distinguished from those who deal with or in toddy. He is found in most provinces, and in Upper India has furnished one throne with a dynasty. On the Western Presidency his place is taken by the Pársi, but above the Gháts he begins soon to settle down to his traditional calling and to thrive on it. The butchers are of two classes, Brahmanic, *Khatik*, and Musulman, *Kasái*. They are most numerous, of course, amongst the martial tribes of the north and elsewhere in places where Musalmáns congregate. Some, however, the Hindus, for instance, do not in the present day kill cattle, but deal in the flesh of sheep and goats only.

GROUP 6. *Distillers and Toddy Drawers.*	4,785,210
1. Kalál	1,195,097
2. Sháha (*Súnri*)	525,698
3. Shána	690,434
4. Tiya	538,075
5. Bhandári	170,014
6. Idga	196,901
7. Iluva	703,215
8. Gamalla	122,322
9. Gaundla	235,902
GROUP 7. *Butchers*	605,890
1. Kasai	302,612
2. Khatík	293,771

The class of leather workers and lower village menials is, next to the agriculturists, to whom they are subordinate, the most numerous body in India, and includes all the tribes of the darker race, who preferred a foreign yoke to exile from the tract they formerly possessed. The first group comprises all who avowedly work in leather and other *exuviæ* of defunct cattle, but the first and third castes, at all events, combine agricultural and village labour with their traditional function to such an extent that they mingle greatly with the group which follows them on the list. The *Móchi* is distinctly an artisan, mostly found in towns, where his occupation is specialised. In villages there are distinctions recognised. Some will mend shoes, but not make them; others devote themselves to making the leather bags in which water for irrigation is drawn from the well. A third only manufactures leather pots in which to store clarified butter, and so on. The fourth item, *Sakilia*, is the caste known as Chucklers to Anglo-Indians in Madras. The Mádiga is a Kanarese and Telugu caste of the same nature, combining tanning with shoe-making, and the Bámbhi is the specially Rajputána community of the same description. From very early Brahmanic times the leather worker has been a member of the village community, and always in his present degraded rank. It would appear from Aristophanes that it was much the same in Athens, where the hemp weaver, the Máng, as it were, had to give place to the Chamár, who, in turn, was to be dispossessed by a still lower caste, the Chúhra, or pig-breeding scavenger, before the degradation of the State was complete. The next group, that of watchmen, &c., is a trifle higher, and several of the castes named, such as the *Pási*, *Dhánúk*, *Bérád*, *Mutrása*, and *Rámosi*, occupy a more reputable place in public estimation than the rest. The *Mahár*, however, of whom the *Dhed* is the northern and the *Holár* the Kanarese variety, and the *Máng*, are practically in the same rank as *Chamárs* and other leather workers, as they mostly serve as tanners, though they do not work up the hides they prepare. Their enterprise in going far a-field from their native village for work,

Class VII. Leather Workers and the Lower Village Menials.	**30,795,703**
GROUP 1. *Leather Workers*	14,003,100
1. Chamár	11,258,105
2. Móchi	961,133
3. Mádiga	927,339
4. Sakilia	445,366
5. Bámbhi	220,596
GROUP 2. *Watchmen and other Menials.*	12,808,300
1. Dosadh	1,284,126
2. Ghátwál	167,089
3. Pási	1,378,344
4. Arakh	85,522
5. Dhánúk	883,278
6. Méhra	226,216
7. Mahár	2,960,568
8. Dhéd	508,310
9. Holár	880,441
10. Máng	690,458
11. Berad	659,863
12. Rámosi	63,991
13. Mutrása	296,743
14. Paraiya (*Pariah*)	2,210,988
GROUP 3. *Scavengers and Miscellaneous.*	3,984,303
1. Mehtar	727,985
2. Chúhra	1,243,370
3. Mégh	148,210
4. Bhuinmáli	231,429
5. Bhuinhári	316,787
6. Dóm (*Dúmna*)	1,257,826

and the demand for hides and skins for export to Europe, together with a strong local demand for tanners, &c. in some parts of India, where, as has been already remarked, European capital has been invested in this industry, tends to raise the position of this class above that of the ordinary village menial, and as money is acquired, the demands for recognition as of a higher caste become more worthy of consideration, elementary schools are started, and the marriage field is restricted, and in a few generations a totally new social stratum is firmly established, based, of course, on one of the heroes of the Brahmanic epics. As regards the territorial designations quoted in the marginal table, the *Dúsadh* is found chiefly in Bihár and parts of Hindustán. The *Dhánuk* extends into Rájputána and the Panjáb, but it is chiefly in Bihár. The *Pási* is a watchman, &c. in the North-West Provinces, as a rule, and more of a toddy drawer across the frontier, and the *Arakh* is his kinsman. Like the *Bérads*, or Bédar of the South Deccan, they were originally hunters and fowlers. The latter are well known for their prowess under the Mysore Sultáns, with whom they enlisted in considerable numbers. Their head-quarters were at Shorápúr in Haidrabád territory, the downfall of the Chief of which State is told by Colonel Meadows Taylor, in his autobiography. The *Rámosi* is a small caste of the Deccan proper, not far removed from the Kóli, but of more southern origin. The *Mutrása* is the village watchman proper of Telingána. As regards the Paraiya, or Pariah, the well-known Tamil caste of labourers, it has before been remarked that his position is generally that of an agricultural labourer, but under special restrictions as to function and residence, like the Mahár of the Deccan. He has, however, no prejudices to overcome, and makes himself at home in any miscellaneous employment; so, like the Chamár of the north, his sphere is extending, though not proportionately to his numbers. As Bráhmanic rules are more widely diffused amongst the peaceful Dravidians, who received them later, than amongst the more varied and frequently disturbed commonalty of Hindustán, where they originated, the opposition to Paraiyan exaltation is more marked. The third group, again, is composed of the lowest grades of the pre-Áryan classes, though the last, the Dóm, is of a very varied constitution, and rises to occupations not attained by the rest. The *Mehtar*, or Bhangi, is found under that title in Hindustán and Western India. In the Panjáb the *Chúhra* takes his place. Both these castes are of fine physique, and very different in appearance and stamina from the Dravidian type of the south. The *Mégh*, or *Meghwál*, is also found in the Panjáb and Sindh, and is said to be of a still more northern origin, as he is accredited by Sir A. Cunningham to a Skythian parentage. The *Bhuinhári*, or *Bhuinmáli*, represent the Bengal and Assam scavenger. Their name clearly denotes the same connection with the land as that of Bhúmio, which is given to the corresponding class in Gujaráth. In the *Dóm*, with its varieties, we have a far more interesting community than that of mere scavengers. In the first place, it is a generic title, the derivation of which is uncertain; but the term must be one of considerable antiquity, as it is used in the "Rája Tarangini," or "Annals of Kashmér," one of the early neo-Bráhmanic productions. There are one or two sections of the caste who are, no doubt, not far above the village scavenger, but most of the tribes have adopted subdivisional names which obscure their affinity to the parent stock, because the latter has but a poor reputation amongst the settled population of the plains of Hindustán. Here the Dóm is a vagrant, and nominally does cane work for a living. He also makes leaf platters and blows horns at marriages, which is a performance never attempted by any but the lowest castes. In Assam he is a fisherman. In the Sewálik and Lower Himálayan valleys, as far west as Kashmér, the Dóm, or Dúmna, is also an artisan or exorciser, and in the latter capacity again associated with musical instruments. But the highest type of Dóm is the *Mirási*, or genealogist, of the lower Brahmanic castes, and, as such, their bard or minstrel, so that his musical gifts, especially with reference to the drum and timbrel, again come to his service. In the South Deccan and northern portions of Madras, the Dómba is, generally speaking, an acrobat, but some few of them seem to be weavers of coarse fabrics. There are many links showing the connection in race of the Dóm with the Máng, Mahár, or Dhéd of further south on the one hand, and on the other, with the various tribes of semi-criminal vagrants of Upper India, such as Sánsi, Bédia, Báwari, Kanjár, Changar, &c., and to the foreign investigator the chief interest in their ramifications lies in the probability of tracing to some of them the parentage of the gipsies of Europe. With the exception of certain classes of the Báwari, the above-mentioned tribes are all vagrant, whereas the Mahár and Dhéd are all settled, and of the Mángs only the small section addicted to snake charming and conjuring still take to the road. But the question of the origin of the gipsies of the west appertains rather to this part of the subject than to that of the vagrant group of castes, because attempts have been made to derive from the title Dóm the universal appellation of Róm given to their community by the gipsies, and meaning, of course, according to their interpretation, "the man." There is every reason to believe that the gipsies are really the descendants of the 12,000 or so of musicians and earthworkers, &c., transported to Persia, probably from Sindh, in the time of Behrám Gaúr, about 400 A.D., and in the section of this chapter dealing with languages, it was stated that the title Egyptian was probably derived from Jat, the prevailing caste of Sindh and the Lower Panjáb at that time. The reason for adopting this root is mainly the insufficiency of evidence for the alternative derivation. In all the varieties of the gipsy language in Europe we find lots of low Prakritic words, a good deal synonymous with those in use in Upper India in the present day, but scarcely any Arabic. Again, there is no tradition regarding the passage of the gipsies to Europe by Egypt, whilst there is a very definite one as to their migration from Mesopotamia and Persia to North Syria, and from thence to the shores of the Bosphorus. Now, in Syria the gipsies are called Zatti, or, in the plural, zatt, to this day, and Arabic authors derive this term from "Jat, an Indian tribe," and give the same title to a particular kind of cotton cloth woven by the gipsies. There is, again, the statement, though the foundation for it is not given, that in olden times, Bithynia, where the gipsies undoubtedly settled, was called Little Egypt, but it does not seem that this derivation of the word is required, in the light of the evidence available as to the connection between the gipsies and India. Language, customs, caste-exclusiveness and all, point to their origin in the Indus Valley, though, as Browning says of them:

> "North they go, south they go, trooping on lonely;
> And still as they travel far and wide,
> Catch they and keep hold a trace here, a trace there,
> That puts you in mind of a place here, a place there."

But though we admit this much regarding the Indian origin of the gipsies, the alleged connection between Dóm and Róm seems to be doubtful. It is open to question, in the first place, whether the interchange of R and a palatal D can take place at the beginning of a word, though it obviously can in any other position. Then, again, there is no reason to affiliate the gipsies to the Dóm rather than to the vagrants more specially given to the performances for which the gipsies are celebrated, who are found in the tracts from which the latter were historically recruited.* From another point of view, that of language irrespective of ethnology, we find that Róm means, not only man, in the general, but, as in German, married man or husband, in the particular, so we may connect it with the Prakritic Raman, a husband or lover; or the same word, in its earlier signification, of restless wandering; or, once more, in its sense of sport, amusement, as the change of a vowel costs less than that of a consonant. Mr. Leland's authority,† John Náno, maker of curry powder in London, but by origin a "Mahometan Hindu" of Calcutta, seems to have been akin to the "certain persons of Kyréné," who favoured Herodotus in a somewhat similar manner.

A great portion of the trading community returns itself by the title of *Bania*, *Vaïshia*, or *Mahájan*, which are simply functional designations, and ignore the real subdivisions of caste which underlie the above. Thus, the full strength of many of the items shown in Table XVII. (A.) under this group is not that given in the return, but something considerably above it, the balance being included under the general title. We have, however, a few definite entries. *Aróra*, for instance, is the great trading and shopkeeping caste of the Western Panjáb. The *Khatri*, its neighbour to the east, is not so exclusively given up to trade, and, like the corresponding class in Gujaráth, furnishes a considerable portion of the staff of employés in the offices of the local government. The commercial element of Telingána is supplied by the *Kómti* and *Balija*, and possibly some of the former have

Class VIII. Traders, &c.	**12,270,973**
GROUP 1. *Traders* - -	12,148,597
1. Mahájan and Bania (*unspecified*).	3,186,666
2. Agarwál - - -	354,177
3. Khatri - -	686,511
4. Aróra -	673,695
5. Komti - - -	545,206
6. Balija -	804,307
7. Chetti - -	702,141
8. Mappila -	916,436
9. Labbé - -	364,293
10. Lohána - -	530,468

* A brave attempt has been made to derive conjure from Kanjar.—J. A. B.
† Gipsies, p. 337.

been included in the latter, which has a wider application. In the south, the inland tracts are served by the *Chetti*, as the Kanarese are by the Banjiga, again a general term, covering numerous subdivisions. On the south-east coast of the peninsula we find trade much in the hands of the *Labbé*, a Musalmán tribe, of mixed origin, and, on the Malabar tract, the *Mappila* occupy a like position. The latter, however, are, in great measure, agriculturists, and having acquired estates have abandoned commerce, but, as a class, they may still be considered to follow the latter. Their disputes with the Nair and other agricultural classes, due probably, as in Eastern Bengal, to their origin amongst the lowest Brahmanic castes, and their religious zeal, have brought them into serious trouble on several occasions during the last few generations; so much so that special legislation had to be applied to their case, and the "Moplah" outbreaks were the main political feature of the coast. For the last 10 years, however, matters have been quiet, though the devotion of the community to their faith is no less marked than before.

The *Lohána* of Sindh are by no means a well-defined body, and probably many of those shown under this title are not of the commercial subdivisions. Like the Khatri, they fill the Government offices, as they are almost the only literate community in the whole province. Amongst the smaller trading castes of the west coast, we find the Bhátia, located chiefly in Kachh and Sindh, with some brethren of the same name in the Panjáb. They are celebrated for their enterprise in foreign trade, especially that with East Africa, and for their sectarian orthodoxy with regard to the Wallabhachárya denomination, of which they are amongst the chief supporters. Then, again, the Méman, a Musalmán body, converted from Brahmanism, is found side by side with the Bhátia, whilst the Khója, who are of the same origin, but different in their Musalmán form of faith, extend well into the Panjáb. It is doubtful, however, whether the Khója of the Peshάwar valley and its neighbourhood are of the same race as the merchants of this name on the Bombay coast, though they may have the same reverence for the deified descendant of the "Old Man of the Mountain" of the time of the Crusades, who has been for a couple of generation or so domiciled in Bombay. In Gujaráth and the North-West Provinces, the subdivisions of what is returned as Bania are exceedingly numerous. The best known are the *Agarwál*, from the north, and the Oswál and Porwál, from Rajputána, with local varieties, such as the Kasárwáni, Shrimáli, and so on. The Deccan, again, has its own variety of trader, in the Lingaiat and its subdivisions, and the Konkan coast sends out three or four subdivisions returned under the question-begging epithet of Vaishya. As a rule, however, the more extensive operations in the Maratha country are in the hands of Bania from Gujaráth or Márwár. In Bengal there seems a great reluctance to retain local variety, so most appear as Bania or Vaish. The pedlars are a small and scattered group. The only large caste is that of the bead and bangle sellers, *Manihár*, and these, too, contain both Brahmanic and Musalmán families. Peddling, however, is now carried on by many of the trading class and by Musalmáns who do not return the caste.

Group 2. *Pedlars*	122,376
1. Manihár	90,131
2. Thoria	9,097

The hieratic castes, to which our attention is now directed, constitute anything but a homogeneous group. In the first place, the vast majority of the population herein included belongs to conventional, not functional, bodies. The other four, it is true, are recruited with reference to the duties they perform for their respective communities. The Jangam, for example, is the sacerdotal class of the Lingaiat sect, and owes his name, it is said, to the practice of the votaries of that sect of wearing the emblem of Shiva, their eponymic deity, in a locket, on their persons, instead of being satisfied with locating it in a temple or shrine. They thus make it "jangam," moveable, instead of "sthάwar," fixed. But their religious guides are not in the present day entirely dependent on their congregation

Class IX. Professional	**21,652,422**
Group 1. *Priests*	15,467,752
1. Bráhman	14,821,732
2. Jangam	396,598
3. Ulama	50,165
4. Gárúdi	41,412
Group 2. *Devotees and Ascetics*	2,717,861
1. Gosáin	231,612
2. Bairági	275,604
3. Sádhu (*unspecified*)	376,130
4. Báwa „	66,115
5. Vaishnav	469,052
6. Fakir	830,431
Group 3. *Temple Service*	320,530
1. Gurao	110,529
2. Satáni	88,354
3. Séwak, &c.	121,647

for their support, and are well known as industrious traders in grain and other village produce throughout the South Deccan. The Ulama are the religious teachers of the Panjáb Musalmán, and are not found returned under this title in other provinces. The Gáruda is a small body, but has been mentioned as representing the priesthood of the village menial, who is prohibited from participation in the ceremonial of the classes above him. The caste seems to be confined to Rajputána and the tract immediately to the south-west thereof. In Madras there are over 50,000 persons returned as Pandáram by caste, which title probably represents those who are the hereditary or elected administrators of large temples, or who perform religious services in connection with the deities in honour of whom the temple was erected. It has been already mentioned that very early in the Indian portion of the history of the Árya, the Bráhman ceased to perform these functions, and the few that continued to participate in them were held to be thereby degraded. Some of these sub-castes of Bráhmans are still in existence, but, as a rule, the working staff of the temple is not Bráhman, though, somehow, the latter caste is always at hand when largess is in question. In the Bráhman caste, returned as such, we have every sort and grade of subdivision. In the Panjáb there is the Muhiál, whose aim is military service, like the Pándé of the Gangetic basin in Hindustan. The cultivating classes of the Desai of South Gujaráth and the corresponding class in Orissa are both termed Mástán, and this title is shared by other castes of cultivating Bráhmans in Upper India. Some of these last perform the whole cycle of operations connected with tillage, whilst others draw the line at holding the plough, and employ their serfs on that task. There is a considerable number of Bráhmans engaged as family and village priests, but the majority has taken to secular pursuits and been subdivided accordingly. In Hindustán the number of Bráhman cultivators is very large, and on the west coast, both in Malabar and along the Konkan, this caste, in various distinct communities, is prominent amongst the landholders. In the Deccan, again, the Bráhman almost monopolises the occupations, barring trade, that require reading and writing. In law and education they are everywhere to the fore. Some have taken to the surveying and outdoor work of civil engineering, but medicine, for ceremonial reasons, has not yet made much way amongst them, and the few that have advanced any way in that profession are scarcely regarded as orthodox. But whatever may be the means that a Bráhman adopts for gaining his livelihood, and however it may be regarded by his fellow-Brahmans, his attitude towards the rest of the community remains unchanged, and the distance between them is never allowed to be diminished. The caste is seen to differentiate in all directions within itself, but towards outsiders it presents a homogeneous and unbroken front, and claims the privileges of birth, *semper, ubique*, and *ab omnibus*. In its capacity of the literary caste of the people, it will be discussed in the next chapter.

We have, then, the devotees and ascetics, of whom there are many groups, none, probably, represented in the returns at its full strength, by reason of the attraction of the general title of "holy man," "brother," and so on. Out of the whole group, nearly a third are Musalmán, chiefly found in the Panjáb and Hindustán. The bond between the fraternity, of whatever subdivision, is the rule not to live except on charity. In the case of the Gosai, however, it is not always the case that *cucullus facit monachum*, and we find that the horsehair plait, and the portentously large rosary belong to a shrewd trader, an industrious cultivator, and, in the pre-British time, to a fanatic and indomptable fighter. But, as a rule, the caste goes from shrine to shrine, living on alms, and giving in return the blessing to which this course of life seems to impart such efficacy.

The temple servant is returned as a caste almost entirely from the Deccan and Madras. In the former, the Gurao has also the monopoly of making the leaf platters used at caste feasts, and so on. The Satáni of the south is apparently a cultivator also, and is found in considerable numbers in the returns from Burma, whither he immigrates as one of the numerous seasonal labourers. In Upper India and Bengal the services performed by these castes are relegated, apparently, to others, who were not specially given up to these occupations at the time the caste was first evolved.

The next group comprises the numerically small but interesting and widely-spread castes who are engaged in retailing by tradition the ballads recounting the annals of the line of chiefs at whose courts they are entertained. In this way they are the genealogists of such families, and such is the veneration of their profession, or,

GROUP 4. *Genealogists*	590,412
1. Bhát	481,119
2. Chăran	99,090

perhaps, the dread of the loss of the tradition in question, that their persons are as inviolable as the laws of Manu would make that of the Bráhman. There are two castes of note in this category. First, the Bhát, or Bhárót, who is sometimes further distinguished by the addition of Ráj, or Royal, bard. It is curious to see that he is not found in such profusion in the heart of Rajasthán, where reside the descendants of the heroes of many of the most renowned of his ballads, as in the North-West Provinces, where the Rájpút is twice as numerous, and in Bihár, in both of which the blue blood of the Kshatria has suffered grievous dilution. The Cháran is in all probability an off-shoot of the Bhát, differentiated when the latter took to genealogy alone, and got above ballad singing, for, in Northern India, at least, the last-named function is appropriated by the Cháran. In many parts of the country, too, the Bhát has taken to agriculture and trade, but he is not found far from the castes that most call his traditional functions into exercise. In a former paragraph of this section it was pointed out how the genealogies of the middle classes of Northern India were kept, and their ballads sung, by the superior divisions of the Dóm caste, but neither they or the Cháran seem to enjoy the personally sacred character of the Bhat.

The writing castes are mainly functional, and have come into prominence with the British system of administration. In old days they were in existence, no doubt, but were kept well in subordination by the Bráhmans. For instance, Manu, whose code embodies the aspirations of the Bráhman of the revival of that religion, ordains that a Shudra, when other occupations fail, should take to writing for a living, and there are other quotations to the same effect, whilst popular proverbs, too, attest the general distrust of the man who lives by his pen. But a naturally intelligent community have lost no time in taking advantage of their opportunities, and the castes that are not merely the village scribes, as are some of those in the south of India, have not only risen in wealth, but have devoted a good deal of research and ingenuity to proving their right to Kshatria origin. In fact, there seems to be a good deal of truth in the presumption that in Northern and Western India, at all events, the position of the writer at the courts of native chiefs in old times was duc to their left-handed connection with their patron's family. But such a connection has not been acknowledged by the rest, and one of the complaints most loudly and frequently heard from the well born of the community is that under the present system of administration,—

GROUP 5. *Writers* - -	2,555,867
1. Káyasth - -	2,239,810
2. Karan -	146,053
3. Karnam	54,177
4. Kannakan -	41,013
5. Prabhu -	29,559
6. Vidhúr -	33,437

"The beggar's book
"Outworths the noble's blood,"

so that the affairs of State are falling into the hands of castes, who, in private life, are not even admitted within the portals of the social leaders of the people. Of the writing castes of this class the most important is that of the Káyasth, which is found chiefly in Bengal and the North-West Provinces. From the former it has migrated into Assam, and in both it is used as synonymous with writer, and is thus recruited from the lower castes, who, as education spreads, take advantage of the term to escape from their origin. In the north-west the caste seems to be more exclusive, but is not altogether devoted to the pen, and furnishes some proportion of the grain parchers and tailors. In the struggle for recognition in the social rank to which it aspires, the Káyasth caste does not return its full strength at the census, but the Kshatria, under various general titles, such as Surajbansi, and so on, gives shelter to a good many. The Karan, or Mohant, of Orissa, is a caste of the same nature as the above. In the west of India we find not only the Káyasth as a strictly maintained caste, but the Prabhu, an entirely local development, though assigning to itself a Kshatria descent. A still smaller caste goes still further in this direction, and calls itself Brahmakshatria. None of these castes are functional, and as they are well-to-do, they have been able to maintain their position without admixture with writers of other origin. The Vidhúr of the North Deccan and Central Plain is, no doubt, a comparatively recent offshoot from the village Brahman. The Kannakan, sometimes adding to his caste the quasi-surname of Pillé, is the descendant of the Conicopillay of Orme. The Karnam is the caste of village accountants in the South and East Deccan, which succeeds, in those tracts, the Deshasth Bráhman of the Maratha Deccan.

The class we have now to deal with is the minor professional, such as the musician, as he is found in India, and singers and dancers, the two being combined, as stated in the chapter on occupations. The first group, however, in the class is of a different type, and comprises the village astrologer or horoscope caster, with the hail averter, and, in Bengal, the medical caste, which does not seem to be found, as a separate entity, elsewhere. There is little to be said of this group, as the main castes are probably functional, and recruited from subdivisions of others. For instance, the Joshi is sometimes a sort of Bráhman, and so, in Upper India, is the Dakaut. The hail averter, Gurpagári, is chiefly found in Berar and the Nágpur or Maratha districts of the Central Provinces. The next group is a large, and, as mentioned in connection with the Dóm, a disreputable one, without being criminal. The Mirási is found almost entirely in the Panjáb, Rajputána, and the North-West Provinces. The Daflé and Dholi, called so from their instruments of predilection, are the village drummers in most provinces of the north and centre. In the south, others, from the Paraiya and allied castes perform on this instrument. The Gondhali are the ballad singers of the Marathas, and do not go beyond the tracts occupied by the latter caste. In the next group, that of singers and dancers, no items are shown, because the body is recruited from many castes, properly so called, and the general title used largely in the census schedule is simply that of the function, as Tawáif, Kaláwant, or Kanchan. In like manner, the small class of the mimes and puppet-show keepers is made up of a number of names which are purely local, with the exception of the two mentioned first in the marginal table, which are found in minute communities in most of the northern provinces.

Class X. Arts and Minor Professions.	4,153,275
Group 1. *Astrologers, &c.*	299,776
1. Jóshi	85,306
2. Vaidya	87,193
3. Dakaut	16,062
4. Kanisan	27,198
Group 2. *Drummers and Ballad Singers.*	645,214
1. Mirási	316,422
2. Daflé, &c.	147,364
3. Gondhali	18,034
Group 3. *Singers and Dancers.*	145,778
Group 4. *Mimes, &c.*	62,507
1. Bahurupia	4,940
2. Bhánd	9,783
3. Bhária	24,539

The next class consists, practically, of two castes, and probably the second of these is but an offshoot of the first. The Banjára, otherwise known as Brinjari and Wanjára, seems to be traceable to the forest grazing lands at the foot of the Sewálik range, and along the base of the Himálaya, in the north of Rohilkhand. Their origin is unknown, but they appear in literature in about the 10th century of the Christian era. Their name is said to be the same as that of the Kanarese castes of traders, Banjiga, from the Sanskrit Banijia-kára, merchant. All over Hindustán and Rajputána they carry loads on their bullocks to and from the coast. In the North Deccan they have settled down as agriculturists, though here this caste denies its connection with the wanderers. In the Panjáb the caste most prevalent is that of the Labáni, which is probably only a subdivision of the Banjára. The same term is used throughout the South Deccan and the central portions of Madras. It is curious that the name should be the same as that of the writing and merchant class in Sindh, and of a caste of shopkeepers in Gujaráth, and that the Labána of Central India should assert their Gujaráthi origin. The coincidence seems to indicate a connection with the Gujar Skythians before the latter had been dispersed across the desert. There is a further distinction between the Labáni and Banjára of the north and the same caste in the south, namely, that the former are either settled residents or well-behaved characters, whilst the latter are of very evil repute, and constantly on the move to avoid intimacy with the local police. The few Pendhári that appear in the return are all that are found to return themselves by this once celebrated title. They seem to be carriers by origin, and to have affected the Deccan and Central India. Near the latter tract, and partly in it, the marauders of the beginning of the present century founded a small State, which is still in the occupation of their leader. They are Musalmáns by religion, and have no doubt returned themselves chiefly under one of the foreign titles.

Class XI. Carriers	973,626
1. Banjára	561,644
2. Labána	327,748
3. Pendhári	6,751

In this next class we have a very varied collection of castes, some of them reputable and useful members of society, and others just the reverse. As a rule, the latter predominate. Most of the items are small, and on comparing the various titles it appears that many are but linguistic varieties of the same tribe, or that in changing his sky the vagrant has also shifted his occupation. The first group is respectable, in spite of his use of the donkey in carrying his wares. In a country where grain and pulse form the staple diet, the grindstone and the curry tablet and roller are too important implements not to be well looked after, and the two castes named in the margin do not represent the full strength of those who keep these articles in order. The second group includes the stone quarriers and earth-workers. The Od, or Waddar, is probably the parent caste of both, and where it is prevalent, as in the South Deccan, it is subdivided into those who dig and those who quarry, or split rock *à la* Hannibal, but using a less costly liquid. The origin of the caste is uncertain, but if not from Od, the old synonym for Orissa, it is likely that Telingána gave it birth, as even in the Panjab this caste preserves its southern habits, and wears the black blanket peculiar to the Deccan. The name of Beldár is evidently a northern one, and has extended south with the migrations of the tribe which use the implement it represents, a peculiarly shaped spade or mattock. The knife grinders are represented by one caste, and that a small one. The occupation is carried on in towns by subdivisions of the blacksmith castes, and the Shikligár is the only vagrant, and even he is said to be settling down in fixed abodes. The next two groups are hardly separable one from the other. Mat making is too often a cover for nefarious observation of the habits of the villagers of the place where the caste in question pitches its camp. The fowler, too, has the reputation of being a noted snapper-up of unconsidered trifles. The cane worker, pure and simple, such as the Burúd, is often respectable enough, and leaves his village only for the travelling season, returning during the rains. Many of the rest travel for purposes distinctly immoral, and are constantly being "moved on" at the request of the resident population. They are, moreover, closely connected with the great tribe of Kanjar, or Sansi, in Upper India, with the Bedia, in the tracts more to the east, and to the Jogi, who, under this philosophical appellation, travels all over India, telling fortunes, singing songs not over decent, and swindling the cultivating public by most palpable frauds. Marco Polo says they live to 150 and 200 years, but, fortunately, the receipt for the draught of sulphur and mercury, by which they achieved this longevity, has apparently been lost. The last group comes from exactly the same stock, and many of them have all the aptitude of hereditary training for conjuring and acrobatic feats, in which they are remarkably proficient.

Class XII. Vagrants	**3,457,666**
Group 1. *Grindstone Makers*	18,996
1. Tákankar	9,508
2. Khúmra	6,554
Group 2. *Earth and Stone Workers.*	1,124,357
1. Od, or Waddar	793,516
2. Béldár	152,515
Group 3. *Knife Grinders*	18,980
Shikligár	16,781
Group 4. *Mat and Cane Workers.*	639,150
1. Korvi	207,045
2. Burúd	53,413
3. Bansphor	89,955
4. Basór	73,345
5. Changár	36,569
6. Ghásia	46,077
Group 5. *Hunters and Fowlers*	948,870
1. Wágri	179,070
2. Bahelia	39,203
3. Mahtam	56,984
4. Móghia	146,667
5. Valaiya	289,411
6. Aheria	36,320
Group 6. *Miscellaneous Vagrants.*	400,969
1. Jógi	214,546
2. Sansia	30,704
3. Kanjar	29,486
4. Barwála	63,856
Group 7. *Jugglers and Acrobats.*	306,344
1. Bedia	65,194
2. Nat	139,068

It is superfluous to enumerate all the items, mostly small, that come under this head, but they will be found in Table XVII. (A.). The comparatively large group of castes, the titles of which are either unrecognisable or so indefinite that they could not be classed, concludes the list of Indian social divisions. In the last category, it may as well be explained, for the benefit of the readers who are acquainted with India, are placed such entries as Madrasi, Bengali, Zamindar, Outcaste, and so on.

Class XIII. Indefinite Indian Titles.	**3,079,204**

The rest of the table needs but little comment. The 14th class, showing the Indian Christians, contains, as explained in the end of the preceding section, only a portion of that community, and the Goanese have only been distinguished in Bombay and a few other places. The class of Musulmán that returns a foreign title includes nearly 12 per cent. of the population, so that it comes next to the Agricultural group in numerical strength. In the marginal statement the chief items are shown.

Class XV. Musulmans of Foreign Title.	34,348,085
1. Shaikh	27,644,093
2. Pathán	3,225,521
3. Moghal	333,114
4. Saiad	1,430,329
5. Balóch	971,835
6. Túrk	50,503
7. Arab	39,338

Out of the 27½ millions of Shaikhs nearly 21 millions are returned in Bengal, the reason for which concentration has been already given. The Pathán, as he is called east of the Indus, comes next in order, and, probably, most of the 970,000 returned in the Panjáb are really of this race, or nearly akin to it. The rest, with the exception of a few colonies in Rohilkhand, have little claim to transfrontier descent. Like the Pathán, the Balóch haunts only the frontier provinces of Sindh and the Panjáb. There are, however, a few bodies of Makráni, with a good tinge of African in them, in many of the native courts of Western and Central India. The Saiad, or descendant of the adherents of the prophet, is found in all provinces and States. In the West Panjáb the title is given to any holy man of that faith, and means simply a religious teacher, supported by the alms of the believer. Elsewhere the title is assumed on conversion, or, according to the proverb, on the acquisition of the proper amount of worldly goods. In the case of the Moghal, the strain of foreign blood is more traceable than in that of the Shaikh or Saiad in the north of India, and amongst the mercantile classes of the west, where it often means anyone of Persian descent. The Túrk is found chiefly in the north-west corner of the Panjáb, where several tribes of the race are returned. In Bombay and Haidrabád there are said to be a few members of the Othmánli community, and in the Rámpur State, in Rohilkhand, there seems to be a considerable colony of this title. Here, however, it is not certain that, as in Madras and formerly in Burma, the name Túrk is not given to any Musalmán of foreign origin. The Arabs are returned mostly in Aden and Bombay. In the former they come from the mainland, and in the latter from the Persian Gulf, either with horses from the northern parts of Arabia, or from Maskat. Along the Malabar coast, too, there are settlements of traders of this race, which have been in existence for many centuries. The Arabs in the Panjáb are either merchants from Bombay, who have entered into business at Multán, or at Peshawar, where India meets Central Asia, or else are local Shaikhs, who have adopted their ancestry more thoroughly than the rest.

Class XVI. Himalayan Mongoloids.	244,722
1. Ladákhi	30,672
2. Bhóti	25,670
3. Lepcha	9,745
4. Khámbu	33,490
5. Tháru	53,875
6. Newár	4,979
7. Limbu	15,079
8. Gúrúng	10,894
9. Mangar	19,383
10. Súnúwár	5,210
11. Múrmi	21,889
Class XIV. Indian Christians	**1,835,848**
1. Native	1,807,092
2. Goanese	28,756
Class XVII. Assamese and Burmese.	**7,297,618**
1. Burmese	5,408,984
2. Karen	540,876
3. Shán	182,745
4. Chinese	41,832
5. Arakanese	452,164
6. Yau	12,934
7. Món	467,885
8. Ahóm	153,518
9. Cross breeds	19,821

The great tribes of the Himálayan Mongoloid race are but poorly represented in the census returns. In the west we have the Ladákhi of Kashmér, a title which includes, probably, the Bálti, of Skárdu, who is found in Simla for a great part of the year. The Bhóti, which is the general name given to those of Thibetan origin, comprise both the people from the British Himálayan districts beyond the first snowy range, as well as the inhabitants of Bhotán, who come in small numbers to Dárjiling and the Assam markets. Between these two come the Nipáli tribes, of whom we have only the settlers in the submontane tracts and the Tarái grazing lands and forests, together with the comparatively few soldiers in so-called Gúrkha regiments, many of whom return their caste as Kshatria. There are also immigrants for labour to be found in the tract round Darjiling. The Lepcha are mostly from

Class XVIII. Western Asiatics	—
1. Jews	16,951
2. Armenians	1,295
3. Pársis	89,618
Class XIX. Eurasians	81,044
Class XX. Europeans	166,428
Class XXI. Africans	18,775

Sikkim, now resident in Dárjiling. Of the Tarái settlers, the Khámbu and Limbu admit their Kiránt or Himálayan origin, whilst the Tháru apparently repudiate it, and it is possible that their Mongoloidic type of feature is due to cross-breeding with the Méch and other forest tribes, after they were expelled, as they assert themselves to have been, from their realm in the Gangetic basin. The Newár are the people of the Nipál Valley displaced by the Gúrkha, and the Gúrúng, Súnúwar, and Mangar belong to the military tribes of that State. The Múrmi, like the Newár, seem to have been once powerful in the higher valleys, and to have succumbed to the rule of the new-comers from the plains. Of the rest of the classes sufficient has been said above, in connection with language and religion, so with this may be concluded a very lengthy, albeit inadequate, description of the chief elements in the heterogeneous mass that is known as the "people of India."

CHAPTER VI.

The Distribution of the Population by Literacy.

The waves of the ocean, before reaching the child, break against four walls, which encompass the water of his education or crystallisation—father, mother, brothers and sisters, and a few extra people, are his forming-world and mould. But, all this deducted, we must remember in education that its power, like that of the spirit of the age, which must not be measured by individuals but by the concentrated mass or majority, must be judged, not by the present, but by the future.—*Richter*.

Where the task of public instruction is undertaken by the State to the extent that it is in India, the function of a census of Literacy is to supplement the current record of progress in regard to this important matter. This can be done either by taking stock of the results on the given date, so they may be shown cumulatively, instead of merely by annual instalments, or by bringing to book the out-turn of institutions which are territorially or departmentally beyond the scope of the annual reviews. How far the census fulfils this object will be discussed in the course of this chapter. The first point to be considered is the scope of the inquiry made at the census. With respect to the tracts brought under enumeration, it was not thought worth while to attempt this detail in the wild country on the eastern frontier of Bengal and Assam, or in the very similar tract to the south-west of Orissa. Then, again, in Rajputána and Central India, the establishments available had to be treated, as explained above in connection with the return of mother tongue, with the utmost leniency, so the schedule was relieved of this column also. Lastly, in Kashmér, as the census was being taken systematically for the first time, it was held that more important statistics than those of instruction should alone be recommended. We have thus to deal with a population of 261,838,926, detailed in Table IX. of the Imperial series. In 1881, nearly the same omissions as on this occasion were allowed in the Hill tracts of Eastern Bengal and Orissa. The Malabar States and those under the Central Provinces, as well as Khairpur under Sindh, and the Nága and Gáro Hills in Assam, were also excluded, but have been brought on to the record of the present census, in addition to Quettah, Aden, and the Andaman settlement and the newly acquired territory of Upper Burma.

To show the nature of the information asked for, the rules for filling up this column are here reproduced :—

1881.	1891.
"Col. 12. Against those under instruction write 'is learning'; against those not under instruction but able to read and write, enter 'knows'; against those who cannot either read or write, or who can read but cannot write, or can sign their names but cannot read, write 'does not know.' Only those should be shown as able to read and write who can do both."	"Col. 12. Enter in this column against each person, whether grown up, child or infant, either 'Learning,' 'Literate,' or 'Illiterate.' Enter all those as Learning who are under instruction, either at home or at school or college. Enter as Literate those who are able to both read and write, but are not under instruction as above. Enter as Illiterate those who are not under instruction, and who do not know how to both read and write, or who can read but not write, or can sign their name but not read." "Col. 13. Enter here the language which those shown as literate in col. 12 can both read and write, and if a person knows how to read and write English as well as a vernacular, enter English also." "This column is to be left blank for those shown in col. 12, as Learning or Illiterate, and, except when English is known, only one language should be entered, namely, that best known."

Thus three classes were distinguished. First, those who were under instruction; secondly, those who had finished their schooling; and lastly, those who had not had any. Special provision was made to exclude from the category of the pupils those who attend what are known as "Rote Schools," which are numerous in the Panjáb, and are found nearly all over India to some extent. In such establishments reading and writing are not taught, and the curriculum is confined to the inculcation of portions of the Kurán, with the appropriate enunciation and gestures, or of some Puránic lore, both entirely by oral tradition. Then, again, in the present day so many messengers, porters, and other menials find it to their advantage to be able to sign their names, that they acquire this amount of literature without ever advancing beyond it; and it was held advisable to specially exclude this class from the category of literate. So far, the instructions in 1891 followed those of the preceding census. But it was thought worth while to attempt a further step by adding to the return of the literate, supplementary information regarding the number that were conversant with the English language. This information, it will be observed, was not called for in respect to those still under instruction, whether at school or college, as the object was to include only such as were, so to speak, out in the world. Taking the instructions as a whole, experience in every Province has shown that the distinction between those under instruction and those able to read and write, but no longer in a state of pupilage, is one which it is advisable to abandon at a future enumeration, since there is a general tendency to disregard it. The former class is considered inferior to the latter, and as India is, according to Jacquemont, "l'Utopie de l'ordre "social à l'usage des gens comme il faut," the dignity of the castes to whom literacy, according to that social ordinance, should be restricted, revolted at the notion that the half-naked urchin set to drive his father's cattle as soon as he has completed the fourth vernacular standard should be entered as Literate, whilst the Bráhman reading for his degree in Arts was relegated to the category of Pupils. The feeling is well expressed by the Census Superintendent for Mysore, himself a Bráhman and experienced in educational matters, who writes :—

> "Moreover, the enumerated persons returned themselves in a vast number of cases as *learned,* though they were still *learning,* probably in a spirit of bravado. For it is a notorious characteristic of the student of the period that he is generally too obtrusively and superciliously self-conscious of the superior educational advantages enjoyed by himself, and as his contemporaries and seniors of the old school were returned as *literate,* his personal vanity was not unnaturally tickled, and many of his class returned themselves at the enumeration as *learned,* although still *learning,* thereby exaggerating the ranks of the *literate,* at the expense of the numbers under tuition."

The results of the enumeration were tabulated by the three age-periods, (*a*) under 15, (*b*) 15 to 25, and (*c*) 25 and over; so it was not difficult to see that Mr. V. N. Narsinghaiangar is right in his facts, whilst his professional knowledge of the class in question allows the presumption that he is not wrong as to the motives he attributes. It is not only in Mysore that the egg, to use a German proverb, holds itself wiser than the hen, and not alone in the Rome of Persius.

> *Ingenium et rerum prudentia velox*
> *Ante pilos venit.*

Thus the really trustworthy division of the population in respect to literacy, so far as the census return is concerned, is into those who do not know how to read and write and those who do, whether the latter be still under instruction or have ceased to be so. But for the sake of comparison in a later part of this chapter with the annual statistics published by the State Educational authorities, the three groups, as collected from the schedules, are shown in the marginal abstract of the general return now under review. But the depth to which literacy has filtered through the community can be better appreciated when the figures are set forth proportionally, especially if the above-mentioned age-periods are also recognised. This is done accordingly in the following statement :—

TABLE A.—General Summary.

—	Total.	Males.	Females.
Learning -	3,195,220	2,997,558	197,662
Literate	12,097,530	11,554,035	543,495
Illiterate -	246,546,176	118,819,408	127,726,768
Total	**261,838,926**	**133,371,001**	**128,467,925**

TABLE B.—Proportional Abstract.

—	Total.				Under 15.		15 to 25.		25 and over.	
	Both Sexes.	Males.	Females.	Females to 1,000 Males.	Males.	Females.	Males.	Females.	Males.	Females.
Learning -	1·22	2·25	0·15	68	4·74	0·36	1·96	0·06	0·09	0·01
Literate - - -	4·62	8·66	0·42	47	1·27	0·18	13·10	0·85	13·73	0·47
Illiterate - - -	94·16	89·09	99·43	1,075	93·99	99·46	84·94	99·09	86·18	99·52

Now, the salient facts illustrated by these relative numbers are, first, that in the whole population dealt with only 58 persons in every thousand can read and write, or are learning to do so, and, secondly, that of those 58, 53 are males and five are of the other sex. If we consider, first, the males only, it will be seen that of those under 15 years of age, 94 in every 100 are neither learning or literate, but if we omit from the calculation all boys under five, assuming them to be below the age at which instruction may be held to begin, the ratio of the illiterate falls to 90 per cent. After the age of 15 instruction begins to have an appreciable weight, and between that age and 25, 15 per cent. instead of 10, are, to put it negatively, not illiterate. It is in this period that the confusion between pupils and literate is perceptible, and the two classes are therefore considered together. The next division of the table treats of men of full age, and the proportion of the illiterate rises a trifle. The comparatively large number of pupils in this period may be attributable in part to the technical and training institutions, or, at least in Upper India, to the adults attending religious lectures in connection with masjid (mosques) in the case of Musalmáns, and charitable institutions of a corresponding character for Sanskrit studies in the case of Bráhmans. The technical name for the former, which would no doubt be returned at the census, is "Seekers after Knowledge" (Tálib ul 'ilm), while the latter would in like manner be termed "Disciples."

Literacy of males.

Another light in which to view these figures is that thrown by the relative distribution of the learners and literate by age, instead of that of the age of literacy, which we have been considering above. The marginal table gives this information. Of the male pupils, 84 per cent. are under and 16 over the age of 15 years. The literate of 25 years and over bear the proportion to the total literate of $69\frac{1}{3}$ per cent., which indicates, as it were, the cumulative results of the system of instruction. Were it not for the intrusion of the literate-pupil element above noted; this ratio would no doubt reach 72 or 73 per cent. The figures for females will be discussed below.

TABLE C.—Instruction by Age.

—	Males.		Females.	
	Learning.	Literate.	Learning.	Literate.
Under 15	84·01	5·84	89·82	16·15
15 to 25	14·27	24·76	6·89	34·55
25 and over	1·62	69·36	3·29	50·70

What has preceded this chapter in the present review has no doubt prepared the reader for the great prevalence of illiteracy indicated by the above statements. First of all, we have the occupational bias of the mass of the population, which is set steadily away from literature. The agriculturist in India is in this respect probably not much below his compeers in far more civilised countries, only his numbers are more preponderant in the community. However well his affairs may prosper, it is long before the landowner gives over personal participation in all the operations by which he has thriven, and after a long course of early rising and late return from the field, the "swinkt hedger" is seldom in the psychological conditions for the assimilation of more abstruse knowledge than is current in the friendly circle that every evening squats down to discuss the húkka and pán of village sociability. Interested as he is in every novelty that his eye has learnt to perceive, the average raiat is not given to going a step out of his way to discover any; but when the three R's are brought within his reach, he is often quick enough to appreciate their advantages in dealing with the grain dealer and money lender, so he sends his son to school accordingly. Unfortunately, however, as the census and departmental returns show—and experience too often confirms them—the necessities of the farm generally lead to the lad's removal at a rudimentary stage in the curriculum, and by the time he is 18 years old he has forgotten most of the little he learnt when he was 11 or 12. In the towns the state of affairs is a little better, but then, as we have seen, their influence extends to less than a tenth of the population.

The second influence antagonistic to a more general spread of literacy is the long continued existence of a hereditary class whose object it has been to maintain their own monopoly of all book-learning as the chief buttress of their social supremacy. Sacerdotalism knows that it can reign over none but an ignorant populace. The opposition of the Bráhman to the rise of the writer castes has been already mentioned, and the repugnance of both, in the present day, to the diffusion of learning amongst the masses can only be appreciated after long experience. It is true that the recognition by the British Government of the virtue and necessity of primary education has met with some response on the part of the literate castes, but it is chiefly in the direction of academic utterances, which cannot, in the circumstances, be well avoided. It is welcomed, too, in its capacity of affording the means of livelihood to many of these castes, as they have to be engaged as teachers, and are bound accordingly to work up to the State standard of efficient tuition. The real interest of the castes in question is centred on secondary education, of which they almost exclusively are in a position to reap the advantage. This, however, is a topic that will recur in connection with the distribution of literacy by caste, which forms the subject of a later section of this chapter.

We can thus see that the field in which the seeds of literacy have to be sown consists of a few square yards of what we may term relatively good soil, prepared to receive all the seed it can get, and thirsting for the whole of the attention of the husbandman. Then comes the vast stony waste of labour and menial offices, without sufficient depth of soil to allow the seed to strike root, and lastly, the many miles of arable mark, so taken up with the production of the food and clothing of the whole community, that whatever else is sown in it is inevitably choked before it can ripen.

Literacy of females.

Before taking up the next section of our subject, a glance has to be given at the return of the literate amongst the weaker sex. The outlook in this direction is, if possible, more dreary than in that from which we have just turned. It is by the position of women in it that we judge to a great extent of the relative progress made by a community towards the complete life that we call civilisation; as the Comte de Ségur has it, "leur sort est un boussole sur pour le premier regard d'un étranger qui arrive dans un pays inconnu." Though, as Burma may be said to show us, there may be no intimate or direct connection between the status or influence of woman and her acquaintance with the three R's, a very great divergence, in this last respect, between the two halves of the community more often than not implies the relegation of the wife and mother to the position either of the queen termite, immured for life in the most remote chamber of the ant hill to fulfil her function of replenishing the numbers of the community, or to that of the household drudge enslaved to the caprice of her mother-in-law. It has been said, and we see the truth of the adage not only in India, but in the west also, that she who rocks the cradle rules the empire, and of what sort must the influence be of those, however shrewd and staunch to the better customs in which they have themselves been brought up, who are unable to stray beyond their immediate and narrow surroundings, or get into touch with anything that may help to elevate them on to a higher level? Their utmost aim is to rear the Telemachus, of whom his father spoke in terms so affectionately depreciatory :—

> Most blameless is he, centred in the sphere
> Of common duties, decent not to fail
> In offices of tenderness, and pay
> Meet adoration to my household gods
> When I am gone.

According to the current theory, the first duty of a woman is to produce and rear a son to perform the funeral obsequies of her husband; and, second, to see that satisfactory meals are ready for her husband, and the third, to keep her husband's family gods in good order for his worship. Into such an ideal, intellect can scarcely be said to enter, but faith pervades the whole. On the other hand, it is to intellect alone that an appeal is made by the State system of education, under which come more than 80 per cent. of the whole body of learners, and amongst nations, writes the author quoted at the beginning of this chapter, the head has at all times preceded the heart. But how if the head of the man persists in advancing, whilst that of the women and the heart of both refuses to stir? The head is a notorious sapper of creeds based as are those of India, and the "dual life" in that country, of which a good deal has been written of late, is not a feature that one would desire to see extended further than its present sphere, where, amongst the fraction of the 6 per cent. of writers and literary Bráhmans whom it affects, it is comparatively harmless. The social reformer possesses, as Carlyle has it, a prehensile tail. He returns home from his meeting or lecture in full panoply of occidental ethics and political catchwords "up to date," to cast off all these alien swaddling-bands as easily as he divests his shapely foot of its patent leather covering, and his person generally of other encumbrances that interfere with his free enjoyment of home comfort. He performs, moreover, all the ceremonies at births and deaths required by the custom of his caste, keeps his brother's widow in the orthodox servitude, and marries off his daughter at eight years old, provided he has no bridegroom ready for her at seven. "Once he has come to forty year," if by mishap he be a widower, he accepts from his friend and co-reformer a bride of as nearly as possible the same age as his daughter, and thus tradition is maintained. In these circumstances, there is practically no breach in domestic life caused by the intellectual advance of the master of the house. His studies are regarded as no more than the proper equipment in life of the class that at the festival of the Diwáli pays homage to its pen as the family bread-winner, just as the trader does to his ledger, and they affect his relations with the outer world only. His indoor life is still regulated by the customs to which he duly conforms, like the philosopher of imperial Rome, who "approached with the same inward contempt, and the same external reverence, the altars of the Lybian, the Olympian, or the Capitoline Jupiter." There is thus no want in that life which the education of his wife is needed to supply. Still less is illiteracy felt in the houses of the mass of the population, where the education of the men themselves is, at the best, but surface deep. Against the above remarks there will be urged, of course, the case of the Parsis, amongst the women of which race literacy is far more prevalent than in other Indian communities. The record of the State Educational Department, too may be brought up to testify against the return of the literate and pupils of the fair sex at the census, which is less by nearly one half than the former. This last argument will be examined in a later section of this chapter. As to the Parsis, they form a small homogeneous community of foreigners, who owe everything but bare existence to another race, equally alien to the country, any part of whose customs to which they may be attracted can be assimilated by them unhindered by caste or tradition. There is obviously no analogy between this case and that of a vast and heterogeneous population that has grown up within the country itself, and has by gradual and historical process, not by imitation or foreign impulse, hemmed itself in by centuries of the most exclusive prejudices and inviolable custom the world has ever seen.

Referring again to Table B., it will be seen that the females imbued with some tincture of literacy come to about six in the thousand, or, as we are dealing with such small fractions, it will be more correct to put the number at 57 in 10,000. Under the age of 15, they come to 54, and the pupils are nearly double the number of those who have ceased their schooling. If we deduct the girls under five years old, the ratio rises to 93, approaching one in a hundred. In the next period, between 15 and 25 years old, the proportion is nearly the same, or 91 per 10,000, and the literate exceed the pupils. This follows of course, the fact that at this age, amongst the classes that mainly contribute to the returns, a girl, sane and sound, who is not married by the age of 15 is an exception, and would certainly not be paraded at school, even if returned at the census at all. The actual pupils in this period are probably, to a great extent, in Normal and Medical establishments, or widows, and the return shows, too, that a good many are returned from the Christian community, where the age of marriage is later. Lastly, amongst women of 25 years old and over, the proportion of the not illiterate drops to 47 per 10,000, leaving over 99½ per cent. illiterate. This seems to indicate that the stimulus to female education was imparted little earlier than the beginning of the present generation. Table C. confirms this view, as not many more than half the literate females come within this age-group. It may be noticed that the proportion of pupils in this group is higher than amongst the males. This may be partly explained by the preference shown by females, in returning their age, for the year 25 over any year between 20 and 24. Then, again, there are the special and technical institutions above mentioned, and the Zanána teaching, all of which are, probably, at work in Bengal and the Malabar States, where the bulk of the class in question is to be found.

A few words more about the proportions of the two sexes amongst the literate and pupils will not be irrelevant to what has just been said. In the population with which this return deals, there are 963 females to every 1,000 of the other sex. To put it in another way, in a thousand of the whole population, there will be, on the average, 509 males and 491 females. The females under instruction number 63 to 1,000 males in the same stage, but to a thousand literate males, there are but 47 females similarly endowed. The illiterate are more on an equality, for we find only 1,075 females to the 1,000 males, a ratio that would represent an excess of the former sex of about 116, if the total number of the two were the same.

The marginal Statement D. gives the figures for 1881 compared with those for 1891 in the same tracts. There will be noticed a slight difference between the latter as here proportionately shown and those in Table B., because from the former have been omitted the returns for Upper Burma and the Malabar States, where literacy is more prevalent than in most of the tracts dealt with, but which did not come within the scope of the census of 10 years ago. As the table stands, the rate of increase of the not-illiterate is considerably above that of the population at large, and is especially marked in the case of females. But in relation to the whole population of each year, the leeway that has to be made up is enormous. Where there were four females in a thousand who are not illiterate, there are now five; and in a thousand males, in place of 91, we now have 104. In a later section, the variation in the different Provinces and States will be shown.

TABLE D.—Comparison of 1891 and 1881.

		Population		Distribution per Cent.		Percentage of Variation.
		1881.	1891.	1881.	1891.	
Males.	Learning and Literate.	10,526,283	13,416,398	9·05	10·42	27·45
	Illiterate	105,838,357	115,454,733	90·95	89·58	9·08
	Total	116,364,640	128,881,131	—	—	10·75
Females.	Learning and Literate.	432,475	589,256	0·39	0·48	36·25
	Illiterate	111,332,927	122,735,279	99·61	99·52	10·24
	Total	111,765,402	123,324,535	—	—	10·34
Total.	Illiterate	217,171,284	238,190,012	95·20	94·44	9·67
	Total	**228,130,042**	**252,205,666**	—	—	**10·55**

Comparison of Census Return with that of the State Department of Public Instruction.

The next point to be treated of is the comparison of the census return with that published for 1890–91 by the various Directors of Public Instruction in India. This relates to British territory only, except with regard to the small States under Bombay which appear to be included with the rest.

TABLE E.—Comparison of Census with Departmental Returns of Pupils.

	Males.		Females.		Difference of Census.	
	Departmental.	Census.	Departmental.	Census.	Males.	Females.
Madras	556,449	576,079	87,715	59,127	+ 19,630	— 28,588
Bombay and States	551,216	439,360	69,282	30,745	— 111,856	— 38,537
Bengal	1,380,385	883,990	88,558	34,845	— 496,395	— 53,513
N.-W. Provinces and Oudh	275,651	238,440	13,870	8,404	— 37,211	— 5,466
Panjáb	223,056	158,849	22,657	7,834	— 64,207	— 14,823
Central Provinces	105,699	76,306	5,799	3,901	— 29,393	— 1,898
Upper Burma	49,341	99,229	3,811	3,372	+ 49,888	— 439
Lower Burma	100,668	128,269	14,629	14,853	+ 27,601	+ 224
Assam	74,086	49,111	4,698	3,427	— 24,975	— 1,271
Coorg	4,059	4,192	736	610	+ 133	— 126
Berár	48,320	38,502	2,022	976	— 9,818	— 1,046
Total	**3,368,930**	**2,692,327**	**313,777**	**168,094**	**— 676,603**	**— 145,683**

The main feature to which attention is required at present is the fact that the departmental return of pupils exceeds that of the census by 25·13 per cent. in the case of males, and as already remarked above, by about 87 per cent. in the case of females. It is further noticeable that the above feature presents itself in every Province, with the exception of Burma and the male pupil element in Madras and Coorg, exceptions which admit of special explanations. The departmental statement is based on the returns from schools and colleges in connection with the State, either directly or indirectly, as by grants-in-aid, or by being under inspection, or financial control. The extent to which non-official schools, especially those of the lower grades, are thus connected, varies in every Province.

In the Panjáb, for instance, the return includes far more than in most other parts of the country. In Upper Burma, on the other hand, the number of monasteries not brought on the departmental books is large, and even in the lower division of the Province there appear to be a good many that are equally ignored. As a rule, every Burmese has to pass a certain period of his boyhood as a "kyaungtha," or attendant at one of these institutions, even if he may not advance to the noviciate, so the number must be enough to place this mode of instruction within the reach of every village. In Madras, the excess shown at the census is attributed in great measure to the same cause, as it occurs in the tracts such as Tanjore and Malabar, in the first of which there are known to be many elementary schools kept by Bráhmans, which are not brought within the sweep of the departmental net, whilst on the Malabar coast, the religious antagonism between the Mappilah community and the rest stimulates the maintenance of many institutions within the precincts of the mosque, which are likewise not brought to the notice of the infidel inspector, whether Christian or Brahmanic. On the other hand, at the opposite extremity of this Presidency, the departmental figures for the Ganjam district show a number of pupils more than 100 per cent. in excess of that found in the census schedules, and this brings us to the second distinction between the scope of the two returns. The census, it is true, includes the pupils of the institutions that do not contribute towards the departmental total, but it excludes, by the definition of pupil adopted in the instructions quoted above, all children who are not learning to read and write. The case of the Kurán-Purán schools has been already mentioned, and in the Panjáb we find 57,397 pupils in them, including over 10,000 of the 22,657 girls departmentally returned. In Bengal, again, this class of institution accounts for over 62,000, and in the whole of the tract covered by the return under discussion, 154,500 come under this category. As few, if any, of these pupils learn how to read or write, they were, of course, ignored in the census. We then come to the departmental return of "public schools," where 809,116 children are shown as "not reading printed books." Finally, there are the "private schools," with about 262,000 pupils in the elementary stage, out of whom probably the same proportion, at least, as in the other class of institution, are not yet advanced enough to study printed books. All these, together with the pupils who patronise the rote schools, give a total of about 1,051,000 children in the most elementary stage of instruction, so far as literacy is in question, and as the departmental total exceeds that of the census by 822,286 only, there remains a balance of 228,770 in favour of the latter. In all probability, the excess is far greater, for in Bengal, where the difference in favour of the departmental return amounts to nearly half a million of boys and over 53,000 of girls, this return is obviously unduly exaggerated by fraudulent entries made by the hedge-schoolmaster who is a more prominent feature in that province than elsewhere. The same feature appears in the return for the Ganjam district of Madras, where the departmental excess, amongst a population notoriously averse from instruction, is most remarkable, and places this tract, in point of education, immediately behind the three foremost districts of the Presidency, Madras, Tanjore, and Malabar. The proximity of Orissa, about which the Educational Inspector writes that "for one case of detection there may be a dozen that go undetected," has probably stimulated the local Pandit to go abroad to some purpose. In the Sháhabád district of Bengal, the district board practically abolished the system of annual rewards in the year under review, because they "encouraged fraudulent practices." In the Dacca district, in 1890, there was discovered "wholesale fabrication of returns in two municipalities." Even under the very shadow of the central authority, in the suburbs of Calcutta, we find it stated that "it is not unusual for unscrupulous men to start schools at the close of the year for the "purpose of earning rewards, which schools melt away as soon as that object is "fulfilled." In one case, the schoolmaster got the reward by showing off a school attended mostly by pupils of his colleagues, lent for the occasion. But the prize for ingenuity is taken by the Chittagong master, who held a school in a village on the frontier of the district, so that, having obtained the reward at the annual examination, he promptly transferred himself with all his pupils to the adjacent village on the other side of the boundary, and reaped his recompense at a second examination held in his new domicile. History stops at this point, but it would be interesting to learn whether the pupils who shared the toil were also admitted to the fruits thereof. It is irrelevant to the present purpose to inquire with whom lies the responsibility for this state of affairs, it is enough that it exists, and that while it exists there is no reason to assume that the difference between the census returns and those of the State department betokens any defect in the former. But apart from intentional fraud, there is the tendency for every village school to attach to itself a sort of kindergarten, where the infants of the lower middle classes disport themselves whilst their elder brothers or sisters, who officiate as caretakers, are possibly really under instruction. In the upper grades of this undisciplined contingent, a plantain leaf, a small board with a supply of sand, or even the mud floor, serves as the medium of communicating the alphabet or the digits, whereupon the pupil is duly entered as "under standard." In the case of females this is a very common practice, and in the Panjáb, for instance, where not only are half the pupils of this sex under instruction in Kurán schools, where they only learn by rote, but in other schools, more than half are under seven years old, it is clear that there is little to complain of in the small show made at the census. Some of that little, too, is explicable, the Superintendent thinks, by the refusal of rural enumerators to recognise instruction in any other character than the Persian, so that Sikh girls learning Gurmúkhi do not appear in the record. Finally, there is always the confusion between literate and learning to fall back upon, but so far as the comparison with departmental figures is concerned, it is not necessary, on the facts shown above, to have recourse to its discussion in detail. In the provincial reports for Bengal, Bombay, and the Panjáb, Messrs. O'Donnell, Drew, and Maclagan have dealt with it in relation to their respective charges.

Literacy by religion.

The general Table IX. is subdivided according to the main religions, and with reference to a few of the items, perhaps, the subject merits a little comment, though the relative spread of literacy in the community can be better appreciated from the caste distribution, the materials for which are to be found in Tables XVIII. and XIX. in Volume II. of the Imperial series. But the proportion of the illiterate amongst the adherents of the main forms of creed will be found in the marginal statement. From this it will be seen that the Parsis hold the first place, both as to females and to males, but, as remarked above, they are only a small and isolated community. With respect to literate males, the Jains come next, as might be expected from their addiction to commerce. But their liberality has not yet extended far in the direction of the instruction of their women, who come fifth on the list, with 14 per 1,000 not illiterate. The second place amongst the females belongs to the Jewess, also the member of a small body, whose male relative comes but third in the roll of his sex. The Buddhist occupies the fourth place, both for males and for the other sex, but in a thousand of the former he shows 474 not illiterate, whereas, owing to the exclusion of women from the Kyaung school in Burma, the corresponding proportion for the sex is but 26. The Christian occupies the fifth place amongst the males, and the third amongst the females. In the former case the not illiterates number 343, and in the latter 136. The four last religions occupy the same order in both sexes. The Brahmanic community comes sixth, with 105 males and 4 females, distinguished from the crowd, but, as was shown in the preceding chapter, the collection of castes that goes by this name represents no uniform feature of importance. It is not very different with the Musalmán, between whom and the Bráhman comes the Sikh. The latter, in the Panjáb, comes between the two in the matter of education only if taken in the lump. Taking separately the larger castes that furnish the Sikh community, these last are more literate than the Brahmanic members, and the balance is restored by the literates amongst the priestly and mercantile classes of the latter. Finally, we have the forest tribes, of whom, as has been explained, only the wilder portions returned their tribal religion. To this section, therefore, literacy can hardly be expected to have extended, so it is not surprising to find but eight in the thousand of the males able to read or write, though it may be unexpected to see that the females are not far from being one in the same category.

Religion.	Illiterate per 1,000 of each sex.	
	Males.	Females.
Brahmanic	895	996
Sikh	904	996
Jain	466	986
Buddhist	526	974
Pársi	223	499
Jew	481	786
Musalmán	929	997
Christian	657	864
Animistic	992	1,000
Total	**891**	**994**

Literacy by provinces, &c.

The next topic in connection with literacy that requires notice is the variety in its territoral diffusion in India. But in anticipation of this, it may be interesting to show how that country stands in this respect in comparison with others of which the returns are available. The marginal statement, accordingly, gives the average number of persons who are not illiterate per thousand of the general population. From this it will be seen that the British colonies in the south head the list, along with the white population of the United States. Less than half the population are literate in Austria, Hungary, Italy, Portugal, Chilé, Ceylon, and amongst the coloured residents of the United States. Unfortunately, census returns for the German Empire, for Scandinavia, and Great Britain, are not available. The return as far as women are concerned, assumes a slightly different order. The greatest divergence is seen in the case of Ceylon, which illustrates the breach between the West and the East in this respect. Portugal, Queensland, and the coloured female population of the States, advance a step, whilst New South Wales and our American cousins go down to that extent. India does not approach within one half of the literacy of even Portugal, so far as its males are considered, and the proportion of its literate females is only just above a fifth of that in Ceylon, and this last, again, does not reach a quarter of that of Portugal, or a seventh of that amongst the negroes and mulattoes of the Western Hemisphere.

TABLE F.

Country.	Number able to read and write per 1,000 of each Sex.	
	Males.	Females.
1. Victoria	755	755
2. New Zealand	748	725
3. United States* (*White*)	725	706
4. South Australia	717	711
5. New South Wales	688	667
6. Queensland	676	691
7. Ireland	554	501
8. Austria	521	467
9. Hungary	408	283
10. Italy	377	236
11. Chilé	281	221
12. Ceylon	269	29
13. United States* (*Coloured*)	254	217
14. Portugal	250	108
INDIA, 1881	91	4
„ 1891	109	6

* The census return for the United States includes only those over 10 years old. The figures here given are therefore approximate.

In Table G., that follows, are shown the component parts of the general total given above, together with the variations in the proportions that have taken place during the last decade :—

TABLE G.—Provincial Statement of Illiterate and others.

Province or State, &c.	Males.					Females.				
	No. per 1,000 Males of—				Variation in Literates in 1891.	No. per 1,000 Females of—				Variation in Literates in 1891.
	Illiterate.		Literate, &c.			Illiterate.		Literate, &c.		
	1881.	1891.	1881.	1891.		1881.	1891.	1881.	1891.	
Ajmer	879	867	121	133	+12	994	992	6	8	+2
Assam	953	924	47	76	+29	999	997	1	3	+2
Bengal	913	892	87	108	+21	997	996	3	4	+1
Berar	938	916	62	84	+22	999	998	1	2	+1
Bombay	883	860	117	140	+23	993	990	7	10	+3
Sindh	921	915	79	85	+ 6	995	995	5	5	—
Lower Burma	539	557	461	443	—18	964	962	36	38	+2
Upper Burma	—	538	—	462	—	—	985	—	15	—
Central Provinces	953	941	47	59	+12	998	998	2	2	—
Coorg	869	844	131	156	+25	990	986	10	14	+4
Madras	862	851	138	149	+11	991	990	9	10	+1
N.-W. Provinces	940	937	60	63	+ 3	998	997	2	3	+1
Oudh	948	942	52	58	+ 6	999	998	1	2	+1
Panjáb	937	926	63	74	+11	998	997	2	3	+1
Total, British Provinces	—	889	—	111	—	—	994	—	6	—
Haidrabad	937	928	63	72	+ 9	999	997	1	3	+2
Baroda	894	856	106	144	+38	998	995	2	5	+3
Mysore	888	895	112	105	— 7	996	993	4	7	+3
Bombay States	900	887	100	113	+13	998	995	2	5	+3
Bengal States	965	945	35	55	+20	999	998	1	2	+1
N.-W. Province States	963	965	37	35	— 2	996	999	4	1	—3
Panjáb States	947	941	53	59	+ 6	999	999	1	1	—
Total, States	—	902	—	98	—	—	993	—	7	—
India	**909**	**891**	**91**	**109**	**+18**	**996**	**994**	**4**	**6**	**+2**

These last are on the side of improvement in every case save those of Lower Burma, Mysore, and the States under the North-West Province Government. As regards the first, the Superintendent finds that in 1881 many families returned as under instruction the boys whom it was intended to send to the monasteries but who had not yet joined, and this misconception accounts for the relative falling off in the number of learners of that sex. The Mysore decrease also occurs amongst the pupils, and is confined to the western division of the State, where it affects the return of both sexes. No explanation is given of the fact in the report, and in the case of the small States of the north no report has yet been submitted. It may be noticed that the ratio of the not-illiterate amongst the females is higher in the States in 1891 than in the Provinces, and this seems to be due mainly to the extraordinary number of this sex returned as literate or under instruction in the Malabar States, which contain nearly one-half of the whole tale of the pupils of feudatory India, and more than that proportion of the literates. As these States were not called upon in 1881 to return literacy, they have been excluded from the table under discussion, but will be found duly entered in the next. The literate males are in considerably higher proportion in the Provinces than in the States at the present census. Upper Burma heads the list with nearly half of this sex not illiterate. In its companion division, the monastery is less frequent, but it will be seen that the provision for female instruction, which is the accompaniment of British rule there, shows a much higher ratio than in any other part of the country. The Superintendent notes, with reference to the Phongi, or Buddhist monk, that there is a tendency to modify the course of instruction in their Kyaung, so as to include the European method of teaching such subjects as mathematics, a fact which indicates anything but the decline of their influence that was feared by some of the State educational authorities. In India proper it will be noted that more than 10 per cent. of the male community are provided with some stock of instruction in Madras, Bombay, Baroda, Ajmér, Coorg, Mysore, and Bengal. Madras and Baroda head the list, the former having inherited this position, the latter having acquired it during the last 10 years. Upper India falls considerably below the average of either the Provinces or the country as a whole. Even Assam exceeds the North-West and the Panjáb, which have only the Central Provinces between them and the bottom of the list. Assam, too, is distinguished by the highest relative increase of its literates, except that in Baroda. The latter lies chiefly in the Gujaráth division of Western India, which has always been the foremost in the Presidency in the matter of education, the Broach and Surat districts coming not far short of Bombay City in the proportion of their literates. The ratio in the city of Calcutta is almost the same as that in Bombay, whilst in Madras, where the unskilled labourer finds less attraction, and educational institutions flourish, holds by far the highest place in this respect. In the Bengal Province it seems that the tract surrounding Calcutta is throughout the best supplied with literates, and that in the Eastern Division it is the dead weight of the Musalmán lower classes that pulls down the average. Bihár, were it not for the hill tracts of Chutia Nagpur, would hold the lowest place in the whole province, whilst Orissa and the north occupy about the middle. In the Madras Presidency, Tanjore, the great Bráhman centre, shows the highest ratio of literate males, but takes a comparatively low place as regards the instruction of its female population. The extreme south and Malabar are the only two districts besides Tanjore that contain less than 80 per cent. of illiterate males. In the Panjáb there is great diversity in the proportion of the literate, and, on the whole, the lowest is found in the Trans-Indus districts of Bannu, Kohát, and Hazára, and on the borders of Rajputána. The western tract of the Central Provinces, bordering on Berar and Bombay, have the largest proportion of literate, and, excepting Jabalpur, the rest of the province gets more illiterate in proportion to the amount of hilly country included in it, until in the Mándla district there are but 29 males per 1,000 literate or under instruction. The details for the North-West Provinces and Oudh are not available for review in the present work. Berar, like Bengal and Bombay, has made considerable progress in the extension of literacy during the 10 years, and nearly reaches Sindh, where, as in Oudh, the progress has apparently been very slow. In the North-West Provinces there seems to have been practically none, as the per-centage of increase is but 3. It is possible, however, that there may be some special explanation of this peculiarity, which will be found in the local report, when published.

The next table deals with the population divided into certain age-periods, as in Table B. On this occasion, however, it has been thought worth while to subtract the infant population, so as to leave a balance of possible school-goers. The result is a difference of 2 per cent. in favour of the literates. In Upper Burma, for instance, the illiterate are reduced by 71 per 1,000; in Madras, by 26; in the Malabar States by 34,

Literacy by age.

TABLE H.—The not-illiterate per 1,000 of each Sex, by Age-period.

Province or State, &c.	Total.		Total over 5.		5–14.		15–24.		25 and over.	
	Males.	Females.	Males.	Females.	Males.	Females.	Males.	Females.	Males.	Females.
Ajmér	133	8	154	9	97	9	191	12	172	9
Assam	76	3	89	4	66	6	114	5	95	3
Bengal	108	4	125	5	96	5	156	7	135	4
Berar	84	2	97	2	104	3	135	3	83	1
{ Bombay	140	10	163	12	149	17	194	14	159	4
{ *Sindh*	85	5	100	6	75	9	119	10	108	5
{ Upper Burma	462	15	533	18	315	15	592	26	620	15
{ Lower Burma	443	38	510	45	290	44	584	67	602	34
Central Provinces	59	2	66	2	54	4	99	3	64	2
Coorg	156	14	175	20	195	37	190	20	162	10
Madras	149	10	175	12	143	18	196	15	185	8
{ N.-W. Provinces	63	3	73	3	41	2	86	4	84	2
{ *Oudh*	58	2	67	2	34	1	79	2	81	2
Panjáb	74	3	89	3	60	4	97	4	125	3
Total, Provinces	111	6	130	7	95	9	155	9	141	5
Haidrabád	72	3	83	3	61	4	97	3	83	3
Baroda	144	5	161	7	128	13	181	7	161	7
Mysore	105	7	118	9	110	14	130	8	118	9
Bombay States	113	5	133	6	110	8	154	8	133	6
Madras States	239	35	273	40	209	49	298	43	273	40
Central Province States	22	1	21	1	17	1	36	4	21	1
Bengal States	55	2	64	2	35	2	76	4	64	2
N.-W. Province States	35	1	40	1	22	1	55	1	40	1
Panjáb States	59	1	66	1	30	1	73	2	66	1
Total, States	98	7	111	8	79	10	129	9	124	6
India	**109**	**6**	**127**	**7**	**93**	**9**	**151**	**9**	**138**	**5**

and in the Central Provinces and the Panjáb by 7 only. The difference, in fact, varies with the prevalence of instruction amongst the younger generation. Another feature in the return brought out by the distribution by age is that, except in Burma, the proportion of the literate males diminishes after the twenty-fifth year, whilst it everywhere increases from the first period to the second. The inference to be drawn is obviously that instruction in India proper is but a plant of tender years, whilst across the Bay of Bengal it dates from some generations.

Literacy by caste or race.

The diffusion of instruction through the community is appreciated more accurately when we have before us the relative extent to which it pervades each of the groups of castes or races under which the population was classified in the preceding chapter. In the provincial volumes this return will be found under the title C., at the end of the Imperial series. In the general series, to which the present review relates, it is numbered XVIII., and will be found in the second volume of tables. In the following proportional abstract, Table J., the leading features are given. It will be noticed that the ratio of the group to the total population is not always identical with that given in the last chapter, partly for the reason stated in the preliminary note to Table XVII., namely, that two Provinces sent in their returns so far in arrears of the rest that the latter had been worked into their proportionate form in anticipation of the incorporation of the former. The reclassification therefore that seemed advisable in the case of some of the castes found chiefly in Bengal and the North-West Provinces, was made only in the portion of the caste returns that was comparatively simple, involving, that is, merely re-addition, irrespective of further computation. Then, again, the return under discussion omits the 25,000,000 or so not returning statistics of literacy.

Table J.—Literacy by Caste.

Caste Group.	A. Both Sexes. Per-centage of			B. Males. Per-centage of			C. Literates knowing English. Per-centage of the English-knowing in each Group on	
	Each Group on Total Population.	Literate in each Group. On Total Literate.	Literate in each Group. On Total Population of the Group.	Each Group on Total Males.	Literate in each Group. On Total Literate Males.	Literate in each Group. On Total Males of the Group.	Total English-knowing Literates.	Total Literates of the Group.
1.	2.	3.	4.	5.	6.	7.	8.	9.
I. Military Agriculturists	9·46	8·10	3·94	9·78	8·01	7·07	2·82	1·55
II. Other Agriculturists	17·48	10·89	2·81	17·43	11·12	5·51	5·83	2·39
III. Cattle Graziers, &c.	4·20	1·01	1·19	4·20	1·12	2·29	0·65	2·65
IV. Field Labourers	3·11	1·25	1·86	3·02	1·28	3·66	0·44	1·55
V. Forest Tribes	5·04	0·44	0·40	4·95	0·45	0·78	0·20	2·01
Class A. Agricultural	**39·29**	**21·69**	**2·55**	**39·38**	**21·98**	**4·81**	**9·94**	**2·03**
VI. Priests	4·90	16·81	15·78	4·96	16·98	29·52	20·29	5·37
VII. Devotees, &c.	0·85	1·00	5·41	0·87	1·01	10·02	0·31	1·38
VIII. Temple Servants	0·11	0·25	10·32	0·11	0·23	18·11	0·07	1·30
IX. Genealogists	0·16	0·20	5·71	0·16	0·20	10·91	0·04	1·00
X. Writers	0·94	4·74	23·37	0·92	4·66	43·59	9·13	8·58
XI. Astrologers and Herbalists, &c.	0·10	0·39	17·58	0·10	0·34	29·72	0·97	11·28
XII. Ballad Reciters and Musicians	0·20	0·06	1·36	0·20	0·06	2·51	0·01	0·53
XIII. Singers and Dancers	0·05	0·06	6·62	0·04	0·03	7·62	0·02	1·19
XIV. Mimes, &c.	0·01	—	3·87	0·01	0·01	7·48	—	0·19
Class B. Professional	**7·32**	**23·51**	**14·80**	**7·37**	**23·52**	**27·53**	**30·84**	**5·84**
XV. Traders	4·11	13·74	15·38	4·15	14·09	29·30	6·60	2·14
XVI. Pedlars	0·05	0·01	1·42	0·04	0·01	2·80	—	0·65
XVII. Carriers by Pack Animals	0·34	0·06	0·81	0·36	0·06	1·51	0·01	0·84
Class C. Commercial	**4·50**	**13·81**	**14·13**	**4·55**	**14·16**	**26·86**	**6·61**	**2·13**
XVIII. Goldsmiths, &c.	0·57	1·20	9·69	0·57	1·24	18·69	0·26	0·97
XIX. Barbers	1·28	0·70	2·51	1·28	0·71	4·80	0·33	2·14
XX. Blacksmiths	0·92	0·50	2·53	0·92	0·52	4·82	0·21	1·87
XXI. Carpenters and Masons	1·13	0·97	3·97	1·14	1·00	7·61	0·24	1·10
XXII. Brass and Coppersmiths	0·11	0·20	8·43	0·11	0·21	16·34	0·08	1·86
XXIII. Tailors	0·23	0·23	4·64	0·23	0·24	8·93	0·14	2·73
XXIV. Grain Parchers, &c.	0·53	0·38	3·29	0·58	0·39	6·46	0·17	1·97
XXV. Betel Leaf Sellers, &c.	0·09	0·13	6·80	0·09	0·14	13·23	0·12	4·12
XXVI. Weavers and Dyers	3·16	2·09	3·03	3·15	2·13	5·83	0·90	1·93
XXVII. Washermen	1·02	0·24	1·08	1·01	0·24	2·08	0·12	2·30
XXVIII. Cotton Cleaners	0·30	0·04	0·64	0·30	0·04	1·25	0·01	0·77
XXIX. Shepherds and Blanket Weavers	1·78	0·39	1·02	1·77	0·41	1·98	0·20	2·28
XXX. Oil Pressers	1·66	1·16	3·22	1·64	1·20	6·32	0·57	2·17
XXXI. Potters	1·14	0·34	1·37	1·15	0·35	2·62	0·26	3·38
XXXII. Glass and Lac Workers	0·05	0·03	2·56	0·05	0·03	5·05	0·04	5·10

TABLE J.—Literacy by Caste—*continued.*

Caste Group.	A. Both Sexes. Per-centage of			B. Males. Per-centage of			C. Literates knowing English. Per-centage of the English-knowing in each Group on	
	Each Group on Total Population.	Literate in each Group. On Total Literate.	Literate in each Group. On Total Population of the Group.	Each Group on Total Males.	Literate in each Group. On Total Literate Males.	Literate in each Group. On Total Males of the Group.	Total English-knowing Literates.	Total Literates of the Group.
1.	2.	3.	4.	5.	6.	7.	8.	9.
XXXIII. Salt and Lime Workers	0·54	0·15	1·29	0·53	0·15	2·49	0·03	0·76
XXXIV. Goldsmiths' Refuse Cleaners	—	—	1·89	—	—	3·90	—	—
XXXV. Iron Smelters and Gold Washers	0·01	—	0·70	0·01	—	1·35	—	0·57
XXXVI. Fishermen, &c.	3·17	0·80	1·13	3·12	0·79	2·17	0·36	2·05
XXXVII. Servants, &c.	0·07	0·02	1·43	0·07	0·02	2·75	0·01	1·14
XXXVIII. Distillers and Toddy Drawers	1·84	2·44	6·11	1·80	2·47	11·87	0·74	1·33
XXXIX. Butchers	0·20	0·03	0·63	0·20	0·03	1·20	0·01	1·64
XL. Leather Workers	4·59	0·53	0·53	4·58	0·55	1·04	0·13	1·13
XLI. Watchmen and Village menials	4·68	0·63	0·62	4·59	0·64	1·21	0·44	3·09
XLII. Scavengers	1·32	0·17	0·59	1·35	0·17	1·11	0·12	3·25
Class D. Artisans, &c.	**30·39**	**13·47**	**2·02**	**30·19**	**13·70**	**3·91**	**5·49**	**1·83**
XLIII. Grindstone Makers	0·01	—	0·51	0·01	—	0·98	—	—
XLIV. Earth Workers and Quarrymen	0·42	0·03	0·33	0·41	0·03	0·62	0·01	1·80
XLV. Knife Grinders	—	—	1·22	—	—	2·29	—	1·97
XLVI. Mat and Cane Workers	0·22	0·03	0·61	0·22	0·03	1·16	0·01	0·79
XLVII. Hunters and Fowlers	0·28	2·04	0·79	0·28	0·05	1·52	0·02	1·56
XLVIII. Miscellaneous Vagrants	0·12	0·03	1·19	0·13	0·03	2·15	0·01	1·31
XLIX. Jugglers and Acrobats	0·10	0·03	1·29	0·09	0·02	2·24	0·03	4·32
Class E. Vagrants	**1·15**	**0·16**	**0·67**	**1·14**	**0·16**	**1·26**	**0·08**	**1·87**
L. Musalmáns of Foreign Titles	12·52	9·46	3·48	12·54	9·56	6·58	6·19	2·91
LI. Thibetan and Nipáli Tribes	0·08	0·10	5·64	0·09	0·10	10·25	0·07	3·09
LII. Burmese Tribes and Chinese	2·79	12·53	20·68	2·72	12·46	39·53	0·58	0·20
LIII. Western Asiatic Races	0·04	0·42	45·50	0·04	0·26	54·89	2·98	33·08
LIV. Mixed Burmese Tribes	0·01	0·01	7·99	0·01	0·01	15·38	—	1·64
LV. Indefinite Indian Castes	1·08	1·40	5·94	1·11	1·37	10·69	1·24	3·95
LVI. Europeans	0·06	0·98	73·24	0·09	0·81	78·67	21·06	95·79
LVII. Eurasians	0·03	0·35	52·18	0·03	0·19	54·73	7·16	91·27
LVIII. Native Christians	0·72	2·05	13·07	0·72	1·67	20·05	7·38	16·28
LIX. Goanese, &c.	0·01	0·05	18·61	0·01	0·04	26·61	0·37	26·18
LX. Africans	0·01	0·01	3·18	0·01	0·01	5·30	0·01	4·98
Class F. Races and Miscellaneous.	**17·35**	**27·36**	**7·25**	**17·37**	**26·48**	**13·17**	**47·04**	**7·67**

Table J. deals with the literate, including those still under instruction, in three sets of ratios. First come the proportions respectively borne to the total population by each of the caste groups. In connection with this is the series showing the proportion of the literate in each group to the total literature, together with a second series, in which is given the ratio between the literate in the group to the total population coming under that group. The second set of proportions deals with the males only, and is added merely on account of the practically universal illiteracy of the other sex. It comprises the same subjects as the preceding set. The third and last set indicates, first, the distribution by groups of the literate persons of both sexes who know English, and, secondly, the ratio between the latter and the total literate of the group. This detail is so far interesting, since instruction above the primary limits is practically conducted in English in all the public schools and colleges. It will be treated, accordingly, along with literacy in general. The following is the way in which the table under discussion is intended to be used:—Group II., Other Agriculturists, contains 17·48 per cent. of the population, with 10·89 per cent. of the literates, the latter bearing a ratio of 2·81 per cent. on the population of the group. Amongst the literates are 5·83 per cent. of the total body of English-knowers, and these, in turn, form 2·39 per cent. of the literates in the group, so that in every 10,000 six know that language, or one in 1,667. With this explanation the figures may be left to speak for themselves, so far as the details are concerned, and it is worth while to bring to notice here only the more prominent features in this curious return. For instance, if both sexes be taken together, as in the first section of the table, it will be seen that in 11 groups only are the literate as high as 10 per cent. on the included population. The marginal extract reproduces the information regarding these 11. They comprise just under 14 per cent. of the population, just over half the literate population, and more than three-fourths of those who can read and write English. If the collection be re-grouped into more minute sections, it will be seen that the Bráhmans, Writers, Traders, Native Christians, Temple Servants and Herbalists, &c., who constitute the strictly native portion of the whole, contain 11 per cent. of the population, 38 of the literate, and 45 of the English-knowers. The Burmese and Parsis with the few Armenians and Jews come next, with 2·8 per cent. of the population, nearly 13 of the literate, and just above 3½ per cent. of those who know English. Finally, we have the European and Eurasian element, which accounts for just under one in a thousand of the population, 13 in the same number of the literate, and 282 of the English-knowing part of the community. Outside this circle is found about 23 per cent. of the latter population, or about the same proportion as is contributed by the Europeans and Parsis, &c., taken together. It will also be noticed that the Bráhmans, Writers, and Europeans monopolise more than half of this class of the literate, and the Traders, Eurasians, and Native Christians, a fifth more. As regards the introduction of the Herbalist and Astrologer, it should be explained that the former is apparently one of the best instructed classes in Eastern Bengal, to which part of the country he is, as a separate caste, confined. The Temple Servant group, again, owes its position to the Sátáni of Madras and Mysore, where this class is most prevalent.

Concentration of literacy in certain groups.

TABLE K.

Caste Group or Race.	Per-centage on total of		
	Population.	Literates.	English-knowing Literates.
1. Priests	4·90	16·81	20·29
2. Temple Servants	0·11	0·25	0·07
3. Writers	0·94	4·74	9·13
4. Herbalists, &c.	0·10	0·39	0·97
5. Traders	4·11	13·74	6·60
6. Burmese	2·79	12·53	0·58
7. Pársis, &c.	0·04	0·42	2·98
8. Europeans	0·06	0·98	21·06
9. Eurasians	0·03	0·35	7·16
10. Native Christians	0·72	2·05	7·38
11. Goanese Christians	0·01	0·05	0·37
Total	13·81	52·31	76·59

We may now turn from the general section of the table to that which treats of males only. Here we find that no less than 20 of the 60 groups returns 10 per cent.

and over of literates in its community. The additions to the former list are the Devotees, Genealogists, Goldsmiths, Brass-smiths, Betel Leaf Sellers, Distillers, Nipali and Thibetan tribes, and the mixed races of Burma, with the group that had to be set apart for indefinite entries, containing a good number of the writing castes serving at a distance from their native province, and thus entered under some misconstrued title. These additions enlarge the scope of the collection considerably. Instead of 14 per cent. of the population we get over 18 of the males, with 58½ per cent. of the literate of that sex and 79½ per cent. of those who know English. The groups in which female instruction is more prevalent take, of course, a lower place in this statement than the last. This remark applies to the Writers, Temple Servants, Herbalists &c., Parsis &c., Burmese, Europeans, Eurasians, Native Christians and Goanese, to all of the former selection, in fact, except to Traders and Bráhmans. In the case of the former, there is no doubt that some of the difference is attributable to the number of literate men who come from Rajputána, &c., to the centres of commerce in British territory without their families, but more to the general cause, namely, apathy, as in the case of the Bráhman. If, again, we take as the standard proportion the ratio of the literate for all India, which we have seen in the beginning of this chapter to be 8·66 for males alone, our roll is increased by one name only, that of the Tailors; but by including the fair sex, the Tailor falls out, and the Nách girl takes his place. It is interesting to compare a few castes selected as the least illiterate of each Province, as is done in the following table :—

TABLE L.

Caste Group, &c.	Per-centage on totals of		
	Males.	Literate Males.	English-knowing Literate Males.
1. Priests	4·96	16·98	20·29
2. Devotees	0·87	1·01	0·31
3. Temple Servants	0·11	0·23	0·07
4. Genealogists	0·16	0·20	0·04
5. Writers	0·92	4·66	9·13
6. Herbalists, &c.	0·10	0·34	0·97
7. Traders	4·15	14·09	6·60
8. Goldsmiths	0·57	1·24	0·26
9. Brass-smiths	0·11	0·21	0·08
10. Betel Leaf Sellers	0·09	0·14	0·12
11. Distillers, &c.	1·80	2·47	0·74
12. Thibetans	0·09	0·10	0·07
13. Burmese	2·72	12·46	0·58
14. Burmese, Mixed	0·01	0·01	—
15. Pársis, &c.	0·04	0·26	2·98
16. Indefinite Indians	1·11	1·37	1·24
17. Europeans	0·09	0·81	21·06
18. Eurasians	0·03	0·19	7·16
19. Native Christians	0·72	1·67	7·38
20. Goanese Christians	0·01	0·04	0·37
Total	**18·66**	**58·48**	**79·45**

TABLE M.

Caste, &c.	Group.	Literate per 1,000 of Sex.	
		Males.	Females.
Madras:			
Bráhman	VI.	722	37
Kannakkan	X.	658	21
Karnam	X.	587	13
Komti	XV.	605	9
Náyar	I.	490	125
Native Christians	LVIII.	218	76
Eurasians	LVII.	786	720
Bombay:			
Bráhman	VI.	645	33
Káyasth	X.	687	212
Prabhú	X.	791	164
Brahma Kshatria	X.	648	268
Bania Shrimáli	XV.	697	15
Bania, Unspecified	XV.	518	18
Berar:			
Bráhman	VI.	638	21
Káyasth	X.	557	160
Prábhu	X.	764	160
Vidhúr	X.	368	—
Bania	XV.	480	—
Kómti	XV.	349	—
Bengal:			
Bráhman	VI.	477	23
Káyasth	X.	555	41
Baidya	XI.	734	139
Karan	X.	604	16
Bania	XV.	280	4
Mysore:			
Bráhman	VI.	678	38
Bania	XV.	819	—
Kómti	XV.	664	12
Central Provinces:			
Bráhman	VI.	317	7
Káyasth	X.	475	16
Vidhúr	X.	342	4
Bania	XV.	388	—
Haidrabád:			
Bráhman	VI.	569	5
Káyasth	X.	438	—
Vidhur	XV.	151	—
Baroda:			
Bráhman	VI.	559	24
Prabhu	X.	790	87
Bania	X.	776	1
Panjáb:			
Bhábra	XV.	453	7
Aróra	XV.	381	6
Bania	XV.	429	3
Khatri	XV.	394	7
Súd	XV.	416	8
Bráhman	VI.	191	2
Kálál	XXXVIII.	164	5
Kayasth	X.	434	68
Saiad	L.	110	6
N.-W. Provinces:			
Bráhman*	VI.	180	5
Káyasth	X.	610	29
Bania	XV.	265	4
Bania Agarwál	XV.	468	6

* The Brahmans in the N.-W. Provinces are largely agriculturists.

The final computation made above brings us to the fact that in India, as a whole, the very moderate average of 46 literate persons in a thousand, is not attained by 81·35 per cent. of the population, but is the result of greater prevalence of instruction amongst the remaining 18·65. In the case of the males alone, the standard rises to 87 per 1,000, but it is not reached by more than 18·89 per cent. of the sex, leaving 81·11 below it.

English-knowing literates.

The return of those who know English shows a ratio of 4·4 per cent. on the tota literate. We must subtract, however, the Europeans and Eurasians from the account, which then amounts to 3·2 only, or 1·4 in every thousand of the community. From the detailed table it will be seen that, excluding the Europeans, Eurasians, Nipáli, Africans, and Pársis, the latter proportion to the literates of the group is achieved only in the case of the Bráhmans, Writers and Herbalists, with the group of the indefinite castes. There are, it is true, four or five other groups that show a per-centage in slight excess of this, but they are all chiefly recruited from Bengal, where this part of the enumeration seems to have been unsatisfactory, since nowhere else do we find the Scavenger, Potter and Acrobat in such exalted company. The entire number returned as knowing English, including Europeans and Eurasians, was 537,811, or 386,032, if the foreign element be excluded. This, too, includes a certain proportion of those who are not yet emancipated from their studies, as has been already remarked in the beginning of the chapter. Some of the Superintendents, on the other hand, seem to think that the return includes, from excess of caution, only those who habitually use English in their daily life, and not the numerous class that learn a certain amount of that language at school, but carry the use of it no further than the last examination before their escape from that stage, and cease to be able to read and write it after the lapse of a few years. The census return seems to compare but poorly with the Departmental record in this respect, for the latter gives an average number of pupils studying English of 290,741 per annum during the last decade, beginning with 187,420, and ending with 353,515. The average period of study is not accurately known, but one would have expected to find at least 700,000 or 800,000 of the above number amongst the English-knowing literates. But apparently the study of English ends in a very rudimentary stage, for with an average annual attendance of nearly 337,000, studying in that language for the last five years, only 15,200 presented themselves for the matriculation examination at the Universities, or 76,000 during the whole period. As English is the language of instruction at the colleges affiliated to the latter institutions, it is presumably an important subject at the matriculation test, if not the most important. But we find from the same returns from which the above quotations are made, that the ratio of the successful for the five years in question was 47·74 in Calcutta, 26·87 in Madras, and 25·41 in Bombay. The other Universities need not be counted, as they are, comparatively speaking, in their infancy. But at any rate the out-turn of 25,680 in five years of youths up to matriculation standard, even with the possible successes under the sixth standard elsewhere, are scarcely results that need make the census returns blush in comparison.

Quality of literacy.

It is interesting, though not arising out of the census returns, to carry this subject a little further, and now that we have seen the concentration of literacy in considerably under a fifth of the population, including foreigners, to give a passing glance at the quality of that acquirement. For this we must resort to the Departmental tables, of which a proportional abstract is given in the margin. To start at the bottom, are 922 pupils in every thousand, in the primary stage, of whom 825 are classed as "elementary" and the rest as "upper." The proportion in the lower section that has not yet got into printed books is not complete, owing to the introduction of the private schools, where the information is not tabulated, but in those under the State it seems that in the total lower primary section 30 per cent. of the boys and 36¼ of the girls are in that stage. The ratio varies from 3·6 in the Panjáb, where the Kurán schools and the like are not in the returns, to 87 per cent. in Upper Burma. Amongst the girls, omitting the Panjáb, Assam comes lowest, with 15, and Berar highest, with 85 per cent. It is remarkable that

TABLE N.

—		Per 1,000 Pupils.
University		4
Normal Institutions		1
Technical Institutions		4
High Schools		15
Middle Schools		54
Upper Primary Schools		97
Lower Primary	Reading Books	492
	Not Reading Books	220
	Not stated	113
Total Pupils		1,000

in the last province and its neighbour to the east, the pupils of each sex not yet up to reading books outnumber those in the advanced stages of instruction. The same table shows the proportion of the lower primary scholars to the total by provinces. It is unnecessary to reproduce it here, but it may be mentioned that in the case of boys, the average is 82 per cent., and Assam heads the list, if we omit Upper Burma, with 90·4, and Bombay comes lowest, with 65½. The figures for girls, averaging 91¼ per cent., rise to 99 in Assam, and fall to 83 in Berar. Out of the thousand, we have left, after the primary scholars, 78 pupils in higher stages. There are 69 in the Middle and High Schools, and four in Technical Institutions, most of which are not specified in the return by the object of their course of training. Normal schoools and colleges account for one in the thousand, leaving four for the University.

Universities. It is worth while to follow the progress of the candidates for matriculation a little further than was done above. It was there shown that an average of 15,200 per annum had presented themselves during the last five years, and that just under 34 per cent. had passed. The accompanying Table N. shows that out of every hundred that were examined in Calcutta 52 failed; in Madras, 73, and in Bombay, 74. In the next section of the table we pursue the successful only, and find that out of every hundred of them, 36 in Calcutta, 2 in Bombay, and 48 in Madras did not attempt to graduate. Of the remaining 64 that came up for a degree in Calcutta, 29 got one. In Bombay, out of 98, 46 were successful, and in Madras, the 52 that tried came out with 26. In the case of Bombay, there is evidently some change of date or system to account for the relative scarcity of those who were content with matriculating, and there may be, in like manner, some special cause for the astonishing proportion of this class in Madras. But so far as the figures go, it seems that out of the four pupils per mille that go up for matriculation, those that get a degree are 1 in 10. The lower test, known as the First Arts, is more popular, and even failure at it is often considered as a certain qualification for salaried employment but the main points brought out by the figures published in these returns seem to be, first, the insignificant number of pupils that carry instruction beyond the rudiments; secondly, the remarkably unprepared state in which the minute remainder appear for matriculation; and lastly, the relatively infinitesimal number that obtain a University degree either in Arts, which is the faculty most favoured, or in more special subjects,

TABLE O.—Results of University Examinations for the five years 1886–87—1890–91.

	Universities.		
	Calcutta.	Madras.	Bombay.
A.—Examined for Matriculation*	100·00	100·00	100·00
Failed	52·26	73·13	74·59
Passed	47·74	26·87	25·41
Examined for Degree in Arts	20·59	10·37	12·87
" " Law	7·06	1·80	2·44
" " Medicine	2·30	1·52	6·66
" " Civil Engineering	0·55	0·16	2·97
Total examined for Degrees	30·50	13·85	24·94
Passed	13·97	6·80	11·78
Failed	16·53	7·05	13·16
Total not appearing for Degrees	17·24	13·02	0·47
B.—Passed the Matriculation	100·00	100·00	100·00
Examined for Degree in Arts	43·13	38·61	50·66
" " Law	14·79	6·68	9·62
" " Medicine	4·83	5·64	26·21
" " Civil Engineering	1·15	0·61	11·67
Total examined for Degree	63·90	51·54	98·16
Passed	29·25	25·32	46·35
Failed	34·65	26·22	51·81
Total not appearing for Degrees	36·10	48·46	1·84
C.—Per-centage of those examined who passed for Degree in Arts.	38·60	55·32	47·69
Per-centage of those examined who passed for Degree in Law.	63·93	28·96	33·79
Per-centage of those examined who passed for Degree in Medicine.	53·78	32·44	48·27
Per-centage of those examined who passed for Degree in Civil Engineering.	47·86	32·14	53·88
Per-centage of those examined for any Degree who passed.	45·77	49·34	47·22

* The actual figures are, Calcutta, 21,238; Madras, 34,393, and Bombay, 14,774.

a number which amounted, in a year of census, to one person in about 213,000 of the population to whom the career was open.

Literature.

In the chapter on occupation it was shown how small a fraction lived by literature, and though the annual returns show an imposing array of publications, the review of the literary activity of the year by the Official Reporter is rather discouraging reading. According to this authority, a few works on Sanskrit texts, with an occasional drama on a historical occurrence or a subject of the day are all that are likely to survive the year of their birth. A good deal of this infant mortality, so to speak, seems to be attributable to the very high proportion of the publications which deal with the text books prescribed for University or School examinations, or other ephemeral works designed for the same market. The most striking characteristic of the outturn seems to be the absence of originality in scientific or imaginative work. The list does not want variety, as will be seen from the marginal statement of subjects, with, of course, the qualification that rather over a third are translations or republications. The language in which the works are issued also is a matter not devoid of interest, and it appears that in English 660 were published, with 955 in polyglot, 2,157 in a vernacular tongue, and 424 in the three Oriental classical languages. But a more favourate outlet for budding talent is found in journalism, of which we find 490 exponents in the list. The largest circulation is stated to be 20,000 in the case of one paper in Bengal; about 6,000 is the maximum in Bombay, and 5,000 in Madras. Elsewhere it seems to rarely reach a thousand. This does not represent, of course, nearly the number of readers, for the economical practice of private circulation, or of perusual at cheap libraries, is far more extended in India than in many other countries. But lithography and disregard for typographical appearance enables an enterprising publicist to start a local broadsheet at a very small cost, and what with the restrictions of career imposed upon themselves by a solely literary caste or two, no country, probably, has more representatives than India of the hero of the Romaic ballad :—

Province.	Books published in 1890–91.
Madras	1,022
Bombay	2,044
Bengal	1,225
N.-W. Provinces	1,107
Burma	149
Assam	22
Berar	13
Central Provinces	13
Total	**5,595**

Subject.	No. of Publication.
Art	80
Biography	58
Drama	185
Fiction	262
History and Geography	128
Languages	682
Law	71
Mathematics	158
Medicine	127
Philosophy	149
Poetry	672
Politics	13
Religion	770
Science	119
Travels	5
Unclassed	2,116
Total	**5,595**

Θερμὸς ἔιμαι πατριώτης, κὰι κουκκουλια 'γω δ'εν βάφω,
Ἢ ὑπουργημα με δίδεις ἢ ἐφημερίδα γράφω.

This digression from the results of the census has been unduly lengthened, but when so much is heard as at present of the literate classes of India, it is just as well to define the limitations of that term. It may thus be judged how far the φῶς ἀφεγγὴς of the handful of people to whom, under the most liberal interpretation, the term can be said to apply, is to be held capable of illuminating the thoughts and conditions of the vast mass from whom the very education, apart from the traditions, of that close corporation, inclines them to stand aloof.

CHAPTER VII.

INFIRMITIES.

"But what we're born for, we must bear;
Our frail condition it is such,
That what to all may happen here
If't chance to me, I must not grutch."—*Ben Jonson.*

The question of how far a return of infirmity should be included within the scope of the census rests mainly on two considerations; first, the social aspect of the inquiry, namely, whether the infirmities selected for the purpose are such as it is possible or advisable for the State effort or private charity to remedy on some general system, and this must be qualified by the condition that these infirmities are not of a sort that their return is likely to be refused or resented by the persons concerned; and, secondly, whether, from a medical standpoint, they are susceptible of being correctly recognised by the layman. In India, it has been the custom at each of the last three provincial enumerations, to restrict the inquiry to four subjects, which may be assumed to fulfil rather better than others the above conditions. In the first place, there are the persons of unsound mind, a term which is held to include both the imbecile and the lunatic. Secondly, the deaf-mute, but only those who have been so afflicted from their birth, a qualification which experience shows to be rather too abstruse for the masses. Thirdly, come the totally blind, and, lastly, the lepers. Before entering further into the subject, it is as well to reproduce the rules for enumeration of the above infirmities :—

1881.	1891.
Column heading :—INFIRMITIES. 1. Unsound mind. 2. Deaf-mutes from birth. 3. Blind. 4. Lepers.	*Column heading :*—NOTE. If any be blind, insane, deaf-mute, or a leper, enter the infirmity below.
Instructions :—Enter as lepers only those afflicted with the true, or eating, leprosy (juzam). Enter as deaf-mutes only those who have been both deaf and dumb from birth. Enter as blind only those who are blind of both eyes.	*Instructions :*—If any person be blind of both eyes, or deaf and dumb from birth, or insane, or suffering from corrosive leprosy, enter the name of the infirmity in this column. Do not enter those blind of one eye only, or who have become deaf and dumb after birth, or who are suffering from white leprosy only.

One of the first points to notice with regard to the above rules is that in most of the vernacular languages of India there are distinct words for "white leprosy" and the true or corrosive disease, and also, as in French, for the "one-eyed," as distinguished from the totally blind. But it is curious to find that in Western India the term for Leukoderma is what is used in the north for true leprosy, when the Arabic name for the latter, which is quoted in the instructions for 1881, is not employed. Again, the the word for one-eyed in the whole of Upper India is said by the Superintendent of the Assam census to be applied in the Bráhmapútra valley to the totally blind. The main object was to frame the instructions so as to exclude these two classes, who appear to have been mixed up with the rest in previous enumerations. As regards the deaf-mutes, there seems to be little doubt that in some tracts those who grew deaf in after years have been included along with the congenitally afflicted. It was desired again, to prevent the excess of zeal that characterised the work of certain enumerators in 1881, who made the entry of "got" or "not got" against each person, without specifying the infirmity in view, and of others, who entered into conscientious detail, such as "cannot see very well," or "is rather hard of hearing, from age," which occurred on former occasions. The results show that, on the whole, the instructions worked well. This fact is manifested chiefly in the decrease in the numbers of the infirm in tracts where there has been no special cause for so great a difference. On the other hand, in Assam, where in 1881 the return seems to have been very deficient, the increase was such as to induce the Superintendent to have a special investigation made, the results of which, it is gratifying to see, confirmed the accuracy of the present figures. In Bombay, too, the difference between the two years was enough to justify inquiry, with the same result.

But, even though we admit the accuracy of the statistics, it is to be feared that the enumeration is prone in too many cases to fail in the matter of diagnosis. For example, in a country where so much disease is put down to fever, there must be numbers of patients who are for a time, at least, "off their head," without being permanently deranged, and some of them are no doubt returned at the census from ignorance on the part of their relatives of the temporary character of the malady. In Europe, there is either medical authority for the case, or the latter is not returned by the householder at all, and it is not Polonius alone, who is puzzled to give a definition of insanity. In the case of leprosy the difficulty of diagnosis is still greater, and, apart from the confusion between the true disease and leukoderma, it is not improbable that a good deal of syphilitic sore is set down by the untrained observer to the former. It seems by no means certain that the confusion of leukoderma is not due to the wording of the instructions in former years, or to the misuse of the vernacular words for it by European professionals, for, whilst in the mouth of the rustic the two maladies are entirely distinct, to the occidental mind there is always a connection between leprosy and whiteness, a casting back to Gehazi or other Biblical characters, and the patches of white seen on the dark skin of a native of India in cases of leukoderma are certainly very striking. It is probable that a good deal of the decrease in the number of lepers returned in 1891 from tracts in which they were formerly remarkably high, is nominal, and due to greater accuracy of diagnosis, and this being so, it is impossible to say for certain whether this disease is, on the whole, stationary or not. In the provincial reports, instances are given by the Superintendents of undoubted decrease, but the assumption that this is the case with the country at large is hardly justifiable at present. The question is one that will be referred to in a later portion of this chapter.

The following statement shows in a proportional form the prevalence of the four infirmities in question, and, for the sake of comparison, the corresponding figures for some western countries are added. As regards the latter, the most striking points

TABLE A.—PROPORTIONAL SUMMARY, showing Prevalence of Infirmities per 10,000 of each Sex.

Country.	Insane.		Deaf Mutes.		Blind.		Lepers.	
	Males.	Females.	Males.	Females.	Males.	Females.	Males.	Females.
India, 1881	4	3	10	7	22	24	8·5	3
India, 1891	3	2	9	6	16	17	6·8	2
England and Wales	31	33	6	5	9	8	—	—
Scotland	38	39	3	2	9	8	—	—
Ireland	38	34	8	7	11	12	—	—
Italy	—	—	6	5	8	7	—	—
Austria	22	19	15	11	10	8	—	—
Hungary	22	18	14	12	13	13	—	—
Portugal	23	17	3	2	21	19	—	—
Ceylon	13	9	2	1	24	18	—	—
Victoria	37	31	4	3	11	6	—	—
New Zealand	33	22	2	2	4	3	—	—
United States	35	32	7	6	10	9	—	—

of difference are, first, the relative freedom of India from insanity, and then the relative frequency in that country of blindness. The former affliction is very markedly prominent in the more advanced of the western countries and in the British colonies in the south. Ceylon, for some reason or other not apparent, stands, in this respect, between east and west. The return for Italy seems to include a smaller class than the rest, so it has been omitted. It is also noticeable that the higher proportion of congenital deaf-mutism amongst males, that has been commented on in the English census, is maintained in India, but in the case of blindness, in Ireland alone, of the western countries mentioned, does the ratio amongst females exceed that in the other sex, as is found to be so often the case in the East. The proportion of deaf-mutes in Austria-Hungary appears from this return, which deals with the figures of 1880, to be higher than that which prevails in India, and in striking contrast to the low ratio in the rest of the European countries selected. Leprosy is returned in India alone, and here we find the proportions in the two sexes to differ more widely than in the case of any other of the infirmities under review, a point that will receive notice further down. The greater prevalence of insanity in western countries is easily accounted for by the difference of life there from what it is in India. We have seen that in the latter the brain-energy of the masses is not overtaxed by literary pursuits, and the struggle for life is not the competition between man and man so much as between man and the soil and sky. In the one case we have almost infinite variety, entailing continual adaptability and change of thought; in the other, monotonous devotion to a certain and lifelong task, based on previous experience. The man of the west runs more and more towards the busy novelty of the town, whilst his Oriental compeer placidly and contentedly chews the cud of village custom. Then, again, though we find that a certain proportion of the insanity of India is attributed by experts to the abuse of hemp drugs or opium smoke, alcoholisation has as yet made no way, except, perhaps, amongst some of the Central Hill tribes and a few of the literate class and the lower strata, who look upon this indulgence as a symbol of their emancipation from former prejudice. This fertile cause of insanity is thus absent. So far as to the men, and much the same arguments will apply to the other sex. It can be seen from the return under discussion how much nearer are the ratios of the two sexes in the West than in the East. The busy household life of the middle class woman in a country where the employment of domestic servants is restricted to the highest families, the seclusion of the upper class within the four walls of the Zanana, away from all chance of active participation in the affairs of the outer world, and the continuous outdoor labour of the lower orders, contain little stimulus towards the over-taxation of the brain, nor does a school life that generally ends at 12 years old, if not earlier, foster any tendencies in the same direction. On the other hand, the prevalence of blindness in India to so much greater an extent than in more temperate latitudes, and amongst women more than amongst men, is a matter that seems to be due to more complicated causes. It has been said that, speaking generally, there is a tendency for this infirmity to increase in intensity as the equator is approached, though the case of Norway is cited in contradiction of the hypothesis, and prevalence of snow in wide expanse may have some influence on the sight in the extreme north; but the returns for India certainly seem to bear out the notion that heat, accompanied by a dry atmosphere, is, other things being equal, inimical to sight. There are facts to be found in the tables that militate against this view, but they refer to restricted areas, where some special local influence may be operative. Taking the country as a whole, however, the hot and dry plain and plateau seem more favourable to the development of ophthalmic defect than the moister, though perhaps warmer, air of the coast and the purer atmosphere of the hill tracts. There seems to be nothing peculiar in connection with the prevalence of deaf-mutism in India. As in many other countries, there seems to be a tendency for this defect to haunt the valleys of certain streams. For instance, the Chenáb, the Gandak, and the Makhua, all three Himalayan rivers, bear a specially evil repute for producing both deaf-mutism and cretinism, with the frequent accompaniment of goitre. In Burma the hill country shows a greater prevalence than the plains, and in Assam the same feature is prominent, and it is by no means improbable that the practice of consanguineous connection that is common amongst the tribes of those tracts has something to do with the spread of the infirmity, for beyond the Gangetic basin, in the Central Belt, the corresponding tribes show no difference from the population of the plain below. Leprosy is a disease with which the East is in the present day credited to an extent beyond, perhaps, its deserts. Its prevalence will be examined in a later portion of this chapter.

We come now to the detailed figures regarding the four selected infirmities which will be found tabulated for each province and State, by sex and age, in Tables XII. to XV. of Volume I. of the Imperial series. The scrutiny of these data is a matter that must be left in great measure to professional experts, and it is not for laymen to draw conclusions from them. It is proposed, therefore, to exhibit the figures here in their proportional form, with a few words of comment or explanation on points immediately connected with the enumeration and kindred operations. The tables that follow are for the provinces only. In the first, marked B., is given the proportion amongst 10,000 of the afflicted found at each age-period, preceded by the corresponding figures for the population, as a whole, similarly distributed.

TABLE B.—Showing the Distribution by Age of 10,000 under each Infirmity.

Age-period.	Males. Total.	Males. Insane.	Males. Deaf Mutes.	Males. Blind.	Males. Lepers.	Females. Total.	Females. Insane.	Females. Deaf Mutes.	Females. Blind.	Females. Lepers.
0-4	1,416	166	457	427	44	1,524	170	528	281	81
5–9	1,433	552	1,445	639	84	1,393	532	1,450	409	180
10–14	1,145	789	1,317	647	236	948	789	1,154	417	399
15-19	836	924	1,070	594	400	817	937	1,024	417	602
20–24	796	1,045	965	609	572	890	988	952	453	735
25–29	866	1,233	897	633	873	900	1,000	859	518	924
30–34	827	1,272	823	662	1,205	833	1,108	801	621	1,186
35–39	613	975	602	563	1,212	556	885	544	541	990
40–44	626	995	620	693	1,516	616	980	622	738	1,292
45–49	369	573	374	565	996	328	608	367	598	788
50–54	404	561	452	785	1,174	421	727	484	868	1,010
55–59	183	287	242	626	495	174	328	252	711	465
60 and over	469	600	729	2,601	1,185	583	911	955	3,422	1,335
Age not stated	17	28	7	6	8	17	37	8	6	13

The mean age of the living, as gathered from the general age-tables, is, roughly speaking, 24 years, and if we divide the population shown under each infirmity at that age, we find the distribution to be as given in the margin. Nearly two-thirds of the insane in both sexes are over the age in question, the deaf mutes are nearly halved. In the case of the blind, there is more divergence between the two sexes, and the males begin to suffer from this affliction at an age considerably earlier than the other sex, whilst as regards leprosy, the reverse is the case, and 20 per cent. of the female lepers are under 25 years of age, as compared with no more than 13 per cent. of the males thus affected. In respect to the more detailed age-periods, it must be borne in mind that the tendency to select multiples of five in returning age, a feature by no means unknown in Europe, is very marked in an Indian census, so that, as the more favoured multiples are the even ones, it is advisable to consider the tables in the decennial periods of

—	Males. 0–24.	Males. 25 and over.	Females. 0–24.	Females. 25 and over.
Insanity	348	652	342	658
Deaf-mutism	525	475	511	489
Blindness	292	708	198	802
Leprosy	134	866	200	800
Total Population	563	437	557	443

Insanity. 25–34, 35–44, and so on. Taken in this way, the figures show a gradual rise in the case of males of unsound mind, from the first five years of life to the period ending at the 35th year, from which point insanity declines with remarkable rapidity. On

the other side, young girls suffering from this defect are a trifle more numerous, relatively to the total number of the insane of their sex, but between 25 and 34 the proportion is less than that which rules at those ages amongst males, whilst after 45 it rises considerably above it.

Deaf-mutism. The deaf mutes exhibit a distribution more in accordance than the rest with that of the population as a whole, but the extremities of the return, especially in the case of the females, indicate the inclusion of the deaf at advanced ages. The first period, if the congenitally afflicted alone had been returned, would have contained the largest number, and there would have been a gradual tailing off, as death, in the ordinary course of events, carried off its victims. It is not so, however, in the table, but the maximum is found in the next period, that between 5 years and 10, and both sexes take a sudden rise after 55 years of age. There are obvious objections on the part of parents to admitting that a young child is deprived of both hearing and speech, especially before completion of the age within which betrothal is possible, and this may account for a good deal of the inconsistency just mentioned.

Blindness. Blindness, in the case of females, is most decidedly the affliction of old age. The table shows that over 40 per cent. of those returning it are past 55, and the increase is continuous, though not regular, through life. In the case of males, there is more irregularity, owing, however, to some extent, to the predilection for returning 25 years, when the actual age is probably anything between 20 and 30. The proportion over 55 is only about a third, and the greater number found amongst the young, as compared with the other sex, is very remarkable. It has been remarked in several of the provincial reports that there was a frequent inclination to return as totally blind persons of advanced age whose sight was dimmed by glaukoma. On the other hand, a few cases were mentioned in which the enumerator, owing to misreading his instructions, tacked on the qualification of "from birth" to this infirmity, as well as to that to which it properly belonged.

Leprosy. Leprosy, in point of distribution between the two main periods of life, corresponds, in the case of females, almost exactly with blindness, but in detail it is very different. There are more than thrice the number of blind girls of tender age than of lepers, the latter are still in a considerable minority between 5 and 15, but the marriageable age being past, they then begin to outnumber the others, relatively, of course, to the respective totals afflicted. The lepers, however, are not recruited, as are the blind, in old age, and their life seems a comparatively short one. Male lepers of less than five years old are still less prevalent than those of the other sex, and it is not till between 25 and 34 that they relatively outnumber the blind. Like the other sex, they maintain their comparative superiority until 55 years of age, when they fall to about the half. Even here, however, they seem to considerably outlast the insane and the deaf mutes.

We may now review the age-return of the afflicted population from another standpoint, namely, in its relation, not to the total of the persons suffering under the respective infirmities, but to that of the entire population of the same sex and age. This ratio is given in Table C., below.

TABLE C.—Showing the number afflicted in 100,000 of each Age.

Age-period.	Males.					Females.				
	Total Afflicted.	Insane.	Deaf Mute.	Blind.	Lepers.	Total Afflicted.	Insane.	Deaf Mute.	Blind.	Lepers.
0–4	86	4	31	49	2	55	2	21	31	1
5–9	186	13	96	73	4	125	9	64	49	3
10–14	240	23	109	93	15	178	19	75	74	10
15–19	310	37	121	116	36	208	26	78	86	18
20–24	337	44	115	125	53	196	25	66	85	20
25–29	341	48	98	120	75	206	25	59	97	25
30–34	385	52	94	131	108	250	30	60	125	35
35–39	444	54	93	150	147	308	36	60	168	44
40–44	509	54	94	181	180	351	36	62	201	52
45–49	600	53	96	250	201	475	41	69	306	59
50–54	666	47	106	297	216	515	39	71	346	59
55–59	939	53	125	560	201	879	42	89	682	66
60 and over	1,285	43	147	907	188	1,179	35	101	986	57
All ages	367	34	95	164	74	277	22	62	168	25

From this statement it appears that, taking all four infirmities together, the average on the whole population begins to be exceeded after the 30th year amongst males, and five years later amongst the other sex, and the general liability to one or other of the four continues to rise from the earliest period. Insanity, in the case of males, reaches its highest intensity in the decade ending with the 45th year, where it amounts to 5 per 10,000. If the accidental variations at quinquennial periods be excluded, this infirmity may be said to remain at this level till old age. Women show the highest ratio between 45 and 54, or 10 years later than the other sex. Deaf mutes of both sexes show that, if correctly returned, they last a considerable time, but the high ratio at the end of life is probably fictitiously swollen by the inclusion of those who are only deaf. In other respects, it is curious to see how the general average is maintained amongst both sexes at all periods except between 10 and 25, and at the extremities of life. Blindness begins to be markedly on the increase after 40 or a few years earlier, but takes its great leap after 55 amongst both sexes. Amongst the very young, though less prevalent than at any other age, it seems from the return to be more than 12 times as prevalent as insanity in the males, and 15 times amongst females. Leprosy, again, seems to pass by the young and to begin its attacks about 25 years of age. Its maximum prevalence is at 50 years, after which those afflicted by it seem to die off. In the case of females, the maximum shown in the table is at 55, but this is a period which is safely taken as conjectural, and is distributable between 50 and 60, without much change of discrimination.

The next series of figures that it is advisable to bring to notice here is that which shows the proportion of females to 1,000 males at each age, in the four returns of infirmity respectively. The general proportion found to prevail amongst the population at large is added in Table D., for the sake of comparison, in anticipation of special notice in a future chapter. The main point is so prominent in the figures as they stand that comment is almost superfluous. In no case but that of the blind does the ratio come anywhere near that found in the general return, and as regards the blind, too, the female element preponderates only after the 40th year. Amongst the insane, at the prime of life, the women are but little above half the men in number, and this is in accordance with a tendency found to prevail not only in India, for the "age of the passions" is more strongly demarcated in the sex which has given itself greater license to indulge them. It will be noted, too, that after the first period, which comprises, probably, the congenitally idiotic, the ages at which insanity in the females approaches nearest the proportion of this infirmity in the other sex, are those of early child-birth, and of the change of life. After the latter period insanity tends to greater sexual equality. Amongst the deaf-mute, as has been already noticed, the small proportion of females is only what is found to be the characteristic of this infirmity in most countries where it prevails, and, indeed, of all congenital defect. It is at its minimum at the age when there is the greatest inducement to conceal it, which is also, it will be noted, that in which the proportion of girls generally is the smallest. From 40 years onwards the ratio begins to rise. The proportion of blind girls to boys similarly afflicted is curiously in consonance with that of the insane for the first three periods shown in the table. It rises, however, continuously from the fifth year, without intermission at the dangerous periods of life, and, as just observed, from 40 years onwards, the blind women are in excess of the blind men. The case of the lepers is very remarkable, so far as the sex proportions are concerned. In the first place, there are three times the number of males that there are of the other sex. Then, again, up to 30 years old this average ratio is exceeded, a fact which is not met with again until the end of life. In the first three periods slightly more than half the number of

TABLE D.—Proportion of Females to 1,000 Males at each Age.

Age-period.	Total Population.	Insane.	Deaf Mute.	Blind.	Lepers.
0–4	1,039	651	728	651	582
5–9	939	614	633	633	685
10–14	799	637	553	638	542
15–19	943	646	603	695	483
20–24	1,079	601	621	737	412
25–29	1,004	516	604	809	339
30–34	972	555	614	928	315
35–39	875	578	569	952	262
40–44	950	628	632	1,054	273
45–49	859	675	618	1,048	254
50–54	1,005	824	674	1,179	276
55–59	922	729	657	1,125	301
60 and over	1,199	967	826	1,125	361
Age not stated	909	850	709	1,231	507
All ages	965	637	630	990	321

lepers are females, but the ratio goes on decreasing till the 40th year, after which it oscillates irregularly, in harmony with the general inaccuracy of the age returns.

Territorial distribution of infirmity.

In treating of the territorial variation in the prevalence of the four infirmities in question, it is necessary to take into consideration the probable effect of relative inaccuracy in the enumeration. To a certain extent this can be appreciated from the comparison of the two last returns, that of 1891 and that of the preceding census. The following statement will give some notion of the differences between the two, as

TABLE E.—Showing the relative Order of the Provinces as regards prevalence amongst Males of Infirmities in 1881 and 1891.

Province, &c.	Insane.		Deaf Mutes.		Blind.		Lepers.	
	1881.	1891.	1881.	1891.	1881.	1891.	1881.	1891.
1. Ajmér	3	11	7	14	3	5	15	15
2. Assam	9	3	12	4	15	9	4	2
3. Bengal and States	5	5	1	2	11	11	2	3
4. Berar	10	14	5	15	4	2	1	1
5. Bombay and States	7	7	10	9	8	8	6	5
6. Sindh, &c.	1	1	3	1	2	4	14	14
7. Lower Burma	2	2	11	13	10	14	3	4
8. Central Provinces	12	12	9	10	7	7	5	6
9. Coorg	13	8	4	7	13	15	12	13
10. Madras and States	8	10	14	6	9	13	7	8
11. N.-W. Provinces and States	15	15	8	5	5	3	8	7
12. Panjáb	4	6	2	3	1	1	9	11
13. Haidrabad	11	13	15	11	12	12	10	9
14. Baroda	6	4	6	12	6	6	11	10
15. Mysore	14	9	13	8	14	10	13	12

it shows the serial order of each province or State with reference to the respective prevalence therein of the four infirmities in the two years. It is not justifiable, of course, to set down the whole of the very large variation that appears to have taken place in some of the items to inaccuracy of enumeration or tabulation alone, as it is no doubt true than in certain parts of the country other causes have been operative, which account for a good deal of the discrepancy. In Madras, for instance, the recuperation of the population since the famine has added so largely to the supply of young children that, except in the case of congenital disease in the affected tracts, the preponderance of that class must have had some influence in bringing down the ratio of the infirm, and it is noticeable that as regards the only congenital disease with which the census has to deal, the variation in the results is least, on the whole, in the tracts where the infirmity was most prevalent in 1881. With the above qualification, the results given in the statement can be best judged by assigning to each item a "figure of merit" according to the stability of its place in the four columns. By this standard, Bengal, Bombay, and the Central Provinces are in a class by themselves, since in two cases they occupy the same relative position in the list at both enumerations, and in the two others they rise or fall by one place only. Below them we find Sindh, which is on a par with them in respect to two infirmities, but changes in the others to the extent of two places each. There follow seven items in which there was identity of position in one case only. Of these the Panjáb comes first, as it has varied but by two places in a couple of columns, and by one in the last. The North-West Provinces come next by one point. Burma and Haidrabad follow at the same interval again. Baroda is worse by two more, as in one case it varies six places, and Coorg, where, as might be expected from the migratory character of a large portion of its inhabitants, there is no instance of identical position on the list, is but two beyond Baroda. There is then a considerable break in the graduation. Mysore and Madras show a variation of 15 places, as compared with the 11 of Coorg, Berar has 16, Ajmer 17, and Assam, of which mention in connection with this point was made above, has no less than 22 points of variance. On the whole, however, it may be said that the results show that, other things being equal, the enumeration was good in all the main provinces; that the variation is probably real in Madras and Mysore, where the conditions are very different in 1891 from what they were 10 years previously, and that in Assam the preceding enumeration was admittedly deficient in accuracy. As regards Ajmér and Berar, it is uncertain which of the two returns is to be trusted. In the former case Mr. Egerton writes, "In 1881 the results showed an unaccountable "increase on the figures of 1876, and the present record shows as remarkable a "decrease on those of 1881. Possibly both enumerations were inaccurate in opposite "extremes. . . . Compared with the figures of 1881 for other provinces, the "proportion of afflicted returned is below the average in about the same degree as "it was above it at the former census." Ajmér is undoubtedly subject to more chance of actual variation than most other parts of the country, as it lies embedded in foreign territory, is a place of passage between two or three large tracts on each side, and lies conveniently for expeditions to several centres of Brahmanic pilgrimage, which are always the favoured resort of the infirm of all religions, who lie in wait by the sacred pool without thought as to the troubling of the waters. It is worthy of note, too, that both here and in Berar instances are mentioned of the application by the enumerating agency of the qualification of congenitality to blindness and insanity, as well as to deaf-mutism. This misunderstanding tends, obviously, to the reduction of the number returned. In Berar, on the other side of the account, it has been found that in 1881 persons were returned as deaf and dumb who had become so in later life, so that the enumeration having been more careful on the occasion under review, the diminution is in the direction of greater accuracy. This part of the subject may be concluded with the remark that the statement we have been considering shows that whilst in the case of all the other infirmities, a number of the items, varying from three, as regards the return of lepers, to six, in that of the blind, occupy the same position in the list that they did 10 years ago, the column for the deaf-mute return does not contain a single instance of identity in the respect, thus proving the difficulty of obtaining a consistent application of the definition of that infirmity.

In considering Table F., opposite, in which is shown the prevalence of the four infirmities to the uniform base of 100,000 of the population, it is, perhaps, more interesting to take the infirmity rather than the territorial item, as the text for comment. In place, therefore, of considering the diffusion of the four infirmities over any particular political unit, information on which point is available in the provincial volumes, the local prevalence of each infirmity will form the subject of the next few paragraphs.

Insanity. To begin with insanity, it appears that at both enumerations Sindh and Lower Burma came first and second respectively in the order of prevalence. In the case of the former, the cause of its bad pre-eminence is not ascertainable from the returns, as they do not distinguish idiotcy from lunacy, so that we cannot say if the climate or water of the river, or the drought, or the indulgence in hemp smoking, or all or any of these are responsible for the results. In Burma, it is said, the people are excitable and self-indulgent; and the returns show that the Môn, a more phlegmatic, or, perhaps, abstemious race, is comparatively free from taint. The population, too, as a whole, is better educated. There seem other considerations, moreover, to which weight must be attached. For instance, in Upper Burma the ratio is higher than in Lower, and as there is not yet an asylum in the former, there was possibly less concealment of domestic cases from fear lest the sufferer should be removed to a place of refuge by the State officials. Then, again, the high ratio amongst the Forest tribes in the Lower Province indicates the probability of much of the return being taken up by the cretinism that seems to follow mountain streams. There is one more fact connected with the Burma return that calls for remark, namely, that the woman adult is apparently more prone to mental derangement than the male. If this were due to ordinary physical change, we should find it more prevalent, but it is peculiar to the upper portion of this particular province, and is unexplained. Third on the list comes Assam, where, no doubt, the greater part of the malady returned is cretinism of the description just mentioned, which follows the main river. In 1881, Ajmer enjoyed this rank, but, as remarked above, its decadence is unexplained. We find the Panjáb and Baroda have changed places, and the former is now sixth instead of fourth, and *vice versâ*. The Baroda report is not yet to hand, and so comment on the figures is inadvisable, in the absence of the local experience of the Superintendent. The chapter on infirmities written by Mr. MacLagan in his Panjab report is well worth perusal, as he has treated the subject with care and in detail, reviewing the circumstances of his large and varied charge from a high standpoint. It appears at least probable that most of the insanity in this Province is connected in some way with special rivers

Table F.—Showing in each Province, &c. the Average Number of Persons afflicted per 100,000 of each Sex, in 1881 and 1891.

Province, &c.	A.—Males.				B.—Deaf Mutes.			
	Males.		Females.		Males.		Females.	
	1881.	1891.	1881.	1891.	1881.	1891.	1881.	1891.
Ajmér	69	22	42	9	80	39	61	24
Assam	38	62	26	49	68	96	41	76
Bengal and States	53	41	36	28	153	117	94	71
Berar	36	19	26	14	104	21	81	15
Bombay and States	41	30	22	17	77	64	54	46
Sindh and Khairpúr	162	109	107	64	133	128	95	75
Burma, Lower	114	83	84	51	72	42	48	34
„ Upper	—	124	—	127	—	79	—	66
Central Provinces and States	27	21	14	12	78	58	59	43
Coorg	23	26	18	25	108	80	85	63
Madras and States	38	25	28	18	62	83	50	62
North-West Provinces and States	19	16	9	8	78	84	48	50
Panjáb and States	59	38	36	22	141	115	92	76
Haidrabád	30	18	16	10	49	46	29	30
Baroda	51	43	34	27	93	45	62	30
Mysore	22	25	14	19	68	77	56	61
Rájputána	—	32	—	19	—	—	—	—
India	**43**	**33**	**27**	**21**	**104**	**90**	**68**	**59**

Province, &c.	C.—Blind.				D.—Lepers.			
	Males.		Females.		Males.		Females.	
	1881.	1891.	1881.	1891.	1881.	1891.	1881.	1891.
Ajmér	355	181	588	208	9	6	3	3
Assam	76	108	60	106	100	183	40	61
Bengal and States	186	100	144	96	122	93	41	31
Berar	330	226	402	241	215	193	59	58
Bombay and States	217	140	273	149	84	77	31	26
Sindh and Khairpúr	391	209	561	221	13	7	10	6
Burma, Lower	152	89	162	99	101	92	33	31
„ Upper	—	317	—	416	—	160	—	81
Central Provinces and States	218	156	296	188	89	66	41	33
Coorg	92	49	90	50	25	12	23	14
Madras and States	153	97	170	99	68	54	25	18
North-West Provinces and States	270	216	290	224	63	54	16	13
Panjáb and States	488	338	538	368	61	29	21	11
Haidrabád	128	100	110	84	42	38	19	13
Baroda	248	161	351	235	89	32	17	15
Mysore	89	106	98	104	16	21	9	11
Rájputána	—	272	—	380	—	21	—	7
India	**217**	**164**	**243**	**171**	**85**	**68**	**29**	**23**

such as the Chenáb in particular, along which cretinism is rife, from the Himálayan valleys to the plains of Multán. This hypothesis receives some support from the experience given by the returns for Bengal, which province comes next on the list. Here, too, the Himálayan rivers seem to form the chief centres of mental unsoundness. On the other hand, so far as Multán is concerned, it is noted that the neighbourhood contains more than one shrine of repute for its curative virtues in such afflictions, so that the local idiots may well be reinforced by those brought to the locality by faithful relatives. There is also the fact that amongst a Musalmán population, such as that of the Western Panjab, there is greater latitude as regards consanguineous marriage than amongst the Brahmanic clans. But, taking the whole of the circumstances into consideration, there seems every reason to think that a specially baleful influence on the mind is exercised by mountains, whether the Himálaya or the Salt range, in Upper India. The detailed returns for the North-West Provinces have not yet been received in the Central Office, so there is a gap in this argument that has to be filled up by the local census Superintendent, whose province enjoys the honour of being, according to the results of his enumeration, the sanest in India. In Bengal, Mr. O'Donnell seems to think that the distribution of insanity is racial or professional rather that local, and that the Mongoloid strain in the eastern portion of the province, together with the wider expansion of instruction and the notoriously litigious temperament of the population in that tract, make, on the whole, a more favourable seed-bed for mental derangement than the stolid ploughman of Bihár, or the Dravidian hill-man of Chutia Nagpur. This may be so, but the details show that the cretin element is by no means unimportant, as the ratio of insanity is far above the provincial average in the sub-Himálayan districts and is remarkably high in the Tarai-bordering State of Kochh-Bihár. That the return, however, is not altogether free from suspicion is shown by Mr. O'Donnell's discovery of an attempt made by a righteous Hindu scribe to cast a stigma on the followers of the Prophet by entering all the infirm of his subdivision as Saiads by tribe. The errors due to fraud or otherwise seem, all the same, to have neutralised each other, for the province, like Sindh, Burma, Bombay, the Central and the North-West Provinces, takes the same place in the list as it did in 1881. As regards Bombay, there is nothing special in the distribution to call for remark, save that the general feature of the variation seems to show that enumeration on this occasion was more correct than that of 1881. It may be here noted that there certainly seems to be some connection between the returns of insanity and the general condition of the people during the intercensal period, for wherever the decade has been one of normal prosperity, the persons thus afflicted have fallen out of the census roll to a remarkably large extent, and this may be noted in Bombay, Bengal, the Panjáb and Madras, as well as in smaller tracts. To a comparatively small extent, too, the spread of hospitals, and of dispensaries in the rural parts of the country must have tended to check the growth of insanity, since the patient, who perhaps may be only temporarily deranged, or epileptic, can be attended to by trained agency before the disease is confirmed. To return to the tables:—In Madras there are traces, according to the view of Mr. Stuart, the Superintendent, of a racial tendency, or predisposition to insanity, as the Uria and Tamil seem to be less subject to this infirmity than the Telanga or the Malabári. The difference does not seem to be due to climatic or geographical causes alone, for the prevalence is by no means in general accord with that of the adjacent districts in the coast and Deccan portions of Bombay. There is one curious fact that may be mentioned for what it is worth, in the present state of the study of morbid pathology, and this is, that amongst the six highest ratios of the insane, no less than four appertain to communities of the Malabár coast, out of whom three are still polyandrous to some extent, in their domestic arrangements. Another fact brought out in the returns is that the ratio of insanity decreased during the decade to a greater extent in the worst of the famine districts than in any other portion of the Presidency. There is little that need be said regarding the rest of the provinces. The distribution of the insane in the Central Provinces seems to indicate that apart from cretinism, which is not prevalent there, there is nothing in the hill-country that specially breeds or wards off this infirmity. The Superintendent, indeed, mentions the tendency of the forest tribes to drink to excess, so that here is ready to hand the explanation of the local prevalence of insanity amongst a class which elsewhere seems peculiarly though densely sane.

Deaf-mutism

The next part of the table to come under review is that which relates to the proportion of the deaf-mute. Here we find Sindh, Bengal, and the Panjáb again well to the front, both in 1881 and on the present occasion. Assam comes not far behind.

In all, except Sindh, where the source of the evil is not traced, it appears that the main prevalence is located in the Himálaya or along the rivers flowing directly from that system, so that, as in the mountainous countries of Europe, this infirmity is combined with cretinism and goitre. It is possible that diet may have some effect on the system predisposing the inhabitants of the tracts in question to these forms of malady, for, at all events, in the Panjáb Himálaya the food of the people is very different from the staples in favour in the plains. This, however, does not explain the Sindh case, nor, probably, much of the prevalence in Bengal, Burma, or Assam. It is curious to find the same feature in the Burma returns from the hill tracts, whilst the Môn, as in the case of insanity, are less liable to deaf-mutism than the Burmese, and in Upper Burma, where there is a comparatively dry atmosphere, the ratio is far higher than in the lower division of the Province. Here, however, there is the probability of inaccuracy in the return, as the enumeration was conducted for the first time, and experience indicates that on such occasions the confusion of the deaf with those afflicted in both ways is greater than at subsequent inquiries. Still, the standard of life is lower, and the diet more sparse than in the Delta. In Madras we find the same feature as in Assam, namely, that the ratio of the deaf mutes to the total population has risen. This is attributed apparently, in part, as in the latter province, to bad enumeration in 1881. Beyond a general accordance with the distribution of insanity, and some slight preference for the hot and dry districts of the South Deccan, the return for this Presidency presents no special feature. It is curious, all the same, to find that the increase in the ratio is least in the tract where the increase of population has been highest during the decade, as if the determining factor were the well-being of the masses. At the bottom of the list come Berár and Ajmér, the two in which the variation is most clearly of all due to inaccuracy of return.

Blindness. In the return of blindness we find greater agreement than in the rest between the results of the two enumerations, and the decrease, which is general throughout the returning tracts, with the exception of Mysore and Assam, where the ratio has risen, may accordingly be taken as truly representative of the facts. There are, as already noted, certain defects in enumeration, such as the inclination to enter, on the one hand, senile glaukoma and dullness of sight as blindness, and to include, on the other, those who were not born blind; but it is not unreasonable to assume that these misconceptions are not universal, and, on the whole, are likely to be constant, and to balance each other. If the scale be unevenly weighted, it is probably on the side of excess; that is, the undue entries are more numerous than the undue exclusion. On this hypothesis, the decrease in blindness in the last 10 years is in reality considerably greater than is shown in the returns, and the provincial Superintendents, as a rule, agree that this is the case in their respective charges. The improvement is attributed chiefly to two causes, first, the rapid spread of dispensaries in the smaller country towns, bringing trained assistance within the reach of many classs who have been hitherto obliged to let ophthalmia and similar affections run their course amongst the children of the community. Then, again, though the increased accuracy of death registration somewhat obscures the fact on paper, there has been a notable diminution in the proportion of deaths to seizures in the case of small-pox, and this disease is, in India, one of the most fertile sources of blindness. In Mr. Maclagan's review of the Panjáb statistics these points are well illustrated, as he shows, as to the first, that the number of patients treated for eye affections at the public medical institutions of the province, rose from 90,820 in 1881 to 233,670 in 1891; whilst in connection with the second, the comparative tables he quotes show that the decrease in blindness is greatest precisely in the parts of the Province where mortality from small-pox has most declined, and where vaccination has made most progress. This last fact proves how difficult it is to trace the relative prevalence of blindness in India to any single cause; for if locality alone were the determinant factor, the infirmity would be more diffused amongst the population of the glaring and arid plains of the Indus valley, instead of reaching its maximum in the wooded and well-irrigated tracts of the submontane and eastern divisions of the province. On the other hand, Sindh, hotter and dryer than even the Multán tract, is peculiarly favourable to the development of diseases of the eye, but so appears to be the Malabar coast, where the climatic conditions are vastly different. But, on the whole, the statistics for different parts of the same province—for the latter is far too varied in its component parts to be otherwise than an unwieldy unit—seem to indicate that blindness is more prevalent, as a rule, in hot and dry tracts, and less prevalent in mountain air and within the influence of the heavier rain currents. In the Panjáb, for instance, the Himálayan tracts are markedly favoured as regards eyesight, so are the Chútia Nágpúr and other hill tracts of Bengal. Along the coast, again, Orissa, the Konkan and the littoral tracts of Burma present a marked contrast in this respect to the plains of Bihár, the North Deccan, Upper Burma, Rájputána, and the adjacent and somewhat similarly conditioned tract of Gujaráth. There are, however, the anomalous cases of the Malabár coast and the north-eastern coast tract of Madras to be considered.

The statistics of the rest of the Presidency are in general accord with those for similar tracts elsewhere, that is, the Nilgiris and surrounding hilly tracts show least blindness, and the hot and dry plains of the Ceded Districts return the maximum. Mr. Stuart has accordingly subdivided the coast districts into their littoral and inland tracts, with the result that the former seem to show more blindness than the latter in some cases, though not in all. It is possible that the geographical peculiarities of these tracts may have some influence on the variation, as there is a great difference in the distribution of the rainfall between Malabar, where the Ghâts lie at some distance from the shore, and Kanara, where they come close down to it. In the latter, the coast receives the full current; in the former, it is attracted to some extent, inland. Perhaps there is some feature of this sort in Vizagapatam and its neighbourhood on the opposite coast, but in either case the suggestion is purely conjectural. It is also open to question whether, so far as ophthalmia and cognate disease is concerned, especially amongst infants, the prevalence does not to some extent depend upon what we may call normal agricultural dirt, which in India is often associated with high cultivation. The better the tillage, the nearer is the manure to the master's eye, and the dryer the air, the more numerous and busy are the flies round every source of moist nourishment, from the dunghill to the eye of the sleeping infant. Finally, and as regards the prevalence of blindness amongst women alone, there are the social considerations, such as seclusion within dark rooms often reeking with acrid smoke from the cooking-places, which is customary rather in Upper India, Sindh, the Panjáb, Rajputána, and the North-West Provinces, than in the rest of the country; also the conventional mourning of relatives, which is necessarily very frequent, and is invariably accompanied, as Mr. Maclagan puts it, by much ostentatious squeezing of the eye. Whether either of these two causes is in operation on the Malabar coast is not stated in the Madras report, though no doubt the long rainy season keeps both sexes indoors to a greater extent than in the light fall of the uplands, and may thus serve the same purpose in connection with our present subject, as the zenána system of the north.

Reverting to the consideration of Table F., it should be remarked that in 1881 the ratio of the blind was higher amongst females than males in all parts of India, except Coorg, Assam, and Haidrabád. In the last two the peculiarity has been maintained on the present occasion, and extends to Mysore and Bengal. Looking at this fact, and the tendency in the same direction in Madras, and in the opposite one in the case of Sindh, the Panjáb, North-West Provinces, Ajmer, and Rajputána, it seems that where the sexes are nearest numerical equality, or the women exceed the men, blindness inclines to be less markedly a female affection; and when the males are far in excess, the women are more prone to blindness. It has not been suggested, however, in any provincial report, that the objection on the part of the patriarch to the return of the females of his household at the census does not extend beyond those who are sound in mind and body, which seems a not unnatural inference to be drawn from the above figures. The relative accuracy of the return for the two years has been discussed on general lines above. All that it seems necessary to add is, that apparently Ajmér and Berár, possibly Sindh and Mysore, and admittedly Assam, show differences which can only be ascribed to the enumeration, without basis in fact. It will be noted that in both years the Panjáb heads the list, though with a remarkable decrease in the prevalence of the infirmity. Berár and Sindh have exchanged places as second and fourth respectively, not without suspicions of inaccuracy in both cases, as the ratio in Sindh seems to have receded by one half. A precisely similar movement has been executed by Ajmér and the North-West Provinces for the third and fifth places, in both instances with a diminution in prevalence amounting to over the half. In the last-named tract the improvement is said to be real, and due to the extension of vaccination and the erection of rural dispensaries. The three next—Baroda, the Central Provinces and Bombay—occupy the same position respectively as in 1881, a fact which shows fairly uniform accuracy of return. The decrease in ratio in all three is less, however, than in the tracts where blindness is more prevalent.

Bengal occupies the eleventh place in both years, and Haidrabad the twelfth. From the Central Provinces downwards, in the case of the males, and from Bombay in that of the other sex, the ratio falls below the general mean for India, showing how much more this infirmity prevails in the north than in the centre, south and east. Rajputána and Upper Burma come on to the list for the first time, and, as in respect to other infirmities, no doubt show a fuller return than will be the case at future enumerations. Both, however, are hot and dry in climate, so that the ratio, though likely to decrease, is not to be expected to descend to the level of that of coast tracts.

Summarising the results of the two returns, it appears that blindness tends to be more prevalent in hot and dry plains away from the hills and sea; that in the north of India social customs are specially favourable to its spread amongst women, but that whether the infirmity be due to congenital or infantile ophthalmia or to small-pox, it is everywhere on the decrease owing to greater facilities for obtaining timely surgical assistance, and to the diminution of small-pox due to the extension of vaccination.

Leprosy.

The subject of leprosy has been brought very prominently before the public during the last three or four years, and so far as India is concerned, has been exhaustively treated by a special commission of qualified experts who have analysed all available statistics in the report recently published.* The record of the results of their investigations, therefore, will necessarily supersede anything that may be written on the subject by a layman, so that a short shrift and sharp execution is all that the statistics require in the present work. Table E. shows that in only three cases do the positions of the territorial items correspond in the two years. Berár still heads the list, and the small variation in its ratio, both amongst males and females show that if inaccuracy there be, it is constant, and therefore statistically insignificant. Sindh and Ajmér again occupy the two last places, each with a considerable proportional decrease in the prevalence of their lepers. As regards the rest, it will be noted that none but Assam has altered its position by more than a single place, and the explanation as to the variation in this last has been already given. It is doubtful how far locality is connected with the prevalence of leprosy. From the fact that the ratio is high in the hill tracts of the Panjáb, and in the corresponding portions of the North-West Provinces and Bengal, and on the Yoma tracts of Burma, it appears that mountainous country is favourable to its development and a dry if not hot, atmosphere inimical. There is some evidence, too, of its affinity to coast tracts; but here, again, the Malabar figures are inconclusive, for those of South Kanara contradict their companions of the next district. In another direction, it appears that this disease finds a poor and ill-nourished population more accessible to its inception than one whose average condition is higher; and it is also stated that there seems to be some connection between the circumstances giving rise to cholera and those favourable to the development of leprosy. The Report of the Commission just mentioned, of which a summary is all that is at present available for the purpose of the present work, is decidedly encouraging in some of its conclusions, and, speaking generally, there seems reason for anticipating that most of the influences which predispose the population to the attacks of this disease are such as are likely to give way as the standard of maintenance advances.

Infirmities by caste groups, &c.

There is only one further point in connection with this subject with which it is necessary to deal here. It is the respective affinity between the four infirmities selected for investigation and social circumstances, so far as the latter can be judged by caste or race. We must first, however, revert for a space to what was said above as to the influence exercised on certain forms of disease by climate and locality. These, it will have been seen, affect, to a greater or less extent, all four of the selected infirmities, so that, looking at the varied territory comprised within the limits of a single Province or large State, it is most probable that distinctions of caste in respect to such matters will be outweighed by physical conditions. As a striking instance of this we may take the prevalence of deaf mutes amongst the two widely different castes of the Bráhman and the Chamár, or leather worker in the Panjáb. The ratio is about the same in both, but more than a third of the total number of affected persons are returned from a single district in the hill tract. But if we compare the proportions amongst the different caste groups for all India, we obliterate,

* A copy of this Report only reached me on the 14th June 1893, so the contents could not be fully adopted in this chapter.—J. A. B

in turn, local influence, and any distinctions there may be are most probably inherent in the social, not the geographical or climatic circumstances in which the caste in question is situated.

The figures on which the following remarks are based will be found in the different sections of Table XVIII. in Volume II. of the Imperial returns. It was necessary to split up this table into three, because the same detail was not tabulated in every one of the constituent tracts. Rájputána, for example, tabulated three of the infirmities by caste, but not deaf-mutism, whilst Central India and Kashmér omitted this portion of the schedule for all but the cantonment population, &c. It is not proposed to enter into territorial detail in respect to the results of the tabulation, for the reason just given above, nor does it seem worth while to reproduce the whole table in its proportional form, as its bearings can be adequately exhibited by the following extracts. Table G.. below, for instance, gives the 12 caste groups in which the total number of afflicted is highest relatively to the total strength of each sex in the group. It should be explained that betel leaf sellers and brass-smiths are amongst the 10 highest in the case of males only, and their place amongst those of the other sex is taken by the leather-working castes and the barbers. The first

Castes showing a generally high ratio of infirm.

TABLE G.

Caste Group, &c.	Males.					Females.					
	Insane.	Deaf Mutes.	Blind.	Lepers.	Total.	Order.	Insane.	Deaf Mutes.	Blind.	Lepers.	Total.
1. Indefinite Castes	130	194	358	128	810	1	79	146	440	53	718
2. Devotees	40	103	305	82	530	7	24	70	227	31	352
3. Scavengers	33	110	281	95	519	3	21	78	310	39	448
4 (*a*). Betel Leaf Sellers	27	105	224	144	500	10 (*a*)	15	65	203	38	321
5. Miscellaneous Vagrants	32	106	318	37	493	2	13	73	355	22	463
6. Burmese	103	62	184	131	480	4	83	51	233	54	421
7. Grain Parchers	26	182	191	79	478	6	12	99	213	30	354
8. Genealogists	28	88	258	82	456	5	16	51	285	35	387
9 (*a*). Brass-Smiths	48	156	156	84	444	10 (*a*)	28	80	173	46	327
10. Hunters and Fowlers	33	98	223	77	431	8	24	72	222	28	346
10 (*a*). Barbers	29	108	210	73	420	9	19	72	215	28	334
10 (*a*). Leather Workers	19	79	215	47	360	10	12	51	251	15	329
Total Population	**33**	**90**	**164**	**68**	**355**		**21**	**59**	**171**	**23**	**274**

place belongs in both sexes to the Indefinite, which probably includes not only wandering nondescripts, but the inmates of asylums, whose caste was not correctly ascertained. The next group, that of Devotees, is necessarily high, as in many cases the affliction is the reason for joining the fraternity. The women are better off in this respect than the men in this category. Thirdly, in both sexes, come the Scavengers, a hereditarily dirty, and often a foul-feeding crew. The Burmese come higher amongst the female groups than on the other side of the table, owing to a high ratio in all four infirmities, with the exception of the deaf mutes. The miscellaneous Vagrants, too, are similarly situated, but owe their position to this infirmity as well as to blindness. The sellers of Betel leaf, who are in many cases agriculturists, show a remarkably high proportion of the blind and leprous amongst the male members of their community, and though the corresponding proportion in the other sex is nothing like as high, the fact that the ratio of lepers is considerably above the average, seems to indicate some uniform predisposition to this malady. The next group, that of the Grain parchers and confectioners, depends upon its deaf mutes for its position in the case of both sexes. The blind are the predominating element amongst the infirm in the category of Genealogists. The Brass-smiths seem to be peculiarly subject to three out of the four infirmities in question, but their eyesight is exempted, and the females, though affected beyond the average in the three cases, do not fall within the 10 groups most afflicted. The Hunters and fowlers, one of the vagrant sections of the community, form the last group which is thus included for both sexes. Then follow, to complete the tale of high ratios in the case of females, the two groups of Barbers and Leather workers, each of which shows a proportion amongst the males above the general average, though not falling within the selected rank. The same remark applies to the two groups included amongst the males, but falling short in their proportion of afflicted females. It should also be noted that the figures in italics signify that the group falls within the 10 highest in their ratio of those afflicted by the infirmity marked in the heading of the column. In illustration of the selection, we may draw attention to the fact that the unfortunate Scavengers and Brass-smiths enjoy this unenviable pre-eminence in three out of the four cases, and the Leather workers in the case of the blind only, whilst the Devotees are prominent in two, of which only insanity is common to the two sexes to that extent. Omitting the Indefinite group, it will be seen that at least four, and probably five, of the rest are of decidedly dirty life, devotees, scavengers, vagrants, hunters, and leather workers, two, the brass-smith and the grain parcher, exercise a very special occupation. Of the whole 12 mentioned in the table, there are four of the insane groups amongst the males and five in the other sex which fall within the 10 at the top of the list for that infirmity. The corresponding figures for the deaf mutes are five and seven; for the blind, eight and six, and for the lepers, six and seven.

Insanity.

The next process is to take the infirmities singly, and see the distribution of the classes affected in the highest degree. Table H. on the next page will show this. In the first section are given the 10 groups containing the highest ratio of the insane. It should be explained with reference to this collection, that two items, the Eurasians and the Pársis, contain less than 100,000 members respectively; but there is a special reason for recognising them along with larger communities. It is that they are the only two with a distinct and predominant foreign strain in their blood, and they are the only two in which education may be said to have really permeated the community, so that both sexes are, comparatively speaking, on an equality in this respect. They thus stand out from the rest, and serve as a landmark, as it were, between the high ratios that we have seen prevail in western countries and the dead level of sanity amongst the masses of the dwellers of the plains in the East. The next point to note in the return under discussion is that amongst the eight remaining groups in this category, the Writers, Herbalists and Traders are found, all of them far above the average in education, as was shown in the last chapter. Still more striking is it to find that amongst the women of the trading castes insanity is much less prevalent than in the other sex, and to note that whilst the latter come high in the ranks of the literate, the former are not far, if at all, above the lower classes. We have then the Brass-smiths, whose occupation is perpetually and indissolubly connected with monotonous noise, which fact may account for their high place amongst the deaf-mute also. The women of this caste do not take an active part in the work, so the prevalence to such an extent of insanity and deaf-mutism amongst them opens out an interesting question of hereditary predisposition to such infirmities. As regards the Musalmáns returned under such titles as Shaikh, Saiad, and so on, it is to be feared that a good deal of the mental alienation returned amongst them is due to indulgence in preparations of hemp, some, no doubt, more deleterious to the faculties than others, but all taken in the most injurious form, that of smoking. The case of the Devotees has been mentioned above, and there is little difficulty in accounting for the prevalence in those orders of mental defect, a quality that is so often regarded by the lay mind as a token of divine interest in the person who manifest it. Finally, the Burmese, who come so high in the list, are said to be as a race more nervous, excitable, and prone to indulgence than the natives of India, as a whole. As they are not distinguished in the returns by any more minute subdivision than that of race, their predisposition to unsoundness of mind is all the more remarkable. It is curious, however, to find the women of the race so high in their ratio, and it is not unlikely that in Upper Burma, where the fair sex is in numerical predominance, a good many have been entered in this category whom greater experience would have excluded.

Deaf-mutism.

The table for deaf-mutes introduces us to an almost new set of people. Writers and Brass-smiths are again present, and, amongst women, the Hunting and fowling castes. In the same sex, too, besides the low life of the latter, we find the Scavengers and the Vagrants, who have the reputation of exceedingly dissipated proclivities. The Mongoloid of the Western Himalaya is here represented, and we have seen that his native tract is peculiarly liable to the infirmity under consideration. The Blacksmith and the Grain parcher, and, amongst the smaller groups not entered in the summary, the Glassblowers and Iron smelters are all groups in which the male workers spend most of their busy hours over the fire, as the Weaver and Oil-presser do

TABLE H.—Showing the Proportion of afflicted Persons per 100,000 of each Sex, in the 12 Caste Groups, in which the Infirmities are respectively most prevalent.

Males.		Females.	
Caste, &c.	No. per 100,000.	Caste, &c.	No. per 100,000.
A. Insane :—*Average*	**33**	**A. Insane** :—*Average*	**21**
1. Indefinite Castes	130	1. Burmese	83
2. *Eurasians*	112	2. Indefinite Castes	79
3. Burmese	103	3. *Eurasians*	69
4. *Parsis, &c.*	91	4. *Parsis, &c.*	57
5. Writers	64	5. Musalmán Races	35
6. Brass-Smiths	48	6. Writers	35
7. Musalmán Races	46	7. Herbalists, &c.	31
8. Herbalists, &c.	45	8. Brass-Smiths	28
9. Traders	42	9. Devotees	24
10. Devotees	40	10. Hunters and Fowlers	24
B. Deaf Mutes :—*Average*	**90**	**B. Deaf Mutes** :—*Average*	**59**
1. Indefinite Castes	194	1. Indefinite Castes	146
2. Grain Parchers, &c.	182	2. Thibetan and Nipáli	104
3. Brass-Smiths	156	3. Grain Parchers	99
4. Blacksmiths	117	4. Brass-Smiths	80
5. Thibetans and Nipáli	114	5. Scavengers	78
6. Scavengers	110	6. Blacksmith	73
7. Weavers	109	7. Miscellaneous Vagrants	73
8. Writers	109	8. Hunters and Fowlers	72
9. Barbers	108	9. Barbers	72
10. Oil Pressers	107	10. Washermen	71
C. Blind :—*Average*	**164**	**C. Blind** :—*Average*	**171**
1. Indefinite Castes	358	1. Indefinite	440
2. Miscellaneous Vagrants	318	2. Scavengers	310
3. Devotees	305	3. Miscellaneous Vagrants	355
4. Scavengers	281	4. Genealogists	285
5. Genealogists	258	5. Servants, &c.	267
6. Betel Leaf Sellers, &c.	224	6. Tailors	256
7. Hunters and Fowlers	223	7. Butchers	252
8. Tailors	222	8. Leather Workers	251
9. Leather Workers	215	9. Burmese	233
10. Traders	212	10. Drummers, &c.	233
D. Lepers :—*Average*	**68**	**D. Lepers** :—*Average*	**23**
1. Betel Leaf Sellers, &c.	144	1. Burmese	54
2. Burmese	131	2. Indefinite Castes	53
3. Indefinite Castes	128	3. Brass-Smiths	46
4. Scavengers	95	4. Field Labourers	42
5. Field Labourers	95	5. Temple Servants	40
6. Oil Pressers	90	6. Scavengers	39
7. Temple Servants, &c.	90	7. Betel Leaf Sellers	38
8. Brass-Smiths	84	8. Forest Tribes	38
9. Genealogists	82	9. Genealogists	35
10. Writers	82	10. Oil Pressers	35

inside the house, and it is worth note that the females amongst the last two groups do not show the prevalence of deaf-mutism to anything like the extent that their mates do, whilst in the former set of caste occupations there is more tendency to equality. Amongst the Writers, too, the females do not appear in the first 10 groups of their sex, though the prevalence of deaf-mutism amongst them is above the average. But the Parsis, who do not reach the minimum population fixed for the table, return a high proportion in both sexes. This distinction may be due to the greater prevalence in this community of consanguineous marriages. There is no explanation apparently for the high ratio of this infirmity amongst the Barbers and Washerwomen.

Blindness. Amongst the blind the Vagrants are again well to the front with the Scavengers. As to the Genealogists, their position is possibly due to the fact that the greater number are returned from Upper India, where blindness is generally more diffused than further south. Some explanation of the same sort may apply to the case of the Leather workers, who are, in addition, uncleanly in food and habits. The Tailors, again, may have their sight affected by their occupation, especially if a large number of embroiderers is included amongst them. It is noticeable that no less than five out of the 10 groups in this section of the table differ in the male column from those that appear on the female side of the return. It is, perhaps, to the higher numbers dealt with in the ratio than to any special or inherent peculiarity of social custom that this discrepancy is due.

Leprosy. Finally, as regards leprosy, it seems that the Commission found that there was no evidence of special predisposition in one caste over another, but that prevalence was generally determined by locality. This opinion appears to be confirmed by the results of the census, as summarised in the table under consideration, with the qualification that the higher ratios are found, as a rule, amongst the lower and poorer castes. The Genealogist, and in the case of males only, the Writer, are exceptions to this rule, and the latter seems to indicate a tendency on the part of the higher or more educated castes to conceal the existence of women and girls thus afflicted. The figures for the Bráhmans and Goldsmiths are in favour of this hypothesis. The Burmese, it will be noted, stand high both in males and the other sex, but, as mentioned above, for the purposes of this table, they cannot be taken on the same footing as a comparatively restricted item, such as the Indian caste, or other occupational or social group. It does not seem advisable to enter into further analysis here in the case of a disease of which so little is known, and regarding which the returns are possibly inaccurate.

CHAPTER VIII.

THE POPULATION ACCORDING TO SEX.

"Oh! Fruitful grief, the world's disease!
And vainer man, to make it so,
Who gives his miseries increase
By cultivating his own woe."—*Cotton.*

Of the many problems that come to light in the course of reviewing the results of the census of an Indian province, none is more perplexing than that of having to account for the varying proportions of the two sexes in different parts of the country. The general outlines of this question as it arises in connection with the present enumeration can be appreciated from the following table, in which are shown the proportions under discussion, both in India and in certain foreign countries in various quarters of the globe. In the case of the former, too, the corresponding figures for 1881 are added.

TABLE A.—Showing the general Proportion of the Sexes.

I. INDIA.						II. FOREIGN COUNTRIES.			
Province, &c.	Females to 1,000 Males. 1881.	Females to 1,000 Males. 1891.	Province, &c.	Females to 1,000 Males. 1881.	Females to 1,000 Males. 1891.	Country.	Females to 1,000 Males.	Country.	Females to 1,000 Males.
Panjáb	847	854	Bengal -	1,010	1,006	England and Wales	1,064	Spain	1,038
" States	828	834	" States	961	970	Scotland	1,072	Portugal	1,091
Kashmér	—	879	Bombay -	955	951	Ireland	1,029	Denmark	1,051
Sindh	833	831	" States	943	956	France	1,005	Sweden	1,065
Khairpúr	826	814	Baroda	917	928	Belgium	1,005	Norway	1,071
N.-W. Provinces	918	923	Haidrabád	968	963	Holland	1,023	Canada	929
" " States -	896	912	Mysore	1,007	991	Germany	1,043	United States (White).	961
Oudh	946	949	Coorg	775	804	Prussia	1,037	United States (Coloured).	993
Rajputána	849	891	Madras	1,020	1,022	Bavaria -	1,049	Chilé	1,000
Ajmér	851	881	" States	1,012	996	Saxony	1,059	Japan	977
Central India	896	912	Upper Burma	—	1,084	Austria	1,044	Victoria	909
Central Provinces	984	998	Lower "	877	892	Hungary	1,015	New South Wales	830
" " States	970	984	**Total, Provinces**	**962**	**965**	Bulgaria	965	South Australia	872
Berár	936	942	**" States**	**922**	**932**	Switzerland	1,040	Queensland	706
Assam	949	942	**INDIA -**	**956**	**958**	Italy	995	New Zealand	856

Except in Italy, where the proportion of females is a little below that of males, and in Bulgaria, which borders on Asiatic conditions, every country in Europe returns more of the former sex than of the latter. In North America immigration from the Old World tends to lower the ratio of the fair sex, but amongst the coloured population of the United States, who were largely indigenous at the census of 1880, there is a nearer approach to equality. The five last countries on the list are given merely to illustrate the results of immigration in new colonies. But in India, as we have seen, immigration is an insignificant factor in the constitution of the community, and, nevertheless, to every 1,000 males there are returned only 958 females. Put in another way, the tables show us that there are in the country fewer females than males to the number of, speaking roundly, 6¼ millions. The table given above indicates how irregular is the distribution, territorially speaking, and from the marginal extract it will be seen that of the deficiency, by far the greater part is to be looked for in the northern portions of India. In the three provinces of Bengal, Madras, and Upper Burma alone, do we find the females in excess, and the aggregate number by which they surpass the males in those tracts is but something under three quarters of a million. The above remarkable discrepancies must represent a state of fact or a state of feeling. That is, the difference between the two sexes in point of numbers must be real, and thus due to some general and widespread cause, natural or social, or else it must exist only in the census returns, and be due to the estimation in which women are held by their male relatives. It is better to consider the latter before entering into the other, which is a more contentious matter. In the third chapter of this work, on page 73, it was stated that the census return appeared to be deficient as regards young women and unmarried girls of nubile age, and that the tendency to conceal these classes at the time of enumeration was stronger in Upper India than in the rest of the country. In addition to this sentiment, there is also the inclination on the part of some classes of householder, not, moreover, of any special position in society, high or low, to assume that an inquiry such as the census, instituted by the Government, is very unlikely to be applicable to individuals of so little public importance as girls and women, so that the latter are simply ignored in making the return, without any intent to deceive. Then, again, there comes the third section of the community, who are open to suspicion in this respect, and that consists of the small settlements of forest tribes in the wilder parts of some of the hill tracts, who deliberately conceal the number of their women, not on either of the grounds above-mentioned, but from mere ignorant apprehension of what may follow the acquisition of this information by persons outside their tribe. In nearly every province are traces to be found of one or other of these motives, resulting in the omission of a certain number of women and girls between the ages of about 10 and 20. But though this feature in the returns is noticed by the Superintendents concerned, few or none of them are inclined to attribute to omission the whole of the difference between the numbers of the two sexes. For instance, in the Panjáb, where, as the above extract shows, the deficiency is greatest, to accept the hypothesis of omission as the sole cause of the above result, is tantamount to asserting that one woman in five escaped enumeration. Looking at the proportions of the sexes in the different grades of society, as shown in the caste statements, it is clear that the deficiency runs through the community, and is found, accordingly, to an almost equal extent in the jealously-guarded household of the local magnate and in the hut of the scavenger, or the mat wigwam of the wandering fowler, whose wife and daughters pass their lives in the open air. In the North-West Provinces, again, it seems to be much the same, though in the absence of the views of the Superintendent it is inadvisable to pronounce a general opinion on the matter. It is to be remembered, however, that in the review of the results of the census of 10 years back, the then Superintendent was of opinion that the omission of women had been very considerable, amounting to nearly all the deficiency. The Census Commissioner for India, too, Sir W. Chichele Plowden, who had personally superintended the census of the Province in question on two occasions, seems to lay more stress on the chance of omission than upon any other cause for inequality in the respective numbers of the sexes. We have, moreover, the undoubted fact that in the majority of cases, the increase during the intercensal decade is shown to be larger in the case of females than in that of the other sex. If the irregularity of rate of advance be very marked, it is reasonable to suppose that a good deal of the excess amongst the females is attributable to more accurate return. If, on the other hand, the rates be not far from identical, it is very doubtful if we should at once jump to the above conclusion. As will be seen below, the subject of sex is a very intricate one, and the more one studies it, the less inclined is a cautious statist to adopt any single explanation. To quote the report on the Panjáb census again, wherein Mr. Maclagan has gone carefully into this important question, it would be more probable that women would be omitted by Musalmán householders than by those with whom the anxiety to ensure seclusion and privacy is less prominent, but the returns prove that the proportion of women

Province.	Females in Defect.
Panjab, &c. -	2,030,027
Kashmér -	162,506
Sindh, &c.	278,955
N.-W. Provinces	1,728,566
Rajputána	690,874
Central India -	472,260
Bombay	453,107
Ajmér - -	34,292

in the exclusively Musalmán tracts is higher than that in the country occupied by Sikhs or Hindus, as the predominant element. Again, the staff available for enumeration was very much better and more intelligently supervised in the centre of the province than in the Himálayan valleys, but the proportion of women brought on to the record was far higher in the latter than in the former. To take an instance in the opposite direction, namely, that of a province in which, as a whole, the female element predominates, in Madras, Mr. Stuart finds reason for believing the omission of females to have taken place to a very small extent in the important tracts in which the general ratio is reversed. He shows that, as in the Panjáb, the relative paucity of women is not confined to the higher, or any other, caste groups, but that it has a tendency to increase amongst the forest tribes of the hill tracts in the north-east of his charge, and to be more marked in the Deccan districts than in those further south. He also shows from the marriage returns that the omission is to be found chiefly amongst the married women. As regards Bengal, Mr. O'Donnell shows that the slight excess of females, taking the province as a whole, is to be found in the west and south only, not in the north and east, and he is not of opinion that in the two last-mentioned divisions of his large and varied charge the deficiency is due to omission at the enumeration, but mainly to local causes and possibly also to the strongly marked racial differentiation of the people, on which comment was made in the fifth chapter of this work. It is certainly very well worth notice that whilst in Oudh and the adjacent tracts of the North-West Provinces there is so great a difference in the numbers of the sexes to the disadvantage of the female, in Bihár, both north and south, that sex should have been found to be in excess far beyond the extent that could be accounted for by the temporary migration of the males to the tracts further to the east. Such a distinction seems to add weight to the argument of the North-West Province census officers that in the case of their charge the deficiency of women is only discoverable in the returns, more especially as the caste-table indicates the omissions to be relatively more numerous amongst the agricultural castes of the military and formerly dominant rank, than in any other portion of the community. It is amongst such classes that the privacy of domestic life is most jealously guarded. Where, on the other hand, the absence of the feminine element from the census return is the result of contempt, or disregard of the importance of the sex in comparison with males, the sentiment is not confined to particular ranks, but generally permeates the whole community; for it is more or less closely connected with the political atmosphere of the country, the lower the form, or, as has been said, the formlessness, of the government, the greater the degradation of women under it. Now, in this respect, the whole country may be said to be uniform, and the affairs of the many have always been in the hands of the few, so there is little reason why one tract should differ from another, so far as the neglect to recognise the position of women is in question.

We must inquire, accordingly, whether there are any special reasons for believing that the deficiency of women in India is a fact, and due to a social cause, such as the neglect, if not the actual murder, of young girls, or to a normally greater mortality amongst this sex than amongst the males, or, finally, to an initial shortness in the supply.

Female infanticide.

Now, it is pretty certain that the deliberate putting to death of female infants is a practice that in the present day, at all events, is confined to exceedingly narrow limits. In former times, no doubt, amongst the Rajpúts and other castes of high social position, it was not by any means rare, and, as we know, its prohibition formed one of the three cardinal tenets inculcated on the leaders of Panjáb society by Sir John Lawrence. In the north of India to the present day, too, certain castes are "under observation" with reference to it, but these are in anything but high ratio to the masses of the people. In the central districts of the Panjáb, for instance, where, as we have seen, the proportion of females is abnormally low, Mr. Maclagan finds reason to suspect that the Jats and other chief constituents of the Sikh community are by no means yet free from suspicion in regard to this offence. But, on the whole, even in Rájputána, the census returns show that the practice must be very restricted in its operation. It is only natural that it should be so, considering that the same results can be obtained by means equally efficient, and not rendering the exponent thereof obnoxious to the suspicions of State officials. The expense of maintaining an infant of either sex is comparatively little; and it is not until, in the castes in question, the arrangements for finding a husband have to be begun that the girl is at a discount. It must be remembered that wherever the Brahmanic system prevails, the main object is to get a husband for one's daughter of higher rank than oneself, whereas the son can honour, in like manner, an inferior family without mésalliance. If a girl dies, therefore, before she arrives at the age when caste custom demands that she should be betrothed, so much the better for the family resources. Many a girl is allowed to die unattended where medical aid would be at once called in if the son were attacked. But this is a cause which is operative in the case of the well-to-do classes only, and is not likely to have serious effect on the census returns of the masses. We have, therefore, to look for another. The age returns show us that in by far the greater part of the country girls predominate numerically over boys during the first few years of life. Whether they do so on entering this vale of tears is a question which will be glanced at later. But in the next five years, taken as a whole, the boys pass them, and the ratio of girls again falls in the five years ending with the fifteenth. In India, omitting from consideration the irregularities of return at the multiples of five, in later life, the Nadir of the female is reached at this period, and in most of the European countries for which normal statistics are available, there seems to be the same tendency. The ratios in France and Germany are excluded for obvious reasons. Now, it has been said that the period in question is diminished at both ends by undue additions to its neighbours. In India, the parents of a girl of marriageable age return her as below it, if she be not betrothed, and above it, for some reason, if she be married, but living with them. In Burma, Mr. Eales holds that the girls return their age as over 16, when they are really below 15, in order that they may escape the consequences of elopement, which is a mode of initiating an engagement by no means uncommon amongst that frisky population. In the same way, in England, it is said to be not uncommon for girls of that age to exaggerate it in order to make themselves out the more eligible for domestic service. The Indian figures, as set forth in Table B. below, do not bear out the hypothesis of over-statement in the case of girls really between 10 and 15, but returned as below the first-mentioned age, except, perhaps, in Berar, to some extent. The period between 15 and 20 yield figures more difficult of appreciation. In the first place, no doubt a good many women as well as men return their age as 20, when it is not more than 19 or even 18, but this practice is more prevalent amongst those of the former sex. Then, too, the omission to return wives, if it exist, is most likely to affect this period than that which precedes,

Mistakes in returning ages.

TABLE B.—Showing the Number of Females to 1,000 Males at each Age.

Age Period.	INDIA.	Bengal.	Madras.	Bombay.	N.-W. Provinces.	Oudh.	Sindh.	Panjáb.	Central Provinces.	Assam.	Upper Burma.	Lower Burma.	Berar.
Under 1	1,020	1,055	1,048	1,016	969	995	932	971	1,014	1,022	1,116	1,024	1,011
Total under 5	1,038	1,081	1,053	1,049	1,018	1,028	959	926	1,076	1,046	1,051	1,014	1,071
5–9	936	951	990	942	900	911	815	845	978	978	1,030	978	1,024
10–14	795	803	871	795	747	761	650	738	830	801	999	884	820
15–19	930	1,031	967	923	815	804	734	887	947	1,074	1,166	1,030	1,047
20–24	1,071	1,187	1,214	1,057	965	1,008	926	869	1,176	1,155	1,065	908	1,195
25–29	989	1,072	1,077	925	947	1,004	856	906	1,083	990	1,052	798	941
30–34	962	1,021	1,093	938	938	978	828	791	977	909	1,054	708	886
35–39	867	882	874	848	891	910	682	921	945	709	993	702	766
40–44	940	982	1,010	945	937	1,011	869	789	891	842	1,082	781	825
45–49	845	878	853	849	866	892	752	855	843	705	1,029	797	714
50–54	993	1,049	1,100	995	994	998	851	705	958	850	1,189	943	838
55–59	908	1,013	907	871	932	884	704	830	1,049	755	1,152	914	744
60 and over	1,187	1,307	1,217	1,218	1,203	1,177	950	774	1,289	1,012	1,416	945	1,033
Total	**958**	**1,006**	**1,022**	**951**	**923**	**949**	**831**	**854**	**998**	**942**	**1,084**	**892**	**942**

TABLE B.—Showing the Number of Females to 1,000 Males at each Age—*continued.*

Age Period	Ajmér.	Rajputana.	Central India.	Kashmér.	Baroda.	Haidrabad.	Mysore.	England and Wales, 1881.	Scotland, 1881.	Ireland, 1881.	Italy, 1880.	Sweden, 1880.	Austria, 1880.	Hungary, 1880.
Under 1	1,012	1,006	980	1,002	1,015	1,072	1,057	998	962	952	956	975	1,001	990
Total under 5	986	977	1,036	988	1,060	1,076	1,054	1,003	976	971	964	976	1,011	1,000
5-9	897	876	915	895	911	959	1,027	1,006	976	977	966	978	1,004	1,003
10-14	765	752	721	733	781	796	898	997	968	957	959	980	1,011	1,012
15-19	816	783	822	876	828	1,038	905	1,008	994	1,040	1,025	990	1,043	1,124
20-24	965	964	1,016	1,033	1,002	1,174	1,098	1,093	1,063	1,060	1,017	1,084	1,046	1,173
25-29	847	863	967	965	921	910	994	1,087	1,105	1,120	1,027	1,066	1,032	1,007
30-34	860	903	900	921	912	983	986	1,077	1,117	1,161	1,027	1,097	1,067	1,045
35-39	805	836	852	810	851	762	867	1,069	1,161	1,128	1,015	1,113	1,055	957
40-44	915	949	882	888	964	917	907	1,079	1,166	1,128	1,010	1,118	1,050	1,000
45-49	691	811	788	715	852	706	852	1,103	1,204	1,047	996	1,113	1,072	950
50-54	945	952	960	763	957	961	1,050	1,104	1,215	1,095	1,020	1,134	1,146	1,097
55-59	706	824	890	683	834	749	960	1,111	1,224	1,058	986	1,144	1,104	1,001
60 and over	1,085	1,146	1,190	766	1,156	1,158	1,246	1,187	1,377	1,075	980	1,289	1,068	1,022
Total	**881**	**891**	**912**	**882**	**928**	**964**	**991**	**1,055**	**1,076**	**1,043**	**995**	**1,061**	**1,047**	**1,030**

or that which follows it. Both these causes tend to reduce the proportion of the women in the period in question, and there is also to be taken into consideration the probability mentioned above, of the omission altogether of a girl of this age who has not been provided with a husband, or who, in Upper India, is attached in some intimate capacity to the zanána of the richer classes. But in addition to these artificial reductions of the number of the females of this age, it is not at all improbable that there is a real deficiency, due to the fact that amongst the great majority of the population the five or six years in question include the first child-bed, an occurrence notoriously dangerous to female life, especially where the wife is as immature, physically, as she too often is in India, and where the obstetric methods in vogue there tend to restrict survival to the fittest only. It must be borne in mind that at this time of life no less than 83·30 per cent. of the women are married, whilst only 36·80 of the males are in the same condition, and in spite of the general deficiency of the former sex, which here amounts to over 850,000, the wives are more than twice the number of the husbands. Carrying this train of inquiry back to the preceding period, where the disproportion is, as observed above, at its height, we have included but a year, or, at most, two, of possible child-bearing, but the arrival of the girl-bride at puberty, an event that is almost invariably accompanied with certain ceremonial rites of a somewhat exciting character, and which entails also other demands on the constitution, which are not, in the circumstances, duly recognised, must have its weight in considering this question. The discussion that arose in the course of last year's legislation regarding what is commonly known as the "age of consent," amply shows that the practice of premature cohabitation is more or less local, or restricted to certain castes, as is indicated by Mr. O'Donnell in his report on the Bengal returns of marriage, but none the less is this period a critical one for girls in India, if only on the ground of the demand on the nervous system, for we find that irrespective of the second and later part of the conjugal arrangement in that country, out of the 13 millions or so girls between 10 and 15 years of age, 49½ per cent. are married in the Indian acceptation of that term, and nearly 1½ per cent. are widows. The conditions under which the other sex has to struggle onwards at this time of life are far less importunate on the constitution in this respect, for only 15½ per cent. are husbands, and less than ½ per cent. widowers. Entirely apart, therefore, from any question of concealment or other cause of omission, and of errors in statement of age, so extensive and remarkable a divergence of practice between the two sexes in reference to such an important and universal factor in social circumstances as marriage is not at all likely to be without its influence on the distribution of the sexes at the periods under discussion, and this influence, if admitted, must inevitably be cast on the side of the results indicated in the returns of both the last enumerations.* It is not worth while to pursue the analysis of the return in detail, because the preference shown, especially by the fair sex, for the even multiples of five, which has been mentioned already as a grave defect in the age tables, grows more and more apparent with age, and even if we adopt the simple method of combining two periods, as from 25 to 35, and so on, the curve is still "backed like a camel" from the age of 24 downwards. The general tendency, however, in India, as in many other countries, is for the women who have safely weathered the period of early childbirth to outlive the men, but there are exceptions to this rule, as in Sindh, Kashmér, the Panjáb, and, curiously enough, Lower Burma. Then, too, there is no doubt but that the age of the old women are exaggerated, and that, though their life is certainly somewhat better than that of men in advanced years, the difference is not so great as that indicated by the returns. It is obvious, again, that so far as the masses are concerned, the wear and tear of woman's life is much the same in India as that of the man's. She shares in most agricultural operations, barring those in which the plough is concerned, carries the grass and firewood to market, and is largely concerned in all general labour, particularly of the class in which the outside of the head bears the brunt of the toil. There is a strong probability, accordingly, that the deficiency shown irregularly between the ages of 35 and 55, has to some extent a foundation in fact. Amongst certain classes, too, as Mr. O'Donnell points out, remarkable prolificity in the prime of life tends to wear out the the woman at a comparatively early age, and the distribution of the Musalmán population of Eastern Bengal is cited as a good instance of this. In the table on page 179 of the Bengal Report the statistics in question are shown side by side for Hindu and Musalmán. The proportions are slightly in favour of the latter between 10 and 30 years of age, after which period the decline in the case of the convert is remarkably swift, and after 60 years of age, there are but 951 Musalman women to 1,000 males of that faith, whereas the Brahmanic classes number 1,179. The general tendency amongst forest tribes seems to be in the same direction. The women are on an equality at least, numerically, with the men, up to a certain age period which oscillates between 35 and 45, after which the hard work of semi-savage existence, rather than the pain and peril of childbirth, has its revenge. In nearly every province, too, the age tables, even in their uncorrected state, show that amongst Indian women, as elsewhere, but to a more marked extent, the time at which the change of life takes place, which is generally between 40 and 45, is a very critical one.

Climate and Nutrition as influential in sex-distribution.

The above resumé of some of the more obvious factors affecting the distribution of sex in India does not, it may be noticed, take into consideration the influence of two elements to which there is no doubt but that some weight should be attached. The difficulty with regard to them is that they are not mutually exclusive, and the sphere of their influence is, at best, but vaguely definable from the available data. The factors in question are, of course, climate and nutrition. A review of the whole field of statistics resulting from the census inquiries seems to afford ground for the following deductions, which, however, are not put forward for the present as more than conjectural. The ratio of females to males, taking the whole population in existence at one time, has a tendency to be higher along the coast or within the influence of sea air, to an extent beyond what can be accounted for merely by the temporary absence of a certain number of males at sea. It runs higher, too, in hilly tracts, as a rule, than on the plains, and it seems to be depressed by a dry and hot climate, particularly if accompanied by a considerable range of temperature. On the other hand, we find traces of the influence of nutrition, which in some cases may fairly be held to neutralise that of climate. It is difficult to prove beyond a doubt any of the above tendencies, for the reason given in the beginning of this chapter, that in the determination of sex so many factors probably

* It is not improbable, too, that the prevalent custom as regards dress may be prejudicial to female vitality between 5 years old and 10 or 11; since, as a rule, when children take to clothes at all, the boy wears only a jacket, but thus covers all above the waist; but the girl wears only trousers or a petticoat, and leaves the more vital organs unprotected.—J. A. B.

enter that, in the present state of information, the relative influence of each cannot be accurately discriminated. Then, again, in a country like India there must be anomalous cases in every such conjecture, which obscure the view of the operation of the general rule, if one there be. A few instances of this may as well be cited nere, to show the difficulty of dealing adequately with the subject. The coast tracts are, as a rule, highly fertile, so that the general predominance of females in their population is attributable to good nutrition as well as to climate or situation. But where we get a comparatively ill-nourished population in this tract, as in the case of Ratnagiri, on the west coast, and thus eliminate one unknown quantity, we only find that a second is to be tackled, in the shape of the emigration of males to other scenes of labour. In the Panjáb, again, there is a hot and dry tract lying adjacent to Sindh, but the ratio of women is not at its lowest there, but in a fertile and highly cultivated triangle further north, the population of which are suspected of unfair treatment of the weaker sex. Then in Sindh the ratio is at its lowest, and the country is hot and dry, but it cannot be said that there is any failure in the food supply of the province, so unless we accept inaccurate enumeration as responsible for the whole of the inequality, there is clearly some important factor not as yet ascertained. In Rájputána, where the improvement in accuracy between the two enumerations is more marked than in any other part of India, the lowest ratio was not in the desert, but in the fertile plains bordering on the Jamna, where the existence is suspected of causes probably not dissimilar to those that prevail in the Central Panjáb. The inconsistency between Bihár and the upper portion of the Gangetic basin in this respect, has been already brought to notice. Then as regards Bengal, where there is no sterile and no dry tract, for the Chútia Nágpur plateau falls within the belt of light but certain rainfall, further complications enter the problem. Admitting, with Mr. O'Donnell, that the zone of deficiency of females corresponds with that occupied by races of Mongoloid parentage, we have to ascertain whether the difference is inherent in race or attributable to artificial causes, such as that of extreme fecundity and consequent high mortality amongst women at a comparatively early age, for climatic considerations have clearly nothing to do with the case, and those of nutrition tell in a direction opposed to the facts, since, so far as Eastern Bengal is concerned, the standard of living is above that of South Bihár. The tide of immigration in this province sets from west to south-east, so the birthplace returns should throw some light on the conditions. On eliminating the immigrants, it seems that in both Northern and Eastern Bengal the ratio rises from 966 to 996 and 989 respectively, but is still far from the corresponding figure for the rest of the province. But in Assam, again, we find the same deficiency of females as in Eastern Bengal, for, deducting the immigrant population, the ratio is only 969 of that sex to 1,000 of the other, and here, too, the deficiency is in the fertile valleys, not amongst the hill population. This seems to point to some conditions common to this province and its neighbour, probably social or physical rather than racial. In Madras, the difference between the Deccan population and that of the south and west as regards the proportion of females is very marked. Mr. Stuart has shown that it extends to all castes, and points out how a Tamil caste, such as that of the traders (Chetti), returns a considerable excess of females whilst the class exactly corresponding to it in Telingána (Kómti) is in the reverse position. It is the same with both higher and lower castes than this, but it does not seem necessary to invoke racial characteristics to explain the discrepancy, as there is strong differentiation in both climate and nutrition which may account for it. There are two curious facts noted by Mr. Stuart in dealing with this interesting subject. First, that it is the general belief amongst the people of the southern tracts of the Presidency that 50 or 60 years ago there were fewer women than there are now, and that whereas formerly wives were at a premium, in the present day they have to be accompanied by a dower. The returns show that it is true that in those parts the proportion of unmarried women of 15 years of age and upwards is higher than it is in the Deccan districts. Then, again, so far back as the beginning of the century, no less competent an observer than Sir Thomas Munro found ample reason for agreeing with the popular belief in the "Ceded Districts" that there were only nine women to every 10 men. He tested the accuracy of the statement by personal investigation in different parts of his charge, and satisfied himself that, taking the whole of the tract together, the men were in excess of the other sex. Assuming this fact, the higher proportion of women now returned seems to argue in favour of the nutrition theory. We are met, however, by a case supporting the opposite conclusion in the Gujaráth division of Bombay, where the ratio of females is lower than in the Deccan, in spite of the general fertility of the tract and its accessibility to sea air. It is noticeable, however, that the ratio tends to descend in a northward course, and as in that direction the tract is bounded by Sindh and Rajputána, where the great deficiency of the sex cannot be wholly attributed to anything but inaccuracy of return, it is probable that a good deal of the Gujaráth discrepancy also can be accounted for in that way. In Burma there is a great difference between the two divisions as regards sex distribution, as in the upper province females are largely in excess, whilst in the lower they number no more than 892 to 1,000 males. It appears, however, that the latter ratio is due to immigration and temporary sojourners, amongst whom the ratio of females is 694 in the case of those from Upper Burma, and only 230 amongst the Indian-born. The birthplace tables show that the home-born have a preponderance of females, as in the upper province, and that along the coast the ratio is generally higher than inland. In no case, however, does it reach that of the newly-acquired territory, of which a few frontier districts in the north and east, where no doubt there is an influx of temporary visitors from the Shán hills, are the only ones that do not return a considerable excess of females. To some extent this is accounted for by the fact that whilst this tract was under Burmese sovereignty, emigrants to British territory were forbidden to take their women with them, and since annexation, there being no restriction, the proportion of females to 1,000 males in that class has risen from 598 to 694. This movement does not, however, suffice to wipe out the distinction between the two divisions of the province, so that, on the whole, the case tells slightly adversely to both the climatic and nutrition hypotheses.

Summary.

To summarise what has been said above, it seems that in most parts of India proper there is a tendency, in a greater or less degree, to omit from the census record girls of from 9 to 15, and wives of from 15 to 20, or thereabouts, but that in every part of the country, except the north, girls below five years old were returned as more numerous than boys of that age. After that period, apart from wilful or ignorant omission, there is probably a real deficiency in the number of females, extending to about the twentieth year, more or less, and due to neglect, functional excitement, premature cohabitation, and unskilful widwifery. At a later period, hard work, as well as the results of the above influences, and, amongst some classes, excessive fecundity, tell on the female constitution, producing greater relative mortality than prevails in the other sex, though towards the end of life the latter succumb to old age sooner than the survivors from amongst their mates. It is also probable that either from difference or inferiority in nutrition, or from climatic influences, female life is, on the whole, better in India on the coast and hills than on the hot and dry plains.

Sex at birth.

So far we have treated of the circumstances that affect the distribution of the sexes amongst those actually in existence. There remains the question of whether the census throws any light on the determination of sex during the "nine months' ante-natal gloom."* Here we tread on delicate ground. In one of the more recent works on the subject the authors say:—

> "The number of speculations as to the nature of sex has been well nigh doubled since Drelincourt in the last century brought together 262 'groundless hypotheses,' and since Blumenbach quaintly remarked that nothing was more certain than that Drelincourt's own theory formed the 263rd. Subsequent writers have, of course, long ago added Blumenbach's Bildungstrieb to the list; nor is it claimed that the generalisation we have in our turn offered has yet received 'final form,' if that phrase, indeed, be ever permissible in an evolving science, except when applied to what is altogether extinct."

The hypothesis in question, as stated by its authors, is that—

> "Such conditions as deficient or abnormal food, high temperature, deficient light, moisture, and the like, are obviously such as would tend to induce a preponderance of waste over repair,—a *Katabolic* habit of body,—and these conditions tend to result in the production of males. Similarly, the opposed set of factors, such as abundant and rich nutrition, abundant light and moisture, favour constructive processes, *i.e.*, make for an *Anabolic* habit, and these conditions result in the production of females. With some element of uncertainty, we may also include the influence of the age and physiological prime of either sex, and of the period of fertilisation."

Now, in India, as in Europe, the male births everywhere exceed the female, and, looking at the diversity of ratio between the two in countries where registration is fairly accurate and complete, there is no reason to suppose that in the tracts we are now considering, there is more than a slight degree of incompleteness in the data for females as compared with those for the other sex. That there is some failure in this respect is admissible, though, as some of the Superintendents have pointed out, the information is not furnished by the parents of the newly-born infant in rural tracts,

* Geddes' and Thompson's "Evolution of Sex."

but obtained indirectly by the accountant, who knows every house in his charge, and has no more interest in returning boys than girls. Where the vicissitudes of season are very considerable, one must expect to find great irregularities in the birth ratio, and in the case of a large proportion of the masses the average standard of nutrition is decidedly low. The best examples of birth registration are given in the Madras Census Report, and, amongst other noteworthy features, they exhibit the peculiarity of containing the highest ratio of male births in the tracts where the general proportion of that sex is the lowest, and *vice versâ*. The confirmation these returns lend to the theory above quoted is very slight, still there does appear to be in them some ground for holding that male births have the tendency to increase relatively to those of females as the amount of nutrition gets lower, and to decrease, conversely, as times improve. There is, again, the question of how far the respective ages of the parents affect the sex of their offspring. The evidence collected by statisticians in Europe on this point begins with the results of the inquiries by Sadler and Hofacker, who held that the greater the distance between the age of the parents, the higher the chance of the offspring being male. Since 1830, however, investigation on this line has been extended over wider areas and larger collections of people, with the result of severely shaking our faith in this theory. At all events, the statistics with which we have to deal at present do not seem to give fruitful results. Finally, there is the supposed tendency of inherited volition. Where a population has special reasons to desire male or to deprecate female children, it has been said by some that a high preponderauce of male births will probably ensue. But such an influence can only be a feeble one, for the reason that its extension would in time tend apparently to the extinction of the race!

In conclusion, the information on sex distribution in India furnished by the census inquiries indicates that, as in most other countries, more boys are born than girls, but owing to the very much higher mortality amongst the former during the first year of life, the latter predominate in number until their vitality begins to be affected by special sexual influences from which the male is free, so that throughout almost the whole of the prime of life the females are to a greater or less degree in defect, and the balance swings back only towards the end of life, when the total number is insufficient to restore numerical equilibrium.

CHAPTER IX.

The Population by Civil Condition.

" For what secures the civil life
But pawns of children and a wife ?
That lie like hostages at stake,
To pay for all men undertake ;
To whom it is as necessary
As to be born and breathe, to marry.
So universal all mankind
In nothing else is of one mind ;
For in what stupid age or nation
Was marriage ever out of fashion ?
Unless———————————."—*Butler*.

As in the case of languages to the philologist, so as regards the study of the branch of ethnology that concerns itself with marriage custom, there is no field more varied and worthy of research than that presented by the population of India. It is but a minute corner of that field, however, that lies within the sphere of exploration to which the census is restricted. A return of the people by civil condition was first required at the enumeration of 1881, and the inquiry was followed up on as far as possible identical lines in 1891. The instructions for filling up this column in the schedule ran as follows :—

1881.	1891.
Young boys and girls who may have been married should be entered as married, even though they may not have actually begun to live with their wives or husbands. A male or female whose first wife or husband has died should be entered as widower or widow, unless he or she has married again, in which case he or she should be entered as married.	Enter each person, whether infant, child, or grown up, as either married, unmarried, or widowed. This column must not be left blank for anyone, of whatever age. Children who have been married should be entered as married, even though they may not have actually begun to live with their wives or husbands. Persons who have been married, but have no wife or husband living, should be entered as widowed. The enumerator must accept the statement made by the person, or, in the case of children, by their relatives.

The inquiry was thus limited to the simple question of whether the individual was single, married, or widowed. It was above all things necessary to avoid the appearance of any undue curiosity on the part of the State as to domestic details, hence the prohibition at the end of the rules of any controversy on the subject on the part of the enumerator who had to fill up the schedule. The statement of the person concerned was to be taken as final. There are certain special difficulties, however, in obtaining even the apparently simple information sought for under the above instructions. Several of the census Superintendents note one or two points in which there has been confusion of condition. For instance, in Assam, though there are plenty of words for widow, and a special word for bachelor, none was found, in the Bráhmapútra valley at least, for widower, so the two classes of men who had not a wife living, whether they had had one already or not, were sometimes entered under one head, and, curiously enough, that of widower. Where, too, there are special colloquial terms for the widow who has married again, it was sometimes held that the general word ought not to be used, so the second ceremony was ignored, and the wife entered as a widow, or, in Assam, where the case is particularly prominent, under the special title. On the other hand, some men who had lost their wives, are said to have been returned as married, especially if still in the prime of life. The question, again, of how to enter the divorced arose in some parts of the country. In Burma, where the institution is most in vigour, there is a recognised term, which was returned without hesitation. In India proper, though in every form of creed prevailing there the separation of husband and wife, under certain formalities, is condoned or permitted, the *status* is by no means recognised by either sex. It was the intention of the rule above cited that such persons should be entered amongst the widowed, as they had been married, but at the time of the census had no partner living. The distinction, however, was too subtle for the commonalty, and in many parts of India, even those where divorce is not rare amongst the lower classes, the former *status* was returned, and both parties appeared amongst the married. This is not the case, it seems, in some of the hill tracts, where the number of widowers and widows is clearly due to the freedom of closing the conjugal union otherwise than by the strong measure of leaving the world. Finally, in almost every section of the lower classes, particularly where the caste rules regarding marriage expenses are stringent, there are numbers of cases in which the wife is one in fact only, but not united by any of the bonds of ceremonial which play so leading a part in the system at large. This practice of permanent concubinage is necessarily confined to those whose property is either insignificant or of a nature not likely to form the subject of a disputed succession. The woman is returned at the census as married, and as often as not the man who entertains her has lost his legitimate wife, and has thus every title, according to his standpoint, to enrol himself in the same category. We have also to deal with the converse case, of the wife who has, and never had, any husband, but who was formally wedded to a dagger, a fig-tree, or bunch of flowers, in order to give her the more dignified *status*. The above constitute the main points with regard to which the statistics now to be reviewed are to some extent untrustworthy, but, speaking generally, the distribution of the population under the three heads of married, single, and widowed, can be accurately gauged by them. It should be mentioned here that Table VIII. in Volume I. of the Imperial series excludes the population for which these details are not available by reason of the omission from the schedule of the column referring to civil condition. The balance, however, amounts to over 262½ millions, the largest population for which this class of statistic has hitherto been collected.

But though the amount of information thus obtained serves the purpose for which it was intended in connection with the census, especially as it has been tabulated in combination with age, and in some Provinces and States with caste also, its comprehensiveness tends to level the diversity and to obliterate most of the distinctions in which the ethnologist delights to revel. Not to go beyond very general topics, we find in the returns comparatively little that is new on the subject of polygyny, save that it is almost entirely restricted to the richer members of the Musalmán community, on the one hand, and to sundry hill tribes of the Central Belt and the north-east Frontier on the other. The extent to which it exists amongst the Brahmanic sections of the people must be very slight, though we are aware of the fact of its legality, and know that cases are not rare in which a second wife has had to be introduced into the family circle, owing to the failure of an heir by the first. Taking the whole of India, without Burma, there are seven in every thousand Benedicts who have more than one wife. The provincial statistics are liable to be disturbed by migration of married men for the season, as well as by the custom, in so many parts of the country, if not universally, for the wife to return to her father's house for her first childbed, as well as by the custom of dancing girls, &c. to return themselves as married, though their spouse was a dagger or graven image. Balancing the omission of young wives mentioned in the last chapter against the widows and others shown as married, though living in concubinage, the excess of wives over husbands seems to be greatest in the south of India, where it is estimated to amount to nearly 40 per 1,000. But here, too, there is a general excess of women, and it is possible that the census of this sex was more accurate than in neighbouring tracts. In Upper India, where the proportion of wives to husbands is in remarkable contrast to that of women to men as a whole, there is no doubt polygyny to a small extent amongst the richer classes, as stated above. In the Central Provinces, where the sexes are generally much on an equality in point of number, there is a remarkable difference between the forest tribes and the rest of the community in regard to the excess of wives over husbands, showing the prevalence of polygyny amongst the former to the extent of more than even the Madras ratio, and touching, in some cases, 60 in the 1,000. In the neighbouring province the same feature is found.

Polygyny.

Polyandry.

In the opposite direction, too, India has its examples to bring forward of polyandry, or the plurality of husbands. In its patriarchal and simplest form we find it in the Himálayan valleys, chiefly wherever the food supply of the surrounding country is scarce. It is found in the north-west amongst both Buddhists and Brahmanic tribes, so it is not attributable, in these tracts, to religion, though we find it cropping up again at the eastern end of the Himálaya amongst the latter. But in the Panjáb, certainly, if not elsewhere, the custom of the marriage of one woman to the whole family of brothers is on the wane, and is growing to be regarded as disreputable. Peace and plenty may have as much to do with this change of sentiment as conviction. In the northern plains of India, again, there are traces of this custom in certain tribes, and even in the south of the Deccan, Mr. Stuart has heard of its existence amongst a subdivision of the great Reddi caste. But the great stronghold of polyandry in Southern India is on the Malabár coast, where it prevails amongst many of the more numerous castes of different social positions. It probably originated, so far as these castes are concerned, with the Nair, or ruling community on that coast, who follow the matriarchal form, not that of the Himálaya. Here the succession is through the female, and the rules thereof somewhat complicated. In fact, the census officer for the Travancore State considered that the term married was not of itself sufficient to denote that condition in a population under the "Marumakkathayam" system, as the husband by marriage is not the husband by consummation, nor is the wife of the male member of the community the woman to whom he has been united by marriage rite. It is proposed that to meet local peculiarities in this respect the present column of the schedule should be expanded to eight, in the case of males, and nine in that of the other and favoured sex.

As a third instance of the special factors that enter into the consideration of Indian matrimony, we may mention the practice of marrying the widows of near relatives. In its most common form, that of the marriage by the younger brother of the widow of the elder, it prevails very widely over the north and east of the country, and is generally mentioned by ethnologists under its Biblically-derived title of the Levirate. It is less common in the centre and south. In the Panjáb and upper portion of the North-West Provinces it has a special name, and the second marriage is duly accounted as such in the returns, diminishing thereby, to a considerable extent, the proportion of the widows. But amongst the polygynous tribes of Assam, according to Mr. Gait, the census Superintendent, the practice extends far beyond its Panjáb limits. For instance, the heir to a Miri estate inherits with it the whole body of his father's wives, which are numerous in proportion to his means, an exception being made, it is well to state, of the actual mother of the successor. The system reaches its climax, some people might think, amongst the Gáro tribe, where the bridegroom, by his marriage, binds himself to the reversion of—shade of Thackeray!—his mother-in-law! "Le monde s'écroule," cries the hero of a recent popular drama," la belle-mère reste!" **Levirate.**

There are several other topics connected with the marriage systems of India, which are not only interesting from the point of view of the ethnologist, but also probably bound up more or less intimately with the wider questions involved in the consideration of this subject, with which alone the census has to deal. The matrimonial bargain, for example, is found in every stage of its progress, from the buying of a wife, which prevails to a great extent amongst the masses throughout India, to the more advanced transaction, in which the husband is bought, a practice in vogue amongst the higher classes only, in some parts of the country, and elsewhere extends to those below who aspire to social distinction by its means. It seems probable, we repeat, that if the field occupied respectively by these two customs were ascertained, it might be found that there is some connection between the mode of contract and the age at which that contract is completed, and thus some additional light thrown upon the distribution of sex, a subject which, as we saw in the preceding chapter, is sorely in need of such illumination. Then, furthermore, it would be interesting, in like manner, to learn how far the custom extends of the father's marrying his son below, and his daughter above, his own rank, a practice connected with the question of dower and bride-gift respectively. Examples of this sort only show how the study of custom ought to be invoked in aid of mere statistics, in treating of wide questions of social importance, such as the marriage system.

For the purposes of the present work, however, we must dispense with that aid, owing to the fact, on which so much stress was laid in the opening chapter, that India is not so much a single country as a continent, so that the collation of such a mass of detail as is available in sporadic form on the subject in hand would entail the preparation of a volume by itself. There are few topics that come within the scope of the census that are less susceptible of being dealt within in Imperial totals than the figures given in Table VIII. and its subdivisions, since the features common to all provinces are prominent, indeed, but subject to such remarkable variety in different territorial subdivisions, that even a province is far too large a tract to be taken as a unit for analysis. In the reports from the Superintendents that have reached the Central Office up to the present time, a chapter is devoted in each case to the consideration of the local statistics, and in some cases the information is supplemented by the valuable experience of the reporting officer of the country concerned, an experience acquired by work and inquiry amongst the people themselves, and not merely derived from standard works of reference. Amongst those that come under this category, the chapters written in the reports on Assam, Bengal, the Panjáb, and Madras are especially recommended for perusal, and to these may be added the corresponding part of the Burma volume, which deals with a marriage system very different from that of the rest of the Indian Empire. Some of the reports on the census of 1881, too, are perhaps even more valuable, since their authors had to work in virgin soil, and were, in this respect, the pioneers of their successors.

General features.

In the present review, all that is proposed is to deduce, as far as possible, from the similarities in different parts of the country, the general type with which the marriage system of the country at large tends to conform, and to indicate, under the same qualification, from the divergency in various directions, the results that seem to ensue from the adoption of that type. To begin with general features only, the following table gives the relative figures of the population in each of the three conditions for the 16 main territorial divisions of India. To make more apparent the difference between the East and the West in this respect, the corresponding return for a few European countries are added.

Table A.—Showing the Distribution by Civil Condition of 10,000 of each Sex.

Country.	Males.			Females.		
	Unmarried.	Married.	Widowed.	Unmarried.	Married.	Widowed.
India, 1891	4,873	4,647	480	3,389	4,851	1,760
„ *without Burma*	*4,852*	*4,668*	*480*	*3,339*	*4,883*	*1,778*
1. Madras	5,387	4,269	344	3,724	4,361	1,915
2. Bombay	4,514	5,021	465	3,027	5,273	1,700
3. Bengal	4,756	4,826	418	3,111	4,826	2,063
4. N.-W. Provinces	4,483	4,854	663	3,037	5,259	1,704
5. Oudh	4,557	4,891	552	3,160	5,239	1,601
6. Panjáb	5,265	4,106	629	3,750	4,877	1,373
7. Sindh	5,836	3,653	511	4,185	4,426	1,389
8. Central Provinces	4,668	4,890	442	3,560	4,960	1,480
9. Assam	5,622	3,968	410	4,138	4,162	1,700
10. Berár	3,838	5,588	574	2,635	5,769	1,596
11. Ajmér	4,839	4,653	508	3,355	5,094	1,551
12. Haidrabád	4,383	5,204	413	2,932	5,270	1,798
13. Baroda	4,323	5,158	519	2,997	5,517	1,486
14. Mysore	5,390	4,138	472	3,636	4,249	2,115
15. Upper Burma	5,603	3,884	513	4,947	3,574	1,479
16. Lower „	5,563	3,980	457	5,136	3,927	937
1. England and Wales (1881)	6,193	3,463	344	5,928	3,314	758
2. Scotland	6,628	3,044	328	6,285	2,896	819
3. Ireland	6,871	2,750	379	6,344	2,698	958
4. Austria	6,151	3,554	295	5,771	3,416	813
5. Hungary	5,603	4,090	307	4,941	4,050	1,009
6. Sweden	6,233	3,411	356	5,958	3,233	809
7. Holland	6,237	3,392	371	5,940	3,317	743
8. Italy	5,989	3,610	401	5,397	3,672	931
9. Portugal	6,232	3,362	406	6,040	3,119	841

Now, one of the first points that will strike one in the above figures is that in Europe, omitting Hungary, which has a tinge of Orientalism about it, at least 60 per cent. of the males, and of the females nearer that proportion than 50, are unmarried. In India, if we include Burma, which in this matter is less different than in others from the rest of the country as to its male population, no more than 48¾ of that sex are single, whilst the females in this condition come only just above the third. Burma, so far as its single population is concerned, is remarkably similar in its ratio to Hungary, and shows a very much higher per-centage of unmarried women and girls than any other part of India. We may pass on to the married, leaving territorial diversity for future consideration. In Europe, on the whole, about one-third of the men, and a slightly lower proportion of the women are paired off, whilst in India

46½ per cent. of the one, and about 48½ of the other are in that state. As to the widowed, the distinction between Europe and India, though marked enough amongst men, where the proportions are 3·5 against 4·8 per cent., is extraordinary when we compare the figures for the other sex, since where there are eight widows in the temperate zone, there are not far from 18 in the tropics. Looking at the difference in the three conditions proportionately for the two continents, and using round numbers only, it may be said that India is behind Europe in its proportion of unmarried men by about 24 per cent.; that it exceeds the latter in that of the married of the same sex by 46 per cent., and has relatively about 36 per cent. more widowers. As regards females, Europe is 43 per cent. ahead in the matter of spinsters, 48 per cent. behind as to wives, and at least 122 per cent. to the worse—numerically—for widows. That is, men in India are largely, and women very largely, given to matrimony as compared with Europeans, with the consequence that in both sexes the widowed are in far higher proportion.

The marginal table (B.) shows the distinctions in another light, namely, the average number of females to a thousand males in the same civil condition. In Europe, for instance, the unmarried women are usually less in number than the bachelors, though, except in Hungary and Italy, the deficiency is but trifling. In India, on the other hand, they reach but two-thirds of their possible mates. In the case of the wedded, the general excess of wives over husbands in Europe, not being explicable by polygyny, is attributable to migration of husbands, leaving the wives at home. It is also not an unusual occurrence for a woman to describe herself as married at the census, when, in fact, the bond is less durable. In India, as has been explained above, there is a certain amount of polygyny, and also of the concealment of wives. In a few cases, too, migration is undoubtedly to be taken into consideration in connection with this point, as in Madras and Oudh, where the excess is considerable, and, on the other hand, in Assam, Ajmér, and Lower Burma, in which the immigration is of married males only. The excess of husbands in Berar is attributed in part to under-enumeration, but the same feature in Haidrabád and Baroda has not yet been explained, and is certainly remarkable in its extent. The sex proportions amongst the widowed vary more than the rest, as might be expected from the different rules that prevail in India regarding the second marriage of women who have lost their husbands In Europe, there seems to be an average of 2,500 widows to 1,000 widowers; in India the mean proportion is about 3,570, which is considerably above that found in Hungary, the tract most abnormally situated in this respect, in the West. France and Germany have been left out of the table purposely, since the figures for 1880 were affected by the losses of male life 10 years previously. It is worth notice in passing, that of the Indian provinces, Madras, Mysore, and Haidrabad show very high proportions, which may be in some degree attributable to the accidental cause of famine, a calamity before which, as has been remarked already, the so-called stronger sex seem to fall sooner than the

TABLE B.—Showing the Sex Proportion in each Condition.

Country, &c.	No. of Females to 1,000 Males.			
	Unmarried.	Married.	Widowed.	Total.
India, 1891	670	1,005	3,533	963
„ *without Burma*	*663*	*1,007*	*3,568*	*963*
Madras	707	1,044	5,702	1,022
Bombay	637	998	3,480	951
Bengal	658	1,006	4,962	1,006
N.-W. Provinces	625	1,000	2,375	923
Oudh	658	1,010	2,756	949
Panjáb	608	1,014	1,863	854
Sindh	596	1,006	2,260	831
Central Provinces	761	1,012	3,340	998
Assam	693	989	3,903	942
Berar	647	973	2,619	942
Ajmér	611	965	2,688	881
Haidrabád	645	976	4,204	964
Baroda	643	977	2,654	928
Mysore	668	1,016	4,433	991
Upper Burma	957	998	3,126	1,084
Lower „	823	880	1,830	892
England and Wales (1881).	1,009	1.014	2,297	1,055
Scotland (1881)	1,020	1,023	2,688	1,076
Ireland (1881)	963	1,023	2,640	1,043
Austria (1880)	982	1,006	2,882	1,047
Hungary (1880)	844	1,007	3,347	1,017
Sweden (1880)	1,014	1,005	2,413	1,061
Holland (1879)	975	1,001	2,048	1,023
Italy (1881)	897	1,012	2,314	995
Portugal (1878)	1,058	1,013	2,263	1,092

more patient. We have, then, Bengal, where the high ratio is due to the local marriage system, and Assam, where the same cause prevails throughout the more populous tract of the province.

We have now elicited two main facts regarding the marriage system in India; first, the abnormal prevalence of marriage, and, again, the abnormal inequality of the sexes in the condition of widowhood. To the discussion of these, then, with their causes and consequences, the rest of this chapter can be more especially devoted.

Prevalence of the married.

As regards the general tendency towards matrimony, it has first to be seen what are the influences that operate with less force in India than in Europe in repression of the mating instincts of humanity. The first is obviously the cost of the process. The charge of recklessness in regard to the assumption of the responsibilities of family life is too often made without considering the relativity of the imputation, and the only recklessness involved is on the side of those who cast the stone. Looking at the difference in the conditions, it is hardly straining language to say that the line between prudent and improvident marriage is more often overstepped amongst the masses in parts of the United Kingdom than it is in India, relatively, of course, to the respective populations. In the latter country, the material necessaries of life, measured in labour, cost but little. The standard of life, as distinguished from bare subsistence, although it shows signs of rising, is still remarkably low, and, as we have seen in the second chapter of this review, the question of building site and accommodation scarcely enters into the question, and clothing is much in the same stage. There are possibly cases, but they are so rare that they only serve to illuminate the general uniformity, in which the labour of a healthy adult does not suffice to provide food for a wife and child as well as for himself. Then, too, at this point, another factor enters into the calculation. Throughout the masses, and it is with them alone that we must deal in this matter, the wife is in every way the helpmeet of her husband, and the sooner she enters on her functions the better for his material comfort. Either she actually works at the family occupation or one of her own, or else a share of the domestic duties being taken by her off the hands of the bread-winner, he is enabled to devote more attention or time, or both, to his special avocation. This relief is, in India, no slight consideration, even though the duties in question be restricted to cooking, fetching water, and cleaning up the pots and pans used in those processes. Every section of the community, so far as general experience goes, seems to have some other with which it cannot mingle and whose touch is pollution to food or drink. There may be somewhere a bottom to the ocean of caste, and probably the European and Chinaman lie very near it, but, as a rule, the distinction is passed down as far as the inquiry is likely to follow. There is no field, therefore, for the public cook-shop, except in towns, or where Musalmáns abound. The time and ceremonial spent in preparing meals is everywhere considerable and amongst some castes proverbial, in witness whereof we may cite the Hindustani saying, "eight Bráhmans, nine cooking-places." It is thus essential that a man who is in the field all the day should have someone to cook and bring his food; so, too, with the artizan, who has his loom, furnace, or tan-pit to attend to. The modern savage, says Mr. Risley, wants a sturdy young woman who can carry his baggage, cook his food, collect edible grubs, and make herself generally useful, and *mutatis mutandis*, with a bit of the higher animal thrown in, this very fairly represents the whole duty of woman throughout the lower grades of Indian society. It will be seen that in these circumstances, the chief motive for prudential restraint is removed almost beyond sight. We come, next, to another side of the case, which was briefly touched upon in the third chapter. The ease with which a man can provide for a wife, the help and comfort he derives from her presence in his home, and the natural wish to leave behind someone to take his place in the world and carry on his name and tradition, all these, it may be thought, are incentives enough to matrimony; but in India, at least amongst the classes most strongly impregnated with Animism, to the realised expectations of this life is added the inducement of improving by a fertile union one's chances in the next. In Madras, writes Mr. Stuart, the strong tendency to marry has little to do with religious sentiment. This may be true, so far as the orthodox Brahmanic view of the destination of the childless adult is in question, but in the popular belief, the spirit of such an individual, so far from being safely encaged, to his own discomfort, in "the Hell called Pút," is found to be exceedingly vicious and importunate in his visitations to his relatives still on earth. Burying him face downwards fails to keep him below ground, and when he has once got up, strings of leaves, and even silver nails, are insufficient to distract his inconvenient attentions.

Then, again, there is the more tangible ground of objection that if the childless man was in possession of any property, the application to the case by the courts of law of rules of inheritance framed entirely on Brahmanic principles, or on custom stereotyped under the neo-Brahmanic influences, might turn out detrimental to the next of kin. Therefore, we may say with Panurge, it is evidently necessary that a man should marry—in India, that is. Now, let us take the case of the women, which, from the census point of view, is more important, and, sociologically, more interesting. In considering this part of the subject, we must first clear the way by assuming or rejecting the hypothesis that was put forward in the last chapter, namely, that the deficiency in the return of women is due in some degree to an actual shortness in numbers, not solely to omissions from the schedules. If fewer girls, relatively to the other sex, reach a marriageable age, the less, of course, is likely to be the proportion of those left unwedded. The greater the difference in age between husband and wife, the higher, in the ordinary course of events, is likely to be the number of the widows. The examination of the circumstances in the case of the male section of the community, which has just been made, indicate how high is the probability that a girl, at some time or other of her life, will find a partner, and whether she is at a premium or subject to discount is a matter of conventionality only. Now, whatever the laxity of the hold that Brahmanic views on social questions, so far as men are concerned, may have on the popular mind, there can be no doubt as to the influence of such tenets in the case of women. It is superfluous to go over again ground already traversed in Chapter V., but it will be borne in mind what was therein laid down as regards the pervading atmosphere of Brahmanic notions, and how they had grown into a standard, as it were, of respectability in certain social features of the community. In marriage custom above all is this perceptible, for the conventionality on which it is based has its root amongst the sex to which, as in other countries, it is of the most importance, so it is by his conduct as regards marriage that the social aspirant is wont to be judged. It is noteworthy that it is in respect to marriage and widowhood that we can appreciate the advance of Brahmanism amongst the forest tribes of the Central Belt. It is amongst the highly orthodox tribes of the western Jamna basin that the Panjáb Musalman preserves all his former customs. Further south, the Telingána population, which received Brahmanism in a fresher form than that which it assumed on its diffusion amongst the Tamils, surpass the latter in their orthodox adherence to the more striking parts of the Brahmanic system, and contain castes which in these respects are said to be more Bráhman than the Bráhmans. The more southern Dravidians, on the other hand, as Mr. Stuart points out, seem to have rejected all of the above-mentioned system that did not chime in with the most honoured of their own customs, and though orthodox in proportion to their position in society, the general level is decidedly below what strict adherence to the Purán would require of them. Now, it is time to see in brief what are the demands of orthodoxy in respect to marriage. It is evident that in the earliest days of which we have even faint record in Aryan history, the girl was left to be courted pretty much as amongst the forest tribes of the present day. She could be won by prowess in athletic games, in war, or by gambling, and could likewise be gambled away or carried off by force or fraud, or otherwise disposed of. But, from what motive it is hardly necessary to inquire, the Brahmanical framers of the Puranic codes conceived a dislike to the position of an unmarried girl, and when they disliked anything they damned it with more than Athanasian comprehensiveness. Thus we read that "the mother, father, and elder brother of a girl, who let her reach puberty unmarried, go to Hell," the precise section of the locality is not mentioned, but it is probably not the same as that reserved for the childless man. The girl was in a parlous state already, from which marriage alone could rescue her, so the act of omission doubtless made it advisable to separate the family, at least by sexes.*

Prohibitio of widow-marriage.

Then comes the question of widowhood, on which much has been written, but nothing need be quoted here, as the injunctions on the subject are apparently of still more modern origin than those respecting the marriage of daughters, and leaving out of question the Bráhmans themselves, such precepts have no currency amongst the people, save what they derive from their value as rungs of the social ladder. But it is none the less apparent that the forbearance from marrying a widow is the first sign, in most parts of the country south and east of the Panjáb, of the intention of severing oneself from a former unregenerate condition, and becoming incorporated in a higher section of the Brahmanic community. In many parts of Upper India, where the Levirate is in

* This was written before I had seen the controversy on the subject between Drs. Jolly and Bhandárkar, with their exposition of the chances of misinterpretation of the text in question.—J. A. B.

vogue, the thin end of the wedge is the restriction of the marriage to the widow of one's elder brother, but amongst the masses of the people of Central and Southern India, apart from the explicable avoidance of half-worn articles when new are to be had and their price is available, a widow of under 20 years of age has a very fair chance of a second husband, and Wellerism is rampant only amongst the very exclusive, or those who wish to be thought so. But we are speaking of the present day, and unfortunately the rise in the standard of living, which has been mentioned more than once in the course of this review as having ensued upon the state of peace and firm government of the last 30 years or so, has wrought a change in the views of those whom it affects, as regards matrimony. It has been said, on the one hand, that amongst the well-to-do classes, such as Bráhmans and Writers, the taste for high living has led to the postponement of marriage amongst the men, because they cannot get enough whilst quite young to support a wife and keep up their standard of luxury, but against this it may be shown, with some reason, that if there be any signs of such postponement, it may be equally attributed to the rise in the price of food, and, in towns, of house rent, both of which hit the recipients of fixed salaries or cash payments, harder than the rest of the community. At all events, the class in question is a very small one, and is by no means backward in letting the public have an opportunity of sympathising if the world does not go quite smoothly with it, so that if the inability to comply with any conventionality that the caste dictates had caused inconvenience, the foundations of the empire would surely have been shaken ere now, in the usual way. But a far more serious development of the Brahmanic system is indicated by some of the Superintendents in their census reports, and that is the strong tendency in the present day of peace and plenty to manifest their prosperity in the way mentioned above, firstly, by prohibiting the marriage of widows, and then by insisting upon carrying out strictly the Brahmanic injunction above quoted, and save themselves from the place to which the law-maker consigns them, by getting all their girls married before they have reached womanhood. Many cases have occurred within recent years to show that any movement amongst the literate classes in the direction of the abrogation of these two precepts is but mouth deep, whilst their heart is with the observance of them to the utmost. *Longum iter per precepta ; breve et efficace per exempla*, but when opportunities occur for carrying into practice amongst themselves or their families some of the reforms they have been so strenuously endeavouring to impose upon others, it is remarkable to note what an amount of filial piety and of deference to the feelings of those to whom their respect is due comes into play, to prevent them from becoming martyrs to their principles. On the other hand, amongst the castes below the Bráhman and Rájput, who have no education, and make no pretence of being sensible of any defects in their social system, we find continual attempts to conquer society by proving their claim to recognition through the adoption of these very tokens of high rank which, by the admission of many who observe them, are blots on the social arrangements of the community, which it is the duty of men of light and leading to suppress. Thus, whilst the mouth is proclaiming its enlightenment and progress, the trunk is waddling backwards as fast as the nature of the ground will permit.

Age, in connection with the marriage statistics.

This brings us to another section of our subject, and one which is, perhaps, the most important, namely, the relationship between age and the general system on which marriage is regulated in India. This can be exhibited in two forms. First, to put it tersely, the distribution of each condition by age, and, secondly, that of each age by civil condition. In anticipation of the final compilation of these statistics, and as an aid in the review thereof by the census Superintendents, the information collected at the enumeration of 1881, together with that for a good many foreign countries regarding which statistics bearing on this point were available, was reduced to a uniform proportional basis in the central office, and circulated to the officers concerned. It will be found, accordingly, that in all the Provincial and State reports, use has been made of this resource in dealing with the return for the special tract under review. It is superfluous to reproduce here the figures aforesaid in their entirety, as they cover about 10 pages of closely printed matter, but extracts will be given where relevant to the point immediately under discussion.

It must first be remarked with regard to these statistics, that whereas those for European countries begin at the 16th year, it is necessary to carry back those for India to a far earlier age, for reasons that, if they cannot be surmised from what has already been said in this work, will be abundantly illustrated by the selected proportions given in the margin on next page. Here we have the number in 10,000 of the single, married, and widowed respectively of each sex, who are less than 15 years old. Whilst in the European countries, except in Hungary, less than 60 per cent. of the single of either sex fall within this age, in India more than three-quarters of the males and over 94 per cent. of the females have not attained it. Put otherwise, in India only 23 out of every 100 bachelors, and only six out of the same number of unmarried women are over 15 years old. Then, again, as to the married, we find 5 per cent. of the husbands, and $13\frac{1}{2}$ per cent. of the wives are below the age at which the tables for European countries, except those of Austria and Hungary, begin. The proportions of the widowed, too, are very different in the two series. The male ratio, again, in India, it will be noted, is higher than that of the juvenile widows owing to the more frequent remarriage of the former in riper years.

TABLE C.

Country, &c.	Proportion under 15 Years old of 10,000 in each Condition.					
	Males.			Females.		
	Single.	Married.	Widowed.	Single	Married.	Widowed.
India	7,681	506	167	9,432	1,360	111
„ *without Burma*	*7,712*	*518*	*171*	*9,514*	*1,391*	*113*
Burma	6,752	4	2	7,617	15	4
Scotland	5,802	—	—	5,536	—	—
Ireland	5,299	—	—	5,327	—	—
Germany	5,821	—	—	5,956	—	—
Austria	5,631	—	—	5,783	2	—
Hungary	6,665	—	—	7,476	13	2
Holland	5,718	—	—	5,823	—	—
Italy	5,461	—	—	5,866	—	—
France	4,937	—	—	5,301	—	—
Sweden	5,449	—	—	5,256	—	—
Portugal	5,761	—	—	5,270	2	—

We can look at the figures at this age from another standpoint, namely, the distribution of the people of this age, according to their civil condition, irrespective of the relation they bear to their elders in the same condition. The following table

TABLE D.

Country, &c.	Number in each Condition of 10,000 of each Sex under 15.						Proportion of Females per 1,000 Males in each Condition.		
	Males.			Females.					
	Single.	Married.	Widowed.	Single.	Married.	Widowed.	Single.	Married.	Widowed.
India	9,390	590	20	8,247	1,702	51	822	2,703	2,369
„ *without Burma*	*9,373*	*606*	*20*	*8,195*	*1,752*	*52*	*811*	*2,702*	*2,368*
Burma, Upper	9,997	3	—	9,989	10	1	1,027	—	—
Burma, Lower	9,995	4	1	9,982	17	1	960	—	—
Scotland							974	—	—
Ireland							968	—	—
Germany				10,000	—	—	998	—	—
Holland							993	—	—
Sweden	10,000	—	—				978	—	—
France							989	—	—
Austria				9,998	2	—	1,009	1 : 53	—
Hungary				9,985	14	1	1,006	1 : 55	—
Italy				9,999	1	—	953	—	—
Portugal				9,998	2	—	968	1 : 8	—

shows that comparison with countries in Europe is, in this respect, useless, as at the age excluded from their tables, India returns nearly 6 per cent. of the boys and 17 per cent. of the girls as married, with a certain proportion of widows and widowers. As before, Hungary and Austria show a few girls married and widowed, and Italy still fewer, showing that Juliet and Saint Elizabeth have their successors, but the highest of the numbers returned by these countries is insignificant. The concluding section of the table simply compares the sexes as distributed between the three conditions in India. It shows that to every 10 husbands under 15 there are 27 wives, and to every 10 widowers about 24 widows, whilst the unmarried girls would be less by about one in every five.

The above three series of comparative figures serve to set forth more prominently than those already given earlier in the chapter one of the most remarkable points of difference between the East and West, that is, the prevalence in the former of juvenile marriage, with its complement of early widowhood. There is a second point which is well worth notice here, namely, the prevalence of marriage at all ages, of which mention has been made both here and in a previous chapter. The following table, accordingly, shows the distribution of 10,000 of the unmarried of each sex within and beyond the period of which we have just been treating.

TABLE E.

Age Period.	India.		Scotland.		Germany.		Austria.		Italy.		Hungary.	
	Males.	Females.	Males.	Females.	Males.	Females.	Males.	Females.	Males.	Females.	Males.	Females.
0—9	5,715	8,059	—	—	—	—	—	—	—	—	—	—
10—14	1,966	1,373	—	—	—	—	—	—	—	—	—	—
Total, 0—14	*7,681*	*9,432*	*5,802*	*5,536*	*5,821*	*5,956*	*5,631*	*5,783*	*5,461*	*5,866*	*6,665*	*7,476*
15—39	2,170	510	3,768	3,642	3,834	3,523	3,915	3,538	3,959	3,483	3,169	2,382
40—49	84	28	201	319	159	209	212	288	253	266	90	78
50 and over	65	30	229	503	186	312	242	391	327	385	76	65

The figures speak for themselves. The average proportion of the unmarried males, which falls in Europe within the first 15 years, is contained in India in the first 10. The next period, 15 to 40 years, comprises what is in India the prime of life, corresponding, no doubt, to 20 to 45 in Europe. Allowing for the difference of age in reaching maturity and beginning to decline from it, the discrepancy between the two series is not excessive in this sex, but in the next periods, omitting Hungary, the proportion of bachelors in Europe is remarkably higher than that in India, owing partly, of course, to abstinence from marriage, and partly to the superior "staying power" of the European, after passing the prime of life. But when we look at the female side of the table, the difference is enormous, and no readjustment of the age periods will suffice to obscure the preponderance of married women in India at the reproductive ages, and, after 40 years of age, the almost entire absence, relatively speaking, of women who have never entered that condition. It is worth while, perhaps, to illustrate this fact a little more fully, by making use of a table corresponding to the second of those given above in connection with the population of less than 15 years old. The following statement, then, shows by series at four age periods, the relative number in each of the three conditions, with the average number of females to 1,000 males of the same age and condition.

TABLE F., showing the Number in each Condition of 10,000 at certain Age Periods above 15, and the relative Number of Females therein.

Country, &c.	A.—Between 15 and 25 Years old.								
	Males.			Females.			Number of Females to 1,000 Males.		
	Single.	Married.	Widowed.	Single.	Married.	Widowed.	Single.	Married.	Widowed.
India	4,879	4,948	173	806	8,709	485	167	1,775	2,841
„ *without Burma*	*4,798*	*5,029*	*173*	*662*	*8,849*	*489*	*139*	*1,774*	*2,848*
Scotland	9,275	716	9	8,623	1,360	17	954	1,949	—
Ireland	9,660	334	6	9,107	877	16	989	2,752	—
Germany	9,649	348	3	8,754	1,231	15	929	3,624	5,030
Austria	9,541	456	3	8,202	1,775	23	898	4,064	7,298
Hungary	8,331	1,653	16	5,416	4,461	123	696	2,888	8,341
Italy	9,462	532	4	7,870	2,100	30	849	4,082	4,772
Holland	9,536	460	6	8,943	1,047	10	937	2,271	3,025

Country, &c.	B.—Between 25 and 40 Years old.								
	Males.			Females.			Number of Females to 1,000 Males.		
	Single.	Married.	Widowed.	Single.	Married.	Widowed.	Single.	Married.	Widowed.
India	1,106	8,407	487	149	8,191	1,660	129	928	3,248
„ *without Burma*	*1,091*	*8,424*	*485*	*134*	*8,189*	*1,677*	*117*	*929*	*3,302*
Scotland	3,431	6,366	203	3,274	6,339	387	1,074	1,120	2,147
Ireland	5,221	4,636	143	3,767	5,832	401	819	1,429	3,191
Germany	3,148	6,735	117	2,411	7,241	348	806	1,131	3,123
Austria	3,230	6,665	105	2,626	7,029	345	860	1,116	3,486
Hungary	1,337	8,501	162	741	8,475	784	563	1,014	4,906
Italy	3,399	6,441	160	2,152	7,457	391	646	1,181	2,485
Holland	3,534	6,329	137	2,978	6,795	227	869	1,108	1,711

Country, &c.	C.—Between 40 and 50 Years old.								
	Males.			Females.			Number of Females to 1,000 Males.		
	Single.	Married.	Widowed.	Single.	Married.	Widowed.	Single.	Married.	Widowed.
India	410	8,596	994	185	5,612	4,203	228	593	3,916
„ *without Burma*	*408*	*8,595*	*997*	*96*	*5,560*	*4,344*	*214*	*588*	*3,961*
Scotland	1,457	8,016	527	2,001	6,680	1,319	1,626	986	2,963
Ireland	2,095	7,471	434	1,869	6,760	1,371	977	990	3,460
Germany	944	8,712	344	1,134	7,632	1,234	1,287	838	3,838
Austria	1,194	8,516	290	1,484	7,321	1,195	1,338	925	4,437
Hungary	470	9,091	439	375	7,467	2,158	779	802	4,797
Italy	1,366	8,169	465	1,279	7,398	1,323	941	909	2,856
Holland	1,432	8,184	384	1,496	7,693	811	1,070	962	2,164

Country, &c.	D.—Fifty Years old and over.								
	Males.			Females.			Number of Females to 1,000 Males.		
	Single.	Married.	Widowed.	Single.	Married.	Widowed.	Single.	Married.	Widowed.
India	306	7,497	2,197	86	2,452	7,462	299	350	3,635
„ *without Burma*	*302*	*7,498*	*2,200*	*76*	*2,387*	*7,537*	*270*	*340*	*3,662*
Scotland	1,140	7,069	1,791	1,961	4,282	3,757	2,236	787	2,726
Ireland	1,388	6,848	1,764	1,514	4,408	4,078	1,174	683	2,490
Germany	765	7,400	1,835	1,092	4,896	4,012	1,634	757	2,501
Austria	962	7,482	1,556	1,388	4,909	3,703	1,584	720	2,613
Hungary	353	7,806	1,841	269	4,750	4,981	767	611	2,716
Italy	1,096	7,144	1,760	1,165	4,938	3,897	1,056	686	2,198
Holland	1,083	7,096	1,821	1,270	5,333	3,397	1,295	830	2,061

The figures in the first period, that of the early prime, bear much the same testimony as those of the preceding one, though in a more striking degree. Half the men are married and nearly 2 per cent. have already lost their wives. The women show nearly 5 per cent. widowed and 87 married. In Europe about 85 per cent. are still single, and not more than 15 per cent. are married. Hungary, of course, is exceptional. To an Indian statist there is always a sense of comfort in reaching this stepping stone between the primitive figures of the East and the dead level of sweet reasonableness found in the more regular returns of Western Europe. As regards the subsequent periods, it will be seen how the tendency in the case of males is much the same in the West, as in India, though the degree in which it is manifested is far lower. The married men rise in proportion up to 50 years, and then decline in much the same ratio in both hemispheres. The widowers rise gradually to the end of life in India, but in Europe, though the course is the same, the rise, after 50 years, is more marked and more sudden. There is, of course, more divergence in the case of the other sex. The wives begin to decline at 40, and after 50 only a quarter of the women are still mated, and the rest are widows, the proportion never married being negligable. In Europe, on the other hand, the proportion of wives follows that of husbands more closely, and amongst the elders scarcely two-fifths are widows, though the ratio of the unmarried is very much higher than it is in India at any age above 10. The results of the inequality can be appreciated from the sex proportions in the last three columns of each section of the table. We need take little account of the single in connection with the point in question. As to the married, owing to the unions being early amongst both sexes in India, the ratio of wives to husbands, between 15 and 25, is only about 18 to 10, which is far below that prevalent in Europe. In the course of the next period the Indian curves for the two sexes, if the details were set forth by diagram, would be seen to cross between 35 and 40, as many young widowers have remarried, whilst widows are not in demand. In Europe, taking account of later marriages, emigration, and the general tendency from various causes of males to be in defect at these ages, the balance is slightly in favour of the wives, and the proportion of widows is not far below that found in India. Single women, too, are, as in India, at their lowest. We next find a very rapid fall in the latter country between 40 and 50, in the proportion of wives, with a slight one in Europe; and the proportions in the widowed, too, correspond in relative variation, both in direction and degree. Finally, the same distinctions are accentuated in later life, and the divergence in India between the numbers of husbands and wives, widows and widowers respectively, is far greater than in the West, and the unmarried women everywhere, save in Hungary, outnumber the bachelors.

This is all that can be said in the present work about the distinction between the marriage system of Europe and that of India, taking the latter, as a whole. We have now to devote attention to the diversity of practice found in different parts of that country, and, as the subject is one which involves the analysis of a very large amount of detail, far beyond the scope of a general review like this, it is proposed to direct the inquiry chiefly towards the two most important questions only, namely, the relative prevalence of juvenile, or, as it is sometimes termed, infant, marriage, and its complement, the prevalence of widowhood, amongst the two sexes respectively; for, as we have been shown in the tables already given, there is little of the nature of equality between the two. Men, as a rule, marry as early, and remarry, as their circumstances permit. The destiny of the women is regulated by custom, and, more distantly, by ideal conventionality, so that greater variety is found in their circumstances than in those of the other sex. The tendency, however, such as it is, lies in the direction, as has been observed above, of earlier marriage and less widow marriage, according to the greater or less attraction exercised on the multitude by Brahmanic influences. Reviewing the whole field of statistics that is opened to us by the census, it seems to be established that in respect to juvenile marriage, and to an extent but slightly less, to widow marriage, the diversity of practice that appears in not only each Province and large State, but in every large subdivision of such units, is due, in the main, to local, rather than to caste or social, custom. We see, that is to say, the lowest grades of the community in some parts of the country habitually marrying at an age below that of the upper ranks in others, not far distant and *vice versâ.* An exception must be made, of course, to this rule in the case of Bráhmans, who, though they may fall in with the local views as to the age at marriage, invariably prohibit, so far as our information is available, the marriage of widows. It will be seen in the comments on each Province, &c. that follow, how far these general tendencies are borne out, but it must be understood beforehand that the age quoted is, as in all cases where this factor enters, only approximately accurate. A few remarks on the territorial diversity at the principal age periods will not be out of place in connection with this part of the subject. The Imperial tables begin with the return of those under five years old. Of these, only a few over 103,000 boys and 258,000 girls are said to be married, and about 7,000 of the one and 14,000 of the other are returned as widowed. The proportion of the married is abnormally high in Baroda and the Gujaráth States of Bombay, and for this there is the special reason given by the Superintendents in 1881, that in a large local agricultural class it is the rule to contract marriages only once in 12 years or so; every infant, therefore, available at the lucky moment is united to some other, under peculiar regulations, lest the next cycle should begin too late for caste propriety.* In Berar, again, both sexes marry very early, not only in this period but in the next as well. Between 5 and 10 comes the critical time when caste custom is supreme, if the Brahmanical rules be operative. Here Berár comes in an easy winner, with over 35 per cent. of its females wedded, but in the matter of boy husbands Baroda and the Gujaráth States of Bombay are its equals, on account of the continuance of the influence noted above. Haidrabád comes high as regards both sexes, a characteristic, also, of the adjoining tracts in the Madras and Bombay Presidencies; and Bengal, though above the average in both sexes, is more remarkable for the number of its young bridegrooms. The period included between 10 and 15 is, perhaps, the most important of all as regards the marriage of females. It is unfortunate, therefore, that it is also that which, as we have seen in the last chapter, probably includes, to adopt an Irish figure of speech, most of the omissions. Taking the returns as they stand, Berar and Baroda again head the list of males, followed by the North-West Provinces and Oudh, which in this respect overtop the average for the first time. Berar and its neighbour, Haidrabád, crown the female ratio with nearly three-fourths of that sex married, Baroda falling back below Bengal, Bombay, and Upper India. The community under 15, as a whole, such as is given in the preceding tables for all India, presents features which are more useful in considering the case of young men than of girls, for it includes far less of the physically adult in the former case than in the latter. Baroda and Berar are far beyond the rest in their proportion of the married in this period, the North-West and Bengal following. It is superfluous to treat of the rest of the age returns in such detail as the above, so we may take, as the period of maturity, the years between 15 and 40. In this, the average proportion of the married is about 67 per cent. of the males and 85 of the females. Berár again heads the roll with 82 and 89 respectively. Oudh exceeds it as to females, but is far below in respect to males. The ratio of married men is high, again, in the Central Provinces, Baroda, Haidrabad, Bombay, Bengal, and the North-West Provinces, and of married women in much the same area, substituting Sindh and the Panjáb for Bengal. It is in connection with this period that the calculation of the fertility of the population is usually made. With the limited *data* in India this can only be a matter of conjecture. In England and Wales it is probably accurately given as 286 births per 1,000 married women of the reproductive ages. In India the Provincial Superintendents who have touched on this point estimate the figure, variously, between 159 and 317†. At all events the general level of the computation indicates that excessive fertility is not a material cause of the increase of the population, so much as the alternative, that is, the high ratio of married couples. It is superfluous, looking at the limitations we have imposed on the treatment of the subject, to review the higher ages, beyond remarking that Madras husbands are the longest in maintaining their hold on this condition, and, omitting Burma and the Central Provinces, where the forest tribes, whose marriage system is very different, turn the scale, Sindh, Oudh, and the Panjáb have the highest proportion of wives alive after 50. This is the more remarkable, as the husbands in these tracts present the lowest ratios in India. Against an average of 350 wives to 1,000 husbands at this age, we have 456 in Oudh, 439 in its neighbour, 393 in Sindh, and 363 in the Panjáb. On the other side, in Haidrabad, only 268 are shown, in Madras, 287, Mysore, 290, and Bengal, 294.

Widowhood.

We must revert awhile to compare with the above figures for the married, those regarding the widowed. Up to the tenth year the ratio follows, of course, closely that of the married, and Bengal, Berar, Baroda, and Bombay lead the way, and the North-West Provinces and Oudh occupy a higher place than they do with respect to juvenile marriage. The same items appear at the head of the next period, 10 to 15, when, in addition to the immature widows, there is probably a considerable sprinkling of those who have been actually married in the European sense of the term. The highest ratio is found in Bengal, where it reaches $2\frac{1}{2}$ per cent. of the total number

* This caste in Baroda returns as married $82\frac{1}{2}$ per cent. of the boys and $96\frac{3}{4}$ of the girls between 10 and 15, and $51\frac{3}{4}$ and $86\frac{3}{4}$ of those under 10.

† Taking the mean birth-rate at 47·90 per 1,000, and the ratio of married women between the ages of 15 and 40 at 165 per 1,000, the average number of births to each married woman will be 290, or almost identically that of England and Wales, because, against the enormous birth-rate in India, must be set off the remarkable prevalence of marriage.

of girls of this age. In Berar it is 2·13, and Baroda and Upper India fall below Haidrabád. At the riper ages, between 15 and 40, the widow is prevalent in Bengal and Mysore to the extent of 15 per cent. of the women included, and in Madras and Assam to 12½ and 14 per cent. respectively. Widowers, relatively speaking, abound mostly in Berar, and the North-West Provinces and Panjáb. The number of widows to widowers is curiously varied. In Madras it is seven, and in Mysore nearly six times. In Bengal it reaches five, and in Haidrabad and Assam nearly four. Excluding territory much affected by male immigration, the North-West Provinces, Sindh, and the Panjáb show the lowest ratio. It may be presumed that these proportions indicate roughly the inclination towards the marriage of widows in all but Madras, Haidrabád, and Mysore, where the losses of 1876–78 during the famine have not yet been effaced from the return.

Panjáb.

It is now proposed to consider the returns territorially, using much the same material as has been set forth in the preceding remarks, but grouped anew for the main provinces, and illustrated by the comments of the local superintendent in cases where his report has been received. We will begin with the Panjáb, as a province which differs materially from the rest of India in some features of its marriage system. In the first place, throughout the west of the province and amongst certain classes elsewhere, marriage is contracted on the same basis as in Europe, that is, husband and wife begin to cohabit immediately after the ceremony, and there is no juvenile betrothal in those tracts, as is customary amongst a Brahmanic population. The latter prevails in the east and centre of the province, and it is here that juvenile marriages appear most frequently in the returns. There is here strong confirmation of the view set forth in a former part of this chapter that the prevalence of custom in marriage, except amongst Bráhmans, depends upon considerations, not of caste, but of local example, for in the east of the Panjáb, where Brahmanic influence prevails, even the Músalmáns follow the practice of their Hindu neighbours, and *vice versâ* in the west, as is shown by the marginal table. Here we have two districts, one pervaded by orthodox Brahmanic views, the other under Musalmán influence. In the latter the Musalmáns scarcely marry their girls at all under 10 years of age, and the Hindus but rarely. On the other hand, along the Jamna, both religions show nearly 10 per cent. of that age as married. The custom of *Karéwa*, the Levirate, is found in most parts of the province, except amongst a few castes, such as Bráhmans and certain divisions of Rajputs; the Panjáb, accordingly, returns a smaller proportion of widows than most of the larger provinces of India, but still, as Mr. Maclagan points out, a quarter of the Hindu and a fifth of the Musalmán women of 15 years old and over are widowed. There is no doubt that Brahmanic disapproval of the marriage of this class has had some effect on the other religion, wherever the two are on more or less of numerical equality. But, on the whole, the Panjáb population marries at a maturer age, and is less strict as to widow marriage than most other parts of the country, though there is a great difference in this respect between the frontier and western plains and the more settled tracts of the centre and east. The latter tract resembles the general distribution of the population shown in the returns for the North-West Provinces, where the age at marriage is younger than usual. The examination of the returns for other provinces shows, however, the need of local experience in reviewing them, and as this is not at present available, there is little to be said on the subject. There is a return of marriage by caste for this province, which shows remarkable differences in custom, but it has been furnished only for the province as a whole, and without knowing whether the peculiarities are local or not, it is unsafe to draw any conclusions from them, beyond a general remark that religion, as in the Panjáb, appears to be but an insignificant factor in regard to marriage custom where the caste is subdivided into a Musalmán and a Brahmanic section, though the purely Musalmán communities marry, as a rule, later than the bulk of the Hindu population.

——	No. of Married Girls under 10 to 10,000 Girls of that Age.	
	Karnál.	Shábpúr.
Hindu	919	147
Musalmán	824	38

N.W. Provinces and Oudh.

Bengal.

We then come to Bengal, where Mr. O'Donnell has treated the subject in an interesting and valuable chapter, affording much food for reflection. As in the Panjáb, we find locality the main factor in determining the age of marriage, but the tendency to conform more and more to Brahmanic orthodoxy in respect to widow marriage is very marked in this province amongst the castes that are on the borderland of respectability. The enormous population dealt with is subdivided by Mr. O'Donnell into large geographical sections, by which means he shows more clearly how certain customs are purely local, not inherent in the castes that follow them. For example, in respect to the juvenile marriages amongst boys the marginal table gives the proportions in the four great divisions of the province, from which we see how prevalent is this practice in Bihár, as compared to Orissa and Bengal, and how the Brahmanisation of the forest tribes of the Central Belt is making rapid progress. If we take the corresponding return for females, the territorial distinctions are still more marked, and, except in Western Bengal and the two sections of Bihár, the custom of marrying girls below 10 years old is remarkably rare—for India. The contrast between the Brahmanic and the Animistic sections of what is practically a uniform community in Chutia Nágpur is very suggestive, as showing the insidious advance of the former in orthodoxy, as a means of establishing a better social position. But apart from the practical utility of demonstrating how localised is the custom in question, Mr. O'Donnell gives information which must, he considers, overthrow the time-honoured notion of the universality of the prohibition of widow marriage amongst the reputedly orthodox Brahmanic population of the lower Provinces. He finds the proportion of widows to the total female population of between 15 and 40 to be 26¼ per cent. amongst Bráhmans, where it is at its maximum so far as the prohibition in question is concerned, so he takes this figure as the standard whereby to measure other sections of the community. By this criterion, it appears that widow marriage is universal amongst the forest tribes of Orissa and Chutia Nágpur, where only from 5½ to 7 per cent. of the women of the reproductive ages are shown as widowed. The Eastern Bengal Musalmáns and the middle class Hindus of Orissa show but a little higher ratio, but amongst the Musalmáns of Western Bengal, where the Hindus show the high figure of 24 per cent. and over, the proportion creeps up. These deductions are certainly worthy of consideration, though it is, perhaps, inadvisable to adopt them without further scrutiny of the details. For example, it is quite possible that the paucity of widows at the age in question in Bihár may be as much due to the early age at which the boys marry as to the remarriage of young women who have lost their first husbands, since the proportion for Musalmáns is higher than that for Hindus, and we have seen above that the former marry later than the latter in the case of both boys and girls, and the difference is greater amongst the boys, thus indicating the earlier loss of the husband. The details by caste which are given in this chapter of the Bengal report are very full and interesting. Mr. O'Donnell finds reason to attribute the earlier marriage of girls of the lower, or outdoor, castes, in some parts of the Province, to the feeling that their life needs protection earlier than that of the upper classes, whose girls are secluded from harm in the zanánah. The difference, however, between the figures for the two classes is scarcely wide enough for the assumption. The distribution of the proportions in various parts of the Province is unequal, and the fact that in most of the more prominent instances the protection of early marriage is extended to the boys as well as the girls is against the hypothesis, whilst the relative paucity of widows is possibly due rather to the existence of the first husband than the acquisition of a second. Mr. Stuart, like Mr. O'Donnell, has made great use of the tabulation of civil condition by caste in reviewing this subject for the Madras Presidency, and from his analysis it appears that the marriage system in the south of India is subject to variations even more locally restricted than those of Bengal and the Panjáb. Taking the Province as a whole, it is chiefly remarkable for its high proportion of the **Madras.**

Sub-Province.	Number of married in 10,000 Boys under 10.		
	Hindu.	Musalmán.	Animistic.
Bengal	46	67	—
Bihár	926	323	—
Orissa	42	—	36
Chutia Nagpur	287	—	52

Sub-Province.	Number of married in 10,000 Girls under 10.		
	Hindu.	Musalmán.	Animistic.
N. Bengal	678	764	—
E. Bengal	692	486	—
W. Bengal	1,154	788	—
N. Bihár	1,773	866	—
S. Bihár	1,084	677	—
Orissa	193	—	62
Chutia Nagpur	829	—	118

unmarried of both sexes, for the low ratio of widowers, with a somewhat abnormally high one of widows. The unmarried are not most numerous, relative to the total population, in the tracts where children bear the highest ratio, as might be expected, and the distribution seems to strictly follow local custom. The marginal table shows two extreme instances of this. In Tanjore, with a low ratio of girls there is a high one of unmarried women, whilst in Vizágapatam, and, indeed, throughout the north-east coast tract, the reverse is the case. It might be assumed that to some extent Bengal custom had filtered down south, but the returns that were mentioned just above indicate that the proportion of unmarried in the Orissa castes, except Bráhmans and writers, is remarkably high. The distinction seems to be, to a certain extent, racial, as in Bihár, as well as territorial. Roughly speaking, the Telingána population is more married, if the phrase be permissible, than the Tamil or Malayálam, and the Uriya than the Telingána. In Malabár, as has been already mentioned, not only does polyandry prevail, but divorce is more in fashion, and the tie is generally more lax than in other parts of the Province. The diversity between the north and the south is due, presumably, to the greater influence of Brahmanic ideas amongst the Telanga population than amongst the more conservatively Dravidian Tamil, partly owing to the intercourse between the former and Northern India having been closer and of longer duration than that of the southern peninsula. The statistics regarding the female section of the community are those in which the diversity of practice is most apparent, even Bráhmans varying between a per-centage of 5 of their girls married under 10 in the Tamil country and one of 12 in the South Deccan, and the figures for girl widows oscillating in harmony, between 10 and 35 in 10,000 of the age in question. Then again, the trading caste of the Kómti, who affect great orthodoxy in Telingána, show a ratio of 940 married and 26 widowed in 10,000 girls under 10, whilst the Chetti, the corresponding caste further south, is satisfied with 213 and 8. A still greater difference appears between, say, the Ambattan, or barbers of the Tamilian races, where the corresponding ratios are respectively 183 and 4, and the Mangala, who officiates in the same capacity amongst the more northern people, and follows the local tendency, by marrying off 762 of his daughters in the 10,000 before they are 10 years old, and finding 24 of them widowed by that age. By analysing and regrouping the caste statistics, Mr. Stuart arrives at the conclusion that juvenile marriage, or the marriage of girls at an immature age, is "prevalent amongst 25 per cent. of the population, and fairly common amongst " 15 per cent. more, whilst among the remaining 60 per cent. it is rare for a girl to " be married till she has attained puberty." By the same process of regrouping, the prevalence of widow marriage is summarised as follows:—" Among about 40 per cent. " of the population there is no restriction on the marriage of widows; among about " 30 per cent. the practice is forbidden or rarely followed, while regarding the " remaining 30 per cent. the statistics are not conclusive one way or the other. We " shall not be far wrong if we assume that the marriage of widows is permitted and " practised by about 60 per cent. of the total population." To this may be added the remark that as in Telingána boys marry early as well as girls, the high proportion of widows there indicates how strong is the adherence to Brahmanic precept in respect to remarriage. On the other hand, in the breasts of the men of the Madras Presidency, hope triumphs over experience to a greater extent than in any other Province, for the proportion of widowers is the smallest recorded; but they avoid mates in the same bereaved condition, as to every 1,000 widowers there are 5,702 widows. The losses during the famine must be credited with a good deal of this irregularity between the figures for the two sexes, but more is due to the advance of caste feeling in Brahmanism. Mr. Stuart writes, "In nearly every considerable caste there are " some subdivisions which enforce the marriage of girls before puberty, and prohibit " the marriage of widows, and these subdivisions invariably hold a somewhat higher " position in public estimation on this account. It is easy to see that this encourage- " ment must produce a steady tendency towards the adoption of practices which are " in many respects injurious to the well-being of the people. And there is no " movement in the contrary direction. Once a caste has embraced the marriage " customs of the Bráhmans it never reverts to its former position."

	Per-centage of Females.	
	Under 10.	Unmarried.
Tanjore	26·56	36·70
Vizagapatam	28·73	29·26

It is worth noting, too, that the Bombay Karnátak, which adjoins the Telingána tract of Madras, is also conspicuous for the early marriage of its females, and, to a less marked extent, for that of its males also. But Gujaráth is the division of this Presidency where boy marriages generally prevail, and here, again, from the caste returns prepared by Mr. Drew, it is clear that the custom is local, not governed by social position. In at least one caste the rules as to dower are so stringent that till within a generation or two ago girls were freely sacrificed, either at birth or during infancy, and even now there are grounds for suspecting deliberate neglect, if not worse treatment. In another caste the curious custom mentioned above prevails, according to which an auspicious season for marriage is only allowed by the tutelary goddess once in 10 or 12 years. Such rules are doubtless evaded, as by marriage to a dagger or a bunch of flowers, which are then disposed of down a well, and the youthful widow remarried at a cheaper rate, or the ceremony is gone through with the Pipal tree, which can never claim its marital rights or interfere with subsequent arrangements. But, as a rule, the custom of the upper classes filters through to the lower, and we find the village menials of Gujaráth, for instance, marrying earlier than the landed aristocracy of the Deccan. The figures for Baroda give a very good notion of the special features of the former, especially in the caste returns. The Sindh figures partake of the nature of those for the West Panjáb. The age at marriage is far later than elsewhere, and there are more widowers and fewer widows. The age return is probably more inaccurate than usual, even at an Indian census. **Bombay.** **Sindh.**

Crossing India, we have the return for Assam to discuss. Mr. Gait has examined the figures with some minuteness, and gives an interesting review of the marriage system in his Province. It appears that Brahmanic views as to the marriage of widows are confined in the Assam valley to Bráhmans and writers, but in the Súrma valley, which is practically a corner of North-Eastern Bengal, only the lowest castes disregard them, and it is said that even amongst these, widow marriage is annually increasing in disrepute. The same remark applies to the Bráhmapútra tract, though the population there is slower to move. The thin end of the wedge is found, not in the restriction of the permission to the widow of a deceased elder brother, as in Bihár, but in allowing only a virgin widow to remarry. As to the Hill tribes, we find very primitive marriage customs in force. The rule is generally to purchase, with the feint of a form of capture, but there are at least two tribes which do not purchase. The wives are invariably grown up, and so, of course, are the husbands. There are more women than men in most of the tribes, and men marry young, owing to the moderate price demanded for a girl. There appears to be little or no restriction, at present, on divorce or widow marriage, but as girls are plentiful, widows, except whilst young, are not in demand. **Assam.**

The position of woman in Burma is, as is well known, very much higher than that which she occupies in any Indian province. There is no juvenile marriage; divorce is available to both parties alike, and is apparently more often initiated by the wife than the husband, though reunions of pairs once divorced are frequent enough to show that the process is not a very serious one. Life is easy, and a wife is more often than not a support, instead of being a burden. This being so, the law in Burma, which probably follows at no great distance the popular sentiment, allows the wife a considerable control over the family property, and checks any tendencies towards polygyny, though the latter custom is not technically illegal. In old times, Mr. Eales points out, the Burman was a great slaveholder and polygamist. He seems to have been chastened by experience, but during the term of probation, if the law books are anything more than academic dissertations on what a monk thought ought to be done, man had left to him very little he could call his own. He could possess, if he liked, a head wife and a lesser, and also six concubines, but the law provided for the eight kinds of debts contracted by these without his knowledge, and, moreover, both wives and debts were subdivided into five orders respectively. Even supposing the head of the family had fortified himself by acquiring the knowledge of law requisite to circumvent his female connections in these respects, it appears that he would not be safe from legal clutch unless he also studied what was prescribed in the case of a husband contracting debts without the knowledge of his two wives and six concubines. In these circumstances, no wonder monogyny is the rule amongst the Buddhists of Burma. The general return for the lower division of the Province is disturbed by the large number of immigrants. Those both from the upper division and from India are generally married men without their wives, and amongst the women from India a good many are widows who have to earn their living by labour, along with their male relatives, who bring them across the **Burma.**

bay. In Upper Burma the Buddhists show a high proportion of widows, which Mr. Eales attributes in part to losses during the operations against the dacoits, and partly to husbands having migrated and died in foreign parts. There is no prohibition of widow marriage, but apparently virgin brides are plentiful, so only the younger widows remarry. The proportion of the married of both sexes is low compared to that ruling in India, not because there is less marriage in Burma amongst adults, but owing to there being no marriage at all before the young people are grown up. To start in life a young Burmese couple, as pointed out by Mr. Eales, wants but his *da* and cooking-pot. The universal bamboo provides the material for his house and furniture, his fuel and his water vessels, and when there is need, part of the family food. It is rare, accordingly, to find a youth of 23 years or thereabouts unmarried.

Mean age of the married.

It is noteworthy, also, that in Burma the difference between the mean age of husband and wife is far less than in India, though it is still considerably above that found to prevail in England. The marginal statement must be taken with the qualification that the ages are inaccurate in detail, but as grouped for the purposes of this computation, not far from the mark on general lines.

TABLE G.

Country or Province.	Mean Age of the Married.		Difference in Years.
	Men.	Women.	
England and Wales	43·1	40·7	2·4
{ Upper Burma	40·6	36·6	4·0
{ Lower Burma	38·5	34·2	4·3
Madras	39·0	29·0	10·0
Bombay	35·2	27·7	7·5
Panjáb	31·8	25·8	6·0
Assam	38·8	28·0	10·8
Berar	35·1	26·5	8·6
India	**35·5**	**27·6**	**7·9**

In order to show more clearly what is meant above by the influence of local or territorial fashion in regard to marriage, a table is given opposite in which the marriage statistics are worked up by religions, as well as by provinces. This point has been but cursorily mentioned in the foregoing review owing to the lax meaning attached to the term Hindu, when caste has not been tabulated in connection with this subject. In all cases, except in Burma and the Panjáb, it is this form of religion that determines the provincial average, and it is curious to note in what degree the other religions vary from it. Taking the first section of the return, which groups the religions territorially, we find a few features strongly marked throughout. First, the Musalmáns marry off their girls at a far earlier age than their boys and young men, and are by no means in such a hurry to get rid of either as the Hindus or Jains. Then, again, the line between the forest tribes and the orthodox is very distinct in the matter of juvenile marriage, and though there are a good many married girls of less than 15 years old compared to the boy husbands, both sexes show but a small ratio in this respect, compared to that which prevails higher up in the social scale. The same class, too, with one exception, shows the lowest ratio of widows in the prime of life, whether the proportion of wives corresponds, as it usually does, or not. The Parsis are only given for Bombay, as elsewhere they are both few in number and in many cases not thoroughly domesticated where they were enumerated. They show a very low proportion of juvenile marriages, and even in the prime of life abstain from matrimony to a greater extent than any other Indian community west of Burma.

In the second part of the return the religion is shown in its territorial variation, and from the figures here given it can be judged how, with the general qualification as to the Musalmáns and forest tribes just mentioned, the different communities tend to assimilate to themselves the local colouring affected by the Brahmanic section of the population. The best example of this is found amongst the Animistic, who are more accessible than the rest, excepting, of course, the Jains, to the influence of Brahmanic precept, as they wish to rise in the social scale. Many of the Musalmáns, it has been already seen, are but semi-converted Hindus, and change their habits the less as the antagonism between the two creeds is milder. The Christians follow the fashion as to juvenile marriage, especially in the matter of their girls. In Madras, where the men marry late in the tracts where Christian converts are most numerous, there are 704 brides of under 15 to 100 bridegrooms of the same age. In Bengal, where both sexes marry younger, there are only 254. In Bombay, the reverse is the case, and there are more girl wives in this community relative to boy husbands than even amongst the Hindus. It is probable that some of this discrepancy is due to temporary absence on the part of the youths in service, or on board coasting and

Table H.—Showing the Marriage System in different Religions, by Provinces.

Province and Religion.	Under 15. Married per 1,000 of each Sex. Males.	Females.	Wives per 1,000 Husbands.	Between 15 and 40. In 1,000 Males. Married.	Widowed.	In 1,000 Females. Married.	Widowed.	Wives per 1,000 Husbands.	Widows per 1,000 Widowers.
Section I.									
Madras	**15**	**97**	**6,369**	**611**	**18**	**806**	**125**	**1,628**	**7,216**
Hindu	16	103	6,338	615	17	807	128	1,385	8,022
Musalmán	5	52	10,245	570	13	813	103	1,535	8,325
Christian	5	36	7,043	603	15	794	87	1,411	6,152
Animistic	23	52	2,111	664	39	816	56	1,201	1,405
Bombay	**67**	**235**	**3,306**	**757**	**31**	**871**	**101**	**1,085**	**3,075**
Hindu	70	248	3,310	772	31	873	103	1,079	3,131
Musalmán	42	141	3,125	682	32	872	92	1,171	2,623
Jain	56	227	3,572	644	35	852	139	952	2,817
Pársi	10	32	2,809	507	16	696	52	1,281	2,976
Christian	11	44	3,850	434	16	832	43	1,001	3,104
Animistic	17	65	3,721	763	23	897	42	1,208	1,898
Bengal	**73**	**223**	**2,891**	**738**	**33**	**824**	**155**	**1,162**	**4,944**
Hindu	100	251	2,396	736	38	809	174	1,132	4,744
Musalmán	34	195	5,434	749	23	859	126	1,216	5,727
Christian	16	43	2,586	578	20	762	83	1,199	3,660
Animistic	24	61	2,479	686	24	774	81	—	—
N.-W. Provinces	**93**	**193**	**1,840**	**719**	**51**	**885**	**96**	**1,125**	**1,712**
Hindu	98	200	1,817	702	55	885	99	1,225	1,748
Musalmán	67	151	2,052	714	48	886	74	1,181	1,471
Jain	75	170	1,962	625	79	823	165	1,100	1,741
Oudh	**83**	**165**	**1,802**	**724**	**38**	**905**	**71**	**1,131**	**1,764**
Hindu	88	171	1,750	724	38	906	73	1,172	1,781
Musalmán	47	126	2,466	730	35	904	55	—	—
Panjáb	**42**	**115**	**2,313**	**649**	**53**	**858**	**105**	**1,161**	**1,723**
Musalmán	25	78	2,687	644	47	858	87	1,205	1,694
Hindu	66	171	2,175	665	61	858	129	1,103	1,816
Sikh	55	138	1,817	638	69	866	117	1,153	1,429
Burma, Upper	**—**	**1**	**—**	**528**	**35**	**587**	**89**	**1,191**	**2,725**
Buddhist	—	1	—	529	36	585	89	—	—
Animistic	1	3	—	543	31	712	70	730	1,283
Musalmán	1	5	—	561	33	651	102	480	1,292
Burma, Lower	**—**	**2**	**—**	**559**	**38**	**680**	**61**	**1,023**	**1,364**
Buddhists	—	1	—	520	38	673	61	—	—
Animistic	1	3	—	544	47	692	60	1,141	1,140
Hindu	9	13	—	592	22	850	52	203	334
Christian	—	2	—	495	26	650	49	1,108	1,575
Central Provinces	**70**	**162**	**2,262**	**775**	**36**	**888**	**80**	**1,179**	**2,247**
Hindu	79	182	2,242	792	37	894	81	1,156	2,268
Musalmán	29	100	3,297	671	38	861	98	1,171	2,348
Animistic	30	68	2,258	713	35	864	62	1,333	1,974
Assam	**7**	**85**	**10,584**	**597**	**36**	**791**	**139**	**1,287**	**3,767**
Hindu	7	92	12,160	562	40	764	168	1,275	3,909
Musalmán	7	101	14,443	643	22	860	115	1,312	5,160
Animistic	11	41	3,640	656	44	777	87	1,298	2,174
Haidrabád	**65**	**259**	**3,814**	**783**	**26**	**869**	**104**	**1,090**	**3,913**
Hindu	69	278	3,795	801	27	872	105	1,073	3,879
Musalmán	28	124	4,312	648	21	842	98	1,268	4,483
Animistic	98	216	2,140	850	25	878	43	1,131	1,642
Baroda	**135**	**253**	**1,732**	**749**	**36**	**888**	**81**	**1,076**	**2,024**
Hindu	143	269	1,735	757	36	891	79	1,063	1,966
Musalmán	74	144	1,799	683	36	869	89	1,148	2,317
Jain	82	93	1,074	634	36	843	139	1,205	3,460
Animistic	23	45	1,935	661	25	878	43	1,130	1,466

Table H.—Showing the Marriage System in different Religions, by Provinces—*cont.*

Province and Religion.	Under 15.			Between 15 and 40.					
	Married per 1,000 of each Sex.		Wives per 1,000 Husbands.	In 1,000 Males.		In 1,000 Females.		Wives per 1,000 Husbands.	Widows per 1,000 Widowers.
	Males.	Females.		Married.	Widowed.	Married.	Widowed.		
Berár	**121**	**332**	**2,690**	**824**	**43**	**893**	**89**	**1,055**	**1,774**
Hindu	134	365	2,660	845	44	910	80	1,033	1,723
Musalmán	19	97	4,865	629	31	860	93	1,238	2,668
Animistic	38	102	2,683	753	30	892	49	1,287	1,779
Bombay States	**77**	**184**	**2,256**	**731**	**35**	**880**	**81**	**1,136**	**2,207**
Hindu	85	200	2,227	742	35	881	82	1,114	2,196
Animistic	13	23	1,653	730	19	860	32	1,333	1,974
Musalmán	33	86	2,480	664	35	883	67	1,300	1,886
Jain	44	143	3,190	681	33	858	120	1,205	3,435
Panjáb States	**56**	**161**	**2,425**	**656**	**54**	**868**	**113**	**1,121**	**1,788**
Hindu	68	191	2,404	658	55	867	119	1,111	1,834
Musalmán	37	110	2,536	659	53	869	101	1,151	1,644
Sikh	52	154	2,317	636	47	870	114	1,108	1,936
Central Province States	**46**	**83**	**1,733**	**755**	**28**	**869**	**64**	**1,165**	**2,298**
Hindu	54	105	1,882	777	28	878	66	1,138	2,331
Musalmán	46	111	2,473	720	33	842	112	1,081	3,098
Animistic	18	41	2,159	680	26	805	68	1,270	2,156
Mysore	**7**	**93**	**13,866**	**573**	**25**	**791**	**152**	**1,344**	**5,852**
Hindu	7	96	14,005	576	26	798	148	1,416	5,887
Musalmán	5	61	11,465	550	18	845	106	1,377	15,410
Section II.									
Sikhs:									
Panjáb	55	138	1,817	638	69	866	117	1,153	1,429
" States	52	154	2,317	636	47	870	114	1,103	1,936
Jains:									
Bombay	56	227	3,572	644	35	852	139	952	2,817
" States	44	143	3,190	681	33	868	120	1,205	3,460
Baroda	83	93	1,074	634	36	843	139	1,205	3,435
N.-W. Provinces	75	170	1,962	625	79	823	165	1,100	1,741
Christians:									
Madras	5	36	7,043	603	15	794	87	1,411	6,152
" States	10	41	4,107	715	13	832	43	1,141	3,336
Bombay	11	44	3,850	434	16	770	87	1,001	3,104
Bengal	16	43	2,536	573	20	762	83	1,199	3,660
Lower Burma	—	2	—	495	26	650	49	1,108	1,575
Animistic:									
Bombay	17	65	3,721	763	23	897	42	1,208	1,898
Baroda	23	45	1,935	661	25	878	43	1,130	1,466
Haidrabád	98	216	2,140	850	25	935	41	1,131	1,642
Central Provinces	30	68	2,258	713	35	864	62	1,333	1,974
" " States	18	41	2,159	680	26	841	55	1,270	2,156
Bengal	24	61	2,479	686	24	774	81	1,250	3,666
" States	17	37	—	695	26	805	63	1,248	2,800
Berar	38	102	2,683	753	30	892	49	1,287	1,779
Madras	23	52	2,111	664	39	816	56	1,201	1,405
Upper Burma	1	3	—	543	31	712	70	730	1,283
Lower "	1	3	—	544	47	692	60	1,141	1,140
Assam	11	41	3,640	656	44	777	87	1,298	2,174
Musalmáns:									
Panjáb	25	78	2,677	644	47	858	87	1,205	1,694
N.-W. Provinces	67	151	2,052	714	48	886	74	1,181	1,471
Bengal	34	195	5,434	749	23	859	126	1,216	5,727
Sindh	12	41	2,685	542	39	859	71	1,328	1,542
Madras	5	52	10,245	570	13	813	108	1,585	8,325
Bombay	42	141	3,125	682	32	872	92	1,171	2,623
Haidrabád	28	124	4,312	648	21	842	98	1,268	4,483

fishing vessels, whilst the paucity of husbands at a later age is explicable by the fact that many Christians come from Goa to make their fortune before returning to marry in their native country. In Lower Burma the Karén converts follow the customs of their Buddhist brethren. There is a good deal more to be made out of this table, but it is so apparent that further comment is, perhaps, superfluous. There is also a great temptation to illustrate the principal topics dealt with in the course of this chapter by copious references to the details of the return of marriage by caste, the preparation of which was left to the option of the local authorities, and which, as compiled by the census Superintendents for Bengal, Madras, the North-West Provinces, Bombay, Baroda, and Mysore, contains an amount of valuable and interesting information which will repay weeks of patient analysis. So far, however, as the general bearings of the subject are concerned, and within the limitations set on their treatment in the early part of this chapter, what has been here set forth will prove, it is hoped, sufficiently explicit.

CHAPTER X.

The Age Distribution of the Population.

> " Sad is our youth, for it is ever going,
> Crumbling away, beneath our very feet.
> Sad is our life, for onward it is flowing
> In current unperceived, because so fleet."—*Aubrey de Vere.*

The services that can be rendered by a census are not to be held complete unless the operations include the statement of the population by age; but the statistics on this subject differ from the rest of those then collected by the fact of their value lying not so much in the return itself as in the use made of it in combination with other *data*, independent of the census indeed, but which can best be tested, as a rule, by means of the results of successive synchronous enumerations. The actual figures are not, however, without a special interest of their own, as by them we can measure some of the great social features of the community, the existence of which is already recognised. They show, for instance, how far the population, as it stood at the time of the census, was maintained by the number of births, how far by the viability or "good life," to use the technical term, of those of riper years. They show, again, the extent of the gaps made by war, famine, or emigration, and any abnormal recruitment from outside the territory enumerated, and, finally, through them comparison can be instituted with other countries in the above respects. But the value of the age returns stands out more prominently when the results of an enumeration are applied to those of its predecessor, on the one hand, and to the birth and death registration on the other. From the combination we arrive at the rate of mortality, and at its complement, the proportion of births which maintain the rate of increase found to have prevailed during the decade. From another standpoint the population is regarded as stationary, and all variation in the birth and death rates being eliminated, certain normal factors are deduced of no small value, and which can be ascertained in no other way. Such is the relative mortality at different ages, and, again, the mean after lifetime, or, as it is perhaps better termed, the mean expectation of life, of persons who have attained those ages respectively.

Inaccuracy in the return of age.

Now, as far as the above computations are concerned, it may be said that in very few, if indeed, in any, countries, east or west, is the raw material fit for use as it is dug out of the mine, that is, compiled from the schedules. Even in the countries where literacy is most prevalent, it is found that the return has to be considerably manipulated before it can be presented to the delicate machinery by which the calculation is effected. The normal distribution of a community by age implies a gradual decrease in the number in each year of life, the difference between each year and its predecessor, after early youth, growing wider as the age increases. But apart from abnormal disturbance, such as losses by war or famine, or recruitment or diminution by migration, there are certain tendencies towards erroneous returns which seem inherent in every population. Some instances of this have been already given in previous portions of this review. In England, for instance, the age of women between 25 and 35 is very often understated, whilst that of girls under 16 is returned as above that desirable limit. In India it is alleged that marriageable girls between 10 and 12 are returned in some tracts as below 10, whilst those between 12 and 14 are overstated at 18 or 20. There is no doubt habitual overstatement of age amongst the old of both sexes, especially women, where great age is considered a sort of distinction. Thus, though in every country some allowance has to be made for deliberate error, in India the return is peculiarly liable to be defective. Facts such as creed, language, connubial condition, literacy, and even caste and occupation, are brought home to the persons in question every day of their lives, but when once launched into the busy world, age is to the masses a matter of no importance. Registration of birth, as we have seen, is singularly deficient in accuracy for the most part, and in many tracts, if carried on at all, is only conducted in the most haphazard manner. For the first few years of life the mother is probably able to tell the age of her infant, but when it comes to a question of whether a child is 10 years old or 13, as, for instance, in a factory inspection, recourse has to be had to "mark of mouth," and the teeth are solemnly counted in evidence. In the upper ranks it is otherwise, as the horoscope is usually available. But even the latter, as events have not unfrequently shown, is not unimpeachable testimony in cases where it is to the interest of the producer to make himself out of an age different to what he really is. Then, again, we have, to an exaggerated extent, the usual tendency of an illiterate population accustomed to count by digits, to return their age in multiples of five.

The even multiples are the more favoured, of course, but an exception is made in the case of 25. This habit gave rise to a curious anomaly in the course of the census operations. The general rule in India is to return the age in completed years, but there is no doubt that in many cases the current year is substituted. So much is this the case in the Panjáb, that on the representation of the late census Superintendent, Mr. Ibbetson, the entry prescribed for that province was altered to suit the local practice. But as all the rest of India was enumerated by the completed year, though probably in Madras the Panjáb system would have been more acceptable, it was necessary, of course, to reduce the Panjáb return to uniformity, which was done by shifting back the tabulated results one year. Then it was at once seen that the relative proportions of the quinquennial periods had been entirely thrown into disorder, because, owing to this habit of plumbing on the multiples of five, all the undue excess got shifted back a period. That is, the return of those at 40 years appeared under the heading of 39, and so on. As the inconsistency affected so large a population, it was advisable to correct it, by distributing the excess amongst the periods to which it would belong if due allowance were made for the idiosyncrasies of the people. It is superfluous to enter into the method of adjustment, but the results are as shown in the tables given later on in this chapter. Whilst we are on this subject of preference of particular numbers, it may be noted that in the detailed return given below, which fairly represents the whole of India, there is a curiously uniform sequence of selection. In nearly every single decennium, up to 70, both men and women agree in returning their age in the order noted marginally. The even multiples of 5 head the list easily, except in the case of 25, which, as we have said above, is a special favourite. The uneven multiples follow, except in the second decade, where 12 and 18 are preferred to 15. The third place is taken by 2, very regularly, and the fourth by 8. The least favoured are 1 and 9, the numbers respectively preceding and following the even and most favoured multiple. For instance, we find, out of 100,000 males, 472 returning 29, 301 returning 31, with 5,850 between them. The neighbourhood of 50 and 60 is still more remarkable for its depopulation by those numbers. The same feature, though to a less striking extent, is found in the return of the coloured population of the Southern States across the Atlantic, and is not by any means absent in the returns for most European countries, especially where they are published in their original irregularity. Table A. summarises in a proportional

Order of years.	Order of preference.
0	1
1	8
2	3
3	7
4	6
5	2
6	5
7	9
8	4
9	10

Table A.—Showing the Age Return of 100,000 of each Sex.

Age.	Males.	Females.	Age.	Males.	Females.	Age.	Males.	Females.
0	3,209	3,300	35	3,977	3,463	70	681	879
1	1,780	1,934	36	805	678	71	33	39
2	2,951	3,256	37	335	289	72	51	41
3	3,136	3,613	38	798	706	73	15	14
4	3,021	3,134	39	322	254	74	19	19
5	3,202	3,253	40	5,240	5,210	75	180	228
6	2,923	2,913	41	216	193	76	16	18
7	2,712	2,872	42	684	549	77	24	8
8	3,082	3,008	43	207	170	78	32	17
9	1,857	1,818	44	259	209	79	27	16
10	3,567	3,148	45	2,659	2,339	80	286	389
11	1,112	1,104	46	283	258	81	9	11
12	3,459	2,617	47	194	152	82	9	11
13	1,168	1,006	48	444	391	83	3	2
14	1,656	1,405	49	131	118	84	4	2
15	2,206	1,935	50	3,647	3,865	85	34	37
16	2,151	2,045	51	128	116	86	4	4
17	737	861	52	321	278	87	4	3
18	2,328	2,397	53	106	90	88	3	3
19	668	686	54	135	131	89	3	3
20	4,014	5,052	55	1,142	1,066	90	52	57
21	531	536	56	173	181	91	3	2
22	1,857	1,907	57	105	88	92	3	1
23	639	639	58	210	179	93	—	—
24	998	975	59	98	109	94	1	1
25	5,200	5,657	60	2,269	2,811	95	10	8
26	1,018	951	61	107	112	96	2	1
27	693	629	62	148	152	97	1	1
28	1,560	1,504	63	65	52	98	2	2
29	472	425	64	72	71	99	1	1
30	5,850	6,243	65	493	546	100	12	12
31	301	300	66	59	54	101	1	—
32	1,504	1,346	67	44	47	102 and over.	3	1
33	406	332	68	66	65			
34	532	400	69	28	38			

form the age distribution of about 540,000 people of each sex, taken at random from the schedules of all the main provinces and States, except Rájputána, Central India, and Kashmér. Owing to the comparatively small numbers involved, the irregularities are all the more apparent. In the Imperial returns, which include all but some 583,000 of the population, the law of great numbers asserts itself, and much of the irregularity is obliterated. A summary of the latter is therefore given below, in Table B., with

TABLE B.—Showing the Distribution by Age of 10,000 of each Sex.

1.—MALES.

Age Period.	India.		England and Wales.	France.	Germany.	Austria.	Hungary.	Italy.
	1881.	1891.						
0–4	1,318	1,409	1,391	930	1,318	1,339	1,425	1,228
5–9 -	1,432	1,428	1,241	901	1,210	1,117	1,102	1,373
10–14 -	1,214	1,139	1,109	890	1,088	1,007	1,044	970
15–19 -	811	809	1,003	848	961	944	919	912
20–24 -	799	803	880	922	850	879	779	851
25–29 -	896	861	776	732	757	740	809	736
30–34	885	859	665	690	659	686	726	711
35–39 - -	587	599	589	675	603	646	680	621
40–44	642	657	533	631	555	593	651	626
45–49 - -	344	354	433	591	488	497	495	485
50–54	436	431	385	531	408	430	416	507
55–59 -	161	165	302	474	338	369	315	378
60 and over	475	486	693	1,185	765	753	639	902
Mean age -	24·51	24·48	25·31	30·69	26·57	27·05	26·33	28·66

2.—FEMALES.

Age Period.	India.		England and Wales.	France.	Germany.	Austria.	Hungary.	Italy.
	1881.	1891.						
0–4 -	1,420	1,527	1,322	910	1,257	1,294	1,383	1,190
5–9 - -	1,383	1,396	1,184	891	1,159	1,071	1,073	1,042
10–14 -	1,006	946	1,048	871	1,044	973	1,025	935
15–19 - -	779	782	959	841	934	940	1,002	940
20–24 -	905	897	912	968	844	878	887	869
25–29 - -	925	892	800	696	760	744	791	760
30–34 -	881	869	679	675	661	700	737	734
35–39 - -	527	537	597	666	613	651	631	627
40–44 -	645	651	545	618	567	612	632	636
45–49 - -	317	309	453	588	504	510	450	485
50–54 -	464	451	402	542	429	471	443	520
55–59 - -	157	155	319	478	369	389	306	374
60 and over -	591	588	780	1,256	859	767	634	888
Mean age -	25·16	24·84	25·86	31·19	27·53	27·59	26·81	28·60

the corresponding reduction of the returns of some European countries, and the Indian return of the preceding census. The mean age of the living, which is entered at the foot of each column, is for purposes of comparison only, and does not pretend to be mathematically accurate. It shows, on broad lines, the comparative growth of the Indian population, and the remarkable distinction in this respect between France and the rest of the countries selected for the table. In every case except Italy the mean age of the females is higher than that of the other sex, and the proportion under 15 much lower. But it is noteworthy that in India alone, the proportion under five is higher than amongst the males, whilst that of girls between 10 and 14, on which comment was made in the chapter on Sex, is lower in India than in any country, except in France, where the whole juvenile population is sparse, and in Italy, where the distribution partakes of the irregularity of that in the Indian table. Then, again, towards the higher ages, Italy and Hungary have the peculiarity of a smaller proportion of women than of men, in striking contrast to the other European countries, as well as to India.

But the latter country indicates the shorter life of its population in the ratio of its people of 60 years old and over, both men and women. At the opposite end of the scale we find France, with more than double the proportion at this age. On the whole, we may sum up the main features of the age distribution of the Indian population as consisting in the exceptionally high proportion of the young, with a very small proportion of those past 50 or 55. In connection with a later part of the subject, it will appear that this is due to a remarkably high birth-rate, accompanied by great mortality amongst infants and those past the prime of life. It is also to be noticed that the proportion of each sex falling within what may be taken as the best working ages of population, namely, between 15 and 45, is higher in India than elsewhere, Hungary alone approaching it. It is also remarkable that this proportion is higher in the case of females than amongst the males, except in France, Germany, and Holland, and in this respect, India, as a whole lies between Austria and England. The extremes are occupied by Ireland, on the side of an excess in the ratio of females, and France, with a far smaller divergence in the opposite direction.

Territorial variation in India.

We may now take up the figures for the different parts of India. In Table C., on the next page, will be found the distribution in each of the main territorial divisions reduced to the uniform radix of 10,000 of each sex, so that comparison is easy. The statement is based on the returns as compiled from the actual schedule, and only in the case of the Panjáb, where uniformity was in question, has any adjustment been made by computation. In various provincial reports, such as those for Madras, Bombay, and Bengal, in particular, the large population dealt with has enabled the Superintendent to bring down the crude results to something like the correct graduation, but as the methods employed have not been the same in all cases, it is preferable to discuss in a general review, like that in hand, the raw material itself, in which the defects are probably much the same in every part of the country. One of these general errors, in addition to those mentioned already, should be noticed here. The great difference in all the items, except in the States of Haidrabád and Mysore, between the number of those less than one year old and those who have entered the second year of life cannot fail to attract attention. It is admittedly not all due to the astonishing mortality during the earlier months, though this accounts for a great deal of it; but the remainder is attributable to confusion of terms. In 1881 it was found that the instruction to "enter the age of an infant of less than one year old in months, "adding the word *month* to the figure," resulted in the abstraction of the said figure as years, owing partly to hurry, partly to misreading, and partly to the omission of the word prescribed to prevent such misunderstanding. On this occasion the authorities consulted, who had all experienced the above difficulty, proposed the rule that all children of less than a year old should be entered as *infants*, without specifying the number of months it had lived. Unfortunately, however, the term suggested applies, in nearly all the vernacular tongues, to any unweaned child, and as the period during which the latter is kept at the breast is far longer in India than in more temperate climates, the second year of life was largely absorbed by the first, and the last state of the return was worse than the first. Passing on to the rest of the annual periods in the first quinquennium, it will be seen that there is absolutely no regularity of sequence in the return. The marginal table shows the order in which the years appear in the total of males for all India, and in the next column is given the number out of 17 items in which the same order, in each case, is found. There is unanimity about despoiling the second year, and the first and third seem also selected with some deliberation, but in the case of the two others, only a third of the territorial divisions agree in the results with the aggregate. The birth registers, if analysed in territorial detail less than the mere province, would possibly show how far such eccentric deviations are based on the variations of harvest in the season preceding the birth, an influence to which the Indian population is undoubtedly more sensitive than that of Europe. There is in the irregularity in question none of those manifestations of deliberate choice which have just been described as prevalent in the return at later periods of life, so it is not unreasonable to attribute them, in part, to some better foundation than caprice or ignorance. In the first place, the return for 1881, except in the Panjáb, materially differs from that under review in

Years.	Serial Order in India, Total.	Number of Provinces, out of 17, in which the Serial Order was observed.
0	1	9
1	5	All.
2	4	8
3	2	5
4	3	5

TABLE C.—Showing territorially the Distribution by Age of 10,000 of each Sex.

Province or State.	Under 1.		1.		2.		3.		4.		Under 5.		5–9.		10–14.		15–19.	
	M.	F.	M.	F.	M.	F.	M.	F.	M.	F.	M.	F.	M.	F.	M.	F.	M.	F.
Madras	330	338	171	178	315	327	352	365	314	316	1,482	1,524	1,391	1,346	1,084	923	828	783
Bombay	341	365	169	189	301	340	300	344	304	323	1,415	1,561	1,382	1,350	1,074	898	816	792
Sindh	384	430	106	132	297	369	378	442	408	443	1,573	1,816	1,573	1,543	962	754	682	603
Bengal	319	335	141	151	293	323	334	372	307	317	1,394	1,498	1,551	1,466	1,214	969	818	838
N.-W. Provinces	330	346	144	161	241	278	289	332	277	296	1,281	1,413	1,326	1,294	1,187	961	857	757
Oudh	374	392	180	176	262	291	310	344	227	294	1,383	1,497	1,334	1,280	1,108	888	784	664
Panjáb	409	465	291	319	301	335	302	320	328	332	1,632	1,771	1,406	1,391	1,040	898	701	655
Central Provinces	288	290	194	210	310	342	338	382	322	339	1,450	1,563	1,578	1,546	1,203	1,001	690	656
Assam	339	368	182	203	324	366	339	383	332	364	1,518	1,684	1,508	1,564	1,140	969	747	852
Haidrabad	268	298	220	251	332	374	298	342	311	328	1,429	1,593	1,331	1,325	1,078	890	724	779
Mysore	239	255	191	208	316	338	329	351	309	320	1,384	1,472	1,364	1,414	921	835	867	792
Central India	275	296	142	161	235	272	280	340	293	322	1,225	1,391	1,449	1,453	1,188	939	798	720
Rajputána	328	370	147	159	245	268	286	327	329	340	1,335	1,464	1,387	1,364	1,134	958	858	754
Baroda	314	344	163	186	273	316	282	340	289	324	1,321	1,510	1,424	1,407	1,108	933	865	772
Berar	310	333	177	201	283	328	276	334	264	292	1,310	1,488	1,319	1,434	1,105	962	628	695
Upper Burma	325	335	208	199	252	240	310	295	232	219	1,327	1,288	1,229	1,168	1,199	1,105	887	954
Lower "	255	293	212	245	280	319	314	349	265	302	1,326	1,508	1,259	1,381	1,190	1,179	927	1,070
INDIA	328	347	173	188	287	319	318	354	305	319	1,409	1,527	1,428	1,396	1,139	946	809	782

Province or State.	20–24.		25–29.		30–34.		35–39.		40–44.		45–49.		50–54.		55–59.		60 and over.	
	M.	F.	M.	F.	M.	F.	M.	P.	M.	F.	M.	F.	M.	F.	M.	F.	M.	F.
Madras	820	973	821	865	828	885	591	505	670	661	385	305	427	460	177	157	516	613
Bombay	844	939	958	931	862	851	641	572	629	626	383	342	416	435	180	165	420	538
Sindh	785	875	900	928	968	964	582	461	612	640	305	276	439	450	132	111	507	580
Bengal	702	828	841	895	807	818	648	568	624	608	369	322	394	410	189	170	469	610
N.-W. Provinces	878	918	868	889	902	916	570	550	713	724	338	317	470	507	144	145	467	609
Oudh	802	848	869	919	884	891	550	528	674	718	361	330	519	545	173	161	589	751
Panjáb	927	948	752	816	874	936	465	436	596	675	388	295	458	522	182	142	629	515
Central Provinces	707	833	840	911	923	904	526	498	755	674	280	236	464	446	95	100	489	632
Assam	757	928	882	928	865	835	672	505	623	557	324	242	390	352	136	109	442	475
Haidrabad	807	983	970	916	914	932	558	441	738	702	323	236	406	495	119	92	513	616
Mysore	850	943	901	904	829	825	700	613	656	601	439	378	418	442	220	213	461	568
Central India	799	892	893	946	1,008	993	622	581	764	738	321	277	433	455	115	112	385	502
Rajputána	788	850	882	855	924	936	569	534	708	749	338	308	472	504	171	158	441	566
Baroda	921	995	916	909	886	850	609	559	649	674	327	300	465	480	141	127	388	484
Berar	694	881	911	910	950	893	670	545	763	568	380	288	539	480	155	122	578	634
Upper Burma	859	844	789	766	728	708	884	626	568	567	410	386	378	414	230	244	712	930
Lower "	939	956	931	833	839	667	807	477	545	477	378	338	358	379	218	223	483	512
INDIA	803	897	881	892	859	869	599	537	657	651	354	309	481	451	165	155	486	588

the order of sequence. Then, again, the return for the other sex is by no means uniform with that for males, as will be seen from the marginal statement, and it is the number of this sex, if there be any truth in the well-supported hypothesis started in a previous chapter of this work, that is influenced more than that of males by physical circumstances preceding birth. The second, third, and fifth years alone of the girls agree in their sequence with those of the boys. There is no doubt that in some parts of India the year 1888–89 was a hard one for the masses, which might account for a paucity of births in 1889–90, but it seems scarcely probable that plenty was so abnormally distributed in 1886–87 as to affect the ratio of the sexes in the births of the ensuing year. It is reasonable, therefore, to attribute but a portion of the irregularity to actual variations in the number of births during the five years in question, and the rest must, it is feared, be relegated to the unknown.

Age.	Serial Order in India, Total.	Number of Provinces in which the same Order is observed.
0	2	5
1	5	All.
2	4	6
3	1	9
4	3	8

Comparing the total falling within the above period, in the different parts of the country, we find the highest proportion of children in the Panjáb, Sind, and Assam. All three are very fertile tracts, on the whole, and as the two first named support a considerable burden of old people there is reason to suppose that the relatively high standard of living has something to do with the maintenance of the stream of population at its two extremes. In Assam life seems shorter, and the mean age is but 23·7 and 22·7 years in the case of the two sexes. The shortcoming of the female average is probably due partly to the number of the forest tribes, who work their women to death at a comparatively early age, and in part to deficient returns, as there is a great difference, far more than usual, in the results of the two enumerations in this province, and whilst the old men have proportionately increased, their mates have considerably declined. On the whole, however, this result may be due to better enumeration at more important periods of life. As regards the aged, Upper Burma almost reaches European proportions, whilst the Lower division of the province is slightly below the average. This result is due in some degree, of course, to immigration, as it is in Upper Burma to the loss of men in the prime of life. Oudh and Berár both come high in the list in this respect, probably on the same grounds as Sindh and the Panjáb.

We have next to consider the period we have selected as indicating the prime of life, namely, between 15 and 45. In the case of Indian women it might be held advisable to place the higher limit nearly 10 years lower, but looking at the important part played by widows in the domestic economy of the majority, it is not incorrect to stretch the period so as to include a large section of this class. The working period for men, too, begins lower than it would be correct to place its limit in Europe, and ends earlier, but we are dealing with the prime of life only. Making allowance for these qualifications, the marginal table, which gives the proportion of this period to 10,000 of each sex, shows the generally high ratio throughout India. The adjustment of the tables in the Panjáb has undoubtedly depressed the figure for that province below its due in the case of females, and to some extent in that of males, though there is no doubt a good deal of emigration on the part of the natives of this province, and the ratio of the adjacent State of Kashmér shows that a high proportion is not to be expected.

Province, &c.	15–44. M.	15–44. F.	Province, &c.	15–44. M.	15–44. F.
Madras	4,558	4,672	Central India	4,400	4,595
Bombay	4,749	4,710	Upper Burma	4,515	4,465
Sindh	4,509	4,471	Lower Burma	4,788	4,480
Bengal	4,440	4,555			
N.-W. Prov.	4,788	4,754	India	4,588	4,628
Oudh	4,543	4,568			
Panjáb	4,315	4,466	England and Wales	4,446	4,492
Cent. Prov.	4,441	4,476	Scotland	4,413	4,451
Assam	4,546	4,605	Ireland	4,207	4,408
Berar	4,614	4,592	France	4,498	4,464
Haidrabad	4,711	4,753	Germany	4,385	4,379
Baroda	4,826	4,759	Austria	4,488	4,525
Mysore	4,803	4,678	Hungary	4,564	4,680
Kashmér	4,400	4,595	Italy	4,457	4,566
Rajputána	4,722	4,678	Holland	4,282	4,255

As regards the comparision with the corresponding return for 1881, is must be borne in mind that we are dealing with very imperfect materials, so the deductions drawn can be but very general. The population, as a whole, is, no doubt, younger, owing to its replenishment by natural growth during the period of normal circumstances since it was last enumerated. Excluding the Panjáb, where the difference, as returned, is enormous, we find the greatest increase in Madras, which contains the worst of the famine-stricken tracts. Next comes Bombay, where the circumstances are similar. Oudh follows in much the same conditions, and Sindh is not far behind. Taking the whole of India, there are in every 10,000 males 91 more boys under five than there were in 1881, and in the same number of females, 107 more girls. It is curious that the ratio should have fallen in the Central Provinces, where there is no special cause for it, but as it was abnormally high in 1881, and the circumstances of the population have since been prosperous, probably the difference must be sought for in the enumeration. In Bengal the decrease in the proportion is but slight. In Assam it is very large and must be classed with that in the Central Provinces. If we look at the other end of the table, we find the gradual recovery from famine marked in Madras and Bombay by the considerably increased proportion of the aged of both sexes. Sindh, Assam, and the Panjáb, for some reason not immediately apparent, accompany an increased ratio of old men by a decreased one of the other sex. Bengal shows a small decrease, and both Oudh and the North-West Provinces an increase. On the whole, India is very much where it was 10 years ago in this respect. In the period between 10 and 15 our interest centres on the famine tracts. Mr. Stuart gives a useful table comparing these tracts with those better situated. An extract is given marginally for the period in question and needs no comment. For Bombay, too, a similar table is available, which is subjoined to that for Madras. The conclusions to be drawn from them are the same in both cases, and the selections are fairly parallel in point of prosperity and the severity of famine respectively. Even in so large an aggregate as the provincial total, the difference is very perceptible. The great increase in the ratio of the young children in these tracts has been already described in the third chapter of this review.

District.	1881.	1891.
Madras.		
M. Godávari (non-Famine)	1,356	1,338
M. Cuddapah (Famine)	1,504	832
F. Godavari	1,077	1,075
F. Cnddapah	1,366	728
Bombay.		
M. Khándesh (non-Famine)	1,207	1,180
M. Bijápúr (Famine)	1,622	768
F. Khandesh	1,035	1,028
F. Bijápúr	1,409	651

There is little that need be said here regarding the age distribution of the different religious communities. In the provincial volumes for Madras, the Panjáb, and Bengal, especially the last, the subject is discussed, but no conclusions of more than local application are derivable from the analysis of the figures. As a rule, the differences, where there are any, are due not to distinctions of religion but of locality, such as climate and food supply. In the case of Bengal, however, Mr. O'Donnell shows strong ground for holding the distinction between Musalmáns and Hindus in Eastern Bengal in the matter of fecundity and length of life, to be due to social habits consequent upon change of creed. His analysis of the returns of age by caste is interesting and suggestive. In one point his remarks are certainly applicable beyond the limits of his charge, namely, as regards the fecundity and shortness of life of the forest tribes, though it is open to question whether the latter is not partly due to the inability of such tribes to specify with accuracy any age over a certain number. It is not unusual for them to recognise nothing under a score, after about 35 or 40 years of age. The women of such tribes, on the other hand, undoubtedly die off very fast after all they go through in the course of their ordinary domestic duties and in childbirth.

Computations based on the age-returns.

We must now pass from the statistics actually collected at the census to those which are merely based on them, supplemented by information derived from other sources, and by computation from the two combined. The object in view is to get the approximate value of life in different parts of India, so that it may be compared with that ascertained with greater accuracy in the case of the population of England and Wales. The first point to be investigated on these lines is the mortality-rate in the community, and from it, with the normal rate of increase, can be deduced the birth-rate, and again, assuming a stationary population, the expectation of life at the different ages. If implicit trust could be placed in the census data, all that would be necessary would be to compare the numbers returned at each age period at the last enumeration with those returned as ten years older on the present occasion, and, by adjusting what we have seen to be the minute influence of emigration, to deduce the rate of mortality within the decade. Unfortunately, however, that simple expedient is not within our reach. We have therefore to work on the mean population at each period as the base, and to go to other sources for the rate of mortality. Luckily, there are two communities amongst whom the registration of births and deaths is conducted with special care.

Selected registration

In the population at large, as mentioned in the third chapter of this work, the omissions of both births and deaths is very prevalent. But in towns there is, as is to be expected, much greater accuracy than in rural circles. The difficulty, then, is to find a town of which the component elements are not largely foreign and abnormal, which would provide a population sufficiently numerous to form the groundwork of calculations applicable to any considerable portion of the population outside its limits. Bombay and Calcutta, for instance, are out of the question, since, as we have seen at page 82, more than two-thirds of their inhabitants are recruited from outside. But Madras stands on altogether a different footing. Nearly three-fourths of its population was returned as home-born, and it is well known that this city, from its comparative want of manufacturing and shipping industry, does not attract the adult population of the surrounding country to anything like the same degree that its two sisters do. As the supervision of registration of vital statistics may be assumed to be equally efficient in all three towns, the results in Madras are obviously nearer those for a normal Indian community than those in either Bombay or Calcutta. We thus have in the birth and death returns for Madras the basis for computation of life-values applicable to the greater part of Southern India, and on them Messrs. G. and H. Stuart have worked out the very interesting and instructive results that find a place in the Census Report for that Presidency. But lest the marked climatic and social distinctions between the south of India and the north, which have been insisted upon throughout this review, may have their effect on the age-values of the respective populations, it was advisable to seek for some data as nearly as possible corresponding to those for Madras in their approximate accuracy. These have been found in the returns collected in the North-West Provinces in connection with the supervision of the communities suspected of female infanticide. The registration of births and deaths among the youthful population of the tribes thus placed under inspection is remarkably good. The population is, no doubt, a special one, and from the very fact of being included in the scheme, must be, presumably, abnormal in its customs. But, on the other hand, the number of individuals in question is large and scattered, and the returns show that the practice of which they are suspected is only perceptible with difficulty and over a very small area. Thus the data are, on the whole, fairly representative of a far larger population than that from which they are collected, and, in any case, they are clearly much more accurate than any procurable from other sources. It is also in their favour that they correspond on the whole very fairly with the figures obtained from the Madras registers, and are now available for a series of years that gives them a high value from a statistical point of view. The report on the Census of 1881 contained a valuable and suggestive chapter wherein the above *data*, so far as they were then available, were passed through the sieve of actuarial experience. On the present occasion the same course was adopted, for to whatever extent may be carried the analysis of an amateur in such matters, the results are certain to be inferior, in both matter and arrangement, to those obtained by the professional hand working on the same material. The information bearing on the subject was therefore made over, in its entirety, to Mr. Hardy, F.I.A., whose experience in 1881 could thus be extended over a wider field. Unfortunately for the completeness of this review, though probably Mr. Hardy looks at it from a different standpoint, he is no longer able to devote his full time to the reduction of the figures and the calculation of the required values, so it has been found impossible to include his note in the present volume. It will be found, however, at the end of the second volume of the general returns.*

* It must be mentioned, however, that when the computations were all but complete, and Mr. Hardy brought them to me in consultation, a considerable delay was caused by a suggestion I made regarding a re-adjustment of a portion of the figures for the Panjáb, the early ages of which appeared to me to require such emendation. This put back, of course, the process of combination for the General Table.—J.A.B.

The Life-tables drawn up by Mr. Hardy are based, like the most recent of those for England, on the results of the two last enumerations. That is, as the period between 1881 and 1891 in India may be considered to have been, on the whole, a normal one, unaffected by famine or excessive prevalence of epidemic disease, it is probably more accurate and useful to take it into consideration than to attempt to find a "mean" which the comparatively frequent occurrence of disturbing factors is likely to render of no more than academic value. For the details of construction and of the results, the reader must be referred to the note itself, and it will suffice for the present purpose to mention a few of the more prominent features brought out in the investigation, both by Mr. Hardy and by Professor Stuart.* In the comparison with the English tables, the most striking point in the Indian is the low expectation of life. The male Englishman is likely at birth to have an after life of 41·35 years, but his fellow-subject in India cannot count on more than 25. The corresponding figures for the other sex are 44·62, and just under 26. The expectation is at its best in the one country in the fifth year, where it rises to 51 in the case of males, and to 53 amongst the females. In the East the zenith is attained a year later, and the chance is there of a little under 40 years for a male, and of 37 only for his mate. Not to enter into further detail, the life probabilities in India of a male who has weathered his first decade are, up to the age of 50, about 25 per cent. below those of an Englishman, and about 33 per cent. after that age. There is far more irregularity, as is to be expected, in the corresponding figures for women. Between 10 and 35 years old, they are from 40 to 35 per cent. worse off in this respect than their English sisters. The nearest approach is at 35, where the deterioration is but 32 per cent., and towards the end of life, that is at 65, the difference rises to over one half, or, relatively, double that of the other sex. At birth the difference between the two countries is, as may be seen from the figures quoted above, enormous, and amounts to nearly 70 per cent. amongst males, and nearly 80 amongst females. As the proportion drops in the next year to 43 and 55 respectively, it is to the year of birth that we must look for the explanation of the remarkable difference in the expectation as a whole. It is found in the rate of mortality which in England is about 17·04 per cent. for boys and 13·54 for girls, in the first year of life. In India, however, the corresponding rates are nearer 29 and 26 per cent. The better life of the girl is a feature in both countries. But, again, to sustain a population with such a tendency to drop off young, at even its present level, implies very high birth-rates, and we find that between 1881 and the next enumeration they must have approximated to 48 per mille of the population. The lowest rate is in the North-West Provinces, 44 per mille, and here the growth of the population is but 3¼, normal, and 6½ (including Oudh) during these last 10 years. Madras, Bengal, and Bombay all approximate to 50. In Madras and Bombay there has been, as already mentioned, a special stimulus to increase during the decade, owing to the depletion of large tracts by famine just before the last census. But the normal rate of growth is considerably less than that now indicated, and does not amount to one-half the rate in the former, and to little over two-thirds in the latter, including Sindh. The death-rate is lowest in Bombay, though both Madras and the Panjáb are very near it. Roughly speaking, it may be taken as just under 39 per mille. It must be remembered, however, that the rate of increase thus implied is not likely to be maintained, and that after so many years of average seasons, previous experience in India warrants the expectation of a check to the growth of population such as that which occurred between 1861 and 1871, and 1871 and 1881. The measures to prevent the loss of life that have been briefly touched upon in Chapter III. will, no doubt, mitigate the severity with which this check is applied, so far as its direct action is in question, but, nevertheless, it will not be surprising to those who have even glanced at these statistics, if there be not in 1911, if not 10 years sooner, a considerable readjustment of the age-distribution at the beginning and end of the tables. As life becomes harder, the proportion of those best adapted to provide for themselves will rise, and in spite of a probable relative decrease of infant mortality, the struggle will be keener for those who have escaped the perils of the first few years, as for those, at the other extreme of life, who have lived to be dependent on the exertions of others.

---

* The expectation figures are those, as a rule, of Madras, and the mortality and birth-rates those for India.—J. A. B.

Conclusion.

This review of the results of the census may fittingly close with a few lines on the administration of the operations. As in 1881, the whole control was placed in the hands of a single officer, but acting on the advice of the Commissioner for the preceding census, the Government of India appointed the officer in question at a considerably earlier date than on the former occasion, in order that the general scheme of operations and the details that had to be uniformly observed throughout the country might be matured in anticipation of the beginning of actual preparations in the provinces and States. To aid the Commissioner in this task, the Superintendents of the 1881 census held a conference at Agra in December 1889, at which the rules for the guidance of the enumerators, the subjects to be entered in the schedule, and the tabular forms in which the results were to be exhibited, with many other matters of minor detail, were discussed. The conclusions reached were then submitted for the approval of the Government of India. On the main points in question the views of the local authorities in different parts of the country were obtained, and it is gratifying to those concerned in the organisation of so large and varied a scheme to think that so little was proposed for reconsideration. The subsequent labours of the Commissioner, who attended the conference in his capacity of former Superintendent of the Bombay operations, were so materially lightened by the help thus rendered to him by his colleagues, that he feels that this opportunity must not be lost of thanking them collectively, and more especially Messrs. White, Ibbetson, and Kitts, for all their valuable suggestions.

About 10 months before the census, Superintendents were appointed to direct the operations in each province and large State or Agency. By this time, the standard rules, framed as above, had been finally sanctioned and circulated, so that the local officers could at once start on the work of translation and printing. From Chapter V. of this review some notion can be gathered of the work involved in the former task, but apart from a small issue of schedules in dialects specially confined to a few Hill tracts, 17 languages were all that were found necessary. In the meantime, the local Superintendent, in his turn, was issuing his general instructions, and the District and State officers were mapping out their charges for the purpose of enumeration, and, what always is a trouble in India, estimating the number of schedules required for use in each subdivision, specifying the languages and even the character in which each indent should be printed, and arranging for their circulation throughout the subdivision from the nearest railway station. Frequent and minute inspection of the progress of these preliminaries was made during the four months preceding the census. In illustration of the magnitude of the task, it may be mentioned that, speaking in round numbers, about 290 tons of paper were used for the schedules, and just under a million men and boys were employed as enumerators. In a country where only about 11 males in the hundred can read and write at all, and the standard of that accomplishment is, as we have seen in Chapter VI., by no means a high one, the difficulty of finding enough competent men was got over by the adoption of a plan tried with success in 1881, and mentioned in Chapter I. above, namely, that of entering beforehand in the schedules the whole of the domiciled population of a place, and merely bringing it up to date on the night of the enumeration. If this course had not been adopted, what with an average population of 300 in each enumerator's block, and the general ignorance of the head of a household as to what was required of him, it would have been impossible to take a census in a single night at all. The preliminary record, too, gave an excellent opportunity of scrutiny by superior agency to that engaged in the enumeration, and in this way much error was detected and rectified. The above remarks refer merely to the ordinary or stationary population, but in India, the long through lines of rail, the practice of making night journeys by cart or on foot, the large boating population on the great rivers, the regimental community residing beyond the pale of civil rule, ports and so on, all had to receive special attention and be enumerated under special rules. There is no doubt that the care taken on this occasion to provide for the census of such unusual cases resulted in a considerable increase in the numbers returned, as compared with the corresponding tale of 10 years back, when the matter was in its tentative stage. In fact, such were the precautions, that it is on record that one distinguished military officer on his way from the east to the north of India found that he had been returned three times in the course of about 15 hours. On the other hand, several others whom the census officers would gladly have seen in their Calcutta returns, were driven to publish the fact of their omission. It is superfluous to comment on the actual taking of the check, as above described, on the prescribed night, so we may pass on to the subsequent operations. In the introductory chapter it is mentioned that the results were published within five weeks of the enumeration, a "record" in compilation, considering that nearly a million persons were collected by tens at local centres, and had to make up totals, check them and get them to the District or State headquarters as soon as possible. The Superintendent of the North-West Provinces, Mr. Baillie, and Mr. Drew, his Bombay colleague, ran neck and neck in the race, each getting in their totals, the one of 46, and the other of 18 millions, in 10 days from the census.

The next operation was the abstraction in more detail than by sexes, which was all that was asked for in the preliminary totaling. The rules issued by the Census Commissioner had been in the hands of the Superintendents for some time previously, and in most cases the necessary forms had been printed, so that establishments could be set to work as fast as the trained supervisors could instruct them into proper efficiency. The system followed was practically uniform throughout the country, though the distribution of the work varied. In tracts where the supply of literates was small a central office was organised. Where more favourable conditions ruled, the work was decentralised, sometimes by divisions, as in the Panjáb, sometimes by districts, as in Bengal, Bombay, and the North-West Provinces, and again, by linguistic centres, as in Madras. The decision in this matter was left to the local Superintendent, and the only stipulation by the Commissioner was that the standard rules should be strictly observed in respect to the forms used and the tests taken of all work sent up by the abstractors. The tabulation of the abstracted work by subdivisions was ordered to follow closely on the former part of the operations, but owing to the varying supply of efficient men, and to the fact that tabulation is always found to be beyond the capacity of most of the ruck who can scrape along very fairly in a semi-mechanical task like abstraction, there was much diversity of practice, leading, in some instances, to serious delay when the results came up for final compilation. As each District was completed in any of the tables, or rather in any set of tables, for the series was subdivided for this purpose, the totals were passed by the provincial Superintendent and sent to the central office in Simla. On the completion of a Province or State for the above sets respectively, the compiled results were interchanged by the Superintendent and the Commissioner, so as to ensure agreement. The Panjáb came in an easy winner in this part of the work, and Mr. Maclagan sent in his first 15 tables by the beginning of August, five months after starting. It must be stated, too, in his favour, that no alterations were afterwards found necessary in his results. The same may be said of Messrs. Gait and Drew, who followed in six and seven months respectively. By the beginning of January, or 10 months after the enumeration, all the above 15 tables were ready, with a few exceptions, which came in a month later. But here begin the sorrows of the census, over which the reader will not be surprised if a veil be drawn. In two large Provinces errors in tabulation were discovered, which threw out all the Imperial tables printed between January and March, necessitating their reprint in England, a task which was not completed till November 1892. Then, again, the two last tables, those concerning caste and occupation, were found to entail more labour and scrutiny in their final compilation by the provincial officers than the whole of what had gone before. Messrs. Drew and Narsinghaiangar were the first to finish them, and all but the two unlucky Provinces aforesaid, and one other, followed within a few weeks. The last of the caste statements, however, did not reach the Commissioner till the 11th of May 1893, and until its arrival he was unable to close and send to press the general tables on this subject; nor, of course, could he take up the review of statistics that were not before him in their final and completed shape. In fact, the whole of the delay in finishing off the census work, whether in the provinces or in the central office, can be truly set down to the exceedingly heavy labour involved in the compilation, classification and printing of so vast an array of figures as those collected in connection with these two topics. Most of the Superintendents were able, in spite of the above obstacle, to complete their reviews within 15 months of the enumeration, but unfortunately the difficulties varied with the population and the number of subordinate offices established, so that the three largest provinces were necessarily the most handicapped, especially as they all undertook the complicated, but highly interesting return of marriage by age and caste, which was left optional with the local authorities. On the present occasion, probably, the maximum of detail was attempted that it is safe to undertake with the agency of the quality now available in India, and though part of the same field may easily be covered by simpler or more restricted means, the results seem to those who have had to consider them to be such as it will be unnecessary to secure at intervals so short as

10 years. It will be enough, according to this view of the circumstances, to take stock, as it were, of the prevailing variations from the general average in the matter of caste in relation to education and marriage, at every other census, even if not once only in a generation of 30 years. This, however, is a matter alien to the present subject.

The cursory account of the operations given above will serve to explain how it happened that so long an interval has taken place between the remarkably prompt publication of the preliminary statement of the results of the census and the issue of the final review. There is still to be considered the cost of the whole of the operations. As this review is written in England, so that explanations or supplementary information cannot be obtained without a delay of a couple of months, the statement given on the next page is admittedly not final, and revision of the figures quoted will no doubt be made on audit of the accounts of the last and current year by the Indian Government. It is, however, believed to be approximately correct. In connection with it, one of the first points to bring to notice is, that though India has peculiar difficulties and complications of its own, above those of European countries, in the way of taking a census, it is not without its compensating advantages. The village system provides the greater part of the continent with a supply of men trained in the interpretation of rules, and with a certain and very useful amount of acquaintance with arithmetic. This forms the nucleus of the census staff. Next, and of still more importance, there comes the administrative experience of the District officer, which it is impossible to value too highly when special arrangements, such as those for the enumeration, have to be organised and carried into practice. Then, too, in addition to the village accountant staff, there is the large supply of subordinate clerical agency in the offices of the State and local bodies, all of which is placed at the disposal of the census officers for a day or so, as far as is not incompatible with the fulfilment of the more emergent duties occurring in the routine of business. It is necessary, too, not to omit the great help gratuitously rendered by the literate residents of a place who come forward as either enumerators or supervisors; and, finally, in the not inconsiderable array of the unemployed members of the professional classes, a cheap and fairly efficient supply of clerical labour is obtained for the abstraction establishments.

TABLE A.—Showing the Imperial Charges on account of the Census.

Province, &c.	Actual Charges during the Year.					Grand Total.
	1889–90.	1890–91.	1891–92.	1892–93.	1893–94.	
	Rs.	Rs.	Rs.	Rs.	Rs.	Rs.
Madras	244	72,405	3,51,527	35,917	—	4,60,093
Bombay	—	66,509	1,11,408	8,476	—	1,86,393
Bengal	—	1,08,952	5,52,110	43,083	—	7,04,145
N.-W. Provinces and Oudh	—	92,967	3,64,041	20,264	—	4,77,272
Panjáb	—	69,015	1,22,270	2,381	—	1,93,666
Burma	—	34,154	87,085	26,091	—	1,47,330
Central Provinces	—	24,914	75,715	9,628	—	1,10,257
Assam	—	23,143	47,367	3,117	—	73,627
A.—Total, Provinces	**244**	**4,92,059**	**17,11,523**	**1,48,957**	—	**23,52,783**
Ajmér	—	2,582	6,648	1,000	—	10,230
Coorg and Bangalore	—	229	2,809	833	—	3,871
Quettah and Andamans	—	645	165	—	—	810
Rajputána	—	9,649	6,476	1,813	—	17,938
Central India	—	15,836	22,914	2,779	—	41,529
B.—Total, Minor Tracts	—	**28,941**	**39,012**	**6,425**	—	**74,378**
C.—Census Commissioner, &c.	**17,576**	**42,753**	**47,785**	**41,886**	**20,000**	**170,000**
GRAND TOTAL	**17,820**	**5,63,753**	**17,98,320**	**1,97,268**	**20,000**	**25,97,161**

TABLE B.—Comparison of the Imperial Charges of 1891 with those of 1881.

Province, &c.	Population enumerated (in Thousands).		Charges in 1881.	Per-centage of Increase in		Mean Charge per 1,000 Persons.	
	1891.	1881.		Population.	Charge.	1891.	1881.
			Rs.			Rs.	Rs.
Madras	35,630	30,827	5,00,000	15·6	−8·0	12·91	16·22
Bombay	18,901	16,506	1,69,903*	14·5	9·7*	9·86	10·29
Bengal	71,347	66,691	8,55,647	6·9	−17·7	9·87	12·83
N.-W. Provinces, &c.	46,905	44,108	2,80,145	6·3	70·3	10·18	6·35
Panjáb	20,867	18,843	1,56,000	10·7	24·1	9·28	8·28
Burma	7,605	3,737	76,645†	103·5	92·2†	19·37	20·51
Central Provinces	10,784	9,839	1,67,983	9·6	−52·3	10·22	17·07
Assam	5,477	4,881	39,082	12·2	88·3	13·44	8·01
Total, Provinces	**217,516**	**195,432**	**22,45,405**	**11·3**	**4·8**	**10·81**	**11·49**
Other Heads of Account	—	—	1,78,118	—	—	—	—
TOTAL	**281,615**	**253,793**	**24,23,523**	**11·0**	**7·2**	—	—

* Provincial contribution is excluded.
† The printing in Burma in 1881 is reported to have been only partially debited to the census grant.

Owing to the above advantages, the census in India is taken at a cost to the Imperial Government of only Rs. 10.81, or something a little under 15*s*. per 1,000 persons, in the provinces. Elsewhere, as in the States, the cost was defrayed for the most part by the Chiefs themselves, and the Imperial Government only supplied forms where required, and, in the case of the less wealthy and smaller tracts, undertook the compilation as well. The incidence on the whole country therefore, cannot be ascertained correctly. In British territory, the range per 1,000 was from Rs. 9.28 in the Panjáb to Rs. 19.37 in Burma, where clerical labour is alien to the habits of the native, and has to be paid, accordingly, at fancy rates. It should be borne in mind, however, that the Panjáb did not undertake the more elaborate of the caste tables, so that, looking at the amount of work done, the cheapest rate is found in Bengal and Bombay, and the dearest, as is to be expected, in Assam, where much of the staff of writers has to be imported from its neighbour. It is hardly of much use to compare the above rates with that of the census in England, as the standard of work and wages is so different, but it may be mentioned that in the latter country, the cost in 1881 was about 4*l*. 18*s*. 9*d*. per 1,000, or, at the rate of exchange taken above, nearly Rs. 72, not far, that is, from five times the rate in India. There is considerable difficulty in comparing the cost in India of the last two enumerations, since in several instances it seems that large items, such as printing, were debited in 1881 to one of the ordinary heads of account, whereas on this occasion as much care as possible has been taken to ensure that the whole cost has been properly shown against the census grant. In Assam, Ajmér and Burmah this is particularly noticeable; but making no allowance for the discrepancy, Table B. shows that whilst the population comparable has increased by over 11 per cent., the cost exceeds that of 1881 by no more than 4·8, and the rate per 1,000 persons has fallen from Rs. 11.49 to Rs. 10.81. The most striking difference is in the Central Provinces, where from Rs. 17.07, the rate has receded to 10.22. Next comes Madras, the accounts of which for 1881 are not quite clear. Taking the amount as set forth in the Imperial and Provincial Reports, the difference is between Rs. 16.22 and 12.91. Bengal, again, is a most difficult province to enumerate, owing, in part, to the general absence of village staff, and the lack of information available as to boundaries, area, and so on. Then, too, the system of abstraction in district offices was tried for the first time, necessitating more preparation and supervision than in other circumstances. It is very much therefore to the credit of Mr. O'Donnell that in spite of the above hindrances and the additional statistics prepared by him, he has managed to reduce the expenditure by more than 17 per cent., whilst the population he had to deal with was nearly 7 per cent. larger than that of his predecessor, and he had to cope with an amount of fudging in a few of his offices almost as phenomenally ingenious as that mentioned in Chapter VI. above, as characterising the dealings of the Bengali Squeers with the State inspector of education. The rise in the Assam charges is attributed in great measure to omission from the return in 1881, as well as to the employment of agency already in State service but whose pay was not debited to the census for the period of their deputation on abstraction. In the Panjáb the work was mostly done by the village accountants, who were most efficient. Their scale of pay, however, has been raised since 1881, and the allowances for extra work may have been either more liberal or more generally earned; at any rate, the cost of the operations was raised somewhat above that of 1881. The accounts of the latter, however, do not seem to have been finally recorded, so part of the excess may be nominal only. In the North-West Provinces, with the lowest rate of increase of population of any of the provinces, the charges have risen in nearly the same proportion as those in Assam, which have been explained above, or Burma, where the relative incidence has been considerably reduced. The causes of this unsatisfactory anomaly have formed the subject of a separate correspondence, so they do not require comment here. Berar, where the same disproportion occurred, has been omitted from the return because the charge is not Imperial. Similarly, the contributions from provincial funds for special tabulation prescribed for local purposes have not been taken into account. In regard to the charges on account of the Census Commissioner and his establishment, which show a decided increase over the corresponding items in 1881, it must be remembered that owing to the unforeseen delays above mentioned in the submission of reports and tables, the central office has had thrown upon it the burden of working out all the proportional reduction of the returns, which was probably being worked out simultaneously by the local Superintendent, though his results were not available for use in the former. This entailed the maintenance of a larger staff than would otherwise have been required, and for a longer period. Then, again, the cost of reprinting all the tables that had been rejected for the reasons stated above, was an unexpected addition to the charges, and, finally, under this head are included certain items not connected with the Commissioner's office otherwise than by a sanction issuing from it. The personal charges show a decrease, as compared with those of 10 years back, except in the matter of travelling expenses. These were heavier in 1891, and the increase is not to be regretted, as the means of supervision were thereby much enlarged, and an acquaintance gained by the controlling authority with men and their doings that could not have been obtained by any amount of study and correspondence.

Here this review must end. The census of India is the heaviest enterprise of the kind that has ever been undertaken, especially as the final enumeration of over 250 millions of people was carried out within four hours. It has been shown to have been conducted economically, and considering the unusual variety of the information collected, and looking at the time spent over the census in other countries, the results cannot be fairly said to have been unduly delayed in publication. As to their accuracy, all that need be said is that in this work there has been no attempt to withhold any criticism of them merely because it might show up their statistical defects, and, to put it comparatively, the evidence is strongly in favour of a great improvement in this respect on the work of 1881. As this is due to the increased confidence of the people in the honesty of the purpose of the State in making inquiries of this sort, it is equally indisputable that for many years to come each census will be more accurate than its predecessor, until we get the return of women nearly up to that of men, and education may induce the lieges to admit that in returning their ages there are other numbers available than those indicated by the natural provision of fingers and toes. In the very opening of this review it was stated that the main standpoint was the diversity, not the unity, of the conditions that had to be dealt with, and that India could not be statistically treated as a single whole, so throughout the work it has been ever an object to avoid as much as possible the use of the Indian total otherwise than as a blank wall on which to chalk the differences of the various parts of that country. By this means it has been possible, no doubt, to collect certain similarities into something of the nature of a general average, though not one that can be circumscribed within the crisp conciseness of an arithmetical expression. The most that can be claimed for it is that it represents a point from which the divergencies on each side are probably the least. It is scarcely necessary, therefore, to add that in the eyes of the reviewer, one of the recommendations of this view, and not one of the least, is the chance that it may induce readers interested in the subjects of which it treats to extend their studies to the Provincial volumes published by his colleagues, on which so much of the present work is based.

JERVOISE ATHELSTANE BAINES,
Census Commissioner for India.

India Office, London,
10th July 1893.

APPENDIX.*

SELECTIONS FROM VOLUME I. OF THE GENERAL TABLES.

* For the Parliamentary edition only.

SUMMARY TABLES.

I.—General Statement.

	INDIA.	BRITISH PROVINCES.	NATIVE STATES.
Area in square miles	1,560,160	964,993	595,167
Towns and villages	717,549	537,901	179,648
(a) *Towns*	2,035	1,416	619
(b) *Villages*	715,514	536,485	179,029
Occupied houses	52,932,102	40,463,963	12,468,139
(a) *In Towns*	5,128,395	3,745,408	1,382,987
(b) *In Villages*	47,803,707	36,718,555	11,085,152
Total population	287,223,431	221,172,952	66,050,479
(a) *In Towns*	27,251,176	20,391,129	6,860,047
(b) *In Villages*	259,972,255	200,781,823	59,190,432
Males	146,727,296	112,542,739	34,184,557
(a) *In Towns*	14,446,160	10,895,997	3,550,163
(b) *In Villages*	132,281,136	101,646,742	30,634,394
Females	140,496,135	108,630,213	31,865,922
(a) *In Towns*	12,805,016	9,495,132	3,309,884
(b) *In Villages*	127,691,119	99,135,081	28,556,038

II.—Variation in Population.

			INDIA.	PROVINCES.	STATES.
A. Tracts enumerated in both 1881 and 1891.	Total Population	1891	281,614,934	218,155,115	63,459,819
		1881	253,793,514	198,860,606	54,932,908
		Variation	+ 27,821,420	+ 19,294,509	+ 8,526,911
	Males	1891	143,887,849	111,082,159	32,805,690
		1881	129,899,318	101,324,656	28,574,662
		Variation	+ 13,988,531	+ 9,757,503	+ 4,231,028
	Females	1891	137,727,085	107,072,956	30,654,129
		1881	123,894,196	97,535,950	26,358,246
		Variation	+ 13,832,889	+ 9,537,006	+ 4,295,883
B. Total, including territorail additions since 1881.	Total Population*	1891	287,179,715	221,172,952	66,006,763
		1881	253,793,514	198,860,606	54,932,908
		Variation	+ 33,386,201	+ 22,312,346	+ 11,073,855
	Males	1891	146,704,540	112,542,739	34,161,801
		1881	129,899,318	101,324,656	28,574,662
		Variation	+ 16,805,222	+ 11,218,083	+ 5,587,139
	Females	1891	140,475,175	108,630,213	31,844,962
		1881	123,894,196	97,535,950	26,358,246
		Variation	+ 16,580,979	+ 11,094,263	+ 5,486,716

* The difference of 43,716 between the population of 1891, shown here, and that given in Table I. is due to the exclusion of certain Bhil tracts in Rajputána, not fully enumerated on either occasion.

III.—Towns and Villages classified by Population.

Class and Population.	INDIA.		PROVINCES.		STATES.	
	No.	Population.	No.	Population.	No.	Population.
1. 1—199	343,052	32,625,858	248,564	24,279,022	94,488	8,346,836
2. 200—	222,996	71,180,018	171,938	54,872,157	51,058	16,307,861
3. 500—	97,846	67,475,109	76,338	52,690,492	21,508	14,784,617
4. 1,000—	38,128	51,349,338	30,260	40,741,875	7,868	10,607,463
5. 2,000—	7,906	19,113,616	6,282	15,178,077	1,624	3,935,539
6. 3,000—	3,770	14,059,089	2,977	11,100,332	793	2,958,757
7. 5,000—	1,502	10,048,838	1,050	6,924,151	452	3,124,687
8. 10,000—	366	4,402,062	220	2,659,579	146	1,742,483
9. 15,000—	150	2,541,135	94	1,602,500	56	938,635
10. 20,000—	168	4,925,158	118	3,548,264	50	1,376,894
11. 50,000—	76	9,309,434	60	7,550,172	16	1,759,262
Unclassed: a. *Travellers, &c.*	—	56,334	—	26,331	—	30,003
Unclassed: b. *Not registered*	1,589	137,442	—	—	1,589	137,442
Total	**717,549**	**287,223.431**	**537,901**	**221,172,952**	**179,648**	**66,050,979**

Note.—The last item refers to the Bengal State of Hill Tipperah, where the villages were not classified. The number of towns of 50,000, and over, is less by two here than in the next table, because the two suburbs of Calcutta are there shown in the population of the city though retaining their distinct numbering, whilst in this table they appear in Class 10.

IV.—The Urban Population classified by Towns.

Towns containing a Population of—	INDIA.		PROVINCES.		STATES.	
	No.	Population.	No.	Population.	No.	Population.
1. 100,000 and over	30	6,173,123	24	5,079,350	6	1,093,773
2. 50,000—	48	3,255,175	38	2,589,686	10	665,489
3. 20,000—	149	4,492,113	112	3,417,347	37	1,074,766
4. 10,000—	407	5,487,983	297	4,044,174	110	1,443,809
5. 5,000—	896	6,164,900	577	4,023,339	319	2,141,561
6. 3,000—	301	1,204,767	238	950,605	63	254,162
7. Under 2,000	204	437,259	130	279,999	74	157,260
Unclassed (*Travellers, &c.*)	—	35,856	—	6,629	—	29,227
Total Urban	**2,035**	**27,251,176**	**1,416**	**20,391,129**	**619**	**6,860,047**

V.—Variation in Population of Chief Towns.

TOWN.	POPULATION. 1891.	POPULATION. 1881.	VARIATION.
1. Bombay*	821,764	773,196	+ 48,568
2. Calcutta City*	681,560	433,219	+284,341
„ Suburbs	59,584	251,439	−191,855
N. Suburban Municipality.	34,278	29,982	+ 4,296
S. Suburban Municipality.	69,642	51,658	+ 17,984
Howrah	116,606	105,206	+ 11,400
Bálli	16,700	7,037	+ 9,663
Total Calcutta and Suburbs	**978,370**	**878,541**	**+ 99,829**
3. Madras*	452,518	405,848	+ 46,670
4. *Hyderábád (Deccan)**	415,039	354,962	+ 60,077
5. Lucknow*	273,028	261,303	+ 11,725
6. Benares*	219,467	214,758	+ 4,709
7. Delhi*	192,579	173,393	+ 19,186
8. Mandalay*†	188,815	—	—
9. Cawnpore*	188,712	151,444	+ 37,268
10. *Bangalore**	180,366	155,857	+ 24,509
11. Rangoon*	180,324	134,176	+ 46,148
12. Lahore*	176,854	157,287	+ 19,567
13. Allahábád*	175,246	160,118	+ 15,128
14. Agra*	168,662	160,203	+ 8,459
15. Patna	165,192	170,654	— 5,462
16. Poona*	161,390	129,751	+ 31,639
17. *Jaipur*	158,905	142,578	+ 16,327
18. Ahmedábád*	148,412	127,621	+ 20,791
19. Amritsar*	136,766	151,896	— 15,130
20. Baréli*	121,039	113,417	+ 7,622
21. Meerut*	119,390	99,565	+ 19,825
22. Srinagar*†	118,960	—	—
23. Nágpur*	117,014	98,299	+ 18,715
24. Baroda*	116,420	106,512	+ 9,908
25. Súrat*	109,229	109,844	— 615
26. Karáchi*	105,199	73,560	+ 31,639
27. Gwalior*	104,083	88,066	+ 16,017
28. *Indore**	92,329	83,091	+ 9,238
29. Trichinopoly*	90,609	84,449	+ 6,160
30. Madura	87,428	76,847	+ 10,581
31. Jabalpur*	84,481	75,705	+ 8,776
32. Peshâwar*	84,191	79,982	+ 4,209
33. Mirzápur	84,130	85,362	— 1,232

TOWN.	POPULATION. 1891.	POPULATION. 1881.	VARIATION.
34. Dacca	82,321	79,076	+ 3,245
35. Gaya	80,383	76,415	+ 3,968
36. Ambála*	79,294	67,463	+ 11,831
37. Faizábád*	78,921	71,405	+ 7,516
38. Sháhjehánpur*	78,522	77,404	+ 1,118
39. Farakhábád*	78,032	79,761	— 1,729
40. *Rámpur**	76,733	74,250	+ 2,483
41. Multán*	74,562	68,674	+ 5,888
42. *Mysore**	74,048	60,292	+ 13,756
43. Ráwalpindi*	73,795	52,975	+ 20,820
44. Darbhanga	73,561	65,955	+ 7,606
45. Morádábád*	72,921	69,352	+ 3,569
46. *Bhopál*	70,338	55,402	+ 14,936
47. Bhágalpur	69,106	68,238	+ 868
48. Ajmér	68,843	48,735	+ 20,108
49. *Bharatpur*	68,033	66,163	+ 1,870
50. Salem	67,710	59,631	+ 8,079
51. Jálandhar*	66,202	52,119	+ 14,083
52. Calicut	66,078	57,085	+ 8,993
53. Gorakhpur*	63,620	59,908	+ 3,712
54. Sahâranpur	63,194	59,194	+ 4,000
55. Sholápur	61,915	59,890	+ 2,025
56. *Jodhpur*	61,849	57,211	+ 4,638
57. Aligarh (Koil)	61,485	62,443	— 958
58. Mattra*	61,195	57,724	+ 3,471
59. Bellâry	59,467	53,460	+ 6,007
60. Negapatam	59,221	53,855	+ 5,366
61. Hyderábád (Sindh)*	58,048	48,153	+ 9,895
62. *Bhaunagar*	57,653	47,792	+ 9,861
63. Chapra	56,352	51,670	+ 5,682
64. Monghyr	57,077	55,372	+ 1,705
65. *Bikanér*	56,252	43,283	+ 12,969
66. *Patiála*	55,856	53,629	+ 2,227
67. Maulmain	55,785	53,107	+ 2,678
68. Sialkot*	55,087	45,762	+ 9,325
69. Tanjore	54,390	74,745	— 355
70. Kambakonam	54,307	50,098	+ 4,209
71. Jhánsi*†	53,779	—	—
72. Hubli	52,595	36,677	+ 15,918
73. *Alwar*	52,398	49,867	+ 2,531
74. Ferozpur*	50,437	39,570	+ 10,867

* Including Cantonments and Military Lines.

† Figures for 1881 not available.

VI.—Religion.

Religion.	INDIA.	PROVINCES.	STATES.
Hindu (*Brahmanic*)	207,688,724	155,129,941	52,558,783
„ *Arya*	39,952	39,014	938
„ *Brahmo*	3,051	2,988	63
TOTAL HINDU	207,731,727	155,171,943	52,559,784
Sikh	1,907,833	1,407,968	499,865
Jain	1,416,638	495,001	921,637
Buddhist	7,131,361	7,095,398	35,963
Zoroastrian	89,904	76,952	12,952
Musalman	57,321,164	49,550,491	7,770,673
Christian	2,284,380	1,491,662	792,718
Jew	17,194	14,669	2,525
Animistic	9,280,467	5,848,427	3,432,040
Minor Religions	185	163	22
Religion not returned	42,578	20,278	22,300
Total	287,223,431	221,172,952	66,050,479

VII.—Age.

Age.	INDIA.		PROVINCES.		STATES.	
	Males.	Females.	Males.	Females.	Males.	Females.
0	4,772,871	4,868,171	3,757,485	3,827,244	1,015,386	1,040,927
1	2,536,430	2,633,714	1,915,249	1,989,643	621,181	644,071
2	4,203,315	4,468,349	3,239,481	3,455,796	963,834	1,012,553
3	4,650,886	4,968,439	3,612,038	3,858,675	1,038,848	1,109,764
4	4,467,878	4,471,446	3,409,284	3,424,241	1,058,594	1,047,205
0—4	20,631,380	21,410,119	15,933,537	16,555,599	4,697,843	4,854,520
5—9	20,908,467	19,578,667	16,121,870	15,131,827	4,786,597	4,446,840
10—14	16,680,438	13,265,378	12,882,349	10,295,331	3,798,089	2,970,047
15—19	12,229,892	11,376,709	9,406,350	8,869,857	2,823,542	2,506,852
20—24	11,743,796	12,577,424	8,961,462	9,669,199	2,782,334	2,908,225
25—29	12,828,365	12,680,985	9,742,243	9,776,490	3,086,122	2,904,495
30—34	12,319,747	11,855,489	9,303,660	9,044,517	3,016,087	2,810,972
35—39	8,980,902	7,783,755	6,898,962	6,039,898	2,081,940	1,743,857
40—44	9,338,636	8,782,207	7,041,292	6,689,990	2,297,344	2,092,217
45—49	5,355,522	4,527,071	4,154,570	3,567,288	1,200,952	959,783
50—54	6,015,467	5,970,618	4,551,100	4,574,183	1,464,367	1,396,435
55—59	2,618,702	2,378,652	2,061,145	1,900,719	557,557	477,933
60—	6,769,435	8,032,448	5,282,917	6,332,328	1,486,518	1,700,120
Age not returned	306,547	276,613	201,282	182,987	105,265	93,626
Total	146,727,296	140,496,135	112,542,739	108,630,213	34,184,557	31,865,922

VIII.—Civil Condition.

Age	Condition	INDIA. Males.	INDIA. Females.	PROVINCES. Males.	PROVINCES. Females.	STATES. Males.	STATES. Females.
0–4	Unmarried	18,805,099	19,419,383	15,851,537	16,351,766	2,953,562	3,067,617
	Married	103,069	258,760	76,428	192,009	26,641	66,751
	Widowed	6,945	13,878	5,572	11,824	1,373	2,054
	Total	**18,915,113**	**19,692,021**	**15,933,537**	**16,555,599**	**2,981,576**	**3,136,422**
5–9	Unmarried	18,344,180	15,663,196	15,509,159	13,254,376	2,835,021	2,408,820
	Married	690,803	2,201,404	588,526	1,821,308	102,277	380,096
	Widowed	28,139	64,040	24,185	56,143	3,954	7,897
	Total	**19,063,122**	**17,928,640**	**16,121,870**	**15,131,827**	**2,941,252**	**2,796,813**
10–14	Unmarried	12,778,801	5,977,301	10,802,316	5,003,591	1,976,485	973,710
	Married	2,342,433	6,016,759	2,017,614	5,137,870	324,819	878,889
	Widowed	71,471	174,532	62,419	153,870	9,052	20,662
	Total	**15,192,705**	**12,168,592**	**12,882,349**	**10,295,331**	**2,310,356**	**1,873,261**
15–34	Unmarried	13,622,958	2,133,452	11,455,088	1,738,832	2,167,870	394,620
	Married	29,683,040	38,144,713	24,795,495	32,013,813	4,887,545	6,130,900
	Widowed	1,350,699	4,160,548	1,163,132	3,607,418	187,567	553,130
	Total	**44,656,697**	**44,438,713**	**37,413,715**	**37,360,063**	**7,242,982**	**7,078,650**
35–49	Unmarried	1,025,383	209,539	864,551	158,647	160,832	50,892
	Married	18,649,824	12,034,052	15,656,068	10,155,572	2,993,756	1,878,480
	Widowed	1,858,073	6,996,592	1,574,205	5,982,957	283,868	1,013,635
	Total	**21,533,280**	**19,240,183**	**18,094,824**	**16,297,176**	**3,438,456**	**2,943,007**
50 and over	Unmarried	430,603	128,749	362,724	97,503	67,879	31,246
	Married	10,537,733	3,688,667	8,922,138	3,134,434	1,615,595	554,233
	Widowed	3,087,748	11,224,933	2,610,300	9,575,293	477,448	1,649,640
	Total	**14,056,084**	**15,042,349**	**11,895,162**	**12,807,230**	**2,160,922**	**2,235,119**
Age not returned.	Unmarried	129,405	100,413	92,052	71,841	37,353	28,572
	Married	113,398	104,591	81,860	75,023	31,538	29,568
	Widowed	9,408	22,906	6,703	15,200	2,705	7,706
	Total	**252,211**	**227,910**	**180,615**	**162,064**	**71,596**	**65,846**
Total returning Civil condition.	Unmarried	65,186,429	43,632,033	54,987,427	36,676,556	10,199,002	6,955,477
	Married	62,120,300	62,448,946	52,138,129	52,530,029	9,982,171	9,918,917
	Widowed	6,412,483	22,657,429	5,446,516	19,402,705	965,967	3,254,724
	Total	**133,669,212**	**128,738,408**	**112,522,072**	**108,609,290**	**21,147,140**	**20,129,118**
Not enumerated by Civil Condition.*		**13,058,084**	**11,757,727**	**20,667**	**20,923**	**13,037,417**	**11,736,804**
Total Population		**146,727,296**	**140,496,135**	**112,542,739**	**108,630,213**	**34,184,557**	**31,865,922**

*A. Assam (N. Lushai)	—	—	20,667	20,923	—	—
B. Kashmir	—	—	—	—	1,353,160	1,190,653
B. Rajputána	—	—	—	—	6,342,407	5,656,979
B. Central India	—	—	—	—	5,331,271	4,880,515
B. Mahi Kántha (Bombay)	—	—	—	—	10,579	8,657
Total States	—	—	—	—	13,037,417	11,736,804
INDIA	13,058,084	11,757,727	—	—	—	—

IX.—Instruction.

		India.			Provinces.		States.	
		Total.	Males.	Females.	Males.	Females.	Males.	Females.
All Ages.	Under Instruction	3,195,220	2,997,558	197,662	2,593,887	162,248	403,671	35,414
	Literate	12,097,530	11,554,035	543,495	9,903,664	447,924	1,650,371	95,571
	Illiterate	246,546,176	118,819,408	127,726,768	99,797,906	107,794,481	19,021,502	19,932,287
	Total returning Instruction.	**261,838,926**	**133,371,001**	**128,467,925**	**112,295,457**	**108,404,653**	**21,075,544**	**20,063,272**
Under Fifteen.	Under Instruction	2,695,792	2,518,240	177,552	2,170,695	145,756	347,545	31,796
	Literate	763,120	675,357	87,763	580,210	72,588	95,147	15,175
	Illiterate	99,468,421	49,960,163	49,508,258	42,169,671	41,748,733	7,790,492	7,759,525
	Total	**102,927,333**	**53,153,760**	**49,773,573**	**44,920,576**	**41,967,077**	**8,233,184**	**7,806,496**
15—24.	Under Instruction	441,224	427,595	13,629	379,023	11,484	48,572	2,145
	Literate	3,052,787	2,864,980	187,807	2,460,633	157,797	404,347	30,010
	Illiterate	40,426,673	18,574,203	21,852,470	15,518,799	18,359,483	3,055,404	3,492,987
	Total	**43,920,684**	**21,866,778**	**22,053,906**	**18,358,455**	**18,528,764**	**3,508,323**	**3,525,142**
25 and over.	Under Instruction	58,204	51,723	6,481	44,169	5,008	7,554	1,473
	Literate	8,281,623	8,013,698	267,925	6,862,821	217,539	1,150,877	50,386
	Illiterate	106,651,082	50,285,042	56,366,040	42,109,436	47,686,265	8,175,606	8,679,775
	Total	**114,990,909**	**58,350,463**	**56,640,446**	**49,016,426**	**47,908,812**	**9,334,037**	**8,731,634**
	Not enumerated by education.*	**25,384,505**	**13,356,295**	**12,028,210**	**247,282**	**225,560**	**13,109,013**	**11,802,650**
	Total Population	**287,223,431**	**146,727,296**	**140,496,135**	**112,542,739**	**108,630,213**	**34,184,557**	**31,865,922**
*A.	Assam (*N. Lushai*)	—	—	—	20,667	20,923	—	—
	Bengal (*Chittagong Hills*)	—	—	—	59,566	47,720	—	—
	Madras (*Vizagapatam Agency*)	—	—	—	167,049	156,917	—	—
	Total, Provinces	—	—	—	**247,282**	**225,560**	—	—
*B.	Kashmér	—	—	—	—	—	1,353,160	1,190,653
	Rajputána	—	—	—	—	—	6,342,407	5,656,979
	Central India	—	—	—	—	—	5,331,271	4,880,515
	Hill Tipperah (Bengal)	—	—	—	—	—	71,596	65,846
	Mahi Kántha (Bombay)	—	—	—	—	—	10,579	8,657
	Total, States	—	—	—	—	—	**13,109,013**	**11,802,650**
	INDIA	**25,384,505**	**13,356,295**	**12,028,210**	—	—	—	—

X.—Parent Tongue.

(a) Languages by Linguistic groups.		Population returning.
FAMILY	A. Aryo-Indic	195,463,807
	B. Dravidian	52,964,620
	C. Kolarian	2,959,006
	D. Gipsy Dialects	401,125
	E. Khási	178,637
	F. Tibeto Burman	7,293,928
	G. Môn Annam	229,342
	H. Taic, or Shán	178,447
	J. Maylayan	4,084
	K. Sinitic	713,350
	L. Japanese	93
	M. Aryo-Eranic	1,329,428
	N. Semitic	55,534
	O. Turanic	659
	P. Aryo-European	245,745
	Q. Basque	1
	R. Hamitic or Negro	9,612
Language unrecognisable		363
Return left blank		19,659
Total enumerated by Parent Tongue		262,047,440
Population not enumerated by Parent Tongue		25,175,991
TOTAL		287,223,431

(b) Languages, in order of prevalence in the tracts enumerated.

(1) 1,000,000 and over each.

Language	Population returning
1. Hindi—A.	85,675,373
2. Bengáli—A.	41,343,762
3. Telugu—B.	19,885,137
4. Maráthi—A.	18,892,875
5. Panjábi—A.	17,724,610
6. Tamil—B.	15,229,759
7. Gujaráthi—A.	10,619,789
8. Kanarese—B.	9,751,885
9. Uriya—A.	9,010,957
10. Burmese—F.	5,926,864
11. Malayálam—B.	5,428,250
12. Urdu (*Masalmáni*)*—A.	3,669,390
13. Sindhi—A.	2,592,341
14. Santhál—C.	1,709,680
15. Western Pahári (Panjab)—A.	1,523,098
16. Assamese—A.	1,435,820
17. Gond—B.	1,379,580
18. Central Pahári (Garhwáli, &c.)—A.	1,153,384
19. Márwádi—A.	1,147,480
20. Pashtu—M.	1,080,931

(2) 100,000 to 1,000,000.

Language	Population returning
21. Karên—K.	674,846
22. Múndá (Kôl)—C.	654,507
23. Túlu—B.	491,728
24. Kachhi—A.	439,697
25. Gypsy dialects (Lambáni, &c.)—D.	401,125
26. Oraon—B.	368,222
27. Khand (Khónd)—B.	320,071
28. English—P.	238,499
29. Môn (Talaing)—G.	226,495
30. Balôch—M.	219,475
31. Kachári (Bódo)—F.	198,705
32. Nipali Hill dialects—F.	195,866
33. Kôrwa (Kúr)—C.	185,775
34. Khási—E.	178,637
35. Shán—H.	174,871
36. Bhil—C.	148,596
37. Gáro—F.	145,425
38. Halbi—A.	143,720
39. Khyîn—F.	126,915
40. Tipperah—F.	121,864
41. Nága dialects—F.	102,908
42. Sáwara—C.	102,039

(3) 10,000 to 100,000.

Language	Population returning
43. Méch—F.	90,796
44. Mikir—F.	90,236
45. Kathé (Manipuri)—F.	88,911
46. Kharria—C.	67,772
47. Arabic—N.	53,351
48. Baiga—C.	48,883
49. Lushai—F.	41,926
50. Lálúng—F.	40,204
51. Chinese—K.	38,504
52. Goanese and Portuguese—A.	37,738
53. Kodagu (Coorgi)—B.	37,218
54. Abor (Miri)—F.	35,703
55. Mal-Pahádia—B.	30,838
56. Gadaba—C.	29,789
57. Kashméri—A.	29,276
58. Brahui—B.	28,990
59. Persian—M.	28,189
60. Eastern Pahári (Nipáli, &c.)—A.	24,262
61. Tibetan—F.	20,544
62. Kuki—F.	18,828
63. Minor Kolárian dialects (6)—C.	11,965
64. Lepcha—F.	10,125

(4) 1,000 to 10,000.

Language	Population returning
65. Bhutáni—F.	9,470
66. Negro dialects—R.	9,612
67. Kanáwari—F.	9,265
68. Kôch—F.	8,107
69. Minor Dravidian dialects (3)—B.	7,651
70. Kakhyîn—F.	5,669
71. Minor Bodo dialects (4)—F.	4,314
72. Máhl—B.	3,167
73. Khámti—H.	2,945
74. Palaung—G.	2,847
75. Malay—J.	2,437
76. German—P.	2,215
77. French—P.	2,171
78. Hebrew (Israeli)—N.	2,171
79. Kôta and Tôda—B.	1,937
80. Salôn—J.	1,628
81. Minor North-East Frontier dialects (3)—F.	1,282

(5) Under 1,000.

Language	Population returning
Indian languages (5)	513
Other Asiatic languages (8)	2,195
European languages (23)	2,913

* Urdû is returned as a separate dialect in Southern, Western, and Central India only.

XI.—Birthplace.

Province or State.	Enumerated in the Province or State.				Born in the Province or State.		
	TOTAL enumerated.	Born in the Province or State.	Born in contiguous Territory.	Born elsewhere.	TOTAL.	Enumerated in contiguous Territory.	Enumerated elsewhere in India.
Ajmér-Mérwára	542,358	433,664	83,447	25,247	490,221	52,720	3,837
Assam -	5,476,833	4,961,324	419,562	95,947	5,017,019	53,417	2,278
Bengal* -	71,345,947	70,597,656	508,805	239,486	71,838,732	1,191,123	49,953
Berar	2,897,491	2,446,576	387,198	63,717	2,561,430	113,498	1,356
*Bombay** - -	15,978,463	14,882,954	805,302	290,207	15,985,829	905,540	197,335
*Sindh** - - -	2,871,303	2,665,691	171,254	34,358	2,692,978	18,940	8,342
Burma* - -	7,602,429	7,273,817	150,649	177,963	7,282,348	2,416	6,115
Central Provinces	10,784,294	10,289,405	420,239	74,650	11,313,422	946,870	77,147
Coorg* - - -	173,010	120,110	51,628	1,272	122,772	2,413	249
Madras and Laccadives*	35,326,412	35,029,729	272,398	24,285	35,646,453	412,669	204,055
North-West Provinces*	34,249,210	33,100,077	1,118,045	31,088	34,768,181	1,459,124	208,980
Oudh* - -	12,649,049	12,179,130	444,645	25,274	12,705,441	389,665	136,646
Punjab* - - -	20,866,787	19,780,050	1,008,424	78,313	20,608,421	729,504	98,867
Provinces -	**220,763,586**	**213,760,183**	**5,841,596**	**1,161,807**	**221,033,242**	**6,277,899**	**995,160**
Hyderabad* - -	11,535,480	11,151,767	301,544	82,169	11,539,750	375,405	12,578
Baroda* -	2,415,197	2,103,474	289,852	21,871	2,355,870	246,757	5,639
Mysore* -	4,941,882	4,746,084	183,652	12,146	4,889,617	136,694	6,839
Kashmér*	2,527,056	2,457,799	66,346	2,911	2,548,726	87,545	3,382
Rajputána - -	11,986,196	11,578,814	370,832	36,550	12,478,431	745,607	154,010
Central India* -	10,317,242	9,564,629	680,467	72,146	10,146,485	558,197	23,659
Bombay States*	8,058,299	7,347,901	609,115	101,283	7,950,857	480,184	122,272
Madras States* -	3,700,369	3,596,784	98,910	4,675	3,629,824	32,338	702
Central Province States	2,160,511	1,554,211	572,069	34,231	1,579,582	25,264	107
Bengal States* - -	3,296,125	2,767,707	513,840	14,578	2,878,968	12,118	99,143
North - Western Province States.	792,491	724,327	65,149	3,015	788,135	59,437	4,371
Panjáb States* -	4,263,192	3,761,338	480,375	21,479	4,206,065	443,425	1,302
States -	**65,994,040**	**61,354,835**	**4,232,151**	**407,054**	**64,991,810**	**3,202,971**	**434,004**
Total returning birthplace.	**286,757,626**	**275,115,018**	**10,073,747**	**1,568,861**	**286,025,052†**	**9,480,870**	**1,429,164**
Aden, Quetta, &c. excluded -	89,921	—	—	—	—	—	—
Not enumerated by birthplace.	375,884	—	—	—	—	—	—
INDIA	**287,223,431**	—	—	—	—	—	—

* Those not returning birthplace are here excluded.

† The total number of persons not born in India, including the French and Portuguese possessions, was 661,637. Of these 478,656 returned as their birthplace countries contiguous to India; 60,519 countries in Asia remote from India, including, however, China; 100,551 the United Kingdom; 10,095 other European, American, and Australasian countries; whilst 11,816 were born in Africa, &c., or at sea.

XII.—Infirmities.

A.—INDIA.

Age.	Insane.		Deaf Mute.		Blind.		Lepers.	
	Males.	Females.	Males.	Females.	Males.	Females.	Males.	Females.
0—4	774	522	5,452	4,057	9,426	6,368	426	285
5—9	2,673	1,617	17,086	10,969	14,836	9,521	843	607
10—14	3,728	2,338	15,758	8,787	14,842	9,437	2,285	1,305
15—19	4,293	2,758	12,968	7,845	13,458	9,388	3,857	1,934
20—24	4,791	2,884	11,660	7,263	13,911	10,292	5,569	2,277
25—29	5,599	2,823	10,814	6,569	14,472	11,860	8,342	2,867
30—34	5,741	3,145	9,914	6,123	15,156	14,217	11,481	3,678
35—39	4,333	2,461	7,282	4,175	12,816	12,276	11,495	3,090
40—44	4,482	2,770	7,498	4,803	15,985	17,274	14,474	4,014
45—49	2,543	1,688	4,552	2,793	12,914	13,394	9,488	2,403
50—54	2,557	2,050	5,487	3,698	17,163	20,378	11,065	3,068
55—59	1,264	903	2,953	1,909	14,269	16,003	4,687	1,415
60 and over	2,673	2,558	8,873	7,250	59,772	78,999	11,131	4,023
Age not returned	188	123	200	123	233	208	125	60
Total	**45,639**	**28,650**	**120,497**	**76,364**	**229,253**	**229,615**	**95,218**	**31,026**

B.—PROVINCES.

Age.	Insane.		Deaf Mute.		Blind.		Lepers.	
	Males.	Females.	Males.	Females.	Males.	Females.	Males.	Females.
0—4	633	412	4,871	3,547	7,860	5,118	371	216
5—9	2,103	1,292	15,407	9,745	11,773	7,451	706	484
10—14	3,005	1,916	14,036	7,755	11,917	7,598	1,971	1,069
15—19	3,520	2,273	11,412	6,880	10,941	7,605	3,346	1,615
20—24	3,983	2,398	10,292	6,397	11,208	8,254	4,786	1,973
25—29	4,699	2,427	9,565	5,776	11,668	9,443	7,306	2,480
30—34	4,845	2,689	8,770	5,387	12,202	11,319	10,086	3,181
35—39	3,714	2,149	6,417	3,654	10,362	9,874	10,143	2,656
40—44	3,790	2,378	6,611	4,179	12,761	13,454	12,683	3,465
45—49	2,183	1,475	3,988	2,466	10,404	10,904	8,331	2,115
50—54	2,139	1,764	4,821	3,252	13,532	15,839	9,825	2,709
55—59	1,094	797	2,574	1,692	11,535	12,972	4,143	1,247
60 and over	2,288	2,212	7,774	6,417	47,899	62,416	9,915	3,580
Age not returned	107	91	79	56	108	133	71	36
Total	**38,103**	**24,283**	**106,617**	**67,203**	**184,170**	**182,380**	**83,683**	**26,826**

C.—STATES.

Age.	Insane.		Deaf Mute.		Blind.		Lepers.	
	Males.	Females.	Males.	Females.	Males.	Females.	Males.	Females.
0—4	141	110	581	510	1,566	1,250	55	69
5—9	570	325	1,679	1,224	3,063	2,070	137	123
10—24	723	422	1,722	1,032	2,925	1,839	314	236
15—19	773	485	1,556	965	2,517	1,783	511	319
20—24	808	486	1,368	866	2,703	2,038	783	304
25—29	900	396	1,249	793	2,804	2,417	1,036	387
30—34	896	456	1,144	736	2,954	2,898	1,345	497
35—39	619	312	865	521	2,454	2,402	1,352	434
40—44	692	392	887	624	3,224	3,820	1,791	549
45—49	360	213	564	327	2,510	2,490	1,157	288
50—54	418	286	666	446	3,631	4,539	1,240	359
55—59	170	106	379	217	2,734	3,031	544	168
60 and over	385	346	1,099	833	11,873	16,583	1,216	443
Age not returned	81	32	121	67	125	75	54	24
Total	**7,536**	**4,367**	**13,880**	**9,161**	**45,083**	**47,235**	**11,535**	**4,200**

XIII.—Occupation.

Order of Occupation or Means of Livelihood.	Number of Persons supported by each Order.*		
	India.	Provinces.	States.
I. Administration by State or by Local Bodies	5,600,153	3,839,643	1,760,510
II. Defence, Military and Naval	664,422	334,193	330,229
III. Service of Foreign States †	500,030	38,179	461,851
IV. Provision and care of Cattle	3,645,849	2,472,872	1,172,977
V. Agricultural	171,735,390	135,504,696	36,230,694
VI. Personal, Household, or Sanitary Services	11,220,072	8,505,420	2,714,652
VII. Provision of Food and Drink	14,575,593	12,120,669	2,454,924
VIII. Provision of Light, Firing, and Forage	3,522,257	2,887,525	634,732
IX. Construction of Buildings	1,437,739	1,113,633	324,106
X. Construction of Vehicles and Vessels	146,508	135,627	10,881
XI. Provision of Supplementary Requirements	1,155,267	991,334	163,933
XII. Provision of Textile Fabrics and Dress	12,611,267	9,655,213	2,956,054
XIII. Provision of Metals and Precious Stones	3,821,433	2,897,046	924,387
XIV. Provision of Glass, Pottery, and Stoneware	2,360,623	1,669,019	691,604
XV. Provision of Wood, Cane, Mats, &c.	4,293,012	3,319,170	973,842
XVI. Provision of Drugs, Dyes, and Gums	391,575	319,981	71,594
XVII. Provision of Leather Hides, and Horns	3,285,307	2,224,604	1,060,703
XVIII. Commerce	4,685,579	3,093,056	1,592,523
XIX. Transport and Storage	3,952,993	3,242,281	710,712
XX. Learned and Artistic Professions	5,672,191	4,386,725	1,285,466
XXI. Sport and Amusements	141,180	98,485	42,695
XXII. Earthwork and General Labour	25,468,017	18,414,315	7,053,702
XXIII. Undefined and Disreputable Means of Livelihood‡	1,562,981	704,801	858,180
XXIV. Means of Livelihood independent of Work	4,773,993	3,204,465	1,569,528
Total	**287,223,431**	**221,172,952**	**66,050,479**

* In this return no distinction is drawn between those who work and those whom they support by their work. The whole population depending upon the occupation is included, in order to indicate the respective sustaining power of the different orders.

† Order III. is intended to refer solely to those not in the employ of the State making the return, but it is probable that in some cases the servants of the State itself have been included.

‡ Order XXIII. includes those not enumerated by occupation in certain wild tracts of Rajputána, Kashmér, and the Bombay States.

TABLE A.

GENERAL STATEMENT.

EXPLANATORY NOTE.

In addition to the population shown in this table, which was dealt with in connection with the Census, the following tracts were roughly enumerated under a system of family or tribal registration during the years 1890–91, but the results being approximate only, have not been included in the Census tables. Other tracts on the Upper Burma frontier were duly enumerated, but, as in Manipur, the returns were destroyed in the subsequent disturbances. The population, however, save in Manipur, was roughly totalled at the time of Census, so the results are entered below :—

Tracts.	Approximate Population.
1. Upper Burma Frontier (in Bhámô and Kathá)	42,217
2. British Balôchistán, excluding Quetta and Railways, &c.	145,417
3. Burma Frontier returns, since destroyed -	74,276
Total, British - -	261,910
4. Sikkim - - - - -	30,458
5. Shán States - - - -	372,969
6. Rajputána (Bhils, &c.) - - - -	204,241
Total, States -	607,668
Total excluded - -	869,578

2. Amongst the tracts included in this table are several which were not enumerated at the Census in full detail. The population of such tracts will be found excluded from the returns for which the information concerning it is not available, the necessary explanation being given on the title page of the table in question.

TABLE A.

PROVINCE.	AREA in Square Miles.	TOWNS.	VILLAGES.	OCCUPIED HOUSES.		
				TOTAL.	In Towns.	In Villages.
1.	2.	3.	4.	5.	6.	7.
1. Ajmér Mérwára	2,711	4	741	101,654	25,787	75,867
2. Assam	49,004	18	17,142	1,118,885	22,399	1,096,486
3. Bengal	151,543	146	227,019	13,592,154	656,130	12,936,024
4. Berár	17,718	37	5,785	591,008	79,805	511,203
5. Bombay (*Presidency*)	125,144	216	24,988	3,380,640	594,508	2,786,132
(a) *Bombay*	77,275	192	21,261	2,857,212	522,296	2,334,916
(b) *Sindh*	47,789	23	3,927	516,020	64,804	451,216
(c) *Aden*	80	1	—	7,408	7,408	—
6. Burma (*Total*)	171,430	60	28,709	1,423,604	181,338	1,242,266
(a) *Upper*	83,473	24	10,957	554,472	80,264	474,208
(b) *Lower*	87,957	36	17,752	869,132	101,074	768,058
7. Central Provinces	86,501	52	34,303	2,158,668	162,073	1,996,595
8. Coorg	1,583	5	492	26,806	3,174	23,632
9. Madras	141,189	214	56,867	6,709,990	608,122	6,101,868
10. N.-W. Provinces	107,503	484	105,716	8,225,191	1,013,547	7,211,644
(a) *N.-W. Provinces*	83,286	399	81,437	5,944,230	822,781	5,121,449
(b) *Oudh*	24,217	85	24,279	2,280,961	190,766	2,090,195
11. Panjáb	110,667	178	34,664	3,127,823	393,982	2,733,841
12. Quettah, &c.	—	2	—	4,543	4,543	—
13. Andamans	—	—	59	2,997	—	2,997
Total, Provinces	**964,993**	**1,416**	**536,485**	**40,463,963**	**3,745,408**	**36,718,555**
STATE OR AGENCY.						
14. Haiderabád	82,698	76	20,011	2,283,787	235,426	2,048,361
15. Baroda	8,226	40	3,003	538,967	123,300	415,667
16. Mysore	27,936	98	16,784	894,446	114,182	780,264
17. Kashmír	80,900	8	8,310	447,993	36,252	411,741
18. Rajputána	130,268	124	30,299	2,177,425	293,806	1,883,619
19. Central India	77,808	66	32,415	1,961,771	202,999	1,758,772
20. Bombay States	69,045	119	15,332	1,596,132	244,680	1,351,452
21. Madras States	9,609	14	1,293	726,966	32,826	694,140
22. Central Prov. States	29,435	6	10,401	409,096	8,761	400,335
23. Bengal States	35,834	2	18,804	584,912	3,523	581,389
24. N.-W. Prov. States	5,109	6	2,312	132,815	5,067	127,748
25. Panjáb States	38,299	60	20,055	713,735	82,165	631,570
26. Shan States (Fort Steadman)	—	—	10	94	—	94
Total, States	**595,167**	**619**	**179,029**	**12,468,139**	**1,382,987**	**11,085,152**
INDIA	**1,560,160**	**2,035**	**715,514**	**52,932,102**	**5,128,395**	**47,803,707**

TABLE A.

POPULATION.								
Both Sexes.			Males.			Females.		
TOTAL.	Urban.	Rural.	TOTAL.	Urban.	Rural.	TOTAL.	Urban.	Rural.
8.	9.	10.	11.	12.	13.	14.	15.	16.
542,858	118,631	423,727	288,325	64,466	223,859	254,033	54,165	199,868
5,476,833	102,074	5,374,759	2,819,575	63,495	2,756,080	2,657,258	38,579	2,618,679
71,346,987	3,443,876	67,903,111	35,563,299	1,905,224	33,658,075	35,783,688	1,538,652	34,245,036
2,897,491	360,711	2,536,780	1,491,826	187,965	1,303,861	1,405,665	172,746	1,232,919
18,901,123	3,502,678	15,398,445	9,793,981	1,913,082	7,880,899	9,107,142	1,589,596	7,517,546
15,985,270	3,116,304	12,868,966	8,194,477	1,691,583	6,502,894	7,790,793	1,424,721	6,366,072
2,871,774	342,295	2,529,479	1,568,590	190,585	1,378,005	1,303,184	151,710	1,151,474
44,079	44,079	—	30,914	30,914	—	13,165	13,165	—
7,605,560	946,649	6,658,911	3,876,301	536,797	3,339,504	3,729,259	409,852	3,319,407
2,946,933	371,404	2,575,529	1,414,005	186,371	1,227,634	1,532,928	185,033	1,347,895
4,658,627	575,245	4,083,382	2,462,296	350,426	2,111,870	2,196,331	224,819	1,971,512
10,784,294	739,592	10,044,702	5,397,304	379,728	5,017,576	5,386,990	359,864	5,027,126
173,055	15,511	157,544	95,907	8,630	87,277	77,148	6,811	70,267
35,630,440	3,406,105	32,224,335	17,619,395	1,663,790	15,955,605	18,011,045	1,742,315	16,268,730
46,905,085	5,314,328	41,590,757	24,303,601	2,792,279	21,511,322	22,601,484	2,522,049	20,079,435
34,254,254	4,352,573	29,901,681	17,812,850	2,286,339	15,526,511	16,441,404	2,066,234	14,375,170
12,650,831	961,755	11,689,076	6,490,751	505,940	5,984,811	6,160,080	455,815	5,704,265
20,966,847	2,413,704	18,453,143	11,255,986	1,356,677	9,899,309	9,610,861	1,057,027	8,553,834
27,270	27,270	—	23,864	23,864	—	3,406	3,406	—
15,609	—	15,609	13,375	—	13,375	2,234	—	2,234
221,172,952	**20,391,129**	**200,781,823**	**112,542,739**	**10,895,997**	**101,646,742**	**108,630,213**	**9,495,132**	**99,135,081**
11,537,040	1,090,129	10,446,911	5,873,129	557,071	5,316,058	5,663,911	533,058	5,130,853
2,415,396	483,515	1,931,881	1,252,983	248,643	1,004,340	1,162,413	234,872	927,541
4,943,604	626,558	4,317,046	2,483,451	311,664	2,171,787	2,460,153	314,894	2,145,259
2,543,952	197,743	2,346,209	1,353,229	109,552	1,243,677	1,190,723	88,191	1,102,532
12,016,102	1,530,087	10,486,015	6,353,488	791,514	5,561,974	5,662,614	738,573	4,924,041
10,318,812	964,538	9,354,274	5,395,536	514,289	4,881,247	4,923,276	450,249	4,473,027
8,059,298	1,177,422	6,881,876	4,120,125	592,865	3,527,260	3,939,173	584,557	3,354,616
3,700,622	175,125	3,525,497	1,853,976	88,678	1,765,298	1,846,646	86,447	1,760,199
2,160,511	38,656	2,121,855	1,089,011	20,166	1,068,845	1,071,500	18,490	1,053,010
3,296,879	16,542	3,279,837	1,673,186	9,771	1,663,415	1,623,193	6,771	1,616,422
792,491	103,188	689,303	409,470	54,478	354,992	383,021	48,710	334,311
4,263,280	456,544	3,806,736	2,324,091	251,472	2,072,619	1,939,189	205,072	1,734,117
2,992	—	2,992	2,882	—	2,882	110	—	110
66,050,479	**6,860,047**	**59,190,432**	**34,184,557**	**3,550,163**	**30,634,394**	**31,865,922**	**3,309,884**	**28,556,038**
287,223,431	**27,251,176**	**259,972,255**	**146,727,296**	**14,446,160**	**132,281,136**	**140,496,135**	**12,805,016**	**127,691,119**

TABLE B.

VARIATION IN POPULATION SINCE 1881.

EXPLANATORY NOTE.

In this return a distinction is drawn in the case of both Provinces and States between the tracts included in the Census of 1881 and those now brought under the operations for the first time. The total population for 1891, as here given, falls short of that returned in Table I. by 43,716 persons, belonging to tracts in Rajputána not enumerated on the former occasion. Similarly, in order to get the full total of 1881, 309,380 persons must be added, representing the Rajputána Bhil tracts not enumerated in 1891; and 221,070 representing the then population of Manipur, the returns for which at the present Census were destroyed during the disturbances of March 1891. The Bombay Provincial total for 1881 is increased by 1,908, the population of an alienated village, the return for which seems to have escaped compilation on that occasion, as it was believed to have been included in one of the Deccan States. A small transfer of 105 persons from Madras to Bengal, and another of 66,315 persons from the Orissa Kandh Mahâls to the same Province, have been taken into consideration here. The 1881 population of the Jhánsi territory, ceded by Gwalior since that year, has been deducted from Central India and added to the North-West Provinces. The Chomehla parganah of Jháláwár, which is partly under Central India, has nevertheless been included in Rajputána with the rest of the State; but the Tonk parganahs in Central India, being wholly detached from Rajputána, are taken as part of the former agency. Similarly, in Table A., the detached parganahs of Gwalior and Indore in Meywár are included in Rajputána, though, as the 1881 population is not separately recorded, it has been omitted from Table B. as well as that for 1891.

TABLE B.

PROVINCE.	BOTH SEXES.			MALES.			FEMALES.		
	1891.	1881.	Difference.	1891.	1881.	Difference.	1891.	1881.	Difference.
1.	2.	3.	4.	5.	6.	7.	8.	9.	10.
1. Ajmér-Merwára	542,358	460,722	+ 81,636	288,325	248,844	+ 39,481	254,033	211,878	+ 42,155
2. Assam	5,433,199	4,881,426	+ 551,773	2,796,864	2,503,703	+ 293,161	2,636,335	2,377,723	+ 258,612
3. Bengal	71,346,987	66,750,520	+ 4,596,467	35,563,299	33,204,733	+ 2,358,566	35,783,688	33,545,787	+ 2,237,901
4. Berár	2,897,491	2,672,673	+ 224,818	1,491,826	1,380,492	+ 111,334	1,405,665	1,292,181	+ 113,484
5. Bombay (*Presidency*)	18,901,123	16,505,967	+ 2,395,156	9,793,981	8,529,316	+ 1,264,665	9,107,142	7,976,651	+ 1,130,491
(a) *Bombay*	15,985,270	14,057,284	+ 1,927,986	8,194,477	7,189,751	+ 1,004,726	7,790,793	6,867,533	+ 923,260
(b) *Sindh*	2,871,774	2,413,823	+ 457,951	1,568,590	1,316,830	+ 251,760	1,303,184	1,096,993	+ 206,191
(c) *Aden*	44,079	34,860	+ 9,219	30,914	22,735	+ 8,179	13,165	12,125	+ 1,040
6 (*b*). Lower Burmah	4,658,627	3,736,771	+ 921,856	2,462,296	1,991,005	+ 471,291	2,196,331	1,745,766	+ 450,565
7. Central Provinces	10,784,294	9,838,791	+ 945,503	5,397,304	4,959,435	+ 437,869	5,386,990	4,879,356	+ 507,634
8. Coorg	173,055	178,302	− 5,247	95,907	100,439	− 4,532	77,148	77,863	− 715
9. Madras	35,630,440	30,827,113	+ 4,803,327	17,619,395	15,257,401	+ 2,361,994	18,011,045	15,569,712	+ 2,441,333
10. North-West Provinces	46,905,085	44,150,507	+ 2,754,578	24,303,601	22,934,051	+ 1,369,550	22,601,484	21,216,456	+ 1,385,028
(a) *North-West Provinces*	34,254,254	32,762,766	+ 1,491,488	17,812,850	17,082,396	+ 730,454	16,441,404	15,680,370	+ 761,034
(b) *Oudh*	12,650,831	11,387,741	+ 1,263,090	6,490,751	5,851,655	+ 639,096	6,160,080	5,536,086	+ 623,994
11. Panjáb	20,866,847	18,843,186	+ 2,023,661	11,255,986	10,202,597	+ 1,053,389	9,610,861	8,640,589	+ 970,272
13. Andamans	15,609	14,628	+ 981	13,375	12,640	+ 735	2,234	1,988	+ 246
Nett Variation since 1881	**218,155,115**	**198,860,606**	**+ 19,294,509**	**111,082,159**	**101,324,656**	**+ 9,757,503**	**107,072,956**	**97,535,950**	**+ 9,537,006**

Additions. 2. *North Lushai* - -	43,634	—		22,711	—	.	20,923	—	—
Additions. 6 (*a*). *Upper Burmah* - -	2,946,933	—	—	1,414,005	—	—	1,532,928	—	—
Additions. 12. *Quettah, &c.* - -	27,270	—	—	23,864	—		3,406	-	—
Total Variation (*Provinces*) -	**221,172,952**	**198,860,606**	**+22,312,346**	**112,542,739**	**101,324,656**	**+11,218,083**	**108,630,213**	**97,535,950**	**+11,094,263**
STATE OR AGENCY.									
14. Hyderabád - - - -	11,537,040	9,845,594	+ 1,691,446	5,873,129	5,002,137	+ 870,992	5,663,911	4,843,457	+ 820,454
15. Baroda - - -	2,415,396	2,185,005	+ 230,391	1,252,983	1,139,512	+ 113,471	1,162,413	1,045,493	+ 116,920
16. Mysore - - - -	4,943,604	4,186,188	+ 757,416	2,483,451	2,085,842	+ 397,609	2,460,153	2,100,346	+ 359,807
18. Rajputána - - - -	11,972,386	9,959,012	+ 2,013,374	6,330,732	5,385,175	+ 945,557	5,641,654	4,573,837	+ 1,067,817
19. Central India - - -	10,318,812	9,387,119	+ 931,693	5,395,536	4,949,941	+ 445,595	4,923,276	4,437,178	+ 486,098
20. Bombay States - - -	8,059,298	6,926,464	+ 1,132,834	4,120,125	3,564,441	+ 555,684	3,939,173	3,362,023	+ 577,150
21. Madras States - -	3,700,622	3,344,849	+ 355,773	1,853,976	1,662,540	+ 191,436	1,846,646	1,682,309	+ 164,337
22. Central Province States - -	2,160,511	1,709,720	+ 450,791	1,089,011	867,687	+ 221,324	1,071,500	842,033	+ 229,467
23. Bengal States - - -	3,296,379	2,786,446	+ 509,933	1,673,186	1,420,909	+ 252,277	1,623,193	1,365,537	+ 257,656
24. North-Western Province States	792,491	741,750	+ 50,741	409,470	384,699	+ 24,771	383,021	357,051	+ 25,970
25. Panjáb States - - -	4,263,280	3,860,761	+ 402,519	2,324,091	2,111,779	+ 212,312	1,939,189	1,748,982	+ 190,207
Nett Variation since 1881 -	**63,459,819**	**54,932,908**	**+ 8,526,911**	**32,805,690**	**28,574,662**	**+ 4,231,028**	**30,654,129**	**26,358,246**	**+ 4,295,883**
Additions. 17. *Kashmír* - - -	2,543,952	-	—	1,353,229	—	—	1,190,723	—	—
Additions. 26. *Shán States* (*Outposts only*)	2,992	—	—	2,882	—	—	110	—	—
Total Variation (*States*) -	**66,006,763**	**54,932,908**	**+11,073,855**	**34,161,801**	**28,574,662**	**+ 5,587,139**	**31,844,962**	**26,358,246**	**+ 5,486,716**
INDIA Nett -	**281,614,934**	**253,793,514**	**+27,821,420**	**143,887,849**	**129,899,318**	**+13,988,531**	**137,727,085**	**123,894,196**	**+13,832,889**
INDIA Total -	**287,179,715**	—	**+33,386,201**	**146,704,540**	—	**+16,805,222**	**140,475,175**	—	**+16,580,979**

TABLE C.

THE POPULATION BY RELIGION.

EXPLANATORY NOTE.

The number of persons either not required to return their religion, or who neglected to give the information when asked for it, was only 42,578 out of the whole population. In parts of the Madras Agency tracts and in the Gilgit division of Kashmir religion was not called for. The omissions were chiefly in Bengal.

For the returns by age, civil condition and education, the term Hindu has been held to include the Brahmo or Áryá Somáj as well as the comparatively recently introduced title of Áryá, which was returned (*a*) as a separate religion, (*b*) as a sect of Hinduism, (*c*) of the Vedic religion, and also (*d*) of the Sikh form of faith. In the returns above-mentioned, too, the few cases of Theism, Atheism, Agnosticism, Deism, Positivism, and Unitarianism, have all been included under the title of Minor religions, which also comprises those distinctly stating that they are of no religion, as distinguished from those who were not returned by religion at all. The full number of these cases, however, is not shown under this head, as in Calcutta, 7 Unitarians, 2 Agnostics, a Positivist, a Freethinker, a Specialist, and 23 persons returning themselves as of no religion, have been included amongst Christains in the local return and shown as such in the age, civil condition, and education tables.

The term Animistic has been adopted comprehensively for the religions of Forest tribes who do not accept the Hindu system, and have not been converted to Christianity or Islám. The distinction between some of these tribal forms of faith and Hinduism was, however, by no means clearly drawn at the enumeration, and the caste returns of Rajputána, for example, will be found to show many Bhils as of the Hindu religion, though that tribe is elsewhere generally entered under Animistic.

TABLE C.

Province.	Total Population.	I.—Aryan— (a) Hindu (*Brahmanic*).	(b) Hindu (*Aryá*).	(c) Hindu (*Bráhmo*).
1.	2.	3.	4.	5.
1. Ajmér	542,358	436,831	1,157	—
2. Assam - - - -	5,476,833	2,996,833		239
3. Bengal - -	71,346,987	45,217,618	—	2,506
4. Berár - - -	2,897,491	2,531,791		—
5. Bombay (*Presidency*) -	18,901,123	14,659,892	—	34
(a) *Bombay* - - - -	15,985,270	14,089,643	—	31
(b) *Sindh* - - - - -	2,871,774	567,536	—	3
(c) *Aden* -	44,079	2,713	—	—
6. Burma - - - -	7,605,560	171,577	—	—
(a) *Upper* - - - -	2,946,933	29,055	—	—
(b) *Lower* - -	4,658,627	142,522	—	—
7. Central Provinces	10,784,294	8,831,199	265	3
8. Coorg -	173,055	156,845	—	—
9. Madras -	35,630,440	31,998,245	—	64
10. North-West Provinces -	46,905,085	40,380,168	22,053	14
(a) *North-West Provinces* - - -	34,254,254	29,364,955	21,063	8
(b) *Oudh* - - -	12,650,831	11,015,231	990	6
11. Punjáb -	20,866,847	7,727,810	15,539	128
12. Quettah, &c.	27,270	11,699	—	—
13. Andamans - - -	15,609	9,433	—	—
Total, Provinces - -	**221,172,952**	**155,129,941**	**39,014**	**2,988**
STATE OR AGENCY.				
14. Hyderabad -	11,537,040	10,315,249	—	—
15. Baroda - -	2,415,396	2,137,562	6	—
16. Mysore - - -	4,943,604	4,639,104	—	23
17. Kashmir	2,543,952	691,800	—	—
18. Rajputána - -	12,016,102	10,192,458	371	—
19. Central India - - -	10,318,812	7,735,246	—	—
20. Bombay States -	8,059,298	6,781,065	—	—
21. Madras States	3,700,622	2,759,211	—	—
22. Central Province States - -	2,160,511	1,658,143	10	—
23. Bengal States	3,296,379	2,603,850	—	40
24. N.-W. Province States -	792,491	549,545	23	—
25. Punjáb States - -	4,263,280	2,493,695	528	—
26. Shán States (*Outposts*) -	2,992	1,855	—	—
Total, States -	**66,050,479**	**52,558,783**	**938**	**63**
INDIA - -	**287,223,431**	**207,688,724**	**39,952**	**3,051**

TABLE C.

INDIAN.			II.—ARYAN—NON-INDIAN.		III.—SEMITIC.	
Total, Hindu.	**Sikh.**	**Jain.**	**Buddhist.**	**Zoroastrian (*Parsi*).**	**Musalmán.**	**Christian.**
6.	7.	8.	9.	10.	11.	12.
437,988	213	26,939	—	198	74,265	2,683
2,997,072	83	1,368	7,697	—	1,483,974	16,844
45,220,124	412	7,042	189,122	179	23,437,591	190,829
2,531,791	177	18,952	4	412	207,681	1,359
14,659,926	818	240,436	697	74,263	3,537,103	161,770
14,089,674	98	239,513	671	72,411	1,286,763	151,001
567,539	720	923	2	1 534	2,215,147	7,764
2,713	—	—	24	318	35,193	3,005
171,577	3,164	—	6,888,075	96	253,031	120,768
29,055	2,591	—	2,844,569	9	42,382	8,786
142,522	573	—	4,043,506	87	210,649	111,982
8,831,467	172	48,644	322	781	297,604	12,970
156,845	—	114	—	39	12,665	3,392
31,998,309	128	27,425	1,036	246	2,250,386	865,528
40,402,235	11,343	84,601	1,387	342	6,346,651	58,441
29,386,026	9,740	82,134	1,191	268	4,725,721	49,129
11,016,209	1,603	2,467	196	74	1,620,930	9,312
7,743,477	1,389,934	39,477	5,768	357	11,634,192	53,587
11,699	1,129	—	—	39	11,368	3,008
9,433	395	3	1,290	—	3,980	483
155,171,943	**1,407,968**	**495,001**	**7,095,398**	**76,952**	**49,550,491**	**1,491,662**
10,315,249	4,637	27,845	—	1,058	1,138,666	20,429
2,137,568	11	50,332	1	8,206	188,740	646
4,639,127	29	13,278	5	35	252,973	38,135
691,800	11,399	593	29,608	9	1,793,710	218
10,192,829	1,116	417,618	—	238	991,351	1,855
7,735,246	1,825	89,984	—	837	568,640	5,999
6,781,065	94	314,773	1	2,511	853,892	8,239
2,759,211	—	10	—	1	225,478	714,651
1,658,153	1	568	3	—	11,875	338
2,603,890	5	228	5,595	—	220,756	1,655
549,568	5	202	107	—	242,532	77
2,494,223	480,547	6,206	468	55	1,281,451	322
1,855	196	—	175	2	609	154
52,559,784	**499,865**	**921,637**	**35,963**	**12,952**	**7,770,673**	**792,718**
207,731,727	**1,907,833**	**1,416,638**	**7,131,361**	**89,904**	**57,321,164**	**2,284,380**

TABLE C.—*continued.*

Province.	III.—Semitic—*concluded.* Jew.	IV.—Animistic Religions. Forest Tribes, &c.	V.—Minor Minor Religions.	(a) Unitarians.	(b) Theists.
1.	13.	14.	15.	16.	17.
1. Ajmér	71	—	1	—	—
2. Assam	5	969,765	25	—	13
3. Bengal	1,447	2,294,506	17	—	6
4. Berár	2	137,108	3	—	—
5. Bombay (*Presidency*)	12,465	213,618	27	—	—
(a) *Bombay*	9,429	135,683	27	—	—
(b) *Sindh*	210	77,935	—	—	—
(c) *Aden*	2,826	—	—	—	—
6. Burma	351	168,449	18	—	—
(a) *Upper*	83	19,428	—	—	—
(b) *Lower*	268	149,021	18	—	—
7. Central Provinces	176	1,592,149	9	—	—
8. Coorg	—	—	—	—	—
9. Madras	42	472,808	29	—	4
10. N.-W. Provinces	60	—	3	—	—
(a) *North-West Provinces*	35	—	—	—	—
(b) *Oudh*	25	—	3	—	—
11. Panjáb	27	—	28	5	6
12. Quettah, &c.	23	—	2	—	—
13. Andamans	—	24	1	—	1
Total, Provinces	**14,669**	**5,848,427**	**163**	**5**	**30**
STATE OR AGENCY.					
14. Hyderabád	26	29,130	—	—	—
15. Baroda	36	29,854	—	—	—
16. Mysore	21	—	1	—	1
17. Kashmér	—	—	—	—	—
18. Rajputana	15	411,078	2	—	—
19. Central India	72	1,916,209	—	—	—
20. Bombay States	1,082	97,641	—	—	—
21. Madras States	1,267	—	2	—	—
22. Central Province States	—	489,572	1	—	—
23. Bengal States	—	458,555	16	—	16
24. N.-W. Province States	—	—	—	—	—
25. Panjáb States	6	—	—	—	—
26. Shán States (*Outposts*)	—	1	—	—	—
Total, States	**2,525**	**3,432,040**	**22**	**—**	**17**
INDIA	**17,194**	**9,280,467**	**185**	**5**	**47**

TABLE C.—*concluded.*

AND INDEFINITE CREEDS.

(c) Deists.	(d) Atheists.	(e) Free-thinkers.	(f) Agnostics.	(g) Positivists.	(h) No Religion.	Religion not Returned.
18.	19.	20.	21.	22.	23.	24.
—	—	—	—	—	1	—
2	—	—	10	—	—	—
—	4	—	6	1	—	5,718
1	—	—	1	1	—	2
—	—	—	27	—	—	—
—	—	—	27	—	—	—
—	—	—	—	—	—	—
—	—	—	—	—	—	—
—	18	—	—	—	—	31
—	—	—	—	—	—	30
—	18	—	—	—	—	1
—	—	—	9	—	—	—
—	—	—	—	—	—	—
4	5	—	12	—	4	14,503
3	—	—	—	—	—	22
—	—	—	—	—	—	10
3	—	—	—	—	—	12
2	—	3	3	—	9	—
—	—	2	—	—	—	2
—	—	—	—	—	—	—
12	**27**	**5**	**68**	**2**	**14**	**20,278**
—	—	—	—	—	—	—
—	—	—	—	—	—	2
—	—	—	—	—	—	—
—	—	—	—	—	—	16,615
—	—	—	—	—	2	—
—	—	—	—	—	—	—
—	—	—	—	—	—	—
—	—	—	—	—	2	2
—	—	—	1	—	—	—
—		—	—	—	—	5,679
—	—	—	—	—	—	—
—	—	—	—	—	—	2
—		—	—	—	—	—
—	—	—	1	—	4	22,300
12	**27**	**5**	**69**	**2**	**18**	**42,578**

1 Y 24230.

TABLE D.

THE POPULATION BY LITERACY.

EXPLANATORY NOTE.

The enumerators' instructions, of which this return shows the results, were that each individual should be entered under one of the three titles, learning, literate, or illiterate; the first applies to those under instruction, whether they know how to read and write or not, but children only learning texts or the multiplication table, by rote, were probably excluded. Those who are able to read and write, but are not under instruction of any sort, come into the second category, whilst the last includes all who are neither under instruction nor able to both read and write.

The return was called for from all Provinces and States except those mentioned below, so that the population dealt with amounts to 261,838,926, and 25,384,505 is excluded :—

A.—TERRITORIAL DISTRIBUTION.

Province or State.	Males.	Females.
Assam (*N. Lushai Land*) -	20,667	20,923
Bengal (*Chittagong Hills*) -	59,566	47,720
Madras (*Vizagapatam*) (*part*)	167,049	156,917
Total, Provinces - -	**247,282**	**225,560**
Kashmér - -	1,353,160	1,190,653
Rajputána - -	6,342,407	5,656,979
Central India - -	5,331,271	4,880,515
Bengal (*Hill Tipperah*)	71,596	65,846
Bombay (*Mahi Kuntha*) (*part*)	10,579	8,657
Total, States - -	**13,109,013**	**11,802,650**
Total excluded -	**13,356,295**	**12,028,210**

B.—RELIGIOUS DISTRIBUTION.

Religion.	Males.	Females.
B. Hindu -	9,918,541	8,864,506
C. Sikh - -	7,326	5,784
D. Jain -	253,197	253,726
E. Buddhist -	56,409	52,061
F. Pársi -	197	136
G. Músalmán - -	1,781,189	1,585,672
H. Christian	775	612
J. Jew -	2	1
K. Animistic - -	1,318,693	1,249,897
L. Minor -	—	—
M. Not returned	19,966	15,815
Total - -	**13,356,295**	**12,028,210**

TABLE D.

A. PROVINCE.	Total returning Literacy.		Under Instruction.		Not under Instruction, but can Read and Write.	
	Males.	Females.	Males.	Females.	Males.	Females.
1.	2.	3.	4.	5.	6.	7.
1. Ajmér-Mérwára	288,325	254,033	6,179	470	32,114	1,540
2. Assam	2,798,908	2,636,335	49,111	3,427	162,553	5,761
3. Bengal	35,503,733	35,735,968	883,250	34,130	2,948,794	109,684
4. Berár	1,491,826	1,405,665	38,502	976	87,128	1,722
5. Bombay (*Presidency*)	9,793,981	9,107,142	334,770	24,981	952,172	54,699
(a) *Bombay*	8,194,477	7,790,793	304,176	22,401	843,055	49,976
(b) *Sindh*	1,568,590	1,303,184	29,639	2,489	102,970	4,362
(c) *Aden*	30,914	13,165	955	91	6,147	361
6. Burma (*Total*)	3,876,301	3,729,259	227,498	18,225	1,515,083	89,376
(a) *Upper*	1,414,005	1,532,928	99,229	3,372	553,733	20,093
(b) *Lower*	2,462,296	2,196,331	128,269	14,853	961,350	69,283
7 Central Provinces	5,397,304	5,386,990	76,306	3,901	230,592	6,982
8. Coorg	95,907	77,148	4,192	610	10,747	676
9. Madras	17,452,346	17,854,128	576,079	59,127	2,021,289	120,324
10. N.-W. Provinces	24,303,601	22,601,484	238,440	8,404	1,257,150	38,466
(a) *N.-W. Provinces*	17,812,850	16,441,404	183,737	7,001	937,430	30,610
(b) *Oudh*	6,490,751	6,160,080	54,703	1,403	319,720	7,856
11. Panjáb	11,255,986	9,610,861	158,849	7,834	675,941	18,206
12. Quettah	23,864	3,406	367	86	7,312	383
13. Andamans	13,375	2,234	344	77	2,789	105
Total, Provinces	**112,295,457**	**108,404,653**	**2,593,887**	**162,248**	**9,903,664**	**447,924**
B. STATE OR AGENCY.						
14. Hydrabád	5,873,129	5,663,911	76,522	3,238	343,566	11,066
15. Baroda	1,252,983	1,162,413	39,290	2,256	136,364	4,552
16. Mysore	2,483,451	2,460,153	61,076	6,415	200,495	11,499
17. Kashmér	69	70	8	6	53	51
18. Rajputána	11,081	5,635	465	123	2,951	483
19. Central India	64,265	42,761	2,291	273	15,532	1,148
20. Bombay States	4,109,546	3,930,516	105,545	5,855	362,644	13,404
21. Madras States	1,853,976	1,846,646	82,318	16,160	360,746	48,380
22. Central Province States	1,089,011	1,071,500	4,991	171	18,710	627
23. Bengal States	1,601,590	1,557,347	15,792	503	72,642	2,026
24. N.-W. Province States	409,470	383,021	1,969	38	12,211	318
25. Panjáb States	2,324,091	1,939,189	13,404	375	128,236	2,000
26. Shan States (*Outposts*)	2,882	110	—	1	1,221	17
Total, States	**21,075,544**	**20,063,272**	**403,671**	**35,414**	**1,650,371**	**95,571**
INDIA	**133,371,001**	**128,467,925**	**2,997,558**	**197,662**	**11,554,035**	**543,495**

TABLE E.

THE POPULATION BY BIRTHPLACE.

EXPLANATORY NOTE.

This return was obtained from all Provinces and States, except a portion of the Madras Agency, Tracts of Rajputána, and from the Gilgit division of Kashmér, containing in all an included population of 350,508. There were also 25,376 persons in the rest of India who failed to fill up the return correctly, so that the net population dealt with amounts to 286,847,547.

The demand made was for the entry of the District and State of birth, if in India, and of the Country, if born elsewhere. In some instances a village which could not be identified was substituted for the former, whilst the required detail was omitted for the latter. Thus Roumania and Bulgaria were entered as Turkey: Europe, America, and the United Kingdom, instead of the country, and so on. The term "India," without further detail, may be taken, as a rule, to mean Hindustán, that is, the North-West Provinces and Oudh.

TABLE E.

Birthplace.	TOTAL.	Males.	Females.
1.	2.	3.	4.
(*a*) In India :—			
1. Ajmér-Mérwara	490,221	259,007	231,214
2. Assam and N. Lushai	5,017,019	2,552,409	2,464,610
3. Bengal	71,838,732	35,763,212	36,075,520
4. Berár	2,561,430	1,299,530	1,261,900
5. Bombay	15,985,829	8,130,650	7,855,179
6. Sindh	2,692,973	1,461,150	1,231,823
7. Burma	7,282,348	3,609,127	3,673,221
8. Central Provinces	11,313,422	5,639,959	5,673,463
9. Coorg	122,772	62,836	59,936
10. Madras	35,646,068	17,679,522	17,966,546
11. N.-W. Provinces	34,768,181	18,197,223	16,570,958
12. Oudh	12,705,441	6,572,501	6,132,940
13. Panjáb	20,608,421	11,152,531	9,455,890
14. Quettah	3	2	1
15. Aden	11,713	5,810	5,903
16. Andamans	1,909	1,523	386
17. Laccadives	385	364	21
Total, Provinces	**221,046,867**	**112,387,356**	**108,659,511**
18. Hydrabád (*Deccan*)	11,539,750	5,854,734	5,685,016
19. Baroda	2,355,870	1,221,524	1,134,346
20. Mysore and Bangalore	4,889,617	2,445,278	2,444,339
21. Kashmér and Jammu	2,548,726	1,350,722	1,198,004
22. Rajputána	12,478,431	6,626,158	5,852,273
23. Central India	10,146,485	5,283,139	5,863,346
24. Bombay States	7,950,357	4,089,804	3,860,553
25. Madras States	3,629,824	1,820,108	1,809,716
26. Central Province States	1,579,582	796,879	782,703
27. Bengal States and Sikkim	2,878,968	1,454,697	1,424,271
28. N.-W. Province States	788,135	407,433	380,702
29. Panjáb States	4,206,065	2,278,294	1,927,771
30. Manipur	5,829	3,503	2,326
31. Shán States and Karenni	8,160	5,031	3,129
32. French Settlements	23,113	9,325	13,788
33. Portuguese Settlements	54,333	34,557	19,776
Total States, &c.	65,083,245	33,681,186	31,402,059
34. India, *unspecified*	55,798	31,490	24,308
Total, India	**286,185,910**	**146,100,032**	**140,085,878**

TABLE E.—*continued.*

BIRTHPLACE.	TOTAL.	Males.	Females.
1.	2.	3.	4.
(*b*) COUNTRIES ADJACENT TO INDIA :—			
35. Beluchistán	61,445	34,205	27,240
36. Afghanistán	84,963	55,860	29,103
37. Yághestán	74,671	44,738	29,933
38. Turkestan	816	559	257
39. Tibet	1,641	1,262	379
40. Nipál	236,398	130,354	106,044
41. Bhután	4,353	2,432	1,921
42. Ceylon	5,612	3,622	1,990
43. Straits Settlements, &c.	1,697	1,140	557
44. Siam	7,060	4,160	2,900
Total, adjacent Countries	**478,656**	**278,332**	**200,324**
(*c*) OTHER ASIATIC COUNTRIES :—			
45. China	25,563	22,470	3,093
46. Mongolia (*Tartary*)	172	122	50
47. Japan	125	50	75
48. Hong Kong	8	6	2
49. Macao, Manilla, &c.	42	33	9
50. Jáva and Sumátra	100	59	41
51. Persia	4,411	3,351	1,060
52. Levant and Armenia	1,874	1,337	53
53. Arabia and Bághdád	28,092	22,829	5,263
54. Russian Turkestán	52	45	7
55. Asia, *unspecified*	80	47	33
Total, other Asiatic Countries	**60,519**	**50,349**	**10,170**
(*d*) EUROPE :—			
56. England and Wales	79,172	70,113	9,059
57. Scotland	8,530	7,309	1,221
58. Ireland	12,706	10,587	2,119
59. Channel Islands	141	105	36
60. United Kingdom, *unspecified*	2	1	1
TOTAL, UNITED KINGDOM	100,551	88,115	12,436
61. Gibraltar	104	73	31
62. Malta	199	137	62
63. Cyprus	1	—	1
64. France	1,258	800	458
65. Belgium	214	128	86
66. Holland	123	115	8

TABLE E.—*continued*.

Birthplace.	Total.	Males.	Females.
1.	2.	3.	4.
(*d*) Europe—*continued*.			
67. Denmark and Iceland	142	96	46
68. Norway	212	196	16
69. Sweden	188	171	17
70. Germany	1,458	1,096	362
71. Austria	418	288	130
72. Russia in Europe	262	178	84
73. Roumánia	40	35	5
74. Greece	236	208	28
75. Italy	881	684	197
76. Spain	210	162	48
77. Portugal	168	125	43
78. Switzerland	218	153	65
79. Turkey in Europe	256	106	150
80. Europe, *unspecified*	633	486	147
Total, Europe	**107,772**	**93,352**	**14,420**
(*e*) America and West Indies:—			
81. United States	836	540	296
82. Canada, &c.	274	191	83
83. West Indies	287	176	111
84. South and Central America	418	209	209
85. America, *unspecified*	553	348	205
Total, America	**2,368**	**1,464**	**904**
(*f*) Africa:—			
86. Cape Colony, &c.	77	56	21
87. Natal	186	95	91
88. West Africa, St. Helena, &c.	25	13	12
89. Mozambique	6	4	2
90. Zanzibár	1,311	732	579
91. Somáli Land	6,501	4,231	2,270
92. Abyssinia	456	236	220
93. Egypt	220	152	68
94. Mauritius	1,295	697	598
95. Africa, *unspecified*	1,491	986	505
Total, Africa	**11,568**	**7,202**	**4,366**
(*g*) Australasia:—			
96. Australia	428	291	137
97. Tasmania	8	5	3
98. New Zealand	70	43	27
Total, Australasia	**506**	**339**	**167**
(*h*) Born at Sea	248	151	97
TOTAL, RETURNED	**286,847,547**	**146,531,221**	**140,316,326**
Birthplace unspecified or unrecognisable	25,376	14,106	11,270
Not enumerated by birthplace	350,508	181,969	168,539
TOTAL, POPULATION	**287,223,431**	**146,727,296**	**140,496,135**

TABLE F.

INFIRMITIES.

EXPLANATORY NOTE.

THE return was called for of persons who were (*a*) of unsound mind; (*b*) Congenitally deaf mutes; (*c*) Totally blind; and (*d*) Lepers. Special instructions were issued to exclude from the second group those who were not both deaf and dumb from birth; from the third, the one-eyed, and from the fourth those suffering from leukoderma, which is sometimes called, by misapprehension, white leprosy.

The population dealt with is only 274,323,929, as the return was not required from Kashmér, the Central India States, a portion of Rajputána and of the Mahi Kántha States under Bombay, and North Lushai land, under Assam. Deaf-mutes, too, were not returned in the Rajputána States, so that in the case of this infirmity the population dealt with on that agency is, as for all the four tables in Central India, that of the cantonments and railways only. The following statement shows the scope of the return:—

PROVINCE OR STATE.	TOTAL.	Males.	Females.
INCLUDED IN TABLES*	274,373,929	139,993,379	134,380,550
Excluded:—			
Assam (*N. Lushai land*)	41,590	20,667	20,923
Kashmér	2,543,952	1,353,229	1,190,723
Central India States	10,219,126	5,336,397	4,882,729
Rajputána (*Meywár Bhils, &c.*)	25,598	13,045	12,553
Bombay States (*Mahi Kántha Bhils*)	19,236	10,579	8,657
Total Excluded	**12,849,502**	**6,733,917**	**6,115,585**
Total Population	**287,223,431**	**146,727,296**	**140,496,135**

* In the case of deaf-mutes the total dealt with is only 262,383,425 (133,652,936 males and 128,730,489 females).

TABLE F.

A. PROVINCE.	TOTAL RETURNING INFIRMITIES.				
	TOTAL POPULATION.	Number of			
		Insane.	Deaf Mutes.	Blind.	Lepers.
1.	2.	3.	4.	5.	6.
AJMÉR-MÉRWÁRA	542,358	87	175	1,053	27
ASSAM	5,435,243	3,022	4,681	5,832	6,727
BENGAL	71,346,987	24,165	66,937	70,056	43,986
BERÁR	2,897,491	478	530	6,768	3,698
BOMBAY	18,901,123	6,296	11,624	28,099	10,187
Bombay	15,985,270	3,843	8,614	21,899	9,977
Sindh	2,871,774	2,443	2,994	6,155	209
Aden	44,079	10	16	45	1
BURMA	7,605,560	6,883	3,904	15,234	6,464
Upper	2,946,933	3,708	2,131	10,860	3,504
Lower	4,658,627	3,175	1,773	4,374	2,960
CENTRAL PROVINCES	10,784,294	1,758	5,463	18,567	5,355
COORG	173,055	44	126	86	23
MADRAS	35,630,440	7,687	26,983	36,424	12,617
N.-W. PROVINCES	46,905,085	5,640	33,147	111,039	17,071
N.-W. Provinces	34,254,254	4,102	23,228	75,316	11,768
Oudh	12,650,831	1,538	9,919	35,723	5,303
PANJÁB	20,866,847	6,312	20,240	73,385	4,351
QUETTAH	27,270	4	9	6	2
ANDAMANS	15,609	—	1	1	1
Total, Provinces	**221,131,362**	**62,376**	**173,820**	**366,550**	**110,509**
B. STATE OR AGENCY.					
HAIDERABÁD	11,537,040	1,584	4,419	10,632	2,977
BARODA	2,415,896	845	918	4,751	569
MYSORE	4,943,604	1,075	3,418	5,194	802
KASHMÍR	—	—	—	—	—
RAJPUTÁNA	11,990,504	3,097	*2	38,280	1,708
CENTRAL INDIA (*Railways and Cantonments*).	99,686	*69	*49	*431	80
BOMBAY STATES	8,040,062	1,994	4,697	13,028	2,554
MADRAS STATES	3,700,622	677	1,557	2,309	1,439
CENTRAL PROVINCE STATES	2,160,511	276	977	1,903	1,259
BENGAL STATES	3,296,379	1,053	2,482	2,934	2,048
N.-W. PROVINCE STATES	792,491	157	393	1,024	379
PANJÁB STATES	4,263,280	1,076	4,129	11,832	1,920
SHAN STATES (*Outposts*)	2,992	—	—	—	—
Total, States	**53,242,567**	**11,903**	***23,041**	**92,318**	**15,735**
INDIA	**274,373,929**	**74,289**	***196,861**	**458,868**	**126,244**

* *See* the Explanatory Note

TABLE F.

MALES.					FEMALES.				
Total Males.	Number of				Total Females.	Number of			
	Insane.	Deaf Mutes.	Blind.	Lepers.		Insane.	Deaf Mutes.	Blind.	Lepers.
7.	8.	9.	10.	11.	12.	13.	14.	15.	16.
288,325	64	113	523	20	254,033	23	62	530	7
2,798,908	1,737	2,683	3,031	5,128	2,636,335	1,285	1,998	2,801	1,599
35,563,299	14,357	41,373	35,614	32,957	35,783,688	9,808	25,564	34,442	11,029
1,491,826	280	317	3,380	2,886	1,405,665	198	213	3,388	812
9,793,981	4,130	7,149	14,640	7,684	9,107,142	2,166	4,475	13,459	2,503
8,194,477	2,515	5,132	11,340	7,558	7,790,793	1,328	3,482	10,559	2,419
1,568,590	1,608	2,008	3,277	125	1,303,184	835	986	2,878	84
30,914	7	9	23	1	13,165	3	7	22	—
3,876,301	3,795	2,150	6,681	4,543	3,729,259	3,088	1,754	8,53	1,921
1,414,005	1,753	1,115	4,477	2,262	1,532,928	1,955	1,016	6,383	1,242
2,462,296	2,042	1,035	2,204	2,281	2,196,331	1,133	738	2,170	679
5,397,204	1,127	3,159	8,444	3,575	5,386,990	631	2,304	10,123	1,780
95,907	25	77	47	12	77,148	19	49	39	11
17,619,395	4,463	15,274	17,715	9,439	18,011,045	3,224	11,709	18,709	3,178
24,303,601	3,886	21,384	56,058	14,114	22,601,484	1,754	11,763	54,981	2,957
17,812,850	2,830	14,981	38,466	9,574	16,441,404	1,272	8,247	36,850	2,194
6,490,751	1,056	6,403	17,592	4,540	6,160,080	482	3,516	18,131	763
11,255,986	4,235	12,928	38,034	3,322	9,610,861	2,077	7,312	35,351	1,029
23,864	4	9	3	2	3,406	—	—	3	—
13,875	—	1	—	1	2,234	—	—	1	—
112,522,072	**38,103**	**106,617**	**184,170**	**83,683**	**108,609,290**	**24,273**	**67,203**	**182,380**	**26,826**
5,873,129	1,036	2,729	5,892	2,261	5,663,911	548	1,690	4,740	716
1,252,983	535	568	2,017	397	1,162,413	310	350	2,734	172
2,483,451	618	1,908	2,644	536	2,460,158	457	1,510	2,550	266
—	—	—	—	—	—	—	—	—	—
6,840,443	2,024	—	17,276	1,314	5,650,061	1,073	*2	21,004	394
59,139	*40	*26	*245	*59	40,547	*29	*23	*186	21
4,109,546	1,224	2,801	6,104	1,911	3,930,516	770	1,896	6,924	643
1,858,976	402	875	1,271	1,013	1,846,646	275	682	1,038	426
1,089,011	167	570	923	799	1,071,500	109	407	980	460
1,673,186	663	1,572	1,463	1,471	1,623,193	390	910	1,471	577
409,470	111	245	543	312	388,021	46	148	481	67
2,324,091	716	2,586	6,705	1,462	1,989,189	360	1,543	5,127	458
2,882	—	—	—	—	110	—	—	—	—
27,471,307	**7,536**	***13,880**	**45,083**	**11,535**	**25,771,260**	**4,367**	***9,161**	**47,235**	**4,200**
139,993,379	**45,639**	***120,497**	**229,253**	**95,218**	**134,380,550**	**28,650**	***76,364**	**229,615**	**31,026**

preceding this Table.

TABLE G.

THE CHRISTIAN POPULATION BY RACE AND DENOMINATION.

EXPLANATORY NOTE.

In the instructions accompanying the schedule all Christians were asked to return their denomination, whilst as regards other religions this detail was left optional with the local administration. In order to secure as complete a return of Christian sub-divisions as possible the various missionary bodies were addressed with a view to the issue of instructions from their different centres as to the correct entry to be made by their congregations. In most cases the entry was printed in the vernacular on a card which was to be shown to and copied by the enumerator, but the return makes it plain that this precaution was to a considerable extent disregarded.

TABLE G.

Denomination.	Total Returned.	Distribution by Race.		
		European.	Eurasian.	Native and African.
1.	2.	3.	4.	5.
Abyssinian	41	—	—	41
Armenian	817	366	247	204
Syrian (*Jacobite*)	200,467	15	3	200,449
Roman	1,315,263	35,645	36,089	1,243,529
Greek	400	360	28	12
Church of England	295,016	101,872	29,116	164,028
„ India	6	—	—	6
Anglican Church	3	2	1	—
" Episcopalian "	1,919	220	205	1,494
" Evangelical "	11	5	—	6
Evangelic Union	3	2	—	1
" Evangelist Church "	199	31	1	167
" Reformed "	1	1	—	—
London Mission	20	2	10	8
St. James' Church	6	—	—	6
St. Paul's „	2	1	1	—
Church of Ireland	55	39	—	16
„ Scotland	4,176	1,751	1,293	1,132
„ America	1,014	12	—	1,002
Free Church	145	—	—	145
„ of Scotland	1,010	305	44	661
Presbyterian	40,407	8,418	1,074	30,915
United Presbyterian	82	82	—	—
Reformed Presbyterian	53	—	—	53
American „	454	24	29	401
Irish „	2	2	—	—
Irish Mission	22	—	—	22
Independent	191	45	1	145
Congregationalist	7,703	228	129	7,346
Methodist	9,957	1,036	900	8,021
Methodist Episcopalian	14,503	449	642	13,412
Primitive Methodist	4	4	—	—
Wesleyan	6,388	3,129	684	2,575
Wesleyan Methodist	1,269	743	122	404
Baptist	191,746	2,907	2,352	186,487
Anabaptist	2	—	2	—

TABLE G.

Denomination.	Total Returned.	Distribution by Race.		
		European.	Eurasian.	Native and African.
1.	2.	3.	4.	5.
Plymouth Brethren	32	21	—	11
"Open" Brethren	1	—	1	—
Bible Christian	2	1	1	—
"Nonconformist"	127	26	38	63
"Dissenter"	428	204	142	82
Puritan	2	—	—	2
Society of Friends	4	4	—	—
Quaker	108	28	—	80
"Protestant"	60,713	6,238	5,252	49,223
Calvinist	3	3	—	—
Welsh Calvinist	8	6	—	2
Lutheran	65,376	939	194	64,243
German Church	6	1	—	5
German Mission	1	—	—	1
Swedish Church	1	1	—	—
Reformed Dutch	4	4	—	—
Zwinglian	1	1	—	—
Moravian	2	—	—	2
Catholic Apostolic	6	5	1	—
Salvationist	1,286	114	34	1,138
"Unsectarian"*	2,343	927	347	1,069
"Heathen" (Convert)	3	—	1	2
Swedenborgian	5	5	—	—
New Jerusalem	1	1	—	—
Unitarian (*sic*)	202	69	48	85
Sarweswara Mathá (Unitarian)	3	—	—	3
Theist (*sic*)	1	1	—	—
Agnostic (*sic*)	2	2	—	—
Denomination not returned*	60,352	1,703	758	57,891
Total Christians	**2,284,380**	**168,000**	**79,790**	**2,036,590**

* The entry of "Unsectarian" is here distinguished from the cases where the column for denomination was left blank, since the former is an assertion, the latter may be due to neglect or ignorance.